D1244503

LIVES OF THE
LORD CHANCELLORS
1885–1940

Oxford University Press, Amen House, London E.C.4.

GLASGOW   NEW YORK   TORONTO   MELBOURNE   WELLINGTON
BOMBAY   CALCUTTA   MADRAS   KARACHI   LAHORE   DACCA
CAPE TOWN   SALISBURY   NAIROBI   IBADAN   ACCRA
KUALA LUMPUR   HONG KONG

LIVES OF THE LORD CHANCELLORS 1885–1940

BY

R. F. V. HEUSTON

CLARENDON PRESS · OXFORD

1964

© *R. F. V. Heuston, 1964*

PRINTED IN GREAT BRITAIN IN THE CITY OF OXFORD
AT THE ALDEN PRESS

TO
CUTHBERT RUDYARD HALSALL

PREFACE

THIS work owes its origin to the enterprise, vision, and generosity of Cuthbert Rudyard Halsall. It was he who conceived the idea and he who supported and sustained the author during the period of its making. His patience and tolerance throughout were exemplary, not least when its progress was beset by interruptions and delays. It is to be hoped that the work will be found worthy of the complete confidence which he placed in the author.

The general object of the work is to depict the Lord Chancellors of the years 1885 to 1940 in their legal, political, and personal lives. It takes up the history of the holders of the Great Seal in substance where Atlay left off, for although he dealt with both Halsbury and Herschell, the fact that he published his two admirable volumes while one was still alive and the other only recently deceased necessarily imposed certain limits on his treatment. I have therefore thought it right to assume that there has been no connected account of the Lord Chancellors since Selborne surrendered the Great Seal in 1885. No doubt comparisons will be drawn between this work and the volumes by Campbell and Atlay. It is fashionable today to sneer at the *Lives of the Lord Chancellors*, but as a result of a close acquaintance with the work over the past five years I have developed a deep respect for the author. The faults, especially in the later volumes, are obvious enough; but he did the work, and that in the intervals of public life and in days before such mechanical aids to authorship as the typewriter and the dictating machine. Campbell's *Lives* are a monument to remarkable industry and talent. As for Atlay's *Victorian Chancellors*, I should indeed be happy if my work could be compared for felicity in portraiture and literary grace with his.

Some of the Chancellors of this period, in particular Haldane and Birkenhead, have already been the subject of admirable biographical studies. Here it has not been possible for me to add much to what is already known. But other Chancellors, such as Loreburn, Buckmaster, and Hailsham, are hardly known at all to the present generation, and in their case I have often been able to use material hitherto unpublished. Whenever possible I have allowed this material to speak for itself with the minimum of comment on my part. The location of documents of this kind is described in the Note on Sources.

R. F. V. HEUSTON

Pembroke College
Oxford

ACKNOWLEDGMENTS

I MUST first express my gratitude to Her Majesty the Queen for her gracious permission to have access to the Royal Archives at Windsor and to reprint material from them.

Next I must tender my sincere thanks to the relatives of the twelve Lord Chancellors whose lives are dealt with in this work. I was fortunate enough to be given unrestricted access to whatever documents had survived for all but two of these twelve, and throughout was treated with the greatest kindness and forbearance. I was unable to obtain access to the papers of Lord Herschell or Lord Birkenhead, but the present Lord Birkenhead's masterly biography of his father is based upon a full survey of the documents, and I have naturally made considerable use of it.

A very large number of other people have been kind enough to furnish me with oral or documentary reminiscences, or give permission for the reproduction of copyright material. Besides the relatives of the Chancellors I am grateful to the following:

Earl Baldwin of Bewdley; Hon. Lionel Brett; Lord Bridges; the late Lord Hankey; Lord Coleridge; Sir George Coldstream; the Duke of Devonshire; the late Viscount Dunrossil; Mrs. M. E. Campbell Fraser; Sir Saville Garner; Dr. G. P. Gooch; Dr. A. L. Goodhart; Mr. Alan Harris; Lord Ismay; the Marquess of Lansdowne; Mrs. F. Laski; Lord McNair; the Rt. Hon. Malcolm MacDonald; the late Lord Merriman; Sir Eric Machtig; Mr. Stephen McKenna; Hon. Sir Albert Napier; Dr. R. C. Reid; the Countess of Rosebery; the Marquess of Salisbury; the late Viscount Samuel; Viscount Simonds; Mr. C. Stott; Mrs. C. Tucker; Hon. Mrs. E. Turner; and Mr. Robert Mackworth-Young.

NOTE ON SOURCES

A. UNPUBLISHED

(1) *In Libraries*:

Gladstone papers, B.M. Add. MSS.
Salisbury papers, Christ Church Library.
Campbell-Bannerman Papers, B.M. Add. MSS.
Balfour papers, B.M. Add. MSS.
Asquith papers, Bodleian Library.
Baldwin papers, Cambridge University Library
Haldane papers, National Library of Scotland.
Gosse papers, Leeds University Library.
Milner papers, New College Library.

A*

References are given to the location of each document cited from these collections, except the Asquith and Baldwin papers, which are at present being catalogued.

(2) *In Private Ownership*:

Royal Archives (Windsor Castle).
Halsbury papers (3rd Earl of Halsbury).
Buckmaster papers (Hon. Mrs. Barbara Miller).
Finlay papers (Hon. Mrs. Hayes).
Hailsham papers (2nd Viscount Hailsham).
Sankey papers (Executors of Miss Edith Sankey).
Maugham papers (Executors of Hon. Mrs. K. M. Bruce).
Caldecote papers (2nd Viscount Caldecote).
Simon papers (2nd Viscount Simon).
Jowitt papers (Countess Jowitt).
Cherry papers (Mr. J. Cherry).
Hanworth papers (Hon. Lady Farrer).
Laski papers (Mrs. Laski).
Rosebery papers (Countess of Rosebery).
Uthwatt papers (Mrs. H. S. Deighton).
Lansdowne papers (5th Marquess of Lansdowne).
Williamson papers (Sir Hedworth Williamson, Bt.).
Cozens-Hardy papers (Mr. Basil Cozens-Hardy).

Of these collections, the Royal Archives alone have been arranged on a system which permits precise references to be given to the location of the document. An initial letter indicates the series under which the document has been filed, and a number then indicates the number of the file in that series. There may also on occasion be another number to represent the number of the document in that file—for example, Royal Archives, W. 35 (2).

None of the other collections mentioned have been calendared, indexed or arranged in any way. The sole exceptions are the Halsbury papers and the Hailsham papers. The Halsbury papers are contained in a number of box files. Within each box the papers are in numbered envelopes, and there is a typewritten list containing a rough index to the contents of each envelope. The Hailsham papers are contained in a large collection of unnumbered box files. Within each box the documents are arranged mainly in alphabetical order according to subject-matter.

B. PUBLISHED

The more important works consulted are cited in the footnotes. Full bibliographical details are given on the first citation. The place of publication is London unless otherwise stated.

LIST OF CONTENTS

LIST OF PLATES

The reproduction of these plates is due to the courtesy of the
following persons or bodies:
Radio Times-Picture Post Library (Nos. 3, 4, 5, 6, 8, 9, 14, 16, 17,
and 18); Masters of the Bench of the Middle Temple (No. 11);
The Edinburgh Academy (No. 12); London News Agency
(No. 15); Walter Bird (No. 21); Heinemann, Ltd. (No. 22); Hon.
Lady Inskip (No. 24).

LIST OF LORD CHANCELLORS 1885–1940

Chancellor	Date of Receiving Great Seal	Length of Tenure
Halsbury	24 June 1885	8 months
Herschell	6 February 1886	6 months
Halsbury	3 August 1886	6 years
Herschell	18 August 1892	2 years 10 months [1]
Halsbury	29 June 1895	10 years 6 months [2]
Loreburn	11 December 1905	6 years 6 months
Haldane	10 June 1912	2 years 11 months
Buckmaster	27 May 1915	1 year 7 months
Finlay	11 December 1916	2 years 1 month
Birkenhead	14 January 1919	3 years 9 months
Cave	25 October 1922	1 year 3 months
Haldane	23 January 1924	10 months [3]
Cave	7 November 1924	3 years 4 months [4]
Hailsham	29 March 1928	1 year 2 months
Sankey	8 June 1929	6 years
Hailsham	7 June 1935	2 years 9 months [5]
Maugham	15 March 1938	1 year 6 months
Caldecote	4 September 1939	8 months
Simon	13 May 1940	

[1] Total tenure of Great Seal: 3 years 4 months
[2] ,, ,, ,, ,, ,, 17 years 2 months*
[3] ,, ,, ,, ,, ,, 3 years 9 months
[4] ,, ,, ,, ,, ,, 4 years 7 months
[5] ,, ,, ,, ,, ,, 3 years 11 months

* The figure of 17 years 6 months was given in an official reply to a Parliamentary question (143 H.C. Deb. 5s. col. 2328) but this seems wrong.

INTRODUCTION

THE Lord High Chancellor of Great Britain, to give him his full official title, occupies a position of great antiquity, much dignity and considerable importance.[1]

The antiquity of the office is a subject of some dispute. Claims have been made for an initial date of A.D. 615, but Edward the Confessor (1042–66) was the first English king to have a great seal and a Chancellor to keep it. From Herfast in 1068 to Lord Dilhorne in 1963 there have been some 228 Holders of the Great Seal.[2] The word apparently derives from the 'cancelli' or lattice-work screen behind which sat the clerks for the dispatch of clerical business in a court. After the Conquest the Chancellor, then an ecclesiastic, was in charge of the secretarial business of the King's court. Once it was customary to call the Chancellor 'Keeper of the King's Conscience', but two modern Chancellors have said the phrase[3] is now meaningless.[4] The proper title of the office is therefore that of Chancellor and he is always so referred to in the older and better usage of Whitehall and Westminster. Thus the Chancellor signs official documents with his peerage title followed by 'C'. The Chancellorship of the Exchequer is a comparatively modern office; it can hardly be traced back beyond 1714, and did not attain its present importance until the first quarter of the nineteenth century. The 'Lord' and the 'High' are honorific marks of respect as in the titles of Lord Chief Justice and Lord Chief Baron, which date in usage from about 1485 and 1589 respectively.

The dignity of the office is great.[5] Its holder is the first subject in the

[1] The Introduction to Lord Campbell's *Lives of the Chancellors*, 8 vols. (1848–69) still contains much useful material. The primary historical account of the office is in W. S. Holdsworth, *History of English Law* (7th ed.), vol. i, chap. v. The most authoritative modern description is by Lord Haldane himself, in chapter x of the Report of the Machinery of Government Committee (1918, Cmd. 9230). Of the other Chancellors, Hailsham and Caldecote have each left short accounts, as have their successors Jowitt and Kilmuir, and some of those who have been Permanent Secretary to the Lord Chancellor. See Viscount Hailsham, *The Duties of a Lord Chancellor* (Holdsworth Club, Birmingham, 1936); Viscount Kilmuir, 'The Office of Lord Chancellor' (1956) 9 Parliamentary Affairs 132; Lord Schuster, 'The Office of the Lord Chancellor' (1949) 10 Camb. L.J. 175; A. Napier, 'The Office of Lord Chancellor' (1950) 1 Nisi Prius 88; G. Coldstream, 'The Lord Chancellor's Office' (1962) Graya 13.

[2] The most authoritative list is in *Handbook of British Chronology*, 2nd ed. (Royal Hist. Society, 1961).

[3] First used by Sir Christopher Hatton (1587–91): D. E. C. Yale, *Nottingham's Chancery Cases* (1957), p. xl.

[4] Hailsham, *Duties of a Lord Chancellor*, p. 12; Simon, *Retrospect*, p. 251.

[5] There is much about the ceremonial side of the position in J. Derriman, *Pageantry of the Law* (1955), pp. 154–64.

realm after the Archbishop of Canterbury, and although it is not strictly necessary for the fulfilment of his functions on the Woolsack every Chancellor in modern times has been created a peer immediately upon his appointment. The office of Keeper of the Great Seal, the powers but not the dignity of which were identical with those of the Chancellor, was formerly used when for various reasons it was thought inexpedient to confer the greater dignity. Its holder was customarily a commoner at first; so the last Lord Keeper, Sir Robert Henley, was appointed in 1757 and not made a peer until 1760 and Chancellor until 1761.

On formal occasions such as the opening of Parliament or the Law Courts the Lord Chancellor is attended by a procession of five persons. First comes a tipstaff; then the official who holds the joint offices of Permanent Secretary to the Lord Chancellor and Clerk of the Crown in Chancery; then the Mace-Bearer; then the Purse-Bearer;[6] then the Lord Chancellor himself, and lastly a Train-Bearer. On a State occasion the Lord Chancellor wears a black velvet court suit with knee-breeches, silk stockings, and buckled shoes, lace stock and cuffs (without bands), and white gloves. Over all is a black and gold State robe of flowered damask. On ordinary occasions (e.g. when on the Woolsack) the Chancellor wears a black silk gown over a court suit of black cloth, and the ordinary judicial bands. When sitting as one of the Commission to signify the Royal Assent to Bills, he wears his peer's robes. A Lord Chancellor always wears a full-bottomed wig, occasionally (when in Commission for the Assent or swearing in a new peer) surmounted by a black tricorne hat.

The importance of the office is best shown by an account of its functions, which did not vary greatly during the period covered by this volume. It is familiar that the Lord Chancellor combines within himself the three functions of government, executive, legislative, and judicial. On the executive side he is a member of the Cabinet and one of the chief government spokesmen in the House of Lords. He holds office like all other ministers at the pleasure of the Crown, that is of the Prime Minister of the day. It is generally believed that there is now no legal bar to a Roman Catholic or Jew holding the position.[7] In his legislative capacity the Chancellor is Speaker of the House of Lords. By the Supreme Court of Judicature (Consolidation) Act, 1925, sect. 13, his annual salary of £10,000 (increased to £12,000 by the Judges' Remuneration Act, 1954) is made up of £6,000 as Lord Chancellor and £4,000 as Speaker of the House of Lords. The former sum (but not the latter) is charged upon the Consolidated Fund by the Courts of Justice (Salaries and Funds) Act, 1869, sect. 12,

[6] For the purse and the Great Seal, see below, pp. 32–33, 480–1.
[7] Haldane so advised Russell of Killowen (*Autobiography*, p. 68), and Simon (127 H.L. Deb. 5s. col. 463; *Retrospect*, p. 89) took the same view.

and so does not come up for annual review in the House of Commons when the estimates are presented, and the sums in question granted, by the Appropriation Act of that year. It seems odd that the salary of the Speaker of the House of Commons should be charged upon the Consolidated Fund by permanent legislation (2–3 Wm. IV c. 105 sects. 1 and 3) but not that of the Speaker of the House of Lords. The salaries of the judges of the Superior courts have been immune in the same way from Parliamentary review and criticism since the Act of Settlement, 1701. The pension of the Lord Chancellor was settled at £5,000 per annum by the Lord Chancellor's Pension Act, 1832, and was confirmed at that figure by the Judicial Pensions Act, 1959.[8] Before the salary was fixed at the present level the emoluments were considerably greater: Eldon's average annual income during his 24 years on the Woolsack was £14,718.

The Chancellor does not have the same powers of discipline as the Speaker of the House of Commons. It is the custom for the Peers to address not him but each other ('My Lords') and the maintenance of order is in the hands of the House itself. The Woolsack on which the Chancellor sits is also as we shall see technically outside the limits of the House. The Woolsack is a large square bag of wool covered with red cloth: it has no formal back or sides, but a small temporary back-rest provides some comfort during a long debate. (There is nothing really exceptional in the term Woolsack: sacks of wool were provided for important persons at meetings of medieval Parliaments—for example, the benches on which the Judges sat were so covered. It is commonly said that the term was adopted in recognition of the great commercial achievement of the English wool trade. A simpler view is that those who had to sit long hours on a wooden bench were anxious to be comfortable.)

On the judicial side the Lord Chancellor presides over judicial sittings of the House of Lords and occasionally over appeals to the Judicial Committee of the Privy Council. In this period there seems to have been a convention that the Lord Chancellor should preside on the hearing of appeals raising important points of Dominion Constitutional Law. Loreburn, Haldane, and Birkenhead each regarded this as a most important part of their duties. The Chancellor is also understood to be responsible for manning these tribunals. The selection of the appropriate Law Lords to hear an important appeal may be a difficult task. During this period the normal day of the Lord Chancellor was to preside over the hearing of judicial appeals from 10.30 to 3.45 or 4 p.m. with half an hour break for lunch. After leaving the Woolsack in his judicial capacity the Lord Chancellor returned to it almost immediately at 4.15 p.m. for the dispatch of legislative business, which occupied him until 7.30 or 8 p.m., after which there

8 For the pension, see also below, p. 397.

might be an official dinner as well as the Cabinet papers of the day to be read. Cabinet meetings (usually on Wednesday, but in a crisis more frequently), had also to be fitted in, as well as the mass of administrative business.

After 1945 the judicial side of the Lord Chancellor's work became much less noticeable. The reason for this is curious. The House of Lords has always adopted the theory that at any of its sittings business of a legislative or of a judicial character may be transacted. It is for this reason that the judgments are technically known as speeches (they are delivered standing, as in a debate) and that a motion is made at the end of the proceedings for the affirmation or reversal of the judgment which is under appeal. So too it is no more than a convention of the Constitution, although since 1884 a well-established one,[9] that lay peers do not attend the hearing of judicial appeals. Therefore the hearing of appeals took place on the floor of the House itself although for reasons of convenience the Chancellor and the Law Lords moved down towards the Bar of the House.[1] After the war rebuilding operations made it impossible to sit in the Chamber during most of the day. It was therefore resolved to commit the hearing of all appeals to an Appellate Committee which met in one of the Committee Rooms.[2] Another factor also affected the position. As a result of wartime difficulties the House began its sittings at 2.30 p.m.[3] and not at 4.15 p.m. and the Lord Chancellor was in effect faced with the choice between sitting in committee to hear appeals from 10.30 until 4 p.m. or of sitting on the Woolsack from 2.30 p.m. In practice most Lord Chancellors have taken the latter course, so that a judgment by a Lord Chancellor is now much rarer in the Law Reports than it used to be. This temporary device undoubtedly facilitated the progress of both judicial and legislative work, but it has also meant the functions of the Lord Chancellor have become less obviously judicial. This has several important consequences—not least that the Chancellor's knowledge of leading members of the Bar has lessened at a time when he has to fill an exceptional number of judgeships. 'But it is not out of harmony with the temper of English history that the chance location of a building operation should have had such far-reaching effects. That is precisely how our constitution has always evolved.'[4]

The Lord Chancellor is also the *ex officio* head of the Chancery division

[9] See Hood Phillips, *Constitutional and Administrative Law* (3rd ed.), p. 96.

[1] See the admirable cartoon in *Punch*, 14 February 1891.

[2] See the history of the practice in 162 H.L. Deb. 5s. col. 1326; vol. 166, col. 33; vol. 169, col. 19. The Committee reports back to the House. Conversely, when the House is not disposing of legislative business (e.g. in the parliamentary recess), the Law Lords still sit in the Chamber itself.   [3] Simon, *Retrospect*, p. 250.

[4] F. Cowper, 'The Judicial Jurisdiction of the House of Lords', *Burke's Peerage* (1953 ed.), p. cxxviii.

of the High Court and a member of the Court of Appeal but it is only very rarely that he has exercised his functions in these tribunals.

In his capacity as President of the Supreme Court of Judicature the Lord Chancellor has always been involved in considerable administrative work. He discharges the important public function of recommending High Court Judges for appointment and in practice is also consulted by the Prime Minister even as to judicial appointments falling within the latter's gift, for example the Lord Chief Justice, the Lords Justices and the Master of the Rolls. He also has responsibilities in relation to various minor appointments in the Courts and in relation to the Rules Committee of the Supreme Court. He also appoints County Court Judges and has considerable duties in relation to the proper administration of that branch of Judicature.

He also appoints and removes Justices of the Peace other than those in the Duchy of Lancaster not merely for England and Wales but also for Scotland. The Advisory Committees instituted under Loreburn have saved the Lord Chancellor some but not much work in this department. During this period there were sixty-two counties and 222 boroughs with their own separate Commissions of the Peace and thirty-seven counties in Scotland. There is also administrative work in connection with the office of the Public Trustee and the Land Registry.

He also has considerable ecclesiastical patronage, almost three times as much as the two archbishops together. As the livings in question are those valued at less than £20 a year in the reign of Henry VIII they are mainly the poorer benefices in the Church, so that the task of filling them is often difficult. They amount to twelve canonries and nearly 700 benefices.

It was not until 1934 that Sankey set up a permanent Law Revision Committee. Before that the responsibility of the Lord Chancellor for law reform, although admitted, had been exercised spasmodically. Selborne's great memorial was the Judicature Act of 1875, while Cairns produced the Settled Land Act, 1882, Halsbury the Land Transfer Act, 1897, and the Criminal Evidence Act, 1898. Haldane, Cave, and Birkenhead together steered through the great Law of Property Legislation of 1925. The great achievements in the field of statute law revision and consolidation were the work of Jowitt and so lie outside our period.

During the past twenty years the scope of the Lord Chancellor's duties has greatly widened with the coming of the welfare state. It has been recognized that he has a general responsibility for the exercise of judicial functions by special or administrative tribunals. In 1961 these were some 420 in number. There are also considerable new responsibilities connected with law reform, legal aid, and the Public Record Office. There has also been an increase in the political and legislative burdens of the office. In

1960 the Lord Chancellor was a member of twenty-three Cabinet committees and Chairman of no fewer than sixteen of them. It is surprising that an office of which Herschell in 1895 declared that the strain was too great for any man to bear for more than three years (a remark cited with emphatic approval by Haldane in 1918) should have been held from 1954 to 1962 by the same man, Lord Kilmuir.

All this administrative work has been accomplished with a small staff. Down to 1885 there were three main secretaries in the Lord Chancellor's office, the Principal Secretary, and the Secretaries of Commissions and Presentations, the former dealing with the appointment of magistrates and the latter with the ecclesiastical patronage. Each of these Secretaries was regarded as the personal servant of the Lord Chancellor of the day. To such an extent was this notion carried that when the Chancellor resigned the Great Seal the Secretaries were in the habit of destroying all the files in the office lest a successor might gain an unfavourable picture of how patronage had been exercised. In 1885 when Halsbury succeeded Selborne the Principal Secretary was R. C. Palmer, a relative of the Chancellor. He was induced to become a Visitor in Lunacy. Kenneth Muir Mackenzie was then appointed Permanent Secretary to the Lord Chancellor, an office which he combined with that of the Clerk of the Crown in Chancery. (These are distinct offices, the former being appointed by the Lord Chancellor and the latter by the Prime Minister. It is merely administrative convenience that has kept them joined together until the present day.) The two Secretaries—of Commissions and Presentations— continued in office as before. The only addition to the staff was the appointment of a Chief Clerk. In 1886 this was Adolphus Liddell, who was succeeded in 1916 by the Hon. (Sir) Albert Napier. The Mace-Bearer and the Purse-Bearer also discharged some clerical duties, mainly by courtesy of the House of Lords in appointing them to minor offices on the staff. For example the Purse-Bearer was generally also the Deputy Sergeant-at-Arms. In 1960 the staff was still small, thirteen in number apart from minor clerks and typists, but each of these thirteen held a professional legal qualification.

The political work of the Chancellors of our period, whether on the Woolsack or in Cabinet, will be fully described in the following pages. Lord Campbell rightly said that 'the history of the holders of the Great Seal is the history of our constitution as well as of our jurisprudence'.[5]

It is sometimes asked how far the position of Law Officer is a help to a candidate for the Woolsack. Of the twelve Chancellors during this period, three, Haldane, Sankey, and Maugham, had never been Law Officers at all. Their cases were, however, slightly different, for Haldane

[5] *Lives of the Chancellors*, vol. 1, p. viii.

had been an active politician while Sankey and Maugham had not, though they were known to have political views agreeable to the party in power. Of the remaining nine, four had been Solicitor-General (Halsbury, Herschell, Buckmaster, and Cave), and five Attorney-General (Loreburn, Birkenhead, Finlay, Hailsham, and Caldecote).

If we take the whole period from 1801–1940, there were fifty-one Attorneys-General, of whom no more than twelve became Lord Chancellor.[6] Five of these have been just mentioned; the remaining seven were Eldon, Lyndhurst, Campbell, Chelmsford, Truro, Westbury, and Cairns. Of the others, six never became judges at all—Wetherall, Follett, Atherton, Karslake, Lawson Walton, and Hastings, and one (Horne) rose no higher than a Chancery Mastership.

Of the Solicitors-General of the same period, eight became Lord Chancellor—St. Leonard's, Cottenham, Cranworth, and Hatherley, besides the four already mentioned. Garrow, Keating, and Brett rose no higher than puisne judgeships.

It has sometimes been said that the requirement that the Lord Chancellor should be a member of the government of the day has produced men of less than first-rate ability. It may have been so once. Shaftsbury, 1672–3, was generally regarded as a man of fashion (he was the last layman to hold the Great Seal just as at the beginning of the seventeenth century Williams, Bishop of Lincoln, was the last ecclesiastic) and Bathurst, 1771–8, was spoken of with scorn. But in modern times this has not been so. As Peel said in 1850: 'The political advantage of a Lord Chancellor to a government would be entirely relinquished if he were not a man of the highest eminence in the profession.'[7] Each of the Chancellors in our period had a substantial professional record, in some cases one of real distinction, at the date of his appointment.

In a general review of this period two questions deserve an answer. First, how did the office itself alter in its powers and functions? Secondly, how far did the men who occupied it change? As for the first question, the office of Lord Chancellor was in 1940 very much what it had been in 1885. Its structure had been simplified and improved but in broad outline the functions were the same. The big changes came after the 1945 War under Lord Jowitt.

Secondly, so far as the men are concerned, the fathers of three (Halsbury, Herschell, Hailsham) and the grandfathers of three (Haldane, Hailsham, Maugham) appear in the Dictionary of National Biography. The fathers of three (Halsbury, Loreburn, Birkenhead) had been barristers, of two (Maugham, Caldecote) solicitors and of one (Haldane) a Writer to the

---

6 See T. Mathew, For Lawyers and Others (1937), pp. 61–63.
7 Report of the Select Committee on Official Salaries (1850), C. 6617, p. 28.

Signet. Of the other six, one (Cave) was the son of an M.P., another (Hailsham) of a merchant philanthropist, a third (Herschell) of a non-conformist minister, a fourth (Finlay) of a doctor. Only two came from a background which was not solidly middle class—Buckmaster, the son of an agricultural labourer who later became an inspector in the Science and Art Department, South Kensington, and Sankey, the son of a draper in a provincial town. All twelve were at a public school (or institution which was later classified as such) except Halsbury, who was educated at home, and Herschell, who attended a south London grammar school. (Of the Chancellors from 1837–85 Cottenham was at Harrow, while Cranworth, Selborne, and Hatherley were all Wykehamists—though the last was expelled in 1818 for leading a rebellion.) All twelve Chancellors except one (Hailsham) were at a university, obtaining Firsts or Seconds in their final degree examination, except for Halsbury, who obtained a Fourth, and Caldecote, who obtained a Third. Five were from the Inner Temple (Halsbury, Loreburn, Buckmaster, Cave, and Caldecote), four from Lincoln's Inn (Herschell, Haldane, Hailsham, and Maugham), two from the Middle Temple (Finlay and Sankey) and one from Gray's Inn (Birkenhead).

In one respect the Chancellors of the late nineteenth and early twentieth centuries certainly differed from their predecessors. Most of these had accumulated a fortune while in office. Evelyn said that the predecessors of Cowper (1705–8; 1714–18) made at least £100,000 on the Woolsack. Eldon, who died worth over £700,000, probably made more out of the Great Seal than any other man in English legal history. The magnificent country houses built by eighteenth-century Lord Chancellors and Lord Chief Justices can not be equalled by their successors. If we take only those men who started from nothing in the struggle for success it is impossible to contemplate the architectural achievements of Hardwicke (Wimpole),[8] Mansfield (Ken Wood), Harrowby (Sandon), Kenyon (Gredington) or Eldon (Encombe),[9] without feeling that the worldly rewards of the Bar have greatly diminished in the last two centuries. The change appears to have come with Loughborough, who was content with 'an ugly villa of Baylis, near Slough',[1] partly in order to be close to the royal family. After Eldon it is noticeable that Chancellors cease to build on a splendid scale. Although they were in general men of substance, their wealth was not remarkable. In our period one left £200,000 (Hailsham) but he was a man whose family background was wealthy; another (Herschell) left

[8] Hardwicke paid £100,000 for Wimpole. At the age of 35, when Attorney-General, he paid £24,000 for Hardwicke.

[9] Eldon at the age of 41 paid £22,000 for the estate in Co. Durham from which he took his title.   [1] Campbell, *Lives*, vol. vi, p. 331.

£150,000. Of the others Cave, Loreburn, Halsbury, and Caldecote each left less than £30,000. Two of the Chancellors died unmarried (Haldane and Sankey). Only two of the remainder (Loreburn and Cave) died without issue. The remaining eight all left male descendants to carry on their families, some of whom attained considerable distinction in their own right.[2] In religion two were Presbyterians (Loreburn, Finlay), two professed their own brand of agnosticism (Haldane, Buckmaster), and the others were more or less faithful members of the Church of England. In the Victorian era three successive Chancellors (Hatherley, Cairns, Selborne) taught in Sunday Schools regularly, but in our period only Sankey and Caldecote were notable for their piety.

[2] It was not always so. In the eighteenth century Pope mocked at the sons of Cowper, Harcourt, Macclesfield and King:

> Why all the toils? Your *sons* have learned to sing
> How quick ambition hastes to ridicule—
> The Sire is made a Peer, the Son a Fool
> (*The Dunciad*)

LORD HALSBURY

CHAPTER I

HARDINGE STANLEY GIFFARD was born on 3 September 1823 at 12 Penton Street, Pentonville, then, as now, a small house in a shabby part of London. He was the third son and fifth child of Stanley Lees Giffard, LL.D., by his wife Susanna Meares, daughter of Francis Moran, J.P., of Downhill, Ballina, Co. Mayo.

The Giffards were an unusual family and Dr. Lees Giffard was an extraordinary man. The family were an authentic example of impoverished gentry of truly ancient lineage—a class which exists more in fiction than in history. The Giffards (whose name means 'fat-cheeked', or, according to other authorities, 'liberal') were rooted in Devon from the early twelfth century, at Weare Giffard. Successive cadet branches were settled at Clovelly, Halsbury, and Brightley, at which latter seat the family was resident at the time of the Civil War. This estate was duly ruined as a result of fines imposed for delinquencies and by the mid-eighteenth century John Giffard, great grandfather of the Lord Chancellor and head of the family, had lost his lands and was practising as an attorney and Coroner of the County of Devon. He visited Dublin in 1743 as a key witness in the famous Anglesey peerage series of cases; and while resident there married a widow, who was born Dorcas O'Morchoe of the Mac-Morrogh family that claimed descent from the Kings of Leinster. John died within three years of their marriage, leaving her with a son John barely eighteen months old. Seven years later the mother died. The orphan child was taken into the family of a barrister at the Dublin Bar, one Ambrose Hardinge who had been engaged with John's father in the Anglesey Case, which so excited Ireland in the seventeen-forties. Five generations of Giffards ever since have been christened Hardinge in gratitude for this Christian act. Hardinge fell on financial difficulties and apprenticed John to an apothecary, with a clause in the deed which provided that at the master's expense he should be made a freeman of the Corporation of Dublin, as eventually happened. He married in 1796 one Sarah, daughter of William Morton of Ballinaclash. After a time he prospered and built himself a house in Grafton Street, Dublin, where he seems to have taken up the trade of selling pharmaceutical materials wholesale. He was also active in the formation of the Irish volunteers from 1782 onwards. He then took up, in turn, parliamentary reporting and speculative building. When he was 39 he purchased land outside Dublin and built a house with the name of Dromartin Castle. At the age of 49, in 1794, he became High Sheriff of the city of Dublin. He and Grattan disliked each other intensely. Grattan described John Giffard as 'the dog in office', 'an impoverished ruffian', 'a bully in the senate and a coward in the field'. Giffard retaliated by saying of Grattan, 'False alike to his God and his country, with impartial cowardice he betrayed both'.[1] Giffard also incurred the strong dislike of Curran and of Sir Jonah Barrington, who said, 'he had a great deal of vulgar talent, a daring impetuosity, and was wholly indifferent to opinion'.[2] The evidence seems to show that in 1798 he was responsible for burning the town of Kildare and for the killing of some 500 rebels: on the other side of the account should be entered the fact that his son, William, aged 17, had been murdered by the rebels a few days before in the immediate neighbourhood. He wrote as follows to his wife on 17 June 1798 from Rathdrum in Co. Wicklow:

I trust the great and almighty God who has so often delivered us from the hands of our enemies will still be the defender of the Protestant cause of loyalty, religion and honour, for which your heroic son died a martyr. But Oh, my darling Sally, love my soldiers; they did not leave my hero unrevenged. Five hundred rebels bleaching on the curragh of Kildare, that curragh over which my sweet innocent girls walked so pleasantly with me last summer; that curragh was strewed with the vile carcasses of Popish rebels and the accursed town of Kildare has been reduced to a heap of ashes by our hands. Had they spared my darling young soldier, the town would at this moment be flourishing and perhaps not a rebel would have been sacrificed to his memory; but extermination is now the cry; the soldiers are by no means satisfied with what is done.[3]

He supported the union in 1800 and also managed the *Dublin Journal* and the *Dictator*, which were the leading Protestant organs of the day.

The High Sheriff had in all four sons, including John, who died young, and William, murdered in 1798. The eldest, Ambrose Hardinge, was educated at Trinity College, Dublin, and achieved distinction in the legal service of the Colonies, as so many Trinity men have done since then. He died a Knight and Chief Justice of Ceylon. The youngest son, Stanley Lees, became the father of the Lord Chancellor. The present Lord Halsbury has said[4] that nothing about Stanley Lees Giffard quite makes sense, 'nothing quite adds up', to use a modern colloquialism. He was certainly a very odd and independent person. Born in 1788, he graduated from T.C.D. in 1808, and spent from then till 1810 reading for the Bar in London. He obtained an LL.D. early in life and was always known as 'the Doctor'. In 1811 he was given an appointment in Co. Mayo under the Stamp Office. His father said:

[1] J. Barrington, *Personal Sketches* (1828), p. 154.
[2] Ibid., p. 155.   [3] Halsbury papers.
[4] Ibid.

PLATE 1

Lord Halsbury as Chancellor in 1885

PLATE 2

Lord and Lady Halsbury in later life

This produces him £500 this year but it has now for six months confined him in Co. Mayo settling distributors' accounts and shooting swans, seals and red deer with the rifle. Now, though the post is respectable and competent, yet it is wasting Lees' talents and education so to employ him. I did hope for something which would have allowed him to attend his term in London where he has been called to the Bar.[5]

On Christmas Eve 1812 comes a letter with the phrase 'that very odd fellow, your brother Lees, is still in Connaught impoverished, a great walker and fond of all field sports'. He married in 1814 Susanna Moran of Downhill, near Ballina. Susanna's grandfather had narrowly escaped in the rebellion of 1798. He was curate of Killala where the French landed. The marriage took place in the drawing-room at Downhill. The groom's father offered to settle £300 a year on the couple, but the offer was refused by his independent and cross-grained son. At the time of his marriage Lees was already involved with another woman, Jane Paton, who had borne him an illegitimate son. He seems to have been less than frank with either of the ladies. Also there was some trouble in the Stamp Office, due entirely to his negligence in not checking his predecessor's accounts. Fraudulent conversions, amounting to £4,000, came to light and eventually Giffard was imprisoned at Castlebar. The evidence seems to show that in fact he was quite willing to stay in prison in order to escape from his wife, his mistress, and his father. In the summer of 1816 he was released on the intervention of Robert Peel, then Chief Secretary for Ireland. His father wrote to Hardinge: 'Upon investigating the accounts with the Stamp Office, I think it will appear that they are in his debt, yet so indolent is he that though every facility is afforded him, and though I constantly urge him, he will not bring it to a conclusion nor go to London to pursue his profession.'[6]

There were other serious family difficulties and the correspondence shows a displeasing note of self-pity on Lees's part. Eventually, at the age of 30, he secured a post in London as editor of the *St. James' Chronicle*, a High Tory organ. He was an immediate success and in a few months was earning at the rate of £1,000 a year, though he never saved a shilling. In 1827 the compromising left wing of the Tory party under Canning was felt to be unsound on the subject of Catholic emancipation; and a new paper, the *Standard*, was founded to oppose all compromise on the subject of Catholic claims to emancipation. (The paper, rather surprisingly, lasted until 1916.) Lees Giffard became the editor of this publication as well as of the *St. James' Chronicle* and the *Morning Herald*, which he maintained until within a year or two of his death in 1858. He seems to have been a very curious person—vain, irritable, sulky, and rather dangerous—

[5] Halsbury papers.   [6] Ibid.

although a cultivated and scholarly man. He had a strong feeling of independence and in particular disliked the attitude of various members of the aristocracy towards him. He refused to become a founder member of the Carlton Club on the ground that 'I knew what the Club would become and what it has become, an instrument for paralysing the Conservative democracy at the humour of a few empty and insolent aristocrats aided by the servile class of place-hunters'. Further, 'I had reasons of a more private and personal nature. I hate the mean and vulgar manners of all the Irish gentry of the Lord and Member of Parliament class, and I knew that from the forwardness of these men they would soon give a mean and vulgar tone to the Club, which they have done. I am a poor and humble man, and therefore I hate the promiscuous great.'[7]

Of the various political issues which engaged Lees's attention during the quarter of a century in which he conducted the *Standard*, most were lost: Catholic Emancipation, the Corporation Act, the Irish Education Bill, Disestablishment of the Irish Church, and the defence of the Corn Laws. If these had represented the sum total of his interests he would indeed have been a champion of lost causes and there would be substance in the comment of the *DNB* that 'he was the exponent of an almost antique type of politics'. But in one sphere, that of factory legislation, he was progressive and successful. He regarded with loathing manufacturers and political economists of the Harriet Martineau School and was an early supporter of Shaftesbury.

In 1822-3 he was living at Pentonville where in 1823 his fifth child and third son, the future Lord Chancellor, was born. He was so weak that he was baptized at home by an Irish parson who forgot to register the event. Indeed, until 1916 it was stated in all the books of reference that he had been born on 3 September 1825, and it was only on reference to the books of Merton College that the true date of 1823 was confirmed from a statutory declaration made by his father. In 1828 Susanna died giving birth to her sixth child. At the age of 42 Lees married another girl in her teens, his cousin Mary Anne Giffard from Devonshire. He had four children by her, of whom one, Harry, became Registrar in Bankruptcy of the High Court of Justice. We first hear of Hardinge when a letter of 6 October 1826 informs his family that he has been ill at Margate but is now better. Back in London his childhood was spent at Myddleton Square, Pentonville. He always spoke affectionately of his stepmother. From time to time 'the Doctor' had to send his wife and children out of the country to Boulogne while he faced his creditors in London; nevertheless he successfully avoided bankruptcy. It was during one such exile that young Hardinge saw the pathetically unsuccessful attempt by Louis Napoleon to

[7] Halsbury papers.

acquire the Crown of France. He also acquired the qualification of *maître d'armes*, of which he was always proud. There is preserved in 'the Doctor's' papers a letter of 29 July 1850 from King's College, London, pressing for payment of an outstanding bill of £22. 10s.; it is endorsed in his handwriting: 'I leave this as a warning to my children and to their descendants never to expect gratitude or even decent behaviour from parsons of the Church of England. I was one of the first promoters of King's College and subscribed £25 to its creation'.[8] He also performed the very difficult task of educating his children himself, by getting up at four o'clock in the morning. There was a good deal of correspondence with Dr. Bliss, the Registrar of Oxford University, about sending Hardinge up to Merton, which clearly displays his independence and unwillingness to ask favours of anyone. He seems to have been disappointed by the progress of his elder son John; he wrote on 24 October 1838:

In truth I have been sometimes more than half convinced that I made a great mistake in sending him to a University. Oxford may be, and I doubt not is, for the classes whom assistance suits, an excellent place of education: but my sons do not belong to those classes. Unable from my large family and narrow income to employ a more finished scholar to superintend the education of these boys and abhorring the education of public schools, I have taught them myself precisely as I was taught. I have endeavoured to fit them to earn their bread by hard work, and have therefore laboured chiefly to give them the broad foundations and, as far as I could, the substance of that knowledge which they must use in after life. For all that I have seen, however, this is not the education that fits them for Oxford. The light matter which is picked up at public schools, almost habitually and without effort, if it were not disrespectful I would call it 'the cant of scoring' cannot be dispensed with, and from my elder son's despair I am inclined to think that even two or three years' hard reading (for he has while at home, at least, read very hard) will not accomplish a young man in it if he has been originally deficient.[9]

But in the event Giffard matriculated at Merton in 1842. The father found it necessary to mortgage his library in order to pay his son's battels, for although his journalistic career had brought him notoriety it had not brought him wealth. It is true that in 1840 one of his patrons, the Duke of Newcastle, offered to pay for Hardinge's education in a letter worded with exquisite tact[1] but 'the Doctor's' fierce spirit of independence obliged him to refuse.

Giffard enjoyed himself at Merton. The College was then a very small society—it had only forty resident members, including the Warden and Fellows. Giffard spoke at the Union, rowed in the College boat and made

[8] Halsbury papers.   [9] Ibid.
[1] A. Wilson Fox, *The Earl of Halsbury* (1929), pp. 14–15.

friends—particularly with two brothers, Berkeley and Francis Compton, the latter of whom became a Fellow of All Souls. In the spring of 1846 a letter from the former indicates that undergraduate correspondence does not alter much with the passing years:

Dear Giffard,

Do you remember my respected fraternity Frank lending you, when you were going up for your degree, some papers containing difficulties in Virgil. Now as he is now in the same condition, i.e., sweating himself violently and horribly in reading he has commanded and entreated me to write to you to entreat of you, if you have any bowels of compassion, which I very much doubt seeing that you are a bloody Irish protestant, to send him at once and immediately, the aforesaid papers, for as much as it seems very probable if you do not he will be plucked, as he has no time to get up his Virgil without them.[2] Old Bree is up here now. He is going in next Saturday. He observes a curious regimen, he eats and drinks as much as he can which as you know is no little, takes no exercise, reads like fun, and takes pills every night and a black dose every morning. I hope they will pass this coercion bill and keep you bloody Irishers indoors a little. I should like to see the griffinhoof dressed for an evening party with a sword and two pairs of pistols and not allowed to go out because it past seven o'clock. I hope all the little griffins are all right and have not been forced to come out into the street in their shirts to frighten the lamplighters! . . . Shinbones has got Halsa's rooms, and has done them up much in the style of a palace, with a gold piano in the corner, diamond bookshelf, and silver fire— (irons, you would say, because you are an Irisher) utensils, I say.

Yours truly
B. D. Compton[3]

Academically Giffard's career was not distinguished. He was placed in the Fourth Class in Greats in Michaelmas Term, 1845. The second Lord Halsbury wrote after his father's death:

My father owed his education entirely to my grandfather. The teaching at Dublin University was wholly different from that at the English Universities with the result that my father was taught Latin and Greek as living languages and a considerable amount of Hebrew. To the day of his death my father could read Latin and Greek as the ordinary person of good education today could read French.[4] I do not think that the right phrase is to say that he had a contempt

2 Francis Compton was placed in the Third Class in Greats, and Second in Mathematics.

3 Halsbury papers.

4 On the seventieth anniversary of his call to the Bar and in his ninety-seventh year (25 January 1920) he received a letter of congratulation from Lord Chancellor Birkenhead. The letter (which is printed in Wilson Fox, *The Earl of Halsbury* (1929), pp. 325–6) contained three lines from the Iliad (I, 250–2) in the original: Halsbury at once translated them for the family around the breakfast-table.

for meticulous scholarship as I do not think he had any contempt for honest work, but he took not the faintest interest in fine points of reading and of abstruse grammatical comment: but on the other hand I have never yet found any classical author that he had not read from end to end and remembered. The result of this education was to give my father a very broad view that was quite disastrous for examinations at Oxford, and I have heard him talk with some bitterness of people who he himself had taught taking far higher places than himself.[5]

His uncle, the Rev. Richard Ryan of Dublin, sent a consolatory letter on 27 November 1845:

Allow me to congratulate you upon your success which you undervalue. I know something of College examinations and it is my firm belief that the man who gets a Fourth Class without a tutor is as good, probably better than, the man who gets a First with one. The difference is that the latter is crammed with all the mysterious humbug which may happen to be the fashion for the time being, while the former depends upon his solid learning to carry him through. So it is here and I believe it is at Oxford.[6]

(It is perhaps worth noting that when Giffard became Lord Chancellor for the second time in August 1886 three of his colleagues in the Cabinet had also obtained Fourths at Oxford—although one (Salisbury) was also a Fellow of All Souls, and each of the others (Stanhope, Hicks Beach) had also obtained a First in some other subject.)

For the next five years Giffard led a somewhat unorganized life. From 1845–8 he helped his father edit the *Standard*. (He unsuccessfully urged his father to increase the circulation by reducing the price from 5d. to one halfpenny. It was to be left to the son of another unsuccessful Irish barrister, Alfred Harmsworth, to change the face of England by this device fifty years later.) They were years of great political excitement— the repeal of the Corn Laws, the Irish famine, the growth of Chartism. In 1848 he was sworn in as a special constable and was posted on Black-friars Bridge to defend the City against a revolutionary mob which never materialized. In the same year he began to read for the Bar and entered the Inner Temple. These were difficult years. At one time he collected testimonials from the Merton dons with a view to becoming an assistant master at King's College. Bullock-Marsham, the Warden, and Goulburn, the Senior Tutor, later to succeed Arnold as Headmaster of Rugby, wrote in the glowing terms which are customary amongst Oxford dons when testifying to the capabilities of young gentlemen who have been good members of the College but placed in the Fourth Class in Schools. But there are documents preserved which awaken less pleasant memories.

[5] Halsbury papers.   [6] Ibid.

There is an Oxford County Court summons, addressed to Stanley Giffard, 39 Myddleton Square, claiming £14. 12s. 3d. on a claim for goods sold and delivered by the plaintiff, one A. Williams.[7] The summons is for 26 February 1850. Presumably the claim was satisfied, for no further proceedings have been traced.

[7] Halsbury papers.

CHAPTER II

UPON BEING CALLED to the Bar on 25 January 1850 Giffard shared chambers with his brother John at 26 Chancery Lane. He does not seem to have been a pupil in chambers. The custom then may not have been so fixed as it became later. As was natural for a Giffard, he joined the Western Circuit. But next year he migrated to the South Wales Circuit, on the advice of one of his father's friends, Mr. Morgan, junior partner in Humphreys, Son & Morgan, who had heard that there was some dispute between the solicitors on the Circuit and the Bar, the effect of which was that the solicitors, as a protest against the then existing members of the Circuit, thought it proper to brief only those who had joined after the difficulties had arisen. So Giffard, among others, got a start which he otherwise would not have obtained. The first case in which he appeared in the High Court was before Lord Campbell, then Chief Justice, and he was the victim of an attack of extreme nervousness, hesitation and stammering. After a few minutes Lord Campbell, who was never the most patient of judges, leaned down from the Bench with the remark, 'For God's sake get on, young man'. This so stimulated Giffard that never again was he nervous in court. (It may here be said that Giffard had a horror of swear-words: he was never heard to use them, and was deeply hurt when Montagu Williams, in his notoriously unreliable *Reminiscences*, depicted him as saying 'By God'.) On the day of his call to the Bar he received from a solicitor-friend of his father his first brief—an action for assault in which the allegation was that the defendant had spat twice in the plaintiff's face. In old age Halsbury liked to recall that he obtained a verdict for the plaintiff for one guinea for each spit. He also liked to recall his defence of the man indicted for stealing the handle of the Swansea town pump, when he argued successfully that as the object was attached to the realty it was not capable of being stolen. Soon he felt confident enough of the future to marry at Tottenham, on 28 August 1852, Caroline Louisa, eldest daughter of William Conn Humphreys of Wood Green, Middlesex. His father-in-law was the senior partner in the well-known firm of City solicitors, whose junior partner had already given him good advice, so some work began to flow in Giffard's direction. (The bride's half-brother, it may be noted, was the father of the future Mr. Justice Humphreys.) By May 1855 Giffard's position was sufficiently established for his father to inform his sister Harriet that her nephew 'if the Almighty spare him, is destined to exalt and even ennoble our family.

Though but five years called to the Bar, Hardinge Giffard's name is as well known as that of any man in England'.[1]

Whatever the reasons for this success may have been, it was not due to Giffard's personal appearance. As a writer in the *Solicitors' Journal* said after his death:

He not only possessed little or no influence, but he had the disadvantage of an insignificant personal appearance; he was short in stature and without obvious external indication of his tremendous force of character, solidity of judgment, and practical common sense. Since success at the Common Law Bar depends largely on the impression made on solicitors who see a man in Court or moving about the halls and corridors of the Law Courts, and since our attention is usually drawn to a stranger by external qualities which seem to denote ability, a man of insignificant appearance has always a hard battle to fight.[2]

One physical disability may be recorded, as Giffard concealed it with such success throughout his life that its existence is not widely known. He was blind in one eye as the result of a blow in early life. Oddly enough, after he had passed ninety he gradually recovered the sight of this eye.

A relative who might have been of assistance to Giffard in starting at the Bar had died prematurely in 1845—Sir William Follett, Peel's Attorney-General, who had married a daughter of Sir Ambrose Giffard, the Chief Justice of Ceylon. Follett left behind him the reputation of being 'the greatest advocate of the century' and also an estate of £100,000—surely one of the greatest fortunes ever accumulated at the Bar by a man who started from nothing and died aged 47, worn out by his exertions.

While doing fairly well on circuit, Giffard's practice in London at this time was, strangely enough, mostly confined to the Chancery side. It has often been said that he was an Old Bailey lawyer and made his name at the Old Bailey. In fact it was not till later in his career that he made any success at the Old Bailey. Giffard always attributed his success in London to the remarks that were made about him in the case of *Feret* v. *Hill*.[3] The court were very much against him, and indeed every conceivable prejudice was against his case. A lease of premises had been obtained by a fraudulent misrepresentation that they would be used for lawful purposes. In fact the lessee used them for a brothel, whereupon the lessor forcibly ejected him. In an action for wrongful ejectment Giffard conceded that the lease might have been set aside for fraud, but argued that this did not mean that the lessee was automatically a trespasser. His leader, Massey Dawson, having failed to convince the court, he succeeded, and all the judges were exceedingly complimentary about his argument. It was a distinct achievement for a barrister of 4 years' standing.

[1] Halsbury papers.   [2] (1921) 66 Sol. Jo. 135.   [3] (1854) 17 C.B. 207.

But his appearances at the Old Bailey were not so frequent as has been imagined. This can be demonstrated from an analysis of the Old Bailey Sessions Papers, which are made up of shorthand reports of all trials there during the nineteenth century. If we take volumes 32 to 101, which cover the years 1850 to 1885, we find that his name appears in some 500 cases in all—i.e. approximately fifteen a year. The annual numbers do not seem, on a rough inspection, either to increase or to decrease with the passing years, but remain remarkably steady, though it is on record that he succeeded (Sir) William Henry Bodkin as Junior Prosecuting Counsel in 1859.

The very first case is *R. v. Clark* (1850), in which Giffard was for the defence in a charge of larceny. In *R. v. Hayes* (1853) we find him holding his first brief in a murder trial, and in *R. v. Barford* (1856) his first brief for the Bank of England (whose standing counsel he had become) in a forgery prosecution. In the following years he appeared for the Crown in a number of cases which attracted the customary label 'sensational'— *R. v. Desmond, O'Keefe, and Barnet* (1869), the Fenian Conspiracy to murder prosecution, and *R. v. Staunton* (1877), when, as Solicitor-General, he prosecuted in the horrible Penge murder case.

It may also be recorded here that at the Old Bailey in 1854 an insane clergyman, labouring under some grievance from a recent trial at Cardiff, fired a gun at him in open court. Fortunately the bullet missed its target. The assailant was tried before Chief Baron Pollock and sent to Broadmoor.

Something of Giffard's abilities at the Bar may be gathered from the unpublished reminiscences of his son, the second Earl of Halsbury, K.C.:

My father was a very quick worker, with a wonderful memory and he never made a note, for which reason he had the reputation of not reading his papers. In 1906 I joined the Chester circuit and the solicitor welcoming me asked if I would like to see an old brief of my father's. I was naturally interested and he produced a brief of very large dimensions which I read with great interest. The date was 1855: there was not a single note on it except on the last page there was written, in my father's handwriting, the times of three trains to London. On coming back to London I spoke to my father about that case: he remembered every single witness, he told me what they said, he told me which broke down and which were believed, he told me of the two important letters which won the case; he remembered the judge and every detail of the case[4]. His great admiration as a judge was Erle, and he always considered the great admiration of Lord Wensleydale much exaggerated. As a persuasive advocate he thought that the greatest he had ever heard was the unfortunate Edward James.

In the Tichborne Case (1871–72), he appeared for the claimant and at first believed him and that is a matter which throws great light upon his character. The thing which made him disbelieve in the claimant for the first time was that

[4] Many other instances of Giffard's extraordinary memory are on record.

the claimant did not remember his mother's Christian name. His view was that it was an impossibility for any son to forget his mother's Christian names, and from that moment he ceased to believe in him. The money ran short, and Ballantine wanted to retire from the case. My father pointed out that having taken responsibility for appearing for him it was impossible to retire half way through the case. He also stood out against Ballantine's other method of putting an end to proceedings, namely to consent to a non-suit. He said in terms that if the plaintiff consented to a non-suit he would undoubtedly be indicted for perjury with little chance of an acquittal. On the other hand, Bovill c.j. had given so many questionable decisions as to the admissibility of the evidence that he thought it would be possible to get a new trial, and as everybody had spent so much money if the claimant dropped the matter, nothing further would be done. He went on to Cardiff on circuit for one case and read next morning in the papers that in his absence Ballantine had consented to a non-suit.[5] When the claimant was tried for perjury he was offered the brief, but as already he had lost so much in practice over the case he did not desire to take it, and asked for a fee of ten thousand guineas, knowing that this would be prohibitive. The result of that trial is well known, but my father always maintained that it contained one of the worst bits of law ever decided in this country. The claimant was charged on two counts and found guilty of perjury. The maximum sentence was seven years, but he was sentenced to seven years on each count and for the first time in English law the sentences were declared to be consecutive. This point of law was very badly argued by Benjamin in my father's judgment because, as he pointed out, what earthly right has a judge to say 'you shall be sentenced to seven years' penal servitude, the sentence to begin in ten year's time,' and if you cannot do that, how does another sentence for another offence justify you in doing it?[6,7]

On the other hand, we have the testimony of Sir Harry Poland (1829–1928), who was engaged in practice at the Old Bailey all through this period, and in fact shared chambers from 1852 with Giffard—first at 7 King's Bench Walk and later at 5 Paper Buildings—until Giffard was appointed Lord Chancellor in 1885. His accuracy and sobriety of judgment are known to all lawyers. He must have known Giffard professionally and personally as well as any one in England. (He is believed, incidentally, to have refused a High Court judgeship when his old friend was in a position to distribute patronage.) In a memorandum sent to the Halsbury

[5] Lord Maugham (*The Tichborne Case* (1936), p. 313) says that Giffard allowed himself to be 'over-persuaded' by Ballantine in agreeing to a non-suit. Gilbert (*The Claimant* (1957), pp. 181–2) is critical of the Giffard family's account of events, but it is not easy to see why. Giffard was a singularly truthful and accurate man (much more so than Ballantine), and there is no reason why his son should have distorted anything in transmission.

[6] Halsbury papers.

[7] It is interesting to consider the decision in *R. v. Blake* [1961] 2 Q.B. 377 in the light of this statement.

family after the Lord Chancellor's death,[8] Poland confirmed that Giffard was lazy and often preferred playing billiards to reading his briefs. He also vouched for the truth of a well-known story of Giffard being locked into a billiards-room by a solicitor in order to induce him to read a large brief. When the door was unlocked Giffard was found asleep on the sofa with the brief, still untied, used as a pillow. This trait was also confirmed by F. W. Ashley, who worked as a junior clerk in their chambers: 'he never read a brief a second time, and rarely a first. Of course, his work was devilled, and half an hour's examination of the devil invariably put him in possession of all the relevant facts and points he required.'[9]

The sole pupil recorded as having entered the chambers of Poland and Giffard was Corney Grain, the well-known entertainer (called, Inner Temple, 1866), a relative of Giffard's wife. As Giffard loathed people whistling in his presence, there must have been some tension in their relationship.

In any event, by the middle 'sixties his practice both on circuit and at Westminster had grown considerably. This is shown by the following letter, which also reveals that he was not thought of by his contemporaries as an 'Old Bailey lawyer' pure and simple. John Greenwood, from the Treasury, wrote on 20 February 1864:

I saw the Attorney-General today upon a variety of matters and among others he referred to the application which had been made to him by, or on behalf of, counsel to hold government briefs at the Central Criminal Court in police and Home Office prosecutions. Though your name had been mentioned, I believe that you have not made any application yourself, and you are not put down in the Law List as attending the Central Criminal Court.

Now I have no authority to compromise the Attorney-General who has not yet decided upon his appointments; my object in writing to you is to know whether it suits your arrangements to attend personally at the Central Criminal Court in all such cases, and at the police courts in cases needing the assistance of counsel. Pray understand that these are questions of my own, and that the Attorney-General's appointments may be wholly independent of anything that I may say or report. It is because your name was mentioned from another quarter and I was unable to say whether your attendance at the Central Criminal Court could be always relied on, and whether you desired such an appointment, that I thought it best to get the answers from yourself.[1]

The Attorney-General in the Palmerston Government was Roundell Palmer, later Lord Selborne. Apparently he did not permit politics to interfere with the distribution of Crown briefs, for the previous November

---

[8] Halsbury papers.
[9] F. W. Ashley, *My Sixty Years in the Law* (1936), p. 20.
[1] Halsbury papers.

he had appointed Giffard prosecuting counsel to the General Post Office on the South Wales Circuit.

By now he felt strong enough to apply to Lord Chancellor Westbury for silk. He followed the old practice of writing to the senior members of his circuit to tell them of his intention. The Chancellor's reply, on 24 September 1864, cast in the chilliest prose of Victorian formality, was not exactly encouraging: 'The Lord Chancellor presents his compliments to Mr. Hardinge Giffard. It is not his Lordship's intention at present to submit any names to Her Majesty for promotion at the Bar, but whenever he does so he will take Mr. Giffard's request into his consideration.'[2]

But the following February he received intimation that the silk gown would be given to him. (It cost him £63. 6s. 6d. in fees.)[3] He was now in his forty-second year. The step, so often taken with trepidation, was a distinct success. In his first year in silk he doubled his income. When he went on circuit for the last time in 1874 he had three hundred retainers when he left Paddington station—a fact which vividly shows the changes which have come over the circuit system. But it should be remembered that fees then were very low by modern standards. It is believed that Giffard received only 400 guineas for the Tichborne case, and that the highest fee he ever received on any brief was 450 guineas for a defence in a murder trial.[4]

In 1867 he was retained for the defence of Governor Eyre, who was alleged to have put down a rebellion in Jamaica with excessive severity.[5] The chief allegation concerned a court martial which had sentenced to death Gordon, a local coloured politician. The Jamaican legislature had passed an Act of Indemnity, but as Eyre himself had signified the royal assent to this measure his opponents were not appeased. On his return to England a private prosecution for murder was instituted. It was just the sort of case to enthral the moral conscience of Victorian England. All the great men of the day—Mill, Tennyson, Dickens, Carlyle—took one side or the other. Giffard and Poland went down to stay with Eyre in Shropshire while the preliminary proceedings before the Market Drayton magistrates were being heard in March 1867. A bench of county magistrates in the eighteen-sixties were not likely to take too severe a view of the conduct of a colonial governor engaged in suppressing civil commotion, but the prosecution had produced some impressive evidence and Giffard called upon all his resources to persuade the magistrates to dismiss the case. Poland said that Giffard's speech was so effective that he reduced

[2] Halsbury papers.   [3] Ibid.
[4] Ashley, *My Sixty Years in the Law*, p. 22
[5] See B. Semmel, *The Governor Eyre Controversy* (1962), for further details.

some of the magistrates—and himself—to tears. Men wept easily in Victorian England, but Giffard always denied this.

Later Eyre wrote to Giffard, on 17 April 1867:

What a very satisfactory confirmation of the views of the Market Drayton justices was the action of the Grand Jury in *Nelson* and *Brand's* Cases in spite of the violent and partisan charge of Sir A. Cockburn;[6] you will have seen it formally announced that the Jamaica Committee now intend to proceed against me under the Governor's Act for misdemeanour. I have been trying to find out from Mr. Rose what they can do and his account does not seem very promising, for he states they may avoid going to a grand jury by getting the judges to grant a rule *nisi* on a criminal information and thereby force a trial without a chance of the interposition of the good sense and sense of justice of an English jury. Surely the judges of the court of Queen's Bench or even the partisan Chief Justice himself would not venture to do this when the prosecution can proceed as readily and more properly by indictment and thereby give me the advantage of a Grand Jury. I shall be glad to know what your view is on this subject as I confess I do not like being left to the tender mercy of Chief Justice Cockburn who, I dare say would act as immorally in his public capacity as he is said to do in his private life,[7] and after the specimen we had of his view in his charge to the Criminal Court Grand Jury it is quite clear he would do all in his power and beyond it to further the ends and objects of the Jamaica Committee. Is there no way of objecting to his having anything to do with the matter after his charge, or of insisting upon the prosecution proceeding by indictment, so as to ensure a Grand Jury?[8]

Eventually, however, the prosecution decided to proceed, in June 1868, by way of bill of indictment, which gave Eyre the protection which he sought, for after a favourable charge by Blackburn J., the bill was thrown out.

Giffard now felt secure enough to attempt to enter Parliament at the General Election of 1868. He secured adoption as Conservative candidate for Cardiff but after a rowdy contest was narrowly beaten. This was the last election held under the old system of open voting before the Ballot Act, 1872, came into force with its provisions for a secret poll.

At the end of the Long Vacation of 1873 private calamity overtook him. When he was on holiday with his wife in Switzerland a coach accident occurred on the edge of a narrow mountain road. Caroline Giffard was overcome by shock and died instantly in front of her husband. The happiness of their married life had been marred only by the absence of children.

[6] The Grand Jury had just thrown out a bill of indictment against Lt. Brand, the president of the court martial, and Col. Nelson, who had confirmed its sentence, despite a powerful charge by Cockburn C.J. suggesting that martial law was unknown to the common law.
[7] Cockburn had two illegitimate children. The Queen refused to grant him a peerage because of his reputation.   [8] Halsbury papers.

Giffard was now aged 50. He had taken silk and had a substantial practice in London and on Circuit. But it was not a practice of the highest class, either in quantity or in quality. He was not briefed in the heaviest civil cases arising out of commercial or shipping disputes. Even in the class of business at which he excelled—plain advocacy before plain men about plain matters—he had formidable rivals. There was Hawkins, there was Parry, and there was Ballantine. Further he had failed—albeit narrowly—to become a Member of Parliament; and it was generally agreed that a man had to enter the House of Commons before he was 40 if he was to make a success of it. If he had been the sort of man given to gloomy prophecies, the future would not have seemed encouraging. His claims to a High Court judgeship were not considerable; he might, perhaps, expect a County Court judgeship or even, given great good fortune, the recordership of the City of London. Meanwhile, as a childless widower past 50, with few interests outside his profession, he would become increasingly lonely and irritable.

Yet in a few years his career was to be entirely changed. The most important and interesting period of his life—now only half-spent—still lay ahead.

First he repaired the gap in his private life. Kind friends and relatives offered help. For some months he made his home with the Humphreys, whose calm friendliness helped him to recover his normal spirits. He also repaired a friendship with John Duke Coleridge, just appointed Lord Chief Justice, which had been broken by the tensions of the Tichborne case, in which Coleridge had been leading counsel for the successful defendants.

When the case for the claimant looked like breaking down, Coleridge called upon his counsel to throw up their briefs under penalty of being involved in the guilt of their client, adding that he spoke, 'however unworthily', as head of the Bar. (At that date the Attorney-General could still take private briefs.) Giffard's reply was admirable both in substance and in style as an expression of the independence of the barrister:[9]

In this court [the Attorney-General] is simply the counsel representing one of the parties, and he has no greater authority than any of the more junior members of the Bar present. I utterly refuse to have my conduct dictated, or insinuations made against me, by the Attorney-General or any other member of the Bar . . . I think nine out of ten people would have supposed that the Attorney-General meant to say my learned friends and myself were concerned in what we considered a fraudulent case. I will not characterise that assertion, but your Lordship will well understand how I *would* characterise it.[1]

[9] Giffard held firm views on this point, and supported the well-known argument of Brougham in the *Trial of Queen Caroline*: see an interesting letter printed in Rogers, 'The Ethics of Advocacy' (1899) 15 L.Q.R. 259, 265.

[1] Maugham, *The Tichborne Case* (1936), pp. 285–6.

As far back as November 1872 Coleridge had written to express his earnest desire to restore their former friendship. Now he wrote on 30 December 1873:

Thank you also for your kind words about myself. They are just like the treatment I have always had from you all my life at the Bar. I hope they are true in one thing, but whatever has fallen to my lot has at least not come to me at the price of personal honour and personal independence. So far I will not deny [something illegible] I have known you too long and have looked to you too often and too familiarly for you to doubt my sincerity in saying that in no other sense can I accept it. No man ever, I am quite sure, got to a great office with a lower opinion of his own capacity to fill it. I am often utterly dismayed to find myself where I am, but I hope and pray to keep simple and humble and then if I do as well as I can the profession I know will be very generous judges.

But I thank you most of all for the rest of your letter, for I think you could not have written it except to one whom you could honour by writing to him as your friend. I do feel it a great honour, my dear Giffard, if you will let me always be what I have always been, except for one short, dreary time when my own haste and inconsiderateness put our friendship in danger. Yet it is very hard indeed to be contented, let alone to be cheerful, under desolating sorrow like yours. I never knew grief like yours, but I have had keen sorrow in my time and I know how difficult, nay, well-nigh impossible, it is to find the substance of things hoped for, the evidence in our time of things not seen, in any faith which I at least have ever attained to. That the ordinary [?thoughts] on this awful matter are inadequate and unphilosophical I have thought for many years: but every year every day and hour deepens my conviction of the ineffable goodness and wisdom of our incomprehensible and inscrutable God, and my belief that somehow we are safe in his hands and our dear ones also. As an argument Butler on the 'Analogy' seems to me very sound and cogent. But it is hardly by argument, however grave and religious, that the heart is much affected. Yet I have never opened that great religious work without feeling at once calmed and strengthened by reading him. It is idle however for man to attempt to comfort another at such times as these. Men in earnest will always find comfort from God in ways as different as are the men themselves . . . Don't please think me unfeeling if I say that at any time if you should like to spend a quiet evening here absolutely alone, you will find friends who can understand and respect your sorrow. Only a word, I beg of you *as a favour*, not to address me differently from our old habits; in court, the proprieties must be kept, but out of court it would add much to the regret with which I left the Bar if my friends, you at any rate, made any difference.[2]

A few months later Giffard was at Windsor for the trial of a petition arising out of the General Election of 1874, at which he had once again been an unsuccessful candidate for Cardiff, being beaten by only nine votes. At Windsor railway station he intervened to help two ladies in

[2] Halsbury papers.

trouble with their tickets. The acquaintance prospered and on 14 October 1874 he married the younger one at Twickenham. She was Wilhelmina (Lynie), third daughter of Henry Woodfall of Stanmore by Sarah his wife. The Woodfalls were a solid legal family like the Humphreys, though unlike them in that their careers had been at the Bar rather than as solicitors. They were also related to the printing firm of Henry Sampson Woodfall, who appears in the *Dictionary of National Biography* (together with his brother and his son), and was famous for his publication of the *Letters of Junius*. The bride was 26. Neither she nor the bridegroom ever regretted the decision.

The events of this time were recalled by Sir Edward Clarke at the age of 75 in a letter which he wrote on 1 July 1916:

I have this morning been reading the judgment of Lord Halsbury delivered yesterday in the House of Lords in the case of the German Company. It is a fine, clear, strong deliverance[3] and would do credit to any judge, but Lord Halsbury was born in 1823 and this makes it an incident without parallel in the history of English law. I have written my congratulations to my old chief; I am moved to set down on paper some of my thoughts about him and his great career . . . It is now more than fifty years since I made his acquaintance at the Old Bailey where he had then the most lucrative practice. It was then a rough place and some of the older men had habits of cruel and offensive cross-examination and violent and unscrupulous advocacy, which Giffard's influence and example did much to banish from our criminal courts. He was not a great defender of prisoners: Ballantine and Parry were men in their prime, and had the most important defences; but his father-in-law, Charles Humphreys, had a large practice in criminal cases, in days before the public prosecutor was appointed, and Giffard was constantly appearing in important prosecutions. To listen carefully to the whole of a case when Giffard prosecuted with Poland for his junior and Ballantine appeared for the defence and Russell Gurney[4] was the presiding judge, was the best lesson a young barrister intending to practise in criminal courts could possibly have. There was no waste of time; no introduction of irrelevant matter; the facts were fully and carefully presented and with perfect fairness. Giffard was one of the many counsel I knew in the course of my fifty years at the Bar who had so strong an instinct of fairness and justice that it really was not possible for him to stoop to unworthy methods or take mean advantage of an opponent . . .

The letter, after relating an instance of Giffard's kindness to him at the Bar in the year 1865, continues:

A year or two later Giffard joined the National Union of Conservative

3 Not many will agree with the second of these adjectives. The judgment begins with one of the most involved and turgid sentences in the Law Reports, and is not very convincing: see [1916] 2 A.C. 307, and below, p. 77.
4 Recorder of the City of London, 1857–78.

Associations, and became a frequent speaker on political platforms. There he did very good service to his party. He was by no means an orator and he took very little pains in preparing his speeches. His appearance was not impressive: his voice was strong and clear but not musical; his gestures were violent and ungraceful. But he was always clear and plain-spoken, and obviously in earnest; the directness of his appeal never failed to command the attention of his hearers and often roused them to enthusiasm . . . In 1868 he stood for Cardiff and I went down to speak for him. He made a good fight of it but was beaten by 450. Six years later he fought again, and this time he was only beaten by nine on a poll at which 5,551 electors voted. By this time he had almost ceased to appear in the criminal courts and was in the full tide of a leading practice at Westminster.

So when I met him in London after the election I congratulated him on his defeat much to his astonishment. I explained. 'We have won and a strong Tory government will come in. If you had won by nine instead of losing our people could not have given you law office for fear you would lose the seat on going in for re-election.[5] Now you will have all the best of the election petitions and make a lot of money and when they are over the Party will find you a safe seat and make you Solicitor.'

It turned out as I expected. At Westminster, at Bolton, and at Windsor, he saved Conservative seats which looked almost hopeless and he earned something better than all the money, for at the Windsor trial he met the lady who became his second wife and who has for forty-two years ensured the happiness of his domestic life.

Then when the election petitions were all over he was made Solicitor-General and the borough of Horsham, which was thought to be perfectly safe, was offered him. He took it.[6] The truth was that he was never a good candidate. His speeches were excellent although an absolute lack of humour made them sometimes rather dull. But in canvassing the undecided voter he was a complete failure. He hated the task of going from house to house to ask for votes. Cardiff was too large a constituency for this work to be so important as in a small borough, but there Mr. Sherley his agent, complained bitterly that Giffard would sit at home reading French novels instead of going about to call on the electors, who told the hired canvassers that they wished to see the candidate. And when he did see them he did not always show the suavity and patience which they thought their due . . .

It was fortunate for the country as well as himself that in each of his marriages he had obtained something more than a happy companionship. In the first he had obtained a substantial practice at the Bar; by the second there was assured for his children a provision which enabled him to take without hesitation the peerage with which the highest judicial post in England is unfortunately burdened . . . [7] He was the greatest judge before whom I ever practised.[8]

One further memory of Giffard as a parliamentary candidate has been

[5] See below, pp. 38, 51, 325.
[6] But lost the election.
[7] In the margin here is the pencilled comment 'No'.   [8] Halsbury papers.

preserved in a letter from a Cardiff supporter to the Halsbury family in 1928:

I well remember going with my father to a meeting held in the St. John's Church school rooms to hear Mr. Giffard addressing his constituents shortly before his second combat, when one of the chief planks of the Radical platform was free education, whose supporters vowed would not cost the rate-payers more than a half-penny in the pound, and the National schools under the auspices of the Church of England would be done away with. He said that a half penny in the pound was the thin edge of the wedge—which he dismissed with a sardonic smile of disbelief. But his manner suddenly changed and with the little mannerism or habit which he had when he had something of greater importance to say whether in a court of law or at a public meeting, of slightly shaking his head from side to side and pinching with left hand finger and thumb his collar and raising his right hand with fore-finger extended, solemnly said: 'Gentlemen, if this iniquitous bill becomes law it will be the means of raising up a race of clever devils!' Many years later he repeated to the writer these words saying 'If I said those words I won't withdraw one of them'.[9]

This has the authentic tone of Giffard's political opinions.

One final example of Giffard's advocacy may be quoted, for it illustrates not only his marvellous readiness to seize the advantage of the last word, but also his wide reading and retentive memory. He once appeared for the plaintiff in an action of slander. The defendant was a member of a charitable association. His counsel had cited the text from the Epistle of James (i. 27) which defines true religion as being 'to visit the fatherless and widow in their affliction, and to keep himself unspotted from the world'. 'My friend has forgotten the text which follows',[1] said Giffard. ' "If any man among you seem to be religious, *and bridleth not his tongue*, but deceiveth his own heart, this man's religion is vain." ' Nobody in court was able to weaken the force of this extraordinarily apt reply. Giffard had a complete familiarity with the whole body of authors who are so famous that most people take them for granted—as G. M. Trevelyan has said, 'They are the bullion in the literary bank, bars cast out of coin once current, now stored deep in the vaults, while the affluent society above thrives on short-term paper.'[2]

[9] Halsbury papers.
[1] In fact it is the preceding verse.
[2] (1960) T.L.S. 238.

CHAPTER III

THE EVENTS LEADING to Giffard's appointment as Solicitor-General in the Conservative Government have already been outlined. An exceptionally rapid turnover of Law Officers occurred. First they were Karslake and Baggallay; then the former retired because of ill-health, and the latter, after succeeding him as Attorney-General, was promoted almost at once to the Court of Appeal, whereupon the new Solicitor-General, Holker, succeeded Baggallay as Attorney-General. Who was to be the new Solicitor-General? So many changes had left rather a dearth of Conservative lawyers in the House, though the claims of A. G. Marten, Q.C., lately elected for Cambridge, were well thought of by his friends and by himself. Senior to him was Staveley Hill, Q.C., who had been in the House since 1868 and was Recorder of Banbury and Deputy High Steward of Oxford University. Other Conservative Silks in the House were Bulwer, Lopes, and Forsyth. But the Prime Minister's choice fell on Giffard, as Clarke had predicted. (Giffard, perhaps naturally, thought little of Marten and Staveley Hill: we shall see later how he disposed of their claims to judgeships.)

The position was offered in a letter in October 1875 from the Prime Minister:

2 Whitehall Gardens

Sir,

The office of Solicitor-General being vacant, I shall have pleasure, if consistent with your own wishes, in recommending the Queen to appoint you to that post in Her Majesty's service. The tenure of the office necessarily involves obtaining a seat in the House of Commons, but I trust, an opportunity may be found to accomplish this.

I have the honour to be,
faithfully yours,
B. Disraeli[1]

The offer was accepted and so at the age of 52 Giffard became a Law Officer with the customary knighthood, which was conferred on 27 November.

Disraeli himself seems to have had some doubts, for he wrote to Lady Bradford shortly afterwards wondering 'whether the new Solicitor-General would turn out such a strong man as some of his friends supposed

---

[1] Halsbury papers.

but at any rate I shall have a lawyer of high reputation, who will be able to state his opinions with effect'.[2]

The task of finding a seat was not an easy one. The unsuccessful attempt at Horsham has already been mentioned. Now nearly a year had gone by and the Solicitor-General was still out of Parliament. The Government took alarm, and the Lord Chancellor wrote in polite but ominous terms:

Confidential.   14th September 1876
My dear Solicitor-General,
            A vacancy on the bench will occur on the promotion of Mr. Justice Blackburn and I shall be happy if it is agreeable to you to submit your name for Her Majesty's approval to fill it.

I do not know whether you will be inclined to relinquish for the repose and dignity of the ermine your prominent position at the Bar, but it is only fair to you that I should on an occasion like the present, communicate with you frankly as to the relations between the Government and the Law Officers of the Crown.

It has been a matter of much regret and no small inconvenience to the Government that owing to the difficulty you have found in obtaining a seat in the House of Commons, they have been, during the past session, deprived of the advantage of your aid in Parliament. They would deeply regret that a continuance of this stage of things would lead to a severance of their official connection with you; but it would be absolutely necessary if this connection is to continue, that you should be able to meet Parliament at the commencement of the ensuing session with a seat in the House.

The Prime Minister wishes me to express to you the satisfaction he would feel if both the present Law Officers had seats in the House of Commons, but he is convinced that you will see how indispensable this condition is to the tenure of office.

                         I remain, my dear Solicitor-General,
                                             yours faithfully,
                                                      Cairns[3]

        The reply to this, dated 20 September 1876 says:

Permit me first of all to express to the Prime Minister and yourself, my sense of the kindly tone of your communication. In anticipation of the difficulty which might arise unless I were provided with a seat in the House of Commons, a seat (I believe a perfectly safe one), has been provided for me. The writ will be issued for the first day of the session, and I have myself no doubt of the result of a contest, if a contest there be. Under these circumstances I feel myself justified in declining the great honour your Lordship is good enough to offer me, an honour however, which in my case would involve the most acute feelings of

[2] G. Monypenny and S. E. Buckle, *Life of Disraeli* (1929), vol. ii, p. 738.
[3] Halsbury papers.

disappointment as it would involve the relinquishment of my participation in political life.

It still remains my hope that I may be of some service in the House of Commons, and I certainly do feel with the Prime Minister that without a seat in the House my official connection with the Government could not continue.[4]

A constituency had been found—Launceston—but it required all the arts of the Whips to secure Giffard's return in February 1877. Launceston was dominated by the Warrington Park Estate: 175 of the 795 electors were tenants of its owner, J. H. Deakin, a Lancashire merchant who had acquired it from the Duke of Northumberland. At the 1874 election Deakin had been returned but later unseated for corrupt practices, as he had allowed his tenants to shoot rabbits on the estate on nomination day.[5] His son was then returned in his place, but was induced to retire in Giffard's favour.

The new Member lost no time in making his maiden speech. On 10 April 1877 he opposed a resolution that it was desirable to supervise more closely the funds of city companies on the ground that the proposal amounted to 'a sort of general communistic inquiry'. The great city companies were, he said, unincorporated bodies whose property was vested in trustees. They were not like limited liability companies but were rather analogous to the Inns of Court and the clubs of Pall Mall. A later speaker retorted that Giffard's speech 'would have done honour to the days of Lord Eldon and Lord Lyndhurst'. This comparison, which was to follow Giffard throughout his career, was repeated in June of the same year by Henry James, M.P., in a debate on capital punishment, which Giffard had defended on orthodox lines.

Giffard's time as Law Officer was not exciting. He appeared for the Crown in the case of The Franconia (1876),[6] in which the question was argued before fourteen judges whether the Central Criminal Court had jurisdiction to try an alien for a criminal offence alleged to have been committed within territorial waters. It was held by seven judges to six, one having died, that there was no such jurisdiction. He also appeared at the Old Bailey together with the Attorney-General, Holker, to prosecute the Stauntons in the once notorious Penge murder case, in which Lewis Staunton, together with his brother and his mistress, were indicted for the murder by starvation of Lewis's wife—a wealthy but feeble-minded girl. The defence strenuously argued that her physical condition indicated tubercular meningitis and not starvation. A conviction was secured after

[4] Halsbury papers.
[5] See Drinkwater v. Deakin (1874) L.R. 9 C.P. 626.
[6] R. v. Keyn (1876) 2 Ex. Div. 63.

a summing-up from Hawkins, J., which lasted for 10½ hours, but the prisoners were later reprieved.[7]

There was one other major prosecution in 1877—four detective officers and a solicitor were indicted for conspiracy to commit various frauds and obstruct the course of justice. Both Law Officers again appeared for the Crown and a conviction was obtained.

His relations with Holker, a large and humourless Lancashireman, who had a great reputation in his day as a winner of verdicts, were sometimes strained. During February 1878 in the course of the debates on the Territorial Waters Jurisdiction Act which was passed to reverse the decision in *The Franconia*, Giffard received the following letter:

I shall esteem it a favour if you will inform me whether you have been instructed to reply to Harcourt by Sir Stafford Northcote's directions. I make this inquiry for this reason—the debate which is going on is perhaps the most important debate which has occurred for years, and as Harcourt is the only lawyer in the House who has indicated an intention of raising any points of law against the Government, I naturally, as Attorney-General, prepared myself to reply to him and I felt, I must say, somewhat surprised when I found that you had been deputed to perform this task. Of course I have no desire now to make a speech in answer to Harcourt for under the circumstances I could not do it with any spirit, but I should like to know whether I am indebted to Northcote for the slight which has been put upon me, or merely to the Whips.[8]

The defeat of the Disraeli Government in 1880 led to 5 years in which Giffard consolidated his position at the Bar as one of the foremost jury advocates of the day—in an age when there were at least half a dozen formidable rivals in that class of litigation. His greatest achievement was indubitably the libel action of *Belt* v. *Lawes*,[9] in which he obtained a verdict for the plaintiff under very difficult circumstances. Giffard's client, Belt, was a sculptor aged about 30 who had produced, amongst others, the statue of Byron in Hyde Park. He had for some time served an apprenticeship in the studio of Charles Lawes, the elder son of a wealthy baronet, and there had been for some years rumours that Belt, who had now set up on his own, was a man of no real artistic ability but simply a clever showman who paid others to execute busts, which he then passed off on the public as being his own work. These rumours had their origin in a Belgian named Verhyden who had worked for some years with Belt but later quarrelled with him. Belt's friends provided the funds to enable him

[7] See *The Trial of the Stauntons* (1911), ed. J. B. Atlay (Notable British Trials Series).
[8] Halsbury papers.
[9] Accounts of the case may be found in several places—e.g. J. Dean, *Hatred, Ridicule, or Contempt* (1953), p. 150; T. A. Humphreys, *A Book of Trials* (1953), pp. 3–10.

to sue and Giffard appeared for him. Lawes was represented by Charles Russell, Q.C., and Richard Webster, Q.C., two future Attorneys-General. In his opening speech Giffard stated that Belt was prepared to execute any work supplied by the court in order to show the libel was untrue and Belt, in the witness box, under a ferocious cross-examination by Charles Russell, repeated the offer several times. The presiding judge was Baron Huddleston, who was apt to remind people that he was the son-in-law of the Duke of St. Albans. He permitted his court to be turned into something of a show room for the occasion, the Bench being crowded with ladies and the court room itself ornamented with a large number of busts which were said to be the work of the plaintiff. The trial began on 21 June 1882, but after proceeding for seven days was adjourned for no less than 4 months in order to enable the judge to go out on the summer assizes. It was then resumed before the same jury for 36 days—with a shorter interval from 30 November to 5 December to enable the judge to attend the opening of the new Law Courts in the Strand. There was also another adjournment over Christmas, the verdict not being given until 28 December. Eventually, the plaintiff's offer to produce a bust was agreed to and he began work on it under the supervision of an officer of the court on 16 November, the jury being at liberty to watch him at work during the midday adjournment. On 13 December the bust was finished and produced in court. In the interval the defence had produced no less than twenty-five witnesses from artistic life to say that the plaintiff's works were useless. The bust in question was of a Mr. Pagliatti, who was chosen because there was already in the court a bust of that gentleman done by the plaintiff. When the second bust was produced most of the expert witnesses were recalled to voice their approval of the first bust and their disapproval of the second one. The suggestion was that the first had been finished by another hand, which had imparted to it whatever artistic merits it possessed. But the plaintiff was able to call a number of sitters who swore that their busts were completed in their presence, and the jury eventually disagreed with the opinions of the experts. No doubt they were influenced by the evidence given by Verhyden, who made a particularly bad witness. He produced a diary written, as he said, from day to day 'in case it should be required in the event of a quarrel'. Giffard's final speech, in which he had to make little of the opinions of the Royal Academicians, was an impressive affair. In his peroration he said, 'This is a case to which, I believe, for wickedness of charge, for meanness, for malice in persistence therein, the ingenuity of man has found and can find no parallel—in which you will not measure with a niggard hand the amount you will give against the persons responsible.' The judge summed up in favour of the plaintiff and the jury, after retiring for 35 minutes, returned a verdict in his favour for £5,000. In January 1883 there was a motion for a new trial on the grounds that the damages were excessive and the verdict was against the weight of the evidence. In July the Court of Appeal announced that it was divided on the question—the majority being in favour of a new trial, but not agreed on the grounds on which it should be granted. But formal judgment was not given until the following December, when a compromise was reached, the damages being reduced to £800. The public heard no more of as barren a piece of litigation, involving an unconscionable waste of time and money, as perhaps can be found in the legal annals of any country. Even then the unfortunate Belt never secured his damages because Sir John Lawes permitted his son to file his petition in bankruptcy rather than pay the damages and costs.

But the effect which Giffard's conduct of the trial had on his professional reputation can be clearly seen from the letter which he received from one of the most eminent of City solicitors:

9th February 1883

My dear Giffard,

   If this letter offends you throw it in the fire and light it, if it does not, it may be worth a few moments' thought; probably you have done all that is necessary in the thinking way long ago but I do hope that in consideration of the past you will not consider this present impertinent.

Benjamin is gone and you are without flattery, pre-eminent at the Bar. You are the only man who can tackle and dispose of Horace Davey. Why don't you take the position Benjamin did, throw over all work in Divisional courts and go nowhere but to the Appeal courts under a special fee of one hundred guineas.

You are too good for *nisi prius*, your judgment, power of expression, and utter freedom from talking nonsense for talking's sake, and what is better, your power of grasping all the facts of a complicated case, make you *the man* for the House of Lords, Privy Council and Appeal Courts. My belief is whatever your income may be now, that you would add immeasurably to it by doing little or nothing but Appeal business, and it would save you from the nuisance of having to trot about from court to court. I am not chaffing or joking but I mean what I say.

Now I must apologise for having written as I have done, but you will I know excuse me for fancying the man whom I have known longest of anyone at the Bar and who has fought with me many touch-and-go cases is and must be the best.

Yours very sincerely,
William D. Freshfield[1]

The distinguished solicitor who wrote this clearly did not think that Giffard was simply an Old Bailey lawyer like Poland or Ballantine or Hawkins.

[1] Halsbury papers.

On the parliamentary side, two events in the year 1884 deserve to be recorded. In May he joined the Liberal Solicitor-General, Herschell, in moving a Bill which would have permitted an accused person to give evidence in a criminal case. This was a reform which Giffard always favoured, though it was not until 1898 that, as Lord Chancellor, he was able to secure its enactment in the Criminal Evidence Act of that year.

In October 1884 he made a considerable name for himself by a powerful speech in the House attacking Joseph Chamberlain, then President of the Board of Trade, for his complicity in the Aston Park riots at Birmingham, when a gang of roughs organized by the powerful Liberal caucus of that city had broken up a Conservative meeting amidst scenes of deplorable violence. The roughs may have gone further than their employers had intended, but there was a distinct feeling that the latter might have closed their eyes and ears to facts which it would have been awkward for them to have known. It was the kind of issue which showed Giffard at his best —an acute conflict of evidence on an issue of fact, together with a suspicion of dishonest concealment on the part of the defendants.

So that when Gladstone resigned in June 1885 Giffard's claims upon his party were generally conceded to be strong.

CHAPTER IV

WHEN SALISBURY CAME to fill up the position of Lord Chancellor the two possible candidates were Giffard and Brett, the Master of the Rolls. Of former Conservative Law Officers Baggallay was on the point of retirement after ten years in the Court of Appeal, while Karslake and Holker were both dead. Cairns, who had been Lord Chancellor under Disraeli, had died the previous April at the age of 66. Even if he had lived, it is doubtful if his health would have permitted him to resume office. So Salisbury's choice lay between Brett and Giffard.

A knowledgeable contemporary publication states that Sir Baliol Brett was first selected, but 'in view of a very strong representation from an important section of the older Conservatives'[1] Giffard's claims were preferred and Brett was consoled with a peerage. In truth Brett's claims were not too strong: he had been M.P. for no more than two years and Solicitor-General for only a few months in 1868 and had then accepted a puisne judgeship. He was also personally unpopular with some members of the Carlton Club. But there were some days of agonizing uncertainty before Giffard announced on 18 June, after an interview with Salisbury on the 17th, that he was returning his briefs. The disappointed candidate sent a friendly note of congratulations beginning 'Dear old Boy', but promising to be more respectful in future.[2]

It was often said that Giffard was given the Great Seal instead of Brett as a result of pressure from Lord Randolph Churchill. But when Atlay repeated this story,[3] and his publisher sent a complimentary copy of the work to Halsbury, a letter came from Ennismore Gardens on 29 May 1908 protesting against the statement in strong terms.

Now considering my relations in the last Parliament of 1885 with the fourth party on the one side and with Lord Salisbury on the other, this is absolutely, I had almost said ludicrously, inaccurate. I think I know to what incident the legend, as the writer describes it, refers and how he was misled but I could not write a letter thanking you for the volume just received without protesting against the legend in question.[4]

The best verdict on the appointment is that of Sir Herbert Stephen, who spoke with unusual professional and personal knowledge: 'His claim to

[1] *Annual Register* (1885), p. 108.
[2] Halsbury papers.
[3] J. B. Atlay, *The Victorian Chancellors* (1906), vol. ii, pp. 440, 441.
[4] Halsbury papers.

the Woolsack was admitted on reflection; his ability to occupy it with distinction was widely doubted by superficial observers. Such doubts were laid to rest before the Government went out of office in January 1886.'[5]

So Giffard received the Great Seal on Wednesday 24 June 1885 and was sworn in before the Master of the Rolls on the following day. Various documents attest to the complexity of the changeover from Lord Selborne, who sent a note, couched in somewhat stiff terms, concerning the keys of the various official boxes and safes. Another, more cheerful, arrived from Muir Mackenzie, later Permanent Secretary to the Lord Chancellor: 'Since seeing you I have ascertained that when you leave the Queen's presence, having received the seal, the messenger of the Great Seal as he is called, will meet you and give you the keys of the cabinet boxes and of the seal box and receive the seal from you, it being his duty to look after it.'[6] *Hansard* records that on 25 June 'The Rt. Hon. Sir Hardinge Giffard, Knight, having been appointed Lord Chancellor, sat Speaker'.[7] The next day his patent of peerage had been made out, and Giffard was introduced as a peer under the title of Lord Halsbury, of Halsbury, in Devon—a small place in the parish of Parkham, between Clovelly and Barnstaple, which was one of the former seats of the Giffard family.[8]

It may be permissible to describe here the nature of the Great Seal and the manner of its use, as even lawyers are curiously ill-informed on the subject.[9]

The Great Seal Act, 1884, and regulations made under it, provide for the classes of state documents which must be authenticated by the Great Seal of the Realm. The authority for the affixing of the Great Seal is a sign-manual warrant, prepared in the Crown Office. This is a brief, formal document signed by the monarch and counter-signed by the Lord Chancellor, a Secretary of State, or other appropriate minister. When this is returned to the Crown Office, the Great Seal is affixed to the letters patent, commission of assize, pardon, or whatever the document in question may be.

It should be noted that the Great Seal itself is not a signet seal, but consists of two heavy silver discs or plates, on one of which, the Great Seal proper, is cut the impression for the obverse of the device, and on the

[5] *DNB, 1912–1921*, p. 211.   [6] Halsbury papers.
[7] 298 Parl. Deb. 3s. col. 1631.
[8] Giffard originally intended to take the title of Brightley, an older family property than Halsbury, but desisted on finding that the Brightley estate was owned by another peer (Lord Clinton).
[9] See H. C. Maxwell-Lyte, *Historical Notes on the Great Seal*, H.M.S.O. (1926), pp. 313–20.

other, the Counter-seal, the impression for the reverse. (Much confusion has resulted from a failure to distinguish between the Great Seal as a matrix and the Great Seal as a wax seal.) These designs, which vary for each monarch, are of varying artistic merit. On some occasions the designer has forgotten that finicky detail does not reproduce well in wax.

The wax for the Great Seal is not put directly upon the paper or parchment in question, as in ordinary seals, but is in the shape of a large disc bearing the obverse and reverse impressions of the two silver plates. When a seal is required a large chunk of wax is first softened in hot water (hence the official in charge was once called the Chaff Wax (*chaud cire*)), and then cooled in cold, after which it is placed between the two plates and pressed, emerging in the above-mentioned shape. This disc of wax is then attached to the document by a tag imbedded in the wax. The disc itself is often kept in a tin or plated case. The wax, once a disagreeable khaki shade, is now coloured red.

When a new Great Seal is required, it is customary for the old silver discs to be 'damasked',[1] or formally rendered useless, by being tapped with a hammer by the Lord President of the Council. The seals so 'damasked' are the perquisite of the then Lord Chancellor, though it has been known for one of the discs to be handed over to a sealless predecessor. This happened in both 1830 and 1860, according to Lord Campbell. It was not done in 1930 (Sankey), 1938 (Hailsham), or 1948 (Jowitt), but in 1948 only the Great Seal, as distinct from the Counter-seal, was renewed.

In 1897, a new Great Seal was prepared, the old one being worn out. New seals had been cast during the Queen's reign only in 1838, 1860, and 1878. The cost of the new seal was £400, which compared very favourably with £513 in 1828 and £413 in 1860, for the seal and counter-seal each contained over 130 oz. of solid silver.[2] The new seal was delivered to Halsbury in March 1900, at a meeting of the Privy Council, and the old one became a family heirloom in a way described in the following letter from Muir Mackenzie to Lady Halsbury:

I am very glad indeed that the dear old seal has reached its home at last. Even after we had laid salt on its tail, the slippery monster tried to elude our grasp as I dare say the L.C. told you, but regardless of all constitutional possibilities we held on. The baby seal is a little awkward in its movements just at first but it will soon learn to jump straight.

I certainly think the best thing to do with the old one is to have a case like its own: a sort of bivalve, so it may lie open on a table of interesting and virtuous objects, and close up when it is to lie by.[3]

[1] Pronounce da-másk.
[2] See 83 H.C. Deb. 4s. col. 1512.   [3] Halsbury papers.

This was in fact done, and the case in question is on the desk of the present Lord Halsbury. Unfortunately one of the Lord Chancellor's purses (the history of the purse is considered later[4]) was sold by the second Earl of Halsbury in 1936, and is now in the Cromwell Room of the Association of the Bar of the City of New York at 42 West 44th Street, N.Y. But two others are in the possession of the third Earl, and a fourth in that of Lady Flavia Anderson.

A second Great Seal was similarly acquired after the accession of Edward VII in November 1904. An observer noted that 'The vivacity and agility of the octogenarian Chancellor in performing his genuflexions and supporting the weight of two seals was astonishing.'[5]

Nowadays the ceremony is more simple. When an old seal is superseded its presence in the Council Chamber is deemed to be a sufficient surrender: it is not actually handed over. When the Order-in-Council relating to the new seal has been approved, the monarch moves forward to the table on which the new seal has been placed, followed by the Lord Chancellor, and each in turn places his hand on it.

Another missive from the lively pen of Muir Mackenzie dealt with the entertainment, oddly described as a Breakfast, which the Lord Chancellor gives on the first day of Michaelmas Term.

August 31st 1885

Will you and Lady Halsbury authorise me to make arrangements as to the entertainment at the House of Lords on the 26th of October. I will let you know what the expense will probably be before giving the final orders. There has to be one, a buffet with refreshments of, as you will recollect, a light sort, for the judges and Q.C.s. It may be a question whether it would be better for you to send the *sherry* from your own house or to leave it to the contractor to supply. Two, a feed of some sort for the various retainers, clerks, train-bearers, tip-staves—strange creatures who gather themselves together out of all the forgotten crannies of obsolete jurisdiction for that occasion—this consists I think chiefly of cold beef, not without beer. Thirdly, two loving-cups which are supplied by a customary contractor in which the L.C. and the Lord Mayor-elect pledge one another. Fourthly, one shilling a head to a further legion of coachmen and lesser fry who used to be entertained but had their vested rights commuted by Lord Cairns, I believe, for a shilling . . . The Lord Chancellor receives the Lord Mayor at eleven-thirty and the judges at twelve. It would be quite convenient to receive the Prince in the private room at the House of Lords and not admit him into the general reception room. He is a very dangerous guest: he once got into Lord Cairns' dining room and ate up the judges' luncheon.[6]

[4] See pp. 480-1.
[5] A. FitzRoy, *The History of the Privy Council* (1928), p. 306.
[6] Halsbury papers.

Further advice on this unusual social function came from the same source a few years later: 'The extinct volcanoes never attend the L.C.'s reception. You never invited either Lord Selborne or Lord Herschell, the embarrassment of expectant County Court judges if they met on that occasion both the present and the future L.C. would be too acute.'[7]

The year 1886 saw two changes on the Woolsack. In February, as we shall see, the Salisbury Government went out, and Herschell became Gladstone's Lord Chancellor. But in August Halsbury resumed the Great Seal after the General Election had returned a strong Conservative Government which held office until 1892. In July and August 1886 Halsbury was closely connected with the Prime Minister in his task of Cabinet-making. Salisbury seems to have felt some obligation to Macnaghten, a distinguished Q.C. among the Conservative members, who had been passed over as a Law Officer in the government formed in June 1885. (The Law Officers then appointed were both common law men—Webster and Gorst. The former was not even an M.P. (and so had to be accommodated with Halsbury's own seat at Launceston), and his appointment aroused the indignation of Edward Clarke, who wrote a strong protest to the Prime Minister, of which he characteristically sent Webster a copy.) It was proposed to offer Macnaghten the post of Home Secretary, which had been refused by Webster on the ground that he did not wish to abandon his profession. The Prime Minister wrote to Halsbury on 28 July:

I hope you will not mind seeing Mr. Macnaghten (he is now at his rooms, 3 New Square, Lincoln's Inn) for me. He might be pressed by very different arguments from those which could be used to Webster. He is not in the running now. If he took the Home Office it would put him in the running for the highest prizes of his profession. Again, he is particularly wanted now as we need a man who can speak on Irish measures as a Cabinet minister. I believe the application is not so hopeless in his case for his practice is not so large: and his private fortune is larger. I am very sorry Webster has refused.[8]

It is not every day that a Q.C. of seven years' standing is called upon by the Lord Chancellor of a powerful new Government with an offer of a Cabinet post, but Macnaghten declined to accept the proposal. It is believed that Halsbury offered Macnaghten the reversion to the Woolsack after himself. If true, Macnaghten must in later years have reflected that he was wise to refuse. That same afternoon Halsbury offered the post to Henry Matthews, Q.C. (later Lord Llandaff) by whom it was accepted.

In the late autumn Halsbury offered Macnaghten a puisne judgeship in the Chancery Division, after ascertaining from the Prime Minister that there was no 'reason against opening a North of Ireland constituency at

7 Halsbury papers.   8 Ibid.

this moment'.[9] But this offer too was refused. Eventually Macnaghten was made a Law Lord in January 1887—an unprecedented honour for one still at the Bar. To the vacant Chancery judgeship Halsbury appointed, as we shall see, Kekewich, Q.C.

This is a convenient point in which to consider in more detail the nature of Halsbury's distribution of judicial patronage, for it is on this that his reputation as Lord Chancellor mainly rests.[1] For the sake of convenience, it may be noted that after the Liberal interlude of 1892–5 Halsbury resumed (29 June 1895) the Great Seal in Salisbury's third government, which was formed at Hatfield on 23 June 1895 in less than 48 hours. The appointment was not universally approved. Moberly Bell, the manager of *The Times*, wrote to Algernon West on 24 June: 'Woolsack a great difficulty. Everybody wants to get [?rid of] Halsbury except himself and Salisbury. Webster is willing to leave it to James provided he [W.] gets the Rolls, a peerage, and is not considered out of the running as a future L.C.'[2]

The appointment was certainly a grave blow to Sir Henry James, although he was consoled with a peerage and the office of Chancellor of the Duchy of Lancaster. (In 1890 he had written to Salisbury asking in vain for the position on the Judicial Committee vacant through the resignation of Sir Barnes Peacock.) When Balfour succeeded his uncle in 1902 he continued the 80-year-old Chancellor on the Woolsack, offering the position in a hurried note.[3]

Almost as soon as Halsbury had retired from the Woolsack in 1905 he accepted the invitation of Messrs. Butterworth, the legal publishers, to act as General Editor of the great encyclopaedia of English law which is known to all lawyers simply as 'Halsbury', despite the fact that there have been two editions under the editorship of later Lord Chancellors—Hailsham and Simonds. If there is to be found any one permanent memorial to Halsbury, it is perhaps to be found in this remarkable publishing achievement, for which he received a fee of ten thousand guineas. The surviving documents show that he took the keenest interest in the whole project and was by no means content to regard his position as a sinecure.[4]

---

[9] Salisbury papers.
[1] There is a complete list of the legal appointments of the second Salisbury Government in (1892) 93 L.T. News. 267.
[2] H. S. Hutchinson, *Private Diaries of the Rt. Hon. Sir Algernon West* (1922), p. 311.
[3] Printed in Wilson Fox, p. 195.
[4] Halsbury papers.

CHAPTER V

HALSBURY'S JUDICIAL APPOINTMENTS have been the subject of considerable comment and speculation, mostly of a critical character. The object of the following pages is to trace in some detail how this situation arose and to indicate that most of the criticism has been of an unfair kind. The criticisms are known in outline to most lawyers; they are in effect that Halsbury appointed to the High Court, and to a lesser extent to the county court, men of little or no legal learning whose previous career in public life had been largely in the service of the Conservative Party or else were relations of his own.

So one book of legal reminiscences states: 'At that time appointments to the Bench were made more avowedly for political or personal reasons than in later years. Lord Halsbury had no hesitation in appointing to the High Court or county court judges whose claims rested more on their political or family ties than on their standing at the Bar.'[1] Another states more tersely that Halsbury was 'quite unscrupulous in his appointments'.[2] Again, a Member of Parliament, a solicitor, has averred in the House that 'the well-known habit of appointing to the Bench unsuccessful Tory M.P.s with large majorities and no incomes has added to the judicial ignorance which is sometimes expressed on social matters'.[3] When it was pointed out that this statement could not possibly be true of 1961, when of seventy-three judges (apart from the Lord Chancellor) only six had sat in the House, and two of those had left it in 1924 and 1933 respectively and another two had been Labour Members,[4] it was thought to be a sufficient reply to say that 'the reference was to a well-known and oft quoted remark attributed to the first Lord Halsbury'.[5] Indeed, although it has never been easy to formulate precisely what the criticisms were and of whom they were made, their general tone is familiar enough to anyone who has ever spent an evening in the company of a barrister. The law, as Disraeli noted some time ago, has a larger stock of bad jokes than any other profession in England, and there can be few barristers who have not heard repeated *ad nauseam* stories of how Halsbury replied with genial

---

[1] G. Alexander, *After Court Hours* (1950), p. 140.
[2] R. Bosanquet, *The Oxford Circuit* (1951), p. 33.
[3] L. Hale in 638 H.C. Deb. 5s. col. 78 (11 April 1961).
[4] *The Times*, 16 April 1961.
[5] Ibid., 20 April. The 'well-known remark' was not specified. Similar criticisms of Halsbury will be found in the *Holmes-Laski Letters* (1953), p. 764.

cynicism to some inquirer who asked whether, *ceteris paribus*, the best man would be appointed to the job: '*Ceteris paribus* be damned, I'm going to appoint my nephew'.

This conventional picture received some confirmation from the biographer of Lord Salisbury, who described her father's attitude in the following words:

With regard to many non-political posts, he would be frankly partisan in his selections. Legal promotions did not come under his direct appointment, but he would never apologise for the practice of making them a reward for political 'right thinking'. Within certain limits of intelligence, honesty, and knowledge of law, one man would make as good a judge as another, and a Tory mentality was, *ipso facto*, more trustworthy than a Liberal one. 'We must pay our debts first in the way of judgeships,' he wrote to Lord Randolph when the farewell distribution of places on leaving office in 1885 was being prepared for: 'Legal partisans are as bad as duns even when it is not judgeships they want. G. lies heavy on my soul; I dare not look C. in the face; and I am round the corner if I see S. H.; while the thought of W. keeps me awake at night'[6] (4 December 1885). An incident recorded by Mr. Buckle witnesses to the same point of view. *The Times'* editor called at Arlington Street for the express purpose of impressing upon the Prime Minister the disrepute which the Lord Chancellor was bringing upon the Government by certain partisan legal appointments. Lord Salisbury listened to his budget, and then observed, with meditative detachment, that it was hard on his colleague that he should be so much abused for what was, in fact, his own responsibility: 'I believe it was I who pressed most strongly on him the claims of those who are considered the worst.'[7]

It may seem surprising to try to refute the recorded opinion of so distinguished a witness as the former editor of *The Times*, but the documents which have survived show both the Prime Minister and the Lord Chancellor in a happier light than this anecdote would indicate.

The total strength of the Supreme Court of Judicature (Court of Appeal and High Court of Justice) during this period was twenty-eight; the Lord Chief Justice, the Master of the Rolls, five Lords Justices of Appeal, and twenty-one High Court Judges: fifteen in the Queen's Bench Division, four in the Chancery Division and two in the Probate, Divorce, and Admiralty Division. During his period of office, Halsbury appointed in all thirty judges, eighteen to the Queen's Bench Division, nine to the Chancery Division and three to the Probate, Divorce, and Admiralty Division. Of these thirty, ten later became peers—all except one on the recommendation of Prime Ministers and Lord Chancellors other than Salisbury and

---

6 These initials may be expanded into Gorst, Clarke, Staveley Hill and Webster.

7 G. Cecil, *Life of Lord Salisbury* (1931), vol. iii, pp. 192–3.

Halsbury himself, the sole exception being Jeune in January 1905, who was promoted to the peerage after a very successful tenure of the office of President of the Probate, Divorce, and Admiralty Division. Four of these also became Lords Justices (apart from those who held this office on their way to the House of Lords) and a number also achieved the undoubted distinction of a Privy Councillorship on or shortly before their retirement. Of these thirty, eight were Members of Parliament at the date of their appointment, six as Conservatives (Grantham, Bruce, J. C. Lawrance, Byrne, Darling, and Bucknill), one (Bigham) was a Liberal Unionist, and one (Cozens-Hardy) a Liberal; another one (Ridley) had also been a Conservative Member of Parliament nearly twenty years before. Three others (Kekewich, Collins, and Charles) had been unsuccessful Conservative, and two others (Romer and Phillimore) unsuccessful Liberal, candidates at General Elections at some period during their professional careers. Therefore, approximately one-third of Halsbury's judicial appointments were from the House of Commons (although only six of these were in fact Tory M.P.s at the actual date of appointment), and nearly one-half (fourteen) had been 'political lawyers', in the sense of being either Candidates or Members—but four of these were Liberals. But it would show a naive unfamiliarity with the practical working of the constitution to think that a parliamentary seat was always an advantage to a candidate for the Bench. For if the seat was held by a narrow majority or the time was inopportune for a by-election the party managers might well object to the proposed elevation. So in 1881 Arthur Cohen, Q.C., M.P., was asked by Gladstone to refuse Selborne's offer of a judgeship on the ground that his seat was unsafe. He did so, and for the rest of his life was never again offered promotion, although uniquely qualified to be a judge. It will be seen that in Halsbury's time the greatest attention was paid to this point— the Prime Minister even going to the extent of circulating to the whole Cabinet any proposal by the Chancellor to appoint an M.P. to the bench.[8]

Little research has so far been done on the political background to judicial appointments. The only serious study so far[9] claims that of 139 judges appointed between 1832 and 1906, eighty were M.P.s at the date of their appointment, and eleven others had been candidates (six of them more than once). Of these eighty, sixty-three had been appointed while their own party was in office, and thirty-three of them had been Law Officers. It is worth noting that the average age on appointment of these eighty was less by six years than that of those chosen solely by reference to position at the Bar.

This is hardly the place in which to argue the advantages and disadvan-

[8] See also above, p. 21, and below, pp. 51, 58, 325.
[9] H. J. Laski, *Studies in Law and Politics* (1932), Chap. VII.

tages of parliamentary experience for a High Court judge. On the one hand the main objection is that it may lead to the promotion to the bench of men who, as under the Stuarts, are in some way subservient to the executive or whose promotion is due to factors other than that of pure professional merit. Since 1689 such appointments have not been heard of in England. Modern research has not seriously shaken the severe verdict of the great Whig historians on the judicial bench under Charles II and James II, though it would not support an assertion that the judges then were actuated by a cynical disregard for the rights of the subject and the law of the land.[1] As *The Economist* remarked as far back as 1859:

No doubt it is a sad thing to have fought elections, to have been loyal to one's Party, and to have chosen it wisely at the outset, and yet to be quietly passed over, silently left on the way. But the sooner Parliamentary services are altogether ignored in the appointment of judicial offices, except perhaps those which are the rewards of the highest legal offices of the Government, the better.[2]

Yet on the other side it may be pointed out that much of the work of a Queen's Bench judge is conducted on a circuit in different parts of the country and is of a nature which demands a shrewd assessment of human character and a sturdy common-sense judgment of fact rather than a profound knowledge of legal principles. It therefore follows that a man who has had some parliamentary experience in the course of his life may well be better suited to sum up to a jury in a straightforward case of manslaughter or negligence than one who has never left the Temple throughout his professional career. Indeed, political experience may be valuable even to an appellate judge. So Haldane, whose probity in these matters is beyond question, wished 'to record my strong conviction that, at all events for a judge who is to sit in the Supreme Tribunals of the Empire, a House of Commons' training is a real advantage. One learns there the nuances of the Constitution, and phases of individual and social political life which are invaluable in checking the danger of abstractedness in mental outlook.'[3] There is also the qualification which *The Economist* itself admitted to exist and which all impartial observers of the English constitution agree to be necessary, i.e. that those who have helped to carry on the government of the country by reason of their services as its Law Officers are entitled to expect that they will receive some reward for their efforts. As Lord Salisbury said, in a letter which will be quoted later,[4] this is part of the tacit convention on which politicians and lawyers together have worked the English Constitution since the glorious revolution of

[1] Havighurst, 'James II and the Twelve Men in Scarlet' (1953) 69 L.Q.R. 522.
[2] (1859) 17 *The Economist* 758.
[3] *Autobiography* (1929), p. 69.   [4] See p. 52.

1689. The truth surely is that the phrase 'It is a political appointment' conceals a number of not very clearly formulated assumptions and really, as is often the case with such loose, popular phrases, will not bear careful examination. The most objectionable latent assumption of all is that a man enters the House of Commons only for motives of cynical self-advancement, and never from a legitimate desire to use his talents for the advancement of the whole community. Yet if one thing is certain about the House of Commons it is that it has an uncommon flair for discovering the cynical careerist and preventing his further advancement. This assumption is all the more objectionable if it underlies, as it often does, the critical remarks of a man who has himself taken no part in public life and whose prejudices are nonetheless real for being of an anaemic and academic kind.

Still, the documents which will be cited show that it was customary for the Prime Minister and the Lord Chancellor to take into account political services in a way which today would be thought surprising, if not positively undesirable.

Finally, there is the point that as the Lord Chancellor himself has had a political career, it would be straining human nature very far to expect him to disregard entirely an experience which he, in the nature of things, is likely to look upon as beneficial and proper; for few human prejudices are deeper than that which a man has in the excellence of his own career: 'What was good for me must be good for others as well', runs the feeling at the back of the mind of every successful lawyer who becomes Lord Chancellor.

We may now turn to survey the appointments which Halsbury made during his tenure of the Woolsack. There were, to repeat, thirty such men and their names are as follows: in the Queen's Bench Division: Wright, Channell, Collins, Charles, Vaughan Williams, Bigham, Bucknill, Phillimore, Walton, Jelf, Bray, A. T. Lawrence, Sutton, Grantham, J. C. Lawrance, Ridley, Darling, and Bruce. In the Chancery Division there were: Farwell, Romer, Buckley, Byrne, Joyce, Cozens-Hardy, Swinfen Eady, Warrington, and Kekewich. In the Probate, Divorce, and Admiralty Division there were: Jeune, Gorell Barnes, and Bargrave Deane. Of these thirty names most lawyers would say at once that they fall into two classes, those of good or even excellent reputation in the first class and those of more doubtful reputation in the second. The first class comprises twenty-three names, of whom four or five would rank very high in the estimation of anyone in the common law world, namely, Wright, Channell, Romer, Farwell (later Lords Justices), and Buckley (later Lord Wrenbury). Of the others, some were entirely reputable men admired in their day for their grasp of legal principle and their common-sense approach to fact. Examples of these are Byrne and Cozens-Hardy in the Chancery Division, and Collins and Bigham, each later a Law Lord, on the Common Law side. In the second class there are seven names which seem to require justification; they are Grantham, Kekewich, J. C. Lawrance, Ridley, Darling, Sutton, and Bruce. The simplest way to deal with the problem of their appointments and to try to discover how far the Lord Chancellor or the Prime Minister may have been influenced by discreditable motives is to take all the appointments chronologically.

Halsbury assumed the Great Seal in June 1885. By the following November the country was in the throes of a General Election and Halsbury himself had to find a successor to Mr. Justice Lopes. He informed the Lord Chief Justice, Coleridge, of this and received the following letter written on 28 November 1885:

It is only like your usual courtesy and kindness to let me know that Lord Salisbury intends to make Mr. Justice Lopes a Lord Justice of Appeal. I do not know whether you wish to know my notions as to his successor. They are very simple. If Charles will take it he is the best man at the Bar for it. It is of the very utmost importance to keep up the character of the Judges at first instance, and this is not the first time I have ventured to put Charles' name before a Chancellor.[5]

Halsbury did not make the appointment until after the results of the General Election had been announced. On 29 December the Prime Minister wrote that, after consultation with the Chief Whip (Akers-Douglas), 'We saw no reason for delaying any longer the appointment of the new Judge.'[6] Halsbury thereupon nominated to the position William Grantham, Q.C., the Conservative Member of Parliament for Croydon, who had not, in fact, been able to take his seat after the election as the House of Commons had not yet met. The delay in making the appointment and the person chosen were both the subject of criticism. It looked as if Halsbury was appointing somebody who had been a successful Conservative lawyer (Grantham was in the greatest demand during the election as a platform speaker) and the manner of making it suggested that undesirable political influences were at work. There were indeed many conflicting claims among the Conservative lawyers of the time; in some copies of *Whitaker's Almanack* for 1886 it is interesting to notice that the name of Sir John Gorst, then the Solicitor-General, was printed among the judges instead of that of Grantham. Gorst, of course, had been one of Lord Randolph Churchill's Fourth Party, and as such was anathema to the Prime Minister. In any event Grantham held his seat by a large majority so that the Tories ran no risk of losing it on a by-election, whereas Gorst had only a slender hold on his. Grantham was a country gentleman

[5] Halsbury papers.   [6] Ibid.

of the old school, distinguished for his knowledge of horseflesh—he used to ride to the courts on a grey cob each morning.

On the Bench he showed himself indefatigable and painstaking, and he never failed to clear his list on circuit. He was shrewd in his judgment of character, had a varied assortment of general knowledge, and his manly, downright ways made a favourable impression on juries. He had a competent knowledge of law for the ordinary work of *nisi prius*, and his industry and energy made a strong contrast to the methods of some of his colleagues. But he lacked the breadth of mind and the grasp of intellect necessary for trying great and complicated issues, and he was a very unsatisfactory judge in commercial cases. Among his failings was an inability to refrain from perpetual comment; his *obiter dicta* brought him into collision at one time or another with nearly every class of the community—deans, publicans, chairmen of quarter sessions, the Council of the Bar, the Durham pitmen, his brother judges. His love of talking was not conducive to the dignity of the Bench, and towards the close of his career he was given strong hints in the Press that the public interest would be best served by his retirement.[7]

As we shall see he incurred severe public and parliamentary criticism some twenty years later when trying election petitions arising out of the General Election of 1906; and some years later, in 1911, when he unwisely tried to justify his earlier actions he received from Asquith 'the severest rebuke which has ever been dealt to an English judge by a minister of the Crown'.[8]

The appointment caused some correspondence with Coleridge, who wrote on 6 October 1886:

Thank you very much for your letter, it is what I should have hoped for and indeed expected from you and I need not say that it removes all feeling of annoyance from my mind. You will see, I hope, from Stephen's letter last before yours how it came that it was not unnatural I should feel it. I do not remember anything passing between you and me as to Grantham. I *did*, I remember, mention Arthur Charles to you; but I don't remember any other name—yes, I mentioned Gorst's, but no other I *think*. Certainly I never dreamt of claiming or rather asking for anything but notice in the appointment of a judge—notion to give an opportunity for possible remonstrance in a possible extreme case. I am quite aware of the absolute right and the sole responsibility of the Chancellor in regard to these appointments.[9]

The next vacancy which occurred was after the Conservative Government had resumed office in June 1886. In the autumn of that year Halsbury wrote to the Prime Minister to report that Vice-Chancellor Bacon had

[7] *DNB, 1901–1911*, p. 152. For another picture of Grantham, see E. Graham, *Fifty Years of Famous Judges* (1930), pp. 146–63.
[8] *DNB, 1901–1911*, pp. 152–3.   [9] Halsbury papers.

tendered his resignation: 'I could not truly say he is wrong in doing so. He is 89 years of age and successful as has been his judicial career it is impossible not to acquiesce in his own view that the time has come to make way for a younger man.[1]

In November the appointment was announced of Arthur Kekewich, Q.C. (of the Chancery Bar), who had unsuccessfully contested in the Conservative interest Coventry in 1880 and Barnstaple in 1885. Like Halsbury himself he belonged to an ancient Devon family; his career at the Bar had prospered at first as he had married a daughter of the great firm of City solicitors, Freshfield & Son, but later had dwindled considerably. It was generally thought that there were other Chancery lawyers better qualified and Kekewich's later career was a disappointment even to Halsbury himself.[2]

On the Bench Kekewich showed an expedition and despatch not usually associated with proceedings in Chancery; he had a thorough knowledge of the minutiae of equity practice and was especially conversant with the details arising out of the administration of estates in Chancery. But his quickness of perception and his celerity in decision were apt to impair the accuracy of his judgments, and he failed to keep sufficiently in control a natural tendency to exuberance of speech. Most kindly and courteous in private life, he was apt to be irritable on the Bench. His judgments were appealed against with uncomplimentary frequency, and though he was occasionally avenged by the House of Lords, it was his lot to be reversed in the Court of Appeal to an extent which would have been disconcerting to a judge of less sanguine temperament.[3]

Nevertheless, 'by the legal profession his shrewdness, sense of duty and determination to administer justice with the minimum of delay were fully recognised'.[4] Indeed Halsbury's successor as Lord Chancellor recommended him for a Privy Councillorship.[5] Kekewich seems to have been a man who has suffered unfairly in the public reputation and the appointment was one which was unlucky rather than discreditable.

In the following year, 1887, Arthur Charles, Q.C., was appointed to the Queen's Bench Division thus fulfilling the hopes which had existed in Lord Coleridge's mind. Charles was a competent judge who retired from the Bench after only ten years, in 1897, but did not die until 1921. He was created a Privy Councillor in 1903. At the date of his appointment he had a respectable common law practice. In 1880 he had been unsuccessful Tory candidate for London University. His son, (Sir) Ernest Charles, was a judge of the King's Bench Division from 1928 to 1947.

Then came a gap of three years until 1890 when four vacancies were

[1] Salisbury papers. [2] See below, p. 60.
[3] *DNB, 1901–1911*, p. 386. [4] Ibid., p. 386.
[5] See below, p. 152.

filled by the appointment of R. S. Wright, J. C. Lawrance, Q.C., Robert Romer, Q.C. and Vaughan Williams, Q.C. These were men of very different characters. R. S. Wright was a product of Jowett's Balliol—a most learned and scholarly man whose judgments are always treated with the greatest respect. He was also, it is important to note, an ardent Liberal. His appointment had been pressed on the Lord Chancellor in a letter of 2 February from Coleridge, who stated that he wrote with the concurrence of Mr. Justice Bowen:

We want a strong man in the Queen's Bench very badly, not only a lawyer but a man of force of mind and character and one who can do the duties and functions of a judge with vigour and ability. If you have made up your mind of course there is no more to be said. If you have not, we both wish to put before you for consideration the name of R. S. Wright, he is a very able, probably the ablest, man at the Bar, except four or five men at the very head who don't practically count for this place, a scholar, a man of distinction and for seven and a half years Treasury devil which used formerly to be thought to give a man a claim ... the Chief Justice need not apologise for writing to the Lord Chancellor as to a vacancy in his Division, but I am sure you will believe that I write simply and solely on public grounds.[6]

Halsbury in fact offered the appointment to R. S. Wright, but, it will be observed, not until the very end of the year and in order to fill another vacancy than that with respect to which the Lord Chief Justice had written. This can be taken to indicate characteristic unwillingness on Halsbury's part to take advice, however good, from anyone. When the position was offered to R. S. Wright he replied on 9 December 1890:

Dear Lord Chancellor,
        Gratefully, but with many misgivings, I accept the offer. There were so many grounds on which I might have been passed over without injustice that I had no expectation of being made a Judge for a long time to come.
                                        Very faithfully yours,
                                                R. S. Wright.[7]

Coleridge thereupon wrote on 26 January 1891: 'If you go on making these appointments I shall have to turn Tory. In sober seriousness nothing could possibly be better.' The two vacancies which had arisen earlier in 1890 were filled in February by the appointment of two very different men, Roland Vaughan Williams and John C. Lawrance. Vaughan Williams was the son of a judge and the grandson of Serjeant Williams, the author of a famous commentary on Saunders' *Reports*:

This Welsh family thus furnishes a remarkable illustration of the inheritance of legal genius. In numbers its record has been equalled and surpassed by other

[6] Halsbury papers.   [7] Ibid.

legal families; but in sustaining through three successive generations the highest level of erudition and the ability to apply it in practice, it can claim a pre-eminent position in the annals of English law. . . . By ancestry and by training he was imbued with the best traditions of the Bench; and, without ever lapsing into pedantry, he maintained throughout his long career the high standard of accuracy and refinement of the old common law judges at a time when there was some danger of the relaxation of their old and well-tried principles at the hands of a generation of lawyers less thorough in their methods. Even in his personal appearance, Vaughan Williams, on the Bench, looked a strikingly picturesque survival from a bygone age.[8]

When at the Bar he had been devil to Halsbury when the latter was Solicitor-General, but he had never been an M.P. or even a parliamentary candidate.

The other new judge appointed in February 1890, John Lawrance, had been M.P. for South Lincolnshire from 1880–90. He sat on the Bench until 1912 when he was created a Privy Councillor. The *Law Times* said of his appointment: 'This is a bad appointment, for, although a popular man and a thorough English gentleman, Mr. Lawrance has no reputation as a lawyer, and has been rarely seen of recent years in the Royal Courts of Justice.'[9] Similar criticism appeared in other newspapers at the time. Lawrance's work as a judge did not apparently improve with the passing years. Sir Frank MacKinnon has explained[1] how Lawrance was in effect responsible for the creation of the Commercial Court in 1895. A difficult case on the construction of a charterparty had come before him and he had reserved judgment. After months had passed and no indication had appeared that he was ready to give judgment, the solicitors ventured to drop a hint on the matter, whereupon the case was restored to the list and Lawrance contented himself by giving judgment in favour of the plaintiff but, as he was legally entitled to do, without giving any reasons at all. As the profession had been expecting a well-argued judgment which would dispose of the various legal problems raised, their discontent can be imagined. The dissatisfaction led to the establishment of the Commercial Court under Mr. Justice Mathew. On the other hand, Sir Travers Humphreys, who had unique experience as a High Court judge, has said that he has been surprised to read references to Lawrance as an unsatisfactory judge.[2] Humphreys regarded Lawrance as having a great fund of useful common sense.

[8] *DNB, 1911–1921*, p. 579.   [9] (1890) 88 L.T. News. 305.
[1] See (1944) 60 L.Q.R. 324, where Lord Justice MacKinnon wrote: 'He was not the worst judge I have appeared before: that distinction I would assign to Mr. Justice Ridley; Ridley had much better brains than Lawrance, but he had a perverse instinct for unfairness that Lawrance could never approach.'
[2] T. Humphreys, *Criminal Days*, p. 140.

In November 1890 Halsbury appointed R. Romer, Q.C., to a vacancy in the Chancery Division. Romer was a well-known practitioner with vague Liberal leanings; he had been an unsuccessful parliamentary candidate for Brighton in 1884. He made a very good judge, and was promoted Lord Justice in 1899. His son, M. L. Romer, became a Chancery judge and later a Law Lord, and his son in turn, C. R. R. Romer, also a Chancery judge and later a Lord Justice. The family of Romer thus shares with the Coleridges and the Russells the distinction of having three successive generations on the bench.

In the following year, 1891, Halsbury made two appointments, R. H. Collins, Q.C., to the Queen's Bench Division and F. H. Jeune, Q.C., the son of a former Master of Pembroke College, Oxford, to the Probate, Divorce, and Admiralty Division. (Collins was appointed to the vacancy created by the resignation of Stephen J., whose remarkable distinction as judge and jurist was marred by ill-health, physical and mental, during his last years on the bench. The Halsbury papers reveal that the Lord Chancellor was obliged to ask for his resignation—which he did in a way that wonderfully combined firmness, tact, and courtesy.) Each of these, in turn, became a peer—Collins as Law Lord, and Jeune obtaining an hereditary peerage on his retirement from a very successful tenure of the Presidency of the Divorce Division in January 1905. Although not in the very first rank of English judges, each was a man of distinction whose appointment was thoroughly well deserved and succesful. Collins had been, at one time, an unsuccessful Tory parliamentary candidate, but in his case there was never any allegation that his appointment had been the reward of political services. 'Henn Collins is excellent,' wrote Coleridge on 9 April 1891, 'admirable in every way.'[3]

In June 1892, on the very eve of the retirement of the Government, Halsbury appointed Gorell Barnes, Q.C., to the Divorce Division. The appointment gave rise to some criticism on the ground that the new judge was of only sixteen years' standing at the Bar and aged 44. It was also alleged that he owed his promotion to the fact that Salisbury's son, Lord Robert Cecil, had once been his pupil in chambers.[4] Barnes had had, while at the Bar, a large commercial practice but little experience in divorce or probate work, though some experience on the Admiralty side. But in the result Barnes proved to be an excellent judge who succeeded Jeune as President of the Division and was raised to the peerage on the nomination of a Liberal Lord Chancellor in 1908.

Another appointment in June 1892 was more dubious. It was of Gains-

3 Halsbury papers.
4 Whatever the father may have thought, the son was not enthusiastic about his master: see Viscount Cecil of Chelwood, *All the Way* (1949), p. 52.

ford Bruce, Q.C., who had been Conservative M.P. for Finsbury since 1888 and had just been returned with a reasonable majority at the General Election the previous week. The vacancy in the Queen's Bench Division had existed for over four weeks and it was strongly hinted at the time that the lengthy delay in filling the position was due to the fact that the Party chiefs wished to have available a safe Conservative seat for any Cabinet Minister who was defeated at the election. Some support is given to this by a letter from Halsbury to Salisbury on 4 June: 'I have received Lord Justice Fry's resignation. A. L. Smith will gratefully accept your recommendation to Her Majesty [i.e. for promotion to the Court of Appeal]. As to A. L. Smith's successor in the Queen's Bench Division I am waiting to hear from Balfour what has [happened].[5]

The position was offered in a curious way. No letter was sent, but instead Liddell, the Assistant Secretary (Muir Mackenzie himself being absent) was commissioned to make the offer.

I went down to the Temple swelling with importance, but Bruce was not in his chambers, so I followed him to the Courts of Justice, where he was sitting as arbitrator. I stood in the back of the Court until he saw me, when he turned quite pale, conjecturing my errand. However, he soon recovered when he came out and I gave him my good news, sitting on a bench in the passage.[6]

In the event Bruce's appointment was not welcomed by the Press at the time. The *Law Times* said: 'We believe it possible that Mr. Gainsford Bruce may make a respectable, if not a good, judge, although we cannot but rebuke those who declare that looking for Mr. Bruce's name in the pages of the Law Reports is like looking for a needle in a bundle of hay.'[7] The Lord Chief Justice, Coleridge, was moved to write on 5 July:

I have your letter, which I hereby acknowledge, announcing the appointment, to a seat in the Queen's Bench, of Gainsford Bruce. What I saw of him at the Bench of the Middle Temple and the very few times I have seen him in our courts would not have led me to the judgment you have formed of his abilities but he is a man of high character and one to whom no-one can take personal exception. Moreover the appointment is made and it is useless to say a word. I should not have said so much even as this but that I will own to you I have felt keenly the difference in your practice towards me from, I believe, the practice of every other Chancellor from the time of Lord Eldon, to every other head of a Court. I only say from the time of Lord Eldon because though I was brought up among judges and *know* the practice up to his time, I do not know beyond. I do not believe it was different but I cannot assert it to have been the same. I *know* Lord Lyndhurst, Lord Cottenham, Lord Cranworth, Lord Chelmsford,

---

[5] Salisbury papers.
[6] A. G. C. Liddell, *Notes from the Diary of an Ordinary Mortal* (1911), p. 290.
[7] (1892) 93 L.T. News. 267.

Lord Cairns and Lord Selborne habitually consulted the Chiefs of courts *before* they made appointments in their respective courts. Cairns was not on good terms with Cockburn or Kelly but he consulted me and made me sort of intermediary to the two other Chiefs when I was in the Common Pleas. Not, of course, that a Chancellor would ever allow a Chief a veto, he ought not to allow it; but as desiring not to make an appointment to which there might be a real objection, and sometimes in the case of an unpopular appointment, to have the support of an independent opinion. The man who took the initiative (I mean was asked to recommend) in the appointment of Lindley, Field, Cave, Mathew, Wills, Bowen and who was consulted about every other appointment either Cairns or Selborne made, I do not think can be said to have made an unfair or discreditable use of his privilege. Of course there were several other men made whom I would not have made; but I always felt that everything which custom and reasonable deference required was done in telling me and hearing what I had to say, and that at last the responsibility was the Chancellor's and not mine, and that he must determine for himself in the last resort what he would do.

You, first I believe of the Chancellors of my lifetime, have never done this. It would grieve me to think, and I do not think, it was from personal mistrust, and even if it were you could always, as Cairns and Selborne did, disregard my advice if you thought it bad or prejudiced. And I have felt the change and on public grounds I regret it.

I say a word now, because it looks if you were going out, and before you have your second innings, of which I think you are very sure, it is all but certain that I shall be gone[8]; and therefore there never can, humanly speaking, be the occasion for thinking of me personally in the matter. Perhaps, indeed, of no-one. For the tendency of legislation has been to put more and more power in the hands of the Chancellor, and to destroy any of the fragments left in the Chief Justice so that I do really think the abolition of the office is very probable. The sense of the thing is very much what Vaughan Williams expressed the other day, what is the good of the Chief Justice if he is no different from any other judge. Personally I suppose they won't think it worthwhile to abolish *me*, but on public grounds I should be sorry if the Chief Justice disappears from the legal hierarchy. But I will not trouble you further with considerations which are much more important to the profession than to myself.

Of course, my dear Halsbury, I receive with *uberrima fide* what you tell me as to your own reasons for appointing Bruce. I only wish on public grounds you had appointed him before the dissolution instead of after. But I daresay you had very good reasons for the delay.[9]

In the event Bruce held office until 1904 when he retired because of ill-health. On his retirement he was sworn in as a Privy Councillor at a ceremony at which a very painful scene occurred.[1] He died in 1912.

Then followed three years, 1892–5, during which a Liberal Chancellor

[8] Coleridge resigned in 1894.   [9] Halsbury papers.

[1] A. FitzRoy, *Memoirs* (1923), Vol. I, p. 208. (Bruce had a recurrence of a paralytic stroke.)

was on the Woolsack; when Halsbury returned to office in 1895, we find him writing on the last day of the year to the Prime Minister: 'I was delighted with the opportunity of giving Marten a county court judge-ship since if a vacancy had occurred among Her Majesty's judges on the equity side I should have been pressed to recognize Marten's claims upon the Party'.[2] Marten had been Tory Member of Parliament for Cambridge from 1874–80 when he was defeated at the General Election of that year. His appointment as a county court judge was announced in January 1896 together with the conferment of a knighthood, a distinctly unusual honour to be granted upon appointment to the county court as distinct from the High Court; but no doubt both the Prime Minister and Lord Chancellor were glad to have his claims upon the Party satisfied so easily. There were no appointments during 1896, but in 1897 a series of vacancies occurred; in one year nearly one-third of the judicial bench was changed. A new Master of the Rolls had to be appointed in succession to Lord Esher and, as we shall see, although Lindley was eventually appointed this was only after lengthy correspondence between the Lord Chancellor and the Prime Minister about the respective claims of Webster, Clarke, and Lindley. There were also three promotions, all excellent, to the Court of Appeal, and no fewer than six vacancies in the High Court to fill up. It is on the appointments made in this year that most of the criticism of Halsbury has centred.

The first, in January, was of L. W. Byrne, Q.C., to a vacancy in the Chancery Division in place of Mr. Justice Chitty who had been promoted to the Court of Appeal. Byrne was an extremely sound Chancery lawyer who had been a surprisingly successful Conservative Member of Parliament for Walthamstow since 1892. He turned out to be a good if some-what slow judge; there is no evidence that his political tendencies in any way influenced his decisions and he takes a respectable, if not a very high, place amongst English Chancery judges.

On 31 March the Lord Chancellor wrote to the Prime Minister as follows:

I am almost ashamed to consult you about a comparatively trifling matter but the bar to the selection of anyone in the House of Commons has caused me much searching of heart. [An illegible sentence.]

A successor to Charles J. must shortly be appointed. There are four men in my mind, as to whom I would say they are all competent and not barred by a House of Commons disqualification. Here are the four.

A. M. Channell, Q.C., called June 1863
F. A. Bosanquet, Q.C., called June 1863

C*   [2] Salisbury papers.

Edward Ridley, Q.C., called June 1868
A. T. Lawrence called January 1869.

Of these the one I should myself prefer would be Edward Ridley but there are
two objections to him. He has been for several years Official Referee and he is
the brother of the Home Secretary. On the other hand he is a very experienced
and excellent lawyer . . . an excellent scholar and a man with a very considerable
university record. He is also a poet and has translated Lucan but these I do not
insist on as judicial qualifications.

Channell is the son of old Baron Channell and I think would be a very good
judge. Bosanquet also I have sent more than once as a Judicial Commissioner
and he has done very well. Lawrence I do not know so much about but I have
good recommendations of him. Could you advise me in particular as to the
objections to Ridley.[3]

The Prime Minister replied on 5 April as follows:

The only question you put to me, which I have the slightest competence to
answer, is whether Ridley's long tenure of the Referee's office should be an
objection to his appointment. I do not know what his positive merits are. They
may well be great enough to outweigh this objection which at most is a small
one. But I think it exists. It is one of the *eidola fori* that unless a man comes to the
Bench quite fresh from the Bar, he has not the fullness of capacity which a
judge should have. The perfume of the Bar is evanescent and escapes in the
interval which separates the Bar from the Bench, if it be prolonged. I remember
exciting great wrath in learned and eminent brains by a suggestion that
Matthews[4] should be appointed Lord of Appeal. Do not imagine that I share
this superstition, I only testify to its existence. I do not know anything of the
other names: and therefore manifestly can have nothing to say against them.[5]

The appointment of Ridley aroused an exceptional storm of public and
professional criticism. The *Law Journal* said: 'The appointment can be
defended on no ground whatsoever. It would be easy to name fifty
members of the Bar with a better claim.'[6] The *Solicitors' Journal* stigmat-
ized the appointment as 'a grave mistake' and in a well-argued criticism
said that if the area of selection of High Court judges was to be widened
from the existing number of practising barristers it would be preferable
to bring in county court judges rather than Official Referees.[7] The *Law
Times* said:

Unquestionable as are the virtues of Mr. Edward Ridley, Q.C.—for some years
the favourite Official Referee—no-one will believe that he would have been
appointed to the High Court Bench but for his connections. . . . Such an

[3] Salisbury papers.
[4] Henry Matthews (1826–1913), 1st Viscount Llandaff, Home Secretary, 1886–92.
[5] Halsbury papers.   [6] (1897) 32 L.J. News. 215.
[7] (1897) 41 S.J. 433.

innovation, we repeat, was only possible where the hard-working official, the bearer of so many heavy burdens of the High Court judges, was highly connected. This is Ridleyism. Let it be known hereafter as Ridleyism. It is a curiosity. It is a mixture of a good and evil thing. Had Mr. Ridley been raised because he was a distinguished classical scholar, a good lawyer, a strong judge, and a conscientious worker in the discharge of a duty from which almost every Queen's Bench judge draws back as wearisome and unpleasant, it would be excellent.[8]

Ridley, a brother of the Home Secretary, Sir Matthew White Ridley, and, therefore, a grandson of the great Baron Parke, had been a moderately successful counsel on the northern circuit and a Conservative Member of Parliament for South Northumberland from 1878–80. He had been appointed an Official Referee in 1886. When he died Pollock wrote to Holmes on 15 October 1928: 'Judicial obituary today: Sir E. Ridley, good scholar, Fellow of All Souls, successful, *sicut dicunt*, as an Official Referee, and by general opinion of the Bar the worst High Court judge of our time, ill-tempered and grossly unfair: which is rather a mystery.'[9] It seems possible to draw several conclusions from the exchange of letters between the Lord Chancellor and the Prime Minister and the subsequent comments. First, none of the four names mentioned in Halsbury's letter of 31 March was that of an M.P.—indeed, there appears to have been at that date a definite ruling against the appointment of M.P.s.[1] Ridley had indeed been an M.P. nearly twenty years before, but this seems to have escaped the notice not merely of the public in its subsequent criticisms but also of Halsbury. Criticism centred entirely on the point that he was an Official Referee and the brother of the Home Secretary. But these two objections had been taken by the Chancellor himself in his letter to the Prime Minister and neither of them seems to have been thought insuperable. What apparently happened was, quite simply, that Halsbury did wish to widen the area of selection of High Court judges and that he chose a man who, on his previous record, should have been excellent—as the *Law Times* itself said. For reasons which, to Pollock as well as to everyone else, were a mystery, this turned out not to be so; but the correspondence clearly acquits both Halsbury and Salisbury of any discreditable motives. Secondly, of the three other persons mentioned as possible judges two, Channell and Lawrence, were appointed later and were entirely suitable. Channell, appointed later in 1897, acquired a very great reputation as a common lawyer, and A. T. Lawrence, appointed in 1904, rose to be Lord Chief Justice under the title of Lord Trevethin. Bosanquet, who had been sent

[8] (1897) 102 L.T. News. 572.
[9] M. De Wolfe Howe (ed.), *Pollock-Holmes Letters* (1941), vol. II, p. 232. See also note 1 on p. 45, above.   [1] See above, pp. 21, 38, and below, p. 58.

as Commissioner with success, was a sound lawyer who, in 1900, was appointed Common Serjeant of the City of London by Halsbury and in 1907 was knighted, at the express request of Loreburn, on the occasion of a royal visit to the City. He achieved the distinction, unusual for a person in that position, of a notice in the *Dictionary of National Biography*.

In the long vacation of 1897 more vacancies arose; in particular a new Master of the Rolls had to be found on the resignation of Lord Esher and the search was long and laborious before Lord Justice Lindley was appointed. On 20 August the Prime Minister wrote to the Lord Chancellor suggesting that, as Webster did not desire the position, it should be offered to Clarke 'on party grounds' despite 'your unfavourable judgment as to Clarke's judicial capacities'.[2]

On 19 September Salisbury wrote again:

I am much perplexed about the Mastership of the Rolls. Webster is quite clear that he does not desire it, and indeed refusing it or accepting it does not touch our chief difficulty, which is Clarke. If Webster goes to the Rolls, Clarke must become Attorney,[3] which from your point of view is every bit as bad as his becoming M.R. The M.R. decides the questions in which individuals are interested, and if he goes wrong he has colleagues and a Court of Appeal to set him right. But if the Attorney-General goes wrong in advising the Government far graver interests are affected; and there is no one to set him right except perhaps a remonstrance from his Solicitor-General which he probably disregards. For a choice, therefore, I had rather see Clarke M.R. than Attorney without taking into account that if he is made Attorney he has a claim which could not be passed over to higher possible vacancies. There remains the third course, to throw Clarke over altogether and tell him that the highest point of his career has been reached. I confess that the more I consider this alternative, the more I dislike it. It is at variance with the unwritten law of our party system; and there is no clearer statute in that unwritten law than the rule that party claims should always weigh very heavily in the disposal of the highest legal appointments. In dealing with them you cannot ignore the party system as you do in the choice of a general or an archbishop. It would be a breach of the tacit convention on which politicians and lawyers have worked the British Constitution together for the last 200 years. Perhaps it is not an ideal system—some day no doubt the M.R. will be appointed by competitive examination in Law Reports, but it is our system for the present: and we should give our party arrangements a wrench if we throw it aside. I asked Arthur Balfour what he thought as he is the practical guardian of the party system on our side of the House of Commons. He was clear that the offer ought to be made to Clarke. I have inquired as far as I could safely from other advisers, especially competent in

[2] Halsbury papers. Salisbury added some caustic comments of his own about Clarke's abilities.

[3] It will be recalled that Salisbury had promised Clarke the first refusal of the Attorney-Generalship if it became vacant before the end of August 1897: see below, p. 324.

this matter, with the same result. After all, there have been in our recollection men who have sat in the high places of the law with a very slender garment of legal knowledge to keep them warm. Consider Coleridge, Chelmsford, Romilly. Of course I am not certain that Clarke, if I offer him the Rolls, will accept them.[4]

On 24 September yet another letter came to the Lord Chancellor:

It is an irony of my fate that very possibly after having succeeded in convincing you that Clarke had much better be M.R. than A.G., I may have to recommend him in the latter capacity after all. But so it is. This is what has happened. Last night, concluding that I shall get no further letter from you, I sent in a submission to appoint Clarke to M.R. This morning at F.O., Webster appears and after some circumlocution lets it be seen that he wants me to *press* him on public grounds to accept M.R. This I declined to do because I said that he was the best judge and I did not think that I was entitled to press a man of his position as to the use to which he should put his abilities. After some further conversation he told me that he would send me his definitive decision on Sunday. I thought I had already decided it: but I could not refuse the *locus poenitentiae* at which he seemed to be aiming as I could not, with entire candour, say that Clarke's name had already been submitted to the Queen. That is where the matter rests now. I have telegraphed to Edwards[5] to suspend the submission for a few days. I have troubled you with these lines lest you might think my proceedings strangely zig-zag.[6]

But in fact Salisbury does not seem to have offered the position until the 30th, when he wrote to Clarke:

It is possibly known to you that Lord Esher has intimated that he cannot resume his work in the Court of Appeal after the vacation. In view of some communications which passed between us with reference to vacancies which might take place within two years, you will probably expect that this preface will be followed by a statement that I have offered the Mastership of the Rolls to Webster, and I should be happy to nominate you for the Attorney-Generalship. I have made the offer to Webster—but he has declined.

All therefore that I can do, in pursuance of our understanding, is on the principle of *cy près* to ask you if you will undertake the Mastership of the Rolls. How such an offer will strike you of course I cannot judge. It is enough for me that your eminent ability and your indisputable position at the Bar entirely authorises me to submit the proposal to your judgment.[7]

But Clarke replied on the same day refusing the post on the ground that it would put an end to his political career—though he added that 'If

4 Halsbury papers.
5 The Rt. Hon. Sir Fleetwood Edwards, K.C.B., Keeper of the Privy Purse.
6 Halsbury papers.
7 E. Clarke, *The Story of My Life* (1918), p. 337.

at any time a vacancy should occur for an English Law Lord, and you thought me worthy of the post, I would accept it with pleasure, as I should still be able to take part in those public affairs which are not essentially of a party character.'[8]

Clarke in fact died a private member of the Bar: to the end he remained happily ignorant of the true opinions about him held by the Prime Minister and the Lord Chancellor.

The Prime Minister now sent a desperate note on 3 October to the Lord Chancellor: 'Webster won't have the Rolls, Clarke won't have the Rolls, what am I to do? Webster recommends Lindley, have you any better candidate?'[9]

Halsbury did not suggest one and on 12 October Lindley was appointed. Two days later Sir Henry James wrote to Halsbury: 'I am delighted to hear that Lindley is to be Esher's successor. You have secured by far the best man for the place, all the other Lords Justices will be mightily pleased. They were much alarmed at the prospect of having a new man put over their heads, and they all regard Lindley as the best lawyer.[1]

Clarke himself welcomed the appointment of Lindley—'I have no doubt that the public service gained by my refusal', he wrote later.

Another problem arose when Lopes L.J. (who had been raised to the peerage as Lord Ludlow in the Diamond Jubilee Honours List in June) also suddenly resigned. He was succeeded by Vaughan Williams J., and Lindley by Collins J.

On 27 October the Prime Minister wrote: 'I have sent in Vaughan-(sic) Williams' name. If there had been time I should have talked over Gorell Barnes with you—but there was not. Ludlow took me by surprise: I thought he had promised not to resign until we gave him leave.'[2] (It is interesting to note that a judge may create a problem by resigning unexpectedly as well as by holding on too long.) There were now two vacancies in the High Court and Halsbury filled them by the appointment of J. C. Bigham, Q.C., and Charles Darling, Q.C. The former appointment was an admirable one and 'the applause which greeted Bigham when he walked up the Central Hall of the Royal Courts of Justice on the first day of the Michaelmas Sittings showed that the Bar approved of the Lord Chancellor's choice'.[3] He was a quick, forthright, and clever judge, who on his retirement was elevated to the peerage as Lord Mersey, and promoted a viscount in 1916. It is worth noting that although at the time of his appointment he had been for two years Liberal Unionist Member for Toxteth, he had previously twice been unsuccessful Liberal candidate for a Liverpool constituency.

[8] E. Clarke, *The Story of My Life* (1918), p. 337.   [9] Halsbury papers.
[1] Ibid.   [2] Ibid.   [3] *DNB, 1922–1930*, p. 82.

Darling's appointment was quite a different matter and the *Law Times* said: 'We do not recollect any outburst of indignation and protest similar to that which greeted the bare announcement by a Press agency that Mr. Darling, Q.C., a purely political barrister, had been nominated to fill the vacancy caused by the elevation of Mr. Justice Collins.'[4] *The Times* itself devoted two leading articles at the end of October to criticism of the recent appointments. Darling was a man who was rarely seen in the Law Courts, but he had been appointed a Commissioner of Assize in 1896 and had done well in that office. He had also rendered valuable services to the Conservative Party by winning a seat for them in Deptford in circumstances of peculiar difficulty and holding it for some nine years. Excitement over the appointment rose so far that a petition to the Bar Council was signed by a number of practising barristers. In December of that year Darling went so far as to attend a public dinner in Kensington and to speak in his own defence. At the date of his appointment he was 46 years of age and apart from his Parliamentary and judicial services had earned distinction mainly as the author of some pleasant light verses. The appointment was universally criticised, with the exception of the *Law Journal*, which said: 'He will prove a far better judge than some of his critics believe.'[5] On the other hand the *Solicitors' Journal* said:

Lord Halsbury has never shown his contempt for the opinion of the profession—and, we will add, of the Bench—so markedly as in his appointment of a successor to Lord Justice Henn Collins. The way to the High Court Bench is once more shown to be through contested elections and general service as a political hack. When these claims are present, learning, experience in practice, and the moral qualities which go to make an efficient and trusted judge, are altogether unnecessary. We do not remember a more unanimous or sweeping condemnation than that with which the new appointment has been met by professional opinion.[6]

Subsequent critics have confirmed, on the whole, the severity of these initial judgments. Darling sat on the Bench for many years, but often appeared to be quite unable to conduct himself or the proceedings in his court with the requisite degree of dignified detachment; his conduct of the Pemberton Billing case in 1918 was a public scandal. Although he possessed a ready and pleasant wit, he was incapable of resisting any opportunity of exercising it in public, and his court was filled with guffawing idlers who hoped to hear the latest judicial witticism. (He had the annoying habit of grinning before making his own jokes.) But even

4 (1897) 103 L.T. News. 573. R. T. Reed in *Punch* (November 27) designed an entertaining coat-of-arms for Darling with the motto 'All good things come from above!'
5 (1897) 32 L.J. News. 525.   6 (1897) 41 S.J. 853.

the severest critics recognized that he had some good qualities; he was patently sincere and honest and was, of course, entirely above any hint of corruption. Also, oddly enough, 'in a murder trial he was very good'.[7] A later Chancellor, Hailsham, while admitting that Darling was not distinguished as a lawyer, claimed that he had other qualities. 'He was a kindly gentleman, a lover of England and of the life and pursuits of the English countryside, with a wide general culture, great industry, complete impartiality on the Bench, a dignified bearing, and complete control both of his temper and of himself.'[8] Lord Tucker has also testified to Darling's dignity and impartiality.[9] It will surprise nobody who is familiar with English life that after some twenty-six years on the Bench he should have been raised to the peerage. Three years previously it had even been thought by some, including himself, that he would succeed Lord Reading as Lord Chief Justice for a brief period in order to keep the position open for Sir Gordon Hewart, the Attorney-General, in very peculiar circumstances. When he was passed over in favour of the 77-year-old Mr. Justice A. T. Lawrence, Darling 'is said characteristically to have remarked that he supposed he was not old enough'.[1] Halsbury himself always remained faithful to Darling. When Darling was made a Privy Councillor in 1917 (the first serving puisne judge to be so honoured) Halsbury wrote 'as your friend and admirer' offering warm congratulations and hoping that 'you may long continue as an example of what an English judge ought to be'.[2] In turn Darling wrote an appreciation of Halsbury ('by one who knew him well') in *The Times* for 12 December 1921.

On 1 November there was yet another appointment—of a successor to Vaughan Williams: Arthur Channell, Q.C., the son of Baron Channell, whom, as we have seen, Halsbury had in mind for promotion in March of the same year. The appointment was entirely successful. Channell was an admirable lawyer without any known politics who rendered considerable service to the development of the common law.[3]

At the end of November there was yet another vacancy, to which Halsbury proposed to appoint Thomas Bucknill, Q.C. who had been the Conservative M.P. for the Epsom Division of Surrey from 1892. His practice at the Bar was respectable but not outstanding. When Halsbury informed the Prime Minister of his intentions he received the following reply on Tuesday, 23 November 1897:

[7] *DNB, 1931–1940*, p. 211.
[8] D. Walker-Smith, *The Life of Lord Darling* (1938), p. v.
[9] In a letter to the author in November 1962.
[1] *DNB, 1931–1940*, p. 212.   [2] Walker-Smith, *Life*, p. 97.
[3] 'One of the most eminent judges before whom I ever had the good fortune to practise': *per* Lord Goddard C.J. in *R. v. Kritz* [1950] 1 K.B. 82, at 87.

My dear Chancellor,

Of course we must in any case wait till Saturday's Cabinet before anything is said to Bucknill. I do not like criticising an appointment which is entirely vested in you—but are you not over-doing a good thing? The judicial salad requires both legal oil and political vinegar; but disastrous effects will follow if due proportion is not observed. My feeling is that at this moment some lawyer of good practice—not in the House—who is competent in your judgment, should be appointed: and that the promising political lawyer whom you mention might well wait for next time, which probably is not far off. But follow your own judgement in the matter, my estimate of the public taste is very likely wrong.

Ever yours truly
Salisbury[4]

This wonderful letter, which shows that the public reaction to the appointments of Darling and Ridley had penetrated Salisbury's notorious detachment from affairs, must have caused Halsbury to draw back, for the vacancy was filled by the appointment of Sir Walter Phillimore, Bt., a former Fellow of All Souls, a member of the distinguished legal family which also owned considerable property in Kensington.[5] He had never taken silk though he enjoyed a substantial practice in admiralty and ecclesiastical cases. It may be noted that, so far from being a Tory, he had three times been an unsuccessful Liberal parliamentary candidate; his appointment was welcomed by the contemporary Press as showing that Halsbury could divest himself of political prejudice. We have it on the authority of Lord Chancellor Sankey that 'in summing up his career as a judge of first instance, a place cannot be found for him among the inner circle of great common law judges, but he became a better judge every year he sat'.[6] He was much criticized because his sentences in criminal cases, especially those of a sexual character, were severe to the point of harshness, and his experience at the Bar had given him little experience for dealing with a common jury in ordinary civil cases, though he was quick, learned, and courteous to counsel. In 1913 he was, perhaps rather unexpectedly, promoted to the Court of Appeal. Two years after his retirement he was made a peer in 1918 and in both the House of Lords and the Privy Council he proved a great success. Appellate work was more to his taste and for an English lawyer he had an exceptionally wide degree of learning in Roman law and international law. Indeed he acquired a European reputation in the field of international law, being a member of the committee

4 Halsbury papers.

5 His father was the Rt. Hon. Sir R. J. Phillimore (1810–85), the 1st baronet, Judge of the P.D. & A. Division 1867–81.

6 DNB, 1922–1930, pp. 677–8.

which drew up the statute constituting the Permanent Court of International Justice at The Hague.

So the eventful year of 1897 drew to an end. Whatever the outside world may have thought of Halsbury, the Prime Minister, no doubt satisfied by the effect produced by his tactful reprimand in November, showed his unwavering faith in the Lord Chancellor by recommending him for an earldom. Although there were indeed precedents of Lord Chancellors being promoted to an earldom, most (with the exception of Cairns and Selborne) had served for longer periods than Halsbury who, in all, had been Lord Chancellor for nine years when the dignity was granted to him.

In the following year, 1898, no appointments had to be made though at the end of the year a vacancy in the Queen's Bench Division enabled Halsbury to propose again 'the promising political lawyer'. On 22 December 1898 Salisbury wrote to him: 'I have directed Mr. Bucknill's name and your kind intentions in regard to him, to be sent round the Cabinet in a circulation box. I cannot think there will be any objection, as I am told his seat is quite safe.'[7] Bucknill's appointment was announced in January 1899 and greeted without the criticism which might have met it in the autumn of 1897. He made a respectable but not distinguished judge. The Prime Minister's letter continued:

Hawkins' letter is pathetic. I have had considerable prepossessions against him: but considering that he is 83 and childless I have put the said prepossessions in my pocket, and have sent in his name to the Queen. I comfort my conscience by the reflection that he has a great reputation, though of a peculiar kind: and that after all he is a better man than Coleridge was.

This refers to the promotion to the peerage under the title of Lord Brampton of Sir Henry Hawkins, who was probably the worst judge on the English Bench in the nineteenth century; capricious, unfair and deceitful.[8] It is well known that the customary farewell when he retired from the Bench was dispensed with because Sir Edward Clarke announced that if it was held he would appear and tell the truth about Hawkins instead of producing the customary flattering platitudes. The strain of cynicism in Salisbury's attitude towards human beings is apparent in the way in which he granted Hawkins' request for a peerage.[9]

Later in 1899 two further vacancies in the Chancery Division arose which was filled by the appointment of two well-known Chancery silks,

[7] Halsbury papers.

[8] He had been appointed by Cairns in 1876.

[9] The *Reminiscences of Sir Henry Hawkins*, ed. R. Harris (1904), p. 361, paint a rather different picture.

G. Farwell, Q.C., and H. Cozens-Hardy, Q.C. Of these two, Farwell bears the greater reputation amongst Chancery lawyers though he never rose higher than Lord Justice of Appeal. Cozens-Hardy, who, it should be noted was a Liberal M.P. at the date of his appointment, subsequently became both Lord Justice and Master of the Rolls. The Chancellor offered the position to Cozens-Hardy in a letter of 21 February 1899:

My dear Cozens-Hardy
Notwithstanding your abominable politics I think you are the fittest person to succeed Romer J., who is to be Lord Justice of Appeal. May I therefore submit your name to Her Majesty as that of one who is willing to serve Her Majesty in the office of judge of the High Court?

I am
always truly yours
Halsbury[1]

The incident later stimulated Theo Mathew to produce a cartoon entitled 'Kiss me—Hardy'.[2]

In 1900 two vacancies arose in the Chancery Division as a result of promotions to the Court of Appeal. It is interesting to note that Halsbury had to write to Salisbury on 17 October:

Your secretary is under some misapprehension about the vacancy in the Court of Appeal. You have the responsibility of that appointment which ought to be that of an Equity man as the Common Law men there are in the great majority. I suggested to you to make Stirling who is a very good Equity lawyer and the senior judge of the Equity Puisnes.[3]

Stirling, who had been appointed to the Bench by Herschell in 1886, was duly promoted to the Court of Appeal and his place in the Chancery Division was filled by the appointment of H. B. Buckley, Q.C., who later rose to greater eminence under the title of Lord Wrenbury.

Another Chancery vacancy earlier in the year had been filled by the appointment of M. I. Joyce, an entirely competent lawyer, and Attorney-General's devil on the Chancery side. ('I have nothing to say against your proposed judge' wrote the Prime Minister.[4]) Joyce proved an excellent judge, who revolutionized the method and style of drafting formal documents such as originating summonses and motions. His decisions are cited still with great respect.

In the following year, 1901, the Lord Chancellor wrote to the Prime Minister on 25 October as follows:

I have received two resignations, one from Mr. Justice Day, which I propose to fill by submitting the name of Jelf, K.C., the leader of the Oxford circuit. He is I

---

[1] Cozens-Hardy papers.　[2] *For Lawyers and Others* (1937), p. 70.
[3] Salisbury papers.　[4] Halsbury papers.

think a good man who has always been loyal and is both a good lawyer and thoroughly a gentleman. Do you see any objection? The other resignation is that of Lord Justice Rigby who has really been quite incapable of doing his job for many months and ought to have resigned long ago. I think his best successor would be Cozens-Hardy. The senior of the Chancery judges is Mr. Justice Kekewich. I do not think his would be a satisfactory appointment. He is a friend of mine and indeed he was one of my earliest appointments, but I must candidly say that I think he has not fulfilled the promise of his earlier career. If you should think right to take Cozens-Hardy or indeed any of the Chancery Judges (it ought to be a Chancery Judge) I should offer the vacancy then created to Mr. Swinfen Eady who in my judgment stands quite at the head of the Chancery Bar.[5]

In the result the two men suggested were appointed. Jelf, the 'thorough gentleman', had been born in 1837 near Berlin, his mother being a Maid of Honour to the Queen of Hanover. Lord Esher had written to Halsbury some years before to press the claims of Jelf, who, he said, was admired by the whole Court of Appeal. Jelf sat on the Bench for nine years, resigning in 1910 and dying in 1917. He left behind a respectable but not outstanding reputation. Rather similar in reputation though not in background was C. Swinfen Eady, Q.C., a competent Chancery lawyer who eventually held the post of Master of the Rolls for a short period of two years, claiming and receiving a peerage on his death-bed as a result of the kindness of Lord Birkenhead.

Earlier in the same year Halsbury had promoted to the King's Bench Division Joseph Walton, K.C., a member of an old Lancashire Catholic family. His decisions in commercial cases are still cited with great respect. He had never been a Conservative M.P. or taken any active part in public life.[6] He died in 1910. Salisbury wrote in reference to the appointment on September 30:

Your list of promotions is quite unexceptionable. I am very sorry that we are to lose A. L. Smith. The only question on which I doubted was whether it would not be better to make Walton Lord Justice at once over Mathew's head. Mathew certainly behaved abominably in that Irish case. But it is some time ago and I think your decision is the right one.[7]

(The 'Irish case' was the Royal Commission on Evicted Tenants of 1892. Mathew, a convinced Liberal, was made chairman, and from the outset was involved in clashes with Carson, counsel for the landlords.)

No vacancies occurred in 1902 or 1903. In 1904 two men were appointed

[5] Salisbury papers.
[6] But Lord Robert Cecil had been in Walton's chambers and much admired him: Viscount Cecil of Chelwood, *All the Way* (1949), p. 54.
[7] Halsbury papers.

to the Common Law Bench, A. T. Lawrence, K.C., and R. Bray, K.C. Lawrence was a silk in substantial practice who later rose, as we have seen, to be Lord Chief Justice momentarily under the title of Lord Trevethin. He had powerful support. Thus, Balfour wrote on 23 October 1901:

> If you are thinking of vacant judgeships, let your mind dwell for a moment on A. T. Lawrence, who did some admirable work when my London Government Bill was passed, in working out all the complicated questions to which it necessarily gave rise. *Please do not think I recommend him.* I do not do so: for two reasons, one is that I am quite incapable at judging his competency as a lawyer; the other is that I do not know anything about the other candidates, and thirdly, there may be, for anything that appears to the contrary, some member of the House to whom I ought by precedence to give my support. I merely mention him in order that his name may be before you.[8]

Alfred Lyttleton (Colonial Secretary, 1903–5), later described how

> I sat next to him [Halsbury] in the Cabinet. He never said much there. I had made up my mind to get him to appoint old Lorry [A. T. Lawrence] as a judge. I waited a whole year and then spoke to him. He did not say much, but one day I saw him writing at the Cabinet. He half pushed the paper towards me, and then drew it back, but I had read, 'I think your friend's chances are favourable. I shall make him after I have made Bray', and he did.[9]

R. M. Bray had had an unusually lengthy career as a junior: when he took silk in 1897 at the age of 55 his former pupils gave him a dinner; the hosts numbered over one hundred. He, like Jelf, had support in high places. St. John Brodrick, the Secretary of State for War, had previously written to Halsbury about him, and Brodrick's father, Lord Midleton, assured the Lord Chancellor that 'I can answer for the pleasure his appointment would give to the whole county [Surrey] with which his family have been connected since the day that his ancestor, Sir Reginald Bray,[1] attended King Henry VIII at the Field of the Cloth of Gold.'[2] A wise biographer has said that 'Although this promotion came at an age when many men are seeking retirement, its wisdom was thoroughly justified, for Bray sat on the Bench for nearly nineteen years, during the whole of which period he was considered one of the ablest of the puisne judges.'[3]

In the same year a vacancy on the Chancery Bench was filled by the appointment of G. R. Warrington, K.C., who, after being promoted to the Court of Appeal, was raised to the peerage on his retirement in 1926. He was a thoroughly sound equity lawyer.

[8] Halsbury papers.
[9] Lord Riddell, *More Pages from my Diary, 1908–1914* (1934), p. 96.
[1] Another ancestor was Sir Thomas More.
[2] Halsbury papers.   [3] *DNB, 1922–1930*, p. 106.

In February 1905 Halsbury appointed Bargrave Deane, K.C., to the vacancy in the Probate, Divorce, and Admiralty Division caused by the promotion of Gorell Barnes to the Presidency. He was a satisfactory judge. Bargrave Deane's father, Sir James Parker Deane (1812-1902), was Vicar-General of Canterbury in his ninetieth year, 'the greatest age at which any Englishman since Serjeant Maynard is believed to have exercised judicial functions'.[4] This record was surpassed by Halsbury himself in his ninety-third year.[5]

In the last days of 1905 the pressure to satisfy the claims of the Conservative lawyers was very great. It will be seen that Downing Street was concerned to find a position for Finlay, the Attorney-General,[6] and there was also pressure from Dublin Castle in support of the Irish Unionists. On 29 November J. S. Sandars, the Patronage Secretary, sent a hurried note to the House of Lords:

I have it in command from the Prime Minister to ask you whether you have negotiated Lord Lindley's resignation, and to be so good as to let him know in the course of tomorrow (Thursday) how this matter stands.

As soon as he hears from you he will acquaint you with his views of dealing with the vacancy.[7]

Lindley resigned that very day: it was his seventy-seventh birthday. He had been suffering for some time from the effects of a fall on the Duke of York's Steps. In the event he survived to the age of 93, dying on 9 December 1921 two days before Halsbury himself. After the post had apparently been refused by Finlay it was accepted by J. Atkinson, K.C., M.P., the Irish Attorney-General. Atkinson had been in that office longer than anyone since 1834; he was said to have refused six puisne judgeships. He was not as distinguished a lawyer as Lindley, but he was a good Law Lord.

On Monday, 4 December, the resignation was announced of Mr. Justice Wills. He was the senior puisne judge, having been appointed by Selborne in 1884. It was seven days before his seventy-seventh birthday. He was given the customary Privy Councillorship. He had apparently sent in his resignation on Saturday the 2nd, for the Treasury made his annuity run from that day. Wills had been sitting on the Saturday (as was the custom in those days), and had given judgment in a libel action. On the Monday the appointment was also announced of his successor—Henry Sutton, the Attorney-General's devil on the common law side. Sutton's successor in that office was Rowlatt, and his was William Finlay.[8] Sutton was entitled to promotion *virtute officii*; he was also supported by letters from Lord Alverstone. It is not easy to see why the Prime Minister

---

[4] *DNB, 1901-1911*, p. 486.   [5] See the *Daimler Case* [1916] 2 A.C. 307.
[6] See below, p. 326.   [7] Halsbury papers.   [8] See below, p. 332.

and the Chancellor laid themselves open to the charge of having acted with indecent haste[9] for the sake of someone who was not a party man and whose claims would have had to be recognized by any incoming Liberal Chancellor. In any event, Sutton unfortunately proved to be a weak judge. He 'failed to display the readiness and strength of judgement required of him',[1] and after the unprecedently brief period of five years resigned in 1910.

Balfour had resigned on Monday the 4th; Campbell-Bannerman had kissed hands on the 6th. But Halsbury still held the Great Seal, which was not surrendered until Monday the 11th. On Thursday the 7th Lord Justice Mathew had a stroke at the Athenaeum Club and resigned the following day. On the 8th Balfour wrote to Halsbury: 'I am sorry to hear of the illness of Lord Justice Matthews (*sic*). But I suppose the appointment of his successor rests with the Lord Chancellor, not with the Prime Minister.[2] In any case, neither you nor I can take any action now.[3]

This appointment therefore lapsed to the Liberal Government.

When we turn to the county court judges, we run into a host of names belonging to forgotten men. We hear something about Judge Willis, mainly because he later encountered the sharp sword of the young Mr. F. E. Smith; or Mr. Maconochie who was appointed, at the age of 63, after an undistinguished career at the Bar culminating in the Recordership of Windsor; of Mr. Melville about whom little was known except that he was an equity draughtsman and conveyancer; and of Mr. MacIntyre who had been born in 1821, two years before Halsbury himself, and had a long and undistinguished career on the North Wales Circuit and also in Parliament, but on the Liberal and not on the Conservative side; and of Mr. John Macdonell, who was recommended by Lord Coleridge in glowing terms.

It would today be an impossible task to try to recreate the reputations and characters of men so long dead and forgotten. All that can be said is that if not very distinguished appointments, the county court, at that time, was not an appointment which distinguished men hoped for. For until the rise in the cost of living after 1945 had made it impossible for men in large practice at the Bar to accumulate sufficient savings, an appointment to the County Court Bench was not one which was sought after.

Here, as elsewhere, Halsbury seems to have been the victim of some unfair criticism and two false charges may be disposed of now. One is that

[9] See the strong remarks in (1905) 50 Sol. Jo. 87.

[1] (1910) 14 L. J. News. 246. Sutton is said to have been the model for Theo Mathew's Forensic Fable 'The Judge Who could not Make Up his Mind.'

[2] This was the second occasion on which this mistake was made: see above, p. 59.

[3] Halsbury papers.

he made his eldest brother, J. W. Giffard, a county court judge, and the
other is that he made his brother-in-law, R. Woodfall, a county court
judge also. So far as the first charge is concerned, the truth is that J. W.
Giffard was appointed to the county court Bench by Cairns as far back as
1875. He died in 1888. As for Judge Woodfall, he was a learned man, a
descendant of the author of a leading work on the law of landlord and
tenant which is still referred to by practising barristers, and himself the
author of a book on railway and canal traffic. Finally, it may be remarked,
that two of his criticized county court appointments, Judges Waddy and
Willis, were in fact ardent Radicals.

When we turn to the third branch of the Lord Chancellor's patronage,
the appointment of Q.C.s, the only serious criticism which seems to have
been levied against Halsbury is that he granted silk to too many men during the administration of 1886–92, namely 71 in all. (The total number of
silks made by Halsbury was 239—178 under Queen Victoria and sixty-
one under Edward VII.)

Finally we must consider his appointments to minor offices in and
about the courts and House of Lords. As early as November 1885 there
were criticisms in *Truth* of his appointments to clerical positions in the
Chancery Division, and in November 1888 the matter was again mentioned in the House of Commons.[4] Halsbury vigorously defended himself
against his critics.[5] There was also some criticism of the fact that his nephew,
Hardinge, the son of Judge J. W. Giffard, was his private secretary, but
again there is no evidence that he was other than competent in the
position, which he held from 1886-92 and again from 1895-1900, when
he left to become a Commissioner in Lunacy. A half-brother, Harry
Stanley Giffard (1832-1912), was Registrar in Bankruptcy, but here again
no imputation was made against his professional qualifications. Some
difficulty did arise in 1899 about the appointment of the Reading Clerk
in the House of Lords, when one Edward Alderson, the nephew of the
Prime Minister, was appointed although the Prime Minister himself wrote
to Halsbury suggesting that the appointment be not proceeded with. In
any event it should be remembered that at this date and indeed down to
very recent years, many of the clerical offices in and about the courts were
filled upon the nominations of the Lord Chancellor or the Lord Chief
Justice of the time being; and anyone who cares to glance at a list of, say,
Clerks of Assize for the past fifty years will be struck by the number of
times on which names like Bovill, Coleridge, and Stephen appear.

[4] 330 Parl. Deb. (3rd. ser.) col. 1038.
[5] Ibid., col. 1169. He admitted that he had transferred his second brother, the Rev.
F. O. Giffard, from one Crown living to another 'slightly better in point of emolument and in a more genial climate.'

Making all due allowance for the existence of hereditary talent, the observer may still feel that the eighteenth-century concept of office lingered for longer in the law than anywhere else.

What conclusions are to be drawn from this lengthy survey? First, it is clear that Halsbury is to be judged by the merits of his appointments to the High Court and not by his appointments to any lesser tribunal. Secondly, of the thirty High Court judges whom he appointed, some four or five, e.g. Wright, Channell, Farwell, Buckley, Romer, were men of real distinction who would have lent credit to the Bench at any period in its history. Some eighteen or nineteen were men of competent professional attainments who discharged their duties as best as they possibly could. The worst that could be said of some of them, e.g. Walton, Jelf, and Bray, is that they were dull. Their professional qualifications are not in doubt. There remain no more than seven judges, Grantham, J. C. Lawrance, Ridley, Darling, Kekewich, Bruce, and perhaps Sutton, whose appointments seem dubious. Four of these seven, Grantham, J. C. Lawrance, Darling and Bruce, were Conservative M.P.s at the date of their appointment; Ridley had been a Conservative M.P. briefly nearly twenty years before and Kekewich had twice been an unsuccessful Tory candidate. But in truth the appointment of Kekewich (like that of Sutton) was an unlucky one. There were reasonable hopes of it being good, the judge himself performed as best he could according to his lights, but he seemed to be dogged by misfortune. Equally it can be said of Ridley that he was an unlucky appointment. The suspicion that he was appointed either because he had been an M.P. or because he was the brother of the Home Secretary seems conclusively disproved. The worst that can be said of Salisbury and Halsbury is that they misjudged the strength of the opposition to the appointment of an Official Referee. This does not mean that the Bar was right in opposing such an appointment. Their opposition may well have been due to professional jealousy and there is much to be said for the argument that the field of selection should have been widened. Indeed the Bar as a whole is not much larger than a big public school, and those who are in the age-group eligible for judicial appointments are only a fraction of the whole. It was again Halsbury's misfortune that a man highly qualified on paper, a Fellow of All Souls, should have inexplicably turned out to be such a bad judge.

Grantham, Bruce, and J. C. Lawrance were as undistinguished on the Bench as they had been at the Bar. Although it would have been better if they had not been appointed, yet each has had his defenders. They were not clever men but, especially before the Great War, the English did not always want clever men in public positions. They often preferred an honest gentleman. But for the last of these judges, Darling, little can be said, although he too has had his defenders. He was a cleverer man than Grantham, Bruce or Lawrance, but he was not a good judge. Still it can be said in Halsbury's favour that four dubious appointments out of thirty during a tenure of the Woolsack lasting seventeen years should not weigh too heavily in the scales when making a final judgment.

Finally, one must not forget the number of occasions on which Halsbury fought against the appointment of a man whom he thought would be a bad judge, e.g. Marten, Edward Clarke, and Staveley Hill. The last named, who was eventually consoled with a Privy Councillorship, had often pressed his claims on the Prime Minister; so on 2 August 1888 Salisbury wrote:

Mr. Staveley Hill has just called upon me. He states that—without complaining—so many of his juniors have now been put upon the Bench that he could not take a puisne judgeship. He thinks, moreover, that Hannen will probably give up after this Commission:[6] Hannen's place is the one that would suit him. I promised to lay his views before you. Somehow he was not as gratified by that assurance as I had expected.[7]

In 1891 Staveley Hill was reduced to writing personally to Halsbury to press his claims to succeed Mr. Justice Stephen.

[6] The Parnell Commission, of which Hannen was a member.
[7] Halsbury papers.

CHAPTER VI

THE YEARS ON THE WOOLSACK slipped quietly by in the golden afternoon of Victorian England. During debates Salisbury often used to leave his seat to sit on the Woolsack beside the Lord Chancellor for a whispered conversation on the business of the day. They got on well together—the gifted descendant of the house of Cecil, with his supple, Italianate mind and dreams of Imperial expansion, and the downright, pugnacious old lawyer. Each had a remarkable knowledge of human nature and a power over his fellow-men. In Halsbury's case this owed nothing to his physical appearance—he had a powerful, broad body on exiguous legs, crowned by a large head and an extraordinarily plain and unprepossessing face, without any eyelashes and with an ugly uptilted nose. On the Woolsack his feet hardly touched the floor, his short legs dangling down uncomfortably under his black silk gown.[1] Yet there was no mistaking the force of the personality which radiated from him. One who saw him presiding over the Court of Appeal in an effort to clear off arrears in the lists noted the extreme deference with which he was treated by even the most eminent of Q.C.s—most of whom would have been in their nurseries when he was in the full tide of a busy junior practice. 'The masterly way in which he brushed aside all niggling points, his deftness in getting to the point under discussion, even the snap of his tortoise-shell eyeglasses as he dropped them after perusing a document, were all highly entertaining.'[2]

Another observer noted how he managed the Law Lords—a stronger team, perhaps, at the beginning of his Chancellorship than at the end. Sir Almeric FitzRoy, the gossipy Clerk of the Privy Council, noted in his diary on 31 March 1905:

A characteristic instance of the Lord Chancellor's humour occurred yesterday. An appeal of the Duke of Northumberland on some point touching estate duty was down for hearing in the House of Lords, whereupon Lord James, though of course not in as many words, intimated that his familiarity with Dukes would render it difficult for him to preserve an impartial mind. The Chancellor, who was quite equal to the occasion, sent him to the Judicial Committee to hear an Indian appeal, which James hates as he knows nothing of Indian law and is reduced to a humiliating silence, and brought Davey to the House of

---

[1] See the admirable cartoon in H. W. Lucy, *The Balfourian Parliament* (1906), p. 244.
[2] G. Alexander, *The Temple of the Nineties* (1938), pp. 111–12.

Lords, who knowing the circumstances, took it as an intimation that he was not familiar with Dukes which was wounding to his vanity. The Lord Chancellor scored by exchanging a weak lawyer for a strong one and flouted two colleagues, neither of whom he is particularly fond of.[3]

In all his personal habits Halsbury was a man of extreme simplicity and lack of ostentation. He sometimes surprised visitors by opening his own hall-door, and in Eights Week used to run along the towpath cheering on the New College boat in which his son rowed.

Until extreme old age he never took alcohol before any meal, and imbibed very sparingly during it. He was addicted to none of the recreations common to successful lawyers—field sports, building country houses, or moving in fashionable society. He occasionally played golf at Richmond, but could not be induced to take it too seriously. As he blasted his way slowly from hole to hole a long queue of players built up behind him, for nobody had the courage to play through. After the game he used to cool himself, in defiance of every rule of common prudence, by sitting in an open door at the club-house in his shirt-sleeves. But despite his unconventional simplicity he was aware of what is due to the first subject in the land after the Archbishop of Canterbury. A peer who, perhaps inadvertently, had addressed him in a fashion which might be called condescending received a thunderous rebuke which brought forth an instant apology. Nothing, indeed, affords more striking testimony of the respect in which he was held by the members of the House of Lords than the correspondence relating to the Parliament Act controversy of 1911. In the mass of letters which have survived it is notable how the holders of ancient peerages, whether themselves distinguished or not, adopted a tone of extreme respect and deference when writing to the veteran ex-Chancellor.

Something must now be said about that famous affair, for although there are many admirable accounts of it, the story is of importance in Halsbury's life. The Parliament Bill of 1911 was introduced by the Liberal Government after they had been again returned to power at the second general election of 1910. The Bill proposed to reduce the delaying power of the Lords to two years in respect of ordinary legislation and three months in respect of money bills. The Cabinet believed, rightly it is now held, that it was entitled to take this step in view of the refusal of the Lords to pass the Finance Bill of 1909.

After much uncertainty the Conservatives, led by Balfour and Lansdowne, finally resolved not to oppose directly the Government's proposals. A vital factor in this decision was the fact that Asquith had secured from a reluctant monarch a promise to create sufficient peers to overcome any

[3] FitzRoy, *Memoirs* (1925), vol. i, p. 248.

opposition which the Lords might manifest to the Bill. But there were
peers who were unwilling to accept this decision and at the age of eighty-
seven Halsbury placed himself at their head. He based his opposition on
the simple ground that it was constitutionally wrong to tamper with the
hereditary principle on which the powers of the House of Lords were
based. It was the kind of simple Toryism which old Dr. Lees Giffard
would have understood. Some of Halsbury's supporters were attracted by
different and perhaps less creditable motives. But they formed a group
which was strong enough to cause anxiety not only to the Government
but also to the official leaders of the opposition. The Conservative Party
has always been inclined to stress the importance of loyalty to the leadership: internal disputes are generally conducted in secrecy. So the activities
of Halsbury and his friends were viewed at Whittinghame and Bowood
with no very friendly eye—though at Hatfield Lord Hugh Cecil outdid
all others in the violence of his opposition to the Government. But the
country and the party were in the grip of a curious mood of feverish
excitement. Today one reads with great astonishment what educated
Englishmen said to and about each other in those hot summer months. A
great and wealthy empire was indulging in the luxury of violent internal
disputes. Looking back it is easy to say that the Halsbury party showed a
lamentable indifference to the long-term interests of the House of Lords
itself and the country as a whole. A House containing the 500 gentlemen
whose names the whips had submitted to Asquith as being suitable for
ennoblement would have been the laughing-stock of Europe. The
fascinating list of names is printed in Spender and Asquith's *Life of
Asquith*. But the Halsbury party announced their intention of dying in the
last ditch, and scornfully described those of their colleagues who followed
Lansdowne in refusing to insist on the Lords' amendments as 'hedgers'.
The technical issue on which the final vote was taken was whether the
Lords should insist upon their amendments to the Bill. Those amendments
had been rejected by the Commons on the ground that they in truth
negatived the fundamental proposals of the Bill. A ditch may be a good
place to die in but it is not a very good place from which to see the surrounding country clearly. But if a great statesman like Milner could say
'damn the consequences', too much should not be expected from Lord
Willoughby de Broke, the young fox-hunting squire who was Halsbury's
right-hand man.

As the day of the great debate approached excitement grew. There were
long and crowded meetings at Grosvenor House and Lansdowne House,
at which men who had been dragged up from the shires by an early train
to the heat of London listened impatiently to discussions of constitutional
niceties; and there was a dinner in Halsbury's honour at the Hotel Cecil,

at which excitement rose to such a pitch that only the pleas of his family dissuaded F. E. Smith and his friends from drawing their hero in triumph back down the Strand to Ennismore Gardens. The student of the episode may well feel that he is reading an account of the annual dinner of the Bullingdon Club and marvel that men of age and position should so behave themselves. But there was no doubt about the enthusiasm Halsbury aroused in his audience. They cheered him to the echo. An observer has left a vivid picture:

I see him now. Below the ordinary height, though broad and thickset; age, except when he stooped, had been very generous to him ... Baldness only revealed better the shape of his head, which was very fine. Clear-shaved, his mouth and chin, well shaped, were as determined as his character ... His eyes were deep-set and bright; his forehead broad and rather protruding. Anywhere he would have attracted attention if only by the fact that he looked a great gentleman.[4]

Eventually the critical debate took place in the Lords on 9 and 10 August. In a tense and sweltering atmosphere (the temperature rose to 97° in London that day), each side restated its position. Lord Morley announced with solemnity that every vote against the Government was a vote for a large and prompt creation of peers. Even then the Halsbury party did not weaken. Right up to the moment of the division there was uncertainty about the result.

The difficulty was that if Halsbury could collect more than seventy-five followers the Bill would be definitely lost. The reason for this was that the Government could not count upon more than seventy-five supporters and although over two hundred Conservative peers had signified in writing that they were ready to follow Lansdowne, about fifty had announced that they would take the opposite course. The promises of the two hundred did not of course include any undertaking to vote for the Government, and hence it became necessary to undertake the unpleasant step of ascertaining whether a sufficient number of Unionist peers were prepared to sacrifice themselves by voting for the Government. In the event, some forty or fifty were willing to do this. When the figures, one hundred and thirty-one to one hundred and fourteen, were announced, it was realized that the Bill had only been saved by the votes of Unionist peers who had sacrificed themselves in order to prevent a worse catastrophe. Nobody had really expected the 'Diehards' to number more than seventy.

Afterwards, on 12 August, Halsbury described to his daughter Evelyn how the eventful day had ended:

4 Wilson Fox, *The Earl of Halsbury*, p. 254.

We only arrived last night about 9 o'clock and of course your mother was almost worn out with fatigue and excitement. If she could only catch a recreant Unionist peer or better still a bishop to slaughter, I believe she would get strong again directly. When the seventeen majority was announced, she hissed loudly from the Peeress's Gallery!!!! But in the excitement her irregularity was not observed, or rather it was not discovered who was the culprit. The excitement was very great, and when we were all coming out in the Prince's Chamber, Lord Lansdowne held out his hand to me and said, 'At least, let us shake hands,' but your mother was boiling over with rage, and would not follow my example. Then your mother and I were cheered when we drove away by a mob and your mother from the window of the carriage spoke, saying: 'It was not our fault.' She has been murmuring vengeance ever since, but she has been getting slowly a little more tranquil. I think nothing but Asquith's blood would have satisfied her yesterday, but today I think penal servitude would almost suffice. The night of the decision Galway, one of the recreant peers was hissed in the Carlton Club, at least so says the *Daily Express*, but I have no other authority for it.[5]

In the autumn the Halsbury Club was founded by those who had been prominent in the summer. But the excitement had passed, and the mass of correspondence on the subject which has survived[6] shows mainly that the sponsors were anxious to deny that they were challenging the official party leadership. After a few weeks the Halsbury Club faded away.

[5] Halsbury papers.   [6] Ibid.

CHAPTER VII

IT WAS SAID of Queen Victoria and her eldest son, in contrast to her grandson, that each of them was not only totally unlike the other but also totally unlike any other person in England. What was said of the monarch whom he served might also be said of the Lord Chancellor. There was nobody else quite like him. Halsbury, indeed, like the Queen herself, was not a Victorian: both had their roots in the older, tougher England of George IV. A few words can describe Halsbury's own relations with the monarch whom he served. The Lord Chancellor is 'keeper of the King's conscience'—so far as the phrase has any meaning to-day, it signifies that he is the primary legal adviser to the monarch on matters affecting the constitutional position of the monarch and the royal family. The Windsor archives show that Halsbury was consulted only infrequently, and then on such matters as the effect of the Royal Marriages Act, 1772, or the proposed nuptials of one or other of the Queen's many kinsfolk. Once she wrote a protest against a list of pardons submitted by the Home Office for the exercise of the Royal Prerogative in the customary way: '*Why* are the judgments given if they are continually to be disregarded; perhaps the Chancellor might speak to the judges on the subject?'[1] A suitably tactful reply was sent. One matter of complaint was the Lord Chancellor's handwriting. The Queen's was not good, but Halsbury's was worse. As Sir Arthur Ellis (an Equerry to Edward VII) complained to Knollys on 11 February 1901 when forwarding a letter from Halsbury containing his ruling that the King's head should be covered when reading the speech from the Throne at the opening of Parliament: 'I am glad his opinion (*not* a bad one) coincides with that expressed by the King himself, and I own it is what I thought also. He writes a governess's hand and difficult to read; but no doubt you can make it out.'[2] At times hints were dropped at Windsor that (contrary to custom) it would be acceptable if the Lord Chancellor made use of a typewriter for his official communications: but they were not acted upon.

A comparison is often made between Eldon and Halsbury, but it seems to be based on little more than the fact that each held the Great Seal for an unusually long period, Eldon for twenty-four years, Halsbury for seventeen, and that each was unusually conservative in his political opinions. That they had some characteristics in common cannot be denied; but they appear to be no more than those qualities which every successful

[1] Halsbury papers.   [2] Windsor Archives, X. 37, No. 12.

lawyer who becomes Lord Chancellor in a Conservative Government shares with others who have achieved the same position. Eldon and Halsbury differed not only in their background (one the son of a coal factor at Newcastle, the other the descendant of an old Devonshire family), and in their practice at the Bar (one in Chancery, the other at *nisi prius* advocacy), but also in more fundamental respects.

Eldon never introduced a legal reform himself, and consistently opposed all attempts to do so by others. Halsbury has two major reforms to his credit—the Land Transfer Act, 1897, and the Criminal Evidence Act, 1898—as well as a record of support for well-argued reforms introduced by others, such as the Criminal Appeal Act, 1907. The great legal historian, Holdsworth, who was not a man given to rash judgments, or known for his lack of sympathy with Conservatism, stated that 'The way in which Eldon performed his duties as head of the legal profession is open to serious criticism'.[3] No such judgment can be passed on Halsbury.

Eldon's Toryism was summed-up in a well-known passage by Walter Bagehot:

He believed in everything which it is impossible to believe in—the danger of Parliamentary Reform, the danger of Catholic Emancipation, the danger of altering the Court of Chancery, the danger of altering the Courts of Law, the danger of abolishing capital punishment for trivial thefts, the danger of making landowners pay their debts, the danger of making anything more, the danger of making anything less.[4]

There was in Eldon's Toryism an almost hysterical dislike of change—something, if the expression may be used, of the old woman—which has never been characteristic of the best elements in English Conservatism.

Halsbury, on the other hand, was not a man of an older generation living in the present—an Eldon or a Metternich. It was well said of him that 'In each successive generation of his long manhood he readily adapted himself to the most conservative standpoint of the moment and voiced its creed in plain and unvarnished language.'[5]

Another difference may be noted. Eldon in extreme old age was a pathetic figure—crouched by his fireside complaining that he was never consulted by the statesmen of the day, his only visitors some toadying attornies who were content to hear the same stories repeated *ad nauseam*, and his only reading the daily newspaper. Unlike Halsbury, Eldon had no acquaintance with the classics of ancient or modern literature—a fact which may help to explain why his judgments, though useful as repositories of Chancery learning, are notoriously tedious and exhausting to

[3] Holdsworth, *H.E.L.*, vol 13, p. 616.
[4] Bagehot, *Literary Studies*, vol i, p. 67.   [5] (1921) 66 Sol. Jo. 134.

read. Halsbury's judgments are like the man himself—plain and straight-forward, and replete with quotable *obiter dicta* which illustrate one or more facets of his personality. 'What manly mind cares about pain and suffering that is past', he inquired in *The Mediana* (1900).[6] (It would no doubt have astonished Halsbury if he had been told of the large awards that modern courts constantly make under this heading.) If his judgments are lacking in the literary grace of those of Cairns or Macnaghten, they at least never leave the reader in any doubt as to their meaning. It is true that in later years their style becomes somewhat diffuse, and there is, perhaps, too frequent an appeal to the merits of that common sense which is characterized by the approving epithet 'sturdy'. Difficult questions of statutory interpretation which have vexed lower courts cannot always be answered satisfactorily by saying 'I confess it is to my mind absolutely amazing that anyone can entertain the smallest doubt as to what those words mean', or something similar, as was done rather too often. But on occasion the direct approach cut through a mass of tangled arguments to the simple truth. Thus in *Farquharson Bros.* v. *King* (1903)[7] the Lord Chancellor's speech began with the sentence: 'A servant has stolen his master's goods, and the question arises whether the persons who have received those goods innocently can set up a title against the master. I believe that is enough to dispose of this case.' After that there was really no more to be said. They are certainly very different from the agonizing doubts and delays and the tortuous qualifications and guarded parentheses which mark the reports of Eldon's decisions.

The substance of Halsbury's judgments are not, it is true, as good as the substance of Eldon's. Halsbury had not the same interest in or knowledge of legal principles. He very seldom made a mistake (though there are some peculiar remarks about resulting trusts in *Smith* v. *Cooke* (1891)),[8] but he cannot as a jurist be placed in the foremost rank of English common law judges with Bowen, Willes, and Blackburn. His learning, with the help skilfully supplied by counsel, was sufficient for the disposal of the appeals which came before him. There have been other able men who have sat on the Woolsack—Lyndhurst, Thurlow, Truro—who have been lawyers only so far as it was absolutely necessary.

It may be said here that, with one possible exception, there is no ground for the suspicion that his political views had any influence upon him in the discharge of his judicial functions. He was always ready to listen to an argument for a change in the law, and did not hesitate to over-rule an old decision if convinced that it really was unsound. One instance must suffice. In *Reg.* v. *Jackson* (1891), when sitting in the Court of Appeal, he strongly repudiated the argument that a husband could, if deserted by his

6 [1900] A.C. 21.   7 [1902] A.C. 325.   8 [1891] A.C. 297, 299.

wife, seize and imprison her until she had agreed to restore his conjugal rights. 'Such quaint and absurd dicta as are to be found in the books as to the right of a husband over his wife in respect of personal chastisement are not, I think, now capable of being cited in a Court of Justice in this or any other country.'[9]

The one exception is his decisions in the field of labour law, which have been held to show a bias against trade unions and a refusal to recognize the legitimacy of strike action. This is a difficult and controversial field. One point can be made with confidence at the outset. Halsbury had no bias against working men as such. This is very clearly shown by two decisions —*Smith* v. *Charles Baker & Sons* (1894)[1] and *Powell* v. *Main Colliery Co.* (1900).[2] In the first he agreed with the other Law Lords in holding contrary to an earlier decision of the Court of Appeal that a workman's right of action against his employer for failing to take reasonable care for his safety by (for example) not providing a safe system of work was not defeated by knowledge of the risk which he was required to run. Knowledge might be evidence of consent, so as to exempt the defendant from the duty of care which he otherwise owed, but it was not by itself conclusive. It is difficult to over-estimate the importance of the decision in *Smith* v. *Baker & Sons* in providing adequate legal protection for workmen injured in the course of their employment. Likewise in *Powell* v. *Main Colliery Co.* Halsbury delivered judgment to the effect that the Workmen's Compensation Acts were to be interpreted in accordance with the known intentions of the legislature—i.e. on broad lines and avoiding legal technicalities and subtleties. By no means all the judges in inferior courts had adopted this view, and Halsbury's firm statement undoubtedly helped to avoid an open clash on this point between the courts and the unions.

But when it came to the legal position of trade unions themselves, or the activities of their members during labour disputes, Halsbury adopted a different attitude. It will be seen[3] how he struggled hard and unsuccessfully in *Allen* v. *Flood* (1898)[4] to persuade the majority of the House that a statement by a single trade union official that he would persuade workmen to terminate their contracts of employment lawfully amounted to an actionable tort. It is true that five years later in *Quinn* v. *Leathem* (1901)[5] the House held that if two persons combined to make such a statement their conduct might amount to the tort of conspiracy unless it fell within certain exceptions. It is fair to say that later decisions of the House of Lords, particularly the *Crofter Case* (1942),[6] have emphasized the scope of the exceptions with the result that the tort of conspiracy has ceased to be of importance in labour disputes.

[9] [1891] 1 Q.B. 671. [1] [1891] A.C. 325. [2] [1900] A.C. 366. [3] Below, pp. 119–122.
[4] [1898] A.C. 1. [5] [1901] A.C. 495. [6] [1942] A.C. 435.

Criticism has fastened on the *Taff Vale Case* (1901),[7] in which the House of Lords upheld the lower court's decision that a trade union was, although not incorporated, an entity known to the law so as to be capable of being sued, and therefore liable in damages for the torts of its members committed in the course of a strike. In a very brief judgment, concurred in by four other Law Lords, Halsbury was content to adopt the reasoning of Farwell J. in the Chancery Division. That reasoning had something, though not perhaps very much, to be said in its favour on technical grounds. Its wisdom as a matter of policy on a very grave social issue is another question. As is well known, the triumphant Liberal majority of 1906 reversed the *Taff Vale Case* in the Trade Disputes Act of that year. But a legacy of suspicion and mistrust was left to poison relations between the courts and the unions for many years. One of Baldwin's favourite themes was the folly of the *Taff Vale* decision: 'The Conservatives can't talk of class-war: they started it',[8] he would remark to G. M. Young. Even after discounting something for the easy certitude of hindsight, and something for the exaggeration of table-talk amongst old men, this is a very severe judgment by one well qualified to make it.

Two final illustrations of Halsbury's judicial work may be given—one from the years when he was still Lord Chancellor, the other from his last years.

In July 1901 he presided over 500 peers as Lord High Steward in the trial for bigamy of Earl Russell.[9] After an unhappy married life in England Lord Russell had obtained a divorce in the State of Nevada and then re-married. This divorce, and hence the re-marriage, was not recognized in English law, as he was still domiciled in England. So on his return he was prosecuted for bigamy and, as a peer of the realm, he was then entitled— and indeed obliged—to be tried before his peers in the court of the Lord High Steward. Halsbury privately took the point that the indictment did not allege that the accused was a British subject; no doubt its framers had assumed that a peer of the realm must be a British subject, but there were peers who were not (e.g. Lord Fairfax), and after a Sunday spent in research in the House of Lords library Halsbury concluded that if the point was taken, the indictment would have to be quashed. For although Parliament is competent to legislate for British subjects wherever in the world they may be, it normally has power over aliens only while they are within the realm. But in the event the point was not taken; Lord Russell pleaded guilty and—perhaps to the surprise of everyone—was sentenced to three months' imprisonment.

The accused does not seem to have impressed Halsbury. A year later,

[7] [1901] A.C. 426.
[8] G. M. Young, *Stanley Baldwin* (1952), p. 31.   [9] [1901] A.C. 446.

out of gaol, Russell moved in the House of Lords the Second Reading of a Bill which would in effect have enabled divorce to be obtained by consent. Perhaps it would have been wise to treat it as the act of a man with a grievance, but Halsbury took the view that 'the introduction of such a provision as that is an outrage upon your Lordships' House, something in the nature of an insult to your Lordships'.[1] The Lord Chancellor thereupon, having secured the defeat of the motion for the Second Reading of the Bill, immediately thereafter stamped it thoroughly into the ground, by moving a motion for its rejection. The next day he wrote to his daughter: 'I had a tune-up last night with Earl Russell in the House of Lords and flatter myself that I squashed him. He is an impudent cad, and he brought Molly to come and listen to his impudence.'[2]

Finally, in his ninety-third year, Halsbury took part in the appeal entitled *Continental Tyre & Rubber Co.* v. *Daimler Co.* (1916).[3] The Court of Appeal had held that a company registered in England could not be an enemy company for the purposes of the Trading with the Enemy Acts even though all its directors and shareholders (save one) were Germans resident in Germany. It was a fundamental principle of English company law that the company was quite distinct from its shareholders. The House of Lords held that it was entitled 'to pierce the veil' of corporate personality to look at the economic truth lying behind the statutory artificial person. Halsbury, rather to the alarm of his family, took an active part in the hearing of the appeal. He wrote to his daughter Evelyn on 23 February 1916, while the case was being heard:

Your mother has persuaded me not to go to the House of Lords tonight, wherein I had meditated making a speech, but perhaps it is as well, since it is of no use arguing that the facts complained of are contrary to international law where you are arguing against people who avow that they will break the law in the name of the law and that they will make it all right with their conscience (German conscience!!!) afterwards. Today I have not been sitting, but tomorrow we resume the argument, and I think the argument is going well against the German side. But I have not heard the whole of the argument by the German side, and therefore I am suspending my view till I have heard everything that can be said for the German view.

I am much troubled by my deafness. When counsel are speaking I can hear comfortably, but when they are reading from a book, as they continually are, and put their heads down to read, I have great difficulty in hearing. Of course I can see the book afterwards, but it is very trying to have to strain your ears to hear it and of course you lose the thread of the argument and the strain on you to hear is very great.[4]

---

[1] (1902) 107 H.L. Deb. Col. 408.
[2] Halsbury papers. 'Molly' was the second Countess Russell.
[3] [1916] 2 A.C. 307.   [4] Halsbury papers.

When judgment was eventually delivered in July Halsbury's achievement evoked admiring letters from his friends. It is certainly most improbable that anyone else in the common law world has ever exercised judicial functions at so great an age. The achievement is all the more striking when it is realized that six months previously Halsbury had drafted, and secured the passage through Parliament of, a Bill to give the Board of Trade power to deal with enemy-controlled companies.[5] Nobody seems to have had the courage to argue that Halsbury had thereby disqualified himself from sitting to hear the appeal in the Daimler case.

On one point Halsbury and Eldon were alike. Each were men of inflexible personal probity: no breath of scandal, moral or financial, ever touched either. When Halsbury presided over the committee which the House of Lords insisted on setting up after the Marconi case to investigate the conduct of Lord Murray of Elibank, one of the ministers who had foolishly engaged in the transaction in question, Liberal supporters claimed that this was 'like handing over the Duke of Monmouth to Judge Jeffreys', and that there was something bizarre in constituting Halsbury a judge of a question of political purity.[6] But this is not so. Neither Halsbury nor Eldon, with all their faults, would ever have put themselves in the position in which Rufus Isaacs found himself.

Halsbury died after a very brief illness at 4 Ennismore Gardens on 11 December 1921,[7] and was buried in the churchyard at Stanmore, Middlesex. His will, dated 15 September 1913, is said to have required an affidavit of due execution before it was admitted to probate on 11 February 1922. In fact the will itself seems to have been properly executed; the difficulty arose from the fact that he left in existence, instead of destroying, two earlier wills to the same effect.[8] His estate was valued for probate at £25,009. He was succeeded by his only son, Hardinge Goulburn (1880-1943), who practised at the Bar (taking silk in 1923) before taking up residence abroad in 1935. His son, the 3rd Earl, has achieved distinction as a scientist.

---

[5] The Government after much hesitation, refused to accept the Halsbury Bill, and eventually produced their own legislation in the form of the Trading with the Enemy (Extension of Powers) Act.

[6] A. G. Gardiner, *The Pillars of Society* (1913), p. 216.

[7] Aged 98 years and 99 days—the greatest age achieved by any peer until the 16th Marquess of Winchester died in 1962.

[8] See R. E. Megarry, *Miscellany-at-Law* (1955), p. 171.

APPENDIX

HALSBURY became Lord Chancellor for the first time in June 1885, surrendering the Great Seal to Herschell the following February.

His first judgment of importance seems to have been in *Darley Main Colliery Co.* v. *Mitchell* (1886) 11 App. Cas. 127, in which he dealt adequately with a difficult question in the law relating to easements of support.

In his second Chancellorship he considered a number of important questions relating to *contract and tort*. One of his first and most characteristic judgments was in *Wakelin* v. *London and South-Western Railway Co.* (1887) 12 App. Cas. 41. The dead body of the plaintiff's husband was found lying on the railway line near a level crossing. It appeared that he had been run down by a train which had failed to whistle as it approached the crossing. The House of Lords held that there was no case to go to a jury. Lord Halsbury said: 'One may surmise, and it is but surmise and not evidence, that the unfortunate man was knocked down by a train while on the level crossing; but assuming in the plaintiff's favour that fact to be established, is there anything to show that the train ran over the man rather than that the man ran against the train?'

On assessment of damages there are some good remarks in *Ruabon Steamship Co.* v. *London Assurance Co.* [1900] A.C. 6, and *The Mediana* [1900] A.C. 113 ('What manly mind cares about pain and suffering that is past').

In *Keighley, Maxsted & Co.* v. *Durant* [1901] A.C. 240, he delivered a judgment of undisputed authority on the position of an undisclosed principal—as well as making some interesting remarks on the influence of Roman Law in English courts—while *Farquharson Bros.* v. *King* [1902] A.C. 325 contains an admirable statement, already quoted, on the question which of two innocent parties shall suffer for the fraud of a third.

Other well-known judgments which show Halsbury at his best on a common law question will be found in *Derry* v. *Peek* (1889) 14 App. Cas. 337; *G.W.R.* v. *Bunch* (1888) 13 App. Cas. 31 (negligence); *Smith* v. *Baker* [1891] A.C. 325; and *Lloyd* v. *Grace, Smith & Co.* [1912] A.C. 716 (vicarious liability); *Adam* v. *Newbigging* (1888) 13 App. Cas. 308 (misrepresentation); *Bank of England* v. *Vagliano* [1891] A.C. 107 (negotiable instruments)—a topic also well dealt with in *London Joint Stock Bank* v. *Simmons* [1892] A.C. 201.

We have already considered his judgments in the great *industrial law* cases—*Allen* v. *Flood* [1898] A.C. 1, the *Taff Vale Case* [1901] A.C. 426, and *Quinn* v. *Leathem* [1901] A.C. 495.

Family law. Mention has already been made of his well-known judgment in *R.* v. *Jackson* [1891] 1 Q.B. 671, holding that a husband had no power to force his wife to live with him other than that given by the law courts. In *Russell* v. *Russell* [1897] A.C. 395 he dissented from the decision of the majority that a wife's unfounded accusations of unnatural offences did not constitute cruelty. (The sequel was *R.* v. *Russell* [1901] A.C. 446.)

Real Property. In *Leigh* v. *Taylor* [1902] A.C. 157, there is a sound treatment of the vexed question of fixtures as between landlord and tenant. In *Colls* v. *Home & Colonial Stores* [1904] A.C. 179, Halsbury agreed with the others in holding that the test for determinng whether an easement of light had been infringed was whether sufficient light was left for the convenient use of the plaintiff's house. Halsbury had also considered the law relating to easements in *Gardner* v. *Hodgson's Kingston Brewery Co.* [1903] A.C. 229, in which payment for a licence to use a way defeated the plaintiff's claim that his user had been *nec vi, nec clam, nec precario.*

Equity was not a subject on which Halsbury could be said to be an authority, but he had sufficient self-confidence to write an occasional judgment. In *Noakes* v. *Rice* [1902] A.C. 24 he considered how far it is permissible to clog the equity of redemption of a mortgage, and in *Kingsbury* v. *Walter* [1901] A.C. 187 the complex rules governing class gifts. In *Smith* v. *Cooke* [1891] A.C. 297, 299, there are some *dicta* about resulting trusts which can hardly be correct.

Criminal law. One of the first appeals to reach the House of Lords from the Court of Criminal Appeal set up by the Act of 1907 was *Leach* v. *R.* [1912] A.C. 305, in which it was held that the provisions of the Criminal Evidence Act, 1898, making a husband or wife a competent witness against the other in certain cases (e.g. those of a sexual nature) did not mean that such a spouse was compellable. Halsbury, who was, as we have seen, the author of the Act, remarked that it would have been 'perfectly monstrous' if such a fundamental change had been made by implication.

Conflict of Laws. There are a number of good judgments on this difficult branch of law. In *Cooper* v. *Cooper* (1888) 13 App. Cas. 88, he held that the capacity of an English infant to enter into a prenuptial marriage settlement with an alien domiciled abroad was regulated by English law. The rule has been criticized but its authority is beyond dispute.

In *British South Africa Co.* v. *Mozambique* [1893] A.C. 602, he considered whether an action would lie in England for a trespass to land committed abroad. He again considered the actionability of foreign torts in *Carr* v. *Fracis, Times & Co., Ltd.* [1902] A.C. 176. His judgment in *Winans* v. *Attorney-General* [1904] A.C. 287, on the question of what must be done to prove the abandonment of a domicile of origin and the acquisition of a domicile of choice, is less often cited than the brilliant speech of Lord Macnaghten. In *Janson* v. *Driefontein Mines, Ltd.* [1902] A.C. 484, he dealt with the question how far an alien enemy can sue in an English court—as he was to do again at the age of 92 in the *Daimler Case* (1916), as we have already seen.

In *De Nicols* v. *Curlier* [1900] A.C. 21, the House gave a bold and liberal interpretation to the law governing succession by recognizing the French doctrine of community of property so as to entitle a wife to share in the fortune built up by her husband as owner of the Café Royal after he had changed his domicile from France to England. The even more difficult rules governing bankruptcy in the conflict of laws were well treated in *Cooke* v. *Charles A. Vogeler Co.* [1901] A.C. 102.

Statutory interpretation was a subject on which Halsbury had decided views. In *Leader* v. *Duffey* (1888) 13 App. Cas. 294 he said:

All these refinements and nice distinctions of words appear to me to be inconsistent with the modern view—which is I think in accordance with reason and common sense—that, whatever the instrument, it must receive a construction according to the plain meaning of the words and sentences therein contained . . . But it appears to me to be arguing in a vicious circle to begin by assuming an intention apart from the language of the instrument itself and having made that fallacious assumption to bend the language in favour of the assumption so made.

In *Hilder* v. *Dexter* [1902] A.C. 474 there is an interesting *obiter dictum* that a draftsman is not in modern times the best judge of the true intention of Parliament.

Constitutional law. All students are familiar with Halsbury's Privy Council judgments in *ex parte Marais* [1902] A.C. 109, and *Tilonko* v. *Attorney-General of Natal* [1907] A.C. 93, which lay down with robust emphasis that when actual war is raging and martial law has been proclaimed the ordinary courts have no jurisdiction to interfere with the military in their efforts to restore order.

On the other hand, in *Cox* v. *Hakes* (1890) 15 App. Cas. 506 he refused to give a literal interpretation to a statute so as to deprive a successful applicant for a writ of habeas corpus of his right to immediate release.

It was characteristic of Halsbury that he should have minimized the power of the courts to extend the common law through the concept of public policy. He vigorously denied in *Janson* v. *Driefontein Consolidated Mines, Ltd.* [1902] A.C. 484, 491, 496, that a court could invent a 'new head of public policy', and in the same case remarked approvingly that 'What politicians call expedience often depends on momentary conjunctures, and is frequently nothing more than the fine-spun speculations of visionary theorists'. Later judges and writers have thought that he took a rather narrow view of the matter. It was also characteristic that he should have affirmed in the most emphatic language that the House of Lords was bound by its own previous decisions.

Of course I do not deny that cases of individual hardship may arise, and that there may be a current of opinion in the profession that such and such a judgment was erroneous; but what is that occasional interference with what is perhaps abstract justice as compared with the inconvenience—the disastrous inconvenience—of having each question subject to being re-argued and the dealings of mankind rendered doubtful by reason of different decisions, so that in truth and in fact there could be no real final Court of Appeal? My Lords, 'interest rei publicae' that there should be 'finis litium' at some time and there could be no 'finis litium' if it were possible to suggest in each case that it might be re-argued, because it is 'not an ordinary case', whatever that may mean.

This judgment in *London Street Tramways* v. *L.C.C.* [1898] A.C. 375, at 380, has given rise to much discussion. Most authorities are agreed that it lays down a rule which is unnecessarily strict for modern conditions. The House of Lords is now the only supreme tribunal in the common law world which is unable to review its own decisions, however undesirable the passage of time may have shown them to be.

But it would be erroneous to think that Halsbury regarded the common law as no more than the application of unrationalized common sense. 'I am not much impressed by what the man in the street would say', he remarked in *Costello* v. *Pigeon (Owners)* [1913] A.C. 407, at 413.

LORD HERSCHELL

CHAPTER I

FARRER HERSCHELL was born on 2 November 1837, at Brampton, Huntingdonshire, the son of the Reverend Ridley Haim (later Anglicized to Henry) Herschell of Gloucester Terrace, Paddington, London, and Helen Skirving, his wife, the daughter of William Mowbray, a merchant of Edinburgh. The day of his birth—*cras animarum*—had been the beginning of Michaelmas Term for years, as he liked to recall.

His father was of a Polish-Jewish family which had come to England after many excitements on the Continent at the beginning of the century. He had received considerable kindness from the great legal family of Farrer, after whom the son was named. The father became a Christian after reading a copy of the Sermon on the Mount which had been used to wrap a parcel.[1] The sponsors at his baptism by the Bishop of London at St. James's, Westminster, in 1830, being a Farrer brother and sister, and the husband of another Farrer—the Rev. H. C. Ridley of Hambleden, Haim Herschell took Ridley as his baptismal name. Despite his Anglican baptism, he seems to have moved into his own brand of nonconformity, for at the date of the future Lord Chancellor's birth he was the minister of Mount Zion Chapel, Chadwell Street, Clerkenwell, and in the birth certificate his occupation is given as simply 'gentleman'. Afterwards he was at the Chapel in John Street, Edgware Road. He was a man of dominant personality who impressed all who met him: so successful was his career that he is noticed in the *DNB*. Farrer Herschell was therefore bred in an atmosphere of nonconformity which at that date excluded him from going to either Oxford or Cambridge, though in later life he became an Anglican of a rather high-church kind. Herschell's mother was a fine musician and a good linguist—qualities inherited by her son.

After some years at a grammar school in south London, and a period at the University of Bonn in 1852 (during which his mother died), Farrer Herschell proceeded to London University in 1855 where he graduated B.A. with honours in classics in 1857. While at University College, London, he was a prominent speaker in the Debating Society and together with (Sir) R. D. Littler edited a 'University Review', an article in which attracted the attention of an ex-Lord Chancellor, Brougham, who sent for the young Herschell and presented him with a complimentary copy of his works.

Herschell was admitted to Lincoln's Inn on 12 January 1858 and called

[1] *DNB*, vol. xxvi, p. 274.

to the Bar on 17 November 1860. He became a pupil of the great mid-Victorian common law pleader, Thomas Chitty. With him in the same pupil room were the future Lord Bowen, the future Lord Justice A. L. Smith, the future Mr. Justice Charles (who had been a contemporary at University College), and Joseph Chitty, the son of Thomas, who in his turn enhanced the fame of this great legal dynasty. After his period of pupillage with Chitty, Herschell joined the chambers of James Hannen and also went on the Northern Circuit, from which the North-Eastern Circuit had not yet hived off. For a time he was a reporter on the staff of a short-lived series, *The New Reports*, which nevertheless succeeded in recruiting to its staff some other youthful barristers who later became judges—Davey, Bowen, and Stirling, the last of whom Herschell was to appoint to the Bench.

Herschell was entirely without any advantages of birth or connection, and whatever success he achieved at the Bar was due solely to his own industry and capacity. He was, however, fortunate in achieving a place in Hannen's chambers. At that time Hannen had a huge practice in insurance and mercantile cases. He was so busy that his pupils took their drafts to him on Saturday to be returned on the following Monday, for he had no time to read them during the week. But it was not until Hannen was made a judge in 1868 and several leading juniors took silk in the same year in consequence that business really began to flow in Herschell's direction. At the Liverpool Summer Assizes of 1869 he found no fewer than eighteen heavy briefs waiting for him on arrival. But in the early years things were very difficult. On 19 February 1866 a very new member of the Circuit, Victor Alexander Williamson, the fourth son of Sir Hedworth Williamson of Whitburn, recorded in his diary that

I left Whitburn and went the same afternoon to Carlisle where I arrived in time for the Bar Mess, at which I dined. I sat next to an insignificant shabby-looking little man, with whom I got into conversation upon Eastern travel, he like myself having some years before made the Grand Tour of the East. The acquaintance made that evening developed into the closest intimacy which death alone has ended. He was Farrer Herschell, for whom a brilliant destiny was in store, but at that time of some six years standing at the Bar and as yet doing very little. Just 20 years later I was dining with him when he received the letter from Mr Gladstone offering him the Woolsack.[2]

Later Herschell told a meeting of law students that

He himself had once held very despondent views, and had on one occasion nearly accepted a tempting offer made to him to go to the Colonies. He was very doubtful if he should ever succeed at all, and his success was a very long

[2] Williamson papers. The published account in (1899) J.C.L. 205 differs slightly.

PLATE 3

Lord Herschell as Chancellor in 1886

PLATE 4

Lord Herschell out of office

time in coming; but it came at last, as it would to every man who was determined to get on, and who did not mind working early and late to achieve his
end. The main essential was to fit oneself for the profession and, above all, to
stick to it.[3]

The incident to which Herschell referred occurred when he was in
conversation with Charles Russell and William Gully, two fellow junior
barristers on the Circuit. All three were bemoaning their briefless lot and
were seriously tempted to abandon practice in England in the hope of
obtaining something better abroad. Herschell thought of the Chinese
Consular Courts, and Gully of the Indian Bar. But it was fortunate for
themselves and for the future development of English law that they
should have decided otherwise, for one became Lord Chancellor, one
Lord Chief Justice, and one Speaker of the House of Commons.[4] Another
member of the Circuit at that time who later rose to prominence was
Holker, who became a Conservative Attorney-General and later Lord
Justice of Appeal.

A friend at the Bar who observed Holker, Russell, and Herschell in
action gives the following picture.

Herschell's intellect differed widely from both. In power of logical statement,
in clear and exact reasoning, and in the ability to conduct an argument without
a flaw from start to finish, he was certainly not the inferior of either. But his
nature on the emotional side, so far at least as advocacy was concerned, was
poorly furnished. He lacked the warmth to sway a jury. He was unable to
realize any disability in others that he did not possess himself, and the consequence was that he had often concluded his address to the jury before those
unfortunate gentlemen had apprehended the essential features of the case he was
trying to enforce. And for this reason his appeal as an advocate was far less
potent than that of either of his two great rivals. The cold steel of his intellect
never reached white heat.[5]

There is also evidence to show that at this period Charles Russell had
some respect for Herschell as a possible rival. In later years Russell
remarked to an American friend, G. J. Clark:

My chief contemporaries on the circuit were Pope, Herschell, and Holker.
Holker was a formidable opponent, so was Herschell; Pope was a very able
man, but not a lawyer in the same sense as Herschell and myself. I do not think
that Pope was suited for *nisi prius* business. He was better suited to parliamentary
business. He was certainly suited for politics, he would have been a greater
success in the House of Commons than either Herschell or myself; had Herschell
and I been different men, the work in the Northern Circuit would not have

---

[3] (1890) 88 L.T. News. 349.
[4] See W. C. Gully, 'Lord Herschell' (1900) 15 L.Q.R. 123.
[5] J. Comyns Carr, *Some Eminent Victorians* (1914), p. 55.

gone so smoothly or so quickly as it did. We were both quick; we lose no time in coming to the point, and we keep to it. We understood and trusted each other.[6]

Another judgment on Herschell's capacity as an advocate comes at a rather later date from the future Lord Alverstone who, as Richard Webster, often appeared against Herschell at the Bar. 'He had perhaps a greater power of placing facts before the jury and of representing the effect of evidence than anyone I can remember.'[7] In any event Herschell was a respected member of the Circuit, tenacious in upholding all the rights and privileges of the Bar. At one time he was active in procuring a general protest to the Attorney-General, Coleridge, because the Crown had briefed Charles Russell to prosecute in a sensational murder case on the Circuit instead of a member of the Circuit named Aspinall who was customarily briefed as 'Attorney-General for the County'.

In 1872 Herschell's position at the Bar was sufficiently strong to warrant his taking silk at the early age of 35. His application was backed by every common law judge on the Bench. In 1875 he took into his chambers at 3 Harcourt Buildings Mackenzie Chalmers, the greatest parliamentary draftsman England has ever known. On 8 May 1872 he also became a Bencher of his Inn and two years later was returned as Member of Parliament for Durham in the Liberal interest, on 13 June 1874. The preceding year he had been appointed Recorder of Carlisle, a position which he held until 1880. His Liberalism may not have been a deeply felt conviction from his earliest years, for in the early 'seventies he is known to have stayed with Derby at Knowsley for the week-end, the great Conservative magnate being anxious to recruit for his party one whose reputation in the north was already secure.[8] Indeed, he seems to have taken no part in the General Election of February 1874 which returned a Conservative Government. But afterwards he appeared for the sitting Liberal members in both Durham City and North Durham, against whom petitions had been presented. In neither case was he successful, but the result of his efforts was very curious: he so impressed the local party stalwarts in the city that they selected him and Sir Arthur Monck as their candidates for the ensuing by-election. The opinions of the displaced members for Durham City are not recorded. (It is said that the first choice fell on Charles Russell, who had been counsel for the successful petitioners, but on reflection it was thought that a Roman Catholic would not be a suitable member for a cathedral city.) In later life Herschell always gave to young

[6] G. J. Clark, *Great Sayings by Great Lawyers* (Kansas, 1926), p. 604.
[7] Lord Alverstone, *Recollections of Bar and Bench* (1914), p. 19.
[8] A. G. C. Liddell, *Notes from the Life of an Ordinary Mortal* (1911), p. 139.

men at the Bar the advice to get into the House of Commons as soon as their practice warranted.

The 1870s were a time of expansion in his life, both public and private. On 20 December 1876 he married at Tincleton, Dorset, Agnes Adela, the third daughter of Edward Leigh Kindersley Porcher, of Clyffe House, Dorset, by Fanny Maitland, fourth daughter of Henry Wilson of Stowlangtoft Hall, Suffolk. His close friend Victor Williamson recorded: 'I officiated as Farrer's best man; and thus was sealed a long friendship; and the foundation was laid of a new one which promises to be equally enduring.'[9] This was indubitably an advantageous marriage for a man of Herschell's background. His bride came from a long-established family of landed gentry with extensive banking interests. There was also a legal connection—she was the grand-daughter of Vice-Chancellor Kindersley. In the same year the old Northern Circuit was divided, and Herschell concentrated on Liverpool and Manchester. Two years later he 'went special', and left London for Circuit only for a special fee. Herschell's position was now sufficiently secure to enable him to purchase the lease of a large house at 46 Grosvenor Gardens, where he remained until his death. His son and heir, Richard Rognvald, was born in 1878. This son, whose widow died in April 1961, became a Lord-in-Waiting to Edward VII and George V.

[9] Williamson papers.

CHAPTER II

WHEN HERSCHELL ENTERED PARLIAMENT after the general election of 1874 his party was in a discouraged condition. Not only had it been defeated by the Conservatives at the general election but Gladstone was in a curious state of sullen retirement and for some time it was uncertain whether he was in truth the leader of the party. It was not until January 1875 that he officially resigned and was succeeded by Hartington, who led the party 'with the typical undistinguished merit of a Cavendish'. Herschell, however, maintained an imperturbable demeanour and quickly established a position for himself in the House. Normally it is not easy for lawyers to do this and some thought that it would be particularly difficult for Herschell, both because of his racial background (the first Jew had been allowed to sit in the House as recently as 1858), and also because his manner was undoubtedly somewhat cold and formal. The struggle for success at the Bar had so far left him little time to cultivate the graces of life. But he quickly obtained a respectful hearing. He made his maiden speech on 12 April 1875 on the Committee stage of the Artisan's Dwelling Bill.[1] It was a brief and pointed intervention which received no more than the usual polite welcome. But on 24 February 1876 he made a remarkable speech,[2] without using any notes, as was customary with him, on the problem of how far British warships should receive fugitive slaves when in the territorial waters of countries which permitted the institution of slavery.

In the preceding autumn the Admiralty had issued a circular which stated that a slave who had taken refuge in one of Her Majesty's ships on the high seas was liable to be surrendered if the ship returned within the territorial limits of the country from which he had escaped. Considerable public discussion and criticism followed—Victorian England was rightly proud of the part it had played in the abolition of the slave trade. The matter was referred to the Law Officers (Baggallay and Holker) who advised that 'if a slave gets on board a [British] ship upon the high seas, we think he becomes, *ipso facto*, free'. On the other hand, a slave boarding a British public vessel in foreign territorial waters retained his status of slavery. The opposite view could only be justified on the erroneous theory that a public vessel was a floating portion of the flag state, instead of merely possessing certain immunities from the local jurisdiction. But the strength of public opinion, as expressed in the debate, was such as to procure the

[1] 223 *Parl. Deb.* 3s. col. 760.　　[2] 227 *Parl. Deb.* 3s. col. 820.

appointment of a Royal Commission, which issued a definitive report.[3] Henceforward Herschell's position in the House was secure.

A few months later he spoke again on the second reading of a Private Member's Bill to regulate the fees of barristers and advocates.[4] The promoter of the Bill was mainly concerned to stop the practice whereby distinguished barristers accepted briefs in two or more different courts with the result that when cases came on some clients were inevitably disappointed. Herschell made an effective speech in which, while not denying that there was room for improvement, both in the practice of the profession and still more in the procedural arrangements of the courts themselves, he made the point that counsel did not pledge himself to appear in any court by accepting a brief but only to use his best endeavours to do so. Also, the arrangements for trial were such that he might well have waited some time for the case in which he was briefed to come on and thus he might be faced with the problem of deserting his next client. Fundamentally, however, as Herschell insisted, the problem was really due to the fact that solicitors or their clients insisted on briefing fashionable counsel, who were thus snowed under with work while a large number of promising junior barristers, who could probably have taken the case equally well, were without anything at all. But the tradition of the legal profession has always been 'unto him who hath shall be given' and probably no Act of Parliament could alter this. Herschell did not mention the complaint, which was perhaps capable of remedy, that the acceptance of too many briefs by a prominent barrister was often due to the insistence of his clerk who, of course, was entitled to a percentage of the fee and thus had a financial interest in seeing that his employer received as many briefs as possible.

Later in the same year, Herschell, whose demeanour in public and in private was generally of extreme gravity, enlivened a speech by a small joke. In the debate on Supply on 26 May the appointment of an official Referee was questioned on the ground of inadequacy of legal knowledge. Herschell remarked that every professional man knows that occasionally persons were appointed to inferior judicial positions 'who not only had no reputation as lawyers, but, worse still, had the reputation of being no lawyers'.[5] Two years later, in May 1878, the question of judicial appointments was again considered when there was a debate on whether the Corporation of the City of London should be entitled to continue to elect their judges, the Recorder and the Common Serjeant, as they had been accustomed to do for generations. The Corporation were, as always, extremely tenacious of their privileges and their attitude was defended by

[3] Report of Commission on Fugitive Slaves (1876), C. 1516.
[4] 229 *Parl. Deb.* 3s. col. 343.   [5] Ibid., col. 1321.

the Solicitor-General, Giffard, in spite of some cogent objections by Herschell.[6]

In August 1878 Herschell took part in the debates on the Territorial Waters Jurisdiction Bill which was necessary as a result of the decision of the Court of Exchequer Chamber in *The Franconia*, in which it was held that the Central Criminal Court had no jurisdiction to try for manslaughter an alien on board a foreign vessel within British territorial waters. The decision as Giffard, who had unsuccessfully argued the case for the Crown, remarked, meant that 'the life and honour of any British subject bathing at the sea side—say, of a school girl at Brighton or elsewhere—would be at the mercy of any foreigner on board a foreign ship who choose to take it'.[7] This was just the sort of vivid, practical illustration to appeal to Victorian Members of Parliament and the Bill went through.

In March 1879 the Government brought in a Bill to establish a Director of Public Prosecutions. Some forty years of parliamentary discussion had preceded this Bill which was opposed by various interests, for example, the solicitors. Herschell made an admirable speech in which he said:

Many attempts have been made to deal with the matter; but those efforts have been frustrated, by reason of its always having been attempted not to make use of the present system of prosecution so far as it extended, but to introduce an entirely new system, by which the whole of the prosecutions throughout the country would be carried on by the Government and by a Public Prosecutor. Against such a scheme, whether right or wrong, a host of opponents were raised. All those who conducted prosecutions at the present time, and all others interested in the present mode of conducting the prosecutions, became at once opponents of any attempt to wipe away the existing system ... He believed that there was the greatest possible want in this country of a Public Prosecutor— it was felt every day; but, on the other hand, he must, for his part, frankly confess that the mode in which by far the greater number of prosecutions that went on throughout the country was conducted, was eminently satisfactory; the distinction should be kept in view, between the existence of a Public Prosecutor whose duty it should be either by himself or by his subordinates to see that prosecutions were carried on to the legitimate results, or, when necessary, to institute and carry on the machinery of the prosecution, and placing of all prosecutions in the country in the hands of Government Prosecutors.[8]

This distinction was the one which was ultimately accepted by the Government and Parliament. Criminal prosecutions in England are still in general a matter for police officers or private persons in the locality of of the crime: the Director of Public Prosecutions takes over only in exceptional cases.

[6] 239 *Parl. Deb.* 3s. col. 1923. [7] 242 *Parl. Deb.* 3s. col. 2035.
[8] 244 *Parl. Deb.* 3s. col. 969.

On 6 May 1879 he moved (unsuccessfully) a resolution on a matter on which he always held strong views: the abolition of actions for breach of promise of marriage.[9] Originally he had thought that it would be best to abolish the action completely and on two previous occasions had suggested this to the House but now he agreed to a compromise by which the action was to be abolished except when actual pecuniary loss was proved. Herschell produced a powerful argument in support of his proposal. His experience at the Bar had taught him that extortionate actions were a common occurrence. He also said that it was an action confined to the middle classes being unknown either to the upper class or the working class and that it had been disapproved by a number of eminent lawyers, including the great Lord Mansfield. But Parliament was unconvinced and the law is still unaltered.

On the broader scene Herschell was an unwavering supporter of Gladstone on both Eastern and Irish affairs. It was a difficult time for the party because Disraeli had apparently solved the Eastern question at the Congress of Berlin in 1878, from which he had returned to England amidst almost universal applause. The morale of the Liberal Party was so low that Herschell's clerk remarked to him at this time, 'Don't you think, Sir, in view of the turn events seem to be taking, that our choice of politics was a little premature?' But his clerk had a firm faith in the capacities of his master, for in 1879 he remarked to someone who inquired whether Herschell was accepting a vacant puisne judgeship which he had been offered by Selborne, 'Thank God we haven't fallen as low as that.'[1] (The judgeship was then accepted by Charles Bowen, his old colleague in chambers.) But at the general election of 1880 a change occurred and the Liberal Party was returned to office once more with a large majority. The Queen invited Hartington and Granville in turn to form a government; each declined, and she was obliged to recognize the inevitable and send for Gladstone. Herschell now had expectations of advancement and he was not altogether surprised to receive from the new Prime Minister the following letter:

Secret 18 Carlton House Terrace S.W.
28 April, 1880

My dear Sir,
The Attorney-General of the new Government has just been appointed, and I have hastened to fortify myself with the best opinions as to the choice, almost equally important, of a Solicitor-General.
The result of my consideration is that I can in no way so well serve the public

[9] 245 *Parl. Deb.* 3s. col. 1867.
[1] Lord Alverstone, *Recollections of Bench and Bar* (1914), p. 263.

interest in this grave matter as by asking you to allow me to submit your name to Her Majesty for the office of Solicitor-General.

I remain, my dear Sir, faithfully yours,

W. E. Gladstone[2]

F. Herschell, Esq., Q.C.

Herschell replied at once.

46 Grosvenor Gardens
29 April, 1880

My dear Sir,

I need hardly say that I shall esteem it a very high honour to serve as one of the legal officers of your administration and shall do my best to perform efficiently the duties of Solicitor-General should Her Majesty be pleased to approve of my appointment. I cannot but add an expression of my thanks for the flattering terms in which the offer is conveyed by your letter.

I am, dear Sir,
Yours very truly,
F. Herschell[3]

The Rt. Hon. W. E. Gladstone, M.P.

The appointment of Herschell, which had been pressed on Gladstone by Selborne, the new Lord Chancellor, and Hartington, was, however, a severe disappointment to a Welsh M.P., Watkin Williams, to whom Gladstone wrote as follows:

29th April, 1880

It will not be in my power to offer you that of which you would have been highly worthy, I mean the post of Solicitor-General under the new administration. I am in doubt whether you would be disposed to accept the office of Judge-Advocate-General, the holder of which will probably have more important duties to perform than heretofore. I only place it at your disposal in token of respect and acknowledgment, and so, I am convinced you will kindly interpret my proceeding. You are aware that the office is accompanied with elevation to the Privy Council.[4]

Only the most avid office-seeker would have accepted an offer made in such unwelcoming terms, and it is not surprising that Watkin Williams replied angrily declining the proffered office of Judge-Advocate-General, and saying:

I should not be true to myself or to you if I did not add that your announcement was received by me with feelings of mortification which I know will be shared in by the Welsh people generally, who will consider that my position and standing in the profession and the political services that I have rendered

[2] B.M. Add. MSS. 44463, f. 232.   [3] Ibid., f. 270.
[4] Ibid., f. 289.

to the Party in Wales had earned for me a higher claim to the office which you are unable to offer me.[5]

But elsewhere, at the Bar and in Parliament, Herschell's appointment was universally applauded. He received the customary honour of knighthood on 13 May 1880. His colleague as Law Officer, Sir Henry James (Lord James of Hereford) on several occasions in later life paid tribute to the friendly relations which existed between himself and Herschell during their period of office. It was well that this was so for the work of the Law Officers at this time was exceptionally heavy. After he had become a peer Herschell said that he never went home at the end of a day spent in the House of Commons without a severe headache. It can be said of Herschell that he established an entirely new position for the Law Officers in the House of Commons. Before his time they were seen at Westminster only for debates on legal questions, or for major divisions when every vote counted.

The difficulties started at once in May 1880 with the question of Charles Bradlaugh, a representative of that now forgotten class, the Victorian atheist, who refused to take the necessary oath after his election at Northampton. The controversy did not show the House of Commons at its best. Bradlaugh on several occasions insisted that he was willing to take an oath or even to affirm but the House of Commons eventually resolved that he should be permitted to do neither. The electors of Northampton stood by their Member, consistently returning him to Parliament on every occasion on which their votes were sought.

In the same session there was a lengthy series of debates on the Employers' Liability Bill, which was regarded by more old-fashioned members of the Bar, such as Giffard, as being a complete inversion of the ordinary principles of contract. The Bill to modern eyes was but a very small step forward in protecting the workman from the inevitable hazards of industrial accidents by placing on his employer certain duties of reasonable care in relation to the provision of proper premises in which to work. These duties were such that they could not be avoided by any contract between employer and workman.

In 1881 Herschell was exceptionally busy throughout the summer on the great Irish Land Act, which took many weeks to pass through its Committee stage, the opposition fighting every line of every clause. It must, at the end of the year, have been a great temptation to escape from these parliamentary hardships by accepting an offer which was made to him of a vacant Law Lordship. The existence of two vacancies in the Judicial Committee of the Privy Council as a result of the retirement of

[5] Add. MSS 44463, f. 291.

Sir J. Colvile and Sir M. Smith made it possible to appoint one new Law Lord. Gladstone offered this position to Sir Henry James, who refused, and then in due course offered it to Herschell, who replied on 21 December:

My dear Mr. Gladstone,

I own that the proposal you make is not without its temptations. The office is not only one of dignity but it affords the opportunity for useful work of a kind agreeable to my tastes. But though conscious of the honour I have come without hesitation to the conclusion to remain for the present in the post I now hold. I am most gratified by and grateful for your expressions with regard to the services I have rendered to the Government. I can assure you it has been a labour of love to serve under you. And if I could think I had in any small measure lightened your burthen, that would be sufficient reward. Indeed the consideration that you might perhaps regret losing me as Law Officer and the hope you encourage me to entertain that I may be of some further use to you in the future have weighed not a little in leading me to my present conclusion. I am, dear Mr. Gladstone,

Yours very truly,
Farrer Herschell[6]

At the date of this offer Herschell had just celebrated his forty-fourth birthday. No other member of the Bar, whether Law Officer or not, has been offered a Law Lordship at such an age. (The position was eventually accepted by a man of 66, who had been an Irish judge for twenty-two years—Lord FitzGerald.)

The next two years saw more heavy work in the House of Commons. In the autumn of 1882 Herschell had to make many speeches in an effort to get through the new Rules of Procedure which were necessary to deal with the persistent obstruction caused by the Irish Members. In the same year Herschell secured the passage of the Bills of Exchange Act, drafted by his old friend Mackenzie Chalmers—who, through Herschell's influence, had now been appointed standing counsel to the Board of Trade, and two years later was to become a county court judge.

In the following year, in April, a Bill to establish a Court of Criminal Appeal was brought in by the Government but opposed by Giffard for the Conservatives on the rather surprising ground that it did not go far enough. The Crown, he said, should have a right of appeal as well as the prisoner.[7] The Bill received a second reading but nothing more happened and it was 1907 before Loreburn succeeded in procuring its passage into law. Throughout the summer Herschell was occupied by the lengthy debates on the Agricultural Holdings Bill and the Parliamentary Elections (Corrupt Practices) Bill.

6 Add. MSS 44473, f. 123.   7 277 Parl. Deb. 3s. col. 1191.

Further offers of promotion were made by Gladstone. In March 1883 Herschell might have succeeded Sir George Jessel as Master of the Rolls; and the following November it was suggested to him by the Prime Minister that he might be the Liberal candidate for the office of Speaker in succession to Speaker Brand. This was a position which in many ways was suitable to Herschell's tastes and abilities but after much thought he felt obliged to decline the offer. He is believed to have consulted Selborne whether his acceptance would be a final bar to eventual promotion to the Woolsack. He explained his reasons to the Prime Minister as follows:

17th November 1883

My dear Mr. Gladstone,

I need hardly tell you how sensible I am of the high honour done me in asking me to allow myself to be proposed for the office of Speaker. It is with real regret that I feel impelled to decline so flattering a proposal, and I fear from what you said that my doing so may cause you some disappointment. If I had followed my inclination I should have given this answer at once, as soon as you were good enough to make the proposal. But as you urge that if I accept the office I should render a public service it came before me in the light of a call of duty to which I was bound to yield if I could even at some personal sacrifice. I have therefore given the matter I may say painfully anxious consideration. I have taken such counsel as I could to guide me and with every desire to do what is right and put out of sight if I could all merely *personal* considerations. But there are others dearer to me than myself who would be affected by my decision and whose interests present claims of absolute duty. I cannot be satisfied that I should be doing them justice if I made the change proposed. Besides the mere pecuniary question, I have some apprehension that my health might not stand the new mode of life and this is of course a matter of serious concern. Weighing it simply as a matter of duty I regret to say that I feel these things must turn the scale. I am comforted only by the hope that in my present position I may still render some public service and I feel sure you will appreciate with kindness the motives which have actuated me.

Yours very sincerely,

Farrer Herschell[8]

Herschell at this time was pushing himself almost to the limit of human endurance. He was at the House of Commons all afternoon and evening and often, especially when debates on Ireland arose, far into the night. During the rest of the day he conducted his normal work as Law Officer together with a large private practice, Law Officers not being, at that date, restricted only to Government work.

One of his cases at this time which attracted much attention was the Durham Divorce Case.[9] This was a petition for nullity by the Earl of Durham, for whom Herschell appeared, on the ground that at the time

[8] Add. MSS 44484, f. 79.   [9] (1885) 10 P.D. 80.

of the marriage three years before his wife was hopelessly insane, as she was now admitted to be. For the respondent it was successfully argued that she had only been an exceptionally shy and nervous girl. Her grandfather, the Archbishop of Armagh, stated that 'he regarded her as the most sensible of his grand-daughters', which, as the judge, Sir James Hannen, observed, was 'a statement entirely consistent with her intellectual powers being feebler than those of her sisters, but entirely excluding the idea of her being imbecile'. So Lord Durham, as the law then stood, was tied for life to a hopelessly insane wife.

The strain of all this work was very great, although at first it did not show itself. As his colleague, Sir Henry James, recorded:

He seemed never to weary—neither physically nor mentally. During his Solicitor-Generalship he would commence his forensic labours at ten o'clock; occupied by them until four, he would then assiduously attend in the House of Commons until long after midnight: no twelve o'clock rule existed then. When the House rose he would bid a wearied colleague take some real rest, while he would proceed to deal with 'the cases for opinion'; and so next morning he would have to recommence his labours without the enjoyment of more repose than could be found in an armchair.[1]

Herbert Gladstone, too, described Herschell as 'a marvellous man' for sitting up with a dozen other members to 3 a.m. for an Irish debate.[2]

But overwork has always been a complaint of Law Officers. Lord St. Leonards described his life as Solicitor-General in 1829–30:

I will tell you what my life was as Solicitor-General. I will begin at 3 a.m., when you may imagine me staggering with fatigue up the steps of my house in Guilford Street on my return from the House of Commons, to find Lady Sugden waiting for me with a cup of tea. I then used to go to bed, with strict injunctions to be called at 6. My briefs were brought to me, and I set to work for a couple of hours. I then had breakfast and slept for a short time before I had to attend consultations. At 10 o'clock I went into Court, and there remained until it was time to go to the House, where I stayed answering questions until the small hours of the morning. Often I was called upon to make a speech at the end of the debate, and so on to the next day of toil and troubles.[3]

Herschell's life at this time was much the same. In his private life there was little time for social relaxation although he occasionally enjoyed musical parties at his home, at which he himself was accustomed to play the 'cello. He had, by now, deserted both the Jewish world of his ancestors (although his physical appearance, especially in middle and old age,

[1] James (1899) 1 J.C.L. 201.
[2] Viscount Gladstone, *After Thirty Years* (1928), p. 181.
[3] *Blackwood's Magazine*, February 1857.

unmistakably recalled his central European background) and the non-conformist atmosphere of his childhood, and had become a devout member of the Church of England, attending regularly at St. Peter's, Eaton Square, a haunt of fashionable high-church Anglicanism. At the same time his brother continued to preach to a large congregation at a chapel in the Herne Hill Road.

At about this time Herschell acquired some financial interest in the building of New Court, Carey Street, and in 1881 he removed his chambers from the Temple to 11 New Court.

CHAPTER III

B Y THE SPRING OF 1885 the Gladstone Government was breaking up. The signs of fission which develop in any Government after five years were increasingly noticeable. The Government's unpopularity in the country had increased after the tragedy of Gordon's death at Khartoum. The end came when the Conservatives made cautious overtures to detach the Irish Members under Parnell from their adherence to Gladstone. On 8 June 1885 the Irish supported a Conservative amendment to the Finance Bill with the result that it was carried against the Government in the early hours of the 9th, by 264 to 252. Gladstone at once offered his resignation. Some discussion took place as to the terms on which Salisbury could or would form his minority government, but after securing from Gladstone pledges (necessarily indeterminate in language) sufficient to secure the passage of the necessary financial legislation, he kissed hands on 23 June. His government lasted just seven months in a year of continuous political excitement almost unprecedented in England.

A general election could not take place until the late autumn, as the large Redistribution Bill, a necessary sequel to the Franchise Act, 1884, was not yet through Parliament. The latter Act not only enlarged the electorate from 3 to 5 millions but also abolished the old double-member constituencies. One effect of this was distinctly adverse to the Liberal Party, for it ended their convenient practice of running Whigs and Radicals in double harness. Another effect was personal to Herschell: he was obliged to stand for a new constituency—North Lonsdale in Lancashire, because the Durham party managers preferred his colleague, T. C. Thompson (who was in the event beaten by T. Milvain, Q.C.). In any event Herschell, as the junior Member, felt bound to sacrifice himself. At the election he was defeated by W. G. Ainslie. The Liberals fared badly in all the boroughs at that election, although the county voters were properly grateful to those who had enfranchised them. In the normal course Herschell's position was not at that moment one of strength; he was out of the House, and there were in the party two lawyers with claims senior to his.

But affairs were not normal: some of the most exciting events in English political history with consequences of the most far-reaching character, were about to happen. On the eve of the election Parnell had thrown the Irish vote in England on the side of the Conservatives: the result was to put him in a position of dominance, for the electorate returned 334 Liberals, 250 Conservatives, and 86 Parnellites. The 86 of '86 thus held the future of English government in their hands. Neither of the great English parties could govern without the assent of the cold, proud, Protestant squire from Co. Wicklow. The story of the following months has been so often told that it is only necessary here to record that Gladstone's conversion to Home Rule was announced; that Salisbury then put the matter to the test by proposing a Coercion Bill in the Queen's Speech; that the Government were defeated (26 January) by seventy-nine votes on the 'three acres and a cow amendment'; and that Salisbury resigned, and Gladstone kissed hands on 1 February. But his conversion to Home Rule was too much for the whig magnates: led by Hartington, they refused to join the new Government.

More important than the loss of the whigs was the loss of Joseph Chamberlain—radical in the way in which only a man with a private fortune of a quarter of a million pounds can afford to be, the dissolution of the Union was yet so repugnant to him that he was willing to split his party rather than see Home Rule go through. Unlike Hartington he joined the Cabinet in his old post as President of the Board of Trade, having in vain sought to be Colonial Secretary. ('Oh, a Secretary of State', was the Prime Minister's reply to the request—not forgiven or forgotten.) But on 26 March, when Gladstone revealed the details of his Bill to a hushed Cabinet, the leader of English radicalism left the room, his party, and the prospect of the premiership. It had not always been so. During the titanic struggle of the previous autumn Esher from the bench sent down a note to Charles Russell, an ardent Chamberlainite: 'Will this be the course of business? In five months Lord Chancellor Harcourt sworn in before me as Lord Chancellor to Mr. Gladstone. In ten months Lord Chancellor Russell sworn in before me as Lord Chancellor to Mr. Chamberlain!' [1]

The prophecy was false.

In the difficult task of Cabinet-making Gladstone seems to have thought first of his former Chancellor—Selborne. On 27 January Selborne received a letter in which the Prime Minister said he could not refrain from 'asking himself, inwardly, whether he could again hope for my co-operation'.[2] Rightly interpreting this characteristic statement as an offer of the Woolsack, Selborne nevertheless felt obliged to decline at an interview a few days later. The proposed Irish policy was anathema to him. Indeed, eighteen years before he had refused the offer of the Chancellorship from the same Prime Minister, being unable to acquiesce in his proposal to

---

[1] J. L. Garvin, *The Life of Joseph Chamberlain* (1933), vol. ii, p. 156.
[2] Earl of Selborne, *Memorials, Personal and Political* (1898), vol. ii, p. 182.

dis-establish the Church of Ireland. Selborne was surely one of the most consistent and honourable members of the Bar who have ever interested themselves in politics. Selborne 'shared with Lord James of Hereford the glorious distinction of being one of the two men who have refused the Great Seal of England for conscience' sake'.[3] 'We parted', said Selborne, 'with expressions of affection and regret, but we parted practically for ever.'[4] An offer was then made to Sir Henry James, the ex-Attorney-General, but he was in Hartington's pocket and refused. Gladstone then thought of his ex-Solicitor-General as a prospective Lord Chancellor. Herschell's old friend, Victor Williamson, wrote later:

I was dining with him—Saturday 30th January—when he received Mr Gladstone's note offering him the Woolsack. I well remember the conversation we had after dinner over our cigars. We discussed the title he should assume as a Peer. He wished to take some name which should have some connection with Durham, for which city, in spite of her shabby treatment he had received, he still regarded with affection. I suggested that he should take the title of Lord Elvet, as he used always to lodge in Old Elvet at Assize times; but he objected that he could not assume the name of 'such a dead and alive old street'. Eventually he resolved to retain his own name—Lord Herschell of the City of Durham—and he added 'One thing I am determined on, and that is not to become a pompous bloke'. It was a remark just like him.[5]

Another old friend, W. C. Gully, later Speaker, recalled his memories of the time as follows:

One morning in February, 1886, he sent a message to me in the Courts that he would like to see me when the case in which he was engaged was over. When judgment had been given against him, he said to me as we walked away together, 'That decision was wrong, but I shall never have the chance of proving it. I have argued my last case. I have accepted the Chancellorship.'[6]

It was said that Sir William Harcourt, himself an ex-Solicitor-General, was disappointed the offer was not first made to him.

The new Government was sworn in at Osborne at 3 p.m. on 6 February 1886. Herschell was sworn a Privy Councillor before receiving the Great Seal. It was a fine bright day and as the jovial party crossed over in the steamer from Portsmouth to Cowes they saw, coming in the opposite direction, the ship bearing the defeated Conservative ex-Ministers. Morley remarked that Emerson's famous statement that ships at sea always looked romantic to each other was not true of this occasion.[7] At the

[3] J. B. Atlay, *The Victorian Chancellors* (1908), vol. ii, p. 405.
[4] *Memorials*, vol. ii, p. 203.   [5] Williamson papers.
[6] (1899) 15 L.Q.R. 126.
[7] Viscount Morley, *Recollections* (1917), vol. i, p. 215.

ceremony at Osborne the Queen was in a gloomy mood. The prospect of another Government under Gladstone was not one which appealed to her and the high spirits of the Liberal Ministers suffered a temporary setback. Herschell, however, remained agreeable and pleasant throughout the day, remarking to his colleagues that he was sworn in as Lord Chancellor at exactly the same age as Cairns, in his forty-ninth year (Cairns (b. 27 December 1819) had received the Great Seal on 29 February 1868.)

Two days later he was created a baron with the title of Lord Herschell, of Durham (taking 'celeriter' as his motto), and the same day sworn in as Lord Chancellor in the Court of Appeal before Lord Esher, the Master of the Rolls. The ceremony was described as follows:

Sir Farrer Herschell, attired in the state robes of Chancellor, preceded by the mace but not, as is usual, holding the Great Seal, came in and bowing to their Lordships stood by the central seat, the Lord Chancellor's chair, by the side of which stood Lord Esher, who held the New Testament in his hands ready to administer the oath. The Senior Registrar then read the oath, first the oath of allegiance, the Chancellor repeating the words after the Officer, and Lord Esher as Master of the Rolls, handing Herschell the book which he kissed in the usual way. Then in like manner the terms of the oath of office were read: 'I, Farrer Herschell, swear that I will well and truly serve Her Majesty in the office of Lord High Chancellor and that I will do right to all manner of people, after the law and usages of the Realm, without fear or favour, affection or ill will'. Lord Esher again handed the book to Herschell who once more kissed it in the usual way and then handed it back to Lord Esher and took his seat in the Chancellor's chair.[8]

It will be noted that he was sworn in as Sir Farrer Herschell—no doubt because he did not take his seat in the House of Lords until that same afternoon. Victor Williamson recorded that:

I went on Monday, February 8th, to the House of Lords to see him take his seat, in charge of his boy Dick then aged 8—and held him up on a chair outside the bar for him to view the ceremony, the whole of which did not last above 20 minutes, and after he had resumed his ordinary attire he drove me up to Brooks'. There were in the carriage, besides himself, Lady Herschell, his sister Mrs Cunliffe, Dick and myself. A strange sight presented itself on our arrival in St James's Street. The windows of all the Clubs and most of the shops were smashed, and the pavements littered with the fragments of broken glass. The lower windows of Brooks' were completely wrecked. There had been a meeting of the unemployed in Trafalgar Square, which had resulted in a progress of a disorderly mob through Pall Mall, St James's Street, and Oxford Street breaking windows and looting the shop windows. It was a scandalous incident for which the apathy of the police was much blamed.[9]

[8] (1886) 80 L.T. 270.   [9] Williamson papers.

A few days before the Prime Minister had consulted Herschell about the prospective Law Officers.

3rd of February, 1886

My dear Herschell,
     If you approve, pray send on the enclosed to C. Russell.
  Is Rigby (seat uncertain) the proper man for Solicitor General? or who?

Ever yours,
W. E. G.[1]

The 'enclosed' which was sent on to Charles Russell, was an offer of the Attorney-Generalship which was at once accepted.
    Herschell replied as follows:

3rd of February, 1886

My dear Mr. Gladstone,
     If Davey had been in the House I should have said that his practice at the Bar and the other circumstances of the case pointed him out as the most fit man for Solicitor-General. But I suppose in existing circumstances his having no seat is an insuperable difficulty. Failing him I quite think Rigby is the best man. And I can think of no man with a seat more secure than his who would be suitable.
    I have transmitted your letter to C. Russell. I think he is undoubtedly the man for Attorney-General.

Yours sincerely,
Farrer Herschell[2]

In the event the Solicitor-Generalship was accepted by (Sir) Horace Davey, who held the position without much success until the Government went out of office in July. Davey had lost his seat at the General Election in November 1885, and made several attempts to regain it. He was returned for Stockton in 1888, but beaten at the General Election in 1892. The sole judicial appointment which fell to Herschell was to find a successor to Pearson J. of the Chancery Division. Herschell appointed the Attorney-General's devil, James Stirling (later Lord Justice), who proved a good, but slow judge. (Stirling was the seventh senior Wrangler to be appointed a judge; the others were Wilson, 1761, Littledale, 1787, Pollock, 1806, Bickersteth, 1808, Alderson, 1809, and Maule, 1810.)
    One of the new Lord Chancellor's first duties in the House of Lords was to explain to the Peers the common law rules governing the use of force to suppress civil disorder. Several debates on the subject took place as the result of a series of riots in Trafalgar Square, which were said to

---

[1] B.M. Add. MSS. 44494, f. 125.
[2] Ibid., f. 127.

have been suppressed with unnecessary force by the authorities. Herschell gave a clear and convincing defence of the Government's action.[3]

The new Government was plunged immediately into the bitter debates on the Home Rule Bill, which Gladstone introduced on 8 April 1886 in one of the most striking speeches of his career, lasting over three hours. The Government had to meet the bitter opposition not only of the Salisbury party but also of those within its own ranks who had followed Joseph Chamberlain (who had resigned some days before) under the Liberal Unionist banner.

Many believed that Herschell's acceptance of the Great Seal had been dictated entirely by desire for self-advancement when he saw the unexpected vacancy opening up owing to the withdrawal of Selborne and Henry James, but on 5 April he sent the Prime Minister two letters on the same day, one of them eight pages long, in which he made it quite plain that he had views of his own about Home Rule and regarded with some alarm the position which the Prime Minister had taken up.

When you did me the honour to ask me to join your Cabinet you read to me the basis on which it was to be formed, *viz.*, an inquiry whether a scheme could be passed giving separate Legislative power to Ireland which should comply with certain conditions. Two of them, and in my eyes amongst the most important, were, 1. that it should be equitable as between Ireland and the other parts of the U.K. and, 2. that it should be just and fair to all classes of the community in Ireland.[4]

The proposed Bill, Herschell argued, was objectionable—as to the first point because it did not provide for increased contributions to the armed forces if their cost increased and left the burden of a war entirely on Great Britain, and as to the second point, because the propertied classes as a whole were favourable to the continuance of English rule in Ireland and would be left at the mercy of a Nationalist Legislature under the Bill as it then stood. Herschell also indicated concern about the position of Crown servants and police officers if the Home Rule Parliament came into existence and concluded that he could not, conscientiously, support the measure as it then stood. (This was, indeed, the decisive point on which Chamberlain resigned, though there is no evidence that Herschell ever contemplated following the Radicals in their schism.) Gladstone's reply, however, was sufficiently persuasive to secure the withdrawal of the objections and Herschell spent the next few months in lengthy debates in Committees of the Cabinet. He was even employed in a vain attempt to

---

[3] 303 *Parl. Deb.* 3s. col. 1621. Constitutional lawyers will be interested in a valuable Cabinet paper by Herschell on this subject, to be found in B.M. Add. MSS. 41233, f. 138.
[4] Ibid., 44496, f. 171.

induce Chamberlain to return.[5] He had not to preside over any debate on the subject in the House of Lords because Gladstone was defeated in the House of Commons on the second reading of the Bill. The division— 342 to 312—took place at 1 a.m. on 8 June, and Gladstone at once dissolved. The electorate returned an anti-Home Rule majority and a Conservative Government under Lord Salisbury was formed after Gladstone resigned on 22 July. Victor Williamson wrote:

I have never been able to believe that Herschell really approved this business, but I do not see how he could have acted otherwise than he did. He was in a most difficult position—having just received his Peerage and the Pension attached to the Woolsack—£5,000 per annum—and it would have been impossible for him to have thrown over Mr Gladstone after only a very few weeks of occupying it. Whatever were his own innermost feelings he nevertheless adhered most loyally to his chief, with the result that for the rest of his life he was mostly out of office, and that the Woolsack has been occupied by a far inferior man.[6]

In the last few days of the Gladstone Government Herschell had some correspondence[7] with the Prime Minister about the position of Sir Charles Dilke, who had been cited as co-respondent in the Crawford divorce case.[8] Dilke had been dismissed from the case, the only evidence offered against him being the unsworn statement of Mrs. Crawford. But the nature of that statement, Dilke's failure to go into the witness-box to contradict it, the curiously inept terms in which his counsel (Sir Charles Russell, Q.C.), announced this decision, and his subsequent unconvincing appearance in the box in the (unsuccessful) proceedings brought by the Queen's Proctor to have the verdict set aside, combined to raise such a storm of disapproval that Dilke was forced out of public life. It is still uncertain just what reasons induced Mr. Crawford to act, just as it is still uncertain precisely what reason induced another complaisant husband, Captain O'Shea, to move in 1890. But the result was that in each case a formidable political rival of Joseph Chamberlain was destroyed. In any event, Victorian society had been severely shaken by the revelations and the Prime Minister thought that it was improper for Dilke to hold a Privy Councillorship any longer. This view was shared by Herschell, who suggested that Dilke's name ought to be removed by the Crown. Gladstone then had doubts and thought if this was done it might prejudice any possible prosecution for perjury which Dilke brought against the

[5] Garvin, *Joseph Chamberlain*, vol. ii, p. 229.
[6] Williamson papers.
[7] Add. MSS. 44498, ff. 276–8.
[8] See R. Jenkins, *Sir Charles Dilke* (1958) for a full account of the case.

witnesses in the case. In any event, he said, Dilke himself ought to move
first in the matter. Herschell said that no prosecution for perjury was
likely and that the matter might well be left to the Conservatives to
handle. (Indeed, it seems much more likely that Dilke himself was in
danger of prosecution—Sir Henry James advised him to leave the country.) In the event the new Government did nothing and Dilke retained
his Privy Councillorship.

On 24 July Herschell paid a week-end visit to Algernon West, Gladstone's private secretary, who was living at Wanborough. Herschell
brought the Great Seal with him, remarking to his host that it went
everywhere in his possession although it was only a matter of days before
he surrendered it to the Queen.[9] Herschell was full of good humour
despite the end of his Chancellorship. At the age of 50 he now found
himself in the position of being a peer in receipt of a pension of £5,000 a
year with abundant leisure for the first time in his life. When he had surrendered the Great Seal to the Queen he went off to Austria and Greece for
a lengthy holiday. Travel was always one of his few recreations.[1]

In the House of Lords Herschell took a prominent part in debate,
sitting on the front opposition bench. In 1887 he supported the Appellate
Jurisdiction Act which was passed in order to enable Lord Blackburn to
sit and vote in the House after his resignation as a Law Lord, but in truth
created all the Law Lords life peers. Herschell spoke in glowing terms of
Blackburn's contribution to the development of English law.[2]

Later in the same year he also supported Lord Bramwell's Evidence
Amendment Bill, which was also supported by Lord Halsbury, the Lord
Chancellor. This Bill would have enabled a prisoner to have given
evidence in a criminal case, a reform for which Halsbury had always
fought and which was eventually to be enacted in 1898 by the Evidence
Act of that year. In April the House gave a second reading to the Irish
Land Bill after a lengthy debate marked by a bitter attack by Selborne on
his old associates in which he accused them of 'throwing the shield over
crime'. This produced a dignified reply from Herschell, who remarked, in
the traditional style of Members attacked under the cover of Parliamentary
privilege, that if the words had been repeated outside the House proceedings for defamation could have been instituted in respect of them. He
said that his party did not sympathize with crime in any shape or form
and that he himself held the same views which he had held all his life on
the subject of Ireland. He had not, he repeated, changed them in order to
obtain office in 1886.[3]

Ireland was again to the fore in the following year when the Govern-

9 A. West, *Recollections* (1899), p. 461.   1 V. Williamson (1899), J.C.L. 205.
2 310 *Parl. Deb.* 3s. col. 748.   3 313 *Parl. Deb.* 3s. col. 1577.

ment introduced a Bill to set up a special Commission to investigate the charges made against Charles Stewart Parnell by *The Times* newspaper. It will be recalled that *The Times* had been deceived by a forger named Pigott, who had sold it letters to which Parnell's name was forged indicating that the Irish leader had supported the extremist element of the Fenian Party and in particular had been privy to the assassination of Lord Frederick Cavendish and his Under-Secretary in the Phoenix Park, Dublin, a few days after their arrival. The investigation before the special Commission was a lengthy and cumbrous affair but it resulted in a complete acquittal of Parnell of all the charges made against him and very heavy costs being incurred by *The Times*.

Herschell made what was generally conceded to be the greatest speech of his career when the Bill was given a second reading in the House of Lords.[4] He not merely reviewed the whole Irish problem and showed how improbable it was that the charges against Parnell were true but also prophesied with great truth that the procedure which the Government proposed was entirely unsuitable for what was bound to be in effect an investigation into the whole state of the Irish Government. When the conduct of Sir Richard Webster, the Attorney-General, was attacked some months later, Herschell said that he thought Webster might have been foolish in permitting any conflict to arise between his duty to the Government and his duty to *The Times* as its counsel, but that there was no reflection upon his honesty as distinct from his wisdom.

In March of the same year he delivered a lengthy speech in the House on the working of the Merchandise Marks Act.[5] He had been the Chairman of a Board of Trade Committee on the subject which had revealed serious gaps in the law. Little was done to protect British goods abroad by securing the proper enforcement of the Act in the Colonies and India, and in addition China and Japan were at that date being flooded with false trade marks on German-made goods. This, Herschell argued, was a grave abuse which should be stopped by an international convention. In the same year he supported the proposal to establish a Public Trustee who would benefit the owners of small estates. But the opposition of solicitors was so strong that this very necessary reform was not achieved for nearly twenty years.[6] He also introduced a bill to codify the law relating to sale of goods—an acknowledged masterpiece of draftsmanship by Mackenzie Chalmers—but it was not until 1893 that, as Lord Chancellor, he secured its enactment.

In the remaining years of the Conservative Government Herschell somewhat dropped out of political life. Fowler wrote to Morley in April 1889 a rather petulant letter complaining that Herschell 'had not spoken

4 330 *Parl. Deb.* 3s. col. 262.   5 323 *Parl. Deb.* 3s. col. 1256.   6 See below, p. 146.

in public since his return'.[7] Herschell devoted these years to his judicial work. He sat constantly in the House of Lords and amongst the great cases in which he delivered a judgment was *Derry* v. *Peek*[8] in which his speech is the classical authority for the proposition that in an action of deceit actual dishonesty must be proved, so that a careless man is very far short of being a dishonest man. Herschell's exposition of the reasons which led him to disagree with the opinion of the Court of Appeal that negligence was equivalent to fraud is generally recognized to be one of the masterpieces of the Law Reports. Its importance as a powerful piece of analysis and exposition has not been lessened by later criticism.

He also undertook a variety of public business outside the law. He was the Chairman of a Royal Commission which investigated the Metropolitan Board of Works and in consequence became an Alderman of the London County Council. He also took a very prominent part in the elaborate negotiations which resulted in the setting up of the Imperial Institute in South Kensington and in the affairs of London University, of which he became Chancellor in 1891. He was also prominent in the world of freemasonry and an active supporter of the National Society for the Prevention of Cruelty to Children. It was even noted that he began to take a more active part in social life. Hitherto almost his only relaxation had been to summon round to Grosvenor Gardens on Friday evenings some students from the Royal College of Music to make up a quartet with him, but now he began to be seen more frequently at dinner parties and balls.[9] He was never what might be described as a popular man, although universally respected for his entire integrity and the great capacities which he devoted to the public service. When he was a junior at the Bar 'A certain primness of demeanour which was innate in Herschell, together with a peculiar cut of the whisker, suggested a comparison with an undertaker. The advertisements of George Shillibeer, inventor of the omnibus and pioneer of inexpensive funerals, were a feature of the period, and Herschell was promptly dubbed after him.'[1] Selborne, with what might be described as charming unconsciousness, once said that brilliant success at the Bar tended to make a man arrogant, and there was also indubitably in Herschell a strain of arrogance which tempted him to domineer over other people. It was noticeable as the years went by that he became increasingly talkative when sitting judicially and members of the Bar were apt to complain about his frequent interruptions. His friends ascribed his increasing irritability, even excitability, to overwork.

[7] Viscount Morley, *Recollections* (1917), vol. i, p. 127.   [8] (1889) 14 App. Cas. 337.
[9] See Sir M. E. Grant Duff, *Notes from a Diary 1889-91* (1901), for glimpses of Herschell in society.
[1] J. B. Atlay, *The Victorian Chancellors* (1908), vol. ii, p. 450.

When the great trade union case of *Allen* v. *Flood*[2] was before the House in 1898 Lawson Walton, Q.C., the respondent's counsel, had to stand silent for prolonged periods while Herschell interchanged views with the Lord Chancellor, Halsbury. An observer said that it sounded rather like this:

Lord Halsbury: Mr. Lawson Walton, what would you say to this proposition, etc., etc.,?
Lord Herschell: Wouldn't the answer to that be, etc., etc.,?
Lord Halsbury: In that case wouldn't you say so and so?
Lord Herschell: I suppose the argument would then be, etc., etc.,

After this had gone on for some time one of the other Law Lords was heard to whisper audibly to a colleague, 'Now I can understand what is meant by molesting a man in his trade.'[3] After this Lawson Walton was permitted to continue his argument.

But Herschell as Lord Chancellor is remembered by lawyers today for his judgments. They are of the highest order of achievement and entitle him to a place in the front rank of English judges. His complete mastery of the relevant case-law is combined with an acute mind and a clear, if not very distinguished, style. A list of his judgments[4] shows that during his short time in the House of Lords he touched upon many of the most important subjects in the Common Law. They are professional productions for skilled lawyers: they contain no rhetoric or extravagances. Indeed, it is on record that once he so disapproved of the lightness of touch to which Lord Macnaghten was prone that the latter withdrew his judgment, which was already in print, and contented himself with the conventional 'My Lords, I concur'. Many years after both were dead the judgment was published in the *Law Quarterly Review*,[5] and is highly regarded by all admirers of the learning, wit, and literary skill of the great Ulster judge. Something of Herschell's conception of the judicial function may be gleaned from the following letter which he wrote when Esher, a man of rather different temperament, resigned in 1897. Herschell wrote to him on 3 November.

I have thought much of you since I saw the announcement that you had ceased to be Master of the Rolls. But I cannot let so important an event pass without telling you so. It must have been a great wrench to tear yourself away

---

[2] [1898] A.C.I.
[3] Atlay, vol. ii, p. 461.
[4] See Van Vechten Veeder, 'A Century of Judicature', in *Select Essays in Anglo-American Legal History* (Boston, 1907), vol. i, p. 831.
[5] The case is *Lawrance* v. *Norreys (Lord)* (1890) 15 App. Cas. 10. Macnaghten's judgment will be found in (1938) 54 L.Q.R. 522, or in *A Selection of Lord Macnaghten's Judgments* (1951), p. 12.

from a post you had so worthily filled, from work you had done so long and so well, but if ever a man had earned repose by good work done, you had. No one in modern times has left a greater mark upon the law or a more solid and enduring monument in the Law Reports. There can be no higher praise than this of a Judge when he quits the judgement seat.[6]

[6] Esher papers.

CHAPTER IV

IN THE SUMMER OF 1892 Parliament was dissolved and a general election took place in which the Liberals were returned with a small majority of forty-two. Their parliamentary position was perplexing and unsatisfactory. It was generally recognized that they were obliged to give Ireland some measure of Home Rule but the difficulties in the way of securing the passage of a Home Rule Bill were considerable. The electorate had returned a leader and a party bound morally and politically to undertake a task in which irresistible parliamentary force was indispensable but had denied the party that necessary force. In addition the Queen had by now reached the lowest ebb of her relations with Gladstone. 'The G.O.M. at eighty-two is a very alarming look-out', she wrote in her diary.[1] Nevertheless Gladstone took up the task and on the day on which the Cabinet was sworn in, 15 August 1892, he wrote from Osborne to Herschell a letter cast in characteristically involved prose. 'The important decision about Mr. L. has gone forward. Law Officers have been invited on the footing you recommended. From the outside Asquith and A. Acland are to be brought into the Cabinet, both and the latter particularly in accordance with strong influences considered to operate through the House of Commons.'[2] Mr. L. was Lowther who was being invited to fill the vacant office of Speaker and the Law Officers were Russell, as Attorney-General, and Rigby as Solicitor-General.

Herschell's claim to resume the Great Seal was never seriously in doubt although the Lord Chief Justice, Coleridge, a former Liberal Attorney-General, appears to have dropped a number of hints that he was willing to be considered for the position.[3] This would not, however, have been a popular appointment. Apart from anything else, the administration of the Queen's Bench Division under Coleridge had become something of a scandal. Distinguished as he was in many ways, he was lax and unpunctual in the day-to-day dispatch of business and the professional legal journals of the time are full of complaints about the state of affairs under his Chief Justiceship.

Herschell was plunged at once into the work of drafting the Home Rule Bill where his services met with the highest appreciation. The Attorney-General was somewhat slow and the Solicitor-General apt to

[1] *Letters of Queen Victoria*, Ed. A. C. Benson, 3rd series (1932), vol. ii, p. 120.
[2] B.M. Add. MSS. 44515, f. 156.
[3] C. Yarnall, *Forty Years of Friendship* (1911), p. 145.

take rather fine-spun Chancery points but Herschell was 'consumately skilful in command of appropriate legal words, ingenious terms of sentence, and all the arts for stopping one hole without opening another'.[4] He reminded those who saw him at work of the capacity of another great Jewish judge, Sir George Jessel, the late Master of the Rolls, whose mind was believed to move so quickly that he was said to be able to read both sides of a sheet of paper at the same time. 'Herschell on the Woolsack held his own with the lawyers, and in Cabinet was straight, ready to help, wonderfully handy, and with his full share of wisdom, divided by Aristotle into phrontis and sophia.[5]

In July 1893 it was widely rumoured that Herschell would succeed Lord Lansdowne as Viceroy of India, but Herschell made it quite plain that he had no desire to leave England. In the Birthday Honours List of that year he received the G.C.B. ('Herschell for G.C.B.—not earldom', Gladstone's private secretary, Algernon West, noted in his diary.[6])

So far as questions of judicial patronage were concerned Herschell had a relatively calm tenure of office. He appointed only one High Court judge during his term, A. R. Kennedy (later promoted Lord Justice), in the place of Mr. Justice Denman. This was a thoroughly sound appointment which met with general approval, except amongst a number of Liberal lawyers in the House of Commons who thought that their own claims might have been considered rather more carefully. The same lawyers were also apt to grumble privately that Herschell had pressed Lord Justice Kay to withdraw his proffered resignation, thereby failing to open up a vacancy. Herschell's main problems with the Superior Courts arose out of the lax administration of the Court of Queen's Bench under the easy-going Lord Coleridge. After much argument and difficulty he secured reforms under which at least five Queen's Bench Division judges were always in London to take jury cases. Herschell also tackled the problem of administration in the county court and secured some important reforms whereby the areas were reorganized to bring them into touch with modern conditions. Herschell favoured the promotion of county court judges to the High Court in suitable cases (it was said he wished to promote Mackenzie Chalmers from the Birmingham county court), but at that time in our legal history the county court bench was in general in low repute and it was not until the time of Lord Birkenhead that the first county court judge was thus promoted.

So far as the appointment of Q.C.s was concerned, the only complaint ever uttered against Herschell's methods was by Sir Edward Carson, a

---

[4] Viscount Morley, *Recollections* (1917), vol. ii, p. 360.
[5] Ibid., vol. i, p. 324.
[6] *Private Diaries of the Rt. Hon. Sir Algernon West*. Ed. H. G. Hutchinson (1922), p. 157.

E*

Q.C. in Ireland and a former Solicitor-General for that country, who had
come to England two years previously and already made a name for
himself at the English Bar. When he applied for silk in England he was at
first refused by Herschell on the ground that his standing in England, as
distinct from Ireland, was not sufficiently great. Eventually Herschell was
persuaded to grant Carson what he asked for and Carson went down to
the House of Lords to receive his patent. It was handed to him by the
Lord Chancellor in complete silence.[7] The two men bowed to each other
and the interview was over. Many besides Carson thought that Herschell
had shown a certain lack of generosity.

The real difficulty in Herschell's time came from an unexpected quarter,
the appointment of Justices of the Peace. The practice at that time was
for the Lord-Lieutenant of the county concerned to forward nominations
to the Lord Chancellor. As Sir Henry Hope wrote to the Prime Minister's
secretary ('Pom' MacDonell), in January:

> By long established and inviolable usage he [the L.C.] makes no inquiries
> into the recommendations of the Lords Lieutenant before acting upon them,
> unless there is something on the face of the recommendation pointing to an
> improper recommendation, or unless someone calls his attention to any specific
> disqualification attaching to any particular gentleman whom the Lord Lieutenant
> proposes. I do not think that the fact of a man being one of the small fry [sic]
> would without more induce any Lord Chancellor to interfere.[8]

There were then no advisory committees to help the Lord-Lieutenant.
These were instituted only after the Royal Commission of 1910.[9] As the
great majority of Lords-Lieutenant were Conservatives it was quite
natural that the bulk of the Justices of the Peace should be Conservative
also, and Lord Halsbury was not the man to suggest that they might
include members of the Liberal Party in their nominations. The result
was that when the Liberals returned to power in July 1892 there were a
host of Liberal supporters in the country who expected to be rewarded
for their support by appointment to the magisterial bench. Herschell set
his face inflexibly against any appointment which was not made entirely
on merit. He found that great pressure was brought to bear on him by
the party and especially by the Whips but he refused to do anything which
might be construed as 'packing the Bench'. In May 1893 there was a
debate in the House of Commons on the subject on a motion by Sir
Charles Dilke and by a narrow majority a resolution was passed to the
effect that county magistrates should not, in the future, be appointed
exclusively on the nomination of the Lord-Lieutenant.[1] The figures

---

[7] E. Marjoribanks, *Carson* (1932), vol. i, p. 187.   [8] Salisbury papers.
[9] See below, p. 157.   [1] 12 *Parl. Deb.* 4s. col. 258.

revealed that Herschell was doing what he could within the limits set by his principles to hold the balance between the parties in making his appointments. On coming into office 22 per cent of the Borough Justices were Liberals whereas by November the figure had risen to 36 per cent. The effect of the debate in the House of Commons was to involve Herschell in an immense correspondence with people able to vouch for the merits of candidates proposed otherwise than through the Lords-Lieutenant. An indirect effect was that Lords-Lieutenant began to pay attention to what had been said in making up their lists, but the work of the Lord Chancellor's office increased greatly. But the party was still not satisfied and further trouble arose in November 1893. On 9 November Herschell wrote to Gladstone:

I apprehend that it is clear that it is not for 'Her Majesty's Government' to carry out the resolution. The law has cast on the Chancellor the duty and responsibility of appointing County Magistrates. The only manner in which H.M.G. can interfere is by asking the Chancellor to resign—which he is quite ready to do! The question suggests what is false—namely that the Chancellor has been remiss in not acting on the resolution. All I can say is that the Chancellor *has been* and *is*, acting on the resolution of the House and proposes continuing to do so.

I have been worked to an extent almost beyond endurance in these matters. I have done my best—I cannot endure the situation much longer.[2]

But a week later Herschell was visited by a deputation composed of no fewer than 280 M.P.s who wished to press their views on him. The pent-up irritation which he revealed in his letter to Gladstone burst out and he replied to them in the following words:

From the time when I come in the morning till evening, I have not a moment unoccupied. I am occupied with my secretaries whilst I am eating my lunch, and very often receive deputations whilst I am eating my lunch. I am engaged with my secretaries whilst I am dressing and undressing for the purpose of attending the House of Lords, and it is very often the case that I am at work till 6 o'clock in the evening, and very often much later. During that time I have to discuss every conceivable question. I am constantly receiving letters from lunatics to say they are not lunatics. You cannot put them aside; there may be something that deserves inquiry, and I have to ask for a report about it, and when I receive the report I have to consider it. I am always receiving complaints of this or that thing done wrong by this or that County Court in all parts of the Kingdom; something about what a coroner has done, or questions about the administration of justice throughout the country, complaints of magistrates, and a multitude of other matters. During the whole of this year I have had no holiday at all. There is not a day—at all events, certainly not three days—

2 Add. MSS. 44517, f. 309.

literally in the whole year in which I am not hard at work, and on many days working 10, 11, 12 or 13 hours.[3]

His assistant secretary, Adolphus Liddell, who was present, noted that this appeal *ad misericordiam* rather spoilt an otherwise impressive speech. Nervous irritation due to overwork may well explain the rather petulant tone of the outburst. (The strain of the years of grinding professional toil was undoubtedly felt by a constitution never over-strong. After his death Sir Almeric FitzRoy, a shrewd judge, said: 'But for an unfortunate tendency to distil a spirit of acrimony, which I believe was foreign to his nature, he would have commanded a more ungrudging influence in the House of Lords.')[4] The general reaction in the profession was one of some amusement, as is shown by the following lines:

> Oh, who would be Lord Chancellor,
> These knotty points to crunch.
> He has to work so very hard;
> He has no time for lunch.
> His labour and his daily toil,
> Is really most distressing.
> He's writing letters all the time,
> When washing and when dressing.
> And now, from Members far and near,
> Come threatening and entreating,
> About the persons whom they want
> Upon the Benches seating.
> His case is very hard indeed,
> Upon my work, I'm blest,
> If I think Herschell evermore
> Will now get washed and dres't.

The problem still continued to vex Herschell in the opening months of the new year.

Private   24th February, 1894
My dear Mr. Gladstone.

I cannot admit that I ought to appoint as magistrates all nominees of any member unless I can show them by actual proof to be unfit. So long as the responsibility is cast upon the Lord Chancellor it is impossible for him to take this course. I do constantly communicate with the members on questions raised as to the qualification of candidates for the Bench suggested by them. I am about to do so now with Mr. Conybeare in a particular case.

I do not confine my inquiries to Conservatives or Unionists. I always endeavour to check any information I get from such quarters by seeking

[3] E. Manson, *Builders of our Law* (1904), p. 422.
[4] A. FitzRoy, *Memoirs* (1925), p. 134.

information from those not under any such political bias. But it is of course natural that where a Liberal gives reasons for not appointing one of his own political views, I cannot possibly make known my informant's name as there would be an end of such communications and of my getting the truth.

Mr. Conybeare did give me the name of one Liberal-Unionist who was appointed but I cannot find any trace of his stating that one of his nominees was a Tory. I must have appointed him, therefore, if I did, under the impression that he was a Liberal.

Mr. Conybeare underestimates somewhat the number of Liberal magistrates I have appointed—moreover he takes no account of the fact that several more would have been added to the Commission but for the fact that they had not the requisite qualifications or were unwilling to serve. I cannot refuse to appoint any Conservatives—this would be setting a precedent fatal to any better state of things if we went out of office. Indeed, in some cases a magistrate was wanted and I only appointed a Conservative after I had made inquiries to see if I could find a Liberal, but in vain.

Yours sincerely,
Herschell.[5]

The following month Gladstone himself resigned office as Prime Minister after an uneasy period of negotiations behind the scenes. His tenure of office culminated in the famous interview at Windsor in which the Queen pointedly refrained both from expressing pleasure at the great length of his services to the Crown and from asking him for advice as to his successor. Gladstone was deeply wounded and the closing years of his life were undoubtedly darkened by a feeling that he had been treated with ingratitude by the Queen. Herschell wrote as follows to the retiring Prime Minister:

9th March, 1894

My dear Mr. Gladstone,

I cannot be content to let the official severance of my connection with you take place without an expression of my personal feeling towards you. It is now nearly fourteen years since you first did me the honour of asking me to serve under you and on the whole of that period I can look back with unalloyed satisfaction.

The retrospect calls to my mind much hard work, but the circumstance that I was working with and for you made that trial a pleasure. I can recall nothing but kindness on your part and a most generous appreciation of any services I may have been able to render. The severance of a connection such as this cannot but cause me much sorrow. Nothing can ever drown my grateful sense of your uniform kindness and consideration or lessen the affectionate esteem with which I regard you. It will as long as I live be a source of unbounded

[5] Add. MSS. 44518, f. 55.

satisfaction to me that I have had the honour of regarding you as a friend. It is my earnest prayer that every blessing may attend you in the days yet to come.

Will you allow me to subscribe myself,

Affectionately yours,

Herschell.[6]

The reply on 14 March is as follows: It begins, 'My dear Herschell', and after a paragraph explaining that eye illness had delayed an earlier answer, continues:

There is so much to say on the position in which I have not very spontaneously left you. However, one word I must say—you owed your appointment in 1880 to merit and distinction such as it was impossible (even perhaps for a man with a cataract) to overlook. One discovery remained for me to make; the intensity of your devotion to the discharge of public duty; and that was made when you freely but with the greatest possible advantage, took your place on the Bench beside Law, that admirable man, and me, on what was *then* considered the very prolonged proceedings in committee on the Irish Land Bill. You have supplied a parallel to that truly generous devotion in your recent dealings with the magistracy. Your reward has not fully come; but come it must.

It is indeed delightful to me to think that affection enters into our farewells, and I heartily reciprocate the feeling you express with the sanguine hope that in two respects only you may resemble your well-known predecessor Eldon, the weight of your judicial authority, and the length of your reign at the head of your great profession.

Ever sincerely yours,

W. E. Gladstone.[7]

Herschell retained the Great Seal under Gladstone's successor, Rosebery, who held office somewhat uneasily until June of the following year when his Government was defeated by a snap vote in the House of Commons. The Cabinet debated whether to resign or dissolve, but although only four favoured the former course, it was the one which prevailed. On 22 June Herschell surrendered the Great Seal and on the 29th wrote to his successor, the veteran Halsbury, who had come into office with the Conservative administration, a friendly note: 'I enclose the cabinet keys. I trust that the cordial relations which have existed between us on former occasions may suffer no diminution during your present tenure of the office. Pray accept my hearty wishes for your happiness.'[8]

Unfortunately within a few months a somewhat strained relationship arose between the two men. This occurred as a result of the procedure adopted for hearing the Appeal to the House of Lords in the great trade

[6] Add. MSS. 44518, f. 99.   [7] Ibid., f. 101.
[8] Halsbury papers.

union case of *Allen* v. *Flood*.[9] The issues raised in this case were of fundamental importance in a modern industrial society. The question shortly
was whether it was an actionable wrong to threaten another to exercise
one's legal rights if that other did not act in some way which was legal
but contrary to his interests. The facts were that the respondent Flood
together with another man, Taylor, were shipwrights who were engaged
by the Glengall Iron Company in repairing a ship at the company's
Regent dock in Millwall. A number of boilermakers working on the
same job objected to the employment of shipwrights on iron work and
the delegate of the boilermakers union, Allen, went to the manager of
the Glengall Company and told him that the iron men, or some of them,
would leave their work unless Flood and Taylor were discharged. Flood
and Taylor were employed 'for the job' and their employment was
terminated at the end of that day's work. They were discharged at the
end of the day because the employers feared that the threat to call out
the boilermakers would be carried into effect if they continued to employ
Flood and Taylor on the iron work. Flood and Taylor having sued Allen,
the jury found that he had maliciously induced the employers to discharge
the respondents and not to engage them in the future and awarded them
damages. This judgment was upheld in the Court of Appeal, but in the
end a majority of the House of Lords (Lords Halsbury, Ashbourne, and
Morris dissenting) held that the appellants had violated no legal right of
the respondent, done no unlawful act, and used no unlawful means in
procuring the respondents' dismissal. The majority of the House emphatically affirmed the fundamental principle of the law of torts that if a
man's conduct is lawful it does not become unlawful because he has been
actuated by a malicious or spiteful motive. It will be noticed that the
Glengall Iron Company had committed no breach of contract by discharging Flood and Taylor, who could not therefore sue Allen for the
well-established tort of inducing a breach of contract. What in effect the
plaintiffs were contending was that that tort should be extended to cover
a case where the plaintiff had been deprived of an expected as distinct
from a promised economic advantage. It will also be noticed that no
question of conspiracy was involved in the case because there was only
one defendant. There can be little doubt that if Allen had combined with
another to do what he did his conduct might have been actionable. It is
possible that if Flood and Taylor had sued Allen and the Glengall Company's manager Halkett jointly for conspiracy they might have succeeded.

The appeal was first argued in December 1895 before Lord Halsbury
and Lords Watson, Herschell, Macnaghten, Morris, Shand, and Davey.
From the very beginning Lord Halsbury took a view strongly adverse

[9] [1898] A.C. 1.

to the position of the trade union and expressed his firm opinion that the plaintiffs, Flood and Taylor, were entitled to damages for an interference with their right to work. It was also clear, however, that on this point he would be unable to carry with him a majority of his colleagues, who thought that the Lord Chancellor was attempting to extend the tort of inducement of breach of contract too far. Halsbury thereupon appears to have conceived the idea that the case should be re-argued before an enlarged body of Law Lords and that, in addition, the House should adopt once more the practice of summoning the High Court judges to advise. This ancient practice had been useful and reasonable in the days when there were no qualified Law Lords in the House of Lords apart from the Lord Chancellor and any ex-Lord Chancellors, but it was generally thought to have become obsolete since the passing of the Appellate Jurisdiction Act, 1876. Still there was no doubt about the existence of the theoretical power to summon the High Court judges to attend, for each judge at the opening of Parliament received a Writ of Summons requesting his assistance if necessary. In any event Herschell appears to have thought that the Lord Chancellor was trying, indirectly, to over-rule his colleagues by summoning this great number of judges. The High Court judges at that time, many of whom were Halsbury's own appointments, were not on the whole notable for progressive views on social or industrial matters. Herschell wrote to Halsbury as follows:

I am sorry to trouble you with the accompanying memorandum with reference to *Allen* v. *Flood*. I only learned a few days ago on conferring with some of my colleagues the circumstances under which the motion for re-argument was made. I must frankly say that I feel I have been very unfairly treated. I hasten however, to add that the kindness and courtesy I have habitually received at your hands satisfy me that there can have been no intention on your part thus to treat me. I have ascertained from those who were present when the motion was made and declared carried, that the memorandum correctly represents the facts as far as they are concerned.[1]

No accompanying memorandum has been traced nor has any reply from Halsbury survived but its purport can be deduced from the next letter from Herschell on 16 February 1897:

Beyond saying how heartily I concur in all you say about our harmonious relations in the past, I defer for the moment answering your letter except on one point. You say: 'I do not at all understand your phrase that I led you to suppose that nothing would be done till the meeting of Parliament in January.' The following extract from your letter of the 1st November 1895 will explain why I said what I did. 'With respect to *Allen* v. *Flood* we are, I think, more divided and I conjecture, though I am not certain, somewhat evenly. I think

[1] Halsbury papers.

the question raised is so serious that I am disposed to follow the precedent of *Angus* v. *Dalton* and summon the judges. *This, I think, can only be done by a resolution of the House when Parliament meets.*' I replied to your letter strongly deprecating the step of summoning the judges. I shortly afterwards returned to England and remained there until towards the end of November but never had a hint that your view indicated in the passage I have underlined, had undergone any change.[2]

Then followed three more letters from Herschell in the following terms:

21st February

I have communicated with my colleagues: I found that Lord Davey was informed one day that you contemplated the summoning of the judges but the remark was not made in a way which he thought called for any expression of opinion on his part. Lord Macnaghten tells me that when walking one day to the House you casually raised the question of summoning the judges, and that he pointed out objections to that course. Lord Watson states that he never heard of the matter at all. Let me add that none of them think any more than I do, that the action you took was due to any intention to act discourteously, but the fact remains that a step of grave importance was taken without consultation with the other Lords and a step to which some have grave objections. Would not the best course be that you should call us together to discuss the matter and consider what had best be done.[3]

The next letter is one of 3 March:

I hope you will not think me importunate if I ask for an answer to my request made in the letter I wrote on Monday of last week, that you would summon a meeting of your colleagues who heard the case of *Allen* v. *Flood* to consider the present position of the case and the course which ought to be taken.[4]

Halsbury evidently thought this letter hinted at something akin to mutiny, for Herschell's next letter, 15 March, after an introductory paragraph says:

Most certainly neither I nor your other colleagues desire the meeting in order that we might pass a vote of censure upon you. If you will refer to my memorandum I distinctly stated this and also that in my opinion if, after consultation, the general conclusion was that the resolution should be rescinded, this might be done at your own instance in a manner which would have cast no reflection on yourself. I cannot agree that the judges as such would have any right whatever to resent this course if it had been ultimately determined that they should not be summoned. At the same time I cannot deny that it would be difficult to take this course at so late a date as the present, though I cannot admit that it would have been so at the time I first proposed it. Secondly, I should leave you under a false impression if I were not to state that the objection of my

[2] Halsbury papers.   [3] Ibid.   [4] Ibid.

colleagues to the course taken was not due to any views or to any influence of myself upon them. I found that their objections (except Lord Morris) to the course proposed were just as strong as my own, and before submitting to you my memorandum I asked them to read it in order that it might not contain any incorrect statement. Thirdly, of course I accept without reservation, your assurance that you had forgotten the passage in your letter which led me to believe that you would not take any step in the matter until after Parliament assembled. But it is better, frankly, to state that admitting this, I feel deeply hurt that my words deprecating the summoning of the judges should have been treated with absolute contempt and indifference. I say without hesitation that if I had received from you objections to any course which I proposed to take in relation to legal business, I should before taking it, have stated my reasons and endeavoured to remove objections and have invited a personal discussion of the question. I cannot help feeling hurt that my objection emphatically expressed should have been as much disregarded as if it had never been put before you. I have always acted towards you with complete loyalty, and I feel that I had some claim to treatment different from that which I have received. It will conduce better to good relations in the future to say all this than to feel it and not say it, and so far as it is a mere personal matter, I am quite willing now to forget it. Fourthly, I certainly think it will be desirable to summon a meeting of the Lords of Appeal for the purpose you suggest.[5]

No reply to this admirable letter has been traced. But certainly Halsbury succeeded in his plan and the case was re-argued before the same Law Lords with the addition of Ashbourne and James of Hereford, on 25, 26, 29 and 30 March and April 1 and 2, 1897, together with the following High Court judges: Hawkins, Mathew, Cave, North, Wills, Grantham, Lawrance, and Wright, JJ. They sat in their red robes on either side of a narrow table, 'looking rather like an omnibus full of old ladies'. The result of this wealth of legal talent can be found in Lord Halsbury's dissenting judgment.

My difference is founded on the belief that in denying these plaintiffs a remedy we are departing from the principles which have hitherto guided our Courts in the preservation of individual liberty to all. I am encouraged, however, by the consideration that the adverse views appear to me to overrule the views of most distinguished judges, going back now for certainly 200 years, and that up to the period when this case reached Your Lordships' House there was a unanimous consensus of opinion; and that of eight judges who have given us the benefit of their opinion, six have concurred in the judgment which your Lordships are now asked to overrule.[6]

Apart from his judicial work as ex-Lord Chancellor Herschell took on many more public activities. He was Chairman of the Royal Commission on the highly complicated question of Indian currency, which produced

[5] Halsbury papers.   [6] [1898] A.C. 1 at 90.

a valuable report, and also sat as Chairman of the Royal Commission on Vaccination, and of the Inquiry into the National Society for the Prevention of Cruelty to Children. (Something of his powers of work can be shown by the fact that he dictated the voluminous Report of the Inquiry to relays of secretaries between 10 a.m. one day and 2 a.m. the following morning.) His greatest work, however, was as the representative of the British Government on two major international arbitrations; in 1898 relating to the boundary of Venezuela, and in 1899 relating to the disputes between Canada and the United States over a number of questions including fishery rights off the coast of Newfoundland and the proper boundary line between Alaska and British Columbia.

So far as the Venezuelan dispute was concerned Herschell died before the proceedings had really got under way. In 1895 President Grover Cleveland announced that under the Monroe Doctrine he would appoint an American Commission to define the boundary and enforce its award— by war if necessary. 'This was certainly one of the most unexpected, least warranted, and least excusable steps ever taken in modern times by a Great Power.'[7] Eventually Washington took a more reasonable line— partly because of the diplomacy of Chamberlain, and partly because of a catastrophic fall in the value of American stocks. By the Treaty of Washington (February 1897) the question was submitted to arbitration, the ultimate award being in favour of Great Britain to the disappointment both of Venezuela and the United States, Great Britain receiving all the gold mines and the greater part of the disputed territory.

The Alaska boundary dispute had its source in the fact that when Russia sold Alaska to the United States in 1867 the boundaries were to a large extent unknown, the country in question having been explored only from the sea and such maps as there were being of a fragmentary character.[8] But the discovery of gold in the Yukon in the 1890s produced a serious situation. A flood of immigrants poured into the Yukon through the port of Skagway and the question at once arose as to where the landward limits of the boundary between the United States and Canada were to be found.

On 30 May 1898 an agreement was signed in Washington creating an International Joint High Commission composed of five British representatives, and five American. It was further arranged that of the five British members four should be Canadian. Herschell was the fifth British member. He told Lord James of Hereford that he felt very tired and would like nothing better than a period of complete relaxation, but his

[7] R. C. K. Ensor, *England, 1870–1914* (1936), p. 230.
[8] Good accounts of this are in W. L. King, *Chief Justice Fuller* (New York, 1950), and M. Pope, *Public Servant* (Toronto, 1960).

strong sense of public duty drove him to accept, and he left England in high spirits and apparent good health, having been assured on all sides that his appointment would be welcomed both in Ottawa and in Washington. He travelled first to Quebec and at the first meeting of the Commission was unanimously elected President. He displayed himself a warm friend of Canada at every stage of the negotiations, ever constant in his friendship and in his desire to promote the interests of Canada so far as was compatible with his duty as President of the conference. In fact, at one stage he said that his only hesitation in accepting the Presidency arose from the fact that it might render him of less use to Canada than he might otherwise have been.

On this journey Herschell was accompanied by two secretaries, his son and (Sir) Hedworth Williamson. After the Quebec meeting there was a fairly long adjournment until the conference met again in Washington on 1 November. In Washington he was received with warmth, the Chief Justice, Fuller, who was a notorious recluse, going to the extent of giving a dinner party for him, and inviting him to sit on his right hand at a session of the Supreme Court, a courtesy only once before granted to any foreigner, Lord Coleridge in 1883. Herschell in his turn devoted himself assiduously to persuading the Americans to adopt a more reasonable attitude and spent much of his time trying to establish friendly relations with the members of the American delegation. Some thought that his policy in devoting himself so exclusively to Senator Fairbanks rather than to some other of the members of the Commission was dubious because it aroused jealousy.

The extremely correct Joseph Pope, who was Sir John MacDonald's private secretary, had been shocked when the Commission met in Quebec because the members of the American delegation had, at a dinner party which they gave in honour of the British, failed to observe the proper etiquette as to the giving of toasts and had toasted the President of the United States before the Queen. Pope recorded that he was determined to observe the proper procedure on such matters when the turn of the British delegation came to entertain the Americans in Washington— namely that the first toast should be in honour of the head of the State in which the dinner is being held. So anxious however was Herschell to conciliate the Americans that at the dinner he insisted on the loyal toast being drunk jointly 'President and Queen', thereby irritating Joseph Pope once more.[9]

The Americans however, despite all Herschell's diplomacy, could not be persuaded to moderate their attitude. Victor Williamson recorded in his diary that:

[9] Pope, *Public Servant*, p. 119.

I received a letter from Herschell written from Washington on the 10th, in which he says 'I am labouring away here at the almost hopeless task of negotiating with our American cousins who are all that could be desired in the nice things they say but are almost incapable of seeing that on any point in which we differ they can be otherwise than completely in the right'. He then passes on to ask me, in view of his intention of letting his house (No. 46 Grosvenor Gardens) from the 1st February, to go there and secure any papers I might find in his private drawers. This, upon my return to London on the 26th, I at once proceeded to do. I little knew what was before me; for on going to the house I found both dining-rooms simply a mountain of unopened papers! It is an extraordinary thing, but a fact nevertheless, that he had gone away feeling acutely that he might be absent for many months without bestowing a thought on having his letters looked after and those of importance forwarded to him. It took me nearly a fortnight's hard work to clear this Augean stable.[1]

The conference broke down on 20 February. Herschell was inclined to ascribe some of the blame for this to a leakage of confidential information which had occurred in London, and in a letter to the Prime Minister hinted clearly that he thought Joseph Chamberlain was the culprit.[2]

On the evening of the 21st Pope recorded that he called on Herschell to bid him goodbye and found him lying in bed in his room at the Shoreham Hotel smoking a cigar and reading a novel. 'On knocking on his door I asked if I might come in. "By all means", replied he, "I am always glad to see my friends." I did not expect quite so cordial a greeting as I did not very often meet him and could not be considered at all intimate with him.'[3] Nevertheless Pope spent twenty minutes in conversation with Herschell who told him of the difference of opinion he had had with General Foster at the conference and how in subsequently alluding to it with a desire to smooth things over he referred to General Foster's remarks on the occasion which had the appearance of being offensive. General Foster interrupted, 'They were meant to be offensive', said he. Pope says that 'this amused and I think rather surprised Lord Herschell'.[4]

Herschell was in bed resting because on 15 February he had slipped on the ice while getting out of his carriage and fractured some bones. The doctors regarded his general health as being perfectly satisfactory and advised that all would be well if he rested for some weeks. As the British Ambassador in Washington wrote to Lord Salisbury on 19 February, 'The accident to Lord Herschell is calamitous but he retained all his clearness and vigour of mind.'[5] But on the morning of 2 March, Herschell woke early feeling extremely ill and quite suddenly died within an hour

---

[1] Williamson papers.   [2] Salisbury papers.   [3] Pope, *Public Servant*, p. 122.
[4] Ibid., pp. 122–3.   [5] Salisbury papers.

at about 7 a.m. The American authorities displayed the greatest sympathy and consideration. The President and other functionaries attended a funeral service and the Supreme Court adjourned its sitting for the day. His body was brought back to Plymouth on H.M.S. Talbot.

The funeral service in the Abbey, on the 21st, was most impressive. The church was crowded with men of every political party: for he had been generally respected and beloved. The coffin was covered with his robes of a Peer and of Chancellor of the University of London and the 'supporters of the pall', were the Lord Chancellor as Head of the Law, the American Ambassador, Lord Kimberley, K.G., as head of the Liberal party, Mr. A. J. Balfour (in the unavoidable absence of Lord Salisbury) as representing the Government, Lord James of Hereford, his colleague as Law Officer in the Gladstone administration of 1880–1885, Lord Strathcona and Mount Royal, the Agent-General of Canada, the Speaker, Sir Henry Roscoe, F.R.S., the Vice-Chancellor of the University of London, and Mr. Francis Buxton and myself as his two most intimate friends. The musical portion was similar to that at Mr. Gladstone's funeral, the full Abbey choir being strengthened by the boys of St. Peter's, Eaton Square, of which Herschell had been churchwarden. The anthem was by Wesley, 'He will swallow up death in victory', and Luther's hymn, 'Great God what do I see and hear' with accompanying trumpets and kettledrums was perfectly magnificent. It was a bitterly cold day—the coldest of the winter, and a heavy snowstorm came on as we left the Abbey by the North Transept aisle door for Waterloo station, where, by some stupidity of the railway officials, no preparation had been made for the reception of the coffin or the mourners; the former being left standing with the hearse out in the snow for over an hour until the car arrived with the rest of the train. In Farrer Herschell I lost, with perhaps the exception of Arthur Stanley, the dearest friend I have ever had in this world, and probably no life then in existence would have left so irreparable a void but one, and that one was to follow too soon.[6]

His grave is at Tincleton Parish Church, which lies in a rather ugly part of Dorset, half a mile from his wife's family home of Clyffe.

In the plain little Victorian church he is commemorated by a tablet in the nave, his grave being in a large plot near the east end of the church yard. On the stone cross are the names of Herschell, his wife, who survived him by only two years, his son, the second Lord Herschell, and his three daughters, one of whom died in infancy, and also his sister, Mrs. Cunliffe of London. Around him are the graves of many of the Kindersleys and Porchers.

Herschell was the third ex-Lord Chancellor in English history to die abroad, the others being Cottenham who died at Lucca and Brougham who died at Cannes. His death left no ex-Lord Chancellor living, an unusual state of affairs.

[6] Williamson papers.

The news was a distinct shock to the Liberal Party. Haldane wrote to Rosebery on 29 February (*sic*):

I must write of what has moved me much—Herschell's death—as you know I used not to care for him. But of late I saw a good deal of him over university matters and at the Bar. I had got to like him very much more. About his intellectual qualities and the constant sureness of his judgement there had never been any doubt. And as the smaller side of him receded one came to see how outstanding were his qualities as a man of rare capacity and effectiveness, and what a loyal fighter he was for his party and his chief. His death is a heavy blow to us all, and the country has lost a great public servant.

Beyond all this the question arises into view—which of us next! Well—faith and calmness are what we have to rest on. Of what moment is it what happens— as of a drop in the ocean! Herschell worked with all his strength and 20 years that are cut off are as nought from the standpoint of eternity.[7]

Rosebery replied on 6 March:

I agree with every word that you say of Herschell. Your letter arrived with the news of his loss, which simply stunned me. His loss to any future Liberal government is scarcely reparable. I have often meditated on the variety and strenuousness of his disinterested public labours, and have come to the conclusion that he was the most valuable public servant in Britain. His career should be a real lesson and incentive to those who would serve the country.[8]

Herschell's will was proved at £153,000—a remarkable sum to have been amassed by a man who began life as a penniless and friendless barrister. (It is worth noting that Cairns left £148,000, and Selborne £70,000—but the latter had settled considerable sums on his family.) Much of it must have been accumulated between the age of 35, when he took silk, and 49, when he was appointed Lord Chancellor, and so cut off from further lucrative employment. The price paid was the heavy one of a constitution worn out by years of overwork.

[7] Rosebery papers.   [8] N.L.S. 5904, f. 191.

APPENDIX

Tort and Contract. In *Davis* v. *Shepstone* (1886) 11 App. Cas. 187 (almost his first judgment), he considered the scope of the defence of privilege in a libel action. We have already considered Herschell's great judgment defining the tort of deceit in *Derry* v. *Peek* (1889) 14 App. Cas. 337, as well as his controversial opinion on the scope of inducing breach of contract in *Allen* v. *Flood* [1898] A.C. 1. His judgment in *Smith* v. *Charles Baker & Sons* [1891] A.C. 325 on the duty owed by a master to take reasonable care of the safety of his servants has constantly been cited with approval.

Other important judgments on common law points will be found in *Bank of England* v. *Vagliano* [1891] A.C. 107, in which he uttered some often cited *dicta* on the true method of interpretation of a consolidating statute; *The Bernina* (1887) 13 App. Cas. 1, in which the misleading doctrine of identification was exploded; *Reddaway* v. *Banham* [1896] A.C. 199, and *White* v. *Mellin* [1895] A.C. 154, in each of which the true scope of trade competition and the tort of 'passing-off' was considered; and *Nordenfelt* v. *Nordenfelt* [1894] A.C. 535 (restraint of trade).

In *Henthorn* v. *Fraser* [1892] 2 Ch. 27, he considered the sort of elementary point on which it is often very difficult to find authority—the moment of time at which revocation of an offer first becomes effective. In *Lawrance* v. *Norreys* (1890) 15 App. Cas. 210, he exposed an attempt to set up concealed fraud as a reply to the Statute of Limitations. (In this case, as we have seen, he insisted on censoring Lord Macnaghten's judgment.)

Conflict of Laws. In *British South Africa Co.* v. *Companhia de Mozambique* [1893] A.C. 602, he dealt with the question of the right to sue in England for a trespass to land situate out of the jurisdiction, and proved to general satisfaction that the rule prohibiting such actions was not based on any procedural technicality but on substantial principles of justice and convenience.

Criminal Law. All students and practitioners are familiar with Herschell's great judgment in the Privy Council appeal of *Makin* v. *Att.-Gen. for N.S.W.* [1894] A.C. 57 on the question how far it is proper for the Crown to adduce evidence of similar acts not covered by the indictment in order to show that the accused is guilty of the offence with which he is then charged.

Real Property and Equity. In *Commissioners of Income Tax* v. *Pemsel* [1891] A.C. 531, he dealt with a problem which still vexes the courts—the legal definition of charitable purposes.

In *Taylor* v. *Russell* [1892] A.C. 244 and *Ward* v. *Duncombe* [1893] A.C. 369, he produced excellent judgments on vexed questions arising out of the priority of mortgages—the former case dealing with the protection afforded (under the pre-1926 practice) by getting in the legal estate, the latter considering how far notice to one only out of several trustees was sufficient to secure priority for an equitable charge. He dealt with vexed points in the law of rating in *L.C.C.* v. *Erith* [1893] A.C. 562 and *Lambeth Overseers* v. *L.C.C.* [1897] A.C. 625. A point of revenue law is discussed in *Lord Advocate* v. *Wemyss* [1900] A.C. 48—a judgment prepared before but delivered (31 July 1899) after his death.

Company Law. In *Salomon* v. *Salomon & Co.* [1897] A.C. 22, he asserted a fundamental principle of jurisprudence governing the legal personality of incorporated bodies. Such entities are juristic persons entirely distinct from the shareholders or corporations.

Herschell was firm about the necessity for maintaining intact the nominal capital of a company. In *Trevor* v. *Whitworth* (1889) 12 App. Cas. 409, he held a company could not purchase its own shares, and in *Ooregum Gold Mining Co.* v. *Roper* [1892] A.C. 125, he finally precluded the possibility of issuing shares at a discount. In *Bloomenthal* v. *Ford* [1897] A.C. 156 he prevented an injustice being committed under the technical cover of a section of the Companies Act. He was not a party to *Sheffield* v. *London etc. Bank* (1888) 13 App. Cas. 333, by which the House of Lords imperilled the title of banks taking negotiable securities as deposit for advances, but he was a party to the decision in *London Joint Stock Bank* v. *Simmons* [1892] A.C. 210, by which the effect of the earlier case was removed.

Family Law. In *Russell* v. *Russell* [1897] A.C. 395, there is an important judgment on the meaning of cruelty.

LORD LOREBURN

CHAPTER I

JAMES REID, a merchant of Edinburgh, had a son John who became an advocate at the Scottish Bar. He married Helen, the elder daughter of George Cunningham, the Inspector-General of Customs for Scotland, and their son, James John Reid, became the Chief Justice of Corfu in the Ionian Islands. These islands had been transferred to Great Britain in 1815 by Russia, Austria, and Prussia as a protectorate, not so much with the object of conferring any benefit on Great Britain or on the Ionian islanders, but rather in order to keep them out of more dubious hands. In 1864 the islands were ceded to Greece as a result of Mr. Gladstone's mission of 1858 but in 1846 they were still a British Protectorate and Sir James Reid was in residence there as Chief Justice, a post to which he had been appointed by Lord Grey of the Reform Bill, whose supporter he had been in the period before 1832. He had earned the gratitude of Grey by his work as secretary of the Reform Association in Scotland—in particular by ordering the destruction of some hand-bills advocating violence. When James Reid's health later broke down Grey appointed him to Corfu.

On 3 April 1846 there was born to Sir James and Mary, his wife, the daughter of Robert Threshie, of Barnbarroch, Kirkcudbrightshire, a second son, Robert Threshie Reid, the future Lord Chancellor. He thus shares with John Copley, afterwards Lord Lyndhurst, who was born in Boston, the distinction of being born on territory which was no longer British at the time of his elevation to the Woolsack. Like two of the other Chancellors of this period (Cave and Maugham), he therefore spent his early years amongst people whose native speech was not English—in this case, modern Greek.

James Reid returned to Scotland with his family when his tenure of office as Chief Justice expired and settled down at Mouswald Place, Dumfries (a property which he had acquired through his wife, a shrewd woman of masterful character). Robert was sent to school at Cheltenham (his father also had a house at Tivoli Lawn in that town), which was then at the beginning of its career as one of the leading English Public Schools. One of the first pupils there was Henry James, the future Lord James of Hereford, who always took a keen interest in the political and legal career of his fellow Cheltonians. At school Reid did well in work and at games—Senior (Classical) Scholar in 1860, Silver (Classical) Medalist in 1864, Captain of both the cricket and football teams, and in his final year

(1863–4) Senior Prefect. From Cheltenham Robert Reid obtained a demyship to Magdalen College, Oxford, but had the self-assurance to ask the President, Dr. Bulley, if he could stand for a scholarship at Balliol without forfeiting his demyship. To this rather impertinent question the President, not surprisingly, answered, 'No'. Reid nevertheless stood for Balliol and won and went up to that college, then just at the beginning of its great period under Jowett, in 1864.

Here he had a remarkably successful university career, which is almost a copybook example of what the Balliol man of that generation was expected to do. He obtained First Classes in both Honour Moderations (1866) and Greats (1868) and also won the leading university Classical Scholarship, the Ireland (1868). The hard work which he put in for his examinations strained even his sturdy constitution, and at one time his family were apprehensive of a nervous breakdown. A contemporary later gave a vivid picture of him as an undergraduate at a lecture 'who came in late, roughly dressed, with a shock head of light hair, a stubbly chin, and a clear-eyed, fresh-coloured face, which looked as if it had lately been plunged into cold water'.[1] Apart from this he was an outstanding wicket-keeper against Cambridge in each of the three years, 1866 to 1868, and also obtained his Blue for racquets, playing against Cambridge in 1865 and 1867. ('You will get a Third, Mr. Reid', said Jowett when he heard of these achievements.) Reid's interest in cricket was maintained to the end of his life, and visitors to Deal recall him walking up and down the promenade with a small, tattered Oxford Blue cap on the top of his large head. He is said to have been disappointed at not obtaining a fellowship with his outstanding academic record. His ambition was the Bar despite the further discouragement provided by Jowett, who remarked: 'You will do no good at the Bar.' In later years when, risen to eminence, Reid ventured to repeat the second of these erroneous prophecies to the formidable Master, the reply simply was, 'I beg your pardon; good morning.'

Reid was called to the Bar at the Inner Temple in June 1871, marrying in the same year Emily Douglas, the daughter of Captain Fleming of the 1st Dragoon Guards. Captain Fleming was a rather mysterious personage, whose daughters were brought up by the Hicks-Beach family in Gloucestershire. In order to subsidize the marriage, Robert Reid obtained a position as inspector of schools. But his father, approving of the former step but not of the latter, soon produced sufficient money to enable his son to survive the early years in the Temple.

At the Bar Reid devilled for (Sir) Henry James and soon acquired a solid if unremarkable practice. He is said to have made several hundred

[1] A. G. C. Liddell, *Notes from the Life of an Ordinary Mortal* (1911), p. 63.

PLATE 5

Lord Loreburn leaving Westminster Abbey after the Service at the beginning of Michaelmas Term

PLATE 6

Lord Loreburn (wearing cape) engaged in conversation

pounds in his first year. He was much sought after in commercial cases, where his Scottish shrewdness was particularly valuable in unravelling the intricacies of commercial frauds. His open, cheerful demeanour, unlike that normally ascribed to Balliol men, made him universally popular. He was 'Bob' Reid to all at the Bar in an age when Christian names were far less commonly in use than now. Amongst his bigger cases were *Capital and Counties Bank* v. *Henty*,[2] and *Balkis Consolidated Co.* v. *Tompkinson*.[3]

In 1882, only eleven years after being called, he took silk at the age of 36—an exceptionally early age. His interests had by now turned towards politics, in which he was a devoted supporter of Gladstone. Through the influence of Sir Henry James at Hereford he was returned as a second Liberal Member for that constituency at the general election of 1880. At first, however, he made little mark in the House. His brief maiden speech, on 2 September 1880, was on the Committee stage of the Employer's Liability Bill, in which he opposed a Lords amendment limiting the operation of the Act to two years. In the following year he spoke a few times, mainly on Irish affairs, in which he showed himself an ardent supporter of Home Rule, but also on leasehold enfranchisement and vivisection. His name in politics was made rather as a speaker in the country than on the floor of the House.

On 22 April 1885 he supported in the House a Bill to alleviate a serious difficulty under which prospective Irish barristers laboured. Although there had been an Inn of Court in Dublin since the time of Henry VIII, the King's Inns, Irish law students were required to eat six dinners in London at one of the English Inns before they could be called in Ireland. For many years an agitation had been carried on to abolish this expensive and tiresome imposition; but the suggested reform was opposed by the Benchers of the King's Inns. Still, as Reid said in his speech, 'If they had to wait until they had the opinion of judges and Benchers for legal reform, they would have very little reform indeed.'[4] The Bill was passed and Irish law students could thus complete their professional training entirely inside Ireland.

It is a coincidence that on the same day he wrote the only letter which has survived from him to Gladstone.[5] It dealt with an incident on the North-west frontier of India at Penjdeh, where English and Russian troops had come into conflict. The frontier then was a sensitive area and for some weeks it looked as if an Anglo-Russian war was likely to add to the many other difficulties of the Government. Reid wrote that he felt strongly about the prospect of further deterioration in the relationship between the two countries as a result of the incident, for the English and

[2] (1882) 7 App. Cas. 741.   [3] [1893] A.C. 396.
[4] 297 H.C. Deb. 3s. col. 422.   [5] B.M. Add. MSS. 44960, f. 143.

Russian Governments would naturally support their own officers, and made the suggestion that the matter be arbitrated by the German Emperor or some other eminent personage. 'If the future be accommodated surely the past may be honourably adjusted in such a way?' Gladstone sent a formal letter of thanks stating that no effort would be spared to procure a peaceful settlement.

At the general election of the same year Reid made an unsuccessful effort to be returned for a Scottish instead of an English constituency, being narrowly defeated at Dunbartonshire. But in the July election of 1886 he was returned for Dumfries Burghs, for which he sat continuously for the next twenty years, and of which he was elected a Freeman in 1894.

Back in the House he took up the cause of Ireland once more, strongly opposing the Criminal Law Amendment Act of 1887 under which the Conservative Government proposed to take the widest powers for the suppression of civil disorder. The Act, he complained in the following year, had been worked in the interests of the landlord class and in a spirit of persecution. Years later these remarks awakened the spirit of gratitude in T. M. Healy, who came to Loreburn's aid when he was hard pressed by his own party over the appointment of magistrates, saying, 'Loreburn stood by Ireland in the old days'.[6] Reid also appeared for the Irish Members before the Parnell Commission, with Russell, Lockwood, and Asquith.

In 1887 Reid took a prominent part in the debates of March of that year on the right of public meeting in Trafalgar Square. This area had long been used by the public for meetings of various kinds but in the previous autumn a series of disorderly meetings had culminated in a mob smashing the windows of the clubs in Pall Mall. Reid suggested that the disorder had been much exaggerated. There was no reason, he said, why a practice which had been continued successfully for forty years should be stopped because of exceptional disorder on one or two occasions. In June of the same year he opposed the Law of Libel Amendment Act on the ground that it would enable the press to libel private persons with impunity.

In the years which followed his practice at the Bar grew slowly but not sensationally. An acute observer of the period remarked that Reid had something of a reputation amongst solicitors but made a poor show in court as advocate. 'I thought he was much more at home when, on one occasion, I came upon him in the market place of Dumfries, his constituency, surrounded by local bailies, chatting, and laughing gaily.'[7] But in the Liberal Government of 1892 to 1895 there opened up for the first time prospects of promotion leading to the highest level. In the summer of 1894 several changes occurred in the judicial scene. Sir Charles Russell,

[6] Lord Beaverbrook, *Men and Power* (1956), p. 296.
[7] G. Alexander, *The Temple of the Nineties* (1938), p. 114.

the Attorney-General, was appointed a Law Lord, Sir John Rigby becoming Attorney-General in his place, and Reid being appointed to the vacant post of Solicitor-General in place of Rigby. Rigby's appearances in debate were often greeted with howls of laughter by the younger Unionist back benchers, who regarded him as a typical pedantic Chancery lawyer. But Reid had always been treated with respect.

So he might have stayed for the rest of the short period of Rosebery's Government, but in the Long Vacation of the same year the Lord Chief Justice, Coleridge, resigned at last and Russell of Killowen was appointed Lord Chief Justice in his place, after serving as Law Lord for only a couple of months. Lord Justice Davey who, as Solicitor-General, had been a somewhat unpopular Law Officer for a few months in 1886 under Gladstone, was then promoted to the House of Lords in the place of Russell and Sir John Rigby to the Court of Appeal in place of Lord Justice Davey. It followed that, as a matter of course, Reid succeeded Rigby as Attorney-General and thus, after only a few months, he had been raised from the position of a somewhat obscure Q.C. and M.P. to one who had within his grasp the highest positions in the legal profession. In the House his main duty was to aid Harcourt in piloting through the Finance Bill with its novel Death Duties.

When it came to filling up the post of Solicitor-General which Reid had vacated, rather elaborate intrigues occurred which were to foreshadow the events of ten years in the future. There were two contestants for the vacant office, each of whom strongly pressed his claim upon the enigmatic and brilliant Prime Minister—Frank Lockwood, Q.C., M.P., and Richard Haldane, Q.C., M.P. Haldane socially and politically moved in the Prime Minister's innermost circle and he must have felt that the position was one which was likely to come to him, for Lockwood's reputation at the Bar had been obtained largely as a good companion and as a cartoonist of considerable brilliance. Everyone who knew Lockwood liked him but not many felt for him the respect which is the due of a future Law Officer. It was also known that the Lord Chancellor, Herschell, took a somewhat unfavourable view of Lockwood's abilities. Some of the story is told in the letters which the unsuccessful candidate received. Sir Edward Grey wrote from Fallodon on 14 October:

My dear Richard,
 I am glad that Asquith has told you what passed at Dalmeny; I thought it was better that he should do it. Everything was said by us that could be of any use but my impression was that R. was simply breaking a piece of news to us gently, which he knew would be disagreeable. He did it of course very kindly, both as regards you and us, but the hearing of it depressed me very much and made me rather angry, not so much with him as with the sort of

way in which these things are approached, discussed and settled by Cabinets and human nature at large. We will talk it over when we meet in London. Meanwhile I hope you will prosper amongst briefs; the idea of course is that Lockwood should take the first judgeship: R. said that was what he (L.) wanted, but I have not the heart to trust any conditional hopes of that kind. I think R. is your very good friend, but that Cabinets, if left to their way, oscillate between mediocrity and meanness.

Yours ever,
Edward Grey[8]

The following day Rosebery himself wrote from Balmoral:

My dear Haldane,

      I must add one word more—and I know you won't think it unkind or indelicate. I have a terrible choice to make with regard to a certain office now vacant. I would ask you to prepare yourself for disappointment. Should it be so, I feel that I may lose your friendship. With many it would certainly be so, but I retain a lingering hope that you may be different.

AR.[9]

Reid himself was delighted to have Lockwood as his Solicitor-General. The two were close personal friends: some of the best of Lockwood's inimitable cartoons are of Reid himself.

---

[8] N.L.S. MSS. 5904, ff. 10–11.
[9] Ibid., ff. 13–14. To his intimates Rosebery signed himself with this hieroglyph.

CHAPTER II

THE FALL OF THE ROSEBERY GOVERNMENT in the summer of 1895 meant that Reid had to return to his life at the Bar with the dubious precedence of an ex-Attorney-General. The position is often not an enviable one, as solicitors are apt to feel that one so distinguished should not be briefed in minor matters, and there is little doubt that Reid's practice in the subsequent years was not outstanding. But he never worried; he had the same Scottish composure as Finlay and those who visited him in his Chambers in Temple Gardens where he sat day after day surrounded by thick fumes from a black clay pipe or who met him on the Oxford Circuit found only the familiar, cheerful, undisturbed 'Bob' Reid.

He was, however, pleased by two events. The first was that in 1897 Sir Richard Webster, the Conservative Attorney-General, asked for the assistance of his predecessor in the Venezuelan Arbitration, as had been done before in the Behring Sea Case. For his work on this heavy and difficult case Reid received, in 1899, the G.C.M.G. Another international arbitration in which he took a prominent part, the Alaska Boundary Dispute of 1903, has already been described.[1] On the domestic side, Oxford University greatly pleased him in 1899 by appointing him its standing counsel. In the years which followed 1900 his name began to appear with increasing frequency in the Appeal Cases as counsel for one side or the other in appeals before the House of Lords or the Judicial Committee, such as *Russell* v. *Russell*[2] and *Neale* v. *Gordon-Lennox*.[3]

It was on the political side, however, that the greatest development took place in his career. The outbreak of the Boer War in 1899 split the Liberal Party sharply. There were those led by Campbell-Bannerman ('the Little Englanders') who regarded the war as wrong in every respect and refused to support it in any way. To this faction Reid was a devoted adherent. The others, under Rosebery, Asquith, and Grey, came to be called the 'Liberal Imperialists' and ranged from those who disagreed with the policy which had led to the outbreak of war but thought once in it was the duty of the country to be united behind the Government, to those, like Haldane, who were suspected, with more or less justice, of supporting the pro-consul Alfred Milner in his efforts to extend the British Empire in the Cape. The two factions disliked each other bitterly. Political differences were accentuated by personal animosities and these in their turn

---

[1] See pp. 123-5. [2] [1897] A.C. 395. [3] [1902] A.C. 479.

made the political dispute harder to settle. 'Campbell-Bannerman viewed with suspicion all communications between his Liberal colleagues and Milner and Milner's intimates in South Africa and spoke impatiently of the *religio milneriana* of which he supposed Balliol men to be the special devotees, Milner also being a son of Balliol.'[4] (Reid was, of course, an outstanding exception to this in Campbell-Bannerman's eyes.)

Reid's relations with his old college had always been friendly. When a junior barrister he had joined A. G. C. Liddell, who later (1909-15) became private secretary to the Lord Chancellor, in forming a Balliol dining club which met at the 'Cheshire Cheese'. Another member of the 'Little Englander' group was Bryce, once Regius Professor of Civil Law at Oxford and later to be Ambassador in Washington. Bryce had been up at Trinity a few years before Reid was at Balliol. As young men they had met in the rooms of R. W. Raper of Trinity, and rather disliked each other. But in later life they were on terms of close personal and political friendship.

Haldane, writing to Rosebery, on 3 October 1900, gives a glimpse of affairs at the time.

I saw Reid tonight. He is very friendly, a good deal anti-Harcourt, but wants peace—on the ground that the causes of differences are over. I do not think they are, but I agree with him that the aggression of the Liberal Imperial Council has not done good. We ought to be (forgive the legal metaphor) defendants and not plaintiffs in ejectment. But Reid spoke quite satisfactorily.[5]

Two years later, on 27 August 1902, Alfred Lyttelton wrote to Milner:

I think the pro-Boers are extinguished. The best of them such as R. T. Reid are definitely abandoning all criticism of the past and looking straight ahead . . . C.-B. has re-affirmed all his most objectionable sentiments, and though his party dislikes him, the Briton's loyalty to a man who has taken work in hand, not sought by himself, and of a thankless character, makes him really impregnable.[6]

In January 1904 Reid's life was saddened by the death of his wife. In their homes at Eaton Square and Deal they had been extremely happy, although their marriage had not been blessed with children. Those who knew her say that if Lady Reid had lived she would have been able to prevent the growth of the tendencies to moroseness and self-pity which became increasingly noticeable in her husband's later years. On 6 January Reid replied to the condolences of Bryce, refusing a kindly worded invitation to stay with him: 'This has been a very heavy blow and I find that it is best to be in a crowd in London at clubs and hotels.'[7]

[4] J. A. Spender, *Life of Campbell-Bannerman* (1923), vol. i, p. 264.
[5] Rosebery papers.   [6] Milner papers, vol. xxxviii.   [7] Bryce papers.

By the end of 1904 and the beginning of 1905 a considerable intrigue was taking place behind the scenes of the Liberal Party. It had become evident that it was hopeless to expect the two sections to coalesce in real sentiment however friendly their statements of policy towards each other might seem to be on the surface. Each section therefore in turn began to marshal its forces and consider what claims it might have upon positions of power when, as must inevitably take place, the Balfour Government collapsed within the near future.

Most of the surviving records of the period come from the Liberal Imperialists—that is, the Asquith-Haldane-Grey group. Not so much has survived to record the opinions of Campbell-Bannerman and his friends, though in the event, as we shall see, it was the less loquacious section who were successful.

In the old days you would see many a Lord Provost in a City like Glasgow moulded on the same lines as Campbell-Bannerman—pawky, shrewd, genial and a keen judge of character. When Asquith, Grey and Haldane tried to push the old man out of the way into the House of Lords, he saw through their game at once. It was just such a situation as many a Lord Provost would have had to tackle and he tackled it in the same way. Without any fuss he put them all in their places and went quietly on his way.[8]

He was amused by the fact that 'They were to serve *under* me, but on condition that they were not to be *with* me!'[9]

The agreement, named the Relugas Compact (after a fishing lodge on the Findhorn in Nairn owned by Grey), was to the effect that Asquith, Grey, and Haldane would refuse to join any government over which Campbell-Bannerman presided unless he went to the House of Lords after, at the most, a preliminary period of a few months in the Commons. The story of how this arrangement was made, of how the King himself was drawn into a somewhat cautious approval of it, and how the conspirators were eventually defeated by the inflexibility of Campbell-Bannerman (and still more of Lady Campbell-Bannerman, a woman of strong character) has been told elsewhere.[1] It is enough here to say that the three conspirators overvalued their own importance to the party which showed disconcerting signs of being able to get along very well without them. For in the event, Campbell-Bannerman, as a result of one of Balfour's characteristic actions, was obliged to form a government before the general election rather than after it, and there was no guarantee that a party weakened in the public eye by the defection of a considerable section of it would be returned in sufficient numbers to justify the attitude which the conspirators had taken up.

[8] Alexander, *The Temple of the Nineties*, p. 264.
[9] Lord Shaw, *Letters to Isabel* (1921), p. 262.   [1] See below, pp. 198-9.

So far as the disposition of the Woolsack itself was concerned, there were three candidates, Reid himself, Davey, now a Law Lord, formerly a not very successful or popular Solicitor-General, and Haldane, whose position at the Bar was greater than Reid's but who had never held office and belonged to a section of the party which was odious to Campbell-Bannerman. Intrigues began at least as early as January 1905, when Morley recorded that he visited Campbell-Bannerman at Belmont and, after a discussion about the composition of the Cabinet, found him 'particularly resolute about the Woolsack'. Shortly afterwards, on 27 March, Edmund Gosse recorded a conversation with Haldane:

It is an open secret between us now that he hopes, but without any confidence, to be the next Lord Chancellor. But he tells me that Lord Davey has claims which he has actually presented, in confidence, to Lord Spencer. Lord Spencer, who is of course of Lord Davey's own generation, has answered rather favourably. But it would be a very unpopular appointment in the Party. Lord Davey's intellect is still brilliant, still almost supernatural in its feats of rapid penetration. But he has been out of politics too long to be thought of in the running, and his person is extremely unsympathetic. His long, melancholy nose is drawn up in a perpetual sneer, his parchment cheeks and stealthy hyena-like tread freeze conversation whenever he makes an appearance, and I can hardly think he makes a dangerous rival to our delightful, our inspired and inspiring Haldane, *homo teres et rotundus*. The play of Haldane's intellect is the most wonderful factor now in my daily life. What would it be if he were Chancellor? But, alas! There is Sir Robert Reid in the way . . . [2]

In the event Davey's claims disappeared from sight, perhaps because Spencer was taken ill in October and played no part in the formation of the Government.

Reid's position rested not only on his status as an ex-Law Officer but also on the simple and, as it turned out, impregnable fact that he enjoyed Campbell-Bannerman's complete confidence and friendship. But at this stage neither Asquith nor Grey quite realized the strength of the opposition against them and they pressed forward eagerly with the fight to have Haldane appointed to the Woolsack. Grey wrote to Asquith on 24 November 1905:

I think (1) that a letter should be written to C.-B. and (2) that this [not found] is an excellent letter. All that occurs to me is that the direct reference to the present Lord Chancellor should be left out; it might however be suggested that the general feeling of the highest legal authorities on the Supreme Court should go for something. Our Lord Chancellor should be a man who has their legal respect and I believe that they are Haldaneites except Alverstone. It might be worth putting the point definitely that by taking office Haldane sacrifices

[2] Gosse papers.

£15,000 a year (he told me that in one year he had made that and returned £5000 of briefs besides) and Reid I suppose doesn't sacrifice anything—his income from the Bar must be trifling.[3]

Asquith, both by letter and personal interview, strongly pressed these and other arguments in favour of the appointment of Haldane on Campbell-Bannerman. Meanwhile, Reid himself had written to Campbell-Bannerman on 29 October as follows, giving some views on the Irish question as it affected the Liberals:

I agree entirely with John Morley and am very glad he spoke as he did. In fact it is evident that Rosebery and his friends have laid their plans to try and get Home Rule in all its possible phases (including Home Rule all round) absolutely excluded by a preliminary bar from the work of the next Parliament. And I think it is equally evident they are also trying to get the Liberal Unionists to join hands with them on this footing . . . I have no sort of complaint against men who wish to bring back the Liberal Unionists if they say so openly. What I am sure of is that it will wreck our Party if we assent to an ordinance that during the next Parliament nothing is to be done for Ireland in the way of self-government beyond administrative reform.

I have been at five meetings already in different parts of the country and have spoken to many people. Our people are very keen about social reform and economy. It seems absurd to expect much of that if you enter upon the duty of government tied by previous statements not to delegate business from the House. For a statement that you will not delegate to Ireland means that you will not delegate to any part of the U.K.: since it would be impossible to do it for any part if denied to Ireland. I have always held and expressed the opinion that no system of Home Rule or devolution is possible unless it applies all round and that view is now very widely held. . . .

I confess my gorge rises when I think of this worn out handful of Liberal Unionists, who in the main will not even support us, requiring an abandonment *pro tem.* of the old policy as a condition of their worthless assistance. But I believe the assistance of most of them would be given just the same whether you accepted Rosebery's demand or not.[4]

The pressure of office-seekers on Campbell-Bannerman now became so great (although the Balfour Government had not even resigned) that he was obliged to rent a house in Belgrave Square for the conduct of negotiations. On 13 November Asquith had an interview with Campbell-Bannerman in which the latter stated definitely that Reid would be Lord Chancellor and repudiated strongly the proposal that he himself should accept a peerage. In fact Reid was the first member of the party to whom Campbell-Bannerman offered a Cabinet post on Tuesday, 5 December. When the King sent for Campbell-Bannerman on that day and commissioned him to form a government he dropped a hint to the effect that

[3] Asquith papers.   [4] B.M. Add. MSS. 41222, f. 141.

perhaps the new Prime Minister would find his life in the Commons rather tiring. But if Campbell-Bannerman's mind had ever hesitated it was finally made up when his wife reached London on the evening of the following day. On the 7th Asquith wrote to Haldane: 'I was empowered this morning to offer the Foreign Office to E. Grey and an offer of the War Office will soon be on its way to you. The Woolsack being, in spite of all my arguments and efforts, elsewhere. I judge from our talk the other day that this would be the place which you would like best, better, e.g., than the Home Office.'[5] Grey and Haldane, finding themselves deserted by Asquith, who had accepted the Chancellorship of the Exchequer, joined the Government. The Relugas Compact was finished.

On 22 December the story closes with the indefatigable diarist, Edmund Gosse, recording a conversation with Haldane in which the latter is quoted as saying: 'Then C.-B. wrote to Haldane; first he said that Bob Reid wanted the Woolsack very badly and that as he was Haldane's senior he did not see his way to refuse it, although he quite felt sure that H. would do it, on the whole, better.'[6] No such letter seems to have survived, but possibly Campbell-Bannerman did sugar the pill in some such polite way.

In the event Reid became Lord Chancellor when the Great Seal was delivered to him on 11 December. He was sworn in before the Master of the Rolls three days later, and took as his title for the customary peerage Loreburn (a corruption of 'lower burn'), a war cry in faction fights in his constituency of Dumfries. (In a window in the Town Hall there is a representation of St. Michael, the patron saint of the burgh, with the inscription 'A Loreburn' underneath.)

His old friend, Adolphus Liddell, now Deputy Clerk of the Crown, noted in his diary on 1 January:

Drew the warrant for the King's signature, authorising the affixing of the Great Seal to the Letters Patent making 'Bob Reid' Lord Loreburn. How wonderful is the irony of fate that he of all men should be driven into a peerage with all its pomps and vanities! A smaller man might have made a fuss, like a Judge did a few years ago about his knighthood, but Reid accepts it all with dignity, which silences one's tongue inclined to mock.[7]

On 13 February the same friend described the traditional ceremony accompanying Loreburn's introduction as a peer ('Kneeling before the throne, laying his patent of peerage upon it, and then taking it off himself') as 'a curious bit of mumbo-jumbo for the twentieth century'.

---

[5] Haldane papers.   [6] Gosse papers.   [7] Liddell, *Notes*, pp. 352-3.

CHAPTER III

LOREBURN BEGAN HIS WORK AS LORD CHANCELLOR with confidence. He quickly established a remarkable ascendancy over one of the most difficult audiences in the world. In a vivid passage Archbishop Benson reflected on the peculiar difficulties which impede anyone who attempts to secure an audience for himself in the House of Lords.

It is painful, very painful to see the Lords always so unappreciative of the Bishop of London [Temple] yet because his voice is a little harsh, and his accent a little provincial (though of what province it is hard to say) and his figure square and his hair a little rough, and because all this sets off the idea of his independence, he is not listened to at all by these cold, kindly, worldly wise, gallant landowning powers.[1]

Loreburn's rugged, plain-spoken Scottish common sense was, however, much to the taste of the peers, and although he belonged to a party which was in a tiny minority in that House and was its main spokesman at a time when political passions rose to unprecedented heights, he retained the affection and esteem of all its members. ('Dear Bob Reid', he was always called by the 6th Earl Spencer.) In 1912, when he retired, the peers paid him the exceptional tribute of a presentation of a portrait which today hangs in the hall of Balliol, of which he had been elected Visitor in 1907.

His success as a debater, greater in the House of Lords than in the House of Commons, was due not only to his evident sincerity but also to the fact that at this time his private affairs took a turn for the better. After his wife's death in 1904 he undoubtedly found his status as a widower a sad one, but on 13 October 1907 he wrote to the Prime Minister:

I write you a line not on any official business but on a private matter of my own in which I hope as a friend you will take a friendly interest. I am going to be married, but that is not all. It is to Miss Hicks-Beach, niece of the redoubtable Sir Michael! They are very old friends of mine and she was a dear friend of my wife. I hope that the unbearable loneliness and desolation in which I have been living, with no one in the world, will pass away.[2]

On 3 December 1907, he married Violet Elizabeth Hicks-Beach, the elder daughter of W. F. Hicks-Beach, of Witcombe Park, Gloucestershire, by special licence in St. Stephen's Chapel. The preceding day he had

[1] *Memoirs of Archbishop Temple*, Ed. E. G. Sandford (1906), vol. ii, p. 76.
[2] Add. MSS. 41222, f. 124.

F*

executed a settlement of the estate at Kingsdown at Deal which he had acquired some years before, and on 3 January 1908, he made a further settlement in Lady Loreburn's favour of various investments and insurance policies amounting to some £40,000. The trustee under both settlements was the Public Trustee, an official who had recently been established under the Public Trustee Act, which received the Royal assent only on 21 December 1906. It had first been introduced by Sir Howard Vincent on the first day on which he was sworn in as a Member of Parliament in 1886, as he was convinced of the necessity for it by his own experience in the Department of Criminal Investigation. The facts were that over 95 per cent of English solicitors at that date kept no proper accounts and cases of embezzlement of the whole of a small trust estate were sadly frequent. The Bill, however, though taken up by Halsbury in 1889 and 1890, and by him steered through the House of Lords, was vehemently opposed in the Commons by spokesmen for the solicitors and country bankers. In 1905 Carson, together with Reid, eventually got the Bill through the Grand Committee of the House of Commons, but it was talked out when it went back to the floor of the House. The passage of the Bill in December 1906 was entirely due to Loreburn's energy and initiative and it was only right that his Account should have been number one in the office of the Public Trustee.

So Loreburn began work as Lord Chancellor, though there was the usual delay while his patent of peerage was being made out. During this time he sat in the Judicial Committee of the Privy Council, because although the Lord Chancellor need not be a peer, the Woolsack not being technically part of the House of Lords, he cannot do more than move that an appeal be allowed or dismissed; he has no vote in the matter and any expression of his opinion would be merely in the form of advice to the Peers and would not be recorded until he himself had been made one of their number. This is the reason why, when the House invites the attendance of the judges, as in *Allen* v. *Flood* (1898), they express their opinions confidentially to the Lord Chancellor and no record of their views is entered or made known in any way upon the formal records of the House, although they are printed in the Law Reports. Thus when in 1827 Alexander C. B. and Leach M. R. heard appeals from Scotland, 'their lordships generally communicated their opinions in a private room to the parties.'[3]

One of the first questions with which Loreburn was confronted was that of judicial patronage, both in the House of Lords and in the lower tribunals. The long reign of Halsbury combined with the general air of laxity in the Balfour Government had produced a serious situation. At

---

[3] See 2 W. & S. 558. For an exception, see below, p. 400.

the beginning of 1905 there were only three Supreme Court judges who had not been appointed by Halsbury: Lord Justice Mathew, Mr. Justice Wills, and Mr. Justice Kennedy, and by the end of the year Wills and Mathew had resigned in circumstances which have already been described.[4] The House of Lords and also the Judicial Committee were under-manned and the county benches of magistrates were almost overwhelmingly Tory. The Liberals in the country were aching for twenty years of injustice to be made up to them.

Loreburn first turned his attention to the problems in the superior courts. A vacancy had arisen in the Court of Appeal. He wrote to the Prime Minister on 22 December 1905 about the appointment of a new Lord Justice:

Moulton would be a very proper appointment in my view, though of course it is for you to determine. But if you think of any M.P. or candidate it is well to remember that he *ought* to take his seat on 11 January, 3 days after the Dissolution, and in view of the certainty of a vacancy very soon by Mathew it might be as well to give the hint to any M.P. or candidate you should fix upon or the constituency would be left in the lurch.[5]

Fletcher Moulton, K.C., the Liberal Member for Launceston, was duly appointed a Lord Justice the following January. The appointment was criticized on the ground that Fletcher Moulton had been the unsuccessful defendant in an action by his step-daughters seeking an account of moneys received by him as their sole trustee,[6] but proved to be entirely justified, the new Lord Justice making a remarkable reputation for himself both as a jurist and as a scientist. In October 1906 Lord Justice Romer's expected resignation occurred and Loreburn wrote to Campbell-Bannerman:

The duty of appointing his successor lies with the Prime Minister. I think I mentioned to you that Mr. Justice Buckley is the man whose appointment would be most approved in the legal profession and with justice I think. He is a first rate man and has proved a very fine judge of the Chancery Court in all ways. It may be that you have other views, in which case I will give you the best information I can if you let me know.

In the event of your choosing Mr. Justice Buckley a vacancy will be created in the Chancery Division, which is customarily filled by the Chancellor's selection. The best man, I think, is Parker, a man of about 45, I should suppose, perhaps a little more.[7] He is on the whole the ablest lawyer at the Bar and will go a very long way. He is a stuff gownsman and counsel to the Treasury in the Chancery Division, a post which traditionally leads to the Bench. I am sure his

---

[4] See above, pp. 62-63.   [5] Add. MSS. 41222, f. 147.
[6] *The National Review*, March 1906. See *In re Moulton* (1906) 22 T.L.R. 380 in which the Court of Appeal allowed the plaintiff's appeal, but making it plain that there was no imputation against Moulton's honour.   [7] Parker was in fact aged 49.

appointment would be received with acclamation. He is a Liberal. I do not know what Buckley is in politics.[8]

Parker was accordingly appointed to the Bench later in October. It is interesting to note that Loreburn's prophecy as to his future eminence was fulfilled, for in February 1913 he was appointed a Law Lord in the place of Lord Macnaghten. Asquith recorded the appointment in the following note to Crewe: 'I have just offered Macnaghten's place (with Haldane's approval) to Mr. Justice Parker, who is the best Chancery lawyer on the Bench. His politics are, I suspect, those of an equity drafts-man.'[9] (On this matter Asquith does not seem to have been as well informed as Loreburn.)

Lord Parker of Waddington, as he now became, was the father of a Lord Chief Justice of England.

Towards the end of 1908 Loreburn turned to grapple with the weakness of the final appellate tribunals which had been giving him and all serious observers much anxiety. Hints had already reached him from several quarters that feeling in the Dominions was particularly strong at the inadequacies of the Judicial Committee. As far back as 10 June 1905 Alverstone, the Lord Chief Justice, whose cast of mind was not attracted by appellate work, wrote to Halsbury:

> I venture to trouble you with a letter upon a subject upon which although it does not directly concern me, I feel the greatest interest. I refer to the present condition of the appellate tribunals of the House of Lords and Privy Council. It is, in my judgment, impossible to exaggerate the importance to the country and to the empire that the Privy Council as well as the House of Lords as Courts of Appeal should be constituted in a manner which will command respect. I know how keenly this is felt in the colonies, and even with reference to appeals from our own Courts of Appeal.[1]

Loreburn sent to the Prime Minister in December 1908 and January 1909 two long, well-argued and acute letters dealing with the problem and making suggestions for reform.[2] The position was that there were available for hearing appeals the Lord Chancellor himself, four Law Lords, one ex-Lord Chancellor, Halsbury, who in the nature of things was expected to attend less frequently now that he was in his eighty-sixth year, and one ex-Lord Chancellor of Ireland, Lord Ashbourne, of whom Loreburn said that, 'I have to keep him away ... useless or worse.' Sir Arthur Wilson was available to hear Privy Council Appeals only. A number of retired judges were also available but in practice those that were willing to come lent little strength to the tribunal and those that

---

[8] Add. MSS. 41222, f. 186.   [9] Asquith papers.
[1] Halsbury papers.   [2] Asquith papers.

would have lent the most strength could not be induced to come up from the country. The position, therefore, was that if the House of Lords and Privy Council were sitting at the same time the House could only muster a judicial strength of three, which was clearly totally inadequate for the final disposition of appeals from the United Kingdom.

The proposal made was that Sir Gorell Barnes, the President of the Probate, Divorce, and Admiralty Division, who had been appointed to that office in 1905 after thirteen years as a puisne judge in the Court, should be made a peer. He was still in his prime, as he had been appointed at the age of 44 by Halsbury[3], but he had earned his pension. Loreburn informed the Prime Minister that he was 'a *very* able judge' and 'I don't know his politics, if he has any. He is a very liberal minded man, whatever his party may be.' At the beginning of the New Year, Barnes was approached on the matter and indicated his reluctant willingness to accept the arrangement.[4] He was accordingly made a peer under the title of Lord Gorell, and served as a successful but not outstanding Law Lord for the next few years. The question of his successor was a subject of discussion. Loreburn wrote to Asquith on 10 January 1909:

> The practice has been for the Presidency of Probate Division (*sic*) not to be treated as a Chiefship but to be offered in a Chancellor's letter like a Puisne. This, however, is a matter of no importance, as to which I am a Gallio. I think it is most desirable that all these judgeships in the High Court should be considered between the Prime Minister and the L.C. was as the way with C.-B.[5]

Eventually the presidency was offered to Mr. Justice Bigham with the cheery remark by Loreburn that he was glad 'there were no damned politics about the appointment'.[6] Bigham's vacant place was filled by the appointment of J. A. Hamilton, K.C., afterwards the distinguished Law Lord, Lord Sumner.

Unfortunately, in the same month, the unity which had so far marked the relationship of Prime Minister and Lord Chancellor was seriously marred by the appointment by the Prime Minister of Thomas Shaw, the Lord Advocate for Scotland, to the Lordship of Appeal vacant by the sudden death of Lord Robertson (the only man in the House of Commons, it was said, of whom Gladstone was afraid). Loreburn wrote protesting strongly that Shaw was not a lawyer of stature and that he simply wished to 'cut a figure' in the House of Lords.[7] Any discontent at his being passed over, he argued, would be entirely local and amongst the ignorant. The

---

[3] See above, p. 46.
[4] J. E. G. De Montmorency, *John Gorell Barnes* (1920), pp. 2–3.
[5] Asquith papers.
[6] Viscount Mersey, *A Picture of Life 1872–1940* (1941), pp. 227–8.
[7] Asquith papers.

appointment was, however, made, and in circumstances described by the
contemporary press as 'not particularly auspicious'. When the vacancy
occurred 'Shaw, who was at the time engaged as a leading counsel for
one of the parties in a divorce case which had attracted much public
notice and was then being heard in the Court of Session, abandoned his
client at a critical stage of the proceedings, and departed to London in
order to urge personally upon the Prime Minister his claims to the vacant
office.'[8] His journey was successful: but it is interesting to note that in
May 1921, Asquith, in reminiscent mood, wrote to Haldane: 'I hope you
have looked at Tommy Shaw's book. To those who remember the
circumstances, his account of how he entered the Gilded Chamber in
reluctant submission to the Will of God, is a prime specimen of unconscious
humour.'[9]

In January 1907 Lord Davey died and Loreburn advised Campbell-
Bannerman to appoint Sir Richard Collins, the Master of the Rolls, to
the vacant position rather than the Attorney-General, Lawson Walton.
The latter would indeed have been tempted by the offer but he might
also have recognized that the Lord Chancellor was correct in urging the
appointment of someone with an established reputation rather than an
Attorney-General of moderate repute who had only been in office for a
year. 'The Chancellor's integrity is all the more to be commended [in]
that no severe criticism need have been expected if the appointment had
been decided by political considerations.'[1] The Prime Minister took
Loreburn's advice and Collins became a Law Lord, Lord Justice Cozens-
Hardy taking his place as Master of the Rolls, Mr. Justice Kennedy then
being promoted to the vacant place in the Court of Appeal and Pickford,
K.C., to the vacant seat in the King's Bench Division. Pickford was
Loreburn's first judicial appointment and it was indubitably a good one.
In all, Loreburn appointed eleven High Court judges, eight of them to
the King's Bench: Pickford, Coleridge, Hamilton, Bankes, Scrutton,
Avory, Lush, and Horridge. The last four of these were appointed in the
Long Vacation of 1910. (Scrutton and Avory had been induced to go as
Commissioners of Assize in January 1910 by a promise from Loreburn
that they would be appointed judges when the Supreme Court of
Judicature Act, 1910, which authorized the appointment of two additional
judges, had passed Parliament.[2] In the event Scrutton was appointed to
the vacancy created by the death of Walton J., and Avory under the Act.)
Each of these, with the exception of Horridge, was a perfectly sound, and
in some cases (Hamilton and Scrutton) a distinguished, appointment.

[8] *DNB, 1931–1940*, p. 807.
[9] Haldane papers. 'Tommy Shaw's book' was his *Letters to Isabel*.
[1] A. FitzRoy, *Memoirs* (1925), vol. ii, p. 315.   [2] Royal Archives, W. 66, 105.

Horridge had risen to fame as a solicitor (afterwards a member of the Bar) who had defeated Balfour at Manchester in the general election of 1906. When the ex-Prime Minister succeeded in returning to the House it is recounted that he chose to enter at the moment when his victor was making his maiden speech. Neither the style nor the contents were to the taste of Balfour and turning to a friend he remarked, 'Who is that person?' On being informed somewhat apologetically of the name, Balfour made the comment, 'He seems to be very pleased with himself.' The appointment was, if not a success, at least not disgraceful. Horridge aroused the amusement rather than the contempt of members of the Bar by taking with extreme literalness and lack of humour the technical precedence given to him as judge of Assize as a representative of the monarch in the county. In the Chancery division Loreburn made three good appointments: Neville, Parker, and Eve.

Judicial appointments again came to the front in August 1910 when Lord Collins was advised to resign on account of ill health. He had been, as Loreburn wrote to Asquith, 'really past his work' for some time. 'And I do hope', the Lord Chancellor went on, 'that Jelf also will retire, though I cannot be sure of this. He is quite beyond usefulness.'[3] (Mr. Justice Jelf in fact retired a few weeks later.) The vacant Law Lordship was thereupon offered by the Prime Minister to the Attorney-General, Robson, and accepted by him. He wrote to the Prime Minister pointing out that the Lord Chancellor was mistaken in thinking that he and four Law Lords together with the voluntary help of Lords Gorell and Mersey, were enough to dispose of judicial business. Two of the Law Lords were Chancery men, a third Irish, and another Scotch. An English common lawyer was, as Robson said, badly needed.

The Lord Chancellor is no doubt anxious to exclude from his Court any appointment he believes to be political, but the political complexion of the Court cannot be altogether ignored especially in view of future developments. The tribunal would have to play a great part in disputes that are legal in form but political in fact, and it would be idle to deny the resolute bias of many of the Judges—there and elsewhere. That bias will probably operate more than ever in cases that touch on labour, educational, constitutional and, for the future I might perhaps add, revenue questions.[4]

These were wise remarks in the year that gave rise to the famous Osborne judgment. Robson unfortunately had to resign in 1912; he had been worn out by overwork as Attorney-General.

Loreburn's retirement from the Woolsack in June 1912 left at least one disappointed man behind. Sir Henry Dickens, K.C., a son of the famous

[3] Asquith papers.   [4] Ibid.

novelist, published in 1934 his autobiography in which there is a chapter headed 'My Great Disappointment'. In this the author records that in January 1912 Loreburn asked him to go as Commissioner of Assize on the Midland Circuit with the clear hint that if the author made a success of this position he might expect a vacant High Court judgeship.[5] Before the next vacancy occurred Haldane succeeded Loreburn on the Woolsack and the next judgeship was given by him to Bailhache, K.C.

One more letter from Loreburn to Campbell-Bannerman may be quoted to show that he took a rather different view of the ability of Mr. Justice Kekewich than that generally prevalent in the profession.[6] On 14 June 1906 Loreburn wrote:

> I have not suggested to you any name for Honours. Will you let me suggest *one* and leave it to your own better judgment.
>
> Mr. Justice Kekewich is the senior Judge of the Chancery Division. He has been twenty years on the Bench and has been repeatedly passed over in the appointments to the Court of Appeal of judges in the same Division much junior to himself. This he has taken with the most exemplary good humour and without the smallest resentment, conformably with the best instincts of a scholar and kindly gentleman, as he is.
>
> The reason of others being preferred to him is not that he is an incapable Judge. On the contrary, in the most important part of a Chancery Judge's duty, such as looking after wards and management of business affairs, he is quite admirable, a perfect 'heavy father'. In the decision of purely law points, though learned and good, he has been surpassed by other Judges, and that is the main business of the Court of Appeal.
>
> I think it would be a singularly graceful compliment if he were made a Privy Councillor. If he were to retire he would, in the ordinary course, be so appointed a P.C. So it is merely anticipating a little and would I am sure be most highly appreciated by the legal profession. Of course in asking him (if you thought it fit to do so) you would take care not to let him suppose it is meant as a hint to retire. His retirement would be a real misfortune.[7]

This request by Loreburn was not granted.

In one other aspect of his patronage, Loreburn was open to some criticism. He took a very long time to consider applications for silk with the result that very often the practice of the applicants suffered in the interval before his decision was known. Often more than a year elapsed between the application and the decision. In the case of H. A. McCardie the lapse was so harmful to his practice that he withdrew his application and then, when the Lord Chancellor offered him a silk gown, refused it, so that he was still a junior barrister when promoted to the Bench some

[5] H. Dickens, *Recollections* (1934), p. 233.   [6] See above, p. 43.
[7] Add. MSS. 41222, f. 175.

ten years later.[8] But if the decision was long delayed it was usually wise, and when he conferred the patent of appointment on the new K.C. it was always accompanied by a friendly word of encouragement. F. E. Smith, not personally much attracted to Loreburn, always recalled how the Lord Chancellor had whispered to him, 'I predict that this will be a great success and that one day you will sit in my place', to which F. E., with a readiness of tongue which his contemporaries had already learnt to admire, replied, 'If I do, Lord Chancellor, I hope that I will always be as kind to young men as you have been to me.'[9]

When we turn to consider the appointment of Justices of the Peace, we find a less happy situation.[1] Indeed, at one time Loreburn's relations with his party were so seriously strained that a number of Liberal M.P.s never forgave his actions. The problem, in essence, was simple. Halsbury had very seldom appointed anyone to the Commission of the Peace but a Conservative and although there had been a Liberal Government from 1892 to 1895, Herschell had always strongly taken the view that it was not the duty of the Lord Chancellor to pack the magistracy with party supporters, no matter how strong the pressure from Members of Parliament; the task of the Lord Chancellor was simply to secure the most suitable man.[2] Nevertheless the Liberal Party would have been less than human if they had not expected Loreburn to make wholesale appointments of Liberals when the party was swept back to power in 1906. But in this they overlooked two important facts. The first was that Loreburn himself was inflexibly opposed to political jobbery or corruption in appointments. The second was that even if he had wished to appoint properly qualified Liberals as magistrates there was the very greatest difficulty in securing the names of such persons. It was customary for the Lord Chancellor to act on the nomination of the Lord-Lieutenant of the particular county involved not so much in his capacity of Lord-Lieutenant, but because as *custos rotulorum* he was the chief magistrate for the county. Until 1910 the Lord-Lieutenant forwarded such names as he himself chose to select, without the help of the advisory committee which was set up only in that year. But because of the long tenure of power by the Conservatives together with the fact that after 1886 the Liberals had lost the support of the great Whig landowners, nearly all the Lords-Lieutenant of the eighty-five counties were themselves Conservatives. Also until 1906 there was a property qualification of £100 for county magistrates. The result was that very few Liberal names filtered through to the Lord

---

[8] G. Pollock, *Mr Justice McCardie* (1935), p. 25.

[9] Earl of Birkenhead, *F.E.* (1959), p. 97.

[1] J. M. Lee, 'Parliament and the Appointment of Magistrates' (1959), 13 *Parliamentary Affairs* 85.　　[2] See above, pp. 114–16.

Chancellor's office except by devious and sometimes undesirable means. But Loreburn was anxious to work through, rather than against, the Lords-Lieutenant—his open character had won him the friendship of many, and he was confident of being able to appeal successfully to their sense of fair play.

Finally, so far as the 220 boroughs were concerned, as Loreburn later told the House of Lords:

> There is no one to advise me or give assistance of any sort, kind, or description. There is no Lord Lieutenant in any borough . . . Personal knowledge I can have none, nor can any Lord Chancellor have it, and through this open gap—open because there are no resources to obtain the proper and necessary information—party claims on both sides are thrust forward, constantly with clamour, and sometimes with menace.[3]

A question in the Commons revealed that between January 1906 and November 1909 Loreburn had appointed 7,000 magistrates, of whom only 3,197 were known to be Liberals.[4] The difficulties and exasperations which both sides to the dispute were involved in are clearly revealed in the following correspondence. On 22 November 1906 Loreburn wrote to Ponsonby, the Prime Minister's Secretary:

> As to the question of Mr. Henry relating to Shropshire Justices, I wish to add to the answer I have suggested the following remarks: (1) I do not know and can't say without further inquiry if it is true that 8 out of 15 in the new batch are Unionists. I don't believe it, but it is *very* difficult to get Liberals who are suitable and are willing to do the work from men like Mr. Henry.
>
> (2) This Mr. Solomon Henry[5] has asked a number of questions and been constantly about my office. He always speaks of the disparity in the county. But he sent me only 14 names, all in his own division, of them only 6 or 7 were of men whom I ought to put on. The others were conspicuous only as his backers, and after twice going into the names at personal interviews with the Lord Lieutenant I was unable to take the rest. The Lord Lieutenant wished, as I wished, to place Liberals on the roll but we could not see our way to these names.
>
> (3) I venture to think there has been enough of offensively framed questions by Mr. Henry. If anything goes wrong in the appointments, as it did in Herschell's time, I alone am to blame and am responsible. The duty of J.P. has very serious sides to it. They deal out justice to the poorest and with little appeal in practice. I should be a coward if I made what I think unsuitable appointments to appease the clamour of M.P.s; all who complain, and they are few, are new M.P.s. And from this little group I receive offensive letters and a scarcely concealed demand that I should act as their Registrar and put on whomsoever they nominate, which I will never do.

[3] 2 H.L. Deb. 5s. col. 670.   [4] 32 H.C. Deb. 5s. col. 2724.
[5] Liberal M.P. for Wellington, Shropshire; created a baronet, 1911.

Now the work is largely judicial and I treat the appointments as in a great degree judicial appointments. I most firmly believe it is necessary to appoint Liberals, but the grumblers when they come privately to my office confine themselves to urging the claim of a few persons who are their supporters and to whom they have in some cases promised the appointment on their own responsibility. I have already appointed about three times as many Justices as have been appointed on the annual average of 10 years and I believe have appointed twice as many as have been appointed in any single year, with infinite labour and trouble, the vast majority being Liberals.

I venture to think that this should be considered from a wider point of view. It is impossible for me to give my reasons as to individuals or to render an account of my actions to individual members. No man can be more anxious to redress the balance than I am but those who complain make it difficult by sending me names, not of the best men, but of the snob and the hacks whom they wish to reward.[6]

This however did not satisfy the Party and the Chief Whip, Whiteley, felt obliged to take the matter up himself. On 3 December he wrote to the Prime Minister:

May I say that it is impossible to exaggerate the mischief being done in the Country by the action of the Lord Chancellor in his magisterial appointments.

I *most* carefully and advisedly use the phrase that he is upsetting and most seriously damaging our Party.

I do not know quite what is my duty in the matter. We have honestly tried to keep our people quiet. But they are indignant beyond restraint, and I do not wonder at it.

May I enclose you the third remonstrance by this morning's post, this from no less a Liberal than George Cadbury ... As I do not wish to go behind the Lord Chancellor's back in writing to you thus, I will send to him a copy of this letter and also Mr. Cadbury's. I know you are aware that our County Members are leaguing themselves to vote a reduction in the Chancellor's salary.[7]

On the same day Whiteley wrote to Loreburn:

Private
My dear Lord Chancellor,
            Nothing is more painful to me than to be thus continually writing to you regarding magisterial appointments. There is no member of the Ministry for whom I have greater personal esteem than yourself, and it is only a strong sense of duty that obliges me to say that you are just rendering my work in the Country and my endeavour to manage things properly, hopeless and heart-breaking ... I am just stranded and beached in the matter, and feel like a man going headlong into bankruptcy. Last time you sat on me when I saw you about these things. I wonder if you would see me again.

Yours sincerely,
Geo. Whiteley[8]

[6] Add. MSS. 41222, f. 194.   [7] Ibid., f. 196.   [8] Ibid., 41239, f. 197.

With this letter was enclosed his letter of the same date to the Prime Minister. This produced the following reply from Loreburn on 10 December:

Dear Mr. Whiteley,

I have only just seen your letter to me about Justices of the Peace. I believe you wish to be friendly to me and I can only say that if the Liberal Party in the Ho. of Commons wants to see done what the complaining members privately asked me to do (*viz.* to job the Judicial Bench), I do not wish any longer to belong to that Party.

I will see you whenever you like, but all I can tell you is that this is an attempt to force upon me what I regard as a prostitution of my office and that I will resign the Great Seal sooner than do it.

Don't you think it might be worth your while to ascertain the facts before you take sides against me?

Yours sincerely,
Loreburn[9]

To this there was a reply on the following day:

My dear Lord Chancellor,

I am the last man in the world to, as you say, 'take sides' against you. There is not a day since we met in October that I have not spent a portion of my time in stoutly defending you, and I shall continue to do so. I am in the position of a good wife who vigorously sticks up for her husband against all the world, but occasionally nags at him across the domestic hearth.

But, with respect—to say that the Party want you to 'job the judicial bench' is contrary to the facts. For twenty years the Tories have done so. The result is that the Bench in various localities is generally composed of from 20 to 10 Tories and 1 Liberal. All that we ask from you is to bear this in mind. We are suffering now the most colossal injustice in these matters. We ask for some rectification of it, and we want *you* to make our magistrates, and not Tory Lords Lieutenant and local Tory Caucuses. We know we are safe with you, but we are galled by the others. I have the exact figures for Shropshire: Previous to this year, 214 Tories, 10 Liberals. Appointed by you, 8 Tories, 7 Liberals. The packed Bench there now consists of 222 Tories and 17 Liberals.

Surely this cries aloud to Heaven for adjustment. I am with most respectful esteem,

Yours sincerely,
Geo. Whiteley[1]

Support for the hard-pressed Lord Chancellor came from his old friend, the veteran Lord James of Hereford, who wrote to the Prime Minister on 31 December:

[9] Add. MSS. 41239, f. 192.   [1] Ibid., f. 193.

I feel that I have exceptional knowledge of the merits of the question as I had to deal with it almost daily during the seven years I was Chancellor of the Duchy—Herschell also was pleased to consult me upon his actions.

Now I think that the Chancellor's proceedings and writings are correct in every respect. He is doing his best to raise the standard of the magisterial benches by requiring the qualification of fitness and by appointing men irrespective of politics who are capable of reading (*sic*) the law and administering justice. But he has all the political wire pullers against him and these gentlemen will doubtlessly influence many Liberal Members of Parliament to join in the cry of condemnation.

I am sure you will feel how deserving the Chancellor is of support. He is making the best Chancellor I have known during my long legal and political life. This is shown by the manner in which he has gained by his strength, courage and courtesy the full confidence of Peers of all parties.[2]

On 20 January 1907 Loreburn wrote again to the Prime Minister: 'All right about the J.P.'s for Stirlingshire—I was obliged last autumn to supersede the Lord-Lieutenant and appoint Mr. Smeaton's men (all suitable) in spite of his protest. I hope he will not make it necessary for me to do so again, but of course I will if necessary as I have done in some other cases.'[3]

Five days later, however, the Duke of Montrose, the Lord-Lieutenant, agreed to the names of six Liberals as magistrates. The matter then petered out in the House of Commons though occasional criticism pursued Loreburn for the next few years, before the appointment of a Royal Commission on the subject in 1910.

Loreburn laid before the Royal Commission proposals which it adopted in its Report and which form the basis of the present system. In each county and borough advisory committees were to be formed. The members were to be appointed by the Lord Chancellor and were to advise him direct. The Lord-Lieutenant was not necessarily to be a member of the committee, but it was contemplated that in practice he would be its chairman (as has happened). When the Royal Commission reported Loreburn put its recommendations into effect without waiting for parliamentary approval. Asquith considered it was worth giving the new system a trial before having another debate in the House of Commons. In this way Loreburn brought about an important change in the con-stitutional structure of the country. It was a change which had great influence on the quality of the justice administered in the ordinary magistrates' court as well as on an important area of political life which had hitherto been the subject of undesirable party patronage. The only major change which has since been made in Loreburn's scheme was that

[2] Add. MSS. 41222, f. 194.   [3] Ibid., f. 199.

in 1925 Cave began to appoint the members of the advisory committees for a fixed term of six years, and to require half the committee to retire by rotation every three years.

There remained, however, a number of M.P.s who were unable to appreciate the courage of Loreburn's stand for the integrity of the judicial bench. Five years later, when the Coronation Honours List was being made up, it was proposed, on the initiative of the King, to promote Loreburn to an earldom. The proposal was greeted with marked coolness in Downing Street. It is true that this was an unusual advancement for someone who had been Lord Chancellor for only five years. Hardwicke had had to wait for eighteen years, Eldon for twenty-two years, Camden for twenty-three years, Cairns for eleven, Selborne for ten, and Halsbury for thirteen years before such a promotion came their way. But the King greatly appreciated Loreburn's simplicity and integrity and pressed the matter. On 9 May 1911 Lord Knollys, his private secretary, wrote to the Prime Minister's private secretary, Vaughan Nash: 'What is the difficulty about the Lord Chancellor being created an Earl?'[4], and also asking why the Prime Minister insisted on Morley being made one. On 24 May Knollys wrote again to say that the King 'is anxious that the Lord Chancellor should be created an Earl and thinks he ought to be made one whatever the Party may think of it'.

---

[4] Asquith papers.

CHAPTER IV

LOREBURN'S WORK AS LORD CHANCELLOR during these years was particularly heavy in view of the large programme of legislation on which the Liberal Government had embarked. The reforms were of a fundamental nature relating to the structure of Parliament, the relationship of the United Kingdom with Ireland and South Africa, and the institution of a rudimentary system of social insurance by the National Insurance Act of 1911. Each of them had to be argued at great length before a hostile audience. It is a tribute to Loreburn and to his audience that he never seemed to lose his temper and, although his health undoubtedly suffered from the strain placed upon it, he retained his good humour and equanimity to the end.

Some reforms of a purely legal nature may be described first. As Sir Robert Reid, he had been appointed Chairman of a committee to consider the amendment of the Companies Act and this committee reported in 1906.[1] Its report suggested several amendments, which were duly enacted in the Companies Act, 1908, which was the basic Statute dealing with the structure of joint stock companies until the Companies Act, 1948, was passed. In such a rapidly developing area forty years is a good life for a Statute.

The history of the Public Trustee Act, 1906, has already been recounted. The remaining change with which Loreburn was associated was the setting up of the Court of Criminal Appeal by the Act of 1907. This was something which had been under discussion for many years. The supporters of the reform pointed to the risk of conviction of an innocent man and their argument was strengthened by the deplorable case of Oscar Slater. The supporters of the existing system stressed the importance of maintaining the sense of responsibility of the ordinary judge and jury, which would be, it was alleged, weakened if a verdict could be set aside on appeal. But eventually the reformers won the day and the Act, which has worked so well that it is almost impossible to imagine the country without it, came into force on 1 January 1908. The Act had the support of Halsbury, who, we have seen, is mistakenly regarded as an arch reactionary in legal matters. Loreburn was particularly careful to conciliate him in every possible way because of the great influence which he had over the Tory peers. On 4 June 1906 Loreburn wrote to Halsbury:

[1] Cd. 3052.

I have been thinking over what you said to me in regard to the members of the Court of Criminal Appeal under the new Bill, being only the judges of the King's Bench Division.

That they should form the court from their numbers, and that the work should practically be done by them (as the Assize work already is done) I quite agree, but when I recall the Judicature Acts and the efforts they made to fuse all the courts and abolish the special and exclusive allocation of particular work by *law* to particular courts, I do feel it would be anomalous to repeat the separation. In law the Chancery judges can go Assizes, though in fact they do not. The Master of the Rolls sat at the Old Bailey some ten or fifteen years ago for one case. I do think it would be a pity now to specialise by Act of Parliament. If you feel strongly in this way I will not fight beyond saying it is a pity, but I hope you will agree with me on this. Many as are the drawbacks of the Judicature Acts (especially as worked by the judges) I think the unification of the judicature was a good thing and this would be a step towards undoing the unification. I hope you will forgive me for disturbing your holiday with this letter on business.[2]

On this particular matter time has vindicated Halsbury rather than Loreburn, for the practice of having the judgment in criminal cases reviewed on appeal by other members of the King's Bench Division sitting as appellate judges *ad hoc* is one which has worked well. There has never been any demand to associate the judges of the other two Divisions with the work.

At the tail-end of the 1907 session a Bill to amend the complex provision of the law relating to patents had to be explained late at night to a House disposed to be hostile. A sidelight on its progress is given in a letter from Salisbury to Halsbury on 26 August:

Sleepily I contended at some unknown hour in the early morning against the professional artillery of the Chancellor—and I contended in vain. I believe I nearly killed him with fatigue—but I had no desire for his blood and his intellect was no longer open to conviction even if my amateur weapons had been more serviceable. So after a futile conversation between an exhausted Chancellor and an ignorant amateur this most important Bill passed through committee at 1 a.m. on the 24th of August. It is thus that we legislate.[3]

On more political matters, in 1908 the first of the Liberal Government's great measures began to reach the Lords. It was a Bill for the taxation of Scottish land values. It had been considered by a Cabinet Committee on which Lloyd George and Loreburn sat, and when the latter had pointed out to the impetuous Chancellor of the Exchequer the difficulties which he would have in persuading the peers to accept a measure which to them would seem revolutionary, Lloyd George taunted Loreburn with being

2 Halsbury papers.   3 Ibid.

'concerned for your friends the Dukes'.[4] Loreburn left the room in disgust but did not hesitate to use his finest oratorical powers when the House of Lords was asked in March 1908 to give a second reading to the measure. The Peers, it was recalled, listened to him 'with the sort of attention given by men who are familiar with a subject, and are aware that their pockets may be touched by the decision'.[5] Nevertheless much of the burden of this work fell on Loreburn himself, the other Liberal peers in the House, such as Crewe and Morley, being immersed to a large extent in departmental duties. Crewe wrote to Asquith complaining about their weakness on 11 April 1908 saying that for general debate as distinct from particular subjects, such as the Scottish Land Bill, 'The Chancellor can to some extent be relied on but is aggrieved by it and makes difficulties.'[6]

The first real test of Loreburn's control over the peers came when the Lloyd George budget of 1909 was sent up to the House. This contained some proposals for taxation which to the modern generation must seem absurdly mild, but in 1909 were regarded as effecting so fundamental a change that the peers would be justified in departing from a tradition two centuries old and rejecting the Bill completely. The brother of the Master of Elibank, the chief Liberal Whip, thus described Loreburn's speech in support of the Bill on its Second Reading on 22 November 1909:

The Lord Chancellor, who in clear and simple language, preaching like a Saint Augustine to the barbarians, tried to expound to the 'wild men' around him the elements of the British Constitution. First, they smiled and laughed, but, gradually, they began to listen. For it was with a touch of that old world, noble enthusiasm that inspired Pitt and Burke that Lord Loreburn spoke of that strange mystic entity, the ancient Constitution of these islands. The phrases fell like blows. 'This unelected Chamber will hold the government of the future in the hollow of its hand'.—'No man of spirit would submit to it'—and then one short sentence which summed it up: 'My Lords, it is a step towards a Constitutional revolution'. Raising a piece of foolscap paper to his eyes he very carefully and slowly read what followed. In these momentous sentences the Cabinet picked up the gage of battle flung down by Lord Lansdowne and returned it. Even the House of Lords realized that, and every sentence that Lord Loreburn spoke was listened to in absolute silence. Lord Loreburn read: 'It is, in my opinion, impossible that any Liberal Government should ever again bear the heavy burden of office unless it is secured against a repetition of treatment such as our measures have had to undergo for the last four years. If we fail in the coming General Election, assuming that His Majesty is pleased to dissolve Parliament, it will only be the beginning of the contest which can end only in one way. If we succeed, I hope we shall not flinch from that which will

[4] T. Jones, *Lloyd George* (1951), p. 36.
[5] Morley, *Recollections* (1917), vol. ii, p. 258.   [6] Asquith papers.

have to follow. We have not produced this conflict. We have not provoked it nor at any time desired it, but we are not afraid of it, and I hope that we shall none of us fail to do our duty in preserving the Constitution of our country'.[7]

This grave warning was not heeded by the Tory backwoodsmen who rejected the Finance Bill by 350 votes to 75. The sequel is well known. The Government at once prepared legislation to cut down the delaying powers of the House of Lords and this measure, the first draft of which was prepared by Loreburn, became the Parliament Act of 1911.

In 1909 Parliament enacted the South Africa Act, which at that date was regarded as a great triumph of Liberal principles, bringing within the British Empire a community of people who had been engaged in a bitter war only ten years before. Loreburn, as an old opponent of Chamberlain and Milner, naturally supported the proposals strongly. The speeches in Parliament make sad reading today, particularly on the question of the protection to be afforded to the Cape coloured population. Loreburn, in winding up the debate on the Second Reading on 28 July, expressed hopes for the extension of native rights which were never fulfilled. 'The real anxiety which exists in Great Britain', he said over these rights, 'is due to obligations of honour.'[8] He hoped for an admission of the native element in good time.

The following year, 1910, saw a temporary lull in the party warfare over the powers of the House of Lords, brought about by the death of Edward VII and the succession of George V. With both monarchs Loreburn had always been on friendly terms. They admired his Scottish honesty and patience. So far as his duties as keeper of the King's conscience were concerned, he was not often asked for advice on the personal legal problems of the monarchy. But in 1906 he advised Edward VII that his consent to the marriage of Princess Ena to the King of Spain was not required by the Royal Marriages Act, 1772,[9] and five years later he was called in to advise upon a dispute which had arisen between the Household Cavalry and the Brigade of Guards as to who had the exclusive privilege of doing military duty, armed or unarmed, within the doors of the royal palaces. Loreburn tactfully advised that the most suitable person to answer the problem was Halsbury, who decided that while both the Household Cavalry and the Foot-guards had proved that they were certainly within the area of selection neither had established a claim to exclude the other.[1] This discreet judgment was sent by Sir Arthur Bigge to the General Officer commanding the London District with the intimation that in future the choice would be made by the King himself.

As we have already seen, George V showed his friendship for Loreburn

[7] A. C. Murray, *Master and Brother* (1945), p. 29.
[8] 2 H.L. Deb. 5s. col. 796.   [9] Royal Archives, W. 64.   [1] Ibid., F. 137.

by pressing his promotion to an earldom upon a reluctant Prime Minister at the time of the coronation.

In 1910 Loreburn was much concerned with questions relating to the nature and functions of trade unions. After the famous decision of the House of Lords in the Taff Vale case in 1901, holding that a trade union was a legal entity capable of being sued in damages, Loreburn had been called in to draft the rules of the Amalgamated Society of Railway Servants.[2] Amongst the provisions were rules which permitted the union to maintain parliamentary representation. The rules further stated that every member should be liable to pay a subscription of one shilling and a penny per year, which would be used to provide a fund for the representation of railwaymen in the House of Commons. It was also provided that all candidates should sign and accept the conditions of the Labour Party and be subject to their whip. A railwayman named Osborne, who was a porter at Clapham Junction, objected to his rule. Osborne, it would appear, was that rare person, a Conservative working man. Litigation was launched, which ultimately reached the House of Lords in December 1909. Loreburn did not sit on the hearing of the appeal, no doubt because of his previous connection with the subject matter of the dispute. The House of Lords unanimously held that there was nothing in the Trade Union Acts from which it could be inferred that unions were intended to have the power of collecting and administering funds for political purposes, and that the rule in question was therefore *ultra vires*.

Two of the Lords Justices in the Court of Appeal, Farwell and Fletcher Moulton, and Lord Shaw in the House of Lords, who was hearing almost his first case as a judge, also delivered themselves of sweeping remarks to the effect that there was a fundamental principle of public policy that no elector or Member of Parliament could bind himself contractually as to the way in which he would cast his vote. Lord Justice Farwell cited Burke's familiar speech to the electors of Bristol in which he said that, 'You choose a member indeed; but when you have chosen him, he is not a member of Bristol, but he is a member of *Parliament*.'[3] Lord Justice Fletcher Moulton said: 'The reason why such an agreement would be contrary to public policy is that the position of a representative is that of a man who has accepted a trust towards the public and that any contract, whether for valuable consideration or otherwise, which binds him to exercise that trust in any other way than as on each occasion he conscientiously feels to be best in the public interest is illegal and void.'[4] Similarly Lord Shaw said:

[2] J. H. Thomas, *Story of my Life* (1937), pp. 23–24.
[3] *Speech to the Electors of Bristol* (1774).   [4] [1909] I Ch. 139, at 186–7.

In regard to the Member of Parliament himself, he too is to be free; he is not to be the paid mandatory of any man, or organization of men, nor is he entitled to bind himself to subordinate his opinions on public questions to others, for wages, or at the peril of pecuniary loss; and any contract of this character would not be recognized by a court of law, either for its enforcement or in respect of its breach.[5]

The reader may feel that it is hardly surprising that foreign nations sometimes accuse the English of hypocrisy. Nobody can doubt that each of these eminent judges sincerely meant what he said, but it is difficult for anyone not brought up in England to understand how three men, two of whom had been in their time Members of Parliament and thus had practical experience of the working of the party machine, should have committed themselves to statements so out of keeping with the real nature of the English constitution in the twentieth century. In any event, the decision itself, quite apart from the *dicta*, was reversed by the Trade Union Act of 1913, which permitted unions to expend their funds upon any lawful object. The decision to introduce legislation of this kind was the subject of a memorandum to their colleagues by Loreburn and Robson, the Attorney-General. Robson, after suggesting that in general this was a favourable moment for the Liberals to fight the Socialists before they had succeeded in building up a large war chest, dealt in particular with the voluntary levy.

The doctrine by which contracts affecting political organization and action may be invalidated on the ground of public policy requires very vigilant watching. It may easily become the means by which the judicial bench may assume the functions of the legislature, and indeed that seems to be the intention, as it is undoubtedly the habit, of Lord Justice Farwell . . . That, however, is a judicial extravagance which may be left out of account when dealing with the judgments as a whole.[6]

Loreburn, after suggesting in general legislation on the lines which eventually resulted in the Act of 1913, said:

I cannot see what considerations of morals or policy ought to prevent trade unions from making it a condition of membership that members shall subscribe for political purposes, always supposing that they became members with knowledge of the terms upon which they joined . . . As individually poor men they all agreed to form a combination which shall have these objects, to unite in confronting the employer, to provide benefits for one another, and to fight parliamentary and municipal elections, subscribing towards each of these objects a prescribed sum. No one pretends that the first and second of those objects are in any way improper. No one, surely, can say that the third object is in itself improper. It is the very spirit of constitutional government that when

[5] [1910] A.C. 87, at 115.   [6] Asquith papers.

men think their class is aggrieved, they should eschew those secret methods which lead to disorder, and, instead of privy conspiracy, should openly state their wrongs and appeal to constituencies to return for them those who will redress them.

If, then, each of these objects is of itself innocent, or even laudable, is it wrong that they should be combined together by the same union? The only ground upon which this can be accounted wrong seems to be that a man may thereby be indirectly constrained to make some sacrifice of his political convictions in order to obtain the protection against the employer and the benefits which the union offers . . . I think the answer is that whenever men agree to be bound by majorities they encounter a risk of having to do something they dislike or to quit the association. Is it real freedom to say that men may not join such an association? Real freedom consists in leaving bodies of men free to combine for objects which are in themselves proper, and leaving each man free to judge for himself whether, having regard to those objects, he chooses to accept the combination and make the sacrifice which acceptance involves, if sacrifice there be. When the sacrifice wounds his conscience, he can quit the union and lose his money, as he knew all along.[7]

The following year found Loreburn faced with the heavy task of presiding over the debates in the House of Lords on the Parliament Bill. In an atmosphere of unprecedented political excitement and in a temperature which in the final days was up in the 90s, Loreburn found this a heavy task. It is not surprising that just before the end a distinct note of irritation appears. On 1 August 1911 he said:

Speaking for myself, I will go on as long as I can doing my best, but I declare that the time is coming and is near at hand when the combination of the duties of Speaker of one of the Houses of Parliament, of a Judge of the highest Court of Appeal, of a Member of the Cabinet, with important and momentous matters to decide, to say nothing of administrative duties relating to lunacy, magistrates, and many other matters, may prove too much for the strength of anybody unless it is mitigated by lightening the burden in some direction.[8]

In the early months of 1912 the pace of political events slackened slightly and the Cabinet were occupied mainly with the question of extending the franchise to women, a proposal to which Loreburn was strongly opposed.

During the Whitsun recess of 1912 Loreburn fell seriously ill and his doctors advised that he should at once resign. An awkward situation then arose, for the Prime Minister was out of the United Kingdom on the Admiralty yacht in the Mediterranean. Loreburn wrote to him on 3 June but was informed by his secretary that the matter must await Asquith's return at the end of the week. But next morning Loreburn felt so ill that

[7] Asquith papers.   [8] 9 H.L. Deb. 5s. col. 752.

he sent the following letter to Haldane, who had just returned from a visit to Germany:

> 8 Eaton Square, S.W.
> Tuesday Morning
> 4 June, 1912
>
> My dear Haldane,
>
>   Will you do me a great favour, *viz.*, to come round to this house as soon as you can and see me this morning. I can then explain why I take this liberty, but I shall be truly grateful if you will be so kind as to come. It is very important.
>
>   Yours sincerely,
>   Loreburn.[9]

The story may be taken up in Haldane's words:

I went at 9:15 and he told me that he had just sent in his resignation of the Great Seal, and wished me to make the communication to the King. He felt, poor man, too unwell to write or go himself. The doctors had advised him to resign as his heart was affected. If he did, they thought he would recover—as he was 66 he felt the time had come for him to cease to be Chancellor, and he had decided definitely and irrevocably.

I saw the King at 10:45. 'Who is to succeed?' said the King. I replied I did not know, as the Prime Minister was away. 'My choice—if the Prime Minister agrees', said the King, 'would be a man who was quite capable of combining three offices—Ambassador at Berlin, Lord Chancellor and War Secretary. I know one who would do them all easily!' (This was his joke.) Of course Asquith will make his recommendation when he returns next week. He has been advised by telephone of the resignation.[1]

Asquith's reply to the message was simple: 'Consult Haldane as to who should succeed him at the War Office.'

The vacancy raised some problems, for it seems to have been felt that no new Lord Chancellor could be appointed and sworn in until the Prime Minister had returned to the United Kingdom on Monday the 10th. Another difficulty was the custody of the Great Seal itself during the interval. Loreburn proposed to leave London for Deal on Tuesday the 4th, and shortly after Haldane had seen the King that morning he received a letter from Knollys inquiring whether it would not be best for Loreburn to give the Great Seal into the temporary safe-keeping of a Cabinet minister. So Haldane kept it in his custody for the next few days. Fortunately the Whitsuntide recess gave everyone a breathing-space, but the House of Lords was due to meet on the following Tuesday, 11 June. It was therefore arranged that there should be a meeting of the Privy Council on the Monday afternoon and that Haldane should be sworn in

[9] N.L.S. 5909, f. 219.   [1] Haldane papers.

by the Master of the Rolls at 11 a.m. on the following morning. Meanwhile complete secrecy was successfully preserved. Haldane tells the story:

Kneeling in front of the King on a cushion yesterday I resigned to him the Seals of Secretary of State for War and received the Great Seal.[2] I then took the oath in his presence swearing in the Scottish fashion with uplifted hand. Immediately afterwards I went to the House of Lords with the Great Seal and assumed office, taking my seat on the Woolsack as Lord Chancellor and Speaker of the House of Lords.[3] One of the first Peers to follow Lord Lansdowne and Lord Halsbury to congratulate me was Lord Eldon, who spoke of our relationship and of my great-great-uncle, his great-great-grandfather. It seems strangely familiar to be in the great Lord Eldon's place.[4]

After he had been sworn in on the Tuesday morning by the Master of the Rolls he dined at Lincoln's Inn with his fellow Benchers that evening.

After dinner I slipped away and crossed into New Square, to look at the staircase of Number 5, where my old garret had been. I went up the stair, and on reaching what once was my door heard barristers at work late, just as I myself more than 30 years before used to stay in chambers to work late. I raised my hand to the knocker, intending to ask to see my old room. But I felt shy and returned down the steep stair unobserved.[5]

A month later he sent Loreburn a friendly letter inquiring how his illness was progressing and received the following reply:

It seems to be a very happy thing that we can write to one another in a friendly spirit, after such wide differences of opinion.

The only thing that makes life worth having is, to my mind, a friendly feeling among men. I think with Sophocles that this alone imparts value to any man's life and the value consists in plain dealing and plain speaking in a friendly sense. Now you and I have been placed in a position of rivalry throughout our lives, not by any wish of mine, for I have never sought it, but by the clash of other men's opinions. I have never had any unfriendly view towards you, nor any complaint that you should have been placed in rivalry with myself. I am very glad to find that at the balance in the end you have so friendly and indeed so partial an opinion of myself. These opinions, among men who have been placed in conflict, are most valuable and worthy of respect. I think I should be unworthy if I did not write with full sincerity. As you truly say, we have

---

[2] 'Kneeling was always an effort and I am afraid he forgot to kiss hands!' his sister remarked later.

[3] Haldane's own account of this incident well illustrates how unreliable a man's memories of even important incidents in his own life may be. In fact he did not take his seat on the Woolsack as Lord Chancellor until 4.15 p.m. on Tuesday, 11 June. Haldane also says that he received the Great Seal at six o'clock on Monday evening: but the Court Circular states that the Council was held at 3.45 p.m. that afternoon.

[4] Haldane papers.   [5] *Autobiography*, p. 238.

differed upon very great subjects and have differed very greatly. I have never doubted your complete right to entertain and fight for your own honourable ambitions. Perhaps you ought to have been made Chancellor when C.-B. came into power. I am not qualified to decide on that, and I never said a word to influence C.-B. or any one else, in my own favour. But I accepted the office on distinct pressure by C.-B. and not otherwise. I should not have said a word had C.-B. preferred yourself. My differences with you have always been this, you have been an Imperialist '*au fond*' and always in my opinion it is quite impossible to reconcile Imperialism with the Liberal creed which we professed, and on the force of which we received the support of the country. In this way we became hopelessly estranged on the greatest of all issues. I am delighted that notwithstanding this you can still regard me in a way that expresses affection as well as most generous appreciation. I hope that it will always be so and believe that the best prospect of its being so is that we should continue to regard each other as heretofore, in a spirit of complete sincerity.[6]

On 3 September Loreburn revealed a little more of his soul to his old friend Bryce:

I resigned because I had been suffering from persistent blood pressure due to worry more than work though the latter was excessive. Had I gone on I must have been utterly broken down. I did not leave them because of any difference of opinion but I may say to you, who are a safe confidant, that I certainly should have resigned over the German business had I not believed and been urged by colleagues to believe that I should serve the country best by staying, and trying to get a sensible policy instead of what had been pursued. It was very distasteful for me to remain in and I stayed with great reluctance and only on that ground.

He added some melancholy reflections of a general nature. 'Democracy is probably the least bad form of human government in states which are trustworthy in character, but I am beginning to fear that the least bad is the highest praise that democracy deserves.'[7]

He hoped, he said, to return to normal work after a few months rest, as fortunately he was able to do during 1913.

[6] N.L.S. 5909, f. 283.   [7] Bryce papers.

CHAPTER V

LOREBURN'S RETURN TO PUBLIC LIFE was marked by an important letter which he wrote to *The Times* on 11 September 1913. The position of affairs in Ireland at that time was complicated. The Liberal Government was pledged to secure the enactment of the Home Rule Bill, if necessary under the provisions of the Parliament Act. On the other hand the Unionist Party, or at any rate the extremist wing of it, in which Carson, Bonar Law, and F. E. Smith were prominent, had embarked upon a course of action which had as its effect, if not as its object, the stirring up of armed resistance in Ulster to the Bill. Tension, political and social, had reached such a level in England that the leaders of the parties could barely meet on the easy terms which had been customary in English life for 200 years. In the early part of September negotiations were, however, taking place in Scotland in what Winston Churchill once called 'the delicious autumn of the Scottish highlands'. Churchill was in attendance at Balmoral and there he had much conversation with Bonar Law. The latter made no secret of his fear of possible anarchy in Ulster. Indeed he darkly hinted that the Liberal Government would be glad to see this as the means of forcing a dissolution. He then, to Churchill's surprise, indicated his willingness to enter into a conference to avoid such a catastrophe, the conference to be on the basis of the exclusion (not necessarily permanent) of Ulster from the provisions of the Home Rule Bill. The proposal for the exclusion of Ulster had been, as Churchill told the Prime Minister in furnishing him with an account of his conversation, put forward by himself and Lloyd George in a Cabinet Committee on the matter some years before, but they had been vehemently repulsed by Loreburn who, as long ago as 1909, had argued in support of 'Home Rule all round',[1] which, he said, would link the issue of the veto with other issues in which the powers of the House of Lords were involved. It would not only enable Ireland to govern itself but also effectively destroy the power of the House of Lords in all matters delegated to the local legislatures as well as avoiding the overworking of the House of Commons. These proposals had the support of F. E. Smith, despite the violent language he had used earlier in the year.

By almost the same post Asquith received from Crewe a lengthy description of a conversation which he had with the King, who was deeply perturbed about the whole situation. The King was under severe

---

[1] Asquith papers. See above, p. 143.

pressure at that time from the Unionist Party to use his prerogative either to refuse his assent to the Home Rule Bill before a general election had been held upon it or else to force a dissolution of Parliament. The King had not then received the masterly memorandum on the constitutional position of the monarchy which Asquith had just written and circulated to the Cabinet[2], but as Crewe remarked, 'Proof of the integrity of his constitutional position is not enough to satisfy him, partly because a number of people now will not accept it, whatever history may do; and partly because he is oppressed by the moral obligation incurred by him within constitutional limits as laid down by the strictest critics.'[3]

The King was particularly worried by the prospect of civil war leading to loss of life for which he would be held responsible and also by the personal hatred of him which many of his subjects would adopt, whatever course of action he followed. ('One can't dislike him for it', said Crewe with all the patronizing condescension of a Whig magnate towards a member of the Hanoverian dynasty.) In this tense atmosphere Loreburn filled three and a half columns of *The Times* suggesting in essence a constitutional conference on the whole Ulster question. The letter was written after preliminary discussions with nobody except John Walter, to whom Loreburn insisted that he was still a Home Ruler, 'and an ALL ROUND specimen of that class'. *The Times* itself welcomed the proposal in a somewhat tepid leading article. The Prime Minister himself did no more than make a cautious inquiry from Loreburn as to what practical overtures, if any, might be made by the Government. As Asquith informed his colleagues on September 20:

I wrote to Lord Loreburn asking him to let me know precisely what he meant by his letter in *The Times*. I pointed out to him that, up to now, there was an irreconcilable difference of principle between the supporters and opponents of Home Rule; that the one affirmed, and the others denied, that necessity for a subordinate legislature with a local executive responsible to it; and that neither party was likely to enter into a conference if the abandonment of the position which it had hitherto held was to be a preliminary condition.[4]

The answer which Asquith received was a lengthy memorandum dated 17 September. (A copy was also sent secretly to Redmond in Co. Wicklow.) It suggested that any conference should be preceded by private negotiations instead of by formal or rigid conditions, and 'by a full and confidential communication between the different leaders it should be ascertained whether or not there is any, and what, meaning in the language which Lansdowne used and Redmond used, and even Carson used,

---

[2] Printed in J. A. Spender and C. Asquith, *Life of Lord Oxford and Asquith* (1932), vol. ii, pp. 29-31.
[3] Asquith papers. [4] Ibid.

quite lately about co-operation for the good of Ireland.'[5] Loreburn particularly stressed the fact that Lansdowne, a Unionist leader, had favourably mentioned the prospect of devolution. The all important question, of course, was how to safeguard the peculiar fears of Ulster. (On this point there were many, then and later, who would have agreed with Churchill's pithy summary of the matter: 'I wish it were possible to do two things: 1. treat these Ulstermen fairly and 2. give them a lesson. But I am afraid No. 1 will stand in the way of No. 2.[6]) Here Loreburn made some detailed suggestions for a legislative and administrative enclave within the larger framework of an independent Ireland. 'These suggestions', he said, 'have no claim to originality, but I think in this way Lansdowne would be obliged to show his hand, and that if he did not accept or suggest some reasonable alternative, the country would be dead against him'.

Asquith, however, still remained dubious.

I pointed out that the parties concerned in this controversy . . . are not likely, at the moment, to accept an invitation (from any quarter) to come into a room and sit round a table, for the purpose of talking in the air about the government of Ireland, or about Federalism and Devolution. It is no good blinding one's eyes to obvious and undeniable facts, and one of those facts, relevant to the present case, undoubtedly is, that there is a deep and hitherto unbridgeable chasm of *principle* between the supporters and opponents of Home Rule. It is a question not of phraseology but of substance. Four-fifths of Ireland, with the support of the substantial British majority in the present and late House of Commons, will be content with nothing less than a subordinate legislature with a local executive responsible to it. They insist, moreover, that whatever may be done with Devolution elsewhere, the claim of Ireland is peculiar and paramount in point of time and urgency. A settlement which ignored those conditions would be no settlement. But within those conditions—so I said to Lord Loreburn—there is (so far as I am concerned) no point . . . upon which I am not ready and anxious to enter into conference, and to yield to any reasonable suggestions.[7]

The King, in the course of a lengthy and well-argued reply to Asquith's memorandum on his constitutional position, remarked that he heartily welcomed Loreburn's weighty letter and hoped that some good would come of it. But the reaction from both Liberals and Conservatives was in general unfavourable. T. P. O'Connor was informed by Lloyd George that 'the bitterest indignation' existed amongst Ministers and M.P.s at the ex-Chancellor's intervention. But this was an exaggeration. Birrell, the Irish Secretary, wrote that he doubted the prospects for a conference on

[5] Asquith papers.
[6] Ibid.   [7] Ibid.

the ground that the Unionists would only negotiate on the basis of 'drop the Bill' and followed it up a few days later by another letter:

> I am curious to know what reply you may get from our ex-Chancellor. I attribute his letter to his proximity at *Deal* to *Lord George Hamilton*, with whom Lady Robson found him shut up in an arbour! He is always like that. He never pulls his oar *right through*. The letter did great harm in Ulster, for in that quarter the less *chance* there is of a row, the more recruits will flock to the banner of hypothetical rebellion. The letter was *there* read as a Flag of Fear. *On the whole* I don't think it has done harm to our *rank and file*—it has hardened our hearts— what effect it may have had in *other* breasts, I have no means of knowing.[8]

Redmond complained to Asquith that Loreburn's letter had only encouraged Carson. Despite lengthy discussion in secret, the two sides seemed to be no nearer together as the New Year opened. The King wrote to Asquith on 26 January 1914:

> I had a long conversation with the Lord Chancellor yesterday, but I cannot say that it was very satisfactory from my point of view. He admitted that I was placed in a most difficult position, such as no Sovereign of this Country has experienced for some centuries. But he did not, so far as I could understand him, suggest any means by which it could be changed for the better.[9]

It is not difficult to imagine the conversation between George V and Haldane which caused the monarch to write this letter.

So the final result of Loreburn's letter was to weaken Redmond and not to strengthen him. For the first time separate treatment for Ulster was seriously considered in London. Bonar Law said he was willing to agree to the permanent exclusion of the four north-eastern counties, together with (perhaps) Tyrone and one other. This was something which Redmond could not have conceded; he was already menaced from his left by the formation in November of the Irish Volunteers in Dublin, as a counterblast to the Ulster Volunteers. He could go no further than to say that he welcomed any settlement by consent which would be consistent with self-government for all Ireland. He was worried by Lloyd George's private warning that some offer to Ulster must be made, though inclined to acquiesce in his ingenious proposal that the Bill should be amended by postponing its coming into operation in Ulster for five years. This was the proposal (with the time limit extended to six years to permit a general election in the meantime) which the Government eventually accepted in its Amending Bill of June 1914. It was not acceptable to the Unionists: 'Sentence of death, with a stay of execution for six years', was how Carson described it. Civil commotion in Ireland in the early summer increased the likelihood of civil war.

[8] Asquith papers.   [9] Ibid.

It was not until the eve of the outbreak of war in July 1914 that the Speaker's Conference on Ulster took place in Buckingham Palace and it broke up without reaching any agreed conclusion, the parties being, as Churchill said, unable to agree about the 'dreary steeples of Fermanagh and Tyrone'.

The war found Loreburn inflexibly opposed to the policy which Grey, Asquith, and Haldane had adopted and which he believed had brought about the commitment of England to a totally unnecessary conflict. His view was that these three had systematically concealed from Cabinet and Parliament the information necessary for the formation of an impartial judgment on foreign affairs and in particular the information about the military conversations with France which had begun in 1906. As he wrote to Bryce later: 'The key to the 1914 imbroglio was our position *vis-à-vis* with France. This hampered, as it seems to me, our power to see straight as well as to speak straight of our intentions.'[1]

The story really starts in 1904 when Lord Lansdowne had made an agreement with France whereby we permitted her a free hand in Morocco in return for non-intervention by the French in Egypt. In January 1906 Germany made a claim to a voice in Moroccan affairs and, no doubt with a view to weakening the position of the French, indicated in various ways that an attack on France was imminent.[2] Grey, on the request of Cambon, the French Ambassador, was informed of what was happening and was obliged to answer Cambon's inquiry whether England would stand by France in the event of a German invasion. Grey, on this matter, consulted Campbell-Bannerman and Haldane, then Secretary of State for War; whether he consulted Asquith is more doubtful, But, in any event, he assured Cambon that it was his opinion, but no more than an opinion, that France could rely on English help in the event of an unprovoked German invasion. He indicated quite clearly, however, that he had no power to pledge the Cabinet or Parliament. But, as he later argued ingeniously, England would not have been free to choose whether or not to go to the help of France if it had not first of all fully investigated the military position with relation to the extension of aid to France. Staff conversations were therefore authorized between the military experts of the two countries. The fact of these conversations being held at all seemed to bind Great Britain to France by ties of honour which the French were quick to emphasize in later years.

Loreburn, together with Lloyd George and Burns and to some extent at a later date Simon and Beauchamp, always thought that they had not been told enough about the existence and nature of these military conversations. Loreburn possessed all the radical's distrust of France and her

[1] Bryce papers.   [2] See below, p. 205.

politicians. In this he was different from his close friend, Campbell-Bannerman, who was, as Haldane later remarked, 'pro-French of course'. Loreburn made it a matter of complaint that he had never been consulted about the military conversations by Campbell-Bannerman, although there is evidence that he was told about them by Lord Fitzmaurice.[3] Yet to the end of his life he laboured under a sense of grievance with respect to his colleagues, Grey and Asquith and Haldane.[4] It was suspected that he even went so far as to egg on liberal editors to attack the foreign policy of his colleagues, whom he genially described as 'a Cabinet of Liberal Leaguers'. Rather inconsistently, he also complained that the Cabinet was 'kept in the dark' or deceived. He thought that a great peace party had been converted by the Imperialists into an instrument of war. In later life he even voted for a Labour candidate at an election. As he wrote to Bryce on 14 September 1917 with reference to the statement that in 1911 there was a division in the Cabinet as to supporting France against Germany: 'There would have been a division of opinion no doubt. But where is the authority for saying it was disclosed to the Cabinet?'[5] Three years later he wrote again to Bryce after reading Haldane's volume on the origin of the war:

> It is egotism in excess and very Jesuitical. The book is of such value as it may possess only because of what it does not contain, the absence of either denial or justification for a course of systematic suppression of the truth . . . Haldane's manifest efforts to get into their [Labour leaders] confidence will fail. He is evidently trying to get into the limelight. He cannot live without it.[6]

Loreburn also took the view, and in 1919 published a short volume (*How the War Came*) to emphasize it, that the undertaking which Grey gave to France on 2 August, that Great Britain would regard an act of hostility against the Channel ports as an act of hostility against herself, thereby enabling the French Navy to be concentrated in the Mediterranean, leaving the defence of the Channel to the Royal Navy, was an act of war *vis-à-vis* Germany, for the German fleet could not, in effect, be used against France whereas the French fleet could be used against Germany. Yet Loreburn, from the windows of his house at Deal, must often have looked across to the French coast and reflected on the importance to British interests of a neutral Belgium.

There is something about Loreburn's attitude on this matter which is not pleasing. His annoyance at finding others pursuing a policy different from his seems to have passed over the border into petulance. Three of

[3] Add. MSS. 41252, f. 128.
[4] J. A. Spender, *Life, Journalism and Politics* (1929), vol. i, p. 241.
[5] Bryce papers.   [6] Ibid.

his colleagues (Asquith, Lloyd George, and Birrell) thought that at bottom he was a jealous man. He disliked being overlooked by Oxonians whose career at Balliol had not been as distinguished as his own. (Asquith had obtained a First, but had not won the Ireland or gained a Blue. Grey had been placed in the Fourth Class.) This may account for the rather enigmatic judgment which Asquith later passed on his colleague: 'There was a direct and virile robustness in his creed and his character which was singularly attractive and masked some latent complexities of mind and temperament (as sometimes happens with Scotsmen) which time developed and made more obvious.'[7]

Loreburn was quite correct in emphasizing the decision to enter upon military conversations in 1906 as being one of extreme gravity for the future of British foreign policy. Whatever Grey might have said to his colleagues or thought in private, it surely committed England by an obligation of honour, if not of law, to come to the defence of France in a time of emergency. As the acute Rosebery wrote to Haldane in August 1916: 'I cannot help believing that this was done to test his sympathies, or more probably to entangle him inextricably in an engagement of a compromising character which must inevitably be carried further, and in that they succeeded.'[8] In any event, Grey's attitude that the House of Commons, to which he was responsible, could disown the military conversations, was incomprehensible in Berlin. The Germans could not understand a body of liberal parliamentarians setting aside the General Staff. So there can be little doubt that if Loreburn had been in the Cabinet at the outbreak of war he would have been on the side of those who favoured neutrality and probably would have resigned in consequence of the declaration of war as did Burns and Beauchamp. Yet a neighbour at Deal in August 1914, though finding him 'very depressed and depressing' about the war also noted that he agreed that Great Britain had to fight after the way in which Germany had treated Belgium.[9] A year later Loreburn was again found to be 'very depressed and does not passionately love his old colleagues, but I'm told that is sometimes the way with ex-Lord Chancellors'.[1]

On 19 October 1914 he was writing to Bryce, 'Only one man can make his voice heard now and that is President Wilson.' The following day he wrote again to say, 'The sooner the war ends the better.' The basis of settlement which he proposed was the restoration of the status quo together with the payment of compensation by Germany to Belgium. One of the difficulties of discussing conditions of peace, he remarked, 'is

[7] H. H. Asquith, *Fifty Years of Parliament* (1926), vol. ii, p. 112.
[8] N.L.S. 5913, ff. 54–56.
[9] Viscount Sandhurst, *From Day to Day* (1925), p. 22.   [1] Ibid., p. 305.

that it tends to give people an excuse for continuing the war'. So 'whether it is opportune to mediate or not, it is opportune to say that the whole thing ought to end'.[2] He suggested to Bryce, at that time Ambassador in Washington, that his letter of the preceding day should be shown to Wilson. There is no indication, however, that if shown it influenced the mind of the President.

The opening months of the war found Loreburn busy with a variety of matters. He was concerned with some questions of international law arising out of capture of contraband at sea. This had always been an interest of his. In 1905 he had published a small volume on the subject, which was reprinted in 1913, under the title 'Capture at Sea', and on a presentation copy given to his Oxford friend, F. W. Hirst, he had inscribed the following Latin motto:

idem velle atque idem nolle de republica, ea demum firma amicitia est.

In this volume he argued that peaceful ships and peaceful cargo should be free from capture at sea, and prize money should be abolished. These arguments, which have a somewhat visionary character, did not attract support from the Foreign Office or the Admiralty. Unlike Finlay, Loreburn was a strong supporter of the Declaration of London, 1911.

F. W. Hirst also persuaded Loreburn to argue against a proposed section of the Defence of the Realm Act, 1914, which would have given power to the executive to try British civilians by court martial during the period of war. After consultation with Halsbury Loreburn agreed to do this and succeeded in procuring an amending Act to this effect in 1915.[3] He had further correspondence with Halsbury in 1916 about the propriety of debating the Irish rebellion in the Lords.[4]

Loreburn also sat to hear a number of important appeals during these years. It is indeed notable that some of his best judgments come from the war-time years rather than from his period on the Woolsack. He was a good judge before whom counsel enjoyed a hearing for 'he restored the older and better practice of listening to counsel instead of arguing with them'.[5] 'Some men by the order of their minds are bound to be terse. Lord Loreburn was one of those.' His judgments will not rank with the greatest contributions to English jurisprudence, but they are always sound and sensible productions and, from the point of view of the parties concerned, what is perhaps more important, usually right.

In 1916 he presided on the hearing of an appeal in the *Tamplin Steamship Company* case,[6] which raised the important question of the circumstances in which a court would hold a contract to have been frustrated by a

[2] Bryce papers.   [3] *F. W. Hirst, By His Friends* (1958), p. 89.
[4] Halsbury papers.   [5] *The Times,* 1 December 1923.
[6] [1916] 2 A.C. 397.

supervening change of circumstances of such a nature as to render the obligation a fundamentally different one from that into which the parties had entered. In this case a tanker had been chartered for a period of sixty months at a monthly rental of £750. After the outbreak of war, when the charter party still had nearly three years to run, the tanker was requisitioned by the Crown. A rather curious dispute then arose. The owners contended that the charter party had been ended by the requisition. The charterers, on the other hand, who were quite willing to pay the freight agreed upon, contended that the charter party was still in existence. The reason for this was that they would have been quite unable to procure another tanker elsewhere at a similar freight. The general principle of the English law of contracts is that once parties have entered into a bargain they must carry it out or pay damages. The law takes a strict view of the matter of a contractual obligation. In certain exceptional cases, such as the actual destruction of the subject-matter of the contract, the law may excuse the parties on the ground that performance has become physically or commercially impossible. But as Loreburn said in a much cited passage of this case:

When a lawful contract has been made and there is no default, a Court of law has no power to discharge either party from the performance of it unless either the rights of someone else or some Act of Parliament give the necessary jurisdiction. But a Court can and ought to examine the contract and the circumstances in which it was made, not of course to vary, but only to explain it, in order to see whether or not from the nature of it the parties must have made their bargain on the footing that a particular thing or state of things would continue to exist. And if they must have done so, then a term to that effect will be implied, though it be not expressed in the contract. . . . An examination of those decisions confirms me in the view that, when our Courts have held innocent contracting parties absolved from further performance of their promises, it has been upon the ground that there was an implied term in the contract which entitled them to be absolved. Sometimes it is put that performance has become impossible and that the party concerned did not promise to perform an impossibility. Sometimes it is put that the parties contemplated a certain state of things which fell out otherwise. In most of the cases it is said that there was an implied condition in the contract which operated to release the parties from performing it, and in all of them I think that was at bottom the principle upon which the Court proceeded. It is in my opinion the true principle, for no Court has an absolving power, but it can infer from the nature of the contract and the surrounding circumstances that a condition which is not expressed was a foundation on which the parties contracted.[7]

Applying these principles to the case before him Loreburn, with whom a majority of the Law Lords agreed, held that the interruption had not

[7] [1916] 2 A.C. 397, at 404.

G*

been of such a character as to make it unreasonable to require the parties to go on with the contract.

In 1918 Loreburn presided in the Judicial Committee in the great appeal relating to Rhodesian lands. The judgment in that case was delivered by Lord Sumner and is generally regarded as being a masterpiece of analysis of highly complicated facts.[8] Loreburn dissented from his colleagues in the ultimate result, although this fact does not appear on the face of the Judicial Committee's judgment in accordance with the standing order going back to 1627 which prohibits the disclosure of dissenting opinions. Loreburn agreed with them that the company had no possessory title to the lands in question but would not have given a penny to them for the expense of administration.

This seems to have been the last appeal in which he took part. In December 1918 he resigned half his pension[9] and retired to his house at Deal where he completed his book on the origin of the war. In 1918 there was a conference on House of Lords reform under the chairmanship of Bryce. The committee was a strong one composed of people like Lansdowne, Crewe, and Austen Chamberlain. Loreburn was also a member of the committee which met twice a week for six months. But there was such a wide divergence between those who wanted a predominantly hereditary Second Chamber, those who wanted something like a French Senate, and those who wanted no Second Chamber at all, that the report was quite inconclusive and the result was nothing. A copy of his book was sent to Lord Lansdowne with whom, although an ardent Tory, he had always been on friendly terms, with the following letter:

27th of April, 1919

My dear Lansdowne,

You were good enough to say I might send you the print of a volume I have written about 'How the War Came'. My reason for asking you to let me send it was that your name and your actions necessarily form part of the story. There is no adverse comment. Indeed I agree with what you did before the war. But I thought it fair to let you see it, if you thought it worth while to read it, before going to press.

I need hardly say that I will gladly correct any error and shall very highly value any criticism of any point.

I am hopeful, because I think President Wilson and Lloyd George are really as one and will make short work of the Italian mendicant.

Italicus esuriens in coelum, jusseris, ibit.[1] Bid him go to hell, to hell he goes. So that the end of this horror is in sight, unless the Germans take the line of telling us to govern Germany for ourselves, which I rather fear.

Every day that passes makes me more certain that you were right when you took your stand on the unwisdom of a blank negative to the advances for peace.

[8] [1919] A.C. 211.   [9] 143 H.C. Deb. 5s. col. 2328.   [1] See Juvenal, III, 77–78.

We could have made a more lasting peace then and made it more easily and saved countless lives if we had acted on your advice. It must be a source of happiness to you in this trying time that you acted as you did. I am coming to think that there are only two qualities of supreme value at a crisis. One is courage and the other is sympathy. Lloyd George has both and for that reason he will hold his own and will make a tolerable peace, though a less good peace in the true sense than we could have made two years ago.

Will you forgive me if I make a suggestion, which I know I have no right to make? But when this peace comes, is there no chance of your bringing about a settlement with Ireland? You know more about it and could do more than anyone else. *Beati pacifici.*

Ever yours,
Loreburn[2]

Lansdowne replied as follows on 28 April:

My dear Loreburn,

[This letter is set out on pages 484 to 485 of Newton's Life of Lord Lansdowne but has the following final paragraph which Newton omits.]

As to Ireland I am very hopeless unless the situation undergoes a change. I had a long talk to Horace Plunkett two or three weeks ago. You have no doubt seen the letter which he wrote to *The Times* soon after. It does not seem to be possible for us to impose anything upon Ireland as we see it today. If it is true, as Dunraven and others think, that the Sinn Feiners really do not represent the feeling of the country, is it too much to hope that before we are much older the country will turn from them to some more far seeing and less irresponsible body? People here would, I believe, be quite ready to make a reasonable settlement giving many things which they do not like, if they had any reason for believing that it would find acceptance and be loyally carried out.

I should like to have a talk to you about this question when we meet, as I hope we shall before long, in the House of Lords.

Yours,
L.[3]

But later in the same year Loreburn seems to have viewed the Treaty of Versailles and the progress of events in general with increasing distaste. On 12 June he wrote to Bryce to say that he had the impression that the Bolsheviks would make good terms. 'Perhaps too good for the capitalists of France and England who want to save the millions they have lent or invested . . . I can't help suspecting that these monied interests are preventing our Governments from coming to terms with the *de facto* government there.'[4] The peace treaty, he thought, was one of which Louis XIV might have been proud. 'We have given in to France as we did when we let her embroil us in her Franco-German quarrel.' He went on to remark that, 'I am not attracted either by the men who are coming on or by the ways they have adopted.'

[2] Lansdowne papers.   [3] Ibid.   [4] Bryce papers.

A few days later, on 25 June, he wrote again to Bryce rejecting the latter's suggestion that he should return to public life. He felt too old and weary of London. Also, 'I should be in perpetual antagonism with the Old Gang, who have sold and deceived us, without being able to agree with the other side whose intelligence is as poor as is the character of the others . . . My whole life has been a long struggle with men and measures alien to all I value.'[5] To F. W. Hirst he wrote often in the same strain.[6] But the struggle was now in effect over and Loreburn remained in almost complete retirement at Kingsdown House, Deal, where, it is recalled, he employed a butler who had witnessed one of the last public executions in England—that of the twelve *Flowery Land* mutineers at Newgate in February 1864, a case in which Hardinge Giffard had appeared for the Crown. Loreburn died there on 30 November 1923. His body was cremated at Golders Green on 4 December after a Church of England service and the ashes were taken to Mouswald for burial. The small kirk at Mouswald looks out over the Solway Firth to the Cumberland hills. The grave is at the end of the churchyard beside the road, and also contains the remains of Loreburn's first wife and her sister, Clementine Fleming. The plain stone cross is inscribed: The Earl Loreburn (Robert Threshie Reid) 1846–1923.

Loreburn's will, dated 20 May 1915, together with a codicil of 6 September 1919, left all his property after various small legacies (including one to his old friend, John O'Connor, M.P.) to his wife absolutely if she survived him. (Lady Loreburn died on 5 February 1931.) If these trusts failed then he left the whole of his estate to the Chancellor of the Exchequer in order to avoid an intestacy. The value of his estate was just under £16,000.

[5] Bryce papers.
[6] F. W. Hirst, 'Lord Loreburn', *Contemporary Review*, January 1924.

APPENDIX

In the field of *tort and contract* Loreburn's best-known judgment is probably that in *Hulton & Co.* v. *Jones* [1910] A.C. 20, in which he held that the fact that the defendant in an action of libel had never heard of the plaintiff was no defence if reasonable men could think that the words published referred to him. The decision is still law although deprived of much of its effect by the Defamation Act, 1952, sect. 4. In truth neither Loreburn nor the other Law Lords appear to have realized the fundamental problems raised by the case. It is significant that later the House of Lords adopted a rule of practice of always reserving its judgment, however simple the case might appear to be at the conclusion of argument. Loreburn was perhaps too ready, especially in his early years on the Woolsack, to dispose of a case by enunciating the relevant rule and applying it to the facts. A party to an appeal before the final tribunal is entitled to a reasoned explanation of why his claim is being admitted or rejected: a judgment in the House of Lords is not the same thing as an opinion furnished by a busy counsel on a case sent to him in the Temple. Thus the very difficult problems raised in *Cavalier* v. *Pope* [1906] A.C. 428 are hardly solved satisfactorily by a judgment of seven lines.

But when his personal interest or experience was involved he could produce an admirably full and well-reasoned judgment on the approved traditional lines. So in *Conway* v. *Wade* [1909] A.C. 506 he gave an authoritative exposition of the effect of the Trade Disputes Act, 1906, on the tort of inducing a breach of contract.

As might be expected, Loreburn was not the sort of judge who is a slave to the maxim *stare decisis*. To him previous cases were illustrative of principle and should not be permitted to stand in the way of doing substantial justice. He considered the problem in one judgment (*West Ham Union* v. *Edmonton Union* [1908] A.C. 1, 4) which has often been cited with approval:

Great importance is to be attached to old authorities, on the strength of which many transactions may have been adjusted and rights determined. But where they are plainly wrong, and especially where the subsequent course of judicial decisions has disclosed weakness in the reasoning on which they were based, and practical injustice in the consequences that must flow from them, I consider it is the duty of this House to overrule them, if it has not lost the right to do so by itself expressly affirming them.

This judgment confines the misleading maxim *communis error facit ius* within proper limits.

Nor did Loreburn fall into the error of confusing questions of law with questions of fact, as has been done even recently by the most eminent of judges. He delivered good judgments on this matter in *McCartan* v. *Belfast Harbour Commissioners* [1911] 2 I.R. 143 and *Shrimpton* v. *Herts C.C.* (1911) 104 L.T. 145.

His judgment in the well-known frustration case of *Tamplin Steamship Co., Ltd.* v. *Anglo-Mexican Petroleum Products Co., Ltd.* [1916] 2 A.C. 397 has already been considered.

In *Wallis, Son and Wells* v. *Pratt and Haynes* [1911] A.C. 394 an important question arose relating to the construction of the Sale of Goods Act, 1893, as it affected sales by description. Loreburn was content to deliver a brief judgment affirming the decision which the Court of Appeal had reached after a lengthy examination of the authorities. In *Lloyd* v. *Grace Smith & Sons* [1912] A.C. 716 he was likewise content to concur briefly.

Other judgments on common law will be found in *Lowery* v. *Walker* [1911] A.C. 10 (duty owed to a trespasser); *Pearson & Son, Ltd.* v. *Dublin Corporation* [1907] A.C. 351 (principal's liability for fraud of agent); *Addis* v. *Gramophone Co., Ltd.* [1909] A.C. 488 (damages for wrongful dismissal); *Robinson* v. *Balmain Ferry Co.* [1910] A.C. 295 (false imprisonment); *Admiralty Commissioners* v. *S.S. Amerika* [1917] A.C. 38; *Adam* v. *Ward* [1917] A.C. 309 (qualified privilege).

In *revenue law* there is a well-known judgment in *De Beers Consolidated Mines* v. *Howe* [1906] A.C. 455, which explains under what conditions it is possible to ascribe 'residence' to a limited company. It has been said by high authority that Loreburn's judgment 'must be treated today as if the test which it laid down was as precise and as unequivocal as a positive statutory injunction' (*Unit Construction Co.* v. *Bullock* [1960] A.C. 351, at 366, *per* Lord Radcliffe).

In *constitutional law* all students of the prerogative orders are familiar with Loreburn's judgment in *Board of Education* v. *Rice* [1911] A.C. 179.

In *Scott* v. *Scott* [1913] A.C. 417 Loreburn agreed with his colleagues in maintaining the important constitutional principle that a court must sit in public save in cases where justice could not be done in open court.

So far as appeals from the dominions and colonies were concerned, the evidence of the Law Reports (and such of his letters as have survived) shows that Loreburn took his duties in the Privy Council very seriously. In *Att.-Gen. for Ontario* v. *Att.-Gen. for Canada* [1912] A.C. 571 he delivered an important judgment, stressing that a broad interpretation of the British North America Act, 1867, should be adopted in order to give the greatest freedom for the organic growth of the Canadian constitution.

LORD HALDANE

CHAPTER I

THERE IS NO VILLAGE AT GLENEAGLES, but there is a station and a well-known hotel. On the opposite side of the railway line, on the road to Dunfermline, there is the ancient castle of Gleneagles. Here the Haldanes have been seated for some seven hundred years, with a direct descent in the male line.[1]

In 1805 Robert Haldane was born to James Haldane and Mary Joass, his wife. Robert was an officer in the Royal Navy who, in later life, turned his interests to evangelical preaching. A sturdy man of dour highland temperament, he married twice; his first wife, Janet Makgill, who died in 1851, left him six children. Two years later he married Mary Elizabeth Burdon Sanderson, of a well-known Northumbrian family. Her father was the nephew of Lord Chancellor Eldon and had for a time worked in the House of Lords as secretary of Ecclesiastical Patronage to his uncle, but eventually resigned, being disgusted with the traffic in advowsons which was carried on, and the extent to which political considerations influenced the gift of Crown Livings. On his resignation he became a Plymouth Brother. This was a religious faith which his daughter shared, so that the Haldane houses in Edinburgh and at Auchterarder were models of Victorian piety.

During the summer the family was accustomed to move to Auchterarder, where in 1851 Robert Haldane had bought a small property called Cloan. On his wife's suggestion, this was renamed Cloanden, a name which still appears on the Ordnance maps of the neighbourhood, although Haldane reverted to the original name for the estate, thinking the Anglo-Saxon suffix inappropriate.

The second child of the marriage, Richard Burdon, was born at 17 Charlotte Square, Edinburgh, on 30 July 1856. Then, as now, this was one of the finest houses in a square renowned for its eighteenth-century architecture. (The house is now the headquarters of the Alliance Insurance Company.) The father's first family were by now out in the world and Richard Haldane's companions in childhood at Edinburgh and in the country were his gifted brothers and sister. (One brother George died in infancy; another, the youngest, William, rose to be Crown Agent in

---

[1] The large collection of Haldane papers in the National Library of Scotland is indispensable. See also Richard Burdon Haldane: *An Autobiography* (1929); Aylmer Haldane, *The Haldanes of Gleneagle* (1935); F. Maurice, *Haldane* (1938); D. Sommer, *Haldane of Cloan* (1960).

Scotland and looked after Richard's business and financial affairs through-out his life. Another brother John became the famous professor of physi-ology at Oxford, and the sister Elizabeth was a woman of remarkable force of character and learning, who contributed much to education in Scotland. Richard, John, and Elizabeth are all noticed in the *Dictionary of National Biography*.)

Richard Haldane appears to have led a somewhat lonely childhood in the Perthshire hills. The atmosphere of the household was sombre, and his own tastes were of a secluded and literary character. Owing to his parents' distrust of episcopacy, school and university in England were out of the question; although at one time it appears to have been suggested that he might have gone up to Jowett's Balliol. It was generally thought, however, that he would follow his great-great-uncle in a career at the English Bar. His first reported appearance on the Woolsack was at the age of six years, when on a visit to London during the Long Vacation his nurse persuaded an attendant to let her place the small boy there, saying: 'One day the bairn will sit there as of right.'

After a brief and unhappy period at The Edinburgh Academy[2] Haldane proceeded at the age of sixteen to the University of Edinburgh. He also attempted external examinations at London University, but failed the First LL.B. He was also afflicted by religious doubts, and on the advice of Professor Blackie he departed for Göttingen, in April 1874, where it was thought Professor Lotze would be able to help him. Haldane spent the following five months at Göttingen, where he appears to have led an enjoyable life, although noticing with displeasure the somewhat unkempt appearance of his fellow students and the dirty and rowdy conditions in which they lived. He talked philosophy with Professor Lotze and had some of his doubts settled. In the intervals he walked vigorously in the Hartz Mountains, and returned to Edinburgh and his family at the end of the summer, much altered in appearance and more at ease in his own mind.

Henceforward he did not regard himself as a subscribing member of any religious faith, although as head of the family he read prayers on Sunday evenings at Cloan. His connection with Germany was maintained throughout his life. In the following year he paid a brief visit to Dresden and, almost annually before the 1914-18 War, was accustomed to walk in the Hartz Mountains with an old friend from Edinburgh University, Professor Hume-Brown, The University of Göttingen conferred an Honorary Doctorate upon him, which was not removed despite the stresses of the war. In turn, Haldane left the University a legacy of £1,000.

In 1876 Haldane obtained First Class Honours at Edinburgh together with various scholarships and prizes, although an attempt to obtain the

2 See below, p. 313.

PLATE 7

Lord Haldane as Chancellor in 1912

PLATE 8

Lord Haldane at a window in Queen Anne's Gate

degree of Doctor of Science was foiled because the then Professor of Botany refused to agree to the award of a doctorate to one who was a professed agnostic.

In 1877 Haldane went south to eat dinners at Lincoln's Inn with a view to being called to the Bar, which happened on 17 November 1879. In the meantime his father had died in 1877, so the task of settling down in London was complicated by numerous practical problems arising out of the administration of his father's estate.

Haldane borrowed upon the reversionary interest to which he became entitled under his father's estate in order to provide himself with funds for his first year at the Bar, 'taking the view that to maintain a good appearance was important'.[3]

He became a pupil of William Barber, a conveyancer of the old school. This was obtained through Farrer Herschell, the future Lord Chancellor, who was the brother of Haldane's aunt by marriage, Ghetal Burdon Sanderson. Later Barber got him into the chambers of Horace Davey, the future Law Lord. For three months one summer he worked in a well-known Edinburgh lawyer's office in order to familiarize himself with Scottish conveyancing. It was difficult to find in London barristers who were expert in this field of the law, and Haldane prudently thought that this might be a way in which he would obtain future clients.

After his period of pupillage with Barber, Haldane went into chambers with Lumley Smith. In 1879 an uncle, Lord Camperdown, 'committed him to Whig politics' by putting him down for Brooks's Club in St. James's Street. In the same year Haldane was called to the Bar at Lincoln's Inn and went into chambers at 5 New Square.

His career at the Bar began as slowly as that of many other barristers. His first case concerned a cellar infested with black beetles.[4] In his first year he earned £31 10s., in his second £109, in his third £160, but in his fourth, £1,100. So slow had been his progress during his first two years, that he thought of going out to Hong Kong to practise before the Consular Court. But in his last years at the Bar from 1903–5, Haldane was earning at the rate of £15,000–£20,000 a year, and had not he taken office in December 1905 there is no doubt that his income would have exceeded £20,000 for that year.

Haldane has left us in his autobiography[5] an unusually clear and interesting account of his struggles at the Bar, and of the qualities required for a successful advocate. He was able to view himself and his capacities in a much more objective way than is common among successful members of the Bar, so it might be interesting to consider here the various capacities

[3] *Autobiography*, p. 31.
[4] Lady Violet Bonham Carter, *The Times*, 30 July 1956.   [5] Chapter II.

which go to make up a great advocate under a number of different headings.

First, as far as physique and presence were concerned, Haldane had not many natural advantages. Although of a good height he was somewhat clumsy in body and as the years went by, put on weight to a disconcerting extent. His voice also was thin and unattractive, and although at one stage he took lessons from an elocution expert, he does not seem ever to have been able to improve it. He was therefore a poor examiner or cross-examiner of witnesses, but as the bulk of his work lay on the Chancery side, and in later years increasingly in appellate courts this was not of so much importance as it might have been for a barrister practising on the Common Law side.

Secondly, Haldane had a remarkable capacity for sustained hard work. This enabled him not only to master his life as a successful barrister, but also in later years, to bear the burden of an astonishingly wide range of public interests. As he wrote to Mrs. Humphry Ward in 1885: 'After all has been said and done, when the highest call has been discharged and we have done our duty to our neighbour, and are free to turn to ourselves, there is no satisfaction so deep and so lasting as that which arises from a sense of concentration in real work. It gives us all our deliverance even when we are dissatisfied with what we have accomplished.'[6] But Haldane never allowed himself to get into the position of Selborne, whose friends used to see him 'quivering with overstrain' at the end of term. As Haldane wrote to another friend some years later: 'I do not propose to leave the Bar. I must live by it. Besides I like it, and I've never before done any work so efficiently as I am doing it now. But I cannot allow it to swallow me up. If I were to become like Lord Herschell or Lord Selborne I should look back on chances wasted of doing really good work in the world.'[7] Haldane was helped in his work by what he called an 'artificial memory' for the details of his briefs. He could remember the facts and the legal principles without effort, whereas by some curious mental freak he had a poor memory for verse or prose.

Thirdly, Haldane had to a greater extent than almost any other English barrister, the ability to seek for and find the principle underlying a complicated mass of detail. This came out very clearly in his conduct of heavy litigation such as the great Free Church of Scotland case in 1904, which will be considered later.[8]

Fourthly, Haldane had the ability to seize whatever opportunities life brought to him. This came out clearly in the first case which put him on the highway to success at the Bar. Horace Davey had been briefed by the Government of Quebec to appear before the Judicial Committee of

[6] Sommer, p. 85.   [7] Ibid., p. 90.   [8] See below, p. 195.

the Privy Council to obtain leave to appeal from a judgment of the Canadian Court. The Solicitor-General of Quebec had been sent over, but had been expressly instructed not to argue himself, but to leave this to Davey. In the evening before the case was heard, Davey was summoned to continue a case in a part-heard appeal to the House of Lords, which imposed on him a higher obligation than that which he owed to the Canadian Government. As no other Q.C. could be found to undertake the task at short notice, Haldane was summoned to a consultation at 10 a.m. next morning at the Privy Council Office. 'I was not used to shrinking from responsibility in things that had to be faced, so I told the clerk that it would be all right. I sat up through much of the night and mastered the real point.'[9]

At the brief consultation before the court resumed at 10.30 a.m. Davey informed the irritated Solicitor-General for Quebec and the managing clerk of Freshfields, the City solicitors who conducted so much litigation on behalf of overseas clients, that the case would be dealt with by Haldane. The Privy Council clerk of Freshfields rose to his feet and said: 'the House of Freshfield has briefed Sir Richard Bethell, Sir Hugh Cairns, Sir Roundell Palmer, and other great men, and none of them has ever treated the firm as Mr. Davey has today.' But it was too late for recriminations and Haldane proceeded to argue as best he could. He was successful, and the Privy Council gave judgment in favour of the Quebec Government.

Neither the Solicitor-General nor Freshfields said a word of thanks to me. They went away as persons aggrieved. But a few days later, who should climb up the narrow stairs to my garret at Lincoln's Inn but old Mr. Wiseman himself, the venerable representative of the great firm of Freshfields. He said that the partners had read the shorthand note of the brief argument at the Privy Council, and now sent me a brief for the Province of Ontario in a great case. There might, he said, be more to follow, and indeed it so turned out. This particular brief was marked 150 guineas, and it introduced me to many Canadian cases.[1]

Fifthly, Haldane displayed considerable skill in psychology; he was a keen student of other men and the way in which their minds worked, and he was adept at turning his knowledge of them to his own advantage. He has given a good picture of his skill in this.

I knew the Judges in the House of Lords and Privy Council so well that I could follow the working of their individual minds. If, for example, Lord Watson, who was by no means a silent judge but who was a man of immense power, started off by being against me, I would turn round to some colleague

[9] *Autobiography*, p. 37.   [1] Ibid., pp. 38–39.

of his on whose opinion I knew he did not set much weight, and who would
be sure merely to echo what Lord Watson had just said. By devoting myself to
the judge who had merely repeated Lord Watson's point I well knew that I should
speedily detach Lord Watson from it and bring him out of his entrenchments.[2]

Again,

I have sometimes stated the point as it had been decided against my side in
the court below before the tribunal could realise on which side I was arguing. I
have done this when I saw that they were in an obstinate mood, with fairness,
but with the result that they jumped from sheer combativeness against the
proposition of law which I intended in the end to overthrow, and it was then
that I gradually disclosed how it was that I was really there to argue the other
way. The results were sometimes good.[3]

By the end of 1887 Haldane's position was sufficiently secure for him
to apply to Halsbury the Lord Chancellor for silk. It is not surprising that
he should have been refused, but when he renewed the application three
years later, he was granted it at the age of thirty-four, one of the most
youthful ages at which any barrister has taken silk.

Haldane practised first in the court of Mr. Justice Kay and then in the
court of Mr. Justice Romer. Under the practice of those days the Chancery
silks attached themselves to the court of one of the Chancery judges. This
had the disadvantage that it produced a somewhat inbred atmosphere,
and sometimes resulted in a weak judge being under the domination of
a strong Bar, but it had the advantage that a litigant knew that the counsel
of his choice would in fact be in the court in question on the day of the
case, and had not, as sometimes happened with a common law leader,
been attracted away by another brief in a different court.

At the age of thirty-seven, Haldane 'went special' which meant that
he refused to appear in court without an additional fee on the brief.
Henceforward he was in the full tide of a busy Chancery practice, and his
reputation as a resourceful and successful advocate was firmly established.

Meanwhile, he had found time to turn to politics. In 1885 he stood
at the general election of that year for East Lothian, a pocket borough of
the Wemyss family, and somewhat to his surprise won the seat. (It would
have been natural for Haldane to have contested West Perthshire where
his family home was, but that had been selected as a constituency by a
senior member, Sir Donald Currie.) Haldane did not make a conventional
maiden speech in the House, his first speech being on the Committee
stage of the Estimates for the Royal Courts of Justice in February 1886.
His first big speech on a political issue was in March 1887, when he
opposed the Government's drastic Crimes Bill for Ireland. His cast of

[2] *Autobiography*, p. 52.   [3] Ibid., p. 53.

mind, however, did not take kindly to strict party discipline. 'I have always cared so much about things and so little about persons that I have never been a very good colleague.'[4]

It is in these years also that we can trace the growth of the legend which attached to Haldane throughout his life, that he was something of an intriguer. If he did enjoy the pleasure of plotting over dinner-parties with Grey and Asquith and Morley, the results were generally harmless, and there can be no doubt that Haldane acted throughout with nothing but the public good in mind. In truth he was always a little uneasy with the orthodoxies of political parties and his biographer has well said that: 'with the passing of the years he became increasingly concerned with the advancement of certain ideas and ideals in which he believed. What particular party was the instrument to bring these changes about was to him of secondary importance.'[5]

We shall see later that it was his interest in education, particularly adult education, which led him into the Labour Party after the First World War, in the belief that it was the only political party which took this subject seriously. Nevertheless his position in the party and in the country was sufficiently strong in 1894 for Rosebery to consider seriously whether he should not be appointed Solicitor-General. As we have seen,[6] Rosebery's choice, mainly for reasons of party policy, fell on Robert Reid, but as Haldane wrote on 15 October to the Prime Minister: 'It is true that I should have liked this office had the course of events made it right that it should come to me. But it was something external—not of the essence of things.'[7]

The following March, 1895, Rosebery sounded Haldane as to whether he would be willing to accept the Liberal Party's nomination for the Speakership. The choice would surely not have been a happy one, for Haldane had not really the attributes of voice and appearance to enable him to control the House successfully. He refused and the office was accepted by an almost unknown barrister on the Northern Circuit who was a close friend of Herschell, W. C. Gully.

Relations between Haldane and the Prime Minister remained friendly. On 26 April Rosebery wrote from the Privy Council office:

My dear Justinian, [his nickname for Haldane]
        I was truly glad to see your handwriting, which I had almost forgotten. You are too apt to use the political potsherd, and I am glad to find you in good heart.
    I am quite cheerful. But we cannot expect to win agricultural constituencies when we have no consolation to give them in the wreck and ruin of their industry, except the assurance that the lower that prices fall the better for

[4] N.L.S., 5923, f. 23.   [5] Sommer, p. 70.   [6] Above, p. 137.   [7] Rosebery papers.

everybody. Even if we can provide no remedy, we can offer sympathy instead of jibes.

Conducting an inherited government with five per cent of one house, and a majority of ten in the other does not exactly represent the exuberance of power, and certainly not its intoxication; but it reminds me, of one of the darker portions of Frederick the Great's campaigns.

Yours ever,
Rosebery

P.S. I see that I have wasted the public note-paper.[8]

In the meantime his private life had seen some development. In March 1890 he had announced his engagement to Miss Valentine Munro Ferguson, sister of an old political friend, Robert Munro Ferguson, who later became Lord Novar. Congratulations poured in, and for a few weeks all went well. But in April Haldane received a sudden note from the lady to say that all was finally over. The effect on him was severe. He was taken in by the Asquith family at their house in Hampstead, where he recovered slowly from something like a nervous breakdown.[9] To a letter of sympathy from Rosebery, he replied on 27 April:

My dear Rosebery,

       I have sometimes differed from you, and in the future shall probably do so again. But I shall never forget that in the time of need you wrote to me words which were right and true. I feel that it would do me good to see you, and though I know that you are busy, I do not hesitate to say that if you can tell me where I may find you—say on Wednesday or Thursday— I should like to come to you for twenty minutes.

I felt what you say from the first moment when I found my feet under an almost physical shock. This is a critical time of my life. I think I have gained. No part of my faith in men and women or in life is gone, and if I begin the world anew, it is with a personal detachment that is good, and not bad. Had what has come demanded less of the individual on whom it has fallen it would have been more difficult to bear. My only ambition now is to set an example in the way in which it is to be born. Shelley is shut and Goethe is open. After all it is well that what has come to me has not come to some poor wretch to whom what is lost had become permanently the whole of life. We have all at times to renounce and turn away, and it is well for me to learn my lesson.

If I cannot see the hand of God in it at least I do not find that of the Devil.

Always yours sincerely,
R. B. Haldane

P.S. I return to work tomorrow.[1]

[8] Rosebery papers.

[9] An attractive picture of Haldane as seen through a child's eyes will be found in Herbert Asquith, *Moments of Memory* (1926).

[1] Rosebery papers.

In writing to his mother, Haldane said briefly that Miss Ferguson's conduct suggested some 'sudden breakdown of feeling which was due simply to some physical cause. There was, if I am right, a mental aberration'.[2] As Haldane's biographer remarks: 'Miss Ferguson died unmarried seven years later and there is not lacking evidence to support Haldane's explanation.'[3] But the loss was severely felt then and later. When she died another letter came from Rosebery to which Haldane replied on 15 September 1897:

My dear Rosebery,
          You have judged rightly. The old love for her remained. It was never broken—it will end, not in her grave, but in mine.
  The thought that I once, for a brief time, held in my hands the fairest and best gift that life could have bought, makes all else seem small just now, and fills me with reverence. But it is heavy to bear.

I am,
R. B. Haldane[4]

Back at work again, Haldane picked up the threads of a social life which was becoming increasingly varied and interesting. His friends now numbered some of the most interesting people in late Victorian England, and he was becoming well known as a constant visitor at the great country houses of the era. Despite the unhappy ending to his engagement and his subsequent resolve never to marry another person, he remained on friendly terms with many women. From 1895 onwards he spent Christmas every year at Mells with the Horner family. With Lady Horner, the centre of a brilliant social circle, he was on terms of great friendship, of which she has left an interesting picture in her autobiography.[5] Like many men of his character, Haldane got on well with American women. Their brightness and gay intelligence appealed to him, and there is an attractive picture of him in the contemporary letters of Lady Jebb, the American wife of the Regius Professor of Greek at Cambridge. In 1894 she wrote to her sister in the United States:

  Mr. Haldane was a joy. Oh how delightfully that man talked, and how able and interesting he is. When only five years at the Bar he became a Queen's Counsel. No-one ever got on faster, and no wonder for he is able beyond most. He is M.P. for somewhere and the rising politician on his side. And lately he has become the favourite of a clever ladies' circle in Town. Mrs. Harry White [the wife of the American ambassador] is a great friend of his.

[2] N.L.S. 5944, f. 125.
[3] Sommer, p. 83. Some of the evidence is in the possession of Mr. Alan Harris.
[4] Rosebery papers.   [5] F. Horner, *Time Remembered* (1933).

I never knew a man such good company in a tête à tête. He took to me, too, and when I said I hope you will come again, he said he would come whenever I asked him. You know, when the company suits me I can generally be good company too. That man will be Lord Chancellor to a certainty some day. He is all round the ablest man I have yet met on this side.[6]

But the main feminine influence in Haldane's life was his mother. To this remarkable lady, who died in 1925 shortly after her 100th birthday, Haldane wrote every day of his life when away from Cloan—as did his sister Elizabeth. Each received daily replies. Most of this vast correspondence is preserved in the Haldane papers.

[6] *With Dearest Love to All* (1960), p. 238.

CHAPTER II

THE PERIOD OF HALDANE'S LIFE between 1902 and 1905 can be divided into three parts: life at the Bar, politics, and other interests. As far as the first heading is concerned, Haldane during these years was supreme among counsel engaged in the heaviest litigation.

One of his big cases before the Privy Council was *ex parte Marais*, in which he argued unsuccessfully that when some civil courts were open it was impossible for martial law to prevail. On 5 November 1901 he wrote:

'I fought my hardest for the Dutch prisoners before the Privy Council this morning, but the tribunal was hopelessly divided, and the anti-Boers prevailed over the pro-Boers. It is bad that so much bias should be shewn, but it is, I suppose, inevitable.'[1]

In the House of Lords Haldane's greatest case was undoubtedly the Free Church of Scotland case,[2] which has already been fully described elsewhere. The central issue was a simple one, though it became submerged under metaphysical distinctions which perplexed the Law Lords: namely, whether the Free Church of Scotland had the power to alter its doctrinal teaching from time to time as changing social conditions required. Haldane argued in vain for this point of view. In his autobiography he has left us an amusing picture of how the Law Lords were perplexed and bewildered by the intricacies of Scottish religious quarrels. As he wrote to Rosebery on 13 March 1904: 'After Tuesday I shall be freed from a three weeks spell of speaking to the House of Lords (you say it is cold, but you know nothing of the arctic and polar conditions into which that House gets when I had it in hand for five hours, and the icy atmosphere has driven its quorum into a wintry slumber.)'[3]

On 23 June Haldane was still arguing before the House and Edmund Gosse's diary gives a vivid description of the course of the case:

Haldane has been making, and is still making, a very fine performance in defending the Free Church of Scotland against the Highland remnant of the Free Kirk before the seven Law Lords. With perfectly unwearying alertness and persistence, in his gentle and persuasive tones, he elaborates the doctrines of predestination and freewill, and shows them to be not indeed consistent

[1] N.L.S., 5966, f. 120.
[2] See *Autobiography*, pp. 70–77. The judgment is reported in [1904] A.C. 515.
[3] N.L.S., 5906, f. 77.

with one another, but to be consistently held by one and the same person. The attitude of the House is highly entertaining. The Lord Chancellor, manifestly hostile to the Free Church's position, is red with the effort, mental and physical, of finding holes in Haldane's polished armour. Lord Alverstone, perfectly blank, with glassy eyes, is an evident Gallio, to whom all this ecclesiastical metaphysic is unintelligible and insane. Lord James of Hereford chafes under it, constantly snapping out, 'I say it without irreverence but', or, 'Well, well, Mr. Haldane, but in the name of common sense—' and Haldane, flapping back the side of his wig, replies, 'My Lord, we deal not with the dictates of common sense, but with a mystery'. Lord Robertson, who probably knows more about it than anybody, sits perfectly still. Lord Davey, with his parchment face puckered up, searches for verbal solecisms. And Haldane, bland, tireless, imperturbable, never taken at a disadvantage, always courteous, always ready, pushes on in faultless flow of language, turning the whole thing into a supplement of his own 'Pathway to Reality.'[4]

Secondly, so far as politics are concerned, Haldane himself has left on record a very clear and fair appreciation of his own advantages and disadvantages as a politician: 'I have no gift of expression and no real capacity for managing men—much less leading them—but I seem to see very clearly at this moment what needs doing and I mean to have my try at helping and encouraging others to do what I cannot accomplish myself.'[5] Perhaps his main disadvantage was his weakness as a public speaker. His voice, like Bismarck's, was high pitched and unattractive, and the substance of his delivery tended at times to read rather like a parody of a novel by Henry James. As A. G. Gardiner said, Haldane was expert at enveloping a speech in a 'lucid fog'. 'No one who has heard Mr. Haldane speak for, say three hours, will deny that there is such a thing.'[6]

As Bryce said,[7] Haldane's speeches were hard to follow because there were no paragraphs in them, only full stops faintly marked. Nevertheless Haldane's position in the country was secure enough for the King to offer him the honour of a Privy Councillorship in June 1901. Haldane wrote: 'The King himself is conferring distinctions on a number of Opposition members, and Privy Councillorships for Edward Grey and myself are among them. It would now be affectation to make any difficulty, although these things are not in my line.'[8]

The grant of such an honour was distinctly unusual and caused some

[4] Gosse papers.

[5] Milner papers, vol. xxxvii. (Letter to Milner of 6 July 1901. The passage is omitted from the version in Headlam, *Milner Papers*, vol. ii, p. 264.)

[6] *Prophets, Priests, and Kings* (1914), p. 82.

[7] A. Chamberlain, *Politics from Inside* (1928), p. 69.

[8] B.M. Add. MSS. 49724, f. 93.

heart burnings among the other Liberal leaders. Lord Davey wrote on 27 January, ostensibly to offer his congratulations:

I was very glad to see your name in the list of honours yesterday though I cannot say that I think the particular distinction very appropriate to a practising barrister. It is only recently that it has been decided that a privy councillor can practise at the Bar of the Judicial Committee. Anyhow I am very glad that your name has been selected for distinction and hope it is only a stage in better and more solid things in the future. I wish you could sit with us on the Judicial Committee. I wonder whether I shall live to sit in the House of Lords under your presidency as Chancellor.[9]

The honour was certainly exceptional for a practising barrister; the only precedent was the case of the Rt. Hon. J. Pemberton Leigh, later Lord Kingsdown.[1] Indeed, until modern times it was most unusual to make even the Law Officers Privy Councillors. So Greville[2] disapproved of J. Stuart Wortley, then a Privy Councillor, being made Solicitor-General in 1856, on the ground that as the Law Officers were official advisers of the Privy Council and were often called upon to sit on the Board as assessors, it was undesirable to confer the honour on them.

Throughout 1904 and 1905 the Conservative Government under Balfour was tottering to its fall. The Liberal Party, however, was not in any very strong position. The party was split, apparently fundamentally, between the Liberal Imperialists on the one hand, and the Little Englanders on the other. Haldane's circle, comprising Grey and Asquith, was also personally hostile to Campbell-Bannerman, the leader of the party and his entourage.

Haldane and Grey acted together. Their animosity against C.-B. was pronounced and undisguised. They thoroughly disapproved of his attitude to the Boer War, despised him as an inferior intellect, and thought how he would discredit the Party. They were constantly thinking how he could be shelved. C.-B. was the obstacle to their ambitions, and as time went on they felt a misgiving that he was becoming popular . . . One objection to C.-B. as P.M. in their eyes was that C.-B. was not 'in society'.[3]

It was therefore peculiarly irritating to Haldane and his friends that Campbell-Bannerman had somehow secured the King's ear, and was favourably regarded at Windsor for (inter alia) his knowledge of French cooking and French literature. On Campbell-Bannerman's side the dislike was reciprocated. 'Haldane always prefers the back-stairs to the

[9] N.L.S., 5905, ff. 207–8.
[1] See Lord Kingsdown's privately printed *Recollections of his Life* (1868), p. 127.
[2] *Memoirs*, ed. R. Fulford (1938), vol. viii, p. 67.
[3] F. W. Hirst, *The Golden Days* (1947), p. 254.

front-stairs; but it does not matter: for the clatter can be heard all over the house.'[4]

In September 1905 the three Liberal Imperialists, Haldane, Grey, and Asquith, made an agreement which was known as the Relugas Compact, after the name of a fishing-lodge on the river Findhorn near Inverness belonging to Grey. The compact was that none of them would take office in a government formed by Campbell-Bannerman unless the leadership of the House of Commons was in other hands. The agreement aimed at procuring the Chancellorship of the Exchequer and leadership of the House for Asquith, the Foreign Office for Grey, and the Woolsack for Haldane. Haldane wrote to Asquith on 27 September: 'We went carefully over the whole ground on Sunday. Grey was a little doubtful of the expediency of approaching the Throne at this stage, but took no exception to what you had written.'[5] The gist of the agreement was communicated to Edward VII.[6] 'It was a private arrangement of a purely defensive character', Haldane wrote in 1916.[7] It is doubtful if anyone ever believed this.

On 2 October 1905 Grey wrote to Asquith:

I adhere to the opinion that it is too soon to put a pistol to C.-B.'s head. If he shows himself willing to discuss the formation of the next government he should be told what we think and feel. But we want it to come to him in a friendly way and not as if we were trying to force him in a way which he might think premature and unfriendly.

All I can suggest is that you should feel your way and use an opening, if you can get it. You can quote my feeling to C.-B. if you think it useful to do so; it may be useful as a peg on which to hang the discussion. My feeling is quite friendly and loyal to him, but I do not mean to go into a government unless the spokesman of the government in one House of Parliament is yourself or Rosebery; and the latter alternative is apparently not the possible one under present conditions.

I think it is too soon in any event to stipulate for definite offices: your leadership in the House of Commons is the most important point and should be made alone first.[8]

Asquith thereupon saw Campbell-Bannerman but found him quite immovable on one point—namely that Reid and not Haldane should be Lord Chancellor in the new administration. Campbell-Bannerman was prepared to consider lightening the load on himself by taking a peerage, at any rate after a token time in the House of Commons; but he refused to commit himself at that stage, and the subsequent arrival of Lady Campbell-Bannerman from Scotland determined him to stand firm in

[4] F. W. Hirst, *The Golden Days* (1947), p. 264.   [5] N.L.S., 5906, ff. 212–13.
[6] See Sommer, pp. 147–8.   [7] N.L.S., 5919, f. 23.   [8] Asquith papers.

face of the conspirators. (Elizabeth Haldane recorded later[9] that her mother had spoken just as definitely about the necessity for standing firm in the opposite sense. But only one of these formidable Scottish ladies was at the centre of power.) Haldane wrote to Asquith when he heard the news of the first interview in mid-November: 'I cannot easily express the sense I have of your affectionate care for my interests. In the relation in which we have stood for so many years it is not necessary that I should. Whatever happens I shall know the utmost has been done.'[1]

On 4 December, at the start of a week of intrigue and discussion, Grey wrote an important letter to Asquith:

Just a line before you see C.-B. to say that I don't want you to risk your personal position more than you think absolutely necessary. C.-B. gave me the impression that he was quite prepared to form a government without any of us: he never once suggested that my abstaining would make the formation of a government difficult, though I had suggested it might raise difficulties as regards yourself.

If you go in without me eventually I shall be quite happy outside and I shan't think it in the least wrong of you to go in.[2]

Asquith took the terms of this letter literally—perhaps a little more so than the other two members of the agreement intended. He was the first to enter Campbell-Bannerman's Government, giving as his reason to the others the important fact that the election lay ahead and not behind them, and there was no certainty that the electorate would return a Liberal majority if the party were weakened by dissension. It was not, however, very easy for the other two to communicate with Asquith during this week, for he had chosen to spend it at Hatfield. Grey and Haldane, after much argument, eventually took the same view as Asquith. One reason which weighed strongly with Haldane was that by staying out they would 'hardly be fair to the King'. This argument (together with others) had been put to him by Lady Horner. Late on Thursday the 7th Haldane called on C.-B. to announce that Grey and he were willing to come in.[3] Haldane wrote to Campbell-Bannerman the next day:

The Times did not help a difficult task this morning, but now that Grey has recognized his obligation he has accepted it very whole-heartedly, and in a spirit which would have given you great satisfaction could you have heard the conversation I have just had with him.

He has conveyed to me your offer of the War Office.[4] This I accept, and

[9] E. Haldane, *From One Century to Another* (1933), p. 214.   [1] Asquith papers.
[2] Ibid.   [3] *Autobiography*, pp. 171–81.
[4] But Haldane's 1916 Memorandum states that it was he himself who had suggested the War Office as a suitable post in conversation with Campbell-Bannerman the previous evening. Haldane also wrote that the first suggestion he should go to the War Office came from the King in the autumn of 1905: N.L.S., 5919, f. 24.

will do all I can to serve you. I am fully aware of the immense difficulties, but it is my own desire to try what close work can do to melt them.[5]

In April 1908 Grey in fact wrote to Campbell-Bannerman to say: 'I have long ago recognized that the difficulties I made when the government was formed were short sighted and ill-judged.'[6] Campbell-Bannerman regarded Haldane's appointment to the War Office with sardonic suspicion, and clearly expected, and perhaps hoped, that the notorious difficulties of that Office would result in the downfall of 'my most philosophical friend'.

Haldane himself wrote to Rosebery on 19 December:

I heard on enquiry that you were still away, so I send a greeting in the shape of a brief letter instead of calling. There is really nothing new to relate, as is, I suspect, usually the case with Ministries we of this one see each other rather less than before we were colleagues. Grey is the exception. He has a flat here and I see him in the evenings. My own work I find very interesting. But the business of reforming the War Office—though it is capable of accomplishment —is one which will need a succession of ministers. My first task has been to get the Generals onto good terms with each other. As they are no longer on deadly terms with the S. of S. this has not been difficult. The second has been to begin the work of a complete survey of the Army as a whole—with a view of getting in the end a definite objective. This is already begun. The past work of the Defence Committee has given a starting ground. I have eliminated from the Council one man who was better for the field than for the office[7] and brought in Sir Wm. Nicholson—an acute big brain but not a very easy man. Still I needed him badly.

As for general politics they remain unchanged. What the electors will do next month no one knows. I do not think much will be heard of Home Rule except from the other side, and Balfour seems now to have broken with Chamberlain. But one cannot be sure of what the country is thinking. A narrow majority would be a great curse.[8]

George Bernard Shaw produced some comments on the new Government on 27 March 1907:

I read your address [as Lord Rector of Edinburgh University] to those unfortunate students very carefully; and I must say that it is like your right honourable cheek to talk to them like that. Why will people not tell the truth? Here are you, the most conspicuous living example in the kingdom of the realisation of all these students' ambitions—a Scotch philosopher who has beaten all the practical men and statesmen at their own game. This you have achieved by doing exactly what you liked; smoking a great deal too many

---

[5] Add. MSS. 41218, f. 161.   [6] Ibid., f. 134.
[7] This was Plumer—'a severe and undeserved blow': DNB.
[8] Rosebery papers.

cigars; eating in a manner that shocks Mrs. Sidney Webb; and generally making the greatest possible success of the world, the flesh, and the devil. And yet you go down and tell those unhappy young people, in lofty and inspiring periods, that you did it all by a life of contemplation, aloof from the world at Weimar.[9]

Haldane may have had these remarks at the back of his mind when he wrote later:

Ever since that time I have avoided being again a candidate for the office of Lord Rector in other Universities, notwithstanding tempting offers. I had said all that I wanted to say in the Edinburgh Rectorial Address, and my work lay for the future more in the direction of organization than of preaching to the students. The Chancellorship of Bristol has not been any real diversion from this resolution.[1]

When Haldane was appointed his first thought was to find himself a suitable assistant. The name recommended was that of Colonel (later General) Ellison, who had been a secretary to the Esher Committee. Ellison tells the story:

I received a telegram from Lord Esher asking me to meet him at Windsor, where he informed me that Mr. Haldane was to be the new Secretary of State for War, and he wanted to know, whether I would be willing to become his Principal Private Secretary if I received the offer of such a post. I asked at once whether Mr. Haldane had any cut-and-dried plan of his own for the Army, and Lord Esher assured me that the new Secretary of State's mind was destitute of any preconceived notions at all about military affairs. This being so I said I would gladly do what I could to help him with the difficult task that lay ahead. Next morning I went with Esher to see Haldane at Whitehall Court and shortly afterwards I took over the duties of my new appointment. I imagine that Esher must have passed on my misgivings about preconceived plans, for at an early stage of our working together Haldane mentioned to me that, during his long practice at the Bar, there were few subjects that he had not had to grapple with in some shape or form, but military affairs were an exception. He confessed that he knew nothing whatever about the elements of military organization, for example, the composition of units, brigades, divisions, etc., and that he relied on me to explain all such details to him.[2]

Ellison was not only versed in detail: he shared Haldane's sense of the importance of principle.

The first task of Ellison was to go to Scotland for Haldane's electioneering. 'During the daytime he was engaged in canvassing and it was not

[9] N.L.S., 5907, f. 143.

[1] *Autobiography*, p. 154.

[2] Ellison's reminiscences are published in his regimental magazine, *The Lancashire Lad*, February 1936.

until after dinner that we got busy with military affairs and then were often at it till one or two a.m. Hour after hour we would walk backwards and forwards in the big billiard room, Mr Haldane on one side of the table smoking the best cigars procurable, I on the other.'[3]

Thirty years later Ellison sent to Harris a letter dated 31 July 1937, describing a lunch with Hore-Belisha tête-à-tête:

Poor chap! I really feel sorry for him. He confesses to absolute ignorance re military matters and is only anxious to learn, but gets precious little information or help from his Army Council. He told me frankly that he wanted someone at his beck and call to be to him what I was to Haldane in the early days. I said at once that it would be too dangerous an experiment now that the Army Council is so much more firmly established than it was in Haldane's time.[4]

The impression which Haldane made on his civilian subordinates is revealed in the following passage:

He was a heavily built man, who never-the-less walked softly and with a cat-like treat: a man with a massive and striking head and beautifully-formed and kept hands. His voice was weak for so strong a frame, but it was suave and kindly. His manner was gentle and courteous: he did not, as some great men have done, think that decision and force of character can only be shown by rudeness and a domineering manner.[5]

With the soldiers he quickly established a most friendly relationship; a well-placed jest which was greeted with guffaws at Aldershot and Windsor immediately won him their affection, and their respect was gained by his obvious devotion to duty and patriotism. Nor did he adopt an air of intellectual superiority. In dealing with his soldiers Haldane appreciated the importance of what a cavalry officer would call 'hands'. Further, all admired his refusal to pull up the plant to see how it was growing. He gave his subordinates a job to do and allowed them to get on with it.

There is no doubt that Haldane picked a strong team to assist him in his War Office reforms. Besides Ellison there was Sir Charles Harris, a distinguished civil servant with long experience of the War Office and a great flair for finance. On the military side Haldane discovered Haig, whom he brought home from India as Director of Military Operations. Haig was consistently praised by Haldane for having a General Staff mind of the highest order, though in some ways he was not a particularly easy person to work with.[6] Last of all, no mention of Haldane's army reforms would be complete without reference to the support afforded by the King. Under King Edward royal influence in politics was a definite

---

[3] *The Lancashire Lad*, February 1936.   [4] Harris papers.
[5] F. Bovenschen, *14th Haldane Memorial Lecture* (1946), p. 19.
[6] See now J. Terraine, *Haig* (1963).

factor, and in something which so much touched the Hanoverian heart as the state of the army, his interest was at its keenest. Haldane moved in the King's innermost circle, accompanying him on the visits to the week-end parties of Edwardian England. Of one visit to Mentmore he wrote:

I have been spending another Kingly Sunday. Yesterday I went to church with the King and sat next him. It was odd to see how nervous the rector of the little parish church was when he prayed for the King in his presence. I saw much of His Majesty in private again. He is very interested in the future of the Liberal Party, which he evidently expects to be in office soon. He is like an old friend now and wants to know how many cigars I smoke and how I arrange my work.[7]

After he had assumed office a keen critic, Sir Almeric FitzRoy, noted approvingly in his diary how Haldane at a meeting of the Privy Council took pains to ingratiate himself: 'Haldane's demeanour at the Council, the first where he had ever taken the leading role, was a masterpiece of deportment. Blandly deferential, his whole being seemed to exhale a subtle flattery most grateful to the senses, and to invoke the royal approval as a matter of kingly grace.'[8]

There is no doubt that the relationship between them was peculiarly warm and even affectionate. Haldane took a laudable pride in which there was nothing sycophantic in his close connection with the monarch.

Campbell-Bannerman wrote to Haliburton on 27 February 1906:

I was pleased (and surprised) to hear from my most philosophical friend the Secretary of State for War the other day that he has been consulting you, and he was able to tell me that you were very sound in your army views—thoroughly Cardwellian. I was glad to hear this from him: and old Bulwer also tells me that Ellison, his Private Secretary, is of the right school. This is hopeful! He had even heard of our Knox and would like to have talk with him: I have told him that I would bring that about if I could.

I never discuss things with him: but I have warned him against talking and speaking in public too much, and above all against dogmatism and swagger; and have advised him whatever he does to give the credit of it to the soldiers and never to seem to be making capital for himself. In short, to be as unlike his predecessors as he can.[9]

There seems to be no evidence to support the idea that Haldane took unnecessary credit to himself for his undoubted reforms. He was indubitably the autocrat of his own dinner table and liked talking about his achievements, but he was scrupulously careful to see the soldiers got their

[7] Maurice, vol. i, p. 146.
[8] A. FitzRoy, *Memoirs* (1927), vol. ii, p. 411.
[9] Add. MSS. 41218, f. 356.

fair share of the credit. By them he was always known affectionately as 'Uncle Richard', and Haig himself paid him a remarkable tribute on a notable occasion.[1]

Haldane sent a memorandum to Campbell-Bannerman on 1 January:

It strikes my mind that the problem of the future reorganization of the British Army can only be considered as a whole, and that it is fatal to try to deal with the parts of which one entire force is made up, without first determining the coordination of the broad principles, according to which they are to be fitted into each other in the scheme as a whole. It is better to take time for this, meantime, to suspend piecemeal reforms; then to start work with a clear conception, from above, of what is to be ultimately worked out.[2]

The reforms which Haldane instituted at the War Office can be considered under two distinct heads: (a) the War Office and the General Staff, (b) the organization of the army itself.

(a) The War Office and the General Staff

The story here begins with Campbell-Bannerman, who when at the War Office in the Rosebery Government, had succeeded in abolishing the post of Commander-in-Chief held by the old Duke of Cambridge. Campbell-Bannerman as a result of this experience knew more about the War Office than about the army but his guidance and help were available to Haldane in the later stages of his plans.

As a result of the grave defects revealed by the Boer War, the Esher Commission abolished the post of Commander-in-Chief, and set up a General Staff on Wellingtonian lines, with a Chief of the General Staff, an Adjutant-General and a Quartermaster-General, the latter two working in watertight compartments of their own. In 1904 Balfour instituted the Committee of Imperial Defence, of which more will be said later. But this new organization had no time to settle down after the Boer War, and Haldane's achievement was to make it plain, first, that the staff was a war staff, its task being to think ahead on the fundamental general principles which should govern the organization and conduct of the British Army in time of war; and secondly, that the staff was not to interfere with questions of administration and finance. (In view of Haldane's later work for the co-ordination of government business, it is interesting to note that he was much taken with the pre-1914 organization of the German Army, under which the General Staff was deliberately located in a building separated from the administration department by at least half a mile.) Haldane also created the post of Chief of the Imperial General Staff, but this title was something of a misnomer, for the Colonies and Dominions were never properly fitted into the general scheme.

[1] See below, p. 212.   [2] Add. MSS. 41218, f. 163.

(b) *The Army itself*

This was made up of three component parts, the Regular Army, the Militia, and the Yeomanry. Since Cardwell in the 1870s no fewer than eleven Secretaries of State had tinkered with it in one way or another. It was in an unhappy and discontented state as a result of the defects in its performance revealed by the Boer War.

So far as the army itself was concerned, Haldane began with some clear thinking on fundamentals. In this his philosophic cast of mind and training were of the highest value. The subjects on which Haldane brooded for some months were these: First, he belonged to the Blue Water school of strategy. The primary defence of Great Britain must rest with the Grand Fleet. Secondly, the objective of any British Army was therefore to keep the Channel ports clear of a hostile force; that hostile force could only be Germany; therefore it was the duty of the British Army to prepare itself to help France in a struggle with Germany. By a conjunction of events this point was uppermost in Haldane's mind in 1906; for, as Grey wrote to him in the midst of the elections: 'Persistent reports and little indications keep reaching me that Germany intends to attack France in the Spring.'[3] As a result of a secret talk between the two friends, the substance of which was later communicated to Campbell-Bannerman and Asquith, the decision was made to begin military conversations with France.

As Haldane wrote to Rosebery on 14 August 1916:

> I think the comment Grey would make is that by 1905 the Naval supremacy of the country over the combined Powers of Europe was in course of inevitable disappearance, and that he had to choose with which group he would range himself. He would further say that it was not safe to range himself with his German group, in so far as German ambitions were not to be trusted.
>
> The wisest course was therefore to do what he did, and to endeavour to give the War party in Germany no cause for inducing the German nation to substitute them for her anti-war party in Germany as an occupant of the saddle. Whether his diplomatism served him very well in this endeavour is another question. It was not an easy task at best. And for a time he succeeded.
>
> When he dispatched me to Berlin in 1912 it was at the Emperor's request. The ordinary channels through which these things were done had somewhat failed and danger was imminent.[4]

A few days later he reverted to the events of 1906. He wrote to Rosebery again on 17 August: 'I believe myself that January 1906 was a really critical moment, and one in which a decision had to be taken. For the ways were parting. Delcassé's resignation and the Morocco pressure brought things to the test.'[5] In other words the Entente was justifiable because British naval policy was meaningless if we stood by ourselves.

[3] N.L.S., 5907, f. 10. See above, p. 173.   [4] Rosebery papers.   [5] Ibid.

As a combination of hostile fleets could overwhelm us, it was necessary to have some friends who would be at least neutral. As Haldane remarked in 1923: 'In international affairs the level of morality has always seemed to me below the level of morality of individuals. There is not a very gentle-manlike spirit between the chanceries as a rule, and you cannot rely on people not taking advantage of you, even when your intentions have been of the best and purest.'[6] But in later years Haldane, in the rather disconcerting manner in which he could hold and express two contradic-tory ideas at the same moment, was accustomed to emphasize another factor. As he wrote to Sir Charles Harris on 20 November 1916:

> The Expeditionary Force had a double purpose from the first. It was intended as a possible help to France if we made an agreement with Russia. But that was a state secret. The Cabinet hardly knew it. But down to 1914 there was little fear of a breach with Germany; it was only an emergency that we were pro-viding against. The strained relations did not occur till the last moment, and they were due to outside causes.[7]

There is no doubt that in 1906 the War Office was also much occupied with schemes for reinforcing India against Russian threats of invasion.

Logically the next conclusion in Haldane's train of thought was that the army, in the shape of an expeditionary force, had to be (a) capable of being mobilized quickly for service in France and the Low Countries; (b) efficient, so as to be capable of standing up to the German war machine; and (c) economical in order to satisfy the Liberals in the Cabinet. There was a strong body in the Cabinet supported, rather surprisingly, by Winston Churchill, which was in favour of cutting down the army estimates.

As the task of the army in war determined its composition in peace, it followed that the Expeditionary Force was to consist of six divisions of infantry and one of cavalry. For the next five years all Haldane's efforts were devoted to achieving the structure of this force, and its perfection in equipment and training.

His achievements have been well summarized by a competent authority who was close to him throughout all this period.

> Before the Estimates for 1907–8 were framed, he had formulated two prob-lems for solution; (a) to produce within the inelastic limits of the voluntary recruit market and of Army Estimates showing a substantial reduction on Arnold-Foster's £29¾ millions, the strongest possible Regular force, not for home defence but capable of taking the field on the Continent, with an adequate second-line army for home defence or expansion in addition; and (b) to make

---

[6] 53 H.L. Deb. 5s. col. 488.
[7] Harris papers.

all necessary preparations for putting the Expeditionary Force in the field with a rapidity equal to that of Germany. And he had found solutions which enabled him at once to reduce the estimates by two millions, to stop expenditure from loans averaging for the last ten years one and a half millions annually, and to announce the general lines on which within three years he organized completely an expeditionary force of 170,000 men (from an establishment of 186,000) which could be (and in 1914 was) put into the field in France in twelve days—a force declared by its first great opponent (von Kluck) to be of 'incomparable' quality—leaving behind it a fully organized second line force of more than twice its size, mobilised for home defence and available (voluntarily) for expansion of the forces overseas.[8]

Sir Charles Harris rightly adds: 'This achievement, by one unversed in military affairs, sounds incredible, and indeed the first reception of his plans by his colleagues and the military critics was one of mingled amusement and incredulity.'[9] This achievement is a clear and permanent refutation of the notion that he was a diffuse and woolly metaphysician incapable of handling a practical problem. It is also a refutation of the notion that lawyers who hold high political office are incapable of initiating and carrying through a policy of their own. When the hour of trial came it was not Haldane who was proved wrong, but his fellow-countrymen with their incorrigible belief in 'common sense' and 'muddling through'. He could not do everything in six years: he could create the machinery of a General Staff, but not a General Staff mind, capable of handling strategic problems of the highest order. Haldane cannot be held responsible for the use to which the generals of the pre-1914 army put the splendid piece of machinery which he had created. The responsibility for the Somme and Passchendaele are not to be laid at his door.

Something more may be said about the organization of the army as it was at the end of Haldane's period of office.

The army consisted of two parts, the Regular Army and the Territorial Army. The Regular Army was to be composed of an expeditionary force of six divisions of infantry and one of cavalry, with a force at home tailored to the needs of this body. The army as a whole was to consist of 5,540 officers, and 154,074 men. The basis of the whole scheme was the linked battalion of the Cardwell era. This arose in the 1870s when Gladstone, on the grounds of economy, had urged a reduction in the army estimates, both in men and in money. He suggested that many of the battalions withdrawn from colonial stations should be abolished forthwith. Cardwell met this demand by laying down the guiding principle that the strength of the home establishment of the army was directly dependent on our overseas commitments, and that for the infantry,

[8] C. Harris, *Lord Haldane* (1928), p. 11.   [9] Ibid., p. 34.

a battalion at home was needed to maintain every battalion abroad. Gladstone and many others argued that depots at home rather than organized units would suffice to meet the needs of foreign service battalions, believing that large sums of money could be saved by substituting depots for draft-finding battalions.

Haldane was faced with identically the same problem and the same difficulties as had been overcome by Cardwell. It was only by basing himself firmly upon the principle of unit feeding unit that he was able to resist the demand put forward by Lloyd George and Churchill for a serious diminution in the number of battalions at home. As Ellison said:

The bedrock principle of the Cardwell system is, I take it, that the number of battalions we are compelled to maintain overseas in peace determine the number we must have at home. Of course, occasionally and temporarily, there may be one or two more abroad than at home, and, very seldom, vice versa. But if by some miracle we could dispense with, say, twenty battalions abroad, logically it would follow under the Cardwell system that twenty would disappear at home. When asked why he had banked on an Expeditionary Force of six divisions, Haldane always replied that under the Cardwell system we had to maintain at home sufficient battalions for such a force.[1]

Having settled the Regular Army Haldane then turned to deal with the auxiliary forces; his matured plans for these bodies appeared in a formidable piece of legislation, The Territorial and Reserves Act, 1908.

The two forces were the Militia, and the Yeomanry or Volunteers. The Militia had always objected strongly to the role assigned to it by Cardwell, but in peace it was subordinate to, and in war was practically an integral part of, the Regular Army. In 1902 the tie between the Militia and the Regular Army had been severed, with the result that the expeditionary force of the future was without any kind of draft-finding machinery. The Militia enjoyed, however, powerful support in high places. When it came to the Yeomanry Haldane was up against the individualistic beliefs of the nineteenth century. Each unit had come to be regarded as the property of some commanding officer, who thought it his duty to preserve intact its status and financial stability. But Haldane was determined to destroy this preposterous notion. Under the old practice all government grants for maintenance in training had been paid directly to the commanding officer, who often supplemented them out of his own pocket; but Haldane decided that the training of the new Territorial Army should be handed over to the Territorial Associations, a term which he had borrowed from the County Association of Cromwell's New Model Army. These two forces, the Militia and the Yeomanry, were in

[1] Harris papers.

1906 in a state of confusion because nobody was clear about their fundamental purposes. Here, as with the Regular Army, Haldane thought hard
and deeply. As home defence was the business of the navy, it followed
logically that these forces were no longer required for home defence. For
what could they then be required? The only logical answer was: to supply
drafts for the Expeditionary Force; so in truth he abolished the Militia
and built the Special Reserve on its ashes, though, with characteristic tact,
he did not say this, in order to spare the feelings of the county magnates
who had regarded the Militia as their own private preserve. The function
of the Special Reserve was to find drafts for the battalions of the Regular
Army.

So far as the Territorial Army was concerned, it was organized on a
county basis, and (this was an essential point) equipped with artillery and
medical services exactly on the lines of the Regular Army itself. The
function of the Territorials was to provide a means for expansion outside
the machinery of the Regular Army. The Territorials were launched with
the personal approval of the King himself, who summoned the Lords-
Lieutenant of England to a meeting at Buckingham Palace in October
1907, and gained their somewhat reluctant support for the new proposal.
So when Haldane left the War Office every part of this great and intricate
structure was in a high state of efficiency, and knew what its purpose was
to be in the war which was inevitably coming. In August 1914 the British
Expeditionary Force was ready for mobilization almost to the last gaiter-
button. Some reservists whose dimensions had altered had to be re-kitted.
All were transported to France without incident. The daily reports which
Kitchener's private secretary provided were on a half-sheet of notepaper.[2]

So when King George V came to the throne in 1910, he found the
defence forces of this country at a higher pitch of perfection than they
have ever reached before or since. There were two massive and well-
organized machines in the Admiralty and the War Office, which had
produced on the one hand the Grand Fleet and on the other the British
Expeditionary Force. Unfortunately the machinery for co-ordinating
these two separate instruments was seriously defective. The Committee of
Imperial Defence was the body charged with this duty, but for various
reasons it was incapable of fulfilling the task.[3] This committee had been
formally created by a Treasury minute on 4 May 1904 as an advisory body
under the Prime Minister with a permanent secretariat. It worked through
various sub-committees, one on coast defences, one on aerial navigation,
another on oversea defences. Since 1910 there had been at attempt to

[2] Information from Sir Herbert Creedy, G.C.B.
[3] See J. P. Mackintosh, 'The Role of the Committee of Imperial Defence before 1914'
(1962) 77 E.H.R. 490.

H*

coordinate the war plans of the various departments. The 'War Book' was annually revised each November for the meeting of the Committee of Imperial Defence the following April. The first revise of the 'War Book' was accordingly ready in April 1913. Since 1909 various other sub-committees set up *ad hoc* had made twenty-nine inquiries, involving one hundred and fifty meetings. The frequency of meetings of the Committee as such was very variable. Intervals of one, two, or even three or six months elapsed between meetings of the full Committee, though in the interval work done by the sub-committees was going steadily forward. It was a body in which Haldane took a most active interest from the first, and constantly attended even when he was Lord Chancellor. But there were several defects. First, comparatively few current problems did in fact find their way to the Committee of Imperial Defence unless the secretariat stirred up individuals or departments to raise them. The secretariat itself had no machinery for laying on the agenda problems of a general character. For example, the C.I.D. never considered either British policy concerning Constantinople, or the effect of opening the Panama Canal on trade and defence. It is indeed almost incredible that such obvious problems of a 'General Staff nature', as Haldane himself would have said, never reached the agenda of the Committee.

A second major difficulty was that the plans of each of the great government defence departments had never been considered as a whole by the Committee. The Admiralty representatives were accustomed to sit in silence, refusing to disclose what was at the back of their minds. This lamentable failure was revealed at a dramatic meeting on 23 August 1911 when, in view of the threatening situation in Morocco, a European war seemed imminent. At the end of a long discussion based upon the sending of the B.E.F. to Belgium, the representatives of the Admiralty, presided over by Lord Fisher, suddenly announced that they were unable to guarantee the passage of the Expeditionary Force, and put forward an entirely different proposal of their own based upon landing the force on the Pomeranian coast eighty miles west of Berlin. The state of affairs revealed by this division of opinion was so serious that Haldane informed Asquith he would resign at once unless urgent steps were taken to intro-duce a naval general staff on the lines of what he had already done for the army. This naval general staff would co-ordinate the work of the Admir-alty with that of the War Office. Lengthy discussions took place as to who should succeed McKenna at the Admiralty. For a moment Haldane pressed his own claims, but in the event, Winston Churchill was appointed First Lord.

August 1914 found the supreme command of the War Office in a somewhat uncertain state. Asquith had been obliged to assume the office of Secretary of State for War in the preceding March, when it became impossible to retain Seely after the Curragh Mutiny. It was, however, unanimously agreed (on the suggestion of Haldane himself) that Kitchener should be recalled to the position. At that time Kitchener's public reputation was such that no other appointment was really possible. But in the meantime, on Sunday, 2 August, Asquith asked Haldane to relieve him by acting as his deputy at the War Office. So all the critical events of the next few days found Haldane in substantial control of the great machine which he had built up a few years before. This met with the emphatic approval of the military. Haig wrote on 4 August: 'No one knows the details of the problems of organization as you do!—This war will last many months, possibly years.[4]'

Yet a few months later it was widely alleged that Haldane had delayed the dispatch to France of the Expeditionary Force which he had himself created. Haldane later stated emphatically that throughout he had been in favour of what had always been planned—the immediate dispatch of all six divisions.[5] Grey supported this assertion. But there is testimony the other way. On 4 August two of the Conservative leaders, Balfour and Lansdowne, talked with Haldane. Each came away with the impression that Haldane was dubious about the need for the immediate dispatch of the B.E.F. Balfour recorded his impression of his conversation (which took place at 11 p.m.) in a contemporary document, according to which Haldane had stated that the B.E.F. should be kept at home to serve as the nucleus of a larger force later, and, in any event, that it might hamper the fleet if the country was denuded of its army. Balfour said that he tried to counter both arguments, but concluded: 'On the whole I was rather depressed by a certain woolliness of thought and indecision of purpose, which seemed to mark his conversation—otherwise very interesting.'[6]

It does not seem possible to reconcile all the statements on this point. It has been plausibly suggested[7] that Haldane may have been trying to inform Balfour of what was in the mind of the Council of War[8] rather than of what his own intentions might have been. But in any event two days later it was decided to send four divisions overseas at once, a fifth to follow later. Still, it has rightly been said to be unfortunate that Haldane, of all men, should have been left to live down the accusation that he delayed the departure of the Expeditionary Force.[9]

---

[4] N.L.S., 5910, f. 253.   [5] *Autobiography*, pp. 277–8.

[6] Add. MSS. 49724. For Lansdowne's version, see Newton's *Life*, p. 440.

[7] Sommer, p. 315. See also Lord Hankey, *The Supreme Command* (1961), pp. 169–73.

[8] Some of whom, according to Haldane (*Autobiography*, p. 278) were 'a little timid' about the departure of the whole B.E.F.

[9] Sommer, p. 315.

The few men, military and civilian, who knew the full extent of Haldane's work for the army remained loyal to him throughout the war. One of the most noteworthy of these was Haig. After the Armistice in 1918 he sent Haldane a generously worded appreciation of his efforts. Some months later he followed this up with a dramatic gesture of loyalty to his old chief—all the more significant because it came from a man who was notoriously undemonstrative. He presented Haldane with a volume of his Dispatches containing this inscription:

To Viscount Haldane of Cloan—the greatest Secretary for War England has ever had.
In grateful remembrance of his successful efforts in organizing our Military Forces for a war on the Continent, notwithstanding much opposition from his Army Council and the half-hearted support of his parliamentary friends!
        Xmas 1919   Haig, F. M.[1]

In his *Autobiography* Haldane stated that the volume of Dispatches was presented by Haig in person, who called at 28 Queen Anne's Gate 'after dark' on 19 July 1919, the day of the Victory March through London.[2] Haldane drew a dramatic contrast between himself, alone and friendless in his house on a day of national rejoicing, and the Field Marshal, 'come from a triumphant ride with his Sovereign along the Mall'. But an ingenious piece of detective work has shown that Haig presented his inscribed Dispatches in December and not in July[3]—as indeed, a reference to the original inscription itself makes plain. It is, however, probable, but not certain, that Haig did call on Haldane after the Victory March. Haig's family testify that he did, even though he was feeling very ill.[4] But the call could hardly have been 'after dark', as the march was over by 3 p.m., and the day was not exceptionally overcast for a London July.[5] It is very probable that Haldane, writing a few months before his death, telescoped into one two distinct visits by Haig. It has been said that Haig made the presentation on Christmas Day, 1919,[6] but Haldane wrote a full account of his doings on that day[7] without mentioning such an event.

---

[1] Preserved in N.L.S., Ry. VII C. 10-11. Note that the version of the inscription given in the *Autobiography*, p. 288, is inaccurate.
[2] Ibid., p. 288.   [3] Sommer, pp. 367-70.
[4] *The Times*, 13 May 1960 (letter from J. Terraine).
[5] Ibid., 21 July 1919.   [6] *Yorkshire Evening Post*, 20 August 1928.
[7] In a letter to Gosse of 30 December 1919.

CHAPTER III

THE MAIN THREAD OF HALDANE'S LIFE may now be taken up again. In October 1910 the resignation of Morley from the India Office was announced, and the post was offered to Haldane. But he felt that his work at the War Office was not yet completed and refused. In the spring of 1911 Asquith was faced with difficulties in the House of Lords. Crewe was unwell and Morley was aged 73, and ahead lay the fierce battle over the Parliament Bill. Haldane was asked to become a peer in order to help the Government in the Lords while retaining his position at the War Office. Asquith wrote to his wife:

> I have just done what I never in this life expected to do—sent a submission to the King that the dignity of a Viscount of the United Kingdom be conferred on the Rt. Hon. R. B. Haldane, Secretary of State for War, with the title of Viscount Haldane of Cloan in the County of Perth.
> When I think of the days when we sat on a Sunday afternoon in the little garden of Eton House at Hampstead—two quite briefless barristers with no apparent or conjecturable future—it is a landmark of what may happen in this strange country.[1]

(It is worth noting that although Haldane constantly signed himself as 'Haldane of Cloan', this was strictly incorrect. Every peerage must be 'of' somewhere, but unless this territorial designation is incorporated into the title of the peerage (as in the cases of Balfour of Burleigh and Montgomery of Alamein, to take two examples) it should not be used as part of the peer's signature. This was clearly settled in the case of Lord Channing of Wellingborough in 1911, full details of which are in the Royal Archives. Haldane may have had in mind the Scots usage which entitles a laird to describe himself as 'of' his estate.)

Haldane's appointment qualified him under the Appellate Jurisdiction Act to sit as a Law Lord; some surprise was expressed at a member of the Cabinet sitting to dispose of appeals in the highest court in the land, but Asquith expressly stated in the House that Haldane did not propose to resign from the Government. His case had an exact precedent in that of Lord James of Hereford, who was appointed to such a position on the Judicial Committee in 1902, while still holding office in the Government as Chancellor of the Duchy of Lancaster. In April 1913 a further honour came to Haldane—he was created a Knight of the Thistle, a distinction

[1] J. A. Spender and C. Asquith, *Life of Lord Oxford and Asquith* (1932), vol. i, p. 293.

much appreciated in Scotland. After the names of several Scottish peers had been canvassed at Windsor, it was clear to all that Haldane should have the honour.

The circumstances under which Haldane became Lord Chancellor in June 1912 have already been described.[2] The appointment was welcomed in the profession, particularly in Lincoln's Inn, as it brought to the Woolsack the first equity lawyer since Cairns. The only discordant note was sounded by the Attorney-General, Sir Rufus Isaacs, who, although not questioning Haldane's personal merits, thought that both he and his office had a grievance. Isaacs represented his grievance to Asquith with such force that the Prime Minister offered him a seat in the Cabinet as a solatium.

On 14 June Haldane replied to Rosebery's letter of congratulations: 'Thank you for a kind letter. I am getting keener about this work now that I have begun the judicial side of it. Sitting and listening to law does not bore me at all. But the clothes business is oppressive.[3]

It is worth noting that on Haldane's accession a change was made in the method of helping the new Chancellor to pay for his elaborate robes. From the reign of George II a new Chancellor had been entitled to a payment of £1,843 10s. from the Civil Contingencies Fund to meet the expenses of first entering office. After 1912 only his actual expenses were borne by the State.[4]

Sir Frederick Maurice said that the months following his appointment to the Woolsack were the one time in his life when Haldane was really popular.[5] Popularity or the lack of it never worried Haldane so long as he could feel his talents were being used to the best advantage. But it was certainly the time in his life when he was at his busiest. Not even in his early days at the War Office had he been kept at full stretch for so long. He was accustomed to quote Herschell's statement that no man could hold the office of Lord Chancellor for more than three years. But Haldane was 56 when he was appointed and his physical and mental powers were at their height.[6] He had always enjoyed hard work and he was happy now.

Haldane left an extraordinarily acute and objective assessment of himself as a judge.

I never considered that I was equipped by nature for the part of a great judge. It was not that I did not know the law. I knew it pretty thoroughly; I had had a long experience at the Bar of the most difficult and miscellaneous kinds of work; and memory had preserved the bulk of my knowledge, notwithstanding absence for over six years at the War Office. But the judicial temperament of the highest order is a very rare gift. Lord Lindley possessed it, and so did Lord

[2] See above, pp. 165-7.   [3] Rosebery papers.   [4] 241 H.C. Deb. 5s. col. 1497.
[5] Maurice, vol. ii, p. 322.   [6] *Autobiography*, p. 255.

Bowen. Lord Watson had it in a notable degree. But I recognised shortcomings
in my own nature which made me despair of rising to their level as regards
the detachment with which they approached the cases which came before them.
Still, knowledge of the law, and the desire to be absolutely just, go for a good
deal, and I had both of these. But I think that a judge, if he is to reach the highest
level, must devote himself, not to many subjects as I did, but to passionate
absorption in the law, as, for example, did the late Lord Blackburn. Lord Cairns
has been almost the only exception to this rule. In our own time such exclusive
devotion to the law is more difficult than it used to be.[7]

Most lawyers would probably agree that this assessment is, if anything,
unfair to its subject. Haldane was not, and did not claim to be, in the class
of Cairns, Blackburn, Jessel, or Macnaghten. But he was only just below
them. Of the Lord Chancellors with whom this volume deals, those
qualified to judge would place Herschell, Haldane, and Birkenhead in a
class by themselves as jurists, with perhaps Maugham and Finlay as well.
In the learned analysis, exposition, and development of legal principles
they are manifestly superior to the other Chancellors. It so happened that
the greatest of Haldane's judgments were delivered in the two years
1914–15. He was rightly proud of the effort and research which had gone
into composing them—and, as he said,[8] an English judge, even in the
House of Lords, has no clerical assistance of any kind, such as is given to
members of the Supreme Court of the United States. These judgments
are considered in detail in the appendix, but two points about them may
be made here. First, they show that Haldane, as might be expected from
the nature of his practice at the Bar, excelled in two fields—equity, and
Dominion constitutional law. Secondly, they make manifest that Haldane
was not only a master of the technical legal learning contained in the
reported cases but was also aware of the social, political, and economic
implications of judicial decisions.

In the field of equity Haldane was particularly strong, not so much in
'pure equity', settlements, trusts, and mortgages (though as *Kreglinger* v.
New Patagonia Meat Packing Co.[9] shows, he could be very good there
when he chose) but in the uncertain area where the principles of common
law and equity overlap. His speculative cast of mind was of peculiar value
here, and it so happened that the accidents of litigation brought before
him during these years two cases which called for the exercise of just such
talents. In *Nocton* v. *Ashburton*[1] he induced his colleagues to agree that the
principle in *Derry* v. *Peek*[2] did not apply to a fiduciary duty such as a

[7] Ibid., pp. 254–5.

[8] Ibid., p. 256. It may be recalled that Hatherley L.C. only twice delivered a written
judgment as 'I find such writing to be positively injurious to my health'. W. R. W.
Stephens, *A Memoir of Lord Hatherley* (1883), p. 87.

[9] [1914] A.C. 25.   [1] [1914] A.C. 932.   [2] (1889) 14 App. Cas. 337.

solicitor's—'in other words, go as near as they dare to saying it was wrong, as all Lincoln's Inn thought at the time', as Pollock triumphantly wrote to Holmes.[3] In his judgment Haldane, in sorrowful terms, hinted that 'if among the great common lawyers who had composed the House' in *Derry* v. *Peek* there had been someone learned in the principles of equity, the result might have been different. The other case was *Sinclair* v. *Brougham*,[4] in which he expounded with masterly learning the circumstances in which equity would permit a beneficiary to trace misapplied trust funds into the hands of third parties when the common law remedy of quasi-contract was not available.

In the field of Dominion constitutional law Haldane made it a point to preside in the Judicial Committee in every important appeal. His influence on the constitutional law of Canada has been profound. Between 1912 and 1929 there were forty-one appeals to the Judicial Committee raising questions concerning the validity of Canadian legislation. In thirty-two of these appeals Haldane was a member of the Board, and in nineteen of them he delivered judgment. These judgments display a remarkably consistent judicial philosophy relating to the nature of Canadian federalism. Their general effect is to deny to the federal parliament and government a number of powers which are usually characteristic of central governments in the twentieth century, even though Haldane also thought that Canada was not a true federation since the constitution created not only a new common government but also new provincial governments.[5]

The British North America Act, 1867, set up a federal form of government in Canada, and by sections 91 and 92 distributed the powers of government between the central and provincial legislatures. Section 91 provided that the Dominion Parliament was empowered 'to make laws for the peace, order and good government of Canada in relation to all matters not coming within the classes of subjects by this Act [sect. 92] assigned exclusively to the legislatures of the Provinces, and for greater certainty, but not so as to restrict the generality of the foregoing, it is hereby declared that (notwithstanding anything in this Act) the exclusive legislative authority of the Parliament of Canada extends to all matters coming within' 31 enumerated sub-heads. Section 92 then assigns sixteen subjects to the Provincial legislatures. In a series of cases the Judicial Committee so interpreted these sections as to cut down considerably the apparently wide powers which they conferred on the Dominion Parliament. It did this in two ways. First, it held that the general power of legislation conferred upon the Dominion by section 91 must be strictly

[3] *Holmes-Pollock Letters*, ed. M. DeWolfe Howe (2nd ed. 1962), vol. i, p. 215.
[4] [1914] A.C. 398.
[5] *Att.-Gen. for Australia* v. *Colonial Sugar Refining Co. Ltd.* [1914] A.C. 237, 252–4.

confined to matters which were undoubtedly of national interest, and must not trench on any of the subjects enumerated in sect. 92 as being within Provincial jurisdiction, unless these have attained such dimensions as to affect the body politic of the Dominion.[6] In effect the residuary power of the Dominion was demoted in favour of its enumerated powers. This decision in the Liquor Prohibition Case was later described by Haldane (who had been of counsel in it) as 'the watershed'.[7] The judgment of the Board was delivered by Lord Watson, whose determination so to interpret the Act as to maintain the independence of the Provinces was revealed with remarkable frankness by Haldane in an obituary notice of Watson[8].

Secondly, after 1896 the Judicial Committee so interpreted the contents of the various powers enumerated in sections 91 and 92 as to grant an exceptional degree of protection to 'property and civil rights in the province', and to minimize the Dominion powers to legislate upon trade and commerce and criminal law. Thus in one judgment Haldane, who throughout was an unswerving adherent of Watson's views, held that the Dominion could not validly enact a statute prohibiting or regulating trade combinations,[9] and in another that it was incompetent to enact compulsory provisions for the investigation of industrial disputes.[1] In the years when Sankey was on the Woolsack it was noticeable that the Judicial Committee adopted a rather more liberal mode of interpretation, but in 1937 the measures enacted by the Bennett Government to counter the economic depression were invalidated in a series of cases.[2] In 1947 the Judicial Committee, presided over by Jowitt, adopted an extremely liberal interpretation in order to uphold the validity of a statute abolishing appeals to the Privy Council.[3] In 1949 the British North America Act was amended so as to permit the Dominion Parliament to amend the constitution for itself, with the important exception that the distribution of legislative powers to the Provinces in section 92 could only be altered by the Parliament at Westminster. Many efforts have been made within Canada itself to secure national agreement for the adoption of an entirely Canadian method of amending the Constitution; but so far they have not been successful because of the determination of Quebec to maintain the privileged position assured to it in 1867 and emphatically reaffirmed in the judgments of Watson and Haldane.

[6] *Att.-Gen. for Ontario v. Att.-Gen. for Canada* [1896] A.C. 348.

[7] In argument in *Toronto Electric Commissioners v. Snider* [1925] A.C. 396.

[8] (1899) Juridical Review 234. Haldane made some similar remarks in (1922) 1 Camb. L.J. 143.

[9] *In re Board of Commerce Act* [1922] 1 A.C. 191.

[1] The *Snider Case* [1925] A.C. 396.

[2] *Att.-Gen. for Canada v. Att.-Gen. for Ontario* [1937] A.C. 326.

[3] *Att.-Gen. for Ontario v. Att.-Gen. for Canada* [1947] A.C. 127.

It is interesting to note that Haldane's only personal contact with the country whose destinies his decisions so profoundly affected was in 1912, when he crossed the Atlantic to attend a meeting of the Canadian Bar Association at Montreal. (An age which prides itself on speedy trans-Atlantic crossings may be surprised to learn that Haldane went for the week-end: he arrived on a Friday and sailed for home the following Tuesday. On his return he received from the King a letter written in his own hand congratulating him on the success of his visit.)

Under Haldane a small but significant change was made in the arrangements of the Privy Council Board Room. Formerly appeals had been heard with members of the Judicial Committee seated at a long table with a vacant chair for the monarch at its end; this table was taken away and replaced by the fine semi-circular piece of mahogany (with no vacant place) which is still in use.

Haldane was helped by a strong team of Law Lords, and in his *Autobiography*[4] he has left interesting pictures of some of them—in particular Lord Moulton, for whose breadth of interests and marvellous swiftness of mind he had real admiration. With his predecessor Halsbury his relations were surprisingly friendly. The minds of no two men in England could have been more unlike than those of Halsbury and Haldane; but the older man constantly encouraged the younger and several times said that he expected to be succeeded by him,[5] while the younger had a genuine respect for the different but very real judicial capacities of the older.

As a law reformer Haldane made a mark. His peculiar talents had already enabled him to reorganize one of the most characteristic institutions of English life—the army. They were now to be devoted to an equally venerable and characteristic structure—the law of real property. The process which culminated in the great series of statutes passed in 1925 to simplify and improve the land law was one in which several Chancellors had a part. Cairns had been responsible for the Settled Land Act, 1882, which introduced the device of over-reaching. It was Haldane who persuaded some of the most eminent conveyancers (Sir Benjamin Cherry and Sir Philip Gregory) to draft a Bill extending the 'curtain principle' further so as to enable third parties to deal with the limited owner of land as if he were the absolute owner while at the same time giving adequate protection to the encumbrancers. Haldane's career had been such as to entitle him to respect from a body of men who are notoriously difficult to impress. When at the Bar he had had a considerable conveyancing practice, and had even appeared for the successful appellant in the great case of *Van Grutten* v. *Foxwell*,[6] in which some most complex and

[4] pp. 257–8.   [5] See N.L.S., 5972, ff. 123 165.   [6] [1897] A.C. 658.

ancient learning had been deployed in an effort to elucidate the *mysterium tremendum* of the Rule in Shelley's case. On his appointment as Lord Chancellor he had been the guest of honour at a dinner of The Institute—the professional body of practitioners in this craft. The Bill which Cherry drafted was introduced in the House of Lords in 1913 and 1914 but made no further progress. After the war it was taken up again, and the co-operative efforts of several Chancellors—Birkenhead, Cave, and Haldane again—succeeded in securing its passage into law.[7]

On the administrative side of his work, Haldane had to make a considerable number of judicial appointments during his first term. (In his second the only appointment was of F. MacKinnon, K.C., who rose to be Lord Justice.) Haldane and Asquith resolved that appointments should be made on professional merit—though, as we have seen,[8] Haldane was fully aware of the value of political experience to a judge. The men appointed were: Younger, Astbury and Sargant in the Chancery Division, and Bailhache, Shearman, Sankey, Low and Atkin in the King's Bench Division. Of these, Sankey became Lord Chancellor, and Atkin rose to be a Law Lord and one of the most distinguished authorities on the common law of the twentieth century.

Haldane also had time to reflect on the curious system whereby the functions of a Ministry of Justice were divided between the Lord Chancellor and the Home Secretary. His thoughts were given expression some years later in the Report on the Machinery of Government.

All this work was carried on at a time when the calls on the Lord Chancellor as Speaker of the House of Lords were exceptionally heavy. The political business of the time was contentious and sittings were often late. Many of Haldane's judgments at this time were written in the early hours of the morning. He also had his work in the Cabinet and as a member of the Committee of Imperial Defence. He was also Chairman of the Royal Commission on the University of London.

Before assuming the Great Seal, in February 1912, Haldane paid a visit to Berlin which was of some significance in Anglo-German relations and of great importance in his own career. In the late summer and autumn of 1911 Anglo-German relations had deteriorated seriously as a result of the Agadir crisis. The prospect became bleaker when it was known that the Germans proposed a substantial increase in their navy. At this moment a hint from Berlin was dropped in London to the effect that a visit from an English Cabinet Minister would be welcome. Haldane always regarded this suggestion as having been made on the authority of the Kaiser himself, who was anxious to support the moderate party as against the war party led by Tirpitz. Haldane was the Minister selected to go. An innocent

[7] See below, pp. 438-40.   [8] Above, p. 39.

attempt was made to pass the visit off as an investigation into German technical education, but this deceived nobody. For three days Haldane had the fullest and most intimate discussions with the Kaiser, Tirpitz, and Bethmann-Hollweg. The essential purpose of the discussions was to discover whether Germany would agree to reduce her fleet in return for a British promise of non-aggression or whether she would stand out (as in fact she did) for a positive promise of neutrality. Haldane made the British position clear. As he wrote to Asquith in 1922: 'Put shortly my cardinal principle—settled before I left London—was that the size of the German Navy made it impracticable to quit the Entente. As Grey always said among ourselves the real reason for the Entente was that it was the only way of retaining command of the sea.'[9]

Although it had proved impossible to secure any formal agreement, Haldane always claimed that his visit had produced a good mood in Anglo-German relations. 'Only', as he wrote in 1917, 'the good mood did not endure long enough.'[1] In June 1912 he wrote to his sister: 'I shall not come again to Germany whilst I am in office except on business. It is too much of a public affair. I seem to have a place in the hearts of these simple people. It is like a journey with Lloyd George in Wales'.[2] But sanguine as he was, he was under no illusions. After his Berlin visit he told the Army Council that they might have three months in which to prepare for war.[3]

There were two further occasions on which Haldane was concerned with German attempts to extract a promise of neutrality from Britain. On 15 September 1922 Haldane wrote to Asquith:

A few months prior to August 1914 I was at Windsor for three days 'keeping the King's conscience'. He said that he did not need help in this matter, but that he did need it in another. Prince Henry of Prussia was coming to visit him at Sandringham—to find out, he felt sure, what England meant to do in case of war—what was he to say? I told him to use the formula we had used before, that if Germany made an aggressive entry into France she could not rely on our remaining neutral. . . . The King appeared to have used the formula with emphasis. The Kaiser was therefore fully warned of what might probably happen.[4]

This statement is supported by other evidence.[5]

A few weeks before war broke out Ballin, the German shipping magnate, an intimate of the Kaiser, dined at Queen Anne's Gate. Grey was present. Haldane said they both told Ballin that peaceful Anglo-German relations depended on Germany not attacking France. On 1 August Ballin wrote to Haldane (in English) expressing the hope that Britain

[9] Asquith papers.   [1] Gosse papers.   [2] N.L.S., 6011, f. 207.
[3] J. Marriott, *Memories of Fourscore Years* (1946), p. 110.   [4] Asquith papers.
[5] Lord Wigram, 'The Word of a King', *The Times*, 2 June 1938.

would be neutral if Germany did not try to 'swallow up' France. Haldane naturally claimed that 'attack' had been the word used. It may be that Ballin's English was not perfect, or it may be that the Germans only heard what they wanted to hear. In any event, the fact of Ballin's letter having been sent got abroad, and Haldane was asked to reveal its contents. He refused to do so, saying that it would not be proper for the Head of the Law to publish a private letter written in peace-time without the writer's consent. Naturally this refusal was construed by Haldane's enemies in the worst possible light. He admitted later that he might have published the letter. 'It was harmless and a little foolish.'[6]

The next episode in Haldane's career reflects discredit on everyone involved except Haldane himself. It is his resignation from office in May 1915. The preceding autumn and spring had seen many attacks on Haldane of an extremely vicious character in *The Times*, the *National Review* and the *Daily Express*, the persons behind this attack being Northcliffe, Beaverbrook, and Leo Maxse. Haldane was accused of a variety of sins ranging from minor follies to something approaching treason. None of these charges, as Haldane's friends well knew, had any substance, but the British public was in a curiously excitable mood, and lent a ready ear to the slanders. Haldane was also personally unpopular with the Conservative Party. Haldane was not the type of man whom the Englishman normally admires; his interests were entirely academic and intellectual. Haldane had on several occasions expressed admiration for what he was accustomed to call the General Staff type of mind. 'He was never a maker of phrases. The only sport in which he took any interest was his shooting in the Perthshire hills. A love of horseflesh is a political asset, but Haldane's devotion to his dogs had no like appeal. He had none of those little human weaknesses and foibles which often endear a leader to his followers.'[7] His own sister-in-law recorded her intense dislike of 'his omniscience, his self-satisfaction and his sneers at the ideas and loyalties of people who disagreed with him.'[8] His un-popularity mounted quickly. At the end of 1914 he was hissed by the aud-ience at a London theatre.

In addition there is the mysterious and important matter (made much of in the Northcliffe Press) of his remark to the effect that Germany was his spiritual home. The true origin of this affair seems to have been a dinner party given by Mrs. Humphry Ward to a number of German professors in April 1913.[9] In the after-glow of dinner, Haldane remarked

---

[6] See *Autobiography*, pp. 270–3.   [7] Maurice, vol. ii, p. 372.
[8] L. K. Haldane, *Friends and Kindred* (1961), p. 150.
[9] G. P. Gooch, *Under Six Reigns* (1959), p. 167, and letter to the author on 25 December 1958. See also Sommer, pp. 318–19.

to one Professor Oncken that 'Lotze's classroom was my spiritual home.'
(Oncken had also been a pupil of Lotze.) After the war broke out this
remark was circulated in Germany and at once taken up by the English
Press. As Haldane himself wrote later, in a remarkably serene and detached
review of the controversy, 'I had gone to Germany too often, and read
her literature too much, not to give ground to narrow minded people to
say that Germany was "my spiritual home".'[1]

The worst that can be said about Haldane's behaviour in this matter is
that he showed a certain tactlessness in drawing attention to the weaknesses of the English character and the strength of the German. 'In truth
all I wanted was to make my countrymen see that there was a problem of
German character raising questions of a very dangerous kind, and that
the organizing power of Germany had to be understood before we could
make ourselves safe. This was not so merely in military matters. In commerce and industry, in regard to which I also had special means of making
myself acquainted with the progress of German advances, the danger
appeared to me not less.'[2] In any event, when the storm broke Haldane was
deserted, not merely by his friends in the Liberal Party who might have
stood by him, such as Asquith and Grey, but also by the more sensible
Conservatives who knew the true state of affairs, such as Balfour and
Derby.

On 18 May 1915 Haldane wrote to his sister:

There have been great rows—Army and Navy. It may be necessary to form
a National Government. We have all sent in our resignations in order to
strengthen the hands of the P.M. I have thought it my duty to tell him specially
that it may be wise to use my office in order to bring in Carson. Anyhow great
changes are likely and I am clear as to everyone's duty, including my own.[3]

It is hardly surprising that Asquith should have replied on 17 May to
Haldane's letter:

Thank you for your letter; which was characteristically true and fine.
I loathe the necessities which seem to confront us. But we must put aside
everything for which we care severally to bring the main thing through.
I should like to have a talk with you some time tomorrow.[4]

The next few days were full of the intricacies of Cabinet-making. On
the 25th Haldane wrote to Gosse: 'I know no more than when I saw you,
though I have been with Asquith several times. He is struggling hard.
But it is on his own account, not mine, for he knows I am well content.'[5]

---

[1] *Autobiography*, p. 285.   [2] N.L.S., 5923, f. 16.
[3] N.L.S., 6012, f. 98.
[4] N.L.S., 5911, f. 37.   [5] Gosse papers.

But it is now clear that on that very day Asquith had offered the Woolsack to Buckmaster.[6]

All that is known is that the Conservative leader, Bonar Law, was inflexible that Haldane's name must not appear in the new Government. He did not claim the Woolsack for the Conservatives although at one time the name of Sumner, a Conservative Law Lord, crossed Asquith's mind as a future Lord Chancellor. The story of how the Prime Minister's choice eventually settled on Buckmaster has been told elsewhere;[7] it is enough to say that on 26 May Haldane himself surrendered the Great Seal to the King, but received in return, quite unexpectedly, the Order of Merit. No more striking proof of the monarch's confidence in Haldane's patriotism could have been given.

Asquith and Grey certainly had the gravest doubts about what they were doing, but they did not press these doubts to the point of resignation. On 26 May Grey wrote to the Prime Minister strongly defending Haldane against the attacks made on him and stating in categorical terms that it was totally untrue that Haldane had first, intrigued with Germany behind the backs of his colleagues, or secondly, weakened the army, particularly the artillery, or thirdly, opposed sending the B.E.F. to France. 'It had, as you know, been my intention not to remain in the Government unless Haldane were included in it. I need not enter into the reasons that have made it impossible for me to give effect to my personal preferences at this moment.'[8]

Asquith replied praising Haldane and agreeing that the attacks made on him were spiteful.

Like you, I more than doubted whether I could find it possible to sit in a Cabinet in which Haldane was not to be included. He is the oldest personal and political friend that I have in the world, and, with him, you and I have stood together amidst all the turbulent vicissitudes of fortune for the best part of thirty years. Never at any time, or in any conjuncture, have the three of us seriously differed.[9]

But Asquith and Grey did not themselves resign: they thought their first duty was to the nation.

Asquith and Grey considered publishing this correspondence, but were advised against doing so by Sir Eric Drummond on the ground that the attacks had in fact ceased and that if the correspondence were now published it would awaken the obvious comment, 'Why did not the Prime Minister keep Haldane if all these facts were true?' Drummond

[6] See below, p. 266.   [7] See below, pp. 265–7.   [8] N.L.S., 5911, f. 106–7.
[9] N.L.S., 5911, f. 145.

said: 'If the true answer is given, it must I am afraid lead to fresh friction between the two parties.'[1]

Asquith's conduct in this matter has been criticized, and in particular his failure to send Haldane at the time any letter of sympathetic defence such as he wrote to Grey. But Asquith did send a letter, couched in terms of unusual enthusiasm, to be read out at a dinner at the National Liberal Club on 5 July at which Haldane was present. In answer it may be said by Asquith's friends that there was no need to send such a letter for Haldane knew perfectly well what the Prime Minister's feelings towards him were, and, in any event, had himself first suggested that his office should be given to a Conservative. But there is testimony to show that Haldane felt hurt that he should have been allowed to depart in silence.[2] There is certainly a touch of acid in the picture Haldane in his *Autobiography* drew of Asquith, with its reference to the attraction which London social life had for him in his later years.[3] It is true that Asquith was a man to whom the open expression of emotion was abhorrent.[4] There is a story that when he saw Haldane during those anxious days, he found himself unable to speak, but stood staring out of the window of his room at the House of Commons into Old Palace Yard.[5] (It is certainly true that at a moment of crisis Asquith's silence could become obtrusive. When Birrell was dismissed from the Irish Secretaryship after the rebellion of 1916, Asquith uttered hardly a word during the interview, though obviously deeply moved at the departure of an old political friend.)

During the days which followed Haldane received scores of letters of sympathy from those who knew the true facts. One of the first came from Halsbury. It was almost totally illegible but its general tone was sympathetic.[6] Simon wrote on 26 May expressing sympathy and disgust:

Your own constant kindness and encouragement to me are among the pleasantest things I have to remember; it was you who first advised me as a junior to seek a constituency. I am honestly glad to feel that it is not I who takes your place (though I know Buckmaster feels as I do and never dreamt of displacing you) and indeed my feelings about the whole thing have been those of your older and closer friends like Grey and Asquith.[7]

Sir George Farwell, the retired Lord Justice wrote on 30 May:

I at any rate remember how you stood aside, regnante Rosebery, to enable him to appoint Lockwood (a Law Officer *pour rire*) instead of you—and how you made way for the worst lawyer of modern times, if you can call such a

---

[1] N.L.S., 5912, f. 28.   [2] Spender and Asquith, vol. ii, p. 167.   [3] p. 103.
[4] Lady Violet Bonham Carter thus explains her father's failure to write: *The Observer*, 22 May 1960.
[5] Told to the author by Lord Samuel.   [6] N.L.S. 5912, ff. 18–19.
[7] N.L.S. 5911, ff. 76–77.

sentimentalist a lawyer at all—on the Woolsack: and now they throw you to the jackals and put Buckmaster (save the mark) in place of the best lawyer we have had on the Woolsack since Cairns.[8]

Rosebery wrote on 6 June:

I dare say you were abused in unscrupulous newspapers which I never see, but that does not seem a sufficient reason. One ought never to do if one can help it what one's foes wish one to do, for that is only giving them pleasure. I have only seen it alleged that in the privacy of a dinner you said to a German professor that your spiritual home was in Germany, and a more inoffensive remark I cannot conceive.[9]

Haldane replied on 9 June:

I thank you for a most kind letter, which has given me much pleasure. It brings back many memories.

There is a section of the public which is full of suspicions and the Unionist leaders thought that they could not control its fury if I remained. They probably judged rightly.

I would not have *refused* to continue to serve, for in these days that would not have been the thing to do. But in my heart I welcomed the decision. The Lord Chancellorship, which takes one away from 10.30 in the morning till six or seven at night, in addition to the time consumed in writing judgments, makes it impossible to keep sufficiently in relation with those concerned to be able to be of full use in War Councils and Defence Committees. And these are the only places that count in critical days.

I am now full of judicial work, and have set to to build up the functions of the Judicial Committee in hearing appeals from India, a starved side of the work where I am now free to help. I have also educational work on hand that much wants pushing on.

So I am busy and quite happy.

When you come to London let us meet as of yore one evening. As I am no longer a servant of the Crown I have ceased to confine myself to soda-water.[1]

It was characteristic of Haldane that at such a moment he should be thinking not of the unhappiness of the past but of the prospect of useful public work in the future. It was also characteristic of him to think of others at such a time, as the following letter from the Permanent Secretary to the Lord Chancellor shows. Writing on black-edged paper, on 1 June 1915, Sir Kenneth Muir Mackenzie said:

My dear Richard,

I was very glad to hear from you: I am very depressed at your absence.

I have just returned from swearing in Buckmaster C. at the Courts: I never thought to do such a thing.

[8] N.L.S. 5911, f. 193.　　[9] N.L.S. 5912, ff. 46–47.　　[1] Rosebery papers.

I have received a notice from the P.M. that I am to be a Birthday Baron. Though I don't care a d- whether I am baron or barren, I do care very much for the honour which you did me and the office by pressing the matter, and I really marvel that you could attend to such a thing in the midst of all your tremendous trials and labours. I cannot afford the fees, and yet I don't think I ought to refuse on that account: I propose moving the Treasury to let me off the payment, as has been sometimes done in cases of meritorious poverty . . . A thousand blessings on you! How I miss you!

Yours ever affectionately,
K. M. M.[2]

Firm support was also expressed by Hankey. He was not yet Secretary to the Cabinet, but at the age of 38 his position in Whitehall was sufficiently strong for him to write thus to Haldane:

I suppose that there is no-one alive who knows as I do what the country owes to you, for I have been on the inner side of official life during the whole period of the Renaissance for which you were so largely responsible. It is in my opinion no exaggeration to say that to your foresight and patient organic reconstruction of our whole defence system, that we owe it that the Allied cause, and with it the British Empire, did not collapse last August.[3]

[2] N.L.S. 5912, ff. 7–8.
[3] N.L.S., 5911, f. 181.

CHAPTER IV

FOR A TIME HALDANE RETIRED from public life. His friends continually urged him to take steps to vindicate his character. But Asquith, on the advice of the Foreign Office, ruled that the papers relating to the Berlin visit should not be published during war time. Naturally it was then hinted that they were being suppressed in order to protect Haldane. Eventually permission was given for a memorandum based on the documents to be circulated privately among friends. But in the nature of things those who would be reached by such a memorandum would not be those who would be influenced by the Northcliffe Press. Still by the end of 1916 it was once more possible for Haldane to take some part in affairs. In December 1916 he was consulted by Buckingham Palace on the important constitutional question whether Lloyd George could obtain from the King a promise of a dissolution as a condition of forming a government. Lord Stamfordham wrote at 10.30 p.m. on 5 December and received an answer written the same night.[1] Haldane emphasized the fundamental principle of the modern constitution that the monarch acts only on the advice of his Ministers. The only alternative to accepting such advice is dismissal of the Ministers. But it followed that the King could not entertain any bargain with a possible Prime Minister before he had fully assumed office. For at such a stage the monarch could not properly weigh the whole parliamentary situation.

In the summer of 1917 Lloyd George appointed Haldane the Chairman of a Committee on the Machinery of Government. 'It is about the best Committee over which I have ever presided', Haldane wrote to his mother.[2] It was a work which was close to his heart. His powers of reflection and organization were now devoted not to the development of one part of the governmental machine, as they had been at the War Office, but to the whole complex structure of government. For the first time the extraordinary artifact of the English Constitution was subjected to logical analysis. The structure of civilian government had never before been examined by the 'General Staff mind'. The results appeared in the Report of the Committee, published in January 1919.[3] As might have been expected, major emphasis was laid on 'the duty of investigation and thought as preliminary to action' throughout the whole field of government business. The Report also reviewed the various principles on which work might be distributed amongst government departments. It had no

[1] Royal Archives, K. 1263.   [2] Haldane papers.   [3] Cmd. 9230.

doubt that allocation according to the kind of service to be performed was the correct principle. It recognized that the adoption of this principle would make necessary a very large reorganization of the existing machinery, under which functions had been distributed according to no rational theory. In particular the functions relating to the administration of justice which were divided between the Home Office and the Lord Chancellor's Office should be allocated to a Ministry of Justice. This section of the Report was drafted by Haldane himself.[4] Haldane wrote to Gosse on 9 January 1919:

The main criticism is that too detailed an exposition has been devoted to the Ministry of Justice and particularly to the office of Lord Chancellor. This is to miss the point, which is that in the case of every other office than that of Lord Chancellor Statutes or Orders-in-Council, or Manuals, or Text-books, explain duties . . . In his case all the knowledge rests on unwritten tradition, which is locked up in the bosoms of about half a dozen men in each generation and passes with them.[5]

The Report also emphasized the importance of a small Cabinet served by an efficient Secretariat. Today this seems a commonplace, but before Hankey had begun to build up such a body in 1916 the Cabinet had not been organized at all. The only serious criticism made of this part of the Report is that it omits to take into account the important political fact that in peace-time a large Cabinet may be a necessity, for it is one of the prime functions of the Cabinet to maintain the ascendancy of the Government in Parliament.

The Report received a somewhat tepid welcome when it was published. The country was in the midst of the post-war general election. Nor have many of its detailed recommendations been adopted. Its real influence lies in the fact that for the first time people were encouraged to think about the structure and functions of government. 'To any student of British government it is such a familiar part of the furniture of the mind that it is hard to see it with detachment.'[6] In particular it became accepted that it was the duty of a government to encourage scientific research. In 1962 it was stated by the Lord President of the Council (Viscount Hailsham) that bodies like the Medical Research Council and D.S.I.R. owed their existence to Haldane.[7] Nothing would have pleased Haldane more than the knowledge that he had been responsible for bringing men of science into the work of the Government, particularly in the field of defence. The contributions of Tizard, Lindemann, and Watson-Watt were made possible by Haldane.

[4] *Autobiography*, p. 253.   [5] Gosse papers.
[6] C. H. Wilson, *Haldane and the Machinery of Government* (1956), p. 17.
[7] 235 H.L. Deb. 5s. col. 710–27.

Haldane's retirement gave him leisure to pursue his many interests outside law and politics. If Haldane had done nothing else in the world his activities in the fields of philosophy and adult education alone would entitle him to a high place in the ranks of British worthies. The catalogue of the Bodleian Library lists no fewer than seventy-four items under his name. Very few of these touch upon law or politics; the majority deal with philosophy or education. Some, indeed, are works by others, edited by or with an introduction by him, but the majority are books and lectures from his own pen.

His philosophy is particularly important for it provides a clue to what appeared to be deviousness in his character. G. M. Young, referring to Cosmo Gordon Lang, and Baldwin, once wrote[8] that he wished there was 'a neutral word for hypocrite'. Some of the puzzlement with which Haldane was viewed may be traceable to his realization of the 'many-sidedness of truth' which came from his philosophical studies. They are difficult to assess. H. G. Wells said of them: 'They are still spoken of with profound respect and a careful avoidance of particulars in academic circles, but they mark no turning point in the history of the human mind.'[9]

His two main books were his Gifford Lectures, entitled *The Pathway to Reality*, delivered in 1902 from elaborate notes made while staying in Scotland, and taken down in shorthand and reprinted. His later work, *The Reign of Relativity*, arose out of his interest in Einstein's Theory in the post-war years. Maugham doubted whether Haldane's mathematical knowledge was adequate for the task,[1] though Pollock gave a more favourable judgment.[2]

Haldane's memory, it may be noted, was always good for the structure of an argument, but poor on quotations and the details of legal cases. He made deliberate efforts to improve this, particularly after he became Lord Chancellor. So that his Gifford Lectures, delivered from memory, mark an interesting stage in this development.

The detailed assessment of Haldane's philosophical work is something that can only be undertaken by a specialist, and much the most valuable contribution on the question was published in a memoir in the *Proceedings of the British Academy*,[3] written by his old friend Professor Pringle-Pattison. Those who are interested in the matter should refer to it for further information. The following letter to Harold Laski, written on 7 April 1920, may serve as an illustration of the power of Haldane's

[8] To Mr. Charles Monteith.
[9] *Experiment in Autobiography* (1947), p. 87.
[1] *At the End of the Day*, p. 33.
[2] *Holmes-Pollock Letters*, ed. M. De Wolfe Howe (2nd ed., 1962), vol. ii, pp. 70–72.
[3] (1928) Proc. Brit. Acad. 405.

mind in these matters, as well as his interest in day-to-day politics. It also shows his courtesy to a then unknown young author.

I have been rereading your 'Authority in the Modern State', after reading the other books you have sent me. I think that you Pluralists make out an excellent case on the facts. Even Bosanquet does not dispute this. The phases of state life are numerous and divergent. But is the controversy a very real one? For my part I have found myself tending to the conclusion that there has been insufficient distinction made between the State and the Sovereignty which is exercised by governments on its behalf. The latter is limited by general opinion, and it expresses only certain aspects of that general opinion. I have no difficulty in recognising a General Will but that Will appears to me to be only partially expressed by governments. It is distributed among groups. To the Govt. is entrusted supreme *legal* power in a country like Great Britain. But the exercise of that power may be itself controlled by opinion, which often insists on the independence of its control of groups like the Church and the Trade Unions. This, however, does not exclude a General Will which may manifest itself as supreme, and may arm Govt. with extended authority on occasions. The New Realists and such Pluralists as Russell appear to me to assume unduly a particular view, under which individuality is atomic substance and not mind. Now mind is capable of genuine correspondence in purpose, even of actual identity in difference of reflection and the volition that is inseparable from it. The New Realists appear to me to fall into a dogmatic form of metaphysics, a metaphysic which is good against a Subjective Idealism, that itself treats an individual as atomic and exclusive, but is not good as against a deeper objective idealism like that of Aristotle and his modern successors. However, this is a divergence. I have been writing about it, and am therefore rather full of it.

The practical situation here is full of interest. Our old Liberalism is for the moment vigorous. But it is moribund. I am trying to find a new outlook which will serve Liberalism and Labour equally, without prejudicing their special programmes. Labour is responding so far much more than Liberalism, and I am overwhelmed with invitations to address Labour meetings. But I am going to address the Liberals of Manchester next week, who have elected me President of their Reform Club and asked me to try to give a lead in the new direction. Still mine is a voice crying in the wilderness. I have no organised party, and am very unpopular with the Old Liberals who look on me as a deserter. But that does not matter. I want to get the Universities on a large scale into the movement for extra mural higher teaching of the working classes, and that of Bristol, of which I am Chancellor, has given me a free hand.

I look forward to seeing you when you come over, and to hearing about your book. You have been wise in avoiding metaphysics. Look at the new edition of Bosanquet's Philosophical Theory of the State. He has come on in it. I addressed a Labour meeting the other day in Surrey under his auspices and at his invitation.[4]

4 Laski papers.

Another interest was higher education. As far back as 1902 Haldane had been the sole member of the Liberal Party to support Balfour's Education Act. To this cause, throughout his life, he devoted much time and labour. For the Workers' Educational Association and the British Institute of Adult Education he delivered more than one thousand addresses in the course of thirty years; many of them in obscure provincial towns, and in the years after he had ceased to be Lord Chancellor, when a certain degree of repose might have been permissible. He also obtained from the millionaire Cassel a very large sum of money to enable the British Institute of Adult Education to carry on its work.

These labours were of a kind which hardly any other public man in English life has undertaken. It was hard work at a low level; the passage of time and the development of the welfare state have made much of his labours during those years unnecessary, and today they tend to be forgotten, but it was admirable work well done.

He also took much part in the re-foundation of London University in its modern guise. The great question at the end of the 1890s was whether there should be two universities or one. The professors thought two, but Haldane was in favour of one large body, and by unwearying negotiation over the years, combined with one of his few really successful speeches in the House of Commons, he obtained the passage of the London University Act of 1898. The keynote of his speeches was the necessity for co-ordination and organization—themes which we find stressed again and again in his speeches on education and politics. His success over London University brought him into the even deeper waters of Irish University politics. At that date Trinity College, Dublin, was pre-eminent in Irish affairs; as Haldane himself said, 'It was the Ark of the Covenant which could not be touched.' Nevertheless the demand from the catholic nationalist majority for a university of their own was so strong that it could not possibly be ignored. Haldane crossed over to Ireland, and after a good deal of intrigue and secret visits to the Catholic Primate of All Ireland, which he much enjoyed, sent an admirable and fully worked out scheme to Balfour. But after much correspondence[5] throughout 1898 and 1899 a timid Unionist Cabinet turned the matter down. It was left for Birrell in 1908 to take Haldane's proposals from their pigeon hole and secure the passage of the Irish University Act of that year.

Haldane's general approach to university education and to several other matters is admirably illustrated by a speech which he delivered at Liverpool:

He would be a pedant who thought that education alone could determine the commercial position of a nation. Yet more than ever, as science tends

[5] To be found in Balfour papers.

increasingly to reduce nature to subjection, education becomes important. In the United States a highly practical people are taking this view, and it is noticeable that the rapid increase there of universities and technical schools is largely due to their faith in their efficiency shown by practical men of business. The millionaire in America seeks to save his soul by building, not churches, but colleges, and if he insists in embodying in their constitution ideas of his own which are not always the highest ideas, this shows his zeal. The British people are not yet a decaying race. The Anglo-Saxon, here as in America, is probably in energy, in courage and doggedness of purpose superior to all his European rivals in commerce . . . But organization and instruction have been carried to a far higher pitch in Germany and in Switzerland than with us, and if we are to hold our position we must furnish ourselves with the discipline and the weapons with which the foreigner has prepared himself for the contest. Now, in suggesting that reform of our education, and particularly of our tertiary education is essential, I am far from desiring to suggest that we ought to wish to see it entirely subordinated to utilitarian considerations. Culture is an end in itself, and if it is to be won it must be sought for its own sake. But the Germans have shown us how the university can fulfil a double function without slackening the effort after culture. In a certain exquisiteness the flowers of scholarship which Oxford and Cambridge have produced are probably without examples to rival them, unless it be in France. But for breadth and understanding who will dare to place the record of work done in Oxford or Cambridge in the department of classical literature above what has been turned out in Germany? Take the editing, and with it the criticism, of Greek philosophy, and compare the shallow formalities which did duty in the English universities up to about thirty years ago, when German ideas began to penetrate, with the work of German scholars . . . The conclusion of the whole matter seems to be that we could establish in Great Britain and Ireland a system of teaching of a university type, with the double aim of Germany, and that without injury to the quality of culture. We are proud of Oxford and Cambridge. They have taken centuries to grow up, they are rooted in splendid traditions which we seek not to disturb. But that does not make the educational reformer desire the less to see the expansion of another kind of teaching which they are not adapted to give, and which is none the less a national necessity.[6]

Indeed it was Haldane's interest in secondary and technical education which in the end led him out of the Liberal Party and into the Labour Party. He wrote to his mother in November 1917 that he found more real interest in these subjects amongst labour men than amongst fellow Liberals.[7] In January 1922 he refused to appear on a political platform with Asquith because of the lack of interest in education shown by the Liberal leaders.

Haldane had a long friendship with the Webbs, who regarded him with a somewhat baffled mixture of affection and suspicion. Mrs. Webb's

[6] Sommer, p. 101.   [7] N.L.S., 5998, f. 145.

diaries are full of references to him—on the whole genial, though there are occasional expressions of wonder at his appetite for the good things of life. Despite this close relationship he did not join the Fabian Society until 1925. It is worth noting that Haldane's interest in social improvement manifested itself solely in the field of adult education. The great scheme for national insurance upon which the welfare state is founded was outside his ken.

The General Election of 1923 brought Haldane out into the open in support of the Labour Party. He addressed several meetings in favour of Labour candidates. The results of the election were declared on 8 December and showed a distinct departure from the traditional two-party system of government. The Unionists formed 41 per cent of the House of Commons, Labour 31 per cent., and the Liberals 28 per cent. After some uncertainty Asquith decided to throw the Liberal vote in support of the Labour Party when the House of Commons met on 15 January. (Baldwin had decided not to resign forthwith but to await the verdict of the representatives of the electorate as declared on the floor of the House.) Fom mid-December it was therefore assumed by all that Ramsay Mac-Donald would be Prime Minister. It was also assumed that he would offer Haldane a post in his Cabinet, and Cave begged Haldane to accept the Woolsack (or any other post) in order 'to save the state'.[8] After some preliminary discussions with the senior members of his party, MacDonald withdrew to Lossiemouth for Christmas. He did not invite any communications from his colleagues as to the composition of the Cabinet; his sole confidant during this period appears to have been Haldane himself, who emerged as the first Labour Lord Chancellor. MacDonald lunched at Cloan on 4 January (it was noted approvingly that he was not a teetotaller), and much discussion took place during the day. Haldane agreed to join the Cabinet as Lord Chancellor, but stipulated that he should be relieved from judicial duties, and should be appointed Chairman of the Home Affairs Committee of the Cabinet. MacDonald also agreed that special consideration should be given to Haldane's interest in defence, It seems that Haldane's lengthy administrative experience was a fact which made MacDonald specially anxious to bring him into his Cabinet [9] Indeed, Haldane was asked to give the traditional dinner-party to consider the King's Speech on the eve of the session. Haldane wrote to his mother: 'The King's Speech Dinner went off remarkably well. At Bay's suggestion I provided both orangeade and lemonade. The unofficial cabinet meeting which followed was a remarkable display of competence and also of conservatism. I never attended a better cabinet meeting'.[1]

[8] Maurice, vol. ii, p. 137.
[9] See Viscount Snowden, *An Autobiography* (1934), p. 608.   [1] N.L.S., 6007, f. 84.

At the first Cabinet meeting proper after the Government was formed on 22 January Haldane 'at once jumped in full of geniality with a lesson in manners'.[2] MacDonald was to be 'Mr. Prime Minister'; other Ministers were to be referred to by their official titles or surnames.

Haldane wrote in January 1925, when he went out of office:

I am glad that I joined the Labour Party. It has made mistakes but its reality rests on this, that it is the party that is most in contact with the democracy of this country. That democracy does not include the whole of the labour leaders, but it includes a very large part of them, and with the growth of education that part is likely to increase. The mistake Tories and Whigs alike made was in failing to see that as the franchise was extended, and as Education permeated further and further, it became vital for any political party which desired to remain effective, to be in the closest contact with people and to break down the gaps which separate class from class unjustly. Labour is the only party that has so far succeeded in giving this faith to its supporters, and I think that will prove in the end to be the party that has really averted upheaval in this country. It may progress slowly but seems to me to be progressing surely.[3]

Haldane wrote to his mother in 1924 that one reason for his joining the Labour Government was 'to allay the wild and unreasoning alarms which prevailed as to what a Socialist Government would do, and so help to kill class prejudice'.[4] The decision necessarily involved some further lessening of contact with his old Liberal friends, especially Asquith. Letters were exchanged on the subject. On 22 January 1924 Haldane wrote:

My dear A.,
            Tomorrow I take office under a government of which you are not the head.

It is with a very real sense of sadness that I realise that. My mind goes back to evenings before either of us could contemplate Parliament for ourselves, evenings in which we were none the less concentrated on ideas. And I think of old days at Cloan, and at Auchterarder, and in London. Nor do I forget how you stood by me, and fought for me over the Chancellorship in 1905, and how you put me there in 1912. Believe me I am not oblivious of these things.

Now it is a new period, and the adventure is both difficult and uncertain. It is not without misgiving that I face it. But I do not consider that I have the right to stand aside in this hour.

None the less, the old sense of personal affection and of gratitude remains with me. But for you I should not have been where I am—whatever that may stand for.

2 J. Webb, 'The First Labour Government' (1961), 32 The Political Quarterly, p. 6.
3 Maurice, vol. ii, pp. 180–1.   4 N.L.S., 6007, f. 26.

And so I will continue to the end to describe myself as
Yours ever affectionately,
H. of C.[5]

Asquith independently described this as a touching letter,[6] and he replied on the same day:

My dear H.,

I was greatly touched by your letter. The memories to which you refer are, and will remain to the end, fresh in my mind. They are associated with the best days of my life.

I share in the fullest degree your regret that after so many years of close cooperation and almost unbroken agreement we should now be called upon to part company.

You are a far better judge than I can be of what, in these strange conditions, is your duty. I confess to a profound distrust, not of the good intentions, but of the judgment of your associates. I sincerely hope I may prove to be wrong.

And as for yourself, as you know, my old feelings never have been, and never will be, the least abated.
Always yours affectionately,
H. H. A.[7]

Haldane worked hard in MacDonald's Cabinet. He viewed some of its customs with amusement and others with puzzlement. He noted that the Cabinets were 'often fixed for hours to which those of us whose ways were not those of the average working man found awkward, 8.45 p.m. for instance'. On the other hand he instigated the practice of smoking in Cabinet, hitherto totally unknown, but as nobody had sufficient experience to check him the practice was adopted with general approval. Haldane cast rather a dubious eye on MacDonald's habit of retiring to Chequers for the week-end, where he was inaccessible to his subordinates.

Haldane was often asked why he had chosen the Woolsack in Mac-Donald's Cabinet instead of the Ministry of Education, as it was education and its problems which had brought him into the Labour fold; but he explained convincingly that he thought that there was an adequate supply of talent in the Labour Party to deal with educational problems, whereas his peculiar asset was long experience of the essential problems of government, particularly as they concerned defence. By taking the Woolsack and by being relieved from the judicial duties of the office Haldane thought he was able to contribute most to the State. He sat constantly on the Committee of Imperial Defence, but some thought that his contribu-

---

[5] Asquith papers.
[6] Asquith, *Memories and Reflections*, vol. ii, p. 209.   [7] N.L.S. 5916, f. 76.

tions were not an entire success. He had reached the age at which a man is entitled to reminisce and the Chiefs of Staff disliked opening up in his presence. Meetings of the C.I.D. therefore, tended to be a failure for the dispatch of business, though the members listened politely to the lengthy monologues from their chairman.[8]

On the administrative side of the Lord Chancellor's office, 'Thanks to Schuster's quick intelligence we have done much in the Lord Chancellor's office for which future Lord Chancellors will bless me.'[9] Haldane, as might have been expected, instituted proposals for a Ministry of Justice to take over the administrative side of the courts from the Treasury on the one hand and the Lord Chancellor's office on the other, but these made little headway. The Government had neither the time nor the power to effect large-scale reforms.

After his retirement from office in November 1924, Haldane reluctantly agreed to lead the Labour Opposition in the Lords. He did not think it right 'to run away from them in their adversity'.[1] He took an active part in the workings of a committee set up to investigate the supply of dye-stuffs and also in the debates over the Central Electricity Board, which set up the grid system, and over the coal dispute.

In 1926 he also published *Human Experience*, a valuable introduction to philosophy in general, and his own in particular. Towards the end he permitted himself some words on the fundamentals of religious belief which give a clue to his own mind on these matters.

In November 1927, he was involved in a somewhat disagreeable controversy with his former leader, Ramsay MacDonald, about his conduct in permitting Austen Chamberlain to quote a memorandum which he had prepared as Lord Chancellor for the information of the Foreign Office. The memorandum expressed the view that many of our problems required consideration from the point of view of the British Empire, and not of Great Britain alone. MacDonald objected to the disclosure of this memorandum on the ground that his permission, as the Prime Minister in office at the time, had not been obtained; more particularly as the memorandum in question was to be used against the Labour Party. The incident ended in an agreement being patched up which, in truth, only concealed fundamental differences.

Haldane's last months were now at hand. For the first time his body failed him. His physical appearance was now that of a very old man. Now he spared himself the task which he had laid upon himself of sitting upon every Dominion appeal raising a point of consitutional law. But he pressed on with his various works.

[8] Information from Lord Hankey.   [9] Maurice, vol. ii, p. 175.
[1] N.L.S., 5923, f. 23.

He was an ideal chief. He expected others to take responsibility, and he was ready and willing to devolve responsibility upon them. His temper was naturally sweet and still unsoured by public obloquy. He attacked his duties with a boyish zest which he communicated to his subordinates. Always courteous, always considerate, he seemed to command affection, and in its enjoyment he expanded. But he knew his own mind, he pressed on to his own goal, undeflected by clamour, undepressed by solitude, unfaltering in the face of death.[2]

The only serious critical reference which has been found to Haldane at this period is in a letter written by Sumner to Buckmaster on 31 August 1928:

All the prophecies when I came away were that we should not see Haldane again. Prophecies are not often so right. I suppose speeches will be made in the House by those who feel called upon to make them, of whom I am not one, but I think most people in the know would agree that he went on, judicially at any rate, too long. As for philosophy, I could never make anything of it: as with Johnson's Pembroke friend, 'Cheer and pleasure would keep breaking through'.[3]

This seems to be one of the less happy examples of Sumner's acute but bitter mind. As president of a tribunal Haldane in his last years may have been a little slower and more reminiscent than he had been. But his judgments show no sign of intellectual exhaustion. His last case was *Medway Oil Co., Ltd.* v. *Continental Contractors, Ltd.*[4] in which shortly before his death he had prepared an elaborate judgment on a difficult question relating to taxation of costs. It is worthy of a place beside his great series of judgments in 1914.

At the end of July 1928 Haldane was very ill and retired to Cloan. It was characteristic of him that he should have sent to a Canadian friend, Professor W. P. M. Kennedy of Toronto, an apology for his inability to receive two young research students who had arrived in London with letters of introduction.[5] Haldane died at Cloan on 19 August 1928. His estate was sworn for probate at £78,000. For the funeral his body was carried down the hill to the family burying ground at Gleneagles at the end of the avenue of great beech trees. The last religious ceremony in the private chapel there had been the baptism of Robert Haldane in 1706. A large contingent of soldiers, Regular and Territorial, attended the service. The grave is marked by a fine stone column. On the right hand side there

[2] C. Schuster, *Lord Haldane* (1928), p. 33.
[3] Buckmaster papers. The quotation from Johnson's friend Oliver Edwards is not quite correct (Boswell, 17 April 1778).
[4] [1929] A.C. 88.
[5] W. P. M. Kennedy, *Lord Haldane* (1929) 6 Can. Bar Rev. 567.

is a memorial inscription to Elizabeth Haldane, on the left one to her brother, John Scott Haldane, the physician. In the centre a finely wrought inscription commemorates their brother.

Richard Burdon
Viscount Haldane of Cloan
K.T., O.M.
Born July 30th 1856
Died August 19th 1928
Secretary of State for War 1905–1912
Lord High Chancellor
1912–1915 and 1924
A great servant of the
State
who devoted his life
to the advancement and
application of knowledge.
Through his work in
fashioning her army
he rendered invaluable aid
to his country in her time of
direst need.

Time has strengthened the claims to truth of this lapidary inscription. The plaque which the London County Council placed on the wall of 28 Queen Anne's Gate commemorates the fact that R. B. Haldane, 'Statesman, Lawyer, Philosopher', lived there. The various facets of Haldane's massive talents are placed in the correct order. As a philosopher he was entitled to a place in distinguished company; as a lawyer he was entitled to rank very high in the small number of gifted equity jurists who have held the Great Seal; but as a statesman he left an achievement which was of permanent value not only to the British people but to the civilized world whose values he had so nobly upheld throughout his life.

APPENDIX

Company Law. Haldane's first reported judgment, delivered on 4 May 1911, after he had been appointed a member of the Judicial Committee under section 1 of the 1833 Act, dealt with the obligations of company promoters: *Att.-Gen. for Canada* v. *Standard Trust Co.* [1911] A.C. 146.

His philosophical training enabled him to deal very convincingly with the problem of corporate personality in *Lennard's Carrying Co., Ltd.* v. *Asiatic Petroleum Co., Ltd.* [1915] A.C. 705.

Real Property and Equity. All students are familiar with a series of great judgments by Haldane which take up many pages of the 1914 Appeal Cases. In *Kreglinger* v. *New Patagonia Meat Co.* (p. 25) he restated the rules relating to clogging the equity of redemption in a masterly fashion. In *Whiteley* v. *Delaney* (p. 132) he handled the problems of priority amongst several mortgagees, and in *Sinclair* v. *Brougham* (p. 398) there is an authoritative survey of the scope of the doctrine of restitution or quasi-contract. Likewise in *Nocton* v. *Ashburton* (p. 932) he dealt admirably with the meaning of 'equitable fraud', and induced the House to place an important limitation on their previous decision in *Derry* v. *Peek* (1889), which, as we have seen, held that in an action of deceit actual fraud must be proved.

In *Ward* v. *Van der Loeff* [1924] A.C. 653, he gave a short but clear explanation of the Rule against Perpetuities.

In *Houston* v. *Burns* [1918] A.C. 337 there is an admirable exposition of the law relating to charitable trusts.

Industrial Law. There is a good judgment in *Vacher* v. *London Society of Compositors* [1913] A.C. 167 holding that the immunity from suit conferred by the Trade Disputes Act, 1906, was not limited to torts committed in the course of trade disputes.

Constitutional Law. Haldane's important judgments on Canadian constitutional law have already been considered. Other important judgments in constitutional cases will be found in *Great West Saddlery Co.* v. *R.* [1921] 2 A.C. 91, and *Hull* v. *M'Kenna* [1926] I. R. 402 in which he explained the principles on which the Judicial Committee would grant leave to appeal from the final court of appeal within a Dominion. A copy was sent to Windsor with the vital passages marked for the King's attention.

In *Local Government Board* v. *Arlidge* [1915] A.C. 120 Haldane delivered a judgment which showed a wise appreciation of the true nature of the relationship between a Minister and his civil servants. An objector to a closing order made in relation to slum property by the L.G.B. was held not to be entitled to see the inspector's report or to have revealed the name of the individual civil servant who had made the decision in the Minister's name. His governmental experience saved Haldane from making a serious error into which a more theoretical judge might have fallen.

Torts. In *Herd* v. *Weardale Steel Co., Ltd.* [1915] A.C. 67 he considered the scope of false imprisonment.

In *G.W.R.* v. *Mostyn (Owners)* [1928] A.C. 57 he concurred with the majority in holding that the Harbours, Docks, and Piers Clauses Act, 1847, s. 74, imposes an absolute liability on a shipowner for damage done to a harbour installation. Haldane's judgment contains some interesting observations on the earlier decision of the House in the *River Wear Commissioners Case* (1877). The *River Wear Case* certainly decided something as between the parties to it, but what general principle, if any, it laid down has been a complete puzzle to later generations. Haldane remarked that 'The very power of rhetoric which Lord Cairns commanded when stating his conclusions about matters of legal principle, makes it the more desirable to see that we are following the substance rather than the form of his propositions.' Other judgments will be found in *Taff Vale Railway Co.* v. *Jenkins* [1913] A.C. 1 (assessment of damages under Fatal Accidents Acts); *Neville* v. *London Express Newspaper* [1919] A.C. 368 (maintenance); *London Joint Stock Bank* v. *Macmillan* [1918] A.C. 777 (duty of customer to bank).

Contract. Good judgments will be found in *Mason* v. *Provident Clothing Co., Ltd.* [1913] A.C. 724 (restraint of trade), a subject also dealt with in *North Western Salt Co.* v. *Electrolytic Alkali Co.* [1914] A.C. 461; *Heilbut, Symons & Co.* v. *Buckleton* [1913] A.C. 13 (sale of goods); *Dawsons, Ltd.* v. *Bonnin* [1922] 2 A.C. 413 (mis-statements in insurance policy); *Lake* v. *Simmons* [1927] A.C. 487 (mistake).

In *Dunlop Pneumatic Tyre Co., Ltd.* v. *Selfridge & Co., Ltd.* [1915] A.C. 847 there is an authoritative survey of the right of a third party to sue on a contract made for his benefit which contains the oft-cited *dictum* 'Our law knows nothing of a *ius quaesitum tertio* arising by way of contract'.

Conflict of Laws. There is an important judgment in *Von Lorang* v. *Austrian Property Administrator* [1927] A.C. 641, holding that jurisdiction to annul a void marriage is possessed by the courts of a foreign country if both parties are domiciled there at the time of the suit.

LORD BUCKMASTER

CHAPTER I

THE SMALL VILLAGE OF SLAPTON, in Buckinghamshire, is really no more than a hamlet. It consists of a group of houses straggling around an old stone church. In the churchyard there are tombstones to Buckmasters who have been resident in the parish and owners of Slapton Mill for at least 200 years, and there are still people of that name resident there today. There is no evidence that any of the family ever owned the right to bear arms. They were mostly content to be agricultural labourers amidst the heavy clayey soil of the Midlands.

To these phlegmatic Saxon labourers there came an Irish girl, Phoebe Price, as the wife of one Thomas Buckmaster. Their child, John Charles, was a remarkable person.[1] Starting life working in the fields at Slapton at the age of 10 for the sum of 2 shillings a week, he rapidly became dissatisfied and at the age of 13 left the hamlet, never to return for fifty years.

After a period of apprenticeship to a joiner he became involved in politics and toured the agricultural counties of England speaking with vehemence against the corn laws. By this time he had acquired not only some education for himself but also a wife, one Emily Anne, daughter of George Goodliffe, of Trumpington, near Cambridge. On the advice of Lord Morpeth John Buckmaster went to a training college for teachers and later was appointed to teach science on its staff; finally he achieved an appointment in the Imperial College of Science and Technology. In his later years he lived at Ashleigh, Hampton Wick, and obtained a seat on the Magistrate's Bench at Spelthorne in Middlesex where for many years he dispensed an unconventional but efficient form of justice.

On 9 January 1861 his third son, Stanley Owen Buckmaster, the future Lord Chancellor, was born at 2 New Road (now Prested Road), off St. John's Hill, Wandsworth, a small yellow-brick house (now demolished) in an undistinguished street in South London near Clapham Junction, where the family was then living. On the birth certificate the father's profession was entered as 'Professor of Chemistry'. The boy was later baptized at Christ Church, Battersea, and confirmed at Watford on 19 June 1877.

By this time he had been sent to school at Aldenham Grammar School near Elstree in Hertfordshire. This was a small but fairly well-endowed Elizabethan foundation which had not, at that period, discreetly trans-

[1] See *A Village Politician: the Life-Story of John Buckley* [J. C. Buckmaster] (1897).

formed itself into a Public School by dropping the word 'Grammar', as it was later to do in company with many other educational institutions of similar character.

When Stanley Buckmaster went to Aldenham, if we may use the modern name for the school, he found it in low water. There were only five boys in the sixth form. The buildings were few and depressing, and the Headmaster was an elderly and unsuccessful parson called Leeman, who spent the day behind the closed doors of his study wearing carpet slippers, only bursting out with a cane in his hand when the uproar became too great. The hardships which the boys endured in these unattractive surroundings made the deepest impression on Buckmaster's mind.[2] It is probable that he would not have survived the rigours of a Victorian Public School had it not been for the devoted efforts of one master, by name Herbert McGill. This admirable man not merely fostered the growing boy's interest in learning with such success that he obtained a Junior Studentship in mathematics at Christ Church in 1879, but also built up a friendly personal relationship with the boy, as is shown by the following letter in 1874:

Your rod ought to make its appearance sometime today, and I hope that it will suit your no doubt fastidious taste. I trust that in the future, when you are even a more experienced fisher than at present, you may often have to thank it for a full basket.

Remember, however, that you have no one to thank for it but your own industry and good conduct. I wish you to let your father know that I never gave this prize with greater pleasure than now, and that your conduct during the past half year has been everything I could wish. I had intended coming down to call on your father yesterday, but, as I am only in town for one day I couldn't find time.

This afternoon I start for Leeds and next week for Scotland, where I shall probably frequently be seen standing up to my knees in water, in the pouring rain, with my rod in my hand and an empty basket on my back. It is lucky that everyone hasn't the same ideas of enjoyment. If everybody fished, there would soon be no fish left. Universal birds nesting would soon leave no birds nests—and perhaps everyone would have to take to butterflies and so on to spiders.[3]

McGill lived long enough to be able to send a letter of congratulation when Buckmaster was made Lord Chancellor.

The arrival of a new Headmaster, the Rev. J. Kennedy, also made a great difference to the school after 1879.

There still survive in the archives at Aldenham all the mark books which

---

[2] *The Aldenhamian* (1882—current) contains much information about the school in the nineteenth century. Many details were also supplied by Mr. C. A. Stott.

[3] Buckmaster papers.

PLATE 9

Lord Buckmaster leaving Westminster Abbey

PLATE 10

Lord Buckmaster in later life

McGill kept for his different classes. They are beautifully illustrated with small coloured cartoons of the boys in the different classes, amongst whom Buckmaster is prominent.

The great day came in March 1879 when his election at Christ Church was announced at Aldenham in the following telegram from H. J. Gerrans, a mathematics tutor at Worcester College. 'You are elected Stop Accept congratulations Stop Write to Sampson and he will send you all particulars Stop Be precise in your questions Stop'.[4] The Christ Church Committee which recommended him for a Junior Studentship was composed of C. L. Dodgson, E. F. Sampson, and R. E. Baynes.[5] In October he went up to the House—buying from Adamson, the tailor in the High, 'A black superfine dress suit' for £5. 5s. 0d.[6] Stanley Buckmaster never forgot the good fortune which he had obtained by reason of his industry in the study of mathematics. Many years later, when he had risen to eminence, and was an Honorary Student of the House, he attended a Gaudy at which he delivered an after-dinner speech. This is notoriously a most difficult form of oratory in which to excel but a passage describing the House of his time may be quoted from it.

The venerable form of Dr. Pusey could still occasionally be seen. Canon Liddon was in constant residence; Liddon, whose face once seen could never be forgotten, whose voice and eloquence could, at a moment's notice, fill to overflowing the vast spaces of St. Paul's. The sermons of Canon Scott Holland poured like hot lava down the cathedral aisles. Canon King was always with us, whose simplicity and saintliness of life inspired the affection and reverence of even the most reckless of us all, and there was also dear old learned Canon Bright, between whom and myself there was a close link of feeling in our common worship of Walter Scott, a link that was a little strained one day when he asked me the name of the man who had been kept in the dungeon where the Duke of Rothesay was starved to death, and whose life was prolonged by a few grains of corn that intermittently fell through the grating. I regret to say I did not know, what is common knowledge to each one of you, that the man's name was Dalwosny.

There was also Dodgson, who attempted to impose on the ignorance of undergraduates by pretending that he was a tutor of mathematics instead of being the immortal author of 'Alice'. And above them all towered the majestic figure of Dean Liddell, whose blessing in the cathedral always made me wish that I could have heard his voice in the rolling magnificence of mediaeval anathema. Dr. Liddell it was who, when a young, shy student, breakfasting at the Deanery, thought the Dean might be interested in a perfectly simple and indisputable scientific fact, thundered the answer: 'Sir, things do not, and never could, exist as you assert them to be.' Science in those days drew bitter and

---

[4] Buckmaster papers.   [5] Information from R. H. Dundas.
[6] Buckmaster papers. All his Oxford bills have been carefully preserved.

perilous breath. It was, by common consent, a study unworthy of the consideration of gentlemen, though it must be admitted that most of the gentlemen found no other study to take its place. . . . There was Talbot, who restored the waning prestige of the House for scholarship by being *proxime accessit* for the Hertford, and it is what might appropriately be described as a cardinal article of faith for Christ Church men that he would have won the prize but for the introduction of an alien influence from Balliol on the board of examiners— Balliol, who was constitutionally unable to appreciate the niceties, and I must admit the rarity, of Christ Church scholarship.[7]

The last few sentences are perhaps characteristic of the man, for devoted son of the House as he was, he was also devoted to the truth and the truth was that in the Oxford of his day, and, above all at Christ Church, the cause of science in general and mathematics in particular was not highly regarded. Buckmaster never forgot that he had left behind him at Aldenham boys who were not even given the chance of undergoing this somewhat despised course of education. Only two of his contemporaries achieved any distinction—W. T. Barnard, who later became a K.C., and Alfred Gilbert, later R.A. and a well-known sculptor. When he was Lord Chancellor he took up the question of Oxford education with some interest and was disappointed to discover how few scholarships in science were available even forty years after his undergraduate time. In a memorandum to his colleagues in October 1916 he said:

Speaking of a school where I myself was educated, it gives an excellent example of what I mean. It was one of the old Elizabethan Grammar Schools. It was intended and stated to be for the benefit of poor boys. It was quite well endowed. There are scholarships from the school to the University, but the boys who do not get these scholarships relax into the humbler forms of commercial life. They become bank clerks, solicitors' clerks and all that large mass of ill paid and ill organized labour which is fed from the mistakes of our educational systems. Oxford ought to set an example at once.

Buckmaster criticized the system under which

nearly all the best minds of the University must necessarily be those of boys whose parents are unable to bear unaided the expense of a University training. For them the thing that is essential is that they should get a scholarship and the masters of the Public Schools satisfy this demand by seizing hold of every bright boy and diverting his intelligence at once to the study of classics in order that he may be certain to win his way by his own work. It is impossible to blame the school master for this. But it not only affects every Public School but it affects all the smaller Public Schools whose boys are also training for the same purpose. It follows that classical masters are sought for at the schools and

[7] J. Johnston, *An Orator of Justice* (1932), pp. 258–9.

thereby an artificial demand is kept up for classical learning which is not justified on its merits.[8]

In spite of the fact that the vast majority of the undergraduates at Christ Church then came from families of a rather different background, Buckmaster led a happy life, mixing freely with his contemporaries by whom he was respected and admired. One of them wrote after his death:

He came up at a somewhat earlier age than did most of us. And he seemed to us to be a little precocious—precocious rather as a moralist and a humanist than as a mathematician and a scientist. In a quite attractive fashion he would—to recall Matthew Arnold's phrase—both Hebraize and Hellenize. Not that he would quote this poet; the antithesis would not have appealed to him; he was a lover of Browning, and it was Browning's synthesis that he made his own.[9] We wondered why he was not going to read for Greats. Getting to know him better, we soon discovered that a slightly supercilious manner was in reality less the expression of, than the effort to veil, a certain consciousness of mission, a consciousness sufficiently serious and assured to afford to be patient and to bide its time.

His noteworthy oratorical gifts were unsuspected by us; I cannot remember him ever to have spoken at the Union. But his thrust and parry in conversation were brilliant and rapid—though never did any venom soil his rapier's point—and foreshadowed the master of today.[1]

His tutor during his first year was W. Warner, and after him E. F. Sampson, under whom he obtained a Second Class in Mathematical Moderations in 1881. Letters of commiseration arrived from friends at the House, among them Ernest Eyre, who had just obtained a Second in Honour Moderations.

We both had d——d, —no, I don't mean that of course—but most 'trying' luck in the matter of Schools. A common contempt for such frivolities shall make us take a wider view of life than that seen through the glass of examiner's verdicts. In my own case I was, I confess, more astonished than disgusted: not by my own failures, as by the success of others, who shall be nameless.

However 'to each man his fate' as says my Algernon! I can forgive, while I despise, the folly of examiners—'Leviora Canamus'. The Fatherland has left me with an admiration for duelling, and a passion for Heine. I think we might introduce the former at Ch. Ch. It was the great excitement of the aristocratic students at Heidelberg: why should not the Bullingdon be induced to try it? A little loss of blood (in a healthy way!) would do them good.[2]

[8] Buckmaster papers.

[9] Amongst Buckmaster's papers is a letter of 1885 to his future wife, in which the young lady received an acute and lengthy essay on the literary achievement of Browning.

[1] Watkin Williams in Oxford (1935), p. 89.   [2] Buckmaster papers.

After 1881 Buckmaster seems—the Christ Church records are defective—to have studied mainly with H. J. Gerrans of Worcester.

Like many an undergraduate before or since hard pressed for money in the Long Vacation he accepted a position as tutor to a young boy, Gerald Lascelles, the son of Sir Frank Lascelles, then British Minister to Roumania. This meant a journey out to Bucharest and then all the excitement of living with a diplomatic family. Before his departure his father sent him a letter of affectionate good advice:

I hope the work will be pleasant and that you will make friends and gain experience. I need not impress upon you the advisability of being cautious and respectful without being servile or obsequious. Your surroundings are, of course, very different to your own home but your education and Oxford connection places you on terms of social equality with the wealthiest.[3]

Amongst his papers, carefully preserved, are letters from the Lascelles family which show the respect and affection which the earnest undergraduate had awakened in them.

When Buckmaster returned from Bucharest to Oxford he at once started working hard for his Schools. Here, unfortunately, he was unsuccessful in obtaining a First, the examiners placing him in the Second Class. The disappointment was the keener as each of his elder brothers, Charles and George, had obtained a First.[4] The sad story is told in a series of letters which begin with one to his father:

You will naturally be anxious to know how I have been faring during the last week and I should have written to inform you what was going on had I been able to do it, but each day's examination left me so tired that I could not set myself to write.

I think I have been the victim of the cruellest fate. The first three days of the exam I felt pretty well, in fact Gerrans was delighted and I reckoned my class secure, but on the fourth the strain began to tell on me and on the fifth—the most important day of all—I was rendered utterly unfit to do even a paper in arithmetic. It was no use trying, my brain simply refused to perform its functions and had my very existence depended on doing the paper before me I could not have done it. It was not that I did not know the work, I did know it and knew it perfectly. It was not that I was nervous, on the contrary I was quite cool, but I could not think and any attempt at it caused me such pain that I was forced to desist from the attempts, so with my face positively in my hands I was compelled to leave the Schools and passed a most awful night. On the last

[3] Buckmaster papers.
[4] Charles became Assistant Secretary in the Board of Education, and George Professor of Physiology at Bristol University after having been assistant to Burdon Sanderson, the brother-in-law of Herschell, at the same time as John Haldane. Another brother, Martin Buckmaster, died in 1961 aged 99 years.

morning I was better but not well and did a good paper again. But in the afternoon I was again baffled and so concluded the examination by giving all the men in—all Scholars—a paper and half's start. I determined not to scratch, it would have been no use, and I awaited the list in expectancy of seeing the six men in the first two classes and myself in the third. The result which was published this morning was better than my expectations but it only served to show how entirely my health had lost what I know my work could have gained.[5]

To these pathetic sentences his parents replied with affectionate understanding. His father wrote:

My dear boy,
        I hasten to acknowledge your letter. I am quite satisfied with the result. My only regret is that you should have been compelled to leave the Schools through your over-work. We are all glad that it is over and you have done well, better than many who have had greater opportunities. Do not let the result trouble you as it will not trouble me. Take things easily. A little rest and agreeable society will soon remove your disappointment which I fear is greater to you than to any of us because we had long settled your class and your future will not be much influenced by the result. It is a position of which many may be proud. If the weather be favourable take a long walk with a friend and don't talk about the examination or the class, or examiners, but the sky, the flowers and anything but mathematics. We look forward to a pleasant Christmas and anything I can do to promote your future happiness and welfare I will do.
        With best love and wishes.

Yours affectionately,
J. C. B.[6]

A letter of commiseration had also arrived from his tutor in the gloomy interval before the results were announced:

My dear Buckmaster:
        I need scarcely assure you that however great your disappointment may be at the untoward result of all your labours, that disappointment does not exceed mine, for I had looked forward to a different end of your mathematical studies. I am not going to weary you with commonplaces: you have had enough already I expect; but I would insist that you have done right in not scratching and that the affect on your after life will differ only infinitesimally from that which might have been expected had our hopes proved true.
        My grief is great, both as friend and as teacher: but it does not blind me and prevent me from seeing great possibilities in store for you. May they be realized!
        For the present take care of your health and busy yourself with your preparations for your mother's visit and your subsequent farewell to the scene of three

[5] Buckmaster papers.   [6] Ibid.

and a half years of your life. If I am not too late, in consequence of my ignorance of the collection customs of Worcester, may I expect you to bring your mother to breakfast on Tuesday at eight thirty? Ever in adversity,

Yours sincerely,
Henry J. Gerrans[7]

A letter also reached John Buckmaster from Dr. E. F. Sampson of Christ Church:

I venture to send you a line about your son. I believe he would have had a 1st if he had not persisted in working too hard:—the only way I can account for his breakdown is that his brain was overwrought. Mr. Gerrans, whom I talked to about him, fully agrees with me. I am most anxious that he should not over tax himself during the next few months. I have talked to him about it—but I feel he is not to be trusted on this matter and so I am troubling you with this letter, that you may know what we think about him here, and if you can see any chance of his doing more than he ought to do, pray, if you think it right to do so, do what you can to prevent it.

Let me add how thoroughly I have learnt to respect the honest and thorough work of your son. He never really cared for mathematics but his readiness to work is all one could possibly ask from a man. I am most sorry that he has not more to show for the hard work he has done, but of the work itself I cannot speak too highly. His fault was over anxiety from work. I am very anxious this fault should not interfere with his career in life.[8]

It is perhaps a pity that no one could foretell the future and console Buckmaster by telling him that another Lord Chancellor, Lyndhurst, had, as an undergraduate at Trinity College, Cambridge, worked too hard for his final examination in mathematics in 1794 and had also exchanged some pathetic letters on the topic with his anxious parents.[9] Despite all the changes in the scope and nature of university education, sad cases of breakdown from overwork still occur, and the remedy is no more obvious than it was eighty years ago.

So Buckmaster went down from Oxford in the summer of 1882, disappointed in not achieving more in the way of academic success, but with a number of sound friends who would be with him throughout his life. During his career at Christ Church he had mixed widely and taken an active part in sporting as well as intellectual activities. In 1881 he had been one of the winners of the Christ Church 'pairs' and in February of the following year rowed number 5 in the college Torpid. In the same year he obtained first prize for throwing the cricket ball, the future Viceroy of India, George Curzon of Balliol, being placed second.

[7] Buckmaster papers.
[8] Ibid.
[9] T. Martin, *Life of Lord Lyndhurst* (1884), pp. 29–32.

The carefully preserved Battels in Buckmaster's papers also perhaps indicate that he had taken part in some of the more traditional pleasures of the Christ Church undergraduate, for moderate as the sums are for each term there is always an entry of a shilling or two under the heading 'damage' and 'glazier'.

CHAPTER II

AFTER GOING DOWN FROM OXFORD in 1882 Buckmaster lost no time in being called to the Bar by the Inner Temple in June 1884. He went as a pupil to Edward Beaumont at 6 New Square, Lincoln's Inn, ordering on 7 July from Ede and Ravenscroft of Chancery Lane, his wig, gown, bands, band case, and blue brief bag, for a total sum of £9. 18s. 0d.[1] He obtained the money to do so from various sources; some from his affectionate family, some from an Aldenham friend called Richard Platt, and the rest by the devices traditional to impecunious young men in the Temple—lecturing, writing, and examining. In later life he used to say that his hardest time was when he found a pile of examination papers waiting for him in the evening. In June 1886, however, life at the Bar was so hard that he applied (unsuccessfully) for the post of Chief Clerk to the City and Guilds Institute. Two Q.C.s whom he consulted told him: 'the prospect is very hopeless'. Edward Beaumont, whose pupil he had been, wrote: 'I will almost guarantee that *in time* you will succeed if you stay with us, but when that time will be is a painful subject for reflection.'[2] He managed to hold on at the Bar, and in 1887 he published a volume on Bills of Sale—a traditionally complex legal subject. But it was difficult: in one year his fees brought in only £46: in another his total income was only £117. He also took some part in politics. In 1884 he went to hear Gladstone speak at Midlothian and in 1886 he felt bold enough to speak himself in support of the Liberal candidate at Evesham in Worcestershire.

By this time he had also acquired a small practice on the Midland Circuit. In 1887 one of the small fruit-growers in the area was sued by a well-known money-lender named Isaac Gordon. Friends of the fruit-grower rallied round and collected five pounds to fight the money-lender and their thoughts turned to the young barrister who had pleased them so well at the elections. Buckmaster came down from London for a fee of three guineas. Amongst his papers is preserved a letter of 9 December 1887 from a firm of solicitors in Evesham enclosing a cheque for £3. 5s. 6d. in the case of *Smith* v. *Gordon* with thanks for his 'attention to the matter and able advocacy'. There is a note in Buckmaster's handwriting: 'One of the first cases I had. I went from London to Evesham and stayed the night, fee three guineas. I wonder what the Bar would think of it today, but it laid a brick for my foundations. I defeated Isaac

[1] Buckmaster papers.   [2] Ibid.

Gordon for the first time.' The character of this money-lender can best be described by an extract from the judgment of Lord Justice A. L. Smith in *Gordon* v. *Street*[3]:

I must here state who the plaintiff Isaac Gordon is; and, in order that there may be no inaccuracy, I will cite only from his own letters and his own admission as to what manner of man he is. He describes himself in writing when pressing the defendant as 'the extortionate and usurious money lender with about a gross of aliases, and that he is the hottest and bitterest of creditors'. He admits that he is not a British subject, but was born in Russia, and has been convicted of fraud, and has charged 3000% interest, but would not say if he had charged 5000%; that he carried on business under six or eight different aliases at Birmingham, Bristol, Bath, Manchester, Liverpool, Oxford, London and Leeds.

On this particular occasion, however, Buckmaster was too much for him. Before the jury he made a great point that Gordon had taken as security articles belonging to the farmer such as silver spoons. His picture of Gordon caught the jury's favourable attention and a verdict was given for the defendant. This greatly enhanced Buckmaster's reputation and in a few months he was again called down to Worcester to champion the cause of a small farmer against the same money-lender. This other farmer had also borrowed a sum and had been sued on his promissory note and had judgment given against him and his house and home sold up by the sheriff, with the result that his wife had been delivered of a child in a barn. Then a legal flaw was discovered. The writ had been served not on the farmer but on someone else and therefore all the proceedings were a nullity. Damages for trespass were claimed against Gordon and he counterclaimed the sums owed on the promissory note. A well-known barrister from Birmingham was briefed for Gordon when the case came on at the Worcester County Court. He took a line which exposed him to a damaging reply from Buckmaster. On cross-examination for the plaintiff he drew from him the comparatively trivial cost of the furniture and other articles which had been sold, thinking that against this loss he could put the far greater sum claimed on the note. But Buckmaster made the point that a home is not to have its value measured by the few sticks of furniture which it contains. This argument prevailed with the jury, who would have awarded a grossly inflated sum by way of damages had it not been for the judge's control over them. One result of all this was that Isaac Gordon's solicitor sent briefs to Buckmaster, and by this means brought him to the High Court in London—for money-lenders in those days were always careful to be represented by counsel of weight and respectability.[4]

[3] [1899] 2 Q.B. 621, at 648.   [4] Johnston, *An Orator of Justice*, Chap. II.

Buckmaster then became a familiar figure in the county courts and police courts around London and seemed to be destined for a successful common law practice, but one day a Chancery brief was offered to him and he accepted, and from that day his Chancery and his common law work began to grow side by side. Then a day came when he had to choose between two cases, one a Chancery brief on the construction of a settlement, the other a criminal case in the country for the defence on a charge of concealment of birth. He hesitated and finally decided by spinning a coin to remain in London and to accept the Chancery brief.[5] Henceforth he remained on the Chancery side.

In his early days in Worcestershire he often came across H. A. McCardie, who was later to be one of the two High Court judges whom Buckmaster appointed. (The appointment was not, however, due to his early friendship. When the vacancy occurred Buckmaster wished to appoint G. J. Talbot, but Asquith, when consulted, suggested McCardie, on the ground that Talbot had had a very specialized practice at the Parliamentary Bar. In later years Buckmaster used to express regret that he had followed the Prime Minister's advice.)[6] He marked his allegiance to the Chancery Bar by becoming a member of Lincoln's Inn, and in 1900 moved his chambers from 1 New Square, to 9 Old Square. As the years went by his position became sufficiently assured for him to take silk in 1902, eighteen years after call. In the same year he attached himself to the court of Mr. Justice Buckley, as was the custom of Chancery silks in those days. The practice, now obsolete, meant that the litigant was always certain of having the services of counsel whom he had briefed in court on the day when the case was called, which was by no means certain to happen if he had briefed a fashionable counsel on the common law side.

The professional life of a Chancery barrister is not such as to attract public attention. Buckmaster's career in those years can be found in the pages of the Chancery Division Law Reports. One case may perhaps be of interest to lawyers and laymen alike. In 1903 Mr. Justice Buckley had before him a case arising out of the golden age of company promoting. The promoter of the company had made gifts of fully paid shares to the directors, one of whom was a M.P. by the name of Hayes Fisher, who, as we shall see, played some part in the career of Lord Birkenhead. Hayes Fisher, for whom Buckmaster appeared, deliberately asked for the opinion of the court on the morality as distinct from the legality of his conduct on the occasion. Mr. Justice Buckley thereupon uttered a famous dictum: 'This court is not a court of conscience.'[7] In other words equity by the

[5] R. Bosanquet, The Oxford Circuit (1951), p. 6.
[6] See MacKinnon, 'An Unfortunate Preference' (1945) 61 L.Q.R. 237.
[7] In re Telescriptor Syndicate [1903] 2 Ch. 174, at 195.

twentieth century had become so set in its ways that it was no longer based upon the principles of natural justice and good conscience which the Chancery of an earlier age had followed. It may, however, be remarked that having said this Mr. Justice Buckley nevertheless went on to criticize in severe terms the conduct of Hayes Fisher and his friends.[8]

We find then, by the beginning of the century, Buckmaster occupying a solid and respectable position in a learned profession. In 1897 there is that rather rare thing—a compliment publicly paid to him in the pages of the Law Reports. In a case entitled *Imray* v. *Oakeshette*, Lord Justice Rigby said, 'Mr. Buckmaster who, I am bound to say, argued the case very clearly, very candidly, and very fairly throughout.'[9]

He had also found time to marry and found a family. In December 1889 he had married Edith Lewin, the fourth daughter of Spencer Robert Lewin, of Widford, Herts. The engagement produced a characteristic letter from John Buckmaster:

I am very glad that you are not engaged to a frivolous, empty headed woman, and there seems no reason why you should not live happily together in a moderate kind of way. You must bear in mind that your income will be liable to fluctuations but if you have your health and concentrate your mind on your profession I think, with the help and kindness of Mr. Lewin, you have a fair prospect. You may not be Lord Chancellor but you may in your own home be equal to him in happiness, which does not consist in the abundance of our possessions, but the fewness of our necessities.

The young couple settled down at 3 Kingdon Road, West Hampstead. In later life Buckmaster maintained a house at Widford, and also became a J.P. for Hertfordshire. By his wife he had a son and two daughters.

[8] See also below, p. 366.
[9] [1897] 2 Q.B. 218, at 230.

CHAPTER III

WITH PROFESSIONAL SUCCESS ASSURED, Buckmaster could now turn again to the promotion of the Liberal cause in politics which had always been so near to his heart. The long reign of the Balfour Government was obviously about to end and it was urgent to secure a constituency. So in 1903 he secured adoption as a Liberal candidate for the borough of Cambridge, a traditional Conservative stronghold. But the tide of politics was running in Buckmaster's favour and he took the fullest advantage of it in a series of speeches which forecast the peculiar species of high-toned oratory of which he was later to be the most acknowledged master in England. Dealing with the question of the use of Chinese labour in the Transvaal he said:

I cannot help thinking that we have made this mistake—we have allowed our eyes to be dazzled by the glitter of gold, and we have not, as we ought to have done, fixed our eyes on a higher vision and looked to an Empire, not set in gold and precious stones, but an Empire that is just and free, right doing and incorruptible, an Empire the vision of which inspired the labours and gladdened the hearts of the great and wise men of old times, whose names we delight to honour.[1]

Again, in the middle of a carefully argued speech dealing with the relative economic position of Great Britain and the United States he suddenly burst out into the following words:

If it were possible for us to sow the sand and plough the furrows of the sea, if we could made the great Atlantic fertile with industry and turn its barren plains into rich mines and waving corn fields, if we could do all that and round it buckle the girdle of our power, we might compare the state of this country with that of the United States.[2]

The people of East Anglia are traditionally phlegmatic folk, but they responded to this oratory and to the mood of the times and returned Buckmaster at the general election of January 1906 by a majority of 308 in an election when no less than 94 per cent. of the total electorate went to the polls.

On the eve of the poll John Buckmaster had appeared to give a final word as a veteran and an enthusiastic Liberal:

I come down here tonight to recommend to you, the electors of Cambridge, my son. I have known him longer than any of you. He has been a good son—he

[1] Johnston, *An Orator of Justice*, p. 21.   [2] Ibid., p. 20.

has never given me one moment's anxiety. He comes to you, not recommended by wealth, not recommended by ancestors, and if he possesses any qualification beyond that of the poorest and humblest elector in Cambridge, it is due to his own work. I think that is a qualification. In addition to that, though he is not a local man, his Mother was one of the best women that Cambridge ever produced. I commend to you my son.[3]

(Whether because of these remarks or because of Buckmaster's own personal qualifications, it is interesting to note that in 1924 a retired hairdresser of Cambridge, one Morton Richardson, bequeathed his whole estate to Buckmaster.) In the hour of his triumph Buckmaster did not forget to congratulate his friends at the Bar who had also been successful. J. M. Astbury, who had been returned as M.P. for Southport and was later to become a Chancery Judge, wrote in extremely warm terms to thank Buckmaster for his congratulations and to express in language unusually moving for a Chancery silk his personal regard for the writer.[4] So too Haldane wrote from the War Office returning thanks for congratulations on his promotion and adding: 'It is true that I have parted with a great income at the Bar and have also refused the Attorney-Generalship'.[5]

The next step was to make his maiden speech. It was characteristic of Buckmaster's strong sense of personal rectitude and disregard for subservience and flattery that he should have chosen to do this by defending a cause and a person upon whom the Liberal Party were pouring the utmost scorn. On 6 July 1906 the House was debating a motion by Swift MacNeill, who at that time possessed some reputation as an authority on constitutional matters, criticizing the conduct of Mr. Justice Grantham on the hearing of two election petitions, one at Yarmouth and the other at Bodmin. In the course of hearing the petitions Mr. Justice Grantham who, as we have seen,[6] was not regarded as one of the strongest of Lord Halsbury's appointments to the Bench, uttered remarks which seemed to indicate that his known Conservative political views had biased his judgment. Buckmaster devoted his time to a careful analysis of the evidence to show that the charge against the judge, whom he did not know personally, might be regarded as not proven.[7] As the careful and dispassionate analysis of the unedifying incidents of the election proceeded, there was a growing murmur from the Liberal hordes on Buckmaster's side of the House. The unusual spectacle was presented of a maiden speech being received not with the customary respectful sounds but with audible protest. This was not a cause of anxiety to Buckmaster, though more time-serving members of the Bar marvelled at the political naivety of

---

[3] Johnston, p. 22.   [4] Buckmaster papers.   [5] Ibid.
[6] See above, p. 42.   [7] 160 H.C. Deb. 4s. col. 378–87.

one who could so afford to disregard popular opinion. But Buckmaster was moved, as he always was to be, by the thought of injustice done to any individual, and also by the sacred duty to maintain in every possible way the prestige and dignity of the High Court judges.

I am not concerned with the man, [he concluded] but for the great system which he represents. It seems to me that the strength of our nation does not depend only upon the strength of our government; it depends far more on the zeal, the fearlessness, and the efficiency with which our public servants in all parts of our vast Dominions administer the affairs of this great state. It is because I believe that our judges, who are the chief of these servants, have through many centuries built up a great tradition of English justice, that I regard this resolution with the uneasiness which I have expressed. I am sure that honourable members will at least remember that, though there may be failings—and if it is true that a high standard must always be maintained on the judicial bench, failings must occur, for the standard must be low if all men always reach it—yet notwithstanding all mistakes I can confidently assert that our great system of English justice is one which commands the respect and confidence of all people throughout the whole civilized world, wherever the English language or the English law is known. It is because I believe that this resolution, if it is passed, will give a check to that system by singling out for attack a man who, as I submit, has been guilty of nothing but folly—to that system whose honour next to the honour of this House, I prize most highly that I trust all honourable members will resist it.[8]

(It is interesting to note that on another occasion Buckmaster defended the payment of judges at a rate lower than the earnings of the most successful barristers on the rather paradoxical ground that a good judge was one who had made some sacrifice to accept the position in the public interest.[9])

His next speech also opposed a project which was dear to his party, though time here has vindicated the judgment of the party. In 1907 Buckmaster opposed the setting up of the Court of Criminal Appeal which had for so long been advocated.[1] His ground was that the solemn responsibility attaching to the position of a juryman would be weakened if he knew that the verdict in which he joined could be reviewed on appeal. Time has shown that Buckmaster was mistaken about this, as he himself recognized in later years. But in the following years in Parliament his voice was heard seldom, and his absences from the House were increasingly lengthy. He spoke once upon the necessity for securing men of high quality for appointment to the judicial bench and again on the then topical subject of the compulsory disclosure of contributions to party funds. A motion on the subject by Hilaire Belloc was defeated as

[8] 160 H.C. Deb. 4s. col. 386–7.   [9] Johnston, p. 64.   [1] 175 H.C. Deb. 4s. col. 204.

the result of an amendment moved by Buckmaster. Belloc later published
a book imputing unworthy motives to Buckmaster for this act, and, on
the advice of the Law Officers, Buckmaster secured an apology from
Belloc.

At the second general election of 1910 Buckmaster lost his rather
precarious seat at Cambridge. He was seen off from the station by a
crowd of over 4,000 shouting encouragement. 'You are too good for
Cambridge', one particularly loud voice asserted. But in September 1911
the Chief Whip wrote that 'in view of possible changes in the government,
I am most anxious to arrange for your speedy return to the House of
Commons',[1] and very soon an invitation came to stand for Keighley, a
Liberal stronghold in Yorkshire. His adoption aroused angry resentment
in Spencer Hemmerde, an able but cantankerous lawyer who wasted his
abilities on futile quarrels. He wrote to a friend at Keighley on 10 October
1911:

> I cannot tell you how amazed I am to see that the Government are attempting
> to get Buckmaster adopted for Keighley. It is difficult to speak or write coolly
> of so scandalous a breach of faith. . . . The matter is aggravated by the fact that
> in my absence from the House it is clearly the intention of the government to
> make Buckmaster Solicitor-General when Rufus Isaacs is promoted. He is not
> only to be given a seat which was promised to me, but solely for the reason
> that I am temporarily out of the House he is to be preferred to me for an office
> which my services to the party give me a greater claim to than do his. I am to
> be punished in this way for my independence. . . . The way to get on is to
> lobby and toady and if the Keighley liberals will put up with an outrage like
> this that will continue to be the path to promotion.[2]

But the angry protest was in vain and Buckmaster was adopted. The
electorate were at first a little astonished at the depth of fire and feeling
in the candidate, who in his turn found some difficulty in understanding
the dour Yorkshire temperament. But each recognized in the other a
fundamental basis of honesty and good will and in a vigorous campaign
Buckmaster was returned with a majority of 825 over his Conservative
opponent, W. M. Acworth, a distinguished authority on transport
economics, with the Labour candidate, W. Anderson, at the bottom of the
poll. Anderson had attacked Buckmaster vigorously throughout the
campaign, not merely for his absence from the House of Commons, but
for his actions when he did attend in speaking and voting, so it was said,
in a way contrary to the wishes of the majority of his party. In particular
Anderson criticized Buckmaster's support for a vote granting public
money to Lord Cromer upon the retirement of that great pro-consul from
his Egyptian career. This drew from Buckmaster a characteristic reply.

[1] Buckmaster papers.   [2] Ibid.

He described to a lively audience the work which Cromer had done in Egypt in transforming a corrupt and poverty-stricken country into one where law and order prevailed.

'Remember,' he cried, 'that he represented England and all that England means.' When this was greeted with interruptions and jeers, he exclaimed:

Does it mean nothing to you here? Have you no pride in your country? This man—Lord Cromer—struck the fetters from the limbs of the slaves and the rod from the hand of the oppressor. He found the country cold and dead with fast sealed eyes, and he made the dead rise up and live again. And this he did, gentlemen, not by the cruelty and desolation of the sword, but by the exercise of the brain and power of one of the greatest administrators who ever shed the light and honour of English liberty on the world. I care not what you do to me at this election, but while breath and strength remain to me I shall protest against meanness and ingratitude to one of the greatest men of our times and for one of the greatest works done for centuries and towards which the contribution of Keighley is the sum of £50.[3]

On his return to the House, Buckmaster's career, both legal and political, became even more active. Although his practice at the Chancery Bar was maintained in full vigour, he found himself increasingly called upon to appear not only in the King's Bench Division, but also in the Judicial Committee of the Privy Council. In 1913 Sir Samuel Griffiths, the Chief Justice of Australia, was in London and as a Privy Counsellor was invited to sit on the hearing of an appeal in which Buckmaster appeared for one of the parties. When the members of the board adjourned for lunch, Haldane, who presided, asked Griffiths his opinion of the argument. 'The best argument I have ever heard in a court of law', replied Sir Samuel.[4] He told his family that at this time he was earning £40,000 per annum.[5] From 1910 to 1913 he was standing counsel to Oxford University. On the political side Buckmaster took an active part in the acrimonious debates which raged in the House in 1912 over the Marconi case in which allegations of the most wounding character were made against the conduct of the Chancellor of the Exchequer, Lloyd George, the Attorney-General, Rufus Isaacs, and the chief Liberal whip, the Master of Elibank. The details of that somewhat sordid dispute need not be rehearsed once more.[6] It has been well said that 'The case was prosecuted viciously and without humility or charity, while the niggardly defence was unredeemed by any act above self-interest.'[7] It is sufficient to say that the sting of the

[3] Johnston, pp. 26–27.
[4] Alexander, *The Temple of the Nineties*, p. 117.
[5] Information from Lieutenant-Commander J. Miller, G.C.
[6] See F. Donaldson, *The Marconi Scandal* (1962), for a full account.
[7] Ibid., p. iv.

allegation against the three ministers was that they had used knowledge which had come to them in their official capacity to make a private speculation in the shares of the Marconi Company. Rufus Isaacs had, in addition, incurred the gravest suspicion amongst laymen by a statement which he had made on the matter in the House of Commons. 'I have had no dealings in the shares of that company', he told the House in the most positive way. The statement was certainly literally true of the English Marconi Company whose affairs were then under consideration, but it was not true of the American Marconi Company, a subsidiary of the English one, in which Isaacs had indeed invested heavily. When the truth was discovered this unhappy answer aroused all the scorn and contempt which laymen reserve for what they describe as legalistic quibbling. 'As thou of all canst try, The truthful well-weighed answer That tells the blacker lie', wrote Kipling in the following year. Buckmaster, however, was entirely convinced of the honesty and good faith as distinct from the prudence of Isaacs and defended him vigorously in the House. His speech undoubtedly won much support for Isaacs from an assembly which realized that the speaker's sense of personal rectitude was so keen that he would never have condoned conduct which seemed to him in the slightest degree shabby or discreditable. Buckmaster moved an amendment which committed the House to accepting the explanations given by the Ministers concerned and to a repudiation of the false allegations which had been made against them. The amendment was carried by a large majority. In the course of his speech Buckmaster, in reference to Isaacs, said:

One of them (i.e., the Ministers) stands in a special and peculiar relation to myself. He is by his official position the head of our profession. It is a profession where competition is pitiless and fierce, a profession where few men win and many fail, a profession where the success of no man can be attained without the closest and most searching investigation of character and honour, and yet no one will dispute that the Attorney-General in gaining the position he has gained has won not merely admiration but esteem, honour, and affection from the men that he has outstripped and outdistanced in the race. I would beg honourable members in this House, who are anxious to maintain a high standard of public honour, and, at the same time, to avoid straining it so as to make their desire to attain that honour a cloak for gratification of party advantage, to see whether this amendment does not meet all that they really desire to achieve. I would ask of them not to persist in their motion which, if it succeeds, cannot fail to mar great public careers and cast upon these men's futures a shadow which no length of succeeding years can ever take away.[8]

It came as no real surprise when in October 1913 Rufus Isaacs was made

[8] 54 H.C. Deb. 5s. col. 472.

Lord Chief Justice that Buckmaster should have been appointed Solicitor-General in the place of John Simon, the then holder of that office, who was promoted Attorney-General. The partnership might perhaps not have been an easy one, for Simon was no less than twelve years younger than his junior colleague as Law Officer and six years younger in standing as a silk. But the co-operation between them was in every way harmonious. Simon later recorded that he only once differed from Buckmaster's opinion and upon reconsideration withdrew his opposition.[9] Letters of congratulation poured in—amongst many others, he heard from his old Christ Church tutor, E. F. Sampson. Two unavoidable customary events followed the promotion—a knighthood, and a demand for fees amounting to £60. 12s. od. from the Crown Office.

At the subsequent bye-election at Keighley Buckmaster was returned obtaining 4,730 votes against Lord Lascelles (Unionist), 3,852 votes, and W. Bland (Lab.), 3,646 votes. 'You have gained a triumph for the whole party as well as for yourself', wrote the Lord Chancellor.[1]

After the outbreak of war, his reputation in the House had risen so high that Asquith felt justified in entrusting to him the extremely difficult office of head of the Press Bureau, the department which supervised the publication of war news. This was a task which would have been difficult for any man. For a man of Buckmaster's meticulous habits and sensitive caste of mind it was something of a nightmare. Neither the armed forces nor the Press had at that date achieved a satisfactory working relationship. In particular, relations with the Admiralty were severely strained, but it would have needed a man of exceptional talents to have satisfied both the desire of the Press Lords and the British public for news and on the other hand the desire of the Admirals to keep matters as secret as possible. Buckmaster had to answer stormy criticisms both in the House itself and in a tedious private correspondence with a Conservative back-bencher, W. Joynson-Hicks.[2] In the Debate on the Address on 12 November 1914 Buckmaster concisely stated his views. 'It has always been my view that the real rule by which this office should be guided is the consideration as to whether the matter that is proposed for publication should be allowed to see the light, tested by whether its publication could afford any assistance to the enemy, whether it could unduly depress our people'.[3] Further he said,

Criticism of the Government or the members of the Government is not that which I have ever stopped, except where such criticism is of such a character that it might destroy public confidence in the Government which at this time is charged with the conduct of the war, or might in any way weaken the confid-

[9] Simon, *Retrospect*, pp. 86–87. [1] Buckmaster papers.
[2] Ibid. [3] 58 H.C. Deb. 5s. col. 129.

ence of the people in the administration of affairs, or otherwise cause distress or disturbance amongst people in thinking their affairs were in a really serious state.

It is not surprising that Mr. Joynson-Hicks should have complained that this really meant that criticism must be suppressed so soon as it became effective. Yet when Buckmaster became Lord Chancellor he received from Gwynne, the editor of the *Morning Post*, a letter saying he had done 'a most difficult and thankless work absolutely fairly and with great success'.

Another difficulty in this office was caused by the activities behind the scenes of the Press Lords, which formed so striking a part of the conduct of public affairs during the First World War. In a memorandum which he wrote later after the break-up of the Coalition Government, Buckmaster recorded this particular problem as follows:

From September 1914, in addition to being Solicitor-General, I was the sole director of the Press Bureau and continued in this office until it was relinquished on the formation of the new Government. During the whole period of the Coalition Government I enjoyed the confidence of the Prime Minister and, in an unusual degree, the privilege of his friendship. My views, therefore, of the causes which led to his overthrow are necessarily liable to the bias of strong personal affection and esteem. I have done my best to recognize and make allowance for this fact in my history of the event.

It was plain during the whole of the time of my control of the Press Bureau, that many of the more powerful newspapers had support and encouragement from within the Government which rendered the proper execution of my duties extremely difficult. On more than one occasion, when strong measures should have been taken with papers like the 'Times' and the 'Daily Mail', my efforts to exercise against them the powers conferred by the Defence of the Realm Act were defeated from within. I could never assign exactly to any person the responsibility for this disastrous consequence: but it was plain that there were people anxious to secure newspaper support who, in return for press favours were friends with the newspapers when difficulties arose. I constantly endeavoured to obtain for myself as Director of the Press Bureau the necessary authority that would place solely in my hands the power of taking all necessary steps to secure an equal observance by all papers, great and small, of the rules which the Press Bureau laid down. In this I was never successful. Again and again, just as I seemed about to accomplish my design, something occurred which led to its defeat. I do not wish to obscure this narrative by any detailed examination of these causes; but I believe this immunity which papers controlled by Lord Northcliffe, by some means or other, contrived to obtain was a prominent factor in the aggregate of events which produced the final catastrophe.[4]

Buckmaster indeed was by this time moving in the innermost circles

[4] Buckmaster papers. For the rest of the memorandum, see below, p. 280.

around the Prime Minister and was a welcome guest at The Wharf, Sutton Courtenay, the then unspoiled village beside the Thames on the borders of Oxfordshire and Berkshire where the Prime Minister found relaxation from the cares of wartime amidst agreeable company, both male and female. By this time Buckmaster's own home was becoming increasingly uncongenial to him (Lady Buckmaster had been an invalid for some years) and he was therefore seen more often both at the Reform Club and at Sutton Courtenay.

CHAPTER IV

IN MAY 1915 Lord Fisher resigned as First Lord of the Admiralty and Bonar Law, the leader of the Conservative Party served notice that the opposition chose to make this issue a trial of strength. Asquith surrendered and agreed to reconstruct his Government. We have already seen the circumstances under which the services of Haldane as Lord Chancellor were dispensed with. The position was that the Conservatives were strong enough to insist that Haldane should leave office, indeed that his departure from office should be the indispensable condition of their joining the Government. They were not, however, strong enough to insist upon the appointment of a Conservative as his successor, although at one time Asquith pencilled on the back of an envelope the name of Sumner, a Conservative Law Lord, as a possible holder of the Great Seal.[1] The claims of Finlay were also advanced by his friends but in the event Asquith was strong enough to insist upon a Liberal holding the position.

The Prime Minister then naturally offered it to Simon, who passed a few days in careful reappraisal of the situation. He took Buckmaster into the closest consultation and they spent the whole of one evening driving around the roads of Hampstead locked in conversation on the momentous offer. The next morning, 18 May, Simon wrote to Buckmaster:

My dear S. G.:

Here is the result of my reflections on the topics you mentioned last night. I will not go to the Lords on any account—the sack rather than the wool-sack! Such qualities as I have are, I think, those of the H. of C. I shall gladly give up the Attorney-Generalship and its emoluments so long as I get *real* work to do. The Board of Trade is the only one of the three you named which offers any such prospect. The Local Government Board I would refuse and Ireland (as the P.M. himself said to me some months ago), is equally idle. I can quite well go back to the Bar but if I am to consider an administrative post the Board of Trade at any rate leaves me in contact with you and the P.M. with the hope of shuffling off this lawyers coil which I have endured for so long.

Yours ever,
J. A. S.[2]

It was said to be 'an open secret that Simon had refused the Lord

[1] Asquith papers.   [2] Buckmaster papers and Simon papers.

Chancellorship on Asquith's advice'[3] as he expected to succeed as leader of the Liberal Party.

A week of silent and agonized speculation on Buckmaster's part then ensued. No definite move came from No. 10 Downing Street where the Prime Minister was locked in the intricacies of cabinet making. On the 24th Buckmaster thought it wise to send a letter which might perhaps be construed as a gentle reminder of his existence:

I know that, with the object of helping you in the work of re-arranging the Government, all of the members of the Cabinet have placed their resignations in your hands. Although not quite in their position, I have constantly thought during the last few days that the disposition of my office might also prove of some assistance and, if this be so, I sincerely hope you will let me place this unreservedly in your hands.

I have always been proud to think that I received my appointment from you. It has been a great pleasure to serve in your administration but it will be the greatest pleasure of all to know that by the use of my post you will be able to remove even the smallest of many difficulties by which I know your work must be beset.

My intimate work and association with Simon has made me feel that the smooth working of our department may be best secured by two men working together, as we have done, with complete unity of opinion and if for this or any other reason, you wish to fill my place, it is yours to fill.

I fear I have expressed myself clumsily, it is not easy to say all that I wish to express.[4]

The following day, however, the Prime Minister wrote:

I have the pleasure of proposing to you that you should become Lord Chancellor in the reconstituted administration.

I should tell you that for the purposes of this combination, and while the war lasts, it is to be agreed that Ministers should 'pool' their salaries, so as to secure as far as possible an equal scale. This will, of course, especially affect your office. As things are pressing, I shall be glad of an immediate reply.[5]

The reply was sent at once.

Official Press Bureau
Whitehall, S.W.
25 May, 1915

My dear Prime Minister:
It is not easy to thank you adequately for the honour you offer me and the expression of confidence which is implied. I want beyond all things to do that which will make your way easy and if this will be accomplished by my saying 'no' I would say it as gladly as I would say 'yes'. If however you have

[3] B. Thomson, *The Scene Changes* (1939), p. 244.
[4] Asquith papers. [5] Buckmaster papers.

decided that my acceptance is what you wish I can only say I am profoundly touched by this mark of your esteem and will do my best to justify your choice. It will be a matter of special satisfaction to know that I shall be enabled to join in political co-operation with yourself.

Yours very sincerely,
Stanley Buckmaster[6]

The same day Buckmaster remembered to send a note of commiseration to Haldane:

You must know that I have been asked to occupy the post you held and I have accepted with the full knowledge that I can never fill it as you did and that but for a spiteful and most unjust intrigue it would not be vacant for me to fill at all.

I cannot let you know all I feel about it, but I think you will understand and know that I should have been happier had you remained where we all wished you to be.[7]

The appointment was generally well received, though *The Times* struck a discordant note by describing it as 'the reward for tolerable success at the Bar, and diligent but commonplace party services'.[8]

Simon wrote as follows to Lady Buckmaster:

May 25, 1915

I must send to you and Miss Buckmaster a word of most hearty congratulations and good wishes. I shall miss the companionship of my dear S. G. more than I can say, but it will be the greatest satisfaction to have him as a Cabinet colleague in his new and exalted post and this is the feeling of all who have been Mr. Asquith's henchmen. It is the just reward of honest purpose and courageous independence and will introduce into the House of Lords a whiff of directness and candour which will do much for our country. And it must be a pleasure for you to feel that *everyone* at the Bar will acknowledge his fitness for these high duties. I expect the day will come when I shall be humbly addressing his Lordship and getting my fallacies exposed with judicial impartiality—but in the meantime it is going to be an interesting time for us in this War Cabinet together. I am simply delighted about it. Keighley and the Press Bureau will mourn and refuse to be comforted.[9]

Lady Buckmaster replied on the 26th:

I cannot tell you how greatly I appreciate your very kind words; the more so that you made time to write them at a moment when you must be overwhelmed with your own correspondence and confronted with a formidable array of new obligations. Your letter will be treasured and I hope handed on as a family heirloom. It is a pleasant antidote to the venom of the 'Times'. And now let me turn the tables and offer you my sincere congratulations on the

---

[6] Asquith papers and Buckmaster papers.   [7] N.L.S., 5911, f. 70.
[8] *The Times*, 25 May 1915.   [9] Buckmaster papers.

fresh distinction conferred on you. You are more popular with the Press and will not be grudged 'the consummation of an astonishingly brilliant legal career'. I rejoice to think that the welfare of my country will be in such good hands and shall hope to approach you whenever I have a reform to put or a spy to pounce on.[1]

Twenty-one years later, almost to the day, Simon wrote again to Buckmaster's daughter:

I am always very glad that I refused the Lord Chancellorship in 1915, and that I pressed Asquith so strongly to appoint your father, who was far more fitted for the post, and who filled it with such distinction. It is not enough to say of your father that he had a passion for justice, it was a burning flame fed by his hatred of everything that was cruel or unfair.[2]

Letters of congratulation poured in upon the Buckmaster family—from Winston Churchill, from Reading, from John Redmond, and from numerous members of the Bar, amongst them his old master in Chambers, Edward Beaumont, who wrote with suitable enthusiasm:

Hurrah. Hurrah. Noble and glorious Being. You know how fond I have always been of you, and how proud I have been of having helped in your education. Do you remember your struggle with those weights in the pupils room? I scolded Lawrence for letting you go on so long, and he said that at the end of a minute and a half you were just as tired as I was, but you would go on for the five minutes—a significant feat, which should be mentioned to your biographer.[3]

A future Lord Chancellor, Maugham, wrote:

26 May 1915

My dear S. O. B.:
          For I really cannot address you in a formal manner of this occasion. My most warm and hearty congratulations. Your post is one of almost absurd eminence, the sort of uncanny position that my instinct tells me no friend of mine ought to occupy. Yet my real feeling is a hope that I have not lost a friend in a Lord Chancellor. And as I am neither a parson nor a politician, nor any sort of place-seeker, perhaps you will believe me when I say, in all candour and selfishness, that I value the friend a d——d sight more than I care about the L.C.
     I hope I shall still see you from time to time, otherwise than on a bit of sheep's skin, and meantime, believe me,
                                        Ever yours sincerely,
                                        F. H. Maugham.[4]

[1] Simon papers.   [2] Buckmaster papers.   [3] Ibid.
[4] Ibid.

Another letter came from the Master of the Rolls.[5]

26 May, 1915

My dear Buckmaster,

       I am sorry, and yet glad, that it will be my duty to swear you in as Lord Chancellor. *Sorry* because I regard Haldane as the victim of an odious newspaper press. *Glad* because if Haldane had to go, it is a pleasure to regard you as my official head. We are Benchers of the same Inn, and I have long avowed my high appreciation of your qualities as an advocate and a lawyer. The Great Seal will be safe in your hands.

       I presume I shall have some notification from Mackenzie of the time fixed for swearing you in. It does not often fall to the lot of a Master of the Rolls to swear in *two* Lord Chancellors.

       There is one matter which I ought to mention. All the judges, without exception, are members of the Athenaeum, and I presume you will wish to be a member. If so, may I have the pleasure of proposing you? There is a meeting of the Committee early next week.

       With hearty congratulations,

Believe me,
Yours very truly,
Cozens-Hardy

P.S. I am not sure how to address you! You are not yet a Peer or a Lord Chancellor,[6] and I am not sure that you have not ceased to be an M.P.

       Buckmaster received the Great Seal on 27 May, being sworn a Privy Councillor on the same day, and was sworn in before the Master of the Rolls on the 30th following. He was aged 54—which has been called 'surprisingly young'.[7] Of the Chancellors of our period only Herschell (49) and Birkenhead (46) were younger. The peers extended to Buckmaster their usual courtly tolerance to a newcomer. He presided over a debate for the first time on 3 June. 'The new Lord Chancellor sat very bolt upright on the Woolsack looking rather nervous, and reminded me of engravings I've seen of Lord Brougham after the very full-bottomed (wigged) figures of Halsbury, Loreburn, and Haldane. Members greeted him very cordially.'[8] He was created a peer under the title of Lord Buckmaster, of Cheddington, on 14 June, and introduced on 22 June. Until then he presided on the Woolsack as a commoner. His manner was judged to be a trifle brusque, and he did not at first acquire control over the House. He himself, although careful to maintain the dignity of his office, found the trappings of knee-breeches and full-bottomed wig

---

[5] Buckmaster papers.

[6] Cozens-Hardy was correct: Buckmaster did not become Chancellor until the moment he received the Great Seal. See below, pp. 336–7.

[7] Blake, *The Unknown Prime Minister* (1955), p. 254.

[8] Viscount Sandhurst, *From Day to Day* (1928), p. 226.

distinctly irksome. He found an outlet for his irritation in walking to
and from his office across Hyde Park—in summer wearing a straw hat,
which some found shocking in a Lord Chancellor.

The new Chancellor was scarcely in office when he had to deal with
some of the consequences of the change of Government. Amongst the
Conservatives who had made a strong case in the bitter struggle for office
of May 1915 was the Right Hon. J. H. M. Campbell, K.C., Solicitor-
General for Ireland from 1901–5, and Attorney-General for a few months
in 1905. Campbell had a high reputation in Ireland as a *nisi prius* advocate
of the old-fashioned kind. He had attempted to imitate Carson's successful
career in London, but found that English judges and juries did not care
for his methods. But he was undoubtedly one of the most prominent and
intelligent of the Irish Unionists. Campbell pressed his claims to the Lord
Chancellorship of Ireland with great vigour, even going to the length of
writing to Bonar Law, the leader of the Conservative Party, every other
day for three weeks, a degree of importunity which shocked his old
friend. Although Bonar Law did his best to help Campbell, the Irish
party, upon whom Asquith still depended for support, were vehement in
their opposition to him, as he had been a member of Carson's 'Provisional
Government' in Ulster in 1913.[9] At one stage it looked as if the formation
of the whole coalition would be prevented by this dispute. Even Campbell
realized that he had more to lose than gain by such an event and withdrew
from the fight, receiving from Asquith a promise of early promotion. 'I
had in my mind an English judgeship, for which he is not badly fitted.'[1]
Then an unsuccessful attempt was made to induce Cherry, the Irish Lord
Chief Justice, to resign in his favour. Cherry had been appointed only the
previous year but his health had begun to fail. It is not often that a judge
has to sustain pressure from the executive comparable to that resisted by
Cherry during the next few months. On 20 June the Irish Secretary,
Birrell, wrote to him:

> The larger sheet I enclose relates to an awkward and painful situation and
> will, I know, be burnt after perusal.[2]
> This has been a horrible time—to some extent even *for me*, and to a really
> shocking extent to our friend the Prime Minister, for whom I am, as I am sure
> you would be, very sorry. I can't pretend to any final opinion as to the wisdom
> of the course—painful to the point of laceration—he has taken. I am very
> uncertain about it—but the *crisis* was stupendous. All I can say is that my
> personal affection and regard for the Prime Minister remains unabated and
> undisturbed—and it is to this feeling and my desire to shield him from any

[9] Spender and Asquith, *The Life of Lord Oxford and Asquith* (1932), vol. ii, pp. 168–9.
[1] Ibid., p. 169.
[2] This request, unlike many others, seems to have been complied with.

imputations that you owe the *infliction* of this and the enclosed letter. After all you have only to say No—and there it ends. Were you able to assist him it would be good *if it suited you*—if it would not suit you—he would understand as well as any man.[3]

Three days later the Prime Minister himself wrote:

My dear Cherry
      You will have already heard from Birrell. I want to add one or two lines on my own account. I am very sorry to hear that the state of your health is not altogether satisfactory. But if—as is possible—you should think this a possible moment for resignation, you would put me under a great debt of gratitude (for reasons which Birrell has indicated), and I should be glad to recommend (in addition to your pension) that you should receive a mark of Royal favour.

Believe me always
Sincerely yours
H. H. Asquith[4]

But Cherry said No. He replied that his health was satisfactory and that he did not intend to resign. He does not seem to have been impressed by the lacerations felt by the circle around the Prime Minister. So Campbell had to be content for the time being with the promises of future promotion which Asquith had given him. He was not, however, the man to leave a promisor in happy idleness and he continued to press his claims with vigour.

September 25th, 1915

My dear Chancellor,
      Campbell again. He now expresses willingness to serve without remuneration on the Judicial Committee, until one of the big things after which he aspires, e.g., Lordship of Appeal or Presidency of the Probate Division, falls vacant and can be given him. He seems to have added Mastership of the Rolls and Lord Justiceship of Appeal, but Carson agrees with me that the English Bar would be up in arms if he were given either of these.
    I suppose there is no technical difficulty in the way of his sitting on Judicial Committee, being first made an English Privy Councillor.

Yours very sincerely,
H. H. Asquith[5]

On 11 January 1916 Asquith wrote once more:

---

[3] Cherry papers.
 [4] Ibid. The delicately worded final sentence of Asquith's letter may be contrasted with the blunter terms in which he had written to the Earl of Elgin ('What about a marquisate?') when removing him from the Colonial Office in 1908.
 [5] Buckmaster papers.

My dear Chancellor:

        Campbell again. Could you now carry out the old suggestion about Darling?[6]

The occupants of the Irish Bench—especially the antiquated and infirm—stick to their places like wax.

Yours very sincerely,
H. H. A.[7]

The following day a lengthy letter came from the Secretary to the Lord Chancellor, Sir Claud Schuster, who had been brought into the office in July 1915 after a distinguished career on the legal side of the Civil Service.

Campbell's business is most unfortunate. You know of course that proposals (or alleged proposals) as to Campbell have been common gossip at the Bar ever since the formation of the present government, and members of the profession have constantly expressed to me the sense of indignation that any such appointment would arouse. I have laughed the matter off, but the impression left on my mind has been unpleasant; and I have formed the opinion that any such appointment would arouse a storm exceeding in intensity that which followed Ridley's appointment years ago. The storm will break on the innocent head of the L.C.: but it would be the worst friendship to the P.M. to allow him to suppose that it will not damage him also. Even if C. were allowed to hold an office for which by universal consent of his fellows he is unfit, any appointment which is obviously political at this moment would be a scandal and might well bring up St. Aldwyn and Middleton (sic)[8] in this House to protest in public with the resulting harm to the judicial office, to the Lord Chancellor, and to the Prime Minister himself. For really there is no possible defence. It is by no means clear that a vacancy in the K.B. ought to be filled at all. To fill it, by the appointment of an unfit man, selected not for his own political services (as has happened before) but as a political manoeuvre and to do so by means of an additional charge of £3500 of the Consolidated Fund at a moment such as this—surely this is outrageous.

Forgive me if I write strongly. I know you do not care for any injury to your personal position if it results in what you think to be right. But the whole administration of the Law and the Public Service are at stake. With what faith can we, after this, bring forward proposals for economies affecting clerks at the courts?[9]

Asquith thereupon saw Reading, the Lord Chief Justice, about the unhappy proposal to appoint Campbell to the English King's Bench

---

[6] The clear inference is that Darling, who had earned his pension by fifteen years' service, was to be induced to retire in Campbell's favour.

[7] Buckmaster papers.

[8] Schuster must have meant the 9th Viscount (and 1st Earl of) Midleton, not the 9th Lord Middleton.

[9] Buckmaster papers.

Division, and it was agreed that Reading was to see the Irish Secretary, Birrell, about prospects of promotion for Campbell in Ireland. Asquith was shown Schuster's letter, and wrote to Buckmaster on 17 January:

Best thanks for your very kind letter of yesterday. I thoroughly realize the force of all you say. We must still try to find another way of getting rid of this millstone.

Preferably, of course, in Ireland.

'*Via prima salutis Qua minime reris, Graia pandetur ab urbe*'.[1]

At least, I think that is how it runs. I will speak to you about it after Cabinet tomorrow; perhaps you could come to lunch.[2]

To this note was a postscript:

Please act on your suggestion as to seeing Carson and Atkinson at once. Birrell tells me that Boyd J. is well over 80 and stone deaf. Madden is well over 70, a distinguished scholar, who might without scandal be made a Baronet. As to Palles, C.B.—Birrell says his best friends wish him to retire. He well deserves a Peerage, but family circumstances make this difficult.[3]

The reference to Atkinson was to a proposal that that distinguished Irish Law Lord (who in his day had been Conservative Attorney-General for Ireland) might be induced to resign in Campbell's favour. But the emissaries were vigorously repulsed. Negotiations were then instituted in Ireland through the agency of Birrell and, upon his report to the Prime Minister, Asquith wrote again to Buckmaster on 16 February:

I hope we are in sight of a better solution to the Campbell problem than in succumbing to the 'unbridled appetency' of old Boyd. Birrell has seen Cherry, whose health is in a bad way, and who is in a mood to resign. At Birrell's suggestion I have written to him a letter, which I hope will produce the desired effect. This would be an excellent outlet from the situation.[4]

The letter on which Downing Street placed such hopes ran thus:

16 Feb. 1916

My dear Chief Justice

I was very sorry to hear from Birrell, with whom I have been talking this morning, that the hopes which you expressed to me some months ago of improvement in your health have not been realised. We (you and I) are

---

[1] *Virgil, Aen.*, vi, 96–97. ('Your way of safety shall first, little as you think it, be opened from a Greek city'.) Asquith was not the first Liberal Prime Minister to use this text. Gladstone cited it when 'the Spanish Government unexpectedly met some bills and so stopped a hole in the budget': G. M. Young, *Portrait of an Age*, p. 483, n. 1.

[2] Buckmaster papers.

[3] For these see V. T. H. Delany, *Christopher Palles* (Dublin, 1960), p. 114. The other Irish judges mentioned are vividly described in M. Healy, *The Old Munster Circuit* (Dublin, 1948).

[4] Buckmaster papers.

K*

old friends and colleagues, and I have the most agreeable and grateful memories of our association in the work of government and Parliament.

If, as I gather from Birrell, you have come to the conclusion that it would be right for you to retire, there will, of course, be no difficulty in the matter of pension. And I should be delighted if there is any honorific mark of recognition which would be grateful to you, to do my best to secure it.

Believe me, dear Chief Justice,

Yours very sincerely
H. H. Asquith[5]

But Cherry still refused to retire, producing medical certificates that his health was satisfactory. Eventually Mr. Justice Boyd resigned on 15 April, being consoled with a Baronetcy, and the then Attorney-General for Ireland, J. H. Gordon, K.C. was appointed to his vacant place on the Irish High Court, Campbell being appointed Attorney-General in place of Gordon. As this was an office which he had held in Mr. Balfour's Government more than ten years before, his ambitions were unsatisfied. He returned to the charge, pressing his claims once more upon Downing Street.

The complicated negotiations came to a conclusion when in December 1916 Cherry finally resigned his position as Lord Chief Justice[6] and Campbell was appointed to succeed him, being made a Baronet at the same time.

Fortunately English judicial appointments did not give rise to the same difficulties. There were only two vacancies, which Buckmaster filled by the appointment of A. F. Peterson and H. A. McCardie. As we have seen, the latter owed his appointment mainly to Asquith's recommendation. He replied as follows to Buckmaster's offer of the position:

11 October 1916

You have offered me a great position.

I accept it with a full sense of the duties and responsibilities it places upon me.

I am most grateful for your letter and for the kind and most generous manner in which you offered me the judgeship.

It is indeed an honour for a junior counsel. Yes, I remember so well the case at the Evesham County Court and I have always been so proud of your brilliant career.[7]

Buckmaster created no K.C.s during his term, for reasons clearly explained in the following letter:

[5] Cherry papers.
[6] Cherry refused any honour and died in 1923.
[7] Buckmaster papers.

13 December 1915

My dear Attorney:

It is true that no appointment has been made to the office of King's Counsel during the last fourteen months. This is not necessarily too long a period to elapse between the dates of such appointments, but as I do not propose to make any further recommendations to the King in the immediate future, I think the Bar may rightly be informed of my intention, and the reason which lies behind. The removal of Juniors in good practice is the opportunity to which all young men rightly look for the purpose of establishing, or improving, their position at the Bar. It is almost the only event which diverts the steady stream of legal business from its accustomed channel, and increases the chance of even the youngest man to gather work. It is unnecessary to tell you what a splendid response has been made by the members of our profession to the national demand; this must be known to all, but it is not so generally realized that in the large majority of cases the men who have gone have left at the most critical moment of their professional career. In these circumstances it is the first and obvious duty of everyone to see that they do not suffer by their patriotism and that no unnecessary opening is made in the ranks of the profession during their absence. Unless, therefore, some unforeseen and special exigency requires an appointment to be made, I do not propose to make any recommendation to the King until the war ends, and I am committed by His Majesty to state that this course meets with his entire approval.

Yours sincerely,

Buckmaster[8]

Ireland also engaged Buckmaster's attention when the Cabinet had to consider whether the sentence of death imposed upon Sir Roger Casement for high treason should be carried out or not. It is not part of Buckmaster's life to consider the events which led up to the trial of that misguided man, but as Lord Chancellor he was naturally closely concerned with the question whether the prerogative of mercy should be exercised.[9] The defenders of Casement have sometimes given the impression that the Cabinet of the period was composed of wicked and scheming men. It is perhaps enough to mention the four men who were most closely concerned with advising the monarch as to whether the prerogative of mercy should be exercised—Asquith, the Prime Minister; Grey, the Foreign Secretary; Buckmaster, the Lord Chancellor; and Samuel, the Home Secretary. It is hard to think of four English statesmen whose reputation for integrity and honour stands higher.

The matter came before the Cabinet on no less than three occasions and it was finally decided to let the law take its course. Buckmaster then received from the Archbishop of Canterbury, Randall Davidson, a letter

[8] (1915) 140 L.T. News. 141.
[9] See below, p. 378.

in which the considerations telling in favour of exercising the prerogative of mercy were so persuasively put that it should be set out in full.

Lambeth Palace, S.E.
11:30 p.m.
August 1, 1916

My dear Lord Chancellor:

I have been thinking over the conversation I had with you a few hours ago upon this wretchedly distressing and perplexing business of Sir Roger Casement.

I think that perhaps in my talk with you, I overmuch concealed the strength of the *instinct* I find stirring within me to the effect that the really *courageous* course for the Government to adopt would be the commutation of the death sentence. The case presents itself to me somewhat thus:

As a question of policy there can I suppose be no doubt that a reprieve would be wiser than an execution. Ireland, America, and possibly other countries would find people to make mischievous capital of the execution, and far more so if they could (as they would) spin a tale to the effect that after hanging a 'political prisoner' the authorities had been privy to the trumping up of an infamous story about the man's immorality, an accusation with which he had never been even confronted; far less had the accusation been proved true after proper investigation. Such would be the shape the accusation against the Government would take. Of course you can, in one sense, afford to ignore all such attacks. But they will, none the less, be mischievous, and in America especially they will do real harm. As a question of pure *policy* therefore, the avoidance of an execution is to be desired.

In the present circumstances of the world, it savours, I think, of pedantry to contend that 'policy' has nothing to do with the decision you should, as a Government, come to, and that 'justice' only has to be considered. The thing is not so simple as that. The object of an execution is to deter offenders. Whom would this execution, as a matter of fact, deter? Whom would a commutation of sentence encourage in evil deeds? No one. What would doubtless happen would be an outcry on the part of a good many people, who would say, 'It is sheer cowardice which has let this man off, after the shooting of weaker or less important rebels. If ever a man deserved hanging it is this man.'

The other rebels were shot, so to speak, red-handed, after court martial. This man was not 'red-handed' in that sense, though no doubt, as the wire-puller, he may be regarded as more guilty than any. I certainly do not attempt to deny that he *deserves* hanging. But when we think of the result which would almost certainly follow, we ought, I believe, to have the courage to be apparently inconsistent, and to send him to Broadmoor instead. The sound argument would, I think, be 'Here is a rebel who has done things worthy of death. But his case is peculiar. For many years, beyond all possibility of doubt, he battled nobly on behalf of the oppressed native folk. He had infinite difficulties to contend with, but at the cost of his health he fought on. He succeeded, and his name will always, and rightly, be held in honour for what he then did, whatever may have happened afterwards. All sorts of complications as to the rebel's real life came subsequently to light. Investigation showed perplexing contradictions in his behaviour, and though not technically (according to the experts) a man out of his mind, he is shown to have been mentally and morally unhinged. In these complicated circumstances we believe that the more sane and fair course is to choose the less irreparable of two evils, and to commute the sentence, and we accordingly do so.'

Of course the more *obvious* course would be to send him to the gallows. But is it not really the less courageous line to follow? It is followed 'lest we seem inconsistent'. I should brave *that*, and do what is really in the truest interests of the country and the Empire. 'Policy' in the largest sense of the word can't be excluded, if those on whose shoulders the responsibility rests are facing their duty from the highest standpoint. After all, the whole thing concerns the well being and safety of the Empire, and nothing less or lower, or more merely *technical*.

I have purposely not dwelt upon all the complexities of immoral morbidities, about which I have so much unpleasing experience every month of my life. Though my experience is abundant and varied, we must *in the main*, be guided, in that field, by professional mental experts. 'In the main', but not to the exclusion of the unprofessional but solid experience of actual facts, that is possessed by some of us, and forms an element (no more) in our consideration of the question.

I feel that I owe you an apology for this intrusion into the field of jurisprudence. But I must plead in defence, by your own encouragement, and your express wish that I should tell you how it all presents itself to me.

And 'jurisprudence' after all, when widely interpreted, shades off into political ethics wherein the most amateurish of us may have a voice.

> I am,
> Yours very truly
> Randall Cantaur[1]

Nevertheless, Buckmaster in an interview with the Archbishop on the following morning, thought that it was not possible for the Cabinet to review the matter once more. He had put his finger on a weak point in Casement's case, namely, that those prisoners of war who had failed to succumb to his persuasions had been treated by their German captors with greater severity. Some prisoners of war had recently been returned from Germany with stories which left him in no doubt of the matter. It was characteristic of Buckmaster's keen sense of honour that he should have viewed with revulsion the efforts of a vain and able man to seduce from their allegiance a number of simple Irish soldiers.

On the wider scene of the war, Buckmaster's personal views were deeply involved in a question which is still unsettled amongst military historians—namely, whether some great effort should not have been made

[1] Buckmaster papers. See also G. K. A. Bell, *Randall Davidson* (1935), pp. 787-9.

in the east to break the monotonous deadlock to which trench warfare in France had led. He was amongst the members of the Cabinet who chafed under the restraints imposed by Kitchener.

In October 1915 the question arose whether an expedition should be sent to Salonika. This proposal was supported with great vigour by Carson and when his views were not accepted he resigned. On 15 October 1915, Buckmaster circulated a memorandum on the question to his colleagues which revealed him to be a convinced westerner.

The questions to which I refer are particularly the proposals to send an army into Macedonia, and the question of the Dardanelles. I do not know what the decision of the Cabinet Committee is on either of these questions. I do not know if in fact they have decided, but it appears from the memoranda of both Mr. Bonar Law and of Mr. Lloyd George that they at least are anxious to undertake the responsibility of sending such a force, notwithstanding the military opinion that such a step would be dangerous in the last degree. It is easy to recognize and to feel inspired by the motives which have prompted Mr. Bonar Law and Mr. Lloyd George. They are obvious, and must appeal to all; but to me there is this far more weighty consideration—the safety of this country and the conservation of its strength.

If history has any value, there is one lesson that it plainly teaches; that the finest military powers can be utterly destroyed if their forces are dissipated away from the centre which it is their first duty to protect. To withdraw two hundred thousand men from France and to starve the remainder of ammunition during the next six months means that, at a moment when, according to Lord Kitchener, the French passed their zenith in the matter of men, we are going to weaken the military position in France and Belgium. The forces there are to be condemned to a defence, to support which reinforcements cannot be sent, and to be exposed to attacks from the Germans, which, if successful, threaten the safety of our shores.

The principle which prescribes concentration of effort and forbids dispersion of forces is especially incumbent upon us and to the geographical position of the central powers.

Hence arise two further considerations which would, in my view, be decisive against the policy of adventure in Serbia. Even the military authorities cannot speak with certainty as to the time it would take to withdraw troops from France or from this country and to dispatch them by sea to Salonika, and the shipping required can only be obtained by further depletion of our already depleted Merchant Service. It is clear that before troops can be brought from the French front, transported by sea, landed at Salonika, and conveyed thence to the battle front, the issue in the Balkans may be decided and the German troops who have decided it may be back again facing our weakened lines in France and Flanders. In that event our army will have played the same part as d'Erlon's forces, wandering between the battles of Ligny and Quatre Bras when their presence on either field would have decided the issue.

Again, what is to be the effect of the diversion of the shipping required for the transport and supply of so great an army? . . . I have no wish to weaken the sense of our obligation to our Allies or the performance of our duties to them. But I protest against the idea that the burden of this war by land, by sea, and in the market is mainly to be borne by us. Such troops as are necessary to render our position in Egypt secure, and to maintain peace in India, should be despatched, and in my opinion no other single man should be sent from these shores or from France.

It must further be remembered that victory in the Balkans will not bring permanent relief to Serbia nor permanently avert the perils arising from the German thrust to the East if it is coupled with defeat in France and Flanders. It would in no way advantage our Allies if the Germans, having been repelled from Serbia, break though in France. France, once mastered, the German forces can again roll down to the south-east and complete the work of conquest which, on the most favourable hypothesis, we shall have arrested temporarily.

As to the Dardanelles, it is surely imperative that without delay we should have a clear statement of the military position and the advice of the military experts. The sick and wounded are now reaching this country, and, making all allowances for the exaggeration due to the weakness of ill health, the stories that they tell shock the public mind and are preparing a condition in which any spark may set fire to the rising popular resentment.[2]

It is not improbable that this powerfully argued statement of a case in an admittedly controversial matter played some part in influencing the Cabinet to abandon the proposal to help Serbia. But as the war moved on through 1916 even the most convinced westerners began to feel despondent. The Battle of Jutland on 30 May 1916 was neither then nor later viewed as a decisive victory for the navy upon which Great Britain had lavished its ingenuity and its treasure for many years; and in July of that year Haig had begun on the Somme his tremendous series of battles which certainly brought no tangible gain in territory or prisoners while costing the country a staggering amount in killed and wounded.

On the first day of the Somme British casualties were 60,000. One who saw Buckmaster at this time found him staring out of his window at a long column of troops crossing Westminster Bridge on their way to the Front and muttering to himself, 'Hateful, hateful.'[3] It was therefore hardly surprising that a movement to change the supreme direction of the war began to gather increasing momentum. There was in England one man who was quite confident that he could save England and nobody else could. It was the Chancellor of the Exchequer—David Lloyd George. It is no part of this history to describe the elaborate intrigues by which

[2] Buckmaster papers.
[3] Information from the Hon. Sir Albert Napier.

Asquith was replaced by Lloyd George in December 1916. They have often been fully recounted elsewhere.

Buckmaster himself was throughout an ardent Asquithian but he seems to have played no active part in the elaborate negotiations beyond attending a meeting on Monday, 5 December, when it looked for one moment as if Bonar Law and his colleagues had overplayed their hands and Asquith might be able to defeat them. The moment passed and the next day the Prime Minister resigned and with him, naturally, the Lord Chancellor.

Buckmaster thought the matter over during the Christmas vacation and in January 1917 he dictated a lengthy memorandum which has so far never been published. It is of such interest that a full extract must be made from it. After a few initial paragraphs dealing with the Press Bureau, which have already been set out, he went on:

... The coalition government started under fair auspices, and for a short time promised well. The Unionist members acted with great loyalty and self restraint, and, excepting on occasions where the dividing line of opinion could not be obscured—as for example on matters relating to Ireland and the franchise, there was never any acute and critical difference of opinion.

In the autumn of 1915, however, difficulty began. The Dardanelles expedition failed. Although all demands for further troops that were required were satisfied, it became more and more plain that it was impossible that the adventure could be carried to a successful conclusion without not only a tremendous sacrifice of life but also of so impairing our strength on the Western Front that the Germans would be able to strike in that field of battle a blow decisive in the fortunes of war. At the same time the introduction of Bulgaria into the war, and the combined attack of German and Bulgarian forces in Serbia, defeated the whole Serbian army and linked up Constantinople and Berlin. The situation was grave and its remedy difficult. Sir Edward Carson and Mr. Lloyd George both violently urged the necessity of saving Serbia from destruction. No one doubted the importance of this step, but most of the Cabinet, of whom I was one, thought that the rescue of Serbia was not in itself the dominating feature in the situation, but that whatever ought to be done should be done with the sole view of so regulating and directing our forces as to secure their use for the one main cause of winning the war. There was no single port at which it could be urged that any large number of troops could be landed for use in the Balkan peninsula, and information as to the means of transport from any port was such as to show that, even if they were landed, it would have been extremely difficult to carry forward any effective operations and at the same time keep the force adequately supplied with men, munitions and stores. At the same time Mr. Venizelos, who represented the more active and patriotic party in Greece, was extremely anxious to persuade the Greek government to honour their treaty obligations to Serbia, and throw the whole of their forces on to the side of the Allies. In this he never succeeded; but, in order to strengthen his hands, he asked that troops might be sent to Salonika, and this request was followed by a definite promise made in the French chamber that the French would support Serbia in her struggle. In the performance of this promise the French required our help and many members of the Cabinet thought we should join. Meanwhile, Sir Edward Carson, unable to secure the performance of his plan, which had not the support of a single military official, withdrew from the Cabinet; and for a moment it appeared as though Mr. Bonar Law, though not agreeing with his position, might feel bound to follow owing to ties of party loyalty. I was throughout strongly opposed to any Salonikan expedition. The information we received was that the port at Salonika was ill adapted for receiving all the vessels necessary to land and maintain a large force. The necessary depletion of our transport, were such expedition undertaken, and the demands it would make upon us in men and money and supplies, appeared to me sufficient reason for rejecting the proposal. We were told that in addition the land between Salonika and the Bulgarian frontier was of such a physical character that the employment of a large quantity of troops was a great difficulty, and every military authority from the Commander-in-Chief downwards looked askance at the plan. Lord Curzon was strongly opposed to it; but the removal of the Dardanelles force having been agreed upon, and the opportunity thereby offered of using that force for the expedition, coupled with their anxiety to preserve the alliance with France, at last prevailed, and the expedition was taken.

I have dwelt on this instance at some length because it was the first sign of any real difference of opinion as to the means of conducting the war. Mr. Lloyd George was throughout passionately and as I think, wholly unreasonably, in favour of making and strengthening this force; and from that date until the time when the crisis arose, he was always complaining of the lack of foresight which caused us to keep our forces in the west instead of attempting to obtain a decisive victory in the eastern theatre of operations. Although he frequently and vehemently referred to this question, he never at any time whatever proposed any plan by which his proposal could be carried into effect, nor did he place before the Cabinet a statement of any military scheme which he desired the Cabinet to adopt.

It is unnecessary to state in detail the important circumstances that occurred in the earlier part of the year 1916; but it became plain as the year advanced that not only was a deliberately organized attack being made upon the Prime Minister in the Press, but also that this attack did not produce resentment, even if it did not obtain support, from some of his colleagues. In particular, Mr. Lloyd George made a speech in the House of Commons, the refrain of which was that everything that the Government had done was too late, and, included among these omissions, I have no doubt, was his view as to the failure to support Serbia. The parliamentary difficulties proceeded to grow and thicken. There were many matters upon which united opinion was quite impossible in a Cabinet constituted from both parties in the State. For some little time there was a severe crisis over the attempt on the part of Mr. Lloyd George to settle the Irish difficulty, and it looked as though that rock would be the one upon which the government would break.

My own personal views could not be expected to be in agreement with those of confirmed Unionists like Mr. Walter Long and the Marquess of Lansdowne; but I do think it right to say that their attitude was one of conspicuous loyalty to the then Prime Minister, and that it was only their desire to avoid the break-up of the Government which led them to continue in office at a moment when it seemed that terms were going to be agreed of which they profoundly disapproved.

After a paragraph of no present interest about amending the electoral register, the memorandum continues:

While matters were in this state, Lord Lansdowne prepared and circulated a memorandum of the very utmost importance. It asked for nothing but a careful consideration of the position in which we stood, a strict and close investigation of all our resources in men, money and goods, a similar calculation with regard to all our Allies, and an attempt to contrast these with what we knew of the enemy's position. This he regarded as essential, because he foresaw —and events have justified his foresight—that by the end of the year Germany would make some proposals for peace; and it was his view—a view which I entirely shared—that those who needlessly prolonged the war would have as heavy a burden to bear as those who needlessly provoked it. It was, I believe, this memorandum that caused the crystallization of the fluid elements of disaffection which were found round and in the Cabinet, and which centred in Mr. Lloyd George. An angry reply was sent to this memorandum by Sir William Robertson, answered again by Lord Grey—Sir Edward Grey as he then was[4]—and Lord Lansdowne. But before all these matters could come up for consideration by the Cabinet, the mine was sprung and the government was overthrown.

The explanation of how this was effected is, I believe, clear. Mr. Bonar Law had always been uneasy and timid about his following in the House of Commons. He had entered the Cabinet as a leader of the Tory Party and with their consent, and he was never quite able to divest himself of the feeling that he was there on their sufferance. I have no doubt that this attitude of his was used by Mr. Lloyd George for attempting to secure an alliance between himself and such Tory members of the Cabinet as would follow Mr. Bonar Law. I believe that for a long time Mr. Bonar Law was not prepared to enter into this alliance, and it is my strong opinion—though I have no evidence—that the alliance was ultimately effected under the agency of Mr. Max Aitkin (sic)—a Canadian financier looked on with much hesitation by most responsible Canadians—who was undoubtedly in the closest daily contact with Mr. Bonar Law.

Mr. Max Aitkin's (sic) position is, indeed, strange. He was a person utterly unknown here and unregarded if not actually distrusted in Canada. Yet he obtained a good seat from the Tory party and was returned as a Tory candidate. He rarely attended the House. I have heard that he once spoke; but if he did he

4 Buckmaster's memory had deceived him here; Grey was made a viscount in July 1916.

made no impression, and I was quite unaware that he had ever done it. He was made a Baronet at the insistence of Mr. Bonar Law for services that no one could divine, and immediately upon the breakup of the Coalition Government, he was created a Peer. To quote the words of the 'Morning Post'—one of the most bitter antagonists of Mr. Asquith and the strongest possible supporter of his opponents—this was 'an honour unworthily bestowed upon an unworthy object'. There could be but one explanation of this behaviour, and that was the service he had rendered in the breakup of the old Government.[5]

Matters reached a head in the week ending December 7th. Mr. Lloyd George was then in the course of making suggestions to the Prime Minister as to the reconstitution of the War Committee. It is unnecessary to go through these negotiations at length: in the main they consisted of the proposal which would have displaced the Prime Minister from his position of authority and forced him to assume an entirely subordinate place. It was, of course, impossible for any man with a sense of honour or dignity to retain the Office of the Premiership and at the same time be regarded in any capacity as a subordinate person. Mr. Lloyd George complained of the delays that took place in decisions, and finally asserted in plain terms that the War Committee had declined to consider his proposal for helping Roumania and that this was one of his main causes for grievance. This last suggestion was wholly apart from the actual facts. Mr. Lloyd George had not in fact made any suggestion before the War Committee and no hint of anything of the kind had ever been before the Cabinet. It is said that he prepared some scheme in the War Office, which the military authorities had instantly rejected without even requiring the opinion of the War Committee upon it.

Matters being in this position, there was a meeting held of all Conservative members of the Cabinet on Sunday, with the exception of Lord Lansdowne, and they passed a resolution that if the Prime Minister would not resign they would be compelled to resign in a body. This resolution was undoubtedly adopted by different people for different reasons. One group thought that by this means the Prime Minister would resign, that Mr. Bonar Law would be unable to form a cabinet—and indeed would not attempt to do so—that Mr. Lloyd George would be equally impotent, and that therefore Mr. Asquith would be once more asked to form a government which he would reconstruct by the elimination of Mr. Lloyd George and possibly of some other members. Mr. Bonar Law, and those who were working with him, had not, however, intended that this should be the result. Their plans had been too well laid, and they intended, on the resignation of the Prime Minister, and the failure of Mr. Bonar Law to form a Cabinet, to support Mr. Lloyd George, and then use all their efforts to bring over the remainder of their Tory colleagues, urging upon them their sense of duty to the country as a reason why they should sink personal difference and join the new government.

This latter plan was the one that succeeded. I doubt if we shall ever know the

---

[5] Lord Beaverbrook's own account (*Politicians and the War* (1932), pp. 328–31) states that his peerage was offered by Lloyd George against the wishes of Bonar Law.

grave reluctance that men like Mr. Long, Mr. Balfour and Mr. Austen Chamberlain had to conquer before they consented to join the new government. I am at any rate convinced that they only did so out of their profound sense of public duty and their desire to carry on the government of the country regardless of their personal feeling in a moment of great emergency.

The plan succeeded—the government fell. Mr. Bonar Law made nothing but an apparent effort to form a government, and Mr. Lloyd George was able to carry out his scheme and to reward every man who had ever raised his tongue against the late government by giving them positions of some kind or another, and creating new posts when the old were not sufficient to go round, in order that he might strengthen as far as possible the hold he could have upon his followers.

This I am convinced is the true story of the causes that led to the overthrow of the Coalition Government. I am certainly not prepared to charge any individual with using the occasion for the gratification of personal ambition. There could be only one person against whom such a charge could properly be brought. I hesitate to bring it. He may have thought that he was better fitted than Mr. Asquith to conduct the affairs of the Nation in the gravest moment of its fate. Few people who knew the two men would agree with him. But this, at least, is sure, that, while most other members of the Cabinet from time to time laid before their colleagues schemes to which they demanded attention—proposals which they desired to carry into effect, I cannot recall a single proposal ever made by Mr. Lloyd George, nor a single scheme that he ever formulated or an attempt to secure the adoption of any policy, apart from the attempt to send a vast army into the East, which he ever laid before the Cabinet for consideration. Had this scheme—which was his only one—ever been adopted I think events show that the opinion then formed by the Cabinet would have been abundantly justified and the whole Allied powers would have been brought down in ruin.[6]

Some comments may be made on this document. One is that it concentrates almost entirely on the question of the Salonika expedition and ignores the other events of 1916, such as the battle of Jutland and the battle of the Somme and the Irish Rebellion. It is really rather remarkable that Buckmaster should dismiss all these with the words, 'It is unnecessary to state in detail the important circumstances that occurred in the earlier part of 1916'; yet it was just those circumstances which seriously weakened the purely Liberal part of the Government in the eyes of their Unionist colleagues. Nobody has yet pronounced a definite judgment upon the merit of the various schemes which were put forward for breaking the deadlock on the western front. Two points may, however, be made. The first was that when the enemy did in fact break in the autumn of 1918 it was the Bulgarian Government which asked for an armistice. The second

[6] Buckmaster papers.

is that quite large armies were in the end maintained through the port of Salonika.

On the whole, though, the document shows Buckmaster capable of judging his enemies, or rather the enemies of Asquith, with considerable fairness and shrewdness. Buckmaster's judgment of Lloyd George was always free from the extreme personal bitterness which prevailed in Asquithian circles—although he (whose only son was serving at the Front) was apt to contrast the war services of Lloyd George's sons with those of Asquith's. He did not charge Lloyd George with personal ambition: 'he may have thought that he was better fitted than Asquith'. This is, of course, perfectly true and the judgment of history probably is that Lloyd George is hardly to be criticized for having held this view and for having striven to give effect to it. On the other hand Buckmaster's remoteness from the day-to-day intrigues of November and December 1916 is shown by his reference to the alleged reluctance which Walter Long and Austen Chamberlain had to conquer before serving under Lloyd George. It is quite true that they were reluctant, but Buckmaster hardly brings out the fact that they were equally, if not more reluctant, to continue serving under Asquith. The discontent which they had felt throughout the summer and autumn of 1916 had come to a head, as is clearly shown in the letter which Lord Robert Cecil sent to Asquith, inquiring whether he did not think he might take a back seat.[7] But Asquith (and his wife) refused to compromise, then or later. There is evidence to show that Lloyd George would have been willing to see Asquith on the Woolsack. But Asquith would not consider it. As Haldane said to Buckmaster on 6 December: 'Asquith is a first class head of a deliberative council. He is versed in precedents, acts on principles, and knows how and when to compromise. Lloyd George cares nothing for precedents and knows no principles, but he has fire in his belly and that is what we want.'[8]

Outside politics Buckmaster, as was often the case with Liberals of his cast of mind, maintained friendly relations with Conservative leaders such as Lansdowne and Balfour. With the latter he found time to institute a correspondence on the topic of Darwin's theory of natural selection.

When Buckmaster finally left office in December 1916 and was replaced by Finlay, he received the following letter from the Permanent Secretary, Sir Claud Schuster:

December 10, 1916

Dear Chancellor,
                    Thus I may address you for the last time for some months. I don't like to bother you with a letter, but I must write a few lines to express what cannot be said face-to-face, that is my deep regret at your termination of office,

[7] See A. Chamberlain, *Down the Years* (1935), p. 120.   [8] Haldane papers.

and my very sincere and lasting gratitude to you. I have much cause for indebtedness to you—your generosity in taking me into your office, untried and unknown to you; your constant backing in every difficulty, your forbearance of stupidity and persistence, your unfailing kindness and readiness to think the best of the little I could do; your readiness to consider and enter into every scheme for improvement and reform. I hope and believe that in your regained freedom you will not lose interest in the office or its officials. In war-time it is difficult to do much, and at any time economy and diligence are drab and uninteresting virtues for the practice of which constant encouragement is needed from outside. I hope you will remember how much is to be done so that when you return to office we may have already advanced and under your guidance may accomplish the remainder.

May I, without presumption, add a word on greater matters? My great fear is lest your party by demanding a definition of our aims, may be represented as a peace party, and so lose its influence just when it is most needed. Free trade, humanity, a respect for settled principles of law, a regard for the rights of others, whether nations or individuals, are the principles which are at stake both in our war with Germany and in our domestic struggles. They are now definitely committed to your care. I am afraid lest in the heat which must arise from the events of this last week and from any such policy as we discussed, the people at large and even your own followers may forget, and you may be involved in a general fog of controversy in which peace and pro-Germanism may look like the same thing. I express myself badly. Please forgive this intrusion, and believe me yours,

Most sincerely and gratefully,
Claud Schuster[9]

[9] Buckmaster papers.

CHAPTER V

OUT OF OFFICE Buckmaster found little to do in the first few years. In March 1917 he was much concerned about the Enemy Titles Act. In October 1917 he had undertaken a piece of war-work at the request of the Prime Minister—he became the third British representative on an Inter-Allied Council to co-ordinate the purchases of the various Allies in the U.S.A. 'You will gather', wrote the Prime Minister, 'that the labours of the Inter-Allied Council are not likely to be very exacting and that the principal object is to satisfy Congress and public opinion in America'.[1]

On the letter of invitation there is a pencilled note by Buckmaster: 'I did as I was asked and worked hard throughout but he never even by his secretary said a word to recognize what we did.'

In December 1917 he wrote to the press in support of Lansdowne's famous letter to the *Daily Telegraph*, in which that statesman had argued in support of a negotiated peace. He had circulated a memorandum to his Liberal colleagues in favour of a negotiated peace as early as the preceding May.

The end of the war found him strongly critical of some of the excesses of the Lloyd George Government. He joined with the veteran James Bryce in opposing the suggestion that the Kaiser should be brought to trial. In 1919 he corresponded frequently with an American friend, Paul Cravath. Buckmaster expressed strong disapproval of the Peace Treaty and admiration for the brilliant book by J. M. Keynes, 'The Economic Consequences of the Peace.' Buckmaster said: 'Its publication is, I think, the best thing that has happened since the Armistice. I regret the too outspoken criticism of Wilson, but it is in no way meant to be unkindly and it really represents an honest man caught in a snare he was not wise enough to avoid.'[2]

In the two following years, Buckmaster was again greatly concerned with Irish affairs. Civil war of a peculiarly bitter kind had broken out in 1919 in Ireland and the Government had resorted to the use of auxiliary forces in an attempt to restore order. These auxiliary bodies of police and military were known by the nickname of 'the black and tans' and their actions gave people in England serious cause for anxiety. In February 1921 a debate took place on the Irish situation in the House of Lords on a motion by the Archbishop of Canterbury, Randall Davidson, who, we

[1] Buckmaster papers.   [2] Ibid.

have already seen, had pleaded for mercy in the case of Roger Casement. Davidson uttered the famous phrase about the black and tans, 'You do not cast out devils by calling in devils.' His speech was strongly supported by Buckmaster who analysed with great care the evidence which showed that the Crown forces had engaged in murder, arson, and robbery. He ended his speech with these words:

I said it is no pleasure to me—it is the exact opposite of pleasure—to recount matters of this kind. Every man's mind must become subdued to his own trade, and I admit that I have a feeling with regard to the administration of justice which, it may be, others might think extravagant. To me it is not merely the exploits of our Army and our Fleet, great and imperishable as they must always be, that really established the enduring power and dominion of the British Empire. It is the fact that at all times, and in all places, under every temptation, in every condition, and between all classes of men, we have attempted to administer justice, we have attempted to be fair . . . It is because the action of the Government has, as I believe, deprived the innocent of her protection and excused the guilty before her Bar that I desire to add my voice in support of the statement of the Most Reverend Primate, and to beg for the return of further information upon this dark spot.[3]

To his American friend he wrote in March of the same year:

I will say no more about Ireland for there is nothing to be said that is good. I can think of few things so discreditable to English statesmanship and the English reputation for fair play and justice as the events that are happening there. The government made the profound mistake of thinking that a great national movement was in fact nothing but the murderous activity of a small knob of criminals and the government is powerless to deal with the situation that has arisen.[4]

Later, in the same year, in October, when there was some prospect of a truce between the two parties, Buckmaster wrote again to Cravath:

Ireland is a naked horror. Things that have been done there by the irregular troops are the counterpart of the things that were done by the Germans in Belgium. Not so gross, nor so extensive nor so indiscriminatingly cruel but in essence and principle they are identical. The armed forces that have been recruited by the Crown are chiefly composed of ex-officers and soldiers out of employment who are offered £1. 1s. 0d. a day for their services. These men go in fear of ambush and sudden assassination—a fate which from time to time overtakes them. They are maddened by the news—and sometimes the sight—of their murdered companions and not being under control they do what all men always have done in the same circumstances. They go wild and burn and kill without investigation or thought.
I do not for a moment think that they intentionally kill people they believe

[3] 44 H.L. Deb. 5s. col. 102.   [4] Buckmaster papers.

innocent—they think they are killing murderers; but we know that punishment inflicted in this way falls far too often on the innocent who cannot escape, than upon the guilty who know how to avoid detection.

The Press here is partially doped and also I think unwilling to proclaim to the world what it is that is happening. We still have at the back of our minds an uneasy feeling that we denounced these things when they were done by other people and the wrath they provoke when the matter is mentioned is the best evidence of the sore place that you have touched.

We had a great meeting at the Albert Hall the other day. Asquith and myself and Margaret Bondfield were the chief speakers. The hall holds from 8000 to 10,000 people and without a single dissentient a resolution was passed condemning what was happening in emphatic terms. Nor had I at least any reason to complain of the enthusiasm of the audience; but practically no reference was made to it in the Press beyond an account of Asquith's speech which met with interruption.

Meetings are being held in many places—almost always with the same result; but you find no record of them in the newspapers nor can we now raise the matter in Parliament, as both the Houses are more than crowded with the mass of work which must be got through before the Session ends. The memory of what we are doing will never be effaced, the evil that day by day grows, is something that we cannot measure. . . .

The Government cannot be overthrown. A majority of something like 500 cannot melt in 5 years. Strangely enough—and it is a bitter satire on democratic Government—many people are turning to the House of Lords. There at least we have some effect. I very nearly succeeded in throwing out the Government Bill for guaranteeing corn prices and I have hopes of making a big attack on their Bill for excluding German dye products. If the House would reject that Bill they would, I believe, immeasurably strengthen their position in this country.

I have only seen Lloyd George once since 1916 and that was two days ago. I met him by accident in one of the corridors of the House of Lords and he instantly asked me to tea, so I went. It is remarkable to see what a change these few years have effected in the man. To me it seemed as though the inspiration he once possessed was gone and I found myself talking to a man uneasy in manner and trying rather to evade events than to control them. One spark of the old time came back when he told me that he heard I had made a very wicked speech on his Corn Bill, and I replied that I liked the compliment as no one was a better judge of a wicked speech than he. This touched one of the old memories and for a moment his face changed. But as a great leader of all that is best in democracy I think his days are done. He will probably remain not for long the most important man in the country, but he will not lead the thing that is best.

Mr. Asquith has thrown himself into the Irish question with great zeal and vigour and made speeches that undoubtedly have had great effect upon the audiences. But he again is not reported, nor has he many effective supporters. I sometimes wonder whether he has any real supporter except myself. I think too he feels the passing away of his power and the effect of that one thing which no one but Gladstone could conquer—the numbing effect of advancing years.

Margot remains unchanged. The same quick affections; the same bitter dislikes; the same fearless indiscretions; but to her too has come the feeling that the days of her husband will not return.

It is a grievous thing to know that Asquith and Grey and the small group of the Liberal leaders could undoubtedly have redeemed this country, The men were there but the country would not have them.

Grey made a magnificent speech on Ireland and came afterwards to dine alone with me and talk things over. But the failure of his sight is terrible. The central vision is completely gone and he can only see from a small area on the circumference of his iris. Nor will he undertake the mere role of critic for he says that such a part is impossible unless the person who plays it is willing to accept the responsibility of government and that he cannot do.[5]

On 6 December, however, to the surprise of many, a Treaty was signed between Great Britain and Ireland under which the twenty-six southern counties of Ireland were established as a Dominion within the British Commonwealth. After a bitter debate the House of Lords finally approved the Treaty. Buckmaster wrote to Cravath on 18 December:

The truth is, I did not think the extreme Ulster Party could be so completely deserted by their Conservative friends who had used the Ulster grievance as a means for pushing their own political interests. It has however been done and if settlement comes to Ireland I rejoice; but I doubt if history ever has disclosed a more shameless betrayal of what people once declared to be their principles. Birkenhead made a very good speech in the House of Lords but its real cleverness consisted in completely ignoring the points made against the Government and diverting the attention of the House by matters that were wholly immaterial.[6]

Buckmaster now found himself caught up once more with the declining fortunes of the Liberal Party and in particular with the bitter personal enmities which were hastening its final collapse. He received in December 1921 a characteristic letter from Mrs. Asquith.

December 19, 1921

Beloved Buckmaster,
    I've ordered the *Contemporary Review*. I agree with every line (so sorry this got torn). What a chance Ll. G. missed in his speech Wednesday. He might have copied Peel who I think pointed to Cobden and said *he* was the man who had done the great thing—but of this we can *all always* be certain, Ll. G. will never do or say a generous thing.

I go to America 18th January, for 8 weeks touring, and finish some Chapters of my 2nd, and thank God, final vol.—entirely for money. With my sister

[5] Buckmaster papers.   [6] Ibid.

Lady Glenconner's death, we lost £2500 a year and it's a bore to be hampered in one's declining years.

You would smile if you saw the offers I've had. £1000 for anything I like to write. Jowett would have been pleased as he told me hundreds of times that I had a perfect ear, and was a master of direct English. I have no illusions, and wonder very much if this is so. How nice of Mr. Parker to write the enclosed. I don't know him, and only saw him that once. (He must be very old now.) You might return his letter at your leisure.

Could you not spend a night or two with us at the Wharf between 9th and 19th Jan.?

My Anthony is such a wonderful little boy. A saint, and so gay and clever.

How cruel that you should ever be ill. If you and I had been married we could sweep this country today. How useless Lord Grey is (*entre nous*), and how self-enfolded, and ungenerous. Why didn't we join up properly. Go to H's 1st meeting at his gates in Newcastle. Why did he ask to speak in the Lords on this late and abominable conversion, to point out, 1. *what* and 2. *who* have converted this rotten lot. 1. Public opinion and failure. 2. The little band of Free Liberals. My blood boils over it all. Let me know if you are ill and I'll come and see you.

Your devoted
Margot[7]

Early in the following year Buckmaster was drawn into discussion with Lord Rothermere, with whom he had had some correspondence on a vaguely formulated idea for restoring the unity of the party. Buckmaster described what happened at the interview in a lengthy memorandum.

1922

On Tuesday January 10th Donald Maclean and myself went, at Rothermere's request, to dine with him at the Ritz and further discussed the proposals that he had made to me before Christmas.

A long and rather tiresome discussion took place which it is impossible to record in any systematized order. Rothermere was very anxious to force an election at the present moment if it could be done. He was well assured that it would result in a breach between the Unionist and the Liberal Coalition, while the diehard group would increase and would, he thinks, be able to secure something like 80 candidates.

He was genuinely concerned about the financial position and said that he was confident that unless very severe measures were undertaken quickly the country would not recover and to use his own expression—in two years time he doubted if it would be possible to dine at the Ritz without risk of assault. . . .

He was obviously suffering from the effects of a bad attack of influenza and he spoke more unguardedly and heatedly, than he formerly had done.

He said that the people in the country would not look to the prospect of having Asquith as a leader and though he himself held friendly feelings towards

---

[7] Buckmaster papers.

him he would in fact let the whole party down. After the Paisley election if he had had any vigour he might have been Prime Minister in six months. He said that in fact quite a few people held the future of the country in their hands if they liked to use their opportunity, and of those few he regarded Donald Maclean and myself as the most important. He said he distrusted Simon, and he waved aside also on party grounds the attacks he made upon our different leaders by saying that he quite understood that we said no to everything that he said and that might be accepted. He wanted to state the position as it appeared to him. He then said once more that the whole of his press would be placed at our disposal if whoever had control of the Liberal Party would satisfy me individually that he was prepared to make as a written part of their programme a statement that would satisfy me. He said he would take nothing else. . . .

He stated that he believed Lloyd George had got at least a quarter of a million out of the four peerages that he had created, that he had very nearly bought the 'Manchester Guardian', that if it went against him he certainly would buy and that he would buy up every Liberal paper that had any effective circulation. He said that Liberals would find themselves absolutely stranded. He added that the power of the newspapers did not consist in booming public men as much as in their power wholly to exclude them from public notice—he added that a favourite statement of Northcliffe was that 'the power of the Press is the power to suppress'.

He wanted arrangements made about his sixty or eighty candidates so that they should not be opposed. He said that they were all fighting seats in the South and West of England where no Liberal had a chance.

Maclean said he was quite willing to consider that if he sent down his representative to Abingdon Street to give him the list of candidates and constituencies to which he referred, he also mentioned the prospect of withdrawing a man from the Isle of Thanet. This made Rothermere very excited. He said Maclean had made a bad mistake in referring to it, that as for his son, he wanted him fought, that his son liked fighting and that he would subscribe £500 towards the expenses of the Liberal candidate in order to put him up. He was obviously much touched by the reference to his son. He said he had lost two sons in the War and that this was a fine boy who cared for nothing and who feared nothing. He added that if we came into power—which he kept on contemplating as possible—we ought to give his son a Secretaryship to which I said your son had better then join our Party. That was the only comment made by either Maclean or myself upon that point.[8]

In the same month Buckmaster received a rather pathetic appeal from a former Liberal Cabinet Minister who had lost his seat before the war and had never been able to regain it. C. F. G. Masterman wrote to him:

January 19, 1922

My dear Buck,

Apologies for this little note. No one was ever more delighted than

[8] Buckmaster papers.

I was, when I heard you were going to speak next Monday. But it is *you* who can make it a success, you only. What we need, and what we lack, said Gladstone to me last week (speaking of the Party but remembering his father and how with such a weapon he would bring cheering audiences to their feet), is moral enthusiasm. Give it 'em. Make them rise to their feet. Denounce the whole concoction and its leader as immoral. Something on the lines of the Swinburne we quoted 'the ever lasting hell shall surely get hold of you'. Neither Asquith nor Grey are capable of this style of eloquence. But without some of it our meeting will be a failure and our people disappointed. And the papers will say, these are the old men. George and Churchill are the new.

Show them up as the cheats, liars, reptiles lepers that they are,
How we drove them to stop massacre in Ireland.
How their promises have ruined Europe.
How George is today selling Liberalism for his own power.
The utter failure of all cursed European conferences.
His killing of the League of Nations.

Ever yours,
C. F. G. Masterman[9]

But all these efforts were in vain. The fall of the Coalition Government after the Carlton Club meeting on 19 October 1922 was welcome to Buckmaster. As an ardent Asquithian he would rather have a government under Bonar Law than under Lloyd George. He offered his congratulations to Baldwin, the new Chancellor of the Exchequer, who had made a telling speech at the Carlton Club in favour of ending the Coalition:

25 October 1922

My dear Baldwin,

It is the duty of all good Liberals to hate Tories but when I sat down after breakfast to my morning hate, I felt all my proper feelings melting on reading your name and in the end I was saying
'For all his tariff hide,
He is white pure white inside.'
and I recognized that your appointment was one that would please all your old companions in the House of Commons and not least myself.

'Duriora canamus.' Cave's appointment leaves a vacancy among the Law Lords.

I want to tell you that to fill that vacancy will be a wanton waste of £6000 a year. We have just the same number for the work as before and, owing to some rather strenuous work, the lists are lighter than they have been for a long time. The Act under which alone the appointment could be made expressly contemplates that it is only in emergency that the numbers are to be kept up. For the moment no such need exists.

The appointment is the P.M.'s, so I cannot write to him but as I shall criticize the appointment if made I thought it fair to write to you.

[9] Buckmaster papers.

It was not however for this that I have bored you with a letter but to say that I wish you luck.

Yours very sincerely,
Buckmaster[1]

He received the following reply:

26 October 1922

My dear Buckmaster,

　　　I value your letter very much and am grateful for your kind words.

A fortnight ago I thought I was out of public life for ever, and now—here I am, if only for a month. It is very strange.

It has been an unpleasant time, and I hope it will be my first and last political crisis: but I could not have acted otherwise.

Thank you for giving me your views on the Law Lords: I will speak to Bonar to-morrow.

Very sincerely yours
Stanley Baldwin[2]

A month later another letter arrived from Treasury Chambers:

19.xi.22.

My dear Buckmaster,

　　　I prize your letter for it is a testimonial from one of the small band of men whose good opinion I value. It was a kind thought to write and I thank you warmly.

Very sincerely yours
Stanley Baldwin[3]

The Liberal Party itself, however, was further weakened by the elections of 1923 and 1924, and by 1926 the party was completely split and discredited after the General Strike of that year.

Buckmaster was asked to support Asquith at a meeting at Greenock but was seriously ill at the time and unable to support his own chief. He wrote a line to tell Asquith this and received a reply which was lengthier than Asquith's normal laconic letters:

October 21, 1926

My dear Buckmaster,

　　　I missed you very much at Greenock as did our old Paisley friends, who were well represented at the meeting. But I knew that your soul was with us.

I am more touched that I can tell you by your pencil letter. I well remember after the Cambridge meeting which you recall, saying on my return to my

[1] Baldwin papers. The vacancy was filled in 1923 by the promotion of Younger L. J. (Lord Blanesburgh).

[2] Buckmaster papers.　　[3] Ibid.

friends in London: 'I have found the best platform speaker in England.' But I did not then know how closely our futures were going to be interwoven, or how much, besides speaking, you were going to contribute to the stock of Liberal ideals, and the effectiveness of our fighting force. Still less could I foresee how deeply I was to be indebted personally to your unfailing loyalty and affection.

These late events have again brought things to a test, and as far as I am concerned to a final test. It had to come to this; that, if I retained my post, I had to choose between leading a section in a squalid faction fight, or submitting to a hollow and humiliating accommodation. I could, of course, do neither; and the only thing that gave me pause was the pain which I knew I should inflict (as my letters everyday abundantly prove) upon countless men and women of tested loyalty; at once the flower and the salt of the Party.

The decision had to be taken—at whatever cost.

I most earnestly hope that you are making substantial and rapid progress. You have been much in our thoughts.

Ever yours,
Oxford[4]

Buckmaster's last contact with the declining affairs of the Liberal Party was in June 1929 when he wrote to William A. Jowitt to commiserate with him on the attacks which he had been subjected to after his decision to join the Labour Party as Attorney-General, although he had been returned to Parliament as a Liberal in the General Election one week before.

8.6.29

My dear Jowitt

     Some people may misunderstand what you have done. I want to write & tell you I understand it thoroughly and that I am overjoyed that the cause which my dear Daughter made her own and to which she gave her life will receive your aid. I feel as you do that the hope & enthusiasm which gave life to the Liberal party is gone. How could it ever be nourished on the spoils of profiteers. My time is over—May you long be able to urge on the only cause that ever made the Liberal Party live—the cause of those who are beaten down & oppressed in the fierce race for wealth.

Yours
Buckmaster[5]

Jowitt replied:

June 11, 1929

Your letter has been a real consolation to me at a time of great stress.

I knew I should be made a target for most bitter abuse, and I knew that the time and manner of my going out would invite criticism.

I have tried for once to show courage and unselfishness—I've funked it previously though I felt it was right.

<hr />

[4] Buckmaster papers.   [5] Jowitt papers.

During this last election, when I was fighting side by side with labour, I noticed the splendid enthusiasm, and idealism which they possess, and I realized what a tremendous force for good that enthusiasm and idealism might prove to be—if wisely led.

I shall use every ounce of my energy and ability to help this government to success.

Only on Sunday last, when feeling utterly wretched, was I saying to Norman Foster 'what will Lord Buckmaster say'? I was so afraid you wouldn't understand—and I am much too sensitive to pretend I didn't mind.

He wanted me to put up for the Garrick Club, and I said I'd like to do so—to see if I should be black-balled. I suppose I'm right in not answering any of the attacks.

I was grieved to hear of your daughter's death. She was a martyr to the cause, which will remain the only cause worth serving, when all our party quarrels are forgotten.

You will like to know that your letter has helped me through these bitter days.

Yours with deep gratitude,
William A. Jowitt[6]

It was, however, in the field of reform, social and legal, that Buckmaster made his greatest reputation at this period. He employed a style of oratory which almost nobody else in England then used. To a modern generation it may seem almost embarrassingly high flown and melodramatic but it is the universal testimony of those who heard him that his audience never felt anything strained or artificial during the delivery.

The reading of old speeches Sir James Stephen once said is like the eating of mouldy wedding cake. That I fear is true of most oratory which owed its success to the excitement of an occasion, or to charms of voice and presence in the orator which we cannot recover. But a speech may have certain artistic qualities of structure and language which delight us even when read in cold blood long after the battle in which it was delivered has been lost or won. . . . Lord Buckmaster seems to be our most finished master of oratory since Lord Rosebery's golden voice was silent. Other orators have gifts of declamation and satire and emotion to which he makes no claim. But he has the supreme gift of persuasiveness. . . . He has two qualities not always found together: he is humane and he is a humanist. He is a hater of injustice and tender to suffering, and he is also filled with the spirit of old good books, and has a fastidious taste and a sensitive imagination.[7]

This judgment of Buckmaster's style of oratory was by a good judge— John Buchan, later Lord Tweedsmuir.

The speeches which Buckmaster delivered to so many audiences had

---

[6] Buckmaster papers.   [7] See Johnston, *An Orator of Justice*, p. ix.

one noticeable characteristic—they were never written out in advance. A few notes, mainly scribbled on the backs of envelopes, were sufficient. It may perhaps be in order to cite a few extracts from typical speeches. A collection which was made of them shortly before his death showed that they ranged over a wide field. He was particularly pleased that his advocacy had secured the passing of an Act for the protection of lapwings. Amongst other causes which appealed to his reforming spirit were birth control, the abolition of capital punishment, the improvement of housing conditions for the poor, female suffrage, and divorce.

With Lord Birkenhead, the then Lord Chancellor, he took a most active part in trying to persuade Parliament to reform the English laws of divorce, thus, incidentally, proving the untruth of the old saying that judges are seldom interested in law reform. This was never Buckmaster's attitude. He was not a man who worshipped tradition for the sake of tradition. When his colleague, Lord Hanworth, once defended an obsolete rule on the grounds that so it had always been, Buckmaster replied, 'I tell your Lordships frankly, that I would as soon worship a gargoyle on the Cathedral of Notre Dame, because it happened to be part of a sacred edifice, as I would pay the least respect to some vicious and distorted anachronism because it happened to be part of the stately fabric of the law. To show reverence where reverence is not due is to rob reverence of its respect and devotion of its grace.'[8]

The background to the story of divorce law reform is briefly as follows:

In 1912 a Royal Commission, under the chairmanship of Lord Gorell, reported in favour of widespread reforms. In November 1918 Buckmaster introduced a Bill to enable divorce to be obtained for desertion, and to give poor people access to the county courts. It was defeated by thirty-nine votes to twenty-nine. In March 1920 Buckmaster moved the second reading of a much weightier Bill, which incorporated all the recommendations of the Gorell Commission. It added five new grounds for divorce to the existing ground of adultery. The Bill eventually passed through the House by a small majority after lengthy and heated debates, but the Government could not find either the courage or the time to take it up in the House of Commons, and so it lapsed. The following year another Bill was introduced but again lapsed for lack of support. In 1923 the law was altered so as to provide that a wife, equally with her husband, could obtain a divorce on the sole ground of adultery. This Bill had been passed first in the House of Commons and when it reached the Lords Buckmaster took charge of it and secured its passage into law. In March 1924 he moved again the second reading of a Bill based on the Gorell Commission Report of 1912, but once again Parliament as a whole showed it was unwilling

[8] Johnston, p. 169.

to move in the matter and it was not until 1937 that the skill of Mr. A. P. Herbert procured a change in the law.

Arguing in favour of recognizing desertion as a ground for a decree of divorce, Buckmaster said:

I had a letter a fortnight ago telling me that two sisters had married two men on the same day and had both been deserted within a fortnight. There they were, left alone; and what is the future before them? Their position is one which the law recognizes as that of married women. The obligation which the law casts on every man to support his wife is utterly denied and can never be enforced. These women are compelled to pass the rest of their lives either in a state of immorality or in a state of embittered loneliness, and to wait until death shall relieve them of the bond from which the law is at present unable to grant release. It is a pitiful thing to contemplate women like these, waiting day by day, while all the time the wine of life is oozing drop by drop, the leaves of life are falling one by one. Noble Lords tell me: 'These of course are grievous cases to which you refer but we have a remedy. You say there is none, but the Church in its thoughtfulness has provided you, for over two hundred years, with a remedy. There is judicial separation.' Judicial separation for a woman deserted by a man that she cannot find! What is the use of that? She is already deserted beyond all possible chance of recall.[9]

Buckmaster went on to ridicule the notion of judicial separation as 'the fruit of compromise, made up of pious doctrine and worldly stupidity'.

The speech made a great impression on the peers. A friend, Lady Frances Balfour, wrote afterwards: 'I have rarely seen the House so enthusiastic—who *clapped*? Some one did, tho' the sound was quickly suppressed! ... Lord Finlay dined with me, and tho' an obstinate old Tory, and an upholder of all established bad laws, he was full of the speech, and said that he never heard yet anything like as good'.[1]

An observer who listened to one of his speeches at this period has left an account of his personal appearance.

He is a man of medium height; and lean. He has a lean face; high cheek bones, hollow cheeks, an aquiline nose, deep set blue eyes, and an earnestness of manner that reaches the quality of solemnity. As he begins to speak he twists a gold ring on his left hand, he twists it rapidly, eagerly; it is the sole indication of nervousness he displays. He speaks with an admirable, clear and easily heard voice, which never falters, which speaks admirable, choicely arranged, finely inflected language ... there is force, precision, care in each syllable; not a slip, not a tremor, not a hesitancy; he finishes his preliminary opening, puts on a pair of heavy-rimmed, thick-stemmed spectacles, and moves into the main section of his address.[2]

[9] 56 H.L. Deb. 5th s. col. 643–4.   [1] Buckmaster papers.
[2] (1925) 3 Can. Bar Rev. 495.

It is interesting to note that Buckmaster was not a tall man—but neither were some of the great nineteenth-century orators, like Bright, Gladstone, and Rosebery.

Another observer of this period remembered how, at a City banquet, when the guests had become impatient and anxious to leave after a succession of heavy speeches from eminent Aldermen, Buckmaster rose at the end to propose a toast to the Judicial Committee of the Privy Council—not a subject which would normally attract an after-dinner audience, least of all one which was anxiously wondering how soon it might escape. But within a few minutes Buckmaster had the guests held in rigid attention.[3] He described a scene in which three chiefs of a West African tribe in their national dress came to lay before the Judicial Committee certain of their grievances.

These men neither worshipped our God nor understood our language. Nevertheless, they were there to discuss a settlement with men whose faces they had never seen, whose voices they had never heard. There we have evidence that London, the centre of the British Empire, is not only the greatest City the world has ever known, remarkable for its Government, its wealth, its various activities, and its venerable buildings, but that it is the centre of a great and living power whose strong pulse throbs and tingles to the far finger tips of the world.[4]

Although a reformer of a distinctly radical cast of mind which became more noticeable as he grew older Buckmaster was not a revolutionary. He was content to work for change within the framework of the established order. His passionate interest in the cause of social justice, which can be ascribed partly to his family background, inclined him towards the Labour Party, and in 1924 there were even some informal soundings to see whether he would accept the Woolsack in Ramsay MacDonald's Government. But eventually, as has been seen, the position was filled by Haldane.

Buckmaster's concern for worthy causes did not mean that he was a sombre or unsociable man. He had many friends in the political and literary worlds of London, and was a popular member of the Garrick Club. 'He seldom said a witty thing and seldom told a good story, but his speeches at the famous Sunday dinners of the club were delightful in their always kindly humour. Perhaps the best of his talk was when, on a fishing holiday beside the Spey, he would be lying on the bank with a friend, often his faithful and much-loved gillie, waiting for the sun to go off the pool.'[5] All through his life he was devoted to the outdoor world and

[3] Information from the Hon. Sir Albert Napier.
[4] Johnston, p. 205.   [5] DNB, 1931–1940, p. 121.

wild life. 'I remember his declaring, with an ecstasy which might seem to be extravagant, but which was not assumed, that one of the most wonderful moments of his life was when, walking in a garden, a robin perched on his hand and sang his song.'[6]

We may turn now to consider Buckmaster's work as a judge in the years after his retirement from the Woolsack. As an ex-Lord Chancellor he was of course in receipt of a pension of £5,000 a year with no more than an obligation of honour to assist when called upon to discharge judicial duties, but his sense of duty and desire for public service were so keen that he sat constantly, either in the House of Lords or Judicial Committee, or even at first instance during the post-war boom in litigation when the lists, particularly in the King's Bench Division and the Divorce Court, were full to overflowing. His sense of duty was so strong that he regarded with contempt the failure of a retired Law Lord like Shaw to sit when necessary. With Lord Birkenhead, who had become Lord Chancellor in January 1919, he was on the friendliest of terms, the new Chancellor having replied in his own hand to a letter of congratulations:

Jan. 14, 1919

My dear Stanley,
  Thank you so much for your most kind letter. You will be surprised to find how much I value and shall rely upon your promise to help me.

You must keep me straight in all Chancery matters. It is to me one of the compensations of the change, which in many ways I regret, that it will renew our friendly association.

Yours ever,
F. E.[7]

There is, however, some evidence that he found the increasing judicial work which he had voluntarily undertaken something of a strain. In February 1923 he received from Sir Claud Schuster, the following letter, in reply to one which has not been traced:

Naturally your letter gave me both pain and anxiety. Consider my position. You taught me to have a zeal for justice and a deep interest in the prompt and effectual dispatch of the business of the Court. I know quite well that so far as you assist in attaining those ends, you are withdrawn from other activities, more pleasant in themselves, and even more profitable. But surely on all your teaching they are not more important. What matters more to a modern state than the maintenance of its supreme court in power and dignity? And, even from your own point of view, I cannot think that there is no sense of satisfaction in doing a thing, in itself worthy of the employment of the highest intellectual faculties, as superbly well as you do this. After all, what is the situation? We

[6] Simon, *Retrospect*, p. 87.   [7] Buckmaster papers.

turn to you in every difficulty, because speaking not otherwise than with respect of your colleagues, you are by far the best president of the Court. The Chancellor cannot always sit. We cannot hope to have the benefit of F. E.'s attendance constantly. Upon whom else, other than yourself, can we depend, either to get through the shorter cases in reasonable time, or to prevent a long case from stretching itself out into a public scandal? Even when the L.C. does sit, he feels very much that another Equity mind besides his own is much wanted for the Equity cases.

Everybody realizes the great judicial qualities which you possess: and I personally cannot imagine a more solid record of accomplishment than to have been recognized universally, as you are, as the person most fitted to preside in the greatest of all tribunals.[8]

This letter does hint at one particular difficulty which Buckmaster felt and which was not remedied for several years. It arose from the fact that when he went out of office after eighteen months of service in December 1916 the then Prime Minister was either unable or unwilling to recommend him for the customary promotion to a viscounty. This produced some difficulties in precedence in the House. The rules were, and are, that in the absence of the Lord Chancellor of the day, an ex-Lord Chancellor takes precedence over other Law Lords not of higher rank in the peerage. But as between ex-Lord Chancellors precedence is according to their rank in the peerage. Hence, in the absence of the Lord Chancellor of the time, Buckmaster was liable, when sitting, not only to be presided over by Finlay, Birkenhead, Cave or Hailsham, all of whom were junior to him in the office of Lord Chancellor, but senior in rank in the peerage, but also to be ranked below Dunedin, Sumner, and Shaw. This was not put right until the New Year Honours List of 1933 when he received promotion to the rank of viscount.

Three judgments may be quoted on his judicial capacities. Two are by colleagues who sat with him in the House of Lords, one by an old friend and distinguished advocate who later himself held the Great Seal. Birkenhead said of Buckmaster that he was 'a consummate judge, perhaps a little premature, but free of petty vanity; and always ready to withdraw if it was shown that he was mistaken. Brilliant, impetuous, learned, a little wayward; a little too sure of himself; in some of his impulses almost like a child.'[9] Lord Dunedin said, after Buckmaster's death: 'I have little sympathy with Buckmaster's political ideas and performances, and think him to be a sentimentalist—unless he is sitting on his arse on the bench; there he is one of the most learned, one of the most acute, and the fairest judge I have ever sat with; and he will leave much in the books.'[1] Simon,

[8] Buckmaster papers. [9] Birkenhead, *Contemporary Personalities*, p. 157.
[1] *DNB, 1931–1940*, p. 120.

after remarking that 'It must be one of the most difficult things in the world to be a really good judge—to have the quickness of mind to see rapidly every variation and ramification of the problem, and at the same time the self-control to keep all this speculation to yourself until arguments on both sides have had their proper opportunity,' went on to say of Buckmaster that he possessed all the attributes of the ideal judge—dignity, learning, and above all a burning sense of justice. 'Occasionally, before the case was over, his brain seemed, as it were, to take fire, and the result sometimes was an outburst, always forceable but always restrained within due limits, followed by a period, not of flame, but of rather sullen smoke.'[2]

A list of the more notable cases in which Buckmaster delivered the judgment will be found in the appendix but the reader who wishes to gain a general impression of his judicial powers may well turn to his judgment in the great case of *Donoghue* v. *Stevenson*[3], in which, on an important point in the law of tort, Buckmaster delivered a judgment remarkable not only for its learning and analytical power but also for the sustained sarcasm of its style.

At the end of 1925 Buckmaster took a step which somewhat alarmed his friends. For some time he had felt frustrated and unhappy—the decline of the Liberal Party had deprived him of a suitable platform for his oratory, and reduced him to supporting causes of social reform which, though meritorious in themselves, lacked the excitement of great political issues. He went into the City in order to right what he thought was a grave injustice to the shareholders of a company called British Controlled Oil Fields. It had had an unfortunate career and its earlier history was rather a mystery. It was alleged that a Peruvian court had been bribed to secure favourable decisions. For some months Buckmaster spent all day in the office investigating a huge mass of accounts. On his advice the directors were sued, but settled the claim by the payment of £100,000. It was characteristic of Buckmaster that he should have surrendered his pension during this period.

Before he left, Buckmaster wrote to his old friend Simon as follows, on 27 November 1925:

My dear Simon,
　　　　　In a few days time I shall leave my old pastures and till new fields. No one would take such a step without feelings of regret, and had it been within my power to do the things that would make our great tribunals greater still, I should not have relinquished the work. But I feel very strongly that it would not help were I to remain. I may even retire, but if I do, it is to you beyond all others I should like to say that the parting is more bitter than many would believe. You have borne with my indecisions which must often have

2 *The Times*, 7 December 1934.　　3 [1932] A.C. 562.

been hard to bear and you have always shown your realization of the fact that I never desired anything but to wrestle with a case in order to gain its secret.

Yours ever,
Buckmaster[4]

Simon replied on the 30th:

My dear Buckmaster,

Your kind and friendly letter is characteristic of you and I am touched by your writing it to me. We are such old colleagues and friends and care so much for the same things that everything that happens to you is of the closest interest to me. I can well understand that after 10 years of the Supreme Tribunals you feel worn and worried at times. If you had not already decided your course I should have prescribed a long holiday as the best cure. But whatever you do I know you do it for high purposes, and with a single mind. We shall miss you sorely in the House of Lords and Privy Council—so often you have been the ray of sanity in a foggy debate.

For all your kindness to me, I am very grateful. I know very well that an S.G. who was a senior man of greater attainments than my own might have made his Attorney-General's life uncomfortable, and you must sometimes have had much to bear. As for the last years, it is I who have sometimes, I fear, been unduly pugnacious—but always with the feeling that I have now, that I am affectionately as well as most sincerely yours,

John Simon[5]

Life in the City however was not entirely to Buckmaster's taste and he returned to his judicial work to be greeted warmly by those he had left behind him.

In February 1928 he wrote a few lines to the veteran Lord Atkinson on his retirement and received the following reply:

Your arguments before me when you were at the Bar had some of the quality of mercy, 'which blesseth him that gives and him that takes'. I fancy you liked delivering them, but I know they always delighted, and almost always convinced me, and I may now say directly to you what I have often said behind your back—that you were the best and most attractive advocate I ever met. Our judicial association and work together was an entire pleasure and help to me, and in the lonely idleness that now awaits me I have no doubt that in a 'vacant chair I'll see your absent image' and bless you for the help you gave me, and the happiness your association afforded me.

I often longed to speak to you for the last month about my resignation, but abstained for this reason. It was arranged many months ago that my resignation should take effect on the 5th of January, 1928. About five weeks ago, when that date was approaching, the Chancellor asked me to postpone my resignation for a month for the purpose of giving them time to carry out their contemplated

[4] Simon papers.   [5] Buckmaster papers.

changes. I acceded to that request, and remained silent, because I thought if I spoke out I might cut across them. My resignation was brought about in a strange way. I had no idea of resigning, as I did not feel unequal to my work, but I did not disguise from myself that a man is not a good judge of his own ability. The Chancellor asked me to call upon him. I did call. He said the scurrilous press of Quebec had abused the Privy Council and said the members were all old fogies, that I was the oldest of the old fogies and had better resign. Of course I would not think of begging not to be dismissed, and assured him that I would resign if he wished it, and I did so. Any other course than that which I took would, I think, have been unthinkable. I never asked to be allowed to remain, and no other reason was given for dispensing with my service. I got some time to arrange my affairs.[6]

The next letters which Buckmaster's files reveal are of a somewhat different character. As Chairman of a Council for co-ordinating the work of various societies opposed to capital punishment, he received the following missive:

March 27, 1930

My dear Lord,
            I read with interest your views on hanging. Everyone seems to give their ideas, except the most important man, the hangman himself. I have been an assistant hangman since 1921, and have assisted at plenty of executions, including Mrs. Thompson, and what is the result, today I am on the dole 17 shillings per week, as no one will employ me because I am the hangman. The public are afraid of me. If I walk out I am pointed out as the man who hung so and so. I don't do it because I like it but for money and what is it. The judge gets thousands, I get £3. 3. 0 *only* when the job is carried out. If he is granted a reprieve, nothing, yet you termed it an office (an office boy gets paid, work or play). If they must carry on executions pay a salary to the men who do the job. After all, if you look the hangmen's record up, you will see they have broken down with shattered nerves—and what for it: nothing, oftener than not suicide, yet a shell-shock soldier gets a pension for life. The sheriff and judges would have to do their own hanging, if someone would give me a decent job. Would it not make a nice headline for the newspapers, English hangman on the dole. I leave you to study this, and you can make use of it at your next meeting. I remain,

Yours faithfully
Thos. N. Phillips,
Assistant Executioner

P.S. I would like a reply, what you think of this.[7]

There is no evidence that Buckmaster took any action upon this strange communication.

In October 1930 he wrote to Baldwin, who was being hard pressed within his own party by the Press Lords. By speech ('They seek power

[6] Buckmaster papers.   [7] Ibid.

without responsibility—the age-old prerogative of the harlot') and action (he secured a decisive vote of confidence from the party), Baldwin decisively routed his enemies. In response to the letter of congratulations from Buckmaster he replied on 25 October:

I have seldom had a letter that has given me more pleasure than yours. It was just like your chivalrous spirit to rush to my side at this moment! I shall always treasure it.

You and I will never be in the same political camp, but please God whenever white men have to stand together we shall be found shoulder to shoulder, wearing our gas-masks and armed with clubs and heavy boots.[8]

Later in the year a signal honour was bestowed upon him—the award of the G.C.V.O., which the King conferred on him privately. Amongst the congratulations which he received was one from his colleague Dunedin, a former Chairman of the Committee on Political Honours, of which Buckmaster himself had been appointed Chairman in 1929 and reappointed in 1931.

Don't be angry with me for writing to compliment you on your ribbon— but at best I do know that it is a thing that cannot be asked for or even hinted at by the recipient. I never sit in certain arrangements in the House of Lords without regretting that you were not made a Viscount. But at least this shows that your services are recognized in high quarters. Not that a Viscounty would have made you happier, but it would me for obvious reasons.[9]

Another colleague, and ex-Lord Chancellor, Hailsham, wrote:

I suppose there is no one who cares less about 'honours' than you do; and certainly no one who deserves them better.

I am heartily glad of a recognition which is long overdue, and I am grateful for the occasion which allows me to say so.[1]

Something of the nature of the work of the Political Honours Scrutiny Committee, which was set up in 1924 after the scandals of the Lloyd George régime, can be seen from the following letter from Lord Macmillan:

4th December, 1930

The P.M. asked me to go and see him this evening and I discussed with him our decisions of yesterday. He understands about E. & appreciates our reasons. But as regards B., he is much perturbed, for he had so little doubt as to his eligibility that he mentioned the matter to him & now of course finds himself badly embarrassed. It seems that the P.M. has known B. personally for many years, that he has given complete satisfaction as the party's solicitor & indeed is acting for the P.M. personally at this moment in his own affairs. I am disposed to reconsider the case in the circumstances. It differs materially from the other

[8] Buckmaster papers.   [9] Ibid.   [1] Ibid.

L*

one, for there is no question of public *fama* or disrepute involved, only professional reputation & if B. has been a useful adviser to the party I think we might stretch a point. If the India Office employ him, that is a reasonable testimonial. I told the P.M. that I would see what could be done to help him out of his difficulty & if you will waive your objection, so will I & so, no doubt, will Barnes.

Please let me know what you think.

An annotation in Buckmaster's handwriting reads:

I answered saying this was exactly what we were appointed to stop; the recommendation was not persisted in.[2]

Buckmaster's reputation in court circles was further shown in the following year when he was asked to undertake a mission of a peculiarly delicate and painful character. A former Liberal Cabinet Minister, a nobleman of ancient family, a Knight of the Garter, was in serious danger of criminal prosecution as a result of revelations arising out of contemplated divorce proceedings. There was a distinct feeling at Windsor that the matter should, if possible, be kept out of the Law Courts and Buckmaster, together with two other peers, Crewe and Chesterfield, the former representative of the Liberal Party, the latter of the world of fashion, called upon the culprit in order to point out to him the necessity for speedy action on his part. Although he had already been warned by Reading of his danger, they found him in a jovial mood, prepared to brazen the matter out, but in a few sentences Buckmaster revealed to him the terrible peril in which he stood and the disgrace which his folly was likely to bring upon his family and, indirectly, upon the monarchy itself. At the end of a distressing interview the nobleman signed a deed agreeing to leave the country and never return. The following week he duly surrendered all his public offices except one and went to live in the United States.

In the 1933 New Year's Honours List Buckmaster's services were further rewarded by the viscounty for which his friends had so often hoped and the veteran jurist Sir Frederick Pollock sent a characteristic letter of congratulations:

My wife's congratulations and mine on your step in the Peerage—you might find some amusement in tracing the history of its designation and therein the ambiguity of *vicecomes*. Professionally learned persons have been known not to be aware that it is also Latin and the only Latin for the sheriff.

Concerning the snail in the ginger beer bottle, I rather think the decision is right, but await the sight of your disinterested opinion in full. Undoubtedly the judgments in *George* v. *Skivington* are weak and of little use—so far I agree.[3]

[2] Buckmaster papers.   [3] Ibid.

In the same month Buckmaster received an honorary D.C.L. from Oxford.

But by now Buckmaster's health was beginning to fail and it was noted that he was losing some of his zest for life. He had, a few years earlier, received a terrible blow in the unexpected death of his daughter Margaret, the wife of Dighton Pollock, the Attorney-General's Junior on the Chancery side, and a man much admired and loved by his contemporaries. Dighton Pollock had himself died two years before his wife. Margaret Buckmaster had been a girl of exceptional ability who had devoted her talents to the cause of social reform and Buckmaster gave a sum of money to Somerville College in her memory.

In May 1934 he wrote to a friend, Sir Lancelot Sanderson:

I have been desperately ill ever since Christmas, and though I am better, it is plain that I shall never get back to my old life and the doctors are firm that I am to make no more speeches. This cuts me off from many things and people but the severance is too recent to destroy my interest in all that goes on. I was therefore greatly pleased at your letter [to *The Times*] about Sumner.[4] He was much misunderstood. He certainly did not carry his heart upon his sleeve but fastened it in a burglar proof safe and woe betide the man who fumbled at the lock. To me he was invariably kind, though we clashed on many things.

He never really had full play for his quality. I have known three men of rare intelligence. Asquith, Sumner, and Moulton (all lawyers). Asquith was the greatest, the others are hard to classify for their fields of thought are widely apart, but Sumner's was a very great mind, a little embittered by early disappointments. I was grieved to see that there was no one but his wife at his funeral service. All this is only meant to say that I am glad you wrote what you did. These things ought to be said.[5]

A month later, in June, he wrote to the same friend:

I fear my race is run and it is a pleasure you cannot realise while the race is on to hear that people whose opinion you value thought the race well run. I feel I ought to have mixed more with the men. My two best and dearest friends, Dighton Pollock and Billy Sheldon, were barristers, but partly from a shyness with which no one would credit me, and partly from the difficulties of a broken home, I never mixed with barristers as I should. . . . As I am to speak no more, I am sending you what was the last, or one of the last. It is at least short so it will not take time. The hills and the moors and the waters I shall see no more except in dreams. I do not mean to complain. I often think of those gallant boys sent back from the war permanently crippled and then I feel ashamed.[6]

To another friend, Elizabeth von Arnim, he wrote in August of the same year:

[4] *The Times*, 29 May 1934.   [5] Buckmaster papers.   [6] Ibid.

My dear Elizabeth,

You are an angel lacking wings. You cannot guess what pleasure your letter gave me. But what a dangerous thing to do! To write to a man who has been desperately ill for eight months and risk his pouring on you all his physiological, psychological, pharmaceutical symptoms and sufferings. I will however refrain, but two things may amuse you. The learned doctors of whom I have had four, attributed my collapse: (*a*) to rowing at Oxford 50 years ago, (*b*) to fishing, (*c*) to making violent speeches. However, whatever the cause, I went down to the edge of the Styx and then Charon refused to take me on board and left me to crawl back. I am still crawling, but alas I never more shall be the cat that I have been.

The other incident is not without interest. For nearly seven months I was continually doped with heroin and became a potential drug fiend. They then said the drug was beginning to disintegrate my internal organs and must be stopped, but Lord Dawson said it must be gradually stopped. I said no, there still is left 'the incomparable will' and the stores of heroin were put down the drain.

I will not try to speak of what I suffered. I still long for it but I have never even asked for it since I left it off, but I now begin to understand drug takers. Heroin gives you no dreams, stirs no imaginations, produces no sleep. It simply floods you with peace and washes all pain away.

I do so often think of you and those happy golden months on the hill, but no more 'bloom last year's roses down the old dead days'. I should love to be a lizard with you but I fear I shall not leave England again. . . . Forgive the pencil, I am not yet advanced to ink, and excuse the dullness of this letter, remembering I have been cut off from life for eight months, but the ravages of sickness have not spoiled my affection for my friends and this is intended to carry to you as much as the import duties will permit to enter.

Yours affectionately,

B.[7]

His death occurred on 5 December 1934 at his house, 1 Porchester Terrace, Hyde Park, and his body was cremated on the 7th at Golders Green, the ashes being deposited in the graveyard of the parish church at Widford in Hertfordshire. The grave, which is beside that of his wife, is on the left-hand side of the pathway under an overgrown tree. Buckmaster was succeeded by his only son, Owen Stanley. Buckmaster's will was proved at a gross sum of £93,000. Lady Buckmaster died on 23 October 1935.

[7] Buckmaster papers.

APPENDIX

Real Property and Equity. A good and characteristic judgment, showing both Buckmaster's technical Chancery learning and his keen awareness of social and religious problems, will be found in *Bourne* v. *Keane* [1919] A.C. 815. He did not hesitate to join with the majority in reversing a direct authority eighty years old and a line of *dicta* some four hundred years old when it was necessary to abolish the obsolete rule that a bequest for masses for the souls of the dead was illegal. It was a logical corollary to his earlier judgment in *Bowman* v. *Secular Society* [1917] A.C. 406, in which the House repudiated the maxim that 'Christianity was part of the law of England'.

In *Matthey* v. *Curling* [1922] 2 A.C. 180, he considered the effect of requisition by the Crown on a tenant's covenant to deliver up the demised premises in good repair. The topic of covenants to repair was also considered in *Murphy* v. *Hurly* [1922] 1 A.C. 369.

In *Boyce* v. *Wasbrough* [1922] 1 A.C. 425 the House divided three to two on a question of construction: did the words 'without having been married' in a settlement made by a divorced woman on the eve of her second marriage exclude the issue of the first marriage? The majority, Buckmaster dissenting in a judgment which contains an apt reference to Thomas Hardy's 'The Laodicean', held that they did.

In *Blackwell* v. *Blackwell* [1929] A.C. 318, he delivered a very full and careful judgment on the vexed question how far it was permissible to adduce parol evidence to prove that property had been bequeathed to a person on terms not disclosed by the will. His judgment is the foundation of the modern law on secret trusts.

Torts. Here Buckmaster's most striking contribution is his great dissenting judgment in *Donoghue* v. *Stevenson* [1932] A.C. 562. The majority of the House created a new head of the tort of negligence, imposing on the manufacturer of products a duty to take reasonable care for the safety of the ultimate consumer or user where there was no reasonable possibility of intermediate examination revealing the defect. Buckmaster dissented in a speech marked by a note of almost passionate sarcasm: he thought the majority had passed the permissible limits of judicial law-making. Time has vindicated the majority rather than Buckmaster: *Donoghue* v. *Stevenson* has been applied in scores of subsequent cases. But his dissent is still of value to the jurist because it makes plain the extent of the change effected by the majority.

Other judgments will be found in *Mersey Docks and Harbour Board* v. *Procter* [1923] A.C. 253, in which Buckmaster dissented from the conclusion of the majority that the Board had discharged their duty of care to a workman who had wandered outside his area of invitation during a fog; *Sorrell* v. *Smith* [1925] A.C. 700 (conspiracy); and *Addie & Sons, Ltd.* v. *Dumbreck* [1929] A.C. 358, and *Excelsior Wire Rope Co., Ltd.* v. *Callan* [1930] A.C. 404 (duty of operator of dangerous machine to children). Later courts have not found it easy to reconcile his judgments in the last two cases.

Other decisions in torts are *Glasgow Corporation* v. *Taylor* [1922] 1 A.C. 44 (occupier's liability); *Rainham Chemical Works* v. *Belvedere Fish Guano Co.* [1921] 2 A.C. 465 (scope of Rule in *Rylands* v. *Fletcher*); *Humphreys* v. *Dreamland (Margate), Ltd.* (1930) 100 L.J.K.B. 13, 137 (occupier's liability); *Minter* v. *Priest* [1930] A.C. 558 (privilege between solicitor and client); *Oliver* v. *Saddler & Co.* [1929] A.C. 584 (negligence in gratuitous bailment); *Tolley* v. *Fry & Sons* [1931] A.C. 333 (libel).

Contracts. Characteristic judgments by Buckmaster will be found in *Grant, Smith & Co., Ltd.* v. *Seattle Construction Co.* [1920] A.C. 162 (marine insurance); *Macaura* v. *Northern Assurance Co., Ltd.* [1925] A.C. 619 (meaning of insurable interest); *Clayton & Waller, Ltd.* v. *Oliver* [1930] A.C. 209 (damages for loss of publicity); *May and Butcher, Ltd.* v. *R.* [1934] 2 K.B. 17n. (uncertainty of terms).

Constitutional Law. He delivered judgments in *Considine* v. *McInerney* [1916] 2 A.C. 102 (status of Crown servants); *Att.-Gen.* v. *Wilts. United Dairies, Ltd.* (1922) 91 L.J.K.B. 897 (illegal taxation); *Roberts* v. *Hopwood* [1925] A.C. 578 (control of discretionary powers); *Engelke* v. *Musmann* [1928] A.C. 433 (diplomatic privilege).

Conflict of Laws. In *Ramsay* v. *Liverpool Infirmary* [1930] A.C. 588, Buckmaster presided on the hearing of an appeal raising the issue whether a testator had abandoned his Scottish domicile of origin as a result of 35 years residence in England. The House held that he had not displaced the strong presumption against the acquisition of a new domicile of choice.

A question relating to domicile also arose in *Ross* v. *Ross* [1930] A.C. 1, which also contains a quotable example of judicial wit: 'Mrs. Dalziel appears to have been one of those enthusiastic sportswomen who demonstrate an interest in nature by seeking to destroy the rarest specimens of her handiwork. She was intrepid, a good horse-woman, a good shot, and had been on sporting expeditions in the Rocky Mountains alone with guides.'

Industrial and Commercial Law. Good judgments will be found in *Carpenters' Society* v. *Braithwaite* [1922] 2 A.C. 440 (construction of penal rules of trade union); *Lloyd's Bank* v. *Savory* [1933] A.C. 201 (negligence by collecting bank).

LORD FINLAY

CHAPTER I

ROBERT BANNATYNE FINLAY was born on 11 July 1842 at Cherry Bank, Main Street, Newhaven, a substantial house on the site now occupied by No. 1 Stanley Road. Newhaven was then a small fishing village near Trinity on the outskirts of Edinburgh where his father, Dr. William Finlay, had a flourishing medical practice.

His mother was Ann, daughter of Robert Bannatyne of Leith. After attending Mr. Oliphant's school in Charlotte Square, then one of the best preparatory schools in Edinburgh, Robert proceeded to The Edinburgh Academy, walking there every morning from Trinity. At The Edinburgh Academy scores of famous Scotsmen had been educated. By a curious coincidence, two of the Chancellors of our period, Finlay and Haldane, were at school there. In those days the practice at the school was for boys to begin at the age of 9 or 10 years and leave seven years later. Each class remained a body throughout its school career, promotion being automatic and not on merit. But within each class there was severe competition stimulated by the serious teaching for which Scottish education has always been famous. Haldane did not recall his school days with pleasure. Speaking of the time when he was there fourteen years later, he said that 'although of a superior type, [it] was not from a modern educational point of view very highly administered in those days'.[1]

Robert Finlay was the eldest of Dr. Finlay's seven sons to attend the school, at which for twenty-five years there was at least one Finlay. All of them, save the future Lord Chancellor, were good rugby players and one, Ninian, a most famous three-quarter, who received his international cap for Scotland while still at school. When Robert Finlay was a young man at the Bar he was introduced to a contemporary who 'listened with languid interest to my remarks but when he was told that I was the brother of Ninian Finlay his whole attitude changed, profound respect for the brother of so great a man took the place of the toleration he had previously been disposed to extend to me.'[2] Amongst his masters was a brother of the mid-Victorian hero, Hodson of Hodson's Horse.

Robert Finlay showed his talents in his very first year by being appointed to the position of *dux* of his class. The first class in those days was known by the nickname of the 'geits'. This honour was one which he held for each of the subsequent seven years (except the fourth) he was at the school, and in 1858, his last year at school, he was *dux* of the whole school. The *dux* of the 'geits' was invited to the breakfast given by the directors of the

[1] Lord Haldane, *An Autobiography* (1929), p. 5.   [2] Finlay papers.

school in the summer of 1852, and the boy of 10 years was placed next to Lord Cockburn of the Court of Session, whose *Memorials of his Time* is one of the most readable and entertaining books of legal memoirs which have ever been published. Cockburn had been born in 1779 and was almost a contemporary of Sir Walter Scott. The old judge and the young schoolboy sitting side by side were between them to cover 150 years of Scottish history. Finlay remembered that Cockburn said to him that Scott had advised the school to abandon the traditional Scottish pronunciation of Latin because many of the boys would go to England and endeavour to make a career at the Bar and in Parliament. 'Why should they be handicapped with what would be regarded, south of the Tweed, as a provincial pronunciation of Latin?' remarked Scott and his hint appears to have been taken by the authorities. The education which Finlay received was the traditional Scottish one firmly based on the classics and to the end of his life he retained a keen and genuine interest in classical literature. He once sent for a copy of Homer in the middle of a consultation about a barge with the name of a Greek hero which had stirred his memory. He was also fluent in French, Italian, Spanish, and modern Greek, and, in his eighties was to astonish the famous jurist Anzilotti on the international court by producing an apt quotation from Dante in the course of a legal argument. Like Halsbury, he was familiar with the best authors in classical and modern literature.

In 1858 he proceeded to Edinburgh University to follow his father's profession of medicine. Here he went through the usual curriculum and graduated M.D. in 1863, obtaining amongst other honours, a gold medal in the classes of midwifery and medical jurisprudence. Then for some reason he abandoned medicine, entered the Middle Temple on 28 January 1865, and was called to the Bar on 18 November 1867. During his university career he was a prominent speaker in the medical undergraduate society, the 'Diagnostic', and also took a leading role in securing Gladstone's election as Lord Rector of the University, being at that stage of his career an ardent follower of Liberalism.

So like many Scotsmen before or since, Finlay went south to seek a successful career in London. It was not so many years since Lord Campbell had written: 'Giving evidence of the profoundest abilities in Scotland is like a flower wasting its fragrance in the desert, or a gem sparkling at the bottom of the ocean, whose lustre is marked only by the stupid inhabitants of the deep.'[3] He joined the South-Eastern Circuit and became a pupil of John C. Day (later a High Court Judge) in whose chambers he stayed even after he was successful at the Bar and to whose biography[4] he was later to

---

[3] *Life of Lord Campbell*, ed. Hardcastle (1881), vol. i, p. 83.
[4] *Sir John C. S. F. Day*, By One of his Sons (1915).

PLATE 11

Lord Finlay as Chancellor

PLATE 12

Lord Finlay in later life

contribute a short introduction. Finlay first met Day in 1867 in the old Court of Common Pleas at Westminster. He was introduced by Maurice Powell, who was the author of works on the law of evidence and the editor of Day's *Common Law Procedure Acts*. Finlay wrote later:

I became Day's pupil, and I have always attributed any success I have had at the Bar to my friendship with Powell, leading, as it did, to my having the inestimable advantage of a training under Day for the practical work of the profession.

Day was at that time a Junior with a very large and a very varied practice. His chambers were the best school of law in the world. Unless he was in court, or engaged in conference or consultation, he spent his whole time in the pupils' room. Every case was discussed by him with his pupils. He had an intuitive insight into legal principles which took him, and his pupils with him, to the very heart of a case at once. Every point was debated by master and pupils with the utmost freedom. These friendly disputes were *a l'outrance*; argumentatively, quarter was neither given nor taken. Authorities, of course, were referred to, but our master never allowed the discussion to degenerate into a mere counting of decisions. Precedents were kept in their proper place as merely guides to principle.[5]

Finlay's period of waiting for briefs in chambers was passed in annotating his law reports (which were later inherited by his son) and, when this failed, in reading Dante for amusement. On circuit he was remembered for his ability to entertain the Bar Mess by declaiming 'Marmion' in a Scots accent.[6]

His professional progress was unspectacular but steady. In 1882 he took silk, although more than one judge advised him to remain a junior in the hope of being appointed Attorney-General's devil with the consequent reversion to a puisne judgeship. But the great step was taken and proved to be a distinct success. Finlay at once stepped into a heavier and more lucrative class of practice and on 24 November 1884 was elected a bencher of his Inn, of which in due course he served a year (1902) as Treasurer. In the same year he married Mary, daughter of Cosmo Innes, sheriff of Moray and Nairn, and a well-known antiquary.

[5] Ibid., pp. 19–20. [6] A. Crispe, *Reminiscences of a K.C.* (1909), p. 64.

CHAPTER II

FINLAY BY NOW felt firmly enough established at the bar to seek further advancement in the field of politics. At that date he was still a member of the moderate wing of the Liberal Party and as such he contested a vacancy at East Lothian in 1883. His efforts were, however, unsuccessful, Lord Elcho, the son of the former M.P., succeeding his father (now Lord Wemyss) in the vacancy. But at the general election of 1885 Finlay was returned for Inverness Burghs, defeating an acknowledged champion of the dissenting interest. At that time the Church of Scotland was in great fear that Gladstone would disestablish it and Finlay, a staunch upholder of the establishment, and all his life a most devout adherent of his Church, tried to bring about an agreement between its supporters on the one hand and the constitutional party in the Free Kirk on the other. His position as Member for a Highland constituency rendered him peculiarly well suited for this purpose and he drafted a short Bill, the Scottish Church Union Bill, which, on 17 March 1886, he tried to pilot through the House in the hope that it might ease consciences and remove the scruples of the constitutionalists on the point of 'spiritual independence'. His maiden speech was clear and full, but a second reading was refused by a majority of twenty-five votes.[1] But the doctrinal niceties of Scottish Presbyterianism were now overtaken by greater events. Gladstone announced his conversion to Home Rule and, over the protests of Hartington and Joseph Chamberlain, he introduced into the House of Commons the Home Rule Bill in which he attempted to do justice to the ancient claims of Ireland. Its plan was to set up an Irish Parliament and executive with control over all but certain reserved subjects, such as foreign affairs and customs. Today these proposals seem mild; then they aroused intense controversy. After Gladstone had made his famous speech introducing the Bill, there arose behind him Finlay, at that stage a slim, keen, sharp-faced man aged 43, looking younger than his years. Speaking slowly and with complete self-confidence Finlay, instead of a general denunciation of the Bill coupled with attacks on the Irish party, took it in his hands as though it were a brief, went into some of its clauses, dissected them coldly and logically, and so in the end proved one of its severest critics.[2] After sixteen days of passionate debate the second reading was defeated on 8 June by 343 votes to 313. Finlay's appearance and

[1] 303 H.C. Deb. 3s. col. 1057.
[2] 305 H.C. Deb. 3s. col. 1679.

manner made a considerable impression on Gladstone, which was not of an entirely favourable kind. When, at the general election of 1886, Finlay was returned as a Liberal Unionist he, along with others in his position, sat for some time in the House on the same side as the Liberal Party itself. Whenever Gladstone rose to speak and, as was his wont, turned round to seek encouragement from his followers, he found right behind him this rigid, unsmiling, Scottish face. It was said that only one other Liberal Unionist Member had the same power of goading Gladstone to a frenzy.[3] The result was to establish Finlay's reputation securely in the ranks of the Unionist Party, a reputation which was increased by the part which he played in the debates on the Crimes Act of 1887, in which he showed himself a convinced supporter of 'strong government'. Apart from Irish affairs Finlay's contributions to debate were not very notable, though in 1888 he supported the Criminal Evidence Bill which was introduced by the Government but failed to pass. In May 1890 he drafted and introduced the Supreme Court of Judicature Act, 1890,[4] which had as its main object the abolition of Divisional Courts. These absorbed much judicial power to little purpose. In future, Finlay proposed, the Queen's Bench judges would have to do as the Chancery judges did, that is, to dispose of every case up to final judgment. Any step beyond would be taken to the Court of Appeal, before which all motions for new trials would also in future be made. Divisional Courts were, however, retained for criminal matters and Crown paper applications. This was because the Bill was vehemently opposed by the officials of the Crown Office, who persuaded Lord Coleridge, the Chief Justice, that the ancient common law of England would be imperilled if appeals from magistrates and county court judges were taken away from the Queen's Bench Division.

Outside the House Finlay took little part in political activity in the country generally and was not widely known as a platform speaker. Perhaps for this reason he lost his seat at the general election of 1892, being defeated by Gilbert Beith, and so was out of Parliament all through Gladstone's last ministry. He regained his seat only at the election of 1895. During these years he was occupied in building up an exceptional position for himself at the English Bar. An observer of the period wrote:

Finlay, in the '90's, was one of the great Victorian figures whether as silk or as Law Officer. In those days certain people were institutions rather than individuals—aere perennius. People regarded Queen Victoria or Gladstone as abiding monuments. It was a profound shock when they passed away. If St. Paul's Cathedral or Westminster Abbey had been swallowed up by an earthquake something of the same sensation might have been experienced. To the

[3] A. D. Elliott, *Life of Goschen* (1911), vol. ii, p. 133.
[4] 144 H.C. Deb. 3s. col. 799.

Bar of the 90's Finlay was a rock—absolutely reliable, solid and trustworthy. He had a slightly rustic air and, with his handsome features, deep set eyes, and good figure, he might have passed as a prosperous Scottish farmer. In later days it savoured of impertinence that one who, in Victorian eyes was almost a youngster, like Lord Birkenhead should usurp the place occupied by so venerated a man.[5]

The Law Reports of these years are full of cases in which Finlay's name appears as counsel before the Court of Appeal, the House of Lords or the Judicial Committee in civil litigation of the heaviest class. Two of the cases in which Finlay made his name in professional circles may be mentioned. The first was *Fry* v. *Tapson* in 1884.[6] In this case the trustees of a marriage settlement, Messrs. Tapson and Benyon-Windsor, were held personally responsible, jointly and severally, to replace the sum of £5,000 in a trust fund which they had advanced upon a mortgage of property which afterwards proved to be worthless. The circumstances were that the trustees were men of the highest character who were genuinely seeking for some means of increasing the income of the life tenant. Their solicitors eventually discovered a possible mortgage investment in a suburb of Liverpool and they recommended as a valuer for the property a person who was in fact the agent of the mortgagor. He was not a Liverpool surveyor and had no specialized local knowledge. In 1875 he went down to Liverpool and inspected the property, describing it in the most glowing terms as being a suitable residence for a Liverpool merchant prince.

This residence is one of the best, if not the best, in the Park, and stands at the end of the road, thus rendering it quite private, commanding lovely views over Sefton Park and the Toxteth Park district. It is detached, of commanding and pleasing elevation, consisting of main building and two wings, with conservatory on either side, is approached by a carriage sweep having two entrances, and contains on the ground floor vestibule and large hall artificially heated, the vestibule paved with encaustic tiles, and the ceiling gilded, and the hall ornamented with marble pillars and handsome mirror.[7]

Unfortunately four years later the mortgagor had become bankrupt and the payments under the mortgage had fallen into arrears. At the trial local surveyors gave evidence that the property was then worth no more than between £3,000 and £4,000 mainly because the neighbourhood had been developed by Lord Sefton with houses of a poor character. In these circumstances the trustees were sued by the life tenant, for whom

[5] G. Alexander, *The Temple of the Nineties* (1938), pp. 117–18.
[6] (1884) 28 Ch. Div. 268.
[7] 28 Ch. Div. 268, at 271.

Finlay appeared. He conducted a masterly cross-examination of the surviving trustee, Tapson, in order to demonstrate the imprudence of lending upon house property more than half its value and also in employing as a valuer of that property the mortgagor's agent who, of course, had a financial interest in obtaining the loan. Mr. Justice Kay held that, although he was reluctant to impose upon trustees acting honestly the consequences of a want of due care on their part, nevertheless in this case it was clear that the trust fund had been diminished if not entirely lost by their fault and they must make restitution. The case, which is a striking illustration of the stringent duties which the law imposes upon a trustee, was regarded at the Chancery Bar and by Finlay himself as being the first really significant success which he had achieved.

In 1889 he appeared, this time for the defendants, in a case which is familiar to every first-year student of law, *Derry* v. *Peek*.[8] The promoters of a tramway in Plymouth issued a prospectus[9] in which they emphasized that a peculiarly valuable feature of the undertaking was the fact that they had obtained power by Act of Parliament to use steam instead of horses as a motive power. This statement was, strictly speaking, inaccurate because the private Act of Parliament in question merely conferred on the President of the Board of Trade power to give permission for the use of steam power instead of horses. In the event this permission was refused on the ground that the streets were too narrow for a steam tramway. The plaintiff, Sir Henry Peek, had bought shares in the company and at the trial, by the skilful management of his counsel, was induced to say that he had bought them because of the statement in the prospectus that the company could use steam power. The question was whether this was a fraudulent statement giving rise to an action in tort for damages for deceit. The Court of Appeal, reversing the trial judge, held that the statement, although made innocently, was nevertheless of a character which attracted the description 'legal fraud' and the promoters were therefore responsible in damages. The House of Lords reversed this decision and emphatically stated that in order to establish fraud actual dishonesty must be shown and that absence of reasonable grounds for a belief in the truth of the statement was no more than evidence from which dishonesty might be deduced if, in all the circumstances, such a deduction was proper. It was emphasized that a careless man was not a dishonest man and that negligence in making statements upon which another acted to his pecuniary loss was not a wrong for which the law gave a remedy. Finlay appeared for one of the directors, Pethick, at the trial and in the Court of Appeal, and it is notable that he convinced the Court of Appeal that his client was

[8] (1889) 14 App. Cas. 337.
[9] Drafted by an experienced practitioner: see (1890) 89 L.T. News. 169.

innocent, and that this particular director was not made a party to the ultimate appeal to the House of Lords in which the order of the Court of Appeal was reversed. It is interesting to speculate on what the result would have been if the House of Lords had had the benefit of Finlay's advocacy, for there is no doubt that the decision, although still the law of the land, was not generally welcome. In 1914 the House of Lords, presided over by Lord Haldane, severely cut down its scope in *Nocton* v. *Ashburton*.[1] On 20 May 1914 Sir Frederick Pollock wrote to Mr. Justice Holmes:

Haldane asked me last week to a tobacco talk on *Derry* v. *Peek* and the possibility of minimizing its consequences. The Lords are going to hold that it does not apply to the situation created by a positive fiduciary duty such as a solicitor's, in other words, go as near as they dare to saying it was wrong, as all Lincoln's Inn thought at the time.[2]

As a former member of the Court of Appeal, Sir George Farwell, wrote to Haldane after the decision in *Nocton* v. *Ashburton*:

Derry v. *Peek* was, in truth, a mere common law action of deceit and the only novelty in the decision was that the House of Lords negatived the existence of any duty (beyond the ordinary duty to avoid lying) due from directors to the British public—and so shocked the poor British public that the Act of 1890 was passed.[3]

This Act, the Directors Liability Act, 1890, the provisions of which have been re-enacted in subsequent Companies Acts, imposes on those who issue a prospectus a duty to take reasonable care that the statements it contains are correct.

Finlay's style of advocacy was not suited to work at *nisi prius* but he did appear in one sensational case which brought him a great deal of publicity, although the outcome was to confirm the view that his talents were better employed elsewhere. This was the Colin Campbell divorce case in 1886. Lord Colin, the 5th son of the 8th Duke of Argyll, had married in 1881 one of the Bloods of Co. Clare. A volume entitled 'A Copious Report of the Colin Campbell Divorce Case'[4] contains the following sentence: 'England has hitherto felt a supreme eminence amongst the nations of the earth in respect to its conjugal moralities. Such a case as this, however, has shaken our reputation on the Continent. We are no longer what we were. France, with her peculiarly constructed system of society, points the finger of scorn at us.' The facts give some support to this statement.

The case was a petition for divorce by Lady Colin Campbell against

[1] [1914] A.C. 932. See *Hedley Byrne & Co.* v. *Heller (Partners) Ltd.* [1963] 3 W.L.R. 301.
[2] *Pollock-Holmes Letters*, ed. M. DeWolfe Howe, 2nd ed. (Cambridge, 1961), p. 215.
[3] N.L.S. 5910, f. 226.
[4] London, 1886. See also T. Humphreys, *A Book of Trials* (1953), pp. 11–17.

her husband on the ground of adultery with a housemaid in their service. Lord Colin cross-petitioned for divorce citing no fewer than four co-respondents—Lord Blandford, Captain Shaw, the chief of the Metropolitan Fire Brigade, General Butler, and Mr. Bird, a well-known doctor. The reason for the institution of proceedings by Lady Colin casts a discreditable light on her solicitor, George Lewis. It seems that the parties had been for some time in negotiation to settle their disputes privately and that at a meeting for this purpose Lord Colin's solicitor, Humphreys, left the room under the impression that George Lewis was going to advise his client again upon the matter. Both sides had prepared petitions but Humphreys waited before presenting his until he had heard the further proposals of his opponent. Lewis, on the other hand, as soon as the meeting was over, sent off his clerk to present Lady Colin's petition before the Divorce Court Registry closed for the day, thus securing the right of his counsel to the first and last words to the jury. In a case where there was little evidence and much prejudice he hoped that Charles Russell, Q.C., whom he had briefed, would be able to secure a verdict by this means. Finlay, who appeared for Lord Colin, described this procedure as 'an ingenious manoeuvre on which I cannot compliment Mr. George Lewis'. When Russell opened the case on behalf of Lady Colin he said very little about the allegations which she was making against her husband, but instead launched into a tremendous tirade against him on the ground of a youthful indiscretion committed while at the university, which had in fact been the subject of previous proceedings resulting in a decree of judicial separation. When the co-respondents, in particular Lord Blandford, went into the witness box they cut a very poor figure. General Butler refused to give evidence, his counsel contending that there was no case for him to answer, but fared no better, for in summing-up Mr. Justice Butt said that if General Butler was innocent it was difficult to exaggerate the meanness of his conduct in refusing to give evidence. The jury returned with the verdict for the respondent in each case and also a verdict in favour of Lord Colin on his wife's petition. They added the rider: 'The jury desires to express the opinion that in not coming forward in the interests of justice, General Butler's conduct is altogether unworthy of an English officer and a gentleman and that he is responsible for the difficulties experienced by the jury in arriving at a conclusion in this case.'

The only other case of this period which now seems of any interest was one of libel in 1890 tried before Mr. Justice Denman in which the judge took the extraordinary course of excluding the public. An opinion was obtained from Sir Richard Webster, Q.C., the Attorney-General, that such a proceeding was entirely void as a court must, save in the most exceptional circumstances, sit in public.

In one respect Finlay's career as a leader of the Bar was different from that adopted by most fashionable advocates. He never overworked. He never worried while not doing work and he never flurried while doing it. He made it a rule never to work on Sundays and to get plenty of sleep. He was accustomed to say that his first duty was to his clients. His recreations were golf (he was captain of the Royal and Ancient Club at St. Andrews in 1903, an honour which gave him peculiar pleasure), and riding. He was accustomed to ride from Kensington to the Temple on an ancient pony whose method of progress and the style of whose rider gave the more fashionable passers-by cause for amusement.

CHAPTER III

IN 1895 THE LIBERAL GOVERNMENT, under Rosebery, was finally defeated on the Army Estimates and the Conservatives took office under Salisbury as Prime Minister. The legal appointments were spaced out at tantalizing intervals. On 29 June the Great Seal was once more entrusted to Lord Halsbury and on 8 July it was announced that the former Attorney-General, Sir Richard Webster, had been re-appointed to his office. But the office of Solicitor-General was the subject of lengthy negotiations between the Prime Minister and its former holder, Sir Edward Clarke. The dispute was a somewhat unedifying one about fees, a subject on which lawyers are traditionally open to public censure. Under the old practice the Law Officers of the Crown had not been paid a comprehensive regular stipend like an ordinary civil servant, but were remunerated not only by a basic salary but also by fees on briefs sent to them by the government departments. In this way it was possible for a Law Officer to amass something in the nature of £20,000 a year. In addition he was permitted to engage in private practice. But the Gladstone Government of 1892 made it a definite rule that a Law Officer must surrender his right to engage in private practice. This ruling was made as a result of the dissatisfaction arising from Sir Richard Webster's appearance before the Parnell Commission in 1888 as counsel for *The Times*. In return for this undertaking the salaries of the Law Officers were increased; that of the Attorney-General to £9,000 and of the Solicitor-General to £6,000 per annum, but they were still entitled to fees on government briefs—a right which lasted until 1946. Clarke, however, contended that he was not or should not be bound by this ruling. Salisbury, supported by the Cabinet (except Halsbury), refused to give way. The final decision was postponed until after the elections, but when neither Salisbury nor Clarke would move from their positions a new Solicitor-General had to be found. Salisbury seems to have inclined at first to the view that Sir Edward Carson should be appointed in place of Clarke. Carson at that date had practised in England for only three years and had only recently taken silk, although he had been a silk in Ireland as well as Solicitor-General there under the Conservative Government. On 19 August Salisbury wrote to Halsbury:

What am I to do with this man? I am now leaning your way about the Solicitor-General. I was so engrossed in repelling the Trade Union doctrines of the Bar which refused to count practice at the Irish Bar as part of a barrister's record, that I omitted to examine into the relative standing of the two candidates, both Bars included. When I looked, I found that Finlay was twelve years older than Carson and has been barrister for 10 years longer than Carson. Even with the howls of the avenging Erinyes of the Carlton in my ears, it strikes me that under these circumstances it would be unjust to pass Carson over Finlay's head. Possibly, however, Finlay may not swallow the Clarke arrangement.[1]

The 'arrangement' to which Lord Salisbury referred was almost certainly the promise which he gave to Clarke on 16 August, that if there was a vacancy in the office of Attorney-General within the next two years it would be offered to him. Finlay, however, swallowed the arrangement and his appointment to the office was announced. It was, in truth, a better appointment than Carson's would have been, for great as Carson's skill as an advocate was, his legal learning was not of a sufficiently high order to be of much value to the Government. In addition, Finlay's appointment was more popular in the party, where Carson had not yet established his position and Finlay's past as a Liberal had been forgiven or forgotten. As Halsbury wrote to the Prime Minister on 23 August 1895: 'I am very glad . . . that Finlay is to have the offer. Although Carson is a very able advocate I am not certain that the day to day work of S.G. . . . would not be done better by a less brilliant but more experienced man.'[2] Clarke himself characteristically said that 'the country lost nothing by the arrangement', and praised Finlay's appointment.

For the next decade Finlay's professional advancement was inextricably bound up with the careers of Webster and Clarke. Something like a block in legal promotion occurred in this decade for almost the first time in modern legal history. In the early years of the nineteenth century the Attorney-General normally filled that office for not more than two or three years. Campbell, it is true, held the office for seven years, but that was in two distinct governments and his nearest rival in point of tenure, Pollock, was Attorney-General for no more than three years. But at the end of the nineteenth century fourteen years passed in which there were only two Law Officers (exclusive of the Liberal Government of 1892 to 1895), namely, Webster and Finlay. In part this was due to the unexpectedly lengthy tenure of the Chancellorship by Halsbury and in part to the somewhat difficult attitudes taken up by Webster and Clarke in relation to the appointments which were at various times offered to them. The problem arose in the long vacation of 1897 when Lord Esher resigned the office of Master of the Rolls. Lengthy negotiations ensued. After the position had been offered to and refused by both Webster and Clarke in turn, it was accepted by Lord Justice Lindley.[3]

[1] Halsbury papers.   [2] Salisbury papers.   [3] See above, pp. 52–54.

But three years later, in June, 1900, Lindley was promoted to the House of Lords and Webster was eventually persuaded to succeed him, Finlay in his turn being promoted to Webster's office of Attorney-General and Carson being appointed to the office of Solicitor-General for which he had been first considered five years before. In October of the same year, however, the unexpected death of Lord Russell of Killowen enabled Webster to secure his real ambition by succeeding to the office of Lord Chief Justice. The new Master of the Rolls was Lord Justice Collins: he first learned of his appointment from the newspapers, and was obliged to write to Halsbury to ask whether the news was true. In November the new Attorney-General was elected Lord Rector of Edinburgh University, obtaining 916 votes against the 621 cast for Sir Edward Grey. In 1905 Finlay had an honorary LL.D. conferred on him by Cambridge University.

The opening years of the twentieth century brought no change in the position. When Salisbury was succeeded by Balfour as Prime Minister in 1902 the veteran Halsbury was continued on the Woolsack. When the Balfour Government began to break up at the beginning of 1905 the question of finding suitable promotions for the Law Officers was much to the fore. On 17 January 1905 Balfour wrote to Halsbury:

I have promised Jeune [the retiring President of the Probate, Divorce and Admiralty Division] his peerage, so that is all settled I hope satisfactorily. Unquestionably Carson, from my point of view, has the first claim to the place if, as I presume, the Attorney-General would not take it. If you make the offer to either of them and it is accepted, I shall be in a considerable difficulty about my new Law Officer. Cripps,[4] I imagine, is the natural candidate, but though he is a very good fellow, I never quite feel that his ability shows to the best advantage in the House of Commons.
P.S. Carson's seat is safe, *Finlay's is not*, but I am sure the latter would not *look* at the offer. I think you would have to circulate the Cabinet your intention of vacating his seat but they would all agree.[5]

Later the Prime Minister wrote again:

It has come to my knowledge since I last wrote to you that Finlay's pecuniary circumstances are not what they ought to be. I had intended when we went out of office, to recommend him for a peerage, partly because I think his seat a very doubtful one, still more because with a slight and uncontroversial alteration of the statutes he might be available for House of Lords and Privy Council work, a most important object. I have now learned, to my dismay, that he does not think it possible to abandon the Bar, he has only £2000 a year, he is 63 years of age, he has been longer Law Officer at a stretch than any man since Lord Mansfield, has throughout all that period been of invaluable service to the government, the nation and the party. I admit that the idea of his resuming

[4] C. A. Cripps, Q.C., M.P., later Lord Parmoor.   [5] Halsbury papers.

the drudgery of his profession (perhaps even deprived of a seat in the House of Commons) and declining into old age without recognition or reward and without even the opportunity of using his great gifts for the public advantage, fills me with a most painful reflection. I fear that no remedy is possible, he hates divorce work and will probably not bring himself to take the vacant judgeship. Still, in the circumstances which I have described, I cannot help feeling that he ought to have the chance. Would you at least think it over.[6]

It has not been possible to discover whether Halsbury offered the vacant post to Finlay or not. In any event if offered it must have been refused because it was certainly offered to and also refused by Carson. Indeed, it later turned out that Carson was not in any event eligible for the appointment as he was not of sufficient standing at the English Bar. But the Government seem to have been concerned about Finlay's position even when breaking up in December 1905: it was said to be 'an open secret' that the Law Lordship left vacant by Lord Lindley's resignation on 29 November was offered to Finlay before it was accepted by Atkinson.[7]

So, Finlay's long career as a Law Officer came to an end, leaving him in the same position as he had been in ten years before; a Q.C. and a private member of the Bar without even a seat in the House of Commons: for, as Balfour had predicted, he had lost his seat at Inverness at the general election of 1906 to Annan Bryce, a brother of Lord Bryce. But solicitors had not forgotten him, despite his ten-year absence from private practice: his first case in the Privy Council was called on the same day as he was arguing one of his last cases as Attorney-General.

It is, in any event, a tribute to Finlay's character that he should have inspired Balfour to write such a letter, for that statesman was not generally considered to number loyalty or devotion to his supporters amongst his virtues. As A. G. Gardiner once said, 'He smiles upon his friends and leaves them to the wolves.'[8] The only tangible reward for his services which Finlay received was the G.C.M.G. which had been given to him in 1904. He was not made a member of the Privy Council until 1905, an unusually late date even at a time when the honour was more sparingly given to Law Officers than is the custom today.

We may now turn back to consider briefly some aspects of Finlay's work as Attorney-General. First, he successfully steered through the House of Commons the Company Act, 1900. Two years later, however, there was severe criticism of his failure to authorize a prosecution of the notorious company promoter, Whitaker Wright. The disappointed shareholders eventually obtained leave from a High Court judge to prefer a voluntary bill of indictment and secured a conviction. The culprit,

---

[6] Halsbury papers.   [7] (1905) 50 Sol. Jo. 87 (9 December 1905).
[8] *Prophets, Priests, and Kings* (1914), p. 34.

however, cheated justice by committing suicide before sentence was passed. Finlay's refusal to authorize a prosecution was the subject of a long debate in the House and Balfour on 19 February 1903 defended his conduct in the following words:

It is due to the Attorney-General to say, in the clearest manner, not only in the interests of the Attorney-General, but in the interests of all, that his position as a director of public prosecutions is a position absolutely independent of any of his colleagues. It is not in the power of the Government to direct the Attorney-General to direct a prosecution. No Government would do such a thing; no Attorney-General would tolerate it being done. Though it is, I believe, peculiar to the British Constitution that political officers, like the Lord Chancellor or the Attorney-General should occupy what are, in fact, great judicial positions, nobody doubts that in the exercise of their judicial or quasi-judicial functions they act entirely independently of their colleagues, and with a strict and sole regard to the duty they have to perform to the public.[9]

In 1901 Finlay was disturbed by legal difficulties arising out of Queen Victoria's death and King Edward's accession. It was so long since there had been a demise of the Crown that precedents on the matter were vague and conflicting; many thought that all the Ministers would, on their re-appointment by Edward VII, be obliged to submit themselves for re-election. Finlay wrote on 7 February to Halsbury:

Mr. Balfour has asked me to write to you as to a suggestion which has been made that ministers on reappointment by the King may have to be re-elected to the House of Commons by virtue of 6 Anne, chapter 7, section 26. The Speaker, with whom I have had some private correspondence about it, says that no one can regard the question as free from doubt and suggests that it might be considered whether there should be legislation. Of course the point need not be raised for 6 months from the date of the demise of the Crown, as during that time offices continue to be held under the Statute of Anne. It might be well to delay the issue of any formal patents to offices till it has been determined whether anything is to be done. In the meantime, if legislation be determined on, an Act could be passed to repeal section 26 so as to provide that the demise of the Crown is not to affect the tenure of office, saving of course the right to dismiss at pleasure. Ilbert has the matter in hand and will send a memorandum upon it early next week. The precedents don't seem to go very far and I suppose no conclusion of the House of Commons will be binding in an action for penalties.[1]

Halsbury wrote to the Prime Minister on the matter on 11 April:

I have been in correspondence with Finlay, he is somewhat anxious about the course he should take when the Demise of the Crown Bill is in Committee. The House of Commons men look to him to make them *quite* safe from penalty

[9] 118 H.C. Deb. 4s. col. 337.   [1] Halsbury papers.

and ask for an indemnity clause now if it is necessary. Of course this makes him very anxious and I think he is disposed to refuse and draw very nice distinctions which I do not quite follow.[2]

In the event the Act which received the Royal assent on 2 July contained a section in broad and simple terms to the effect that 'the holding of any office under the Crown, whether within or without his Majesty's dominions, shall not be affected, nor shall any fresh appointment thereto be rendered necessary, by the demise of the Crown'.

It was in the field of international law that Finlay mainly made his reputation in these years. The course of international affairs produced several events of major importance; the Spanish-American War of 1898, the Boer War of 1899 to 1902, and the Dogger Bank incident of 1904. Some of this work resulted in heavy trials, such as the prosecution of Dr. Jameson of the Jameson Raid in 1899, or Dr. Lynch, the patriotic Irishman who had joined the Boers, in 1903, or else heavy arbitrations such as the Alaska Boundary Arbitration of 1903 when Finlay assiduously but unsuccessfully presented the Canadian case. There was also an arbitration at The Hague arising out of the Venezuelan boundary dispute. All this was on top of the normal advisory work which the Law Officers carried on for the Government.

The Opinions or Reports of the Law Officers of this period have been published by Lord McNair in three volumes.[3] They give a very clear picture of the extremely wide variety of matters upon which an Attorney-General may be asked for an opinion. In the old days it was customary to send the papers first to a personage called the Queen's Advocate, but that office lapsed in 1872, and as at that date the Foreign Office did not, as it does now, employ a full-time legal adviser, the Law Officers of the Crown necessarily had to carry at their fingertips a large amount of international law. The process whereby their advice was asked has been well described by Simon, who was Solicitor-General from 1910 to 1913.

In those early days the typewriter was very little used. In sending papers to the Law Officers the Foreign Office, and some other departments also, did not duplicate their Instructions but often sent a linen bag like a small pillow case with all the original papers inside, tied and sealed around the neck, to the Solicitor-General in the first place. When you broke the seal and cut open the bag, you pitched the papers onto the table and sorted out the contents, which were usually all in original. The Instructions took the form of the Secretary of State 'presenting his compliments to the Law Officers of the Crown and inviting their attention to the circumstances that . . . that . . . etc.,' ending with the question on which advice was sought. It was rather like a judgment in a French court with its series of paragraphs 'Attendu que' or 'Vu que', all in *oratio obliqua*.

[2] Salisbury papers.   [3] *International Law Opinions* (Cambridge, 1957).

When the Law Officers had arrived at their opinion the whole process was repeated in reverse. Mr. James Abbs, who was the Law Officers' Official Clerk for this purpose and worked in the basement of the Law Courts, used to prepare for their signature an equally lengthy document to the Secretary of State, 'acknowledging receipt of his commission informing them that . . . that . . . that', etc., and ending up by saying, 'we have taken these papers and matters into our careful consideration and now have the honour to report that, in our opinion', and so forth.[4]

It seems incredible that all this circumlocution should have prevailed in this branch of Government business down to the beginning of this century.

Mr. Abbs had been appointed Chief Clerk in the Law Officers' Department by Webster and Clarke in the 1886 Tory Government. The Department as such hardly existed, and they had to pay his salary themselves. He was a man of great efficiency who put the business of the Department on a sound footing.

He kept a register of all the papers sent to the Law Officers for their opinion in non-contentious cases, which amounted to several hundreds in the course of the year. The papers being received and the date registered, they were sent alternatively to the Attorney and the Solicitor. When the opinion was written, it was sent to Mr. Abbs, and he, noting the date of the return, passed it on to the other Law Officer. If he concurred in the opinion he added his signature, and it passed again through the hands of Mr. Abbs to the proper department, the date of its delivery being duly registered.

The former casual approach to affairs had indeed produced a serious crisis for the British Government some forty years before when it had failed to prevent the departure of the armed cruiser *Alabama* from Liverpool to join the Confederate navy in the American Civil War. As a result of this unneutral act Great Britain was obliged to pay to the United States some £3,000,000 by way of compensation. The failure to prevent the departure of the ship was due almost entirely to the fact that the papers in question were detained by the Law Officers of the time for a period which prevented speedy action being taken. It is believed that the main cause of that delay was the fact that one of the Law Officers of the time was fishing on the Wye in South Wales when the parcel containing the papers was sent down to him. This fact got to the notice of the spies whom the Confederate Government had in England and they had little difficulty in intercepting the parcel on its return journey through the rural post office. After opening the parcel and seeing what the opinion was, namely that the ship should be seized at once by the Government, they were able to take steps to see that the *Alabama* put to sea without completing her fitting out.[5] (It is interesting to note that in 1897 Finlay

[4] Viscount Simon, *Retrospect* (1952), p. 59.   [5] (1893) 94 L.T. News. 490.

was away in Scotland when the Government urgently required advice as to the position of the Chinese Ambassador, who had imprisoned in the embassy the famous politician, Sun-Yat-Sen. Fortunately Webster, the Attorney-General, gave the correct advice and the prisoner was released.)

Finlay's Reports on questions of international law are notable for two facts. First, the width of the reading displayed. All the leading authorities in the main European languages are referred to, such as Grotius and Pufendorff. His reading in international law was clearly not confined, as that of his colleague Carson appears to have been, to a perfunctory acquaintance with the leading English text-books interpreted in the light of bold common sense. Finlay had a sound and scholarly knowledge of the subject. Secondly, in the words of Lord McNair himself, it is noticeable how often Finlay not only 'told the Government what the law was *but advised them what to do*'.[6] His services in this field were recognized by the award of the G.C.M.G. in 1904.

In his work as Law Officer on problems of an international law aspect, Finlay was much helped by Sir Erle Richards, later the Chichele Professor of International Law at Oxford. Finlay recorded that Richards was

well known as an able and accomplished member of the Oxford Circuit, but had not devoted any special attention to Public Law. He threw himself with his whole heart into this new class of work, and gave one more illustration of the wholesome rule that in looking for help it is much better to be guided by your opinion of a man's general abilities than by his special familiarity with the class of subject which may be expected to come up for consideration. A very distinguished statesman once said to me: 'Believe me, there is no more unsafe guide than a man with special knowledge.' After all, the primary question is always the qualities of the man himself. If he is the right sort of man he will soon familiarize himself with the problems presented by a new field.[7]

Richards assisted Finlay in both the Venezuelan Claims and the North Atlantic Coast Fisheries Arbitrations at The Hague. Finlay recorded later, in an interesting way, the methods whereby he and Richards used to prepare the case.

I think that sometimes there is an inadequate appreciation of the value of the conversational method as a preparation for the conduct of a case in court, whether it be international or municipal. It is an educational process of the most effective kind. I was early habituated to it when I myself worked in the Chambers of my friend, the late Mr. Justice Day, then Mr. Day of the Home Circuit, whose name will go down to posterity as the author of the standard edition of the Common Law Procedure Acts. He was a very busy junior, but when not actually engaged in court or in consultation he spent all his time in the pupils' room, discussing with his pupils all the cases in chambers, and, in effect, carrying

[6] McNair, *International Law Opinions*, vol. i, p. 42.   [7] (1922) 3 B.Y.I.L. 16.

on legal education in the most efficient of all possible ways—by oral discussion. With Richards I repeated the experience which I had with my old tutor, Day, and benefited greatly by the process in both cases.[8]

On the civil side, mention may perhaps be made of one unusual case in which Finlay appeared for the Crown. In 1896 there was found at Broighter, in the north of Ireland, an extremely valuable gold hoard which was packed closely together in a small space on a raised beach by Lough Foyle, which at one time had been submerged. It was argued for the Crown that the articles were treasure trove as being valuables found buried lying together in one place, the presumption being that they were intentionally hidden for the benefit of the depositor. The defendants argued that the articles had not been intentionally deposited but had been thrown into the sea as a votive offering to an ancient Irish sea god. As Mr. Justice Farwell said:

In my opinion the defendants' theory is not even plausible. I desire to speak with all respect of the gentlemen who have been called as witnesses for the defence, but I must express my opinion that the court has been occupied for a considerable time in listening to fanciful suggestions more suited to the poem of a Celtic bard than the prose of an English law reporter. The defendants' suggestion is that the articles were thrown into the sea, which, they suggest, then covered the spot in question, as a votive offering by some Irish sea king or chief to some Irish sea god at some period between 300 B.C. and 700 A.D.; for this purpose they ask the Court to infer the existence of the sea on the spot in question, the existence of an Irish sea god, the existence of a custom to make votive offerings in Ireland during the period suggested and the existence of kings or chiefs who would be likely to make such votive offerings. . . . What magic bag had the Irish sea king which would withstand the action of the waves until the ornaments confided to its care found a safe resting place in the soil formed on the surface of the beach when the sea receded? It was perhaps natural that the defendants should grasp at theories which, in justice to them, I may say were not invented for the purpose of this defence, but it is really little short of extravagant to ask the Court to assume the existence of a votive offering of a sort hitherto unknown in a land where such offerings are hitherto unknown, in a sea not known to have existed for 2000 and possibly 4000 years, to a sea god by a chieftain, both equally unknown, and to prefer this to the commonplace but natural inference that these articles were a hoard hidden for safety in a land disturbed by frequent raids and forgotten by reason of the death or slavery of the depositor.[9]

Finlay's last few months as Attorney-General evoked some serious public criticism when he appointed as junior counsel to the Inland Revenue Commissioners his son, William Finlay, who at that stage was

[8] 3 B.Y.I.L. 16, at 17.
[9] *Att.-Gen.* v. *Trustees of the British Museum* [1903] 2 Ch. 598, at 610–611.

a junior barrister of four years standing. The appointment was a valuable piece of patronage and there was a feeling in professional circles that it had been abused. The timing of the appointment was also a little unhappy.[1] In the very last week of the Balfour Government Mr. Justice Wills resigned. His place was taken by H. Sutton, the Attorney-General's devil on the common law side. Finlay then appointed S. A. T. Rowlatt *vice* Sutton, and his son William *vice* Rowlatt. Rowlatt had once been Finlay's devil on the Oxford circuit, and had by him been appointed junior counsel to the Inland Revenue in 1900: he later became a successful High Court judge. The *Law Times* on 9 December 1905 said of William Finlay:

> Of this gentleman's ability and qualifications for this important and not unremunerative post we confess our entire ignorance—a lack of knowledge that is shared by the profession generally. But we do contend that to appoint a barrister of four years and six months standing to a position of this description can only be described as a job. We are sorry to say that of recent years there has been a growing tendency to fill vacancies, even if on the Bench, without regard to the great responsibilities that rest upon the nominator.[2]

The career of William Finlay again excited notice when in 1924, his father being still alive, he was appointed to the High Court Bench by Lord Cave. The *Law Times* said on this occasion:

> Sir William Finlay must be accounted as a singularly fortunate man. Called by the Middle Temple in 1901, in 1905, being the son of the then Attorney-General, he was appointed Counsel to the Inland Revenue, an important and lucrative post previously held by counsel of standing and experience. Now, after but 23 years at the Bar, for no apparent professional reason, he is passed over the heads of those who have undoubted prior claims for consideration and whose appointment would have strengthened the King's Bench. At the present time it is essential in the highest degree that the best men available should be selected for high judicial office, and there should be no repetition of the methods of some 40 years ago.[3]

Finlay's last few months as Attorney-General were enlivened by an incident when he was a passenger in the motor-car of Sir William Anson, the Warden of All Souls, on his way from Pusey to Oxford. Anson was stopped by the police and successfully prosecuted for speeding.[4] The popular press made the most of the matter.

During the next few years Finlay built up for himself a peculiarly commanding position at the Bar, particularly in work before appellate tribunals. Yet his fees were never very high, and on at least one occasion he astounded the Temple by returning a brief on the ground that the fee

---

[1] See above, pp. 62–63.   [2] (1905) 118 L.T. News. 471.   [3] (1924) 158 L.T. News. 481.
[4] H. H. Henson, *A Memoir of Sir William Anson* (Oxford, 1920), p. 154.

marked on it was too large. There is hardly a reported case of significance in the Appeal Cases for 1906 to 1914 in which he does not appear as counsel on one side or the other. His name is particularly prominent in appeals from the Dominions to the Privy Council. During this period, in which his practice in appellate tribunals was the largest which any English barrister has ever enjoyed, he had only one 'devil', Geoffrey Lawrence, the future Lord Oaksey, who has recorded his impressions of Finlay's advocacy as follows: 'Unlike Simon he did not state every proposition in his argument. He was more compressed and gave his audience credit for understanding the process of a logical argument.'[5] So his work went steadily and happily ahead, saddened only by the death in 1911 of his wife. Thereafter his sister acted as hostess for him in London and at Nairn, where every summer he delighted to entertain a host of friends and relations. Henceforward it was noticed that his style of advocacy, never particularly light or brisk, had become increasingly prolix with advancing years, but so great was his reputation with the Bench that no attempt was ever made to hint that a slightly abbreviated mode of presentation would be preferable. It was noted that he retained his Scottish gravity to the end. He never made a joke, either in court or in the House of Commons.

One small incident from those years may be recalled. In March 1908 the Court of Mr. Justice A. T. Lawrence was disturbed by an outbreak of fisticuffs between two K.C.s, Vesey Knox and Roskill, the former of whom had made disparaging remarks about the latter's ancestry. Finlay had to separate the embattled K.C.s.[6] His last case at the Bar was the defence of Dr. J. M. Bullock, editor of *The Graphic*, on a charge of contempt of court. He had described Roger Casement as a traitor before he had actually been convicted.

[5] Letter to the author, 5 February 1959.   [6] Crispe, *Reminiscences*, p. 64.

CHAPTER IV

IN 1910 FINLAY RE-ENTERED THE HOUSE OF COMMONS as Member for Edinburgh and St. Andrews Universities. Almost at once he became a member of the Unionist Shadow Cabinet. In 1914 he even drafted for that body a proposed amendment to the Army Annual Act which would have had the effect of preventing the Government from using the Army in Ulster until after a general election. It is indeed an indication of the level of party strife over Ireland that the leaders of English conservatism should have contemplated such a reckless interference with the security of the country.

In May 1915 the reconstruction of the Asquith Government, which resulted in the departure of Haldane from the Woolsack, at once raised expectations more in the minds of his friends than of himself that Finlay's long-deferred claims to the Lord Chancellorship would be recognized. The Tories however, although strong enough to secure that Haldane was not re-appointed, were not strong enough to secure the appointment of one of their own men and, as we have seen, Buckmaster was given the Great Seal. The letters which Finlay received on that occasion tell their own story. On 29 May 1915 Carson wrote:

My dear Finlay,

Very many thanks for your kind and indeed affectionate letter. I cannot say I feel the least pleasure in being A.-G. even in the Cabinet and I greatly fear the strain of the work in front of me. But I am also greatly distressed that you are not with us as a Lord Chancellor—it spoils everything and is almost unpardonable. I understand the sole reason given was that as Lord Haldane was being unfairly dealt with they could not have a Lord Chancellor from our side. It is a real matter of disappointment to us all. My wife desires me to thank you for your kind message and sends her kind regards.

Your old and sincere friend,
Edward Carson[1]

On 2 June 1915 Austen Chamberlain wrote:

My dear Finlay,

If you have suffered a great disappointment in the formation of this government—as I feel that you must have done—your old colleagues and friends have suffered a hardly less one in not seeing you in that place which was rightfully yours and where your great abilities would have been at the service of your country and yourself always at hand to help them. You will

[1] Finlay papers.

know that we at least had no doubts as to what was due both to you and to the country and to your profession. And that our leaders did all they could to see that right was done. It is a deep disappointment to us all that they were unsuccessful and not least to your old friend,

Austen Chamberlain[2]

From the newly appointed Lord Chancellor came another letter on the 29th:

My dear Finlay,
          I cannot but value very highly your kind letter of congratulations, for but for the strange whirligig of fortune you would long ago have occupied the seat which I fill now with much misgiving. You have always been to me, as to so many others at the Bar, the man to whom we all looked as our real head and your letter is one that I was proud to receive.

Yours very sincerely,
Stanley Buckmaster[3]

But when the coalition Government finally fell in December 1916 Lloyd George offered the Woolsack to Finlay (after a period during which Loreburn, Carson,[4] and Asquith were all considered as possible holders of the office), but on one condition—that he refused to draw the pension of £5,000 a year to which an ex-Lord Chancellor was entitled. The request was made on the ground that there were four ex-Chancellors living and that in war time the country could not stand the strain of so many pensions. It was undoubtedly true that there were four living—Halsbury, Haldane, Loreburn, and Buckmaster—but although unusual this was not exceptional, for when Westbury became Chancellor in 1861 on the death of Campbell there were five ex-Chancellors living: Lyndhurst, Brougham, St. Leonards, Chelmsford, and Cranworth. In any event, Finlay accepted the condition, which was made effective by the letters patent, which are normally issued on such an occasion granting a pension of £5,000 a year conditional on the recipient ceasing to hold the office of Lord Chancellor, not being issued.

The appointment produced a flood of congratulatory letters. Balfour's former private secretary, J. S. Sandars, wrote on the 18th:

As an old friend who has worked with you in the past years I hope you will allow me to offer my very sincere congratulations to you on obtaining the dignity of Lord Chancellor. You must know well that I was one of those who greatly lamented the accidents which hitherto have hindered the due recognition of those abilities and attainments which alike in your profession and in public service have been conspicuous in your public career. But now justice has been done and the highest dignity has come to you, and with it the abundant rejoicing

[2] Finlay papers.   [3] Ibid.   [4] See H. M. Hyde, *Carson* (1953), p. 413.

of all those who know you, have learned to respect you and have loved you as a friend and a colleague. I write to you in all sincerity; and, as there is no longer any room for me in the field of political and parliamentary service, I shall always cherish the recollection I have of your kindness and co-operation in the work which in earlier days brought us together.[5]

Another letter came on 22 December from a former Conservative Whip, Lord Edmund Talbot:

I have been hoping to meet you personally to convey my most sincere congratulations. I greatly and sincerely regret losing you from the House, as you have always been a pillar I knew I could rely on for help and advice. But it was a genuine pleasure to me when I realized that you would have the offer of the Lord Chancellorship for I was bitterly disappointed, with very many others, when the circumstances of the moment prevented this at the time when the first coalition was formed.[6]

'I saw Finlay yesterday. He is like a boy with pleasure', wrote Haldane to Gosse on 19 December.[7] A large number of other letters from members of the Bench and Bar arrived in similar terms. All said more or less the same thing, that it was an appointment which would have been his long before had it not been for Lord Halsbury's long tenure of the Woolsack. Loreburn, the former Liberal Lord Chancellor, added the statement: 'That this is not meant as any disparagement to Lord Halsbury, the greatest judge we have had for a long time.'[8]

A number of letters from members of the legal profession in Canada and Australia testified to the esteem in which Finlay was enjoyed in those countries as a result of his appearances before the Privy Council.

Finally, there was a letter from the Master of the Rolls:

My dear Finlay,
        I am delighted to see that the current report is well founded and that you *will* be the Lord Chancellor. I say will be, because I suppose you are not fully possessed of all your functions until you have come to be sworn in before me. No appointment could be more popular with the Bench and the Bar. In truth it has long seemed little short of a scandal that you should be arguing cases before me. It is high time that you should be reversing me, and I am sure that you will do this in a manner which will raise no ill feelings. Believe me, my dear Finlay,

                                                Yours ever truly,
                                                Cozens-Hardy[9]

The statement by Cozens-Hardy that the office of Lord Chancellor was not fully vested in Finlay until he had been sworn in is not entirely accurate, and as there was another mistake made at the actual ceremony

---

[5] Finlay papers.   [6] Ibid.   [7] Gosse papers.
[8] Finlay papers.   [9] Ibid.

of swearing-in on Tuesday, 12 December, it may be helpful to set out the correct practice.

The appointment to the Office of Lord Chancellor is made by the Sovereign simply delivering the Great Seal to the person chosen at the same time addressing him by the title of his office, without any letters patent or other document. In 1850 Lord Langdale was appointed Commissioner of the Great Seal jointly with Vice-Chancellor Shadwell and Baron Rolfe, but he objected to receiving the Great Seal as First Commissioner until the Commission had actually been sealed on the ground that the unqualified delivery of the Great Seal would at once make him Lord Chancellor and not Commissioner. The Great Seal is normally delivered to the person appointed at a meeting of the Privy Council and immediately after the delivery the oath of allegiance and the official oath are tendered to the Lord Chancellor by the Clerk of the Council and taken in the presence of His Majesty in Council. Finlay received the Great Seal and took these oaths on 11 December. These oaths are required under the Promissory Oaths Act, 1868, which requires three oaths from a newly appointed Lord Chancellor—first, the oath of allegiance, secondly, the official oath, and thirdly, the judicial oath. The judicial oath is, according to the Statute (sect. 6), to be taken 'as soon as may be after his acceptance of office', and is administered by the Clerk of the Crown in Chancery at a later time and place. It is customary for this ceremony to take place in Appeal Court 1, 'The Master of the Rolls holding the book', according to ancient custom. It is also customary, though not required by the Act of 1868, for the Clerk of the Crown in Chancery to administer the official oath as well as the judicial oath and the oath of allegiance.[1]

When Finlay was sworn in on Tuesday, 12 December 1916, having received the Great Seal the previous day, the customary assembly of judges was seen in the court. The Lord Chief Justice and Lords Justices occupied places on the Bench; the judges of the King's Bench Division and the Chancery Division stood on either side of the Senior Master, Sir John Macdonnell, who was present in his long wig. The Clerk of the Crown, Sir Claud Schuster, duly administered the official oath and the judicial oath, the Master of the Rolls, in accordance with custom, duly 'holding the book'.

Where the error occurred was that Lord Cozens-Hardy took the central place with the Chancellor on his right and the Chief Justice on his left, as he was normally accustomed to sit when presiding in his own court. But properly speaking, the central place should have been left for the Chancellor,[2] who also should himself have ordered the oath to be recorded by

[1] When Lord Dilhorne was sworn in before Lord Denning, M.R., on 17 July 1962 (in Appeal Court 2) all three oaths were taken.   [2] This was done on 17 July 1962.

M*

the King's Remembrancer and not, as in fact happened, for this to be done by the Master of the Rolls on the motion of the Attorney-General.[3] This was the order of business observed at the swearing in of Sir Robert Reid in December 1905 and it seems to be correct in principle, for had the Court of Appeal proceeded with the business of the day it would have required a shuffling of seats to give the Lord Chancellor and the Lord Chief Justice their proper precedence over the Master of the Rolls. For although the Master of the Rolls normally presides in the Appeal Court, his precedence naturally yields to that of the Lord Chancellor and the Lord Chief Justice when present. Furthermore, in any event, the function of the Master of the Rolls at the swearing in of the Lord Chancellor is not a judicial function at all. It is a ministerial rather than a judicial duty, being a survival of his position as the first of the twelve Masters in Chancery. This is shown by the fact that in the absence of the Master of the Rolls the Senior Chancery Master holds the book, as happened when Eldon was sworn in in 1801. The Master of the Rolls as a permanent judge in the Court of Appeal dates only from 1881.

That same afternoon, Tuesday, 12 December, Finlay took his seat on the Woolsack as Speaker of the House of Lords having the unique experience of being congratulated by the four living ex-Chancellors. But Finlay was not introduced as a peer until the following Tuesday, 19 December—the day on which the letters patent for his peerage passed the Great Seal.

---

[3] As was also done on 17 July 1962.

CHAPTER V

So AT THE AGE OF 74, the greatest age at which anyone has been appointed to the Woolsack (with the exception of Lord Campbell in 1859 at the age of 80), Finlay began his career as Lord Chancellor. Eldon, who had the experience of holding the Great Seal in old age once said that, 'Commencing a Chancellorship at 73 is so foolish a business'[1] but in Finlay's case there was no reason for regret at the appointment.

It is true that his mind was never very flexible and in his later years at the Bar he had become somewhat prolix in speech with the result that when he sat on the Woolsack he was apt not merely to be loquacious himself but to refuse to still loquacity in others. His meticulous caution also made him insist on sending for all the relevant authorities: counsel and the Law Lords were quickly surrounded by small mountains of volumes bound in law calf. It was said that neither in pace nor in quality did he improve any tribunal over which he presided. The first part of this judgment may be true but the second is much more dubious. Finlay as a judge was in the first rank of Lord Chancellors. His judgments reflect his own personality: sound, careful, cautious pieces of scholarship. Of all the practitioners in active work at the English Bar he was, at the date of his appointment, the oldest in years, the senior in standing and the foremost in actual business. He fulfilled indeed the requirements for a judge which were set out in the language of medieval Scotland in the Statute of 1579, chapter 93. By this Act, which insisted upon a combination of good living, professional capacity and social status in the judiciary, it was required that a judge was to be 'Ane man that fearis God, of gude literature, practick, judgment and understanding of the lawes, of gude fame, havand sufficient living of his awin, and quha can make gude expedition and despatch of matters touching the lieges of the realm'.

In the dark last two years of the war there was little for the Lord Chancellor to do except maintain in an imperturbable fashion the functioning of the ancient machinery. This task Finlay performed exceedingly well, but as he was not a member of the War Cabinet or indeed much in sympathy with the aims and methods of the Prime Minister, his part in public affairs was not a noticeable one. In the dispatch of the routine work of his department his Scottish prudence and unwillingness to hurry sometimes worried the agile Schuster; but that formidable civil servant was wise enough to know when to restrain his impatience. Finlay disliked

[1] H. Twiss, *Life of Eldon* (1846), vol. iii, p. 16.

appointing women or parsons as Justices of the Peace—the latter he described as duffers at the job. On one occasion he wished to appoint as a magistrate a retired Indian judge who had settled down at Eastbourne but the Lord-Lieutenant of Sussex, the Duke of Norfolk, refused to nominate a person whose only connection with English soil was the occupancy of a villa at a seaside resort. Finlay was pressed to over-rule the Duke but refused: 'We must make allowances for these rustic minds', he said. He appointed four High Court judges—Maurice Hill, K.C., to the Divorce Division (1917), F. A. Roche, K.C., Clavell Salter, K.C. (1917), and P. O. Lawrence, K.C. (1919), to the King's Bench Division.

The dissolution of 1918 did not alarm him for, although he had been appointed at so advanced an age, it had been tacitly understood between him and the Prime Minister that his surrender of his claim to the normal pension was to be in return for a reasonable period of occupancy of the Woolsack. To his great surprise he was displaced. He arrived in his room in the House of Lords one morning to find on the desk a letter from the Prime Minister stating with no very great politeness and with some brevity that the Woolsack was required for another. As Finlay read the letter, his face darkened as if he had been personally insulted, and he slowly tore it across and threw it in the waste-paper basket. Otherwise he did not show his chagrin before his friends or subordinates.

The veteran Halsbury, who sat beside him at a reception at the American embassy early in the New Year, wrote afterwards to his daughter: 'We are all most disgusted at the treatment of the Lord Chancellor, who had done good work in his office. I . . . sat next to the L.C. but did not then know he was an Ex. I doubt whether he did himself, if he did he must have taken it very coolly as no word of discontent escaped his lips.'[2] But to his old friend Haldane, Finlay wrote on 14 January 1919:

My dear Haldane,
          I thank you for your most kind words. I value them very highly as coming from you.
I did not resign and was never more surprised than last Friday when I got my letter of dismissal. Your work in the post must have been killing, with all the Cabinet meetings in addition to everything else. But I was free of that and never felt that desire for 'repose' with which some papers credit me. I liked the work thoroughly and am very sorry to leave it. I mean to sit regularly—we started on Scottish appeals today—and I hope we shall often meet as hitherto in close proximity. Always,

Sincerely yours,
Finlay[3]

[2] Halsbury papers.   [3] N.L.S. 5914, ff. 13–14.

Two months later Finlay received promotion in the peerage to a viscounty.

It may be doubted whether Lloyd George regarded the arrangement of 1916 in the same light as Finlay did. It was not in Lloyd George's character to contemplate anyone holding political office otherwise than at his pleasure. There is in any event evidence that in September 1918 negotiations took place (without Finlay's knowledge) to bring about a reunion between Asquith and Lloyd George. It was suggested that Asquith should enter a reconstructed government as Lord Chancellor (a post for which he was admirably suited but for which he had not much desire), but nothing came of it.[4] Towards his successor, F. E. Smith, a man who was young enough to be his son, Finlay felt no bitterness of any kind. He at once sent him congratulations and the present Lord Birkenhead stated that, 'Probably nothing pleased him more than the brief note in which his veteran predecessor, Lord Finlay, assured him that he would at any rate appreciate the comfort of the Woolsack'.[5] Birkenhead replied in a short, typewritten letter of thanks.[6] That Finlay bore his successor no grudge is shown by the fact that a few years later, when he was sitting judicially together with Birkenhead to hear the appeal in the case of *Admiralty Commissioners* v. *The S.S. Volute*,[7] in which the law relating to contributory negligence was restated by the Lord Chancellor in a famous judgment, Finlay said, after it had been delivered: 'I regard the judgment to which we have just listened as a great and permanent contribution to our law on the subject of contributory negligence, and to the science of jurisprudence.'[8] This is almost the only reported instance in which one judge has publicly complimented a colleague on the quality of his judgment;[9] the compliment is all the more remarkable coming from a man who was as undemonstrative as Finlay normally was.

Towards Birkenhead, indeed, Finlay maintained an attitude of amused and almost paternal admiration. He attended the debate in the House of Lords in which Birkenhead defended the Government's action in signing the Irish Treaty in December, 1921. Birkenhead was obliged to speak to a bitterly hostile audience and to repudiate many of his own former beliefs and friends. This he did in a speech of remarkable power. Walking away from the House afterwards, Finlay met Sir John Marriott and said

[4] A. C. Murray, *Master and Brother* (1945), pp. 175–89.

[5] Earl of Birkenhead, *F.E.* (1959), p. 331.

[6] Finlay papers.

[7] [1922] 1 A.C. 129.

[8] [1922] 1 A.C. 129, at 145. But it is generally believed that Lord Phillimore drafted the judgment: see Lord Wright (1952) 13 M.L.R. 1, 17.

[9] In *Jones* v. *Stevens* (1822) 11 Price 235, 283, Richards C. B. congratulated the 82-year-old Wood B. on his judgment.

to him that he regarded the speech as the most wonderful which he had ever heard.[1]

On one matter though Finlay disagreed with Birkenhead. The question arose in 1922 how far it was proper for the Law Lords to make speeches of a political nature. The question arose in relation to the activities of Carson, who had recently been appointed a Lord of Appeal and who had been delivering throughout the country a series of bitter speeches attacking the Irish settlement in general and Birkenhead's part in it in particular. Birkenhead delivered a pronouncement stating that there was a clear difference between the position of the Lord Chancellor, who was universally recognized to be the chief spokesman of the Government in political matters in the House of Lords, and on the other hand the Law Lords who, although Peers of Parliament and so entitled to speak, should by convention and understanding regard themselves as being entirely impartial and detached from the excitement of daily politics. Their judicial capacity should, he thought, be entirely predominant over their legislative capacity. But Finlay disagreed with Birkenhead and argued, together with Lord Sumner, that Law Lords were entitled to take part in such political debates as they pleased.[2] No doubt in accordance with this view, Finlay in 1920 had moved a motion in the House of Lords[3] deploring the Government's treatment of General Dyer, who had been recalled from India after the incident at Amritsar in which over 400 Indians had been killed or injured by firing from troops under Dyer's command. In extreme Tory circles it was thought that the Government had failed properly to defend one of its military servants placed in a difficult position. Birkenhead later published an essay[4] in which he described Finlay's views as 'unsound in conception, and disastrous if carried into execution'. His careful argument was based on much original historical research.

After his retirement from the Woolsack Finlay embarked almost immediately on a North American tour, speaking at the annual meeting of the Canadian Bar Association in Winnipeg in August 1919. At the meeting he delivered an extremely scholarly and interesting paper entitled 'Reprisals in War and the Indirect Blockade', as well as some general reflections upon the place of international law in the post-war world.[5] This paper, which has not received from international lawyers the attention which it deserves, is of peculiar importance by reason of Finlay's position as a former Attorney-General concerned with such

[1] J. Marriott, *Fourscore Years* (1946), p. 200.
[2] 49 H.L. Deb. 5s. col. 950.   [3] 41 H.L. Deb. 5s. col. 222.
[4] Earl of Birkenhead, *Points of View* (1922), p. 147.
[5] *Proceedings of the Canadian Bar Association* (1919), p. 126.

matters. It deals in a full and careful way with the development of the
doctrine of continuous voyage during the Great War as well as the
question of how far reprisals could be used by way of retaliation against
the Germans for their submarine outrages. He also visited the standard
places of interest in Canada and the United States and sent his family at
home interesting accounts of what he had seen. On his return he plunged
at once into the work of hearing appeals and the Law Reports of the early
1920s contain many judgments in leading cases.

In 1921 there was some speculation that Finlay might be appointed
Lord Chief Justice to hold the position temporarily in succession to Lord
Reading until the Attorney-General, Hewart, could be spared by the
Government from his position in the House of Commons. It has been
stated that Finlay was willing to resign the office whenever Lloyd George
wished.[6] Birkenhead strongly opposed the suggestion on the ground that
it infringed the constitutional principle of judicial independence and in a
letter to the Prime Minister considered other objections.

Lord Finlay is approaching 79 years of age. He has in the past rendered the
most eminent services as Attorney-General and has enjoyed the highest reputation as an advocate. You yourself thought that age unfitted him to hold the
position of Lord Chancellor towards the end of 1918. Since then he has sat
frequently in the House of Lords for the purpose of hearing appeals, and it is
apparent to everyone that the great powers which he once possessed are now
gradually leaving him under the burden of his advancing years. I have no doubt
that even if he were willing to accept office on such conditions, professional
opinion would condemn the appointment, and the public would inquire how
it was that he who was too old to be Lord Chancellor in 1919 was not too old to
enter upon the arduous office of Lord Chief Justice in 1921. But in addition, it
would become apparent to the whole world immediately upon his assumption
of his duties that he had reached an age at which he was unfitted to perform
them.

This letter drew from Lloyd George an angry reply, in the course
of which he said, 'As to Finlay's capacity, Carson, whom you will admit
is the most eminent advocate of his day, told me that the profession would
regard his appointment with great satisfaction.'

Birkenhead replied promptly to this on the same day:

The question has never arisen whether a judge could properly be put under
a condition to retire at the age of 80 because, so far as I know, no one has ever
been made a judge at an age which suggested such a stipulation. Campbell was
70 when he became L.C.J. but his vitality was amazing; he was, I think, a
record. Carson has not practised before Finlay since the latter became Lord

[6] Lord Beaverbrook, *The Decline and Fall of Lloyd George* (1963), p. 36. It is hard to
believe that Finlay would have accepted such an offer from such a source.

Chancellor. I have sat with him continuously. I by no means say that he is unfit for judicial work but he is not the man he was and I do not think he could undertake the office of L.C.J. The appointment is yours and if you appoint him I shall loyally co-operate with him but *I most earnestly hope that if you do you will make him L.C.J. without any condition* relying upon his age to terminate his tenure of office within a reasonable time. If any condition is imposed I am sure that we shall find ourselves exposed to the risks and difficulties suggested in my letter, the suggestion of which was the object of that letter.[7]

Finally, in April the Prime Minister appointed Mr. Justice A. T. Lawrence, aged 77, Lord Chief Justice. In August he was created Lord Trevethin. The appointment was not popular. In March 1922 Hewart succeeded him in the position.

But in the same year, 1921, an even more significant position was offered to Finlay. The League of Nations had just established the Permanent Court of International Justice at The Hague and Finlay was invited to be the candidate supported by Great Britain. After he had been prevailed upon to accept he was amongst the few judges who were elected on the first ballot at the Second Assembly of the League at Geneva.

The appointment of a man aged 78 at first caused some surprise but Finlay's past career as a judge and as an advocate with exceptional knowledge of international law was, as we have seen, one of incomparable distinction. His knowledge of and interest in international law was shown in many ways. Apart from the years of service as Law Officer, in 1903 he appeared as leading counsel on behalf of Canada and Great Britain in the Alaska Boundary arbitration. The award was not satisfactory to Canada but she had no fault to find with the presentation of the case by Finlay. As the Canadian Agent reported after the conclusion of the hearings: 'We are much indebted to Sir Robert Finlay for his opening argument, which in dignity, clearness and mastery of detail was in every respect worthy of the important character of the issues involved.'[8]

A few months later Finlay had appeared at The Hague to argue on behalf of Great Britain, before the Permanent Court of Arbitration, the claim of the three powers which had blockaded the Venezuelan coast to priority over the other powers in the settlement of their claims against Venezuela. His argument was successful and the tribunal gave a unanimous award in favour of the three powers. Again, in 1910, when he had ceased to be either Attorney-General or a Member of Parliament, he delivered the opening speech on behalf of Canada in the North Atlantic Fisheries Arbitration before the same tribunal. This was perhaps one of the greatest forensic triumphs of his life. His argument lasted through sixteen sittings of the tribunal and was spread over a fortnight, to be followed a month

[7] Birkenhead, *F.E.*, pp. 402–7.   [8] (1929) 10 B.Y.I.L. 190, 191.

later by a speech of Mr. Root, the Secretary of State for the United States, who spoke for almost the same length of time presenting the case on behalf of the fishermen of Massachusetts and Maine.[9]

The argument put forward by the United States in the opening speech, a printed copy of which was delivered a few days before the opening of the Session, advanced an entirely novel theory with respect to the interpretation of the treaty of 1818, namely, that the legal effect of the agreement was to constitute a servitude in favour of the United States in regard to which the United States was the dominant member and Great Britain the servient; proceeding upon that theory the argument was elaborated and presented to the tribunal with reference to hundreds of writers upon international law. It was thought by Aylesworth, the Canadian Agent, that, as four members of the tribunal were skilled in civil law, they might be very much influenced by this argument and he went to see Finlay in a state of some agitation.

I consulted Sir Robert Finlay as soon as I could find him and on going up to his house, I found him in his library entrenched behind masses of books on the table, the floor was covered with them, so that one could not get to the spider in the centre of the web without travelling over the volumes of reports with which the floor was covered; almost the first thing I said to him, after social greetings, was 'What on earth are we going to do with this question of servitudes'? and I was very much comforted by Sir Robert remarking quietly in his careful, peaceful, Scottish manner, 'Oh, I am not much frightened at servitudes'.

Some years later Mr. Justice Rowlatt wrote: 'By common consent Sir Robert Finlay's marshalling of the facts was masterly, and his argument on the subject of servitudes notable as well for its learning as for its cogency.'[1]

So, to those who really knew, the appointment was by no means unexpected. Nevertheless Finlay himself, although for personal reasons he was anxious to be elected to the court, hesitated for long before consenting to become a candidate. His hesitation was due not to his great age, the disadvantages of which he regarded with a certain impatience, but because he doubted whether he had the necessary qualifications for the highly responsible task. But as Judge Anzilotti, later the President of the Court, said in an obituary speech marked by the peculiar eloquence and dignity of language of the continental jurist:

It would not be easy to find a man possessing the qualifications necessary for sitting on this court to a greater extent than Lord Finlay. It is only too true to say that often a choice has to be made between persons whose judicial

---

[9] See Scott, *Hague Court Reports* (Washington, 1916), p. 41.
[1] 'The Rt. Hon. Sir. R. B. Finlay' (1916) 16 J.C.L. 4.

experience has been in municipal courts and who have not had an opportunity for profound study and application of international law, and persons who, having devoted themselves to the study of international law, have no experience of judicial duties. Such however was not the case with Lord Finlay who, while holding the highest judicial offices in his country, had also to study and apply international law. . . .

Anzilotti also stressed two other valuable qualities which made Finlay specially suited to the court.

One of these was his knowledge of languages; if his mother tongue alone was familiar in the strict sense of the word, he could, however, not only read and understand but also speak German and French; further, he had a knowledge of Italian and Spanish more than sufficient to read and appreciate even the most difficult authors who have written in those languages. The other quality to which I feel that I must here refer, for I think that it contributed much towards enabling him to acquire and maintain to a very advanced age that broadness and suppleness of mind so necessary to understanding international questions, difficult and complex as they, if any, are—the other quality was his classical and literary culture. I still remember vividly the impression made on me when, a few months after making his acquaintance, I heard him repeat fluently and by heart long passages of Homer and of Virgil, or when, as sole response to certain arguments put forward in the court during a discussion in which he had not taken part, he quoted to me without a single mistake certain remarkably appropriate lines of the 'Divina Commedia'.[2]

In 1924 Finlay was elected President of the Classical Association, and delivered the customary lecture.

Although in his later years he had become somewhat anxious about his health, he insisted on making his own way, a heavily muffled figure, from London to The Hague for the annual sessions of the court. He travelled by ship from Harwich and when he arrived at The Hague was accustomed to go by himself by train and on foot around the town. Amongst his fellow judges, some of them persons of great distinction in their own countries, he at once established a peculiar ascendency. There is hardly any other reported example of a lawyer trained in the common law tradition establishing so quickly easy relationships with lawyers trained under the very different civil law system. As Anzilotti said:

This authority impressed itself from the very outset and never diminished. The opinion of Lord Finlay was always, in the eyes of his colleagues without exception, of the greatest weight; one was pleased to find oneself in agreement with him; if one did not agree, one required time for reflection. And without doubt, the members of this court would have been happy to give him some more striking external mark of their confidence, if this had not been constantly and definitely refused by him.[3]

[2] Anzilotti, (1929) 10 B.Y.I.L. 193, at 195.   [3] 10 B.Y.I.L. at 195–6.

The cases in which Finlay took part during this period are probably of interest only to a specialist in international law, but it may be emphasized that Finlay never hesitated to vote against views put forward by his Government's representatives when he was convinced that right lay on the other side. On at least two such occasions opinions were divided in the court and the continental judges voted in favour of the British Government's contentions whereas Finlay voted against. He viewed his duties in an entirely impartial and detached spirit. But at the end of 1928 when he was in his 87th year, it was noticeable that even his marvellous physical powers were weakening. In particular he was afflicted with eye trouble. He met these difficulties with his usual composure, and merely announced to his colleagues his intention of seeking the most expert advice from the London oculists in order that he might begin reading again and sit at the annual session of the International Court. But after undergoing an operation he weakened rapidly and died at his London home, 31 Phillimore Gardens, on 10 March 1929. After a funeral service at St. Columba's Presbyterian Church, Pont Street, where for years he had been a devout worshipper, he was buried at Nairn in the same grave as his wife and his brother, Alexander Finlay, on 14 March. The grave, on the western side of the cemetery overlooking the river, is surmounted by a plain granite cross. His estate was valued for probate at £95,000. He was succeeded by his only child, William, a judge of the King's Bench Division, who inherited his father's interest in international law, becoming President of the Grotius Society and United Kingdom representative on the United Nations War Crimes Commission. After having been promoted Lord Justice of Appeal in 1938, he died in June 1945 before his expected appointment as British member of the International Court of Justice could be announced.

APPENDIX

Constitutional Law. In *R. (Zadig)* v. *Halliday* [1917] A.C. 260 Finlay delivered the leading judgment holding that the Defence of the Realm Act, 1914, authorized the making of regulations providing for the internment without trial of persons of hostile origin or associations.

There is a good judgment in *Rodriguez* v. *Speyer Bros.* [1919] A.C. 59 (right of co-partner of alien enemy to sue), a topic he had also considered in *Stevenson (Hugh) & Son* v. *Aktiengesellschaft für Cartonagen-Industrie* [1918] A.C. 239. In *Home Secretary* v. *O'Brien* [1923] A.C. 603, he dealt with the rights of an applicant for *habeas corpus*.

In *London & Lancs. Fire Insurance Co.* v. *Bolands* [1924] A.C. 836, he held that armed robbery by four men during the Irish 'troubles' constituted a riot within the classic common law definition of the term.

In *Russian Commercial & Industrial Bank* v. *De Mulhouse* [1925] A.C. 112, he produced a full and valuable treatment of the effect to be given in England to a foreign nationalization decree. In *Duff Development Co.* v. *Kelantan Government* [1924] A.C. 797, he gave a clear exposition of the reasons why the defendants were legally entitled to have the proceedings against them set aside on the ground that they impleaded a foreign sovereign state.

In *Bowman* v. *Secular Society, Ltd.* [1917] A.C. 406, Finlay agreed with the other Law Lords that the crime of blasphemy was not committed by a temperate attack on religion in which the decencies of controversy were maintained, but dissented alone in holding that the courts would not help efforts to undermine Christianity by upholding a bequest to a society of rationalist beliefs.

Contract. In *Morris* v. *Baron* [1918] A.C. 1, he considered the difficult questions of waiver and rescission of written contracts, and in *Metropolitan Water Board* v. *Dick, Kerr & Co., Ltd.* [1918] A.C. 119, the scope of the doctrine of frustration—a subject also discussed in *Bank Line, Ltd.* v. *Capel & Co., Ltd.* [1919] A.C. 435.

He dissented from the majority in a difficult question of third-party rights in *Elder, Dempster & Co., Ltd.* v. *Paterson, Zochonis & Co., Ltd.* [1924] A.C. 522, but concurred in *Glasbrook Bros.* v. *Glamorgan C.C.* [1925] A.C. 270 (promise to perform existing duty).

Finlay delivered good judgments in *Banbury* v. *Bank of Montreal* [1918] A.C. 626, and *London Joint Stock Bank* v. *Macmillan* [1918] A.C. 777, each dealing with important points in banking law and practice.

Torts. In *Neville* v. *London Express Newspaper, Ltd.* [1919] A.C. 368, he dealt with some difficult problems in the law prohibiting maintenance. He held (1) that the success of the maintained litigation was no bar to an action, but (2) that the action will not lie in the absence of proof of special damage, while admitting that there was no real damage where a man was compelled to discharge his legal obligations. As the other four members of the House were equally divided Finlay had a casting vote on each proposition. It is difficult to deny that the result is rather illogical—although Finlay himself next year, in an admirable judgment in *Weld-Blundell* v. *Stephens* [1920] A.C. 956 (libel) suggested two instances where a plaintiff might be able to prove special damage even though he had been unsuccessful in the maintained proceedings. Another libel case, of a more sensational character, was *Sutherland* v. *Stopes* [1925] A.C. 47. In *Adam* v. *Ward* [1917] A.C. 318, he also considered the scope of the defence of qualified privilege. In *Greenock Corporation* v. *Caledonian Railway* [1917] A.C. 556, he agreed with his colleagues that a heavy rainfall in Scotland could not be called a *damnum fatale* sufficient to exonerate the defendants from liability for their interference with the bed of a stream.

Real Property and Equity. In *Leeds Industrial Co-operative Society* v. *Slack* [1924] A.C. 851, he delivered the leading judgment on the vexed question whether there was jurisdiction to award damages in lieu of a *quia timet* injunction.

In *Att.-Gen.* v. *National Provincial Bank* [1924] A.C. 262 Finlay held that a bequest 'for patriotic purposes or objects' was void for uncertainty. The decision has often been followed, as has *Houston* v. *Burns* [1918] A.C. 337, where Finlay held that a bequest for public purposes to be selected by a third party was void for uncertainty even though it was limited to a particular locality.

Conflict of Laws. He considered domicile in *Casdagli* v. *Casdagli* [1919] A.C. 145, and *Lord Advocate* v. *Jaffrey* [1921] 1 A.C. 146.

LORD BIRKENHEAD

CHAPTER I

FREDERICK EDWIN SMITH was born on 12 July 1872 at 32 Pilgrim Street, Birkenhead, a small house in an unattractive quarter of the town.[1] He was the eldest of the five children of Frederick and Elizabeth Smith (*née* Taylor). The father was the son of a north country nonconformist of dominant temperament who had established an estate agent's business in Liverpool. At an early age Frederick had broken away from his family, and joining the Army went to India where he rose to be a sergeant-major. A few years later he returned to England and was called to the Bar at the Inner Temple. It is notable that within a few years he had been elected Mayor of Birkenhead and was recognized as 'one of the finest speakers in the north of England'.[2] Frederick Smith was an intelligent man who realized his son's exceptional capacities. At the age of 9 F.E. (as he will hereafter be called, for so he was universally known in his lifetime) was sent to a small preparatory school in Southport, and before going his father told him that he hoped to see him Lord Chancellor one day. F.E. retold this story to his contemporaries, by whom it was naturally greeted unsympathetically, although thirty-seven years later he was to receive letters from some of his former school friends testifying to the truth of the prophecy and offering their congratulations upon his promotion to the Woolsack.

In 1887 when F.E. was in his sixteenth year his father died suddenly. In later life F.E. was accustomed to draw a gloomy picture of the narrow circumstances in which the family lived both before and after his father's death. In truth there seems to have been no serious shortage of money, and the family were brought up in the solid comfort of a north country middle-class home. In religion the family were Wesleyan Methodists. Some men prefer to depict their childhood in heightened colours. F.E., who later adopted as his motto 'Faber meae fortunae', preferred to paint his early years in blacker colours than was justified in order to draw the contrast between the provincial atmosphere of Birkenhead and the splendours of his later life. After an unsuccessful attempt to gain a scholarship at Harrow (a failure which was always bitterly resented) F.E. went to

[1] The main source for the life of Lord Birkenhead is the biography by his son: *F.E.* The two-volume edition of 1933 has been superseded by the one-volume revision of 1959. The autobiographical chapter in Birkenhead's own *Law, Life and Letters* (1927) is also useful. Most statements of fact not otherwise verified are based on these works.
[2] *F.E.*, p. 17.

Birkenhead School where he had an outstandingly successful career. At 17 he won a scholarship to University College, Liverpool, but his thoughts had already turned towards Oxford. But to get to Oxford it was essential that he should win a scholarship, for although an uncle had promised financial assistance it was not by itself sufficient to meet the expenses of an Oxford education in the days before government grants. In December 1890 F.E. proceeded to Oxford to attempt to gain a scholarship. In those days the group system for scholarship examinations was not so well organized as it later became, and Balliol examined first, followed by a group comprising Wadham and Trinity. F.E., who stayed in the Wilberforce Temperance Hotel (at the suggestion, he said later, of a friend with whom he afterwards lost touch), was unsuccessful at Trinity, but then gained the fourth scholarship of £80 at Wadham. F.E., who had developed to a high degree the quality of associating with his own fortunes any institution with which he became connected, remained to the end a devoted member of Oxford in general and Wadham in particular.

When F.E. came up to Wadham in the Michaelmas Term of 1891 he joined a College some of whose members later achieved great distinction. There was C. B. Fry, the all-round athlete, John Simon, the future Lord Chancellor, A. A. Roche, a future Law Lord, J. Stenning, later Warden of the College, F. W. Hirst, a Liberal publicist, H. M. Giveen, later a K.C. and a Bencher of Gray's Inn, and Campbell Hone, later Bishop of Wakefield. (Simon, Hirst, and Hone were one year junior to F.E.). There is a vivid picture of F.E. seated at the scholars' table in Hall in his first week: 'I saw that his hair was rather untidy, being of the kind that stands upright unless prevented. He had a long lean brown face and an impudent nose, but very remarkable eyes. They were the colour of a peat pool on Dartmoor, full of light, and fringed by luxuriant silky eyelashes.'[3] At the Bar some years later he was described thus: 'His sombre eyes and clear-cut features were lawyer-like enough; only the mouth lacked the set precision of a legal face. The lips were slightly ajar, as if about to close on a cigar; at moments shaped to insolence or disdain; at moments weary.'[4]

F.E. entered into every side of Oxford life with the zest which never deserted him. Academically, he obtained a Second in Honour Moderations in 1893—a disappointment, but he had never pretended to the close exactness which is required for the highest honours in that examination. He then persuaded the college to permit him to read for the Law School instead of Greats. The Final Honour School of Jurisprudence had only recently been established as a separate branch of studies, and its reputation

[3] C. B. Fry, *Life Worth Living* (1939), p. 79.
[4] L. E. Jones, *An Edwardian Youth* (1956), p. 185.

PLATE 13

a. (*Left to right*) Viscount Dunedin, Viscount Haldane, Earl of Birkenhead, Viscount Cave, Lord Moulton

b. Lord Atkinson, Viscount Cave, Viscount Haldane, Viscount Dunedin, Sir Lyman Poore Duff

THE JUDICIAL COMMITTEE OF THE PRIVY
COUNCIL ABOUT 1920

PLATE 14

Lord and Lady Birkenhead return from skating

was still somewhat uncertain. At the top it had some exceptionally distinguished professors (Anson, Dicey, Pollock, and Vinogradoff), but the college tutors who did the bulk of the undergraduate teaching were not as strong as they became later. It was also usual for people to say that the best Oxford lawyers read for one of the traditional Honour Schools, and then, having obtained a First, went to London to pick up their law in the Temple, although the facts do not entirely bear out this view. (Two future Lord Chancellors obtained Firsts in Law during this period—F.E. and Jowitt.) For the first eighteen months after his change of Schools the time passed in a carefree manner. But at the beginning of 1895 F.E. realized that there was less than six months before his Finals and that a First, with the prospect which it opened up of a Fellowship, was essential if he was to make his way in life. (The holder of a junior fellowship at an Oxford college today will learn with amazement that F.E. confidently expected to be able to pay off his debts (which amounted to some £400) out of his fellowship stipend—and succeeded in doing so.) The achievement of a First was to F.E. more than a matter of academic distinction—it was a matter of necessity in the struggle for existence.

Smith handled the situation in his own manner. He isolated himself from his friends, and took rooms in Wellington Square, a grim quadrangle of yellow-brick houses lying little known and seldom visited behind Beaumont Street. He carted a library of law books into his lodgings and began the first great sustained effort of his life. The wonderful concentration which he was so reluctant to employ now came to his aid. For six months he toiled in these dispiriting rooms for fourteen hours a day. He never left them, shunning the world outside, fearful of a break in his rhythm, and the distraction of his friends. From early morning until late at night, when he crawled into bed and fell into a profound coma, his slippers were on his feet. Once each day, at a regular hour, he would come up for air and exercise, pedalling violently round Wellington Square on a safety bicycle, an outing which was, during this period, his sole and pathetic relaxation.[5]

This extraordinary effort had its reward in June 1895 when F.E. was placed in the First Class in the Final Honour School of Jurisprudence. In the Hilary Term of 1896 he obtained the distinction which he prized most in his career, both academic and public—the Vinerian Scholarship, which in those days was competed for in a separate examination and not awarded on the results of the B.C.L. examination as at present. It was not merely an honour in itself but all the more remarkable in that amongst the defeated candidates was W. S. Holdsworth, later the distinguished legal historian. (Holdsworth remained on terms of affection with F.E., to whom he dedicated the first nine volumes of his monumental history, and by

[5] *F.E.*, p. 54.

whom he was consulted when a judgment had to be written on a difficult point.) The modern law student may be interested to know that F.E. ascribed his success to the fact that he had concentrated on Roman Law.

Outside his books F.E. had many interests. On the playing field he was prominent. He became captain of the Wadham Rugby XV, which won all its games against other college sides. He played as a forward and his vigour and dash were respected by all. Despite the fact that he was tried several times for the University he failed to obtain a Blue—perhaps because of his impoliteness in the scrum, perhaps because he did not come from Fettes, or perhaps through ill luck.

F.E. was also a member of the Wadham Soccer Team which under the captaincy of C. B. Fry reached the finals of the Cup. He also took part in long-distance running and here again just missed his Blue. (In 1920 when he was Lord Chancellor he is said to have wagered the famous runner W. R. Milligan that he would run the circuit of Tom Quad after dinner four times before Milligan could run eight. Birkenhead won the bet.)

F.E. had also begun to make a name for himself at the Union as early as the Hilary Term of his freshman year. In March 1892 he made his maiden speech 'on the paper' at a debate on local option at which the principal visiting speaker was Sir Wilfrid Lawson. F.E.'s speech showed much of the cogency and corrosive power which marked his later public utterances, albeit in a rather more gay and youthful form. Lawson, on inheriting his father's title and estate in 1867, had immediately destroyed the stocks of wine in the cellar. F.E. said:

The honourable gentleman inherited a noble cellar, in which the piety of his ancestors had laid to rest delicate clarets, sustaining ports, stimulating champagnes, and warm and ancient brandies. What did the honourable gentleman do with his cellar? He destroyed that priceless heritage of the ages, in which was stored the bottled sunshine of the south—he destroyed it under circumstances of such barbarity that even the thirstiest throat in Carlisle was denied participation! I tell you, Sir, that if in years to come, the honourable gentleman comes to me, when I am nestling in Abraham's bosom, and asks me for a drop of water, I shall say to him: 'No, not a drop! You dissipated greater liquor!'[6]

F.E. rose to be Treasurer of the Union in the autumn of 1893 and President in 1894. To the end of his life he retained a close interest in the affairs of the Union. When living at Charlton, a small country house near Banbury which he acquired in 1907, he was accustomed to drop in unheralded on occasional evenings.

After his First in the summer of 1895 it might have been expected that F.E., whose ambitions were always fixed on London and the Bar, would

[6] *F.E.*, p. 45.

have hastened to qualify himself as a barrister as quickly as possible. But although he had become a member of Gray's Inn in 1894 and had begun to eat dinners, he allowed no less than four more years to elapse before being called to the Bar. It is not easy to explain this delay. It was filled honourably by his election as Fellow of Merton in October 1896, where he enjoyed life and was regarded as a successful and popular tutor. In 1928 Merton gave him a room in College of which he made much use. He also found time to write an admirable short article for the *Law Quarterly Review* on the topic of the measure of damages in contract.[7] (No other Lord Chancellor, or indeed Law Lord, is known to have contributed to this scholarly quarterly at such a youthful age.) But it is hard to picture F.E. as a young law don. Somehow one feels that it would have been more natural for him to have been elected to All Souls and then gone straight to the Bar.[8] But he may have thought that Simon's chances of All Souls were greater than his (Simon was in fact elected in 1897). In *Who's Who* F.E. stated that in 1899–1900 he was 'Examiner in the Final Schools, Oxford'. The University *Gazette* shows that this was not the Final Honour School but Group B(4) in the Pass School. Not many Lord Chancellors would have recorded this fact.

In June 1896 F.E. was placed in the Second Class in the B.C.L., together with Holdsworth and F. Hemmerde, an able but eccentric man whose early promise was not fulfilled. The only First was (Sir) David Maughan, who later had a distinguished career at the New South Wales Bar. The Chairman of the Examiners on that occasion was H. Goudy, the Regius Professor of Civil Law, his co-examiners being J. C. Wilson and W. E. Vernon (two names now forgotten), and Edward Jenks, a well-known academic lawyer. In the folklore of the Oxford Law School it is always believed that Jenks was responsible for the decision to give F.E. a Second, and that F.E. never forgave him and took advantage of several opportunities which life later afforded to humiliate him.[9]

In 1897 F.E. was involved in a riot in the Oxford streets, which occurred when on a visit from the Prince of Wales some police imported from London behaved with unnecessary violence. F.E. found himself in the cells for a night charged with assault and obstruction of a police officer in the execution of his duty. Such charges against a don aroused considerable interest and jurists of the eminence of Dicey and Anson wrote to F.E. with advice and support. In the proceedings which followed before the Oxford magistrates F.E. was acquitted, the brilliance of his cross-

---

[7] (1900) 16 L.Q.R. 275.

[8] As there is a gap in the All Souls records for 1895, it has been impossible to discover whether F.E. competed.

[9] One of the many stories will be found in the *Holmes–Laski Letters* (1953), p. 1271.

examination of the police witnesses being taken as a prophecy of things to come.

F.E. was called to the Bar at Gray's Inn on 14 June 1899. It is interesting to note that he was bracketed equal first in the Bar Final Examinations, for it was not at that time an examination which Oxford candidates took very seriously. Gray's Inn did not then enjoy the reputation which later came its way (to some extent as a result of F.E.'s own career), but F.E. chose it partly because it had some connection with the Northern Circuit which he was to join, and partly because, as he characteristically told Simon, who had joined the Inner Temple, it would mean that he would be (as he was) Treasurer of his Inn ten years before Simon was Treasurer of his.

As soon as he had been called, F.E. went into chambers with Leslie Scott in Liverpool, where there was a strong local Bar. His first brief, in a licensing case, came in August 1899 when Scott was away on holiday. From that time forward F.E. did an extraordinary amount of business for a junior at the Liverpool bar. But even the fiercest rivals in a profession in which competition is keen responded to his frank and generous nature. The first pupil in F.E.'s chambers wrote later:

> I could write almost indefinitely of my recollections of my years with F.E. They are permanently recorded in my memory. I enjoyed them so much, and I hated the separation when he went to town. He was the most engaging and inspiring companion I have ever met. He had the supreme gift of absorbing one in his own ambitions and professional progress so completely that quite unconsciously one felt personally identified with them; no lawyer's success can ever have given greater pride or pleasure to his companions in Chambers, all of whom realized his unfailing generosity and transcendent loyalty.[1]

From August to December 1899 F.E.'s fees amounted to 48 guineas. In the following year, 1900, he made £530, and in the succeeding years his practice increased so enormously that when he moved to London in 1906 he was making £6,000 a year, a remarkable sum for a provincial junior. At first much of this was obtained by licensing work before local magistrates, but after 1901 he built up a large shipping and commercial practice mainly as the result of the appreciation of the Liverpool solicitor George Harley, who handled a lot of work for Houston, the shipping magnate. Another Liverpool magnate whose legal business came to F.E.'s chambers was Lever, the soap manufacturer. In those days the Liverpool solicitors did not employ London agents but went up themselves to the capital bringing with them the barristers whom they had briefed at the local bar. Therefore Liverpool barristers had an exceptional opportunity of appearing in court in London and so becoming known not only to the Bench

[1] *F.E.*, p. 96.

and Bar but also to the solicitors of the metropolis. This was an opportunity of which F.E. took full advantage. He was also fortunate enough at an early stage to be briefed for the appellant in *Wise* v. *Dunning*,[2] since known to generations of students as a leading case on the right of public meeting. This was an appeal to the Divisional Court from a decision of the Liverpool Stipendiary Magistrate requiring the appellant to find sureties for good behaviour. The appellant was an ardent Protestant crusader whose appearance in Catholic districts of Liverpool had given rise to disturbances. F.E.'s argument was that these had not been caused by the appellant but by his opponents. He had in his favour an earlier decision of the Divisional Court, *Beatty* v. *Gillbanks*,[3] in which Field J. had uttered a dictum to the effect that it is not a natural consequence of one person committing a lawful act that another should be led to commit an unlawful act. But the Divisional Court held that in some circumstances the law would pay sufficient attention to the infirmities of human nature to regard a breach of the peace as a natural consequence of a Protestant crusade in the Catholic quarter of Liverpool. Although F.E. lost the appeal he received afterwards a note of congratulation from the Lord Chief Justice, Lord Alverstone, which was promptly framed and hung in his chambers.

F.E. also acquired fame by his defence at the Old Bailey of Goudie, the Glasgow bank clerk who had defrauded his employers of over £160,000. Goudie acquired no personal benefit from this large fraud for he had fallen into the hands of blackmailers. There was never any hope of securing an acquittal, and F.E.'s main task was to make a speech in mitigation of punishment. This is commonly said to be one of the most difficult tasks which can face an advocate at the criminal Bar. F.E.'s speech on this occasion, which had been carefully written out and memorized, was conceded to be a masterpiece even by hardened practitioners of the Old Bailey who had no reason to look with pleasure upon the intrusion of a young man from the provinces.

Other famous cases in which F.E. was concerned in these years were the *Veronica* murders,[4] and the Guinea Gold litigation arising out of a merger in the tobacco industry between Ogdens and the Imperial Tobacco Company, which lasted for over four years and was before the courts more than 1200 times.

Meanwhile in 1901 he had married Margaret, daughter of the Reverend Henry Furneaux, a Fellow of Corpus Christi College, Oxford. The

[2] [1902] 1 K.B. 167.   [3] (1882) 9 Q.B.D. 308.
[4] See the Notable British Trials Series volume *The Veronica Trial* (1952), ed. G. W. Keeton and J. Cameron. F.E.'s own account of the case together with several others in which he was engaged can be found in his volume characteristically entitled *Famous Trials of History* (1926).

marriage was an entire success and F.E. owed much of his happiness in life to the gaiety and resilience of his wife. With her he lived in a comfortable house at Hooton, where he soon began to accumulate the material possessions which were an outward frame for his vivid and energetic personality. Horses, motor-cars, and yachts began to accumulate around him. These good things were shared with a multitude of friends. The beginnings of the legend of the gay roisterer can be traced. If he had known of it, he might have cited the remarkable observation of Lord Campbell, who once said: 'I cannot help thinking that an occasional *booze* has a favourable tendency to excite the faculties, to warm the affections, to improve the manners, and to form the character of youth. Of course it is to be understood that excess is to be avoided, which is not only contrary to morality but inconsistent with true enjoyment.'[5]

[5] *Life of Lord Campbell*, ed. J. Hardcastle (1881), vol. i, p. 96.

CHAPTER II

I T WAS NOW TIME FOR F.E. to consider obtaining a constituency. He never concealed his ambition for a parliamentary career. 'Parliament, after all, is the microcosm of the talent of Great Britain; and no man of great ambition, conscious of great powers, will willingly throughout his career be excluded from its arena.'[1] His first political speech in the north was made in 1894 while he was still an undergraduate. In the years when he was building up his practice at the local Bar he spoke often and attracted the attention of Archibald Salvidge, the Liverpool Conservative leader. F.E.'s big opportunity came when in 1904 Joseph Chamberlain visited Liverpool in the course of his Tariff Reform Campaign. At that time F.E. was canvassing the Scotland Division vigorously but without much hope. At a meeting at the Hippodrome, Liverpool, at which Chamberlain delivered one of his finest speeches, F.E. spoke later in the evening and so impressed Chamberlain that afterwards Salvidge was informed that a safe seat must be found for F.E., who accordingly found himself adopted for the Walton Division. The election took place in January 1906 in an atmosphere of great bitterness. The practice in those days was for the elections to be spread out over some three weeks and polling day at Walton was not until 16 January. Before that date the news had come in of widespread Unionist reverses culminating in the defeat of Balfour at Manchester. But on the day of the poll F.E. was returned by a majority of 709 over his Liberal opponent, Jellicoe. F.E. wrote afterwards: 'This election was incomparably the greatest milestone which I ever had passed—or ever was destined to pass—in my career. I was at least to be afforded the chance of measuring myself with those who were to determine the fortunes of the country.'[2]

The Conservative representation in the House was low in number and morale. Before the election the Unionists had a majority of 134; after it the Liberals had a majority of 356. F.E. then took an audacious decision. He decided to make a maiden speech which would not only revive the halting spirits of his party but also establish his own reputation securely in the public mind. Thanks to the help of Chamberlain he was called by the Speaker at the most favourable moment of the debate—10 p.m. The day was 12 May—just two months before his thirty-fourth birthday.

[1] *Law, Life and Letters*, vol. ii, p. 216.
[2] Ibid., p. 225.

I asked for no indulgence because I was making a maiden speech. The request for indulgence seemed to me could only come gracefully from the lips which made a modest appeal, couched in uncontroversial language, and I had not it in mind to make such an appeal. I spoke for sixty-five minutes, which I believe to be a record for a maiden speech; and I spoke with a degree of calculated insolence and sustained invective which I am quite sure has never been attempted before or since by one who addressed the House of Commons for the first time. As I drove down to the House of Commons with my wife, I said, 'I shall either make a brilliant success or a greater failure than that of Disraeli.' Before I sat down it was obvious that it was a *tour de force*; the speech had at least, whatever its real merits, been a great success.[3]

The passage of time has served only to confirm the characteristic judgment of the speaker on his own performance. His son has rightly said: 'In the long history of first speeches there had been nothing like it, and there has been nothing like it since.'[4] The speech did not contain any serious arguments from principle: it was not intended to do so. It was a fighting speech, cast in language of corrosive power, with occasional flashes of savage wit or irony. One illustration must suffice: 'It is far easier, if one has a strong stomach, to suggest to simple rustics, as the President of the Board of Trade did, that if the Tories came into power they would introduce slavery on the hills of Wales.'[5] Lloyd George fell into the trap and indignantly said that he had never made such a suggestion.

The right honourable gentleman would no doubt be extremely anxious to forget it, but, anticipating a temporary lapse of memory, I have in my hand the *Manchester Guardian* of 11 January 1906, which contains a report of his speech. The right honourable gentleman said: 'What would they say to introducing Chinamen at a shilling a day in the Welsh quarries. Slavery on the hills of Wales! Heaven forgive me for the suggestion.'
I have no means of judging how Heaven will deal with persons who think it decent to make such suggestions.

When F.E. had finished he hurried from the House for he had to catch the midnight train to Chester where he had an important case next day. But he knew his reputation was made. As he sat down he received a note from Tim Healy: 'I am old, and you are young, but you have beaten me at my own game.'
From this day forward F.E. was familiar to every person in England. Stories of his legal and political triumphs became part of the history of the country and anecdotes began to circulate about the more picturesque aspects of his life and character.

The brilliance of his first appearance, the rapidity of his wit, and the ferocity of his attack caused men to take a false view of his character and of his attain-

[3] *Law, Life and Letters*, vol. ii, p. 237.   [4] *F.E.*, p. 133.   [5] 153 H.C. Deb. 4s. col. 1014.

ments. He was regarded as a swashbuckler, witty and courageous, but head-strong and superficial—in the courts, as the man for a crushing cross-examination or a speech to a jury rather than for a serious legal argument, and in the House, for the brilliance, raillery, and rhetorical display of a partisan rather than for the measured view and wise counsel of the statesman. His appearance and manner of life contributed to this view. He was strikingly handsome, six feet one inch in height, of a distinguished figure, slightly marred by sloping shoulders. His clothes, although not in any one particular out of the ordinary, gave the impression that he was over-dressed. The hat worn on the back of his head, the red flower in his button-hole, the very long cigar always carried in his mouth, made him a ready subject for the caricaturist. The great houses in which he stayed, the late hours which he kept, his fondness for gaiety and for gay people, for cards, for horses, and for all the bright and expensive things of life, confirmed the opinion that he was a reckless partisan, fighting hard for his own side, grasping at his own enjoyment and advantage, not a responsible or serious person either as a lawyer or as a parliamentarian. Furthermore, his sharp tongue, his aggressive demeanour, and the cynical attitude which he at times assumed made many enemies and not only among his political foes.[6]

Smith was in part conscious of the effect which he produced, and having moral as well as physical courage he intensified these traits, which were rather of outward conduct than of inward character. Regarding ambition as one of the most powerful spurs to fine action, he gloried in it. He had an artist's pleasure in getting the most out of life as he conceived it.

At the Bar during those years he appeared in a succession of cases which passed into legal legend. (He had by now acquired London Chambers at 4 Elm Court.) One was the Lever libel action in 1906 against the Northcliffe Press, which had accused the Liverpool soap magnate of creating a Soap Trust. The story of F.E.'s Opinion in this case is still told among junior barristers in the Temple. Summoned by telegram to London, when he reached the Savoy he found a stack of papers nearly four feet high in his rooms and was told that an Opinion was required by next morning. 'He ordered a bottle of champagne and two dozen oysters, and began to read the papers. They were of great length and complexity, and he worked on them for eleven hours, all through the night. At 8.30 next morning he wrote the following terse opinion: "There is no answer to this action for libel, and the damages must be enormous. F. E. Smith." '[7] The Opinion was perfectly justified by events for the defendant settled the action by paying £50,000, the greatest sum ever paid in a libel action in an English court.[8] Four years later F.E. defended Ethel Le Neve, the mistress of Dr. Crippen, on a charge of being an accessory after the fact

[6] Sir Claud Schuster in *DNB, 1921–1930*, p. 784.   [7] *F.E.*, p. 100.

[8] In *Lewis* v. *Daily Telegraph Ltd.* [1963] 2 W.L.R. 1063 awards amounting to £217,000 were set aside by the House of Lords.

to the murder of Mrs. Crippen. He was deeply hurt that his successful defence evoked no work of thanks from his curious client. In the spring of 1913 F.E. appeared in the Marconi case as counsel for Herbert Samuel, then the Postmaster-General, in his libel action against the French newspaper *Le Matin*. Carson appeared for Rufus Isaacs, the Attorney-General, Samuel's co-plaintiff. It is curious that Samuel and Isaacs should have chosen that very moment to issue a writ, for the rumours relating to the dealings in the shares of the Marconi Company had been current in the English Press for six months and they had taken no steps to preserve their reputation by an action. They now chose to sue a French newspaper which had already apologized in print, which had refused to defend the action, and which apologized again in open court.[9] They were, however, it appears anxious for an opportunity to make a full public statement of their position and thought that this would be a suitable occasion. As events turned out they made a lamentable error of tactics, for Carson in the course of his speech revealed the fact, until then unknown to the public, that Isaacs had had dealings in the shares of the American as distinct from the English Marconi Company. In April and May F.E. and Carson also appeared for Isaacs in the criminal prosecution against Cecil Chesterton for the statements which he made in his weekly paper *The New Witness*. The fact that F.E. and Carson had appeared for the Liberal Ministers was felt by them to debar them from taking part in the debates in the House of Commons on the matter. They acted as they did after taking advice from Halsbury. This was misunderstood and severely resented by some of their fellow Conservatives. The controversy boiled over in June into the correspondence columns of *The Times*. F.E.'s reply on 17 June was a masterpiece of controversial invective.

I invite our critics to indicate with precision the grounds upon which it is suggested that it was our duty to refuse these retainers. Were we to say 'We cannot accept because the plaintiffs are Liberals and we are Conservatives, and, therefore, the issue being political, the circumstances are special'? I would recommend those who take this view to examine with some care the certain consequences of such an action. Political issues constantly present themselves for decision in the Law Courts. In the overwhelming majority of cases juries have done their duty indifferently between the parties, treating their own views upon politics as immaterial. How long do you think this state of things will endure if every Conservative case is to be presented by Conservative advocates and resisted by Liberal advocates? . . . You speak of the ordinary man. I do not in this connection recognize such a tribunal. May I without incivility add that, if upon a matter requiring some degree of enlightenment and cultivation for its adequate comprehension, the 'ordinary man' is uninstructed upon the function which every civilized country in the world has assigned to the advocate, *The*

[9] F. Donaldson, *The Marconi Case* (1962), p. 94.

Times would be better employed informing his mind than appealing to his judgment.

In *Greenlands Ltd.* v. *Wilmshurst* [1] the Court of Appeal were asked to order a new trial in an action for libel on the ground that the damages were excessive. It was said that the jury had been angered by the attitude of the defendants and in particular by the way in which F.E. had conducted their case. Hamilton L.J. said: 'Still, in my opinion by no formula or manipulation can £1,000 be got at. For any damage really done, £100 was quite enough; double it for the sympathy; double it again for the jury's sense of the defendants' conduct, and again for their sense of Mr. F. E. Smith's. The product is only £800.' The appeal succeeded.

Outside the law courts F.E. during these years was particularly active in the political controversies over the Parliament Bill and the Irish Home Rule Bill. F.E. thought that the House of Lords was guilty of folly in rejecting Lloyd George's Budget in 1909. The consequence was one which he foresaw, namely the general election of January 1910 which showed that the electorate was behind the Liberal Party in its proposals to amend the Constitution so as to reduce the powers of the House of Lords. F.E.'s exasperation was displayed in a remarkable letter which he wrote to J. L. Garvin, the editor of *The Observer* in January 1910.

Under the encouragement of your letter I will write without false modesty. I am conscious of powers which may be made of real service to the Unionist Party and I believe further (promising no other than normal political developments) that if the Party gives me the artificial position and standing which they alone can give me I can win the next election for them. If they will give me *formal recognition* I am certain that in two years I can undertake a considered campaign in the country which will itself win thirty or forty seats. I am assuming of course—a point on which I have no doubt—that I shall maintain and improve my parliamentary position, and that they put me on the front bench. And I add that unless the Party creates someone who can do this there is no reason why we should win the next election at all.[2]

In fact the promotion which F.E. desired came not from his own party but from the Liberal Government. In June 1911 Asquith proposed to insert F.E.'s name in the Coronation Honours List as a Privy Councillor. The news caused some alarm to Balfour, the leader of the Conservative Party, who wrote to Asquith to complain that F.E.'s name had been substituted for that of Hayes Fisher, the Conservative politician recommended for the honour by Balfour when Asquith had consulted him. Hayes Fisher had been a loyal member of the party for many years and as Balfour wrote to F.E. informing him of his objections: 'He has not

[1] [1913] 3 K.B. 507, at 532.   [2] *F.E.*, p. 151.

been over-well treated by fortune,[3] and I feel confident that you would regret as much as I that he should now be disappointed of an honour that he has been led to expect.'[4] Asquith had no personal objection to Hayes Fisher but the chief Liberal whip, the Master of Elibank, had reported to Downing Street that his selection would be very unpopular with London Liberal M.P.s. Asquith wrote to Balfour maintaining his decision to select F.E. The list ultimately published contained the names both of Hayes Fisher and F.E. The latter wrote to the Prime Minister on 16 June to thank him:

When I feel things deeply I find it difficult to write about them, and will therefore only say that I am well aware of the special difficulties which arose in my case and of the special alterations in your original plans which were adopted to meet these difficulties. These facts make it quite impossible for me to attempt any adequate expression of my gratitude. I can only say that it is a paradoxical and singular circumstance that those against whom I have been fighting for fifteen years have paid me the greatest compliment I have ever had in my life; while those on whose behalf I have been fighting did their best to prevent it.[5]

Yet after this letter F.E. was involved a month later in one of the most extraordinary parliamentary outbursts of modern times, when on 24 July the Prime Minister was shouted down in the House of Commons. Asquith had intended to announce to the House the Government's refusal to accept the Lord's amendments to the Home Rule Bill but he was unable to make himself heard over an uproar led by Lord Hugh Cecil and F.E. During this period F.E. was an ardent supporter of the diehard group which gathered itself around Lord Halsbury. He acted as an unofficial whip to this group and worked in the closest contact with Halsbury himself, the Duke of Westminster and Milner. To the latter he wrote in the middle of the crisis on 22 July:

My dear Milner,
        We should be most grateful if you could come to Grosvenor House tomorrow at twelve to discuss things.
    The whole party in the country is behind us and we shall yet show the wisdom of damning the consequences.

Yours sincerely,
F. E. Smith.[6]

---

[3] Hayes Fisher had been obliged to resign office as Financial Secretary to the Treasury in 1903. For his humiliating dismissal by Lloyd George in 1918 see R. Blake, *The Unknown Prime Minister* (1955), pp. 381–3.

[4] Asquith papers.   [5] Ibid.   [6] Milner papers, Box A. III.

Yet at the same time F.E. was active behind the scenes of both parties negotiating with Lloyd George and Winston Churchill (with whom he was now on terms of the most intimate friendship) to see whether moderate men of good will could not come together to form a national or coalition government. This was not the only occasion in F.E.'s life when he displayed a liking for coalitions. It is by no means easy to understand the divergence between some of his public speeches and activities at this period and his private conversations behind the scenes. There is certainly testimony available from those who knew the facts of the moderation, clarity, and common sense which he displayed in private conversations with the Unionist leaders at this date.[7] Yet at the same time he was able in his public speeches at Blenheim and Belfast and elsewhere on the Ulster issue to arouse public excitement to such a pitch of violence as has hardly been seen in England before or since. In July and September 1912 F.E. delivered in Ulster speeches of extraordinary power and vigour. To the end of his life he remained deeply impressed by the determination and steadfastness shown by the enormous crowds which gathered to hear him. On 28 September 1912 he joined with Carson and others in signing the Ulster Covenant in Belfast, whereby the men of Ulster pledged themselves to maintain the Union. F.E. was watched by an observer of exceptional penetration and skill in portraiture, Martin Ross, the joint author with Edith Somerville of *The Reminiscences of an Irish R.M.* 'I have seen a face so inscrutably youthful, so immutably serious, in a deal at the Dublin Horse Show, when a man had so good a horse to sell that he was lifted above any mere trivialities or panegyrics. Sir Edward Carson's speech was like masonry; the speech of Mr. F. E. Smith was like the flight of a strong bird.'[8]

On his return to Liverpool F.E. and his wife were met by a crowd of over a hundred thousand people, the largest gathering ever seen in the city. A year later in September 1913, a second 'Ulster Day' was celebrated in Belfast and on the 25th of the month Smith acted as Carson's 'galloper' at a review of the Ulster Volunteers. For years to come, in Ireland and elsewhere, the nickname 'Galloper Smith' stuck to him. Yet at the same time that he was acting thus in public F.E. was negotiating behind the scenes, mainly with Churchill, to see whether an accommodation would not be found between the views of the various parties based in part on the exclusion of Ulster. These negotiations came to nothing and by March of the following year the country was on the verge of civil war. The Curragh Mutiny in March combined with Churchill's action earlier the same month in ordering the Third Battle Squadron to Lamlash in the

[7] Earl Winterton, *Pre-War* (1932), pp. 218–19.
[8] *F.E.*, pp. 216–17.

Isle of Arran opposite the port of Belfast, had aroused the two islands to a feverish state of excitement. In the same month the Home Rule Bill received its third reading. In the debate on the Curragh Mutiny at the end of the month, F.E. once more indicated the strength of his desire for an accommodation between men of good will.

I do believe that a time has come when men of all parties in this House would be well advised to consider, not where one party is drifting, but where we are all drifting. (General cheers).

We shall not arrive at a conclusion upon this point by long historical arguments and recriminations. Nobody will ever persuade us on this side of the House that we have not been justified in the things we have done. I admit they were very difficult to justify. No one will ever persuade honourable gentlemen opposite that they, equally on their part, were not justified in what they have done. . . . As far as I am concerned I can only say, and I believe as far as many who sit on this side of the House are concerned, late as is the period at which this controversy has arrived—I believe many of us are willing that it should be conducted in those later stages, even though the mischief may be irreparable, with a deep sense of responsibility, and an anxious desire to see, even while the water runs under the bridges, whether nothing can be done by the House of Commons to retain some memory of the patriotism and traditions of the past.[9]

F.E. was in a way fortunate: nobody could say that he was a man born out of his time. The two gifts which providence had bestowed upon him in abundance were for demagogic oratory on the one hand and for intimate conciliatory discussion on the other. In each case the historical circumstances of England when he was in his prime were strongly in his favour. Before the era of television the public meeting was still a recognized and important part of English political life, and Parliament itself was the centre of affairs, where, in his own words, men of ability could pit themselves against each other. Conversely, his liking for conciliation and genius for friendship were aided by the fact that English political society was still a closed group of comparatively few men sharing largely common assumptions and background.

During the following months nothing happened to bring any further light to the Irish scene. The Speaker's Conference in July 1914 broke down and there is general agreement that only the outbreak of war in August prevented civil war in Ireland. For the moment the Irish controversy faded from F.E.'s mind but seven years later he was to return to it and all his gifts as a political tactician and as a conciliator were to be called upon to their utmost to play a part in bringing about the Irish Treaty of December 1921. It is worth noting that F.E. apparently never visited the

[9] 60 H.C. Deb. 5s. col. 890.

south of Ireland until 1928, when he received an honorary LL.D. at Trinity College, Dublin. Yet a detailed and highly-coloured picture has been published of a visit by Birkenhead to Dublin in 1920 to speak at the College Historical Society in Trinity College.[1] If this visit ever took place, it was certainly not with the object of speaking at the College Historical Society, for the Society's records (confirmed by the memories of those who were active in it at the time) disclose no such visit. In 1925 Birkenhead did promise to speak, but at the last minute was persuaded, most reluctantly, by Lord Glenavy, the President of the Society, that it might be inadvisable to come to Dublin.

[1] H. Brust, *I Guarded Kings* (1935), pp. 190–4. The story is accepted by the second Lord Birkenhead: *F.E.*, p. 353.

N*

CHAPTER III

FOR A SHORT PERIOD after the opening of the war, F.E. was charged with the difficult task of organizing the Press Bureau. As he was ignorant both of service life and of journalism it was not one of his happier experiences and on 26 September 1914 he resigned the office and departed for France a few days later. He was promoted captain in his regiment (The Queen's Own Oxfordshire Hussars) on 15 November and later held the temporary rank of major with the staff. He was given the rather curious office of Intelligence and Recording Officer to the Indian Corps which had arrived at Marseilles at this time. Here he met almost the only soldier with whom he was on terms of friendship and understanding throughout the war, Lt.-Gen. Willcocks, the Commander of the Indian Corps. At home, F.E.'s family found this a difficult period. Money had never been saved and they had just moved into a large new house at 32 Grosvenor Gardens. (The house is a strikingly ugly example of Victorian architecture; but F.E. had never shown any interest in the fine arts.) After a period camping out in the enormous rooms his wife was obliged to move to smaller quarters and let the house to the Red Cross. Meanwhile F.E. sent home extremely indiscreet but entertaining letters describing the progress of the campaign in France during the first few months, and in particular the sufferings undergone by the Indian Corps in the unfamiliar mud and damp of Flanders. In May 1915 the Asquith Government was reconstructed. F.E., being at the front, played no part in the intrigues which led to the formation of the First Coalition but his position in the Conservative Party was sufficiently strong for him to be appointed Solicitor-General. He plunged at once into the great mass of work which descends upon the Law Officers in time of war, particularly in the Prize Court. In October the resignation of Carson opened up the Attorney-Generalship and after a brief discussion with Cave, F.E. was appointed to the position with Cave as his Solicitor-General. Under a war-time arrangement the salaries of the Law Officers were reduced to £5,000 each per annum. F.E. later claimed that he was 'The only Attorney-General known to history who has insisted that his Solicitor-General should receive approximately the same fees as himself.'[1] In some ways the period which followed was one in which F.E. rendered the most useful public service of his life. He was at the height of his powers, his constitution not yet sapped by the strains which he placed upon it, and he laboured with

[1] *The Times*, 22 November 1928.

great assiduity to discharge the duties of his office. One case alone during this time brought him such notoriety, namely the prosecution of Sir Roger Casement for High Treason in the summer of 1916, that a full discussion of it is desirable.[2]

Very early on the morning of Good Friday 1916 (21 April) Roger Casement, with two companions, landed from a submarine at Banna Strand on the Kerry coast. Casement, of Irish descent, had had a distinguished career in the Colonial Service. In particular he had exposed atrocities both in the Congo and on the Putumayo in a manner which had attracted public approval and gained him the C.M.G. in 1905 and a knighthood in 1911. The latter honour he had acknowledged in a letter of fulsome thanks, which was to be quoted against him with effect at his trial. Those who admired him regarded him as a man of courage, ability, and sensitivity. Those who disliked him thought him very vain, and without any sense of humour. Certainly he was ardently devoted to the cause of Irish nationalism. It is now clear that his devotion to this cause arose at a much earlier date than was supposed in 1916.[3]

After the outbreak of the war he made his way to Germany. There he had addressed Irish soldiers in prisoner-of-war camps in an endeavour to persuade them to join an Irish Brigade. Casement told them that the object of this brigade was to maintain the rights conferred by the Home Rule Act, 1914, in face of opposition from the Ulster Volunteers. The brigade would be landed in Ireland after a German naval victory permitted this to be done. At that date Irish soldiers had been very little influenced by the doctrines of Sinn Fein. After the 1916 Rebellion it was different, but in 1915 Casement gained only some fifty recruits. Once at least he had to be protected from the prisoners by a guard of soldiers 'provided by a nation which thinks of everything'.[4] By the beginning of 1915, if not earlier, news of these events had reached the British authorities from various sources. There was no doubt that *prima facie* they would have justified the arrest and prosecution of Casement on some criminal charge if he had returned within the jurisdiction.

This he did in the manner already explained a year later. It is still not clear exactly what the purposes, immediate and ulterior, of Casement's return may have been. He declared that he intended to warn the Republican leaders in Dublin, where the Rebellion broke out on Easter Monday

[2] The best account is in the volume in the Notable British Trials Series, edited by H. Montgomery Hyde (1960). Information will also be found in R. MacColl, *Roger Casement* (1956); A. Noyes, *The Accusing Ghost* (1957); B. Thomson, *Queer People* (1922); ibid., *The Scene Changes* (1939); A. M. Sullivan, *The Last Serjeant* (1952); *Irish Times*, 26 April 1956; H. O. Mackey, *Roger Casement* (1962).

[3] G. Costigan, 'Treason of Sir R. Casement' (1955) 60 *Am. Hist. Rev.*, 283.

[4] F.E. in his opening speech for the Crown: *Trial*, p. 11.

(24 April), that they could expect no real help from the Germans. It seems plain that he had reached the limit of his usefulness to the Germans and that they had reached the limit of their usefulness to him. The Germans may well have contemplated his almost certain capture and trial with equanimity. A more security-conscious generation can only view with amazement some of the incidents of the voyage and landing. Casement left on the beach, or easily discoverable, such impedimenta as a pistol, a torch, a code book, and a railway sleeper ticket from Berlin to Wilhelms-haven.

He was arrested hiding in a ruin called McKenna's Fort, and brought over to London under military escort on the night of Saturday. The War Office appears to have thought that a summary court martial and execution at the Tower as a spy would be the right solution, and to have contemplated stopping the Irish Mail at Willesden in order to remove Casement from the train before (as happened) he was taken into the custody of Scotland Yard at Euston. But F.E., though at first prepared to contemplate a court martial if it were held in public, later insisted that the ordinary criminal law administered in public must be predominant.[5] Casement, after a lengthy interrogation by (Sir) Basil Thomson, an Assistant Commissioner and head of the C.I.D. at Scotland Yard, was sent to the Tower, whence he was brought before the Chief Metropolitan Magistrate at Bow Street on 15 May. Until then he had been still in some danger of a court martial. At Bow Street the Attorney-General appeared for the Crown and outlined his case in an objective manner. Casement was committed for trial. Under the law as it then stood a prisoner indicted for treason had to be tried before three judges of the King's Bench Division sitting in the High Court of Justice, and not (as now) before one judge sitting at the Central Criminal Court. This procedure was known as a Trial at Bar.

F.E.'s conduct in relation to the prosecution has been the subject of criticism ranging from the mild to the hysterical. The simplest way to consider these criticisms is to consider the history of the case in its various stages—(1) the decision to prosecute, (2) the Bow Street proceedings, (3) F.E.'s conduct of the prosecution before the King's Bench Division, (4) F.E.'s conduct of the proceedings before the Court of Criminal Appeal, and his consequent refusal of leave to appeal to the House of Lords, and (5) his conduct after the trial, particularly in relation to the attempt to damage Casement's reputation, before and after his execution, by the circulation of his diary. As to the first point, it can hardly be contended that F.E. should have excused himself from fulfilling the duty which law and convention cast upon the chief Law Officer of the Crown of appearing

[5] *Trial*, p. xli.

in person at a State Trial. The evidence is clear that F.E. insisted throughout on the maintainance of the traditionally high standard of English criminal justice, being particularly insistent that the prisoner should be tried in public in the ordinary course of law and not dispatched summarily before a court martial as a spy. As to the second point no serious objection has been or could be taken to F.E.'s conduct of the proceedings before the magistrate at Bow Street.

The third, fourth, and fifth points are inextricably interlocked; throughout there is the common factor that something mysterious happened in relation to Casement's diaries. Between the committal and the trial, the first mention of these documents occurs. A full study of the affair still remains to be written; much of the testimony comes either from Sir Basil Thomson, who gave several different accounts, or from Serjeant Sullivan, who was under severe nervous stress at the time of the trial and reverted to the matter again at the age of 83. It appears, although it has been denied, that the diaries came into the possession of the authorities when Casement's rooms in London were searched some months before his arrest. This may well have been as much as sixteen months before the trial. Those who support the notion of forgery have been concerned to extend the period in order to give adequate time for the considerable penmanship which must have been necessary. Thomson suggests that the significance of the diaries was not appreciated until Casement had actually been arrested.[6] Thomson wrote later that the diary could not have been published in any age or in any language.[7] In 1959 an English edition, of questionable accuracy, was published.[8] The diaries themselves were put in the Public Record Office in the same year by the Home Office, which until then had preserved silence on the matter. Most of those who have seen the diaries are in no doubt that they are genuine. They record details of Casement's life in England, Ireland, and South America. Interspersed with the normal incidents of his life are details of sexual perversion. It has never been alleged that the whole diaries were forged but merely the latter entries. The truth may well be that the diaries are genuine but these incidents are imaginary. It is in any event clear that by the first week in June typescript copies of the diaries were being shown to selected persons in London— an act which shocked both Simon and Haldane.[9]

If one puts aside the charge that the diaries were forged by the British authorities, two distinct allegations of a rather contradictory nature have been made as to the use to which they were put, and to F.E.'s part in these

[6] *The Scene Changes*, pp. 276–8.   [7] Ibid., p. 276.

[8] P. Singleton Gates and M. Girodias, *The Black Diaries*. See the review in the *Times Literary Supplement* for 26 February 1960 (republished in J. Sparrow, *Independent Essays* (1963), p. 150).   [9] *Trial*, p. lxv.

incidents. First, it is said that F.E. caused the diaries to be shown to Serjeant Sullivan, Casement's leading counsel, before the trial, with the object of persuading him to plead insanity as a defence at the trial. (Such a plea is in practice raised only on the first day of the trial, at the moment when the prisoner is arraigned—i.e. called to the Bar by name and asked whether he pleads guilty or not guilty. It might seem unnecessary to mention such a simple point had not an extraordinary theory of a conspiracy been put forward.[1] The conspiracy, allegedly between F.E. and Sullivan to discredit Casement, is based on the entirely fallacious notion that such a plea could be put forward on the third day of the trial.) Secondly, it is said that F.E. procured copies of the diaries to be circulated amongst influential persons after the trial with the object of persuading them that Casement ought not to be reprieved. It is worth noting that these persons apparently fell into two distinct classes—those who disliked Casement so much that they were glad to have an additional reason for his execution, and those who were his ardent supporters, but who were also not anxious as Irishmen to see the reputation of a patriot martyr besmirched by a reprieve which would necessarily involve the publication of the contents of the diaries. The second class were prepared to regard an execution as the lesser of two evils; the first class positively welcomed it.

As to the first allegation, there can be little doubt that F.E. attempted to bring copies to the attention of Sullivan before the trial. (There is also some hearsay evidence that F.E. showed the diaries to C. A. O'Connor, the Irish Attorney-General (later Master of the Rolls), who happened to be in London during the trial and naturally attended it out of curiosity.[2] If true, this was a discreditable act.) There is some conflict of evidence as to the exact circumstances in which F.E. attempted to bring the documents to the notice of Sullivan but the main outlines of the story are clear enough. F.E., directly and indirectly, attempted to bring the diaries to Sullivan's personal attention and the latter refused to look at them; he took the view that there was no question of pleading insanity: he would ask for a verdict of 'not guilty'. Sullivan's conduct in this matter seems to have been entirely correct according to the etiquette of the criminal bar. It is the responsibility of counsel to decide upon the proper line of defence, in the absence of instructions from his client. In old age Sullivan said that 'Freddie Smith was savage' at his refusal to look at the diaries,[3] but this does not appear from two letters which Sullivan wrote to F.E. in July 1916, the first of which specifically denied that Sullivan had any grievance about the diaries and in general expressing his warmest thanks for the kindness shown to him throughout the trial by the Attorney-General.[4] Still, it is not improbable that F.E. felt angry, but that Sullivan

[1] Mackey, sect. 1.   [2] Noyes, pp. 176–7.   [3] F.E., p. 310.   [4] Ibid., pp. 310–12.

did not think it necessary or desirable to refer to the matter in a letter touching on broader themes. The letter is one which might well have been written by a member of the Bar to counsel on the other side after an anxious criminal case.

But there is one difficulty which has hardly received sufficient attention. To any competent lawyer the suggestion that the diaries would be evidence of insanity must seem extraordinary. In 1916 the M'Naghten Rules were applied in a more severe manner than later. But at no time during their existence have the Rules permitted evidence to be given of anything other than the inability of the prisoner to distinguish between right and wrong at the moment when he committed the crime for which he is indicted, the term wrong meaning legally wrong. If we leave aside the point that there is no recorded instance of a prisoner charged with treason raising the defence of insanity, it is difficult to see (as Sir Ernley Blackwell noticed in his memorandum of July 1916[5]) how acts of sexual perversion can be evidence of incapacity to realize that the acts one is charged with having committed are treasonable. In 1916[6] and in 1952[7] Sullivan himself was perfectly clear on the point. F.E. must also have appreciated this, and it is not easy, therefore, to understand what his motive may have been in making the diaries available to Sullivan. He may have hoped or desired that Sullivan would be foolish enough to raise the defence of insanity unsuccessfully and then find that the character of his client had been irretrievably blackened. It would be hard to defend such a course of action. Or in his anxiety to secure a verdict of guilty (whether or not accompanied by a finding of insanity) he may have simply ignored the M'Naghten Rules. On the other hand, if he honestly believed that the defence of insanity could be properly raised, his conduct in making the documents available was entirely in accordance with the high principles which govern the conduct of prosecuting counsel at the Bar.[8]

So far as F.E.'s conduct of the trial itself is concerned, no serious criticism has been levied against him. F.E.'s opening speech was a clear survey, moderate in tone, with few of his characteristically tart phrases. Archibald Bodkin (later Director of Public Prosecutions), who had done much of the work on the brief as one of the junior counsel for the Crown, was somewhat disturbed to find, when he attended a conference with F.E. the night before the trial opened and made various suggestions as to the contents of the Attorney-General's speech, that F.E. had already caused a copy of it to be cabled to the U.S.A.[9] After the trial Serjeant

[5] Printed in *Trial*, p. 310.   [6] *F.E.*, p. 311.   [7] *The Last Serjeant*, pp. 271–2.

[8] In his letter of 16 July 1916 Sullivan expressly said that 'in view of one defence it was right that they should be available for my information' (*F.E.*, p. 311).

[9] R. Jackson, *The Case for the Prosecution* (1962), p. 39.

Sullivan wrote in the warmest terms to express his thanks for the consideration shown to him in what had been a severe ordeal for counsel—briefed before a strange court, in the most serious of cases, involving difficult questions of law, and in an atmosphere poisoned with war-time hysteria and English resentment at the Easter Rebellion in Dublin. It is not surprising that Sullivan should have broken down on the third day of the trial. It is particularly worth noting that F.E. had been so determined to secure a fair trial for Casement that, struck by the apparent disparity of strength between the prosecuting and defending teams, he had in vain tried to persuade Lord Chancellor Buckmaster to grant Sullivan an English silk gown. Buckmaster could indeed hardly have granted the request for he had already publicly stated that he would create no silks during the war. When Sullivan did become an English K.C. in 1919, it was as one of Birkenhead's first batch of creations. Artemus Jones also expressed his appreciation of F.E.'s conduct of the trial[1]—though apparently J. H. Morgan did not,[2] while J. H. Doyle the American lawyer who was also a member of the defence team was always a bitter critic of F.E.[3] The report does not suggest that Casement was fortunate in his counsel. Sullivan's arguments are repetitious and confused: F.E. by contrast was clear and cogent. (Sullivan was only one year older than F.E., yet somehow there is a widespread impression of him as a venerable figure.) The Lord Chief Justice, Reading, who presided, kept a firm control over the proceedings. One of the defence counsel commented that his rather limited vocabulary enabled him to get on terms with the common jury more quickly that the contrasted eloquence of either Sullivan or F.E.[4]

The legal issues involved may be stated quite briefly, although the argument on them occupied two days before the Court of Criminal Appeal. The Statute of Edward III (1351) under which Casement was indicted made it treason for anyone to be 'adherent to the King's enemies in his realm, giving them aid and comfort in the realm, or elsewhere'. The adherence is the essence of the offence, involving as it does the breach of the feudal tie of allegiance which subsists between sovereign and subject. It was argued for Casement that the adherence must be by a person who, being in this country, gives the aid and comfort in question, whether within or without the realm, but the Lord Chief Justice held, and his direction was upheld in the Court of Criminal Appeal,[5] that the words 'giving aid and comfort to the King's enemies' are words in apposition; they are words to explain what is meant by being 'adherent to'. In other

[1] *Without my Wig* (Liverpool, 1944).
[2] See Mackey, pp. 43–45.   [3] Noyes, p. 187.   [4] Artemus Jones, p. 163.
[5] [1917] 1 K.B. 98.

words a man could be adherent to the King's enemies in his realm by giving them aid and comfort in his realm or he could be adherent to the King's enemies elsewhere, that is by giving them aid or comfort elsewhere. Indeed, in an island country adherence to the King's enemies is more likely to occur without than within the realm. The Court of Criminal Appeal thought it clear that from the earliest times to 1868 adherence to the King's enemies without the realm had been held treason. The statute of Henry VIII merely provided machinery whereby acts admitted to be criminal could be tried within the realm. Probably it was never really doubted that the offence could be tried if the offender could be found within the jurisdiction although there may have been some doubts as to the mode or manner of trial before the statute of Henry VIII.

The only point for which F.E.'s conduct during the trial might have been criticized was when Casement made his final speech from the dock after the jury had brought in its verdict of guilty and before sentence had been passed. In an hour-long apologia for his career Casement touched with some effect upon F.E.'s earlier connexion with the Irish Home Rule dispute when he had acted as 'Galloper' to Carson. On hearing this sentence, F.E., who until then had preserved an attitude of boredom, lounged out of court with his hands in his pockets. This can hardly be called anything worse than undignified. It is worth noting that Casement himself had softened various passages in this speech on the ground that 'he did not want to hurt his feelings'.[6]

After Casement's appeal had been dismissed by the Court of Criminal Appeal on 18 July, he applied to the Attorney-General for his fiat for leave to appeal to the House of Lords. This was refused on the 21st. Under the law as it then stood (it has since been altered by the Administration of Justice Act, 1960) it was necessary to obtain the leave of the Attorney-General to appeal to the House of Lords from the Court of Criminal Appeal, and under the Act of 1907 two distinct conditions had to be fulfilled before he gave his fiat—first, a question of law of public importance had to be involved, and secondly, he had to be satisfied that it was in the public interest that a further appeal should lie. The second consideration was as important as the first—in criminal justice speed and certainty are of great public benefit: an authoritative settlement of a disputed legal point by the final tribunal may be of value, but it may also be in the public interest to put a stop to the process of appellate proceedings and allow the law to take its course. Lord Shawcross has stated that he had no reason to think that F.E. had exercised his discretion improperly.[7] It may also be remembered that in 1916 there had been only two appeals to the Lords under the Act of 1907 (the cases of *Ball* in 1911[8] and *Felstead*

[6] Artemus Jones, p. 165.   [7] *Daily Telegraph*, 10 August 1957.   [8] [1911] A.C. 47.

in 1914[9]): the whole idea of appeal in criminal cases was something of a novelty then, and it is not surprising that the practice should have been rather against granting leave to appeal.

F.E. decided for himself to refuse the fiat: it is true that he consulted the other Crown Counsel (whose view in fact coincided with his) but when he had done so he informed them (but only when the Solicitor-General specifically asked him) that his refusal had already gone out. One of the Counsel consulted, Travers Humphreys, later wrote admiringly of this episode.[1] Perhaps it is best regarded as the sort of behaviour which not many men except F.E. could have carried off successfully.

After the trial there is no doubt that copies of Casement's diaries were circulated amongst influential people in England and America with considerable effect. This may well have been done on the private initiative of Thomson and Hall, the Chief of Naval Intelligence, rather than on instructions from their superiors.[2] Another person responsible was G. H. Mair, once literary editor of the *Manchester Guardian*.[3] It is not unknown for inferior officials in the Secret Service to act in this way. So far as F.E. himself is concerned, he can be acquitted of any part in the matter: so far from circulating the diaries, he wrote to Grey on 29 June 1916 to protest that it was 'a ghoulish proposal' and received a distinct assurance that it would not be done under the authority of the Foreign Office.[4] Yet not everyone has agreed that the circulation of the diaries was an inexcusable business: it has been argued that it is sometimes permissible to do a little evil that much good may come.[5]

The Cabinet itself, as the Asquith papers show, considered the matter on three different occasions. Grey and Lansdowne each made the point that it was undesirable to create a martyr by execution. But no competent mental expert could be found to say that Casement was insane, and he was executed on 3 August. At the end the Cabinet seem to have been influenced by a statement that Irish prisoners who had not joined with Casement had had their rations reduced[6]—although Casement himself had denied this at the trial.[7] Certainly no man could have asked for his fate to be considered by a body which comprised men as upright as Asquith, Grey, Buckmaster, and Samuel. (It is not surprising that on 22 July 'Blackwell confessed he did not know, with such a weak Cabinet, what the result would be'.[8]) After the execution there is only one attested occasion on which F.E. showed the diaries to anyone (whatever others

[9] [1914] A.C. 534.   [1] *Criminal Days* (1946), p. 223.   [2] *F.E.*, p. 309.
[3] D. Gwynn, *Roger Casement* (1930), p. 20.   [4] *F.E.*, p. 308.
[5] *Times Literary Supplement*, 26 February 1960.
[6] See above, p. 277. For another possible reason, see *Trial*, p. cxxvii.
[7] Ibid., p. 134.   [8] Ibid., p. cxxii.

might have done), and that was in 1922 when he showed them to Michael Collins, apparently at the latter's request.[9] Another signatory of the Treaty, Eamonn Duggan, also saw them at the same time. Indeed, on some unspecified date which was probably in the early 1920s, F.E. intervened to prevent the commercial publication of the diaries 'at the request of certain people here who did not wish the memory of Casement or anyone associated with 1916 reviled'.[1]

F.E.'s appointment as Attorney-General carried with it a seat in the Cabinet. In this he followed the precedent set by Isaacs and Simon. It was later realized by the Government and also by F.E. himself that it was undesirable for the chief Law Officer of the Government who occupies a quasi-judicial position to be a member of the chief executive body.

F.E. took no prominent part in the intrigues of December 1916—indeed, he expressly let it be known that, as Attorney-General, he made no claim to the Woolsack, although if he had made such a claim no doubt Finlay, as the senior, would have been preferred in any event.[2] Yet he was close to the contenders for power. On the night before Lloyd George assumed office in December, Aitken and Churchill were dining at 32 Grosvenor Gardens. It was at this party that Churchill learnt from Aitken, after the departure of Lloyd George, that he was not to be included in the new Government. His anger flashed out. 'Smith, this man knows I am not to be included in the new Government', he said.[3] Never before had he addressed his old friend by his surname. F.E.'s reticence on this occasion may have indicated that he thought a period of consolidation in his career was desirable, and that this could best be performed by quiet public service in the Attorney-General's office.

His time was fully occupied with the crushing work of his office. Even his powers of delegation to skilled underlings were strained to the utmost in order to keep abreast of the work which flowed through the Law Officers' Department. He appeared for the Crown in two of the leading cases in Prize Law, the *Zamora*[4] and the *Ophelia*[5]. In 1917 he prosecuted the Wheeldons for conspiracy to murder the Prime Minister, and in 1918 he argued the Rhodesian Land Case before the Judicial Committee. He also did much good work as the reviewing authority in court martial cases. Until then there had been almost no system for this important function. Court martials themselves were conducted by military officers without the assistance of a legally trained Judge-Advocate-General, as later became the case. F.E. secured the appointment of a number of skilled

[9] *F.E.*, pp. 307–8.   [1] E. Duggan in *F.E.*, p. 307.
[2] *Law, Life and Letters*, pp. 245–6.
[3] Lord Beaverbrook, *Politicians and the War* (1932), vol. ii, pp. 289–90.
[4] [1916] 2 A.C. 77.   [5] [1916] 2 A.C. 206.

barristers to this position and also set up a small reviewing staff to consider the sentences. It was therefore a peculiarly unfortunate incident when in February 1916 on a visit to France he was arrested by order of the Adjutant-General, Sir Nevil Macready. The arrest was technically justifiable because F.E. was in a military area without the appropriate pass but the folly of it displayed only too clearly the petty-minded attitude which some military leaders had during the First World War towards civilians. F.E. had made a number of enemies at General Headquarters in France who were only too pleased at what seemed a heaven-sent opportunity to get their own back on a formidable and witty person who had used his tongue at their expense. The incident ended with the Attorney-General being asked to lunch by the Commander-in-Chief, Haig, where his consumption of brandy was noted by his host in his diary.

On the domestic front there is a glimpse of the Attorney-General attending a conference at the Ministry of Munitions about industrial unrest. Sir Basil Thomson recorded in his diary on 15 May 1917: 'F.E. Smith, whose manners were bad as usual, talked good sense. He said that as the Cabinet had sent the King and Queen to the strike areas, it would be wrong to prejudice the success of their visit by arresting the strikers until they have left the north.'[6]

At the end of 1917 F.E. paid a quick visit to the United States of America and Canada where his gift for public speaking attracted large audiences anxious to hear the Allied Cause supported. During his absence he was created a baronet in the New Year's Honours List. Shortly before he left, in November 1917, he had been elected Treasurer of Gray's Inn, an honour which he deeply appreciated. In December he was able to entertain the Prime Minister to dinner in the Inn, an occasion on which Lloyd George replied to the Lansdowne Peace Letter recently published in the *Daily Telegraph*. At the general election of 1918 F.E. was returned for the West Derby division of Liverpool, abandoning his old constituency of Walton. He had not even taken his seat in the new parliament when he was summoned to Downing Street by Lloyd George and offered his old position of Attorney-General; but it was indicated to him that it would be impossible for him to retain his seat in the Cabinet because of a strong desire that the number of its members should be reduced. F.E. was unwilling to suffer such a blow to the prestige of his office and told the Prime Minister that he could not accept such a condition, although he was prepared to give independent support to the Government from the back benches. The Prime Minister then replied 'as quick as lightning': 'How about the Woolsack?'[7] The question was accompanied by the statement that an answer was required by 10 o'clock the following

[6] B. Thomson, *The Scene Changes*, p. 338.   [7] *Law, Life and Letters*, vol. ii, p. 245.

morning. As F.E.'s family were away in the country it was impossible to communicate with his wife for her opinion and advice.

I had accordingly to take the decision for myself. I promised the Prime Minister to breakfast with him on the following morning, and to give him my answer at this melancholy meal. I spent most of that night in debating the matter in my mind. I had not reached a complete decision when I arrived at No. 10 Downing Street. Winston Churchill was breakfasting there also. He had hitherto shown himself inflexibly opposed to any proposal that I should leave the House of Commons. But after ten minutes discussion, before our arrival was announced, he greatly weakened. I suppose that I was hardly conscious of having reached a conclusion. I had nevertheless groped my way to one in the long hours the previous night. At any rate, I left the breakfast table on that morning with the knowledge that I was to become Lord Chancellor.[8]

The decision was in many ways a disagreeable one to F.E. It cut him off from the prospect of further political advancement and also from the chance of returning eventually to the Bar. It also, perhaps more seriously, curtailed his income by a considerable degree. Nor were matters improved by the reaction of the public. The King himself wrote to Lloyd George asking for the appointment to be reconsidered on the ground that 'His Majesty does not feel sure that Sir Frederick has established such a reputation in men's minds as to ensure that the country will welcome him to the second highest position which can be occupied by a subject of the Crown.'[9] The King also stressed the youthfulness of the new Chancellor, who was in his forty-seventh year. The Prime Minister replied adhering to his intention to appoint F.E. to the Woolsack and stating, quite inaccurately, that 'Many of the most distinguished Chancellors in our history attained the office between the age of thirty and forty'.[1] The only Chancellor who was certainly younger was Jeffreys, who was aged 43 years when appointed in 1685.[2] *The Times*, in a leading article, stated that the appointment was 'carrying a joke too far' and there is no doubt that at the time it was unpopular both with Bench and Bar. F.E. received the Great Seal on 14 January 1919 and on 30 January as Sir Frederick Smith he presided over the hearing of his first appeal.[3] On 3 February he was created a peer with the title of Baron Birkenhead and on the following day was introduced into the House of Lords.

---

[8] Ibid., p. 247.   [9] *F.E.*, p. 332.   [1] Ibid., p. 333.

[2] It was once thought that Jeffreys was Lord Chancellor at 40: but it has now been settled that he was 43: H. Montgomery Hyde, *Judge Jeffreys* (2nd ed., 1948), p. 19. Cowper (?1664–1723) was Lord Keeper at 41 (1705) and Lord Chancellor at 43 (1707), but the date of his birth is doubtful.

[3] See below, p. 400.

CHAPTER IV

AS LORD CHANCELLOR Birkenhead takes a very high place in the list of holders of that office. From the very start he devoted his great talents to excelling in all three of the aspects of the work of Lord Chancellor, in Cabinet, as head of the judicial system, and as Speaker of the House of Lords. Any fears that he might have behaved in a frivolous or light-weight fashion were quickly dispelled. All opinions about him had to be revised in the light of the extraordinary release of constructive energies which followed his appointment. It was noticed immediately that as President of the Final Court of Appeal his judicial demeanour was above reproach. He was proud of the fact that no observation of his made while sitting on the Bench had ever been followed by the reporter's phrase 'laughter in court'. He realized what other judges have sometimes not realized; that litigation was a serious business to the parties themselves if not to anyone else and his behaviour was a model of sober correctness. He was always anxious to maintain the dignity of the judicial position. In May 1923 he delivered a severe rebuke to Simon for having absented himself from an appeal to the House of Lords in which he was counsel without having first obtained leave.[1] A full assessment of his judgments will be found in the Appendix. It is enough to say here that they show a remarkable width of learning and scholarly research set forth in a vigorous and lively prose style illuminated by his familiar flashes of mordant irony. He had no false pride: he did not pretend to knowledge which he had not got. So he did not disdain the services of a research assistant when necessary (for some years Sir Roland Burrows filled the position) although his judgments in their style and mode of presentation are inimitably his own. Lord Dunedin wrote later: 'The end of it has been that although other eminent judges who had a longer tenure have left more in the books, yet I do not believe that the judgments of any judge taken as a whole would show what I may call a higher level of excellence than his.'[2] Some of the principal cases in which he took part were *Bourne* v. *Keane* (1919) in which the House upheld the validity of a bequest for masses for the souls of the dead; *Sutters* v. *Briggs* (1922) in which an ingenious point was taken on the Gaming Act, 1835; *Admiralty Commissioners* v. *S.S. Volute* (1922) in which we have already seen that his masterly judgment on the subject of contributory negligence was publicly commended by two of his fellow Law Lords; *Director of Public Prosecutions* v. *Beard* (1920)

[1] *Abram S. S. Co. Ltd.* v. *Westminster Shipping Co. Ltd.*, The Times, 2 May 1923.
[2] In *The Times*, 2 October 1930.

one of the rare occasions in which the House had to consider a fundamental point of criminal law, in this case the effect of the defence of drunkenness; and *Wakeford* v. *Bishop of Lincoln* (1921) in which he took great pains to ensure that a just decision was arrived at in a case involving an acute conflict of testimony.[3] On several occasions in 1920 Birkenhead sat at First Instance in the Divorce Court to help dispose of the mass of post-war business. Good judgments on points in matrimonial law will be found in *C.* v. *C.* (1921), *Gaskill* v. *Gaskill* (1921), and *Russell* v. *Russell* (1924). His efforts as a law reformer were considerable; it will be seen that the great property legislation of 1925 was enacted largely as a result of his parliamentary gifts. There were various other legal reforms of a technical and administrative kind. He did much of the preliminary work for the Supreme Court of Judicature (Consolidation) Act 1925 and also he remodelled the rules relating to the conduct of litigation by and against poor persons and provided for the trial on circuit of poor persons' divorce cases. He also attempted to reform the outdated circuit system, but was defeated by the conservatism of local politicians who feared the loss of prestige which would follow the abolition of an assize. He also improved the tenure of office of county court judges and laid the foundation for the County Courts Act, 1924. Indeed one of his first judicial appointments to the High Court Bench was of a county court judge, Edward Acton. Acton had never taken silk but fortunately enjoyed the distinctions of being a member of the Northern Circuit and a former scholar of Wadham College. The appointment was a success and set a valuable precedent for the promotion of county court judges, who until recent years had been a somewhat despised section of the judicial hierarchy. Birkenhead's other judicial appointments were admirable and entirely unmarked by any undesirable political influence. At least twice he stood firm against Lloyd George's attempts to influence appointments—once (unsuccessfully) when the office of Lord Chief Justice was vacant, and again (successfully) when the Prime Minister wished to make Ellis Griffith, K.C., a High Court judge. To the King's Bench Division Birkenhead appointed, besides Acton, Rigby Swift, K.C., another member of the Northern Circuit, F. A. Greer, K.C., a most learned authority on the common law who was eventually promoted to the peerage under the title of Lord Fairfield, and G. A. H. Branson, who had never taken silk but had been Attorney-General's devil on the common law side, a post which traditionally entitled its holder to judicial appointment. In the Chancery Division Birkenhead appointed M. Romer, K.C., and F. W. Russell, K.C., each of whom later rose to be a Law Lord. He also appointed ten judges to the County Court Bench.

[3] See below, pp. 456–8.

One judicial difficulty which faced Birkenhead during these years related to Sir Ernest Wild, the Recorder of the City of London. The Recorder of the City is elected by the Court of Aldermen and not appointed by the Lord Chancellor. Nevertheless his position at the Old Bailey is one of great power and when the usual High Court judge is not present he is competent to try capital cases, unlike the Recorder of any other city. As such it is desirable that he should occupy a position as detached and impartial as that of the ordinary High Court judge. Nevertheless under the law as it then stood the Recorder of London was not formally prohibited from being a member of Parliament and Sir Ernest Wild, who had fought many elections in vain before his return as a Coalition Unionist in 1918, refused to resign his seat when elected Recorder. Birkenhead dealt with the matter in a simple and drastic way. He informed Wild that although the Chancellor had no power to remove the Recorder from office, so long as he retained his parliamentary seat the Lord Chancellor would not insert his name in the Commission which issued for the Old Bailey as for any other assize court. The Commission of Assize was drafted in the Crown Office and although for centuries the Recorder's name had appeared in it, this could be deleted on the instructions of the Lord Chancellor himself. Sir Ernest Wild reluctantly recognized that he had encountered a stronger power and resigned his seat.[4]

In Cabinet Birkenhead was a valuable counsellor. His opinions were generally on the side of moderation and conciliation. It was noticed by many that he seldom spoke and then only when he was certain that he had something to say. His reluctance to venture an opinion on something which he had not studied for himself was equalled only by his rapidity of comprehension when it was necessary for him to tackle a strange subject. He had highly developed the leading barrister's skill in mastering a complicated brief quickly. Thus Lloyd George recalled how at the Peace Conference of 1919 a question involving international law arose and the Lord Chancellor was sent for to advise.

When he arrived Monsieur Clemenceau as President of the Conference submitted to him the issue upon which his opinion was sought. Without a moment's hesitation Lord Birkenhead gave an exposition of his views. The statement lasted ten minutes. It was a model of clarity and compression. At the end of it you felt there was nothing more to be said. Monsieur Clemenceau turned to me and said: 'How wonderfully clear.' I asked him to let us hear what the French jurist, a lawyer of great distinction, had to say. Monsieur Clemenceau replied: 'It is quite unnecessary. The Lord Chancellor's statement has settled the question.'[5]

[4] Report of the Select Committee on Offices or Places of Profit under the Crown (1941), p. 98.   [5] F.E., p. 467.

In the House of Lords itself it was noted how quickly Birkenhead adapted the tone and manner of his public oratory to the very different atmosphere in which the Peers were accustomed to do business. As Churchill remarked, 'For all the purposes of discussion, argument, exposition, appeal or altercation F.E. had a complete armoury. The bludgeon for the platform; the rapier for a personal dispute; the entangling net and unexpected trident for the Courts of Law; and a jug of clear spring water for an anxious perplexed conclave.'[6] It was indeed remarkable how Birkenhead showed himself as skilled at addressing the House of Lords as addressing a crowd of fervent Ulster men in a gale in Co. Antrim. Some of his speeches are notable by any standards. In particular those who wish a sample of his oratory should refer to his speech in the debate relating to General Dyer in which the Lord Chancellor defended the conduct of the Government in placing General Dyer on half pay.[7] Birkenhead emphasized that there could not be one standard for India and another for Glasgow, Belfast or Winnipeg—in each of which riots had recently occurred. Anyone who defended Dyer must also be prepared to defend shooting 400 rioters in those cities. Another admirable speech will be found in the debate on the Government of Ireland Bill 1920.[8] Perhaps his most striking speech of all, prepared for once with the aid of full notes, was on Lord Buckmaster's Divorce Bill of 1920.[9] Birkenhead lent all the powers of his passionate advocacy to support of the Bill. He had been convinced from his experience at the Bar that the existing divorce law gave rise to grave unhappiness. Another speech under circumstances of peculiar difficulty was given in support of the Anglo-Irish Treaty in December 1921. In the late summer of 1921 Birkenhead, until then an inflexible supporter of the Government's policy in Ireland of meeting force with force, had become convinced of the necessity for a settlement. In the protracted and delicate negotiations with the Irish Delegation in November and December he had displayed constructive statesmanship of a high order. It was very different from his intervention in Irish affairs ten years before when he had 'grazed the very frontiers of treason'[1] with Carson. In particular he had quickly established a relationship of mutual trust and confidence with Michael Collins, who said of Birkenhead: 'If all the British delegation had his capacity for clear thinking, capacity for work and getting ahead, things would be much easier. Lawyer, but with a great difference. Concise. Clearness of ideas a great advantage. Refuses to be drowned by the might of others. A good man.'[2] When the Treaty

---

[6] W. S. Churchill, *Great Contemporaries* (1939), p. 176.
[7] 41 H.L. Deb. 5s. col. 264.   [8] 42 H.L. Deb. 5s. col. 421.
[9] 39 H.L. Deb. 5s. col. 663.   [1] *F.E.*, p. 371.
[2] R. Taylor, *Michael Collins* (1961), p. 122.

was debated in the Lords Birkenhead had not merely to persuade a reluctant House to agree to a measure which struck at all the principles of Unionism but had to do so under the shadow of the charge that he had deserted his own personal convictions in order to sign the Treaty. The charge had been made by Carson a few days previously in a speech of extraordinary venom. Carson had said: 'Of all the men in my experience that I think are the most loathsome it is those who will sell their friends for the purpose of conciliating their enemies, and, perhaps still worse the men who climb up a ladder into power of which even I may have been part of a humble rung, and then, when they have got into power, kicked the ladder away without any concern for the pain, or injury, or mischief or damage that they do to those that have helped them to gain power.'[3] Birkenhead had sat through this speech and a somewhat less vicious one by Salisbury pale and motionless on the Woolsack. He took no notes for his reply, which was delivered on 16 December. It was a masterly rebuttal of the charges made against him. 'He was a little over-wrought, but had evidently steeled himself to a great effort. He spoke with intense energy and kept his hands clenched close to his body.'[4] He defended himself from the attacks made upon him.

Neither Lord Salisbury nor Lord Carson has made any contribution to any alternative policy. Lord Salisbury says he is a Home Ruler, but he does not indicate the particular form of Home Rule he intends to honour with his support and what particular body of people he will succeed in persuading to believe in it. As for the speech of Lord Carson, his constructive effort at state-craft would be immature on the lips of an hysterical schoolgirl.[5]

Birkenhead concluded his speech by a general appeal to the Peers to accept the Treaty as the best possible settlement of 700 years of bitterness.

The Irish people are a very strange, wayward, and incalculable people. . . . But of this I am certain: that we have given a population which is overwhelmingly homogeneous the opportunity of taking their place side by side with the other communities in the British Empire. That is an immense moment in history. We believe there is a chance that this settlement will satisfy that sentiment of nationhood, and if it does, year by year the animosities which have poisoned our public life will disappear.

The Treaty was accepted by 166 votes to 47.

In his legislative capacity the Lord Chancellor introduced a Bill to do what he had been unable to do in his judicial capacity—alter the law as to gaming laid down in *Sutters* v. *Briggs* (1922). This decision had produced the absurd result that one who paid a lost bet by cheque, as distinct from cash, could recover the sum so paid from the winner, and the Gaming

[3] 48 H.L. Deb. 5s. col. 44.   [4] *F.E.*, p. 390.   [5] 48 H.L. Deb. 5s. col. 196.

Act, 1922, reversed the decision. On the Second Reading Birkenhead said: 'I very seldom myself visit racecourses—very seldom indeed. I can truthfully say of racecourses that I am *parcus et infrequens cultor*. It is almost equally true to say that I never risked any sum or any wager except on those few occasions on which I have been present at a racecourse.'[6]

1922 was a testing year for Birkenhead. For the first time there began to appear the signs of the discontent which were to lead to the fall of the coalition Government in October of that year. Personally his main pleasure had arisen from the fact that in March he had been appointed High Steward of Oxford University and in June had received the honorary degree of D.C.L.[7]

By the summer of 1922 two main factors had begun to contribute to the weakness of the coalition. One was the dissatisfaction of the Unionist Party with the Irish Treaty of December 1921. The other was the uneasiness over the distribution of honours by the Prime Minister which had culminated in the scandal involving Sir Joseph Robinson in June 1922, when the 80-year-old South African was obliged to write withdrawing his acceptance of a peerage in circumstances which were humiliating both to the Government and himself. In retrospect it may seem curious that such an incident should have weakened one of the strongest governments of modern times, but three of those who were Under Secretaries in the Government have testified to the importance of the incident.[8] As Ernest Pollock, then the Attorney-General, wrote in his hitherto unpublished memorandum: 'In perspective with other events, this matter may seem insignificant, but I am sure that it cut away from Lloyd George the support of a great number. It was a point on which every one could hold and express an opinion and it stirred the blood of Englishmen to find that the Crown and its prerogative of the bestowal of honours was being used to advance the Party, or indeed the personal, ends of the Prime Minister.'[9] Pollock recorded how he and some other members of the Conservative Party met Austen Chamberlain (since April of the previous year the party's leader in the House of Commons) in his room at the House in June 1922. There were present Sir Robert Sanders, G. Gibbs, later Lord Wraxall, Leslie Wilson, the Chief Whip, L. Amery, George Stanley, Sir Arthur Griffith-Boscawen, W. C. Bridgeman, Sir Laming Worthington-Evans and also Sir Leslie Scott, the Solicitor-General. Chamberlain received them sympathetically and expressed his appreciation of the spirit in which, and the purpose for which, they had approached him.

---

[6] 47 H.L. Deb. 5s. col. 145.   [7] See below, p. 445.

[8] Earl Winterton, *Orders of the Day* (1953), p. 114; L. Amery, *My Political Life* (1953), vol. ii, p. 233; E. Pollock, Unpublished Memorandum in Hanworth papers.

[9] Hanworth papers. The quotations which follow are from this memorandum.

He was deeply interested in what we had to say while of course he appreciated —as we did—the delicacy of the situation. It was one thing to learn of the unrest in the constituencies. It was another to tell the Prime Minister that he was no longer wanted. But apart from that, was the unrest well-founded, or based on a renewal of the prejudice which had attached to Lloyd George before the war? Was it wise for us to detach ourselves from a powerful fighter who could wield great power—if and when a general election came?

Pollock recorded that, 'We had not delivered ourselves of an ultimatum, but of news from the constituencies which needed cautious consideration.' The Session proceeded in the normal way and it was not until the end of July that the dubious members of the Unionist Party were told that the Cabinet had been informed of their doubts and that it had determined to hold a meeting with the doubters for consideration of the matter. 'The meeting was arranged for August 3. My memory tells me that it was in the last week of the Session. That is a stage in the Parliamentary Session when nerves are frayed and tempers are not at their best.' The meeting was presided over by Austen Chamberlain and attended by Birkenhead and Balfour. Several accounts of Birkenhead's behaviour at this meeting have survived. Pollock's may be quoted at some length.

I think Lord Birkenhead took the matter in hand at once. He cross-examined Peter Sanders as to his information and Willie Bridgeman upon the deductions to be drawn from it. He poured scorn upon both. He derided the reports from the country as mere gossips' tales, unworthy of credit and not representative of the real feeling of the country. He was severe upon Bridgeman, who said with characteristic courage that he shared the opinions reported, and was anxious to see Lloyd George and what new or divergent policy from that being pursued was possible in the hands of any leader. Lord Birkenhead's attitude was unexpected and both hostile and dictatorial as if addressed to inferiors who had no right to express opinions. A servant must obey his master without question and the manner of Lord Birkenhead was directed to affirm this principle, and put presumptuous and wayward servants in their place. Then he turned upon me as the leading servant who ought to have known better than to allow his fellow servants to disclose this spirit of *hubris*. It is true that as Attorney-General, I was the chief Law Officer of the Crown, and as such was my own master, and was not in a subordinate capacity as were some of those who had joined in the interview with Austen Chamberlain. They were under secretaries and junior whips. Whether this was the reason or not, Lord B. made a very direct attack upon my conduct—the impropriety and folly of it. We had been friends for many years and in his earlier days at the Bar I had seen not a little of him. I liked him and I think he liked me. Indeed I feel sure that he did so. Perhaps that was the reason that when he differed from me, he threw some driving-power—if not acerbity—into his remarks. I replied as the story told above called for. I emphasized the fact that we had, none of us, intended to go beyond a just and proper report and deliberation with our Leader, that Lord Birkenhead had wholly misunderstood our attitude and we had been encouraged, rather than discouraged, by Austen Chamberlain in our discussion with him, that there was no disloyalty on our part, and that we felt we were misunderstood both in our method and in our purpose. It was of no avail. I confessed that we wished that Austen Chamberlain would have reinforced what I had said and explained how matters had reached this stage; but for reasons good or bad, he left the matter in Birkenhead's hands. After I had received a somewhat severe rating, we were told as a body that we were to go away, and not to entertain any ideas of our own as to the personnel of our Leaders, or their policy, and that our whole conduct was a compound of insubordination and stupidity. . . . The meeting broke up. It is idle to pretend that Lord Birkenhead's attitude and language did not create animosity. I have seldom seen men so stirred. They had refrained from words of recrimination, but the very fact that they had done so deepened their feelings of injustice and resentment. I walked away with Balfour, to whom I poured out my story, that the whole position had been misinterpreted and mishandled—that we had been misrepresented and misunderstood. He was always a most kind friend to me, as indeed to us all, and I felt eased by the sympathetic hearing he gave me.

Birkenhead's arrogant and overbearing conduct to the junior ministers on this occasion was bitterly remembered by them (and their wives) not merely for the months but also for the years to come. It is certainly paradoxical that he who was so flexible in reconciling opposing points of view in order to create a coalition should have been so inflexible when it came to maintaining it and his position in it. On the other hand, Birkenhead's intransigent attitude undoubtedly helped to stiffen that of Austen Chamberlain. Indeed during the months to come the two of them moved closer together in both political and personal friendship. Four days before the Carlton Club meeting on Thursday 19 October there was another meeting in the Conference Room at 2 Whitehall Gardens, at which Chamberlain presided, assisted by Birkenhead and one or two others. The meeting listened to a statement by Chamberlain to the effect that support of the coalition was indispensable. Pollock, together with others, thought that a further discussion with Chamberlain might help to keep the party together. 'Some of us felt that if Chamberlain could unbend a little, become more coaxing in manner, the rift might be closed up.' Pollock then led a group composed of himself, Edward Wood and Jock Gilmour to Chamberlain at 11 Downing Street on the following Tuesday evening. But the visit was fruitless. 'Austen was unyielding. He had taken counsel with Balfour and F.E. They had with him thought out and helped to prepare his declaration and from it he would not deflect his course. More than that he seemed to feel that it was not consonant with his position to seek to induce the recalcitrant group to join him. Rather it was for them to offer loyal obedience. It was not a time for cajolery—it was the occasion for the whip.' The evening before the meeting at the Carlton Club was spent by the anti-Lloyd George Conservatives in trying to persuade Bonar Law to attend it and break up the Coalition. At the last moment he agreed to do so and his appearance at the meeting came as a surprise to many.

No hint of this intention was conveyed to Austen. During these days of rapidly changing views, communications between persons and groups had been incessant and rapid. The telephone facilitated them. There would have been time to go and see Austen over night. There was abundant time to see him before the meeting which was timed for 11 o'clock. Yet no approach was made or sent by Bonar Law to Austen. I have never been able to understand or indeed to excuse this silence. Bonar Law thereby placed Austen in a compromising and ambiguous position; and the man who caused this difficulty was the friend with whose guidance, or at any rate with whose approval, Austen had acted as he had done.

The only explanation that I am able to advance is that Bonar Law never really understood English ways—certainly not the ways which are learned at the English public school. I doubt if anyone trained in that arena could have placed his friend in such a difficulty without notice to him.

It is perhaps surprising that Pollock should have been so taken aback at the appearance of Bonar Law at the meeting, for *The Times* for that morning, 19 October, stated that Bonar Law would attend. The editor, Wickham Steed, had inserted this statement on the strength of a late-night telephone call to Bonar Law himself. In the event, as we have seen, the Conservative Party decided to withdraw from the coalition and by that afternoon the Government was out of office.

Birkenhead made no attempt to conceal his disgust at the Conservative Party decision, and left the meeting with a dark scowl on his face. He could not have been described as a good loser. Ahead of him lay vistas of government by men whom he despised and at that moment probably hated, and whom he was to stigmatize bitterly as 'second class brains', deliberately ignoring the fact that among them were three Fellows of All Souls, and a brilliant newcomer, Douglas Hogg, of whose great capacities he was fully aware.[1]

Thereafter Birkenhead was an unwavering supporter not only of Austen Chamberlain but of Lloyd George himself. When at a meeting soon afterwards the meaningless taunt 'Judas' was flung at him he was able to reply 'I had always understood that Judas was abhorred for betraying his master; am I to be blamed for refusing to betray mine?' In the Dissolution Honours List Birkenhead was advanced to an earldom, having previously

[1] *F.E.*, p. 452. Further details of Birkenhead's political activities in 1922 can now be found in Lord Beaverbrook, *The Decline and Fall of Lloyd George* (1963).

been promoted viscount in June 1921, on the recommendation of Bonar Law. During the next year Birkenhead's position in the party and the country slumped sharply.

At the age of 50 he found himself 'powerless, restless, almost alone'.[2] In the quarters in which he was normally accustomed to seek and find political support, the inner circles of English conservatism, he was disliked and distrusted for his support of the Irish Treaty and, above all, for his refusal to desert the coalition. His sneers at the new Government did not add to his popularity. A reference to 'die-hards' met with an effective retort that they might be preferable to 'live-hards'. He was rebuked by his wife for calling Curzon and Selborne 'the Dolly Sisters' of the Conservative Party.[3] Nor had he been able to build up support for himself in other quarters. The Irish have never been noted for the display of gratitude to those English politicians who gave help to their cause (to this day no statue or plaque anywhere in the Republic commemorates the titanic efforts of Gladstone to bring about Home Rule) and for a variety of reasons the name of Birkenhead was as unpopular everywhere in Ireland as it was in England. Even if it had been otherwise, popularity in Ireland would have been of little help to an English Conservative statesman in 1923.

Furthermore, to the English public at large he was still F.E. rather than an ex-Lord Chancellor. It would in any event have taken some years for the true weight of his achievement on the Woolsack to be appreciated by the ordinary man. The learning and wisdom of his judgments, the vigour and good sense of his efforts at law reform, and the essential rightness and wisdom of his opinions on all public issues would eventually have been assessed at their true value. But it would have taken time for this assessment to be made. For these achievements had been accomplished by a man whose previous public reputation was of quite a different kind, and they had been compressed into the short space of three years. In addition Birkenhead himself, by his manner of life after 1923, both in public and in private, did little to help the public form a different judgment of him. The traits of character which in a rising young lawyer politician had been greeted with tolerant smiles somehow seemed less attractive in a former Lord Chancellor in the sixth decade of his life. It had always been true, as The Times remarked after his death, that 'his sociability brought him in touch with circles where other Lord Chancellors would not have been equally welcome'.[4] But now his friends began to note an increasing stridency of tone, and lamented, sometimes with amusement, sometimes with pity, the inability of one who was so wise a counsellor of others to

[2] The Times, 1 October 1930.
[3] In a Lords Debate: 53 H.L. Deb. 5s. col. 576.   [4] 1 October 1930.

manage his own affairs with wisdom. There was still much to admire in 'the unmistakable chic—the flavour of "Max" and "F.E." and the Prince of Wales, of the big table in the Sporting Club, the second magnum and the fourth cigar, of the chauffeur kept waiting hour after hour without compunction'.[5] But it was not admiration of which his true talents were worthy. It is notable how his appearance had changed in the photographs of this period. Although he retained to the end his fine head of dark hair, his features had coarsened and aged. It is particularly noticeable that his clothes often seem casual—yet he had once been famous for his dandyism. (His appearance in Downing Street for a Cabinet meeting in a soft hat and country clothes brought a rebuke from the King and an angry response from Birkenhead.)[6]

The restlessness which afflicted him in these years is vividly illustrated by the Rectorial Address which he delivered at Glasgow University on 7 November 1923. Although he had early, as Churchill remarked, 'reached settled and somewhat sombre conclusions upon a large number of important topics',[7] the reader of this Address is both dismayed and repelled by the bleak cynicism which it displays. Entitled 'Idealism in International Politics', its general tone can be gathered from two sentences —the latter of which has gained a place in the *Oxford Dictionary of Quotations*, and has served as the title of a biography of its author. 'Yet nothing is more apparent than that politically, economically, and philosophically the motive of self-interest not only is, but must be, and ought to be, the mainspring of human conduct.' 'The world continues to offer glittering prizes to those who have stout hearts and sharp swords.' His son refers to the incident very briefly, saying only that 'the ignorant clamour that followed it filled him with foreboding'.[8] In a happier mood Birkenhead might have agreed with the second Viscount Hailsham, who said, 'for the young it is not, oddly enough, the glittering prizes which attract the generous heart of youth; it is, on the contrary, the gleaming sword and the lust for battle'.[9]

Finally, his extravagance had ceased to be a source of mild amusement to his friends and become one of anxiety and irritation to his family.

At the end of his life, when he had left politics for the City, he had his yacht, six motor cars, only three of which were normally used, three chauffeurs, eight horses with three grooms, a large London house in Grosvenor Gardens and a house in Oxfordshire. He refused to attend to his income tax returns, exercised no control over his agents and gradually incurred an enormous overdraft. This rake's progress was prompted by the same *hubris* which led to the downfall, in

[5] E. Waugh, *Brideshead Revisited* (1949 ed.), p. 162.
[6] See *F.E.*, chap. 24.   [7] *Great Contemporaries*, p. 174.
[8] *F.E.*, p. 554.   [9] 239 H.L. Deb. 5s. col. 373.

a different way, of Oscar Wilde. When protests were made to him he bought another car or a new motor launch, and this selfishness and indifference to the interests of his family was undoubtedly the least attractive feature of his character.[1]

At the end of 1923 Birkenhead returned from a visit to America to find that Baldwin the Prime Minister had suddenly adopted a policy of Tariff Reform. The proposal was to fight a general election on this issue at the beginning of December. Some attempts took place to reunite the Conservative Party. Birkenhead and Austen Chamberlain were approached to see whether they would support the election campaign, especially in Lancashire, where Birkenhead's assistance was needed, but they agreed to do so only on condition that they re-entered the Cabinet. Chamberlain told Baldwin that the only office that an ex-Lord Chancellor could accept was the Woolsack and therefore that Cave must be dismissed in order to make room for Birkenhead. He also stipulated that Leslie Scott should be appointed Solicitor-General instead of Inskip, who should be offered a puisne judgeship.[2] The concern which Chamberlain showed for Birkenhead's interests throughout this negotiation was no doubt a reflexion of the gratitude which he felt for the former's support at the Carlton Club in the previous year. So far as Baldwin was concerned Birkenhead was anathema to him at that date. He despised his character and disliked him personally with something approaching bitterness. It was only in later years that this hostility came to an end. The negotiations broke down apparently because of objections made by the stiffer elements in the Unionist Party to Birkenhead's presence in the Cabinet on both political and personal grounds. Birkenhead, however, did, in an unofficial capacity, assist the Government by speaking in Lancashire throughout the election. The disastrous results of that election for the Conservative Party (258 Conservatives, 198 Labour, 158 Liberal) and the formation of a government under Ramsay MacDonald brought the Conservative Party together as nothing else had done. On 6 February 1924 Birkenhead rejoined the Conservative Shadow Cabinet. During the period of the Labour Government much of Birkenhead's time was taken up with writing for the Press a series of articles on general topics of the day. Many of these articles and essays were later reprinted in book form.

Birkenhead took some part in the proceedings relating to the Campbell case in the autumn of 1924, on which the Labour Government fell from office. The major debates took place in the House of Commons but Birkenhead spoke on the matter in the Lords on predictable lines. The

---

[1] F.E., p. 476.
[2] C. Petrie, *Life and Letters of the Rt. Hon. Sir Austen Chamberlain* (1940), vol. ii, pp. 234–5.

O   821312

Labour Attorney-General, Sir Patrick Hastings, later bitterly accused Birkenhead of having told a falsehood to the Director of Public Prosecutions.[3] Hastings alleged that Birkenhead had told the Director that he was authorized by the Attorney-General to see the file of a previous case in which he, Birkenhead, when Attorney-General, had withdrawn a prosecution. Hastings flatly denied that he had ever given any such permission. The case had occurred during the labour disputes in the munitions industry in May 1917. Birkenhead claimed that it illustrated the complete freedom of the Attorney-General as regards both the initiation and the termination of a criminal prosecution. The Cabinet minuted a decision requiring the Attorney-General to prosecute a certain person for sedition. Birkenhead said that he refused to consider the matter until the minute had been rescinded. It offended against the principle that the Attorney-General occupies a quasi-judicial position and as such should be free from political pressure in the discharge of his duties. When the prosecution had actually been commenced F.E. stopped it on obtaining from the strike-leader a signed undertaking that he would abide by the agreement to return to work negotiated by his union. F.E. emphasized that he had consulted nobody before withdrawing the proceedings.[4]

When Baldwin formed his second government in November 1924 Birkenhead was appointed Secretary of State for India. He was the first ex-Lord Chancellor to hold another Cabinet office since Camden in 1784 had been made Lord President of the Council. No similar appointment occurred until Hailsham was made Secretary of State for War in 1931. Caldecote, upon resigning the Great Seal in May 1940, was appointed Secretary of State for Dominion Affairs.

In private life 1924 was a sad year for Birkenhead. Apart from the financial difficulties which were increasingly pressing upon him, both his brothers died during the course of the year. To the younger of these brothers, Harold, who became a K.C., a Knight and a member of Parliament for Warrington, Birkenhead was especially devoted.

At the India Office Birkenhead left behind him a respectable but not outstanding reputation. Although he had never visited that country his quick sympathy with the more romantic side of imperialism had made him familiar with the history and achievements of the British in India and his skill in mastering complicated material quickly enabled him to dispose of the departmental business of the day without difficulty. He was also fortunate enough to be on terms of close personal friendship with the two Viceroys of the period, Reading and Irwin. Birkenhead's Indian policy was in general of a cautious, conservative character. His knowledge of

[3] P. Hastings, *Autobiography* (1948), pp. 243–4.
[4] *The Times*, 2 and 15 October 1924.

the gulf between Catholic and Protestant in Ireland helped him to appreciate the communal division between Hindu and Mohammedan. He realized this problem was at the centre of the Indian difficulty. He regarded Indian self-government as but a faint possibility in the far future. 'I am not able, in any foreseeable future, to discern a moment when we may safely, either to ourselves or India, abandon our trust.'[5] So he said to the House of Lords in July 1925. A few years later he was willing to contemplate a slightly faster pace of constitutional advance. The Simon Commission was set up in 1927 to report whether the Indian situation permitted an extension of self-government. Birkenhead had obtained the services of his old Wadham contemporary as Chairman of the body. He wrote to Irwin on 19 January 1928.

I cannot help thinking that Simon's published decision to abandon practice at the Bar will be regarded as a great proof of earnestness in the task he has undertaken, and of his own realization of its difficulty and importance. He is, of course, a rich man, and I suspect that he was becoming weary of eternal forensic conflicts, and ever since a boy—as you know we were at Wadham together—he has been very honourably, but very strikingly ambitious. Few people have realized it, but my own view has always been that he was more interested in politics than the Bar, though I have always thought that on great decisions he has generally taken the wrong line. This does not, of course, in any way reflect upon his extraordinary suitability for this particular task, which, though it raises immense political problems, is also beset with a number of others with which his clear, penetrating mind is eminently qualified to deal.[6]

In October 1928 Birkenhead ceased to be responsible for the government of India but he always took a keen interest in events in the subcontinent and was both perplexed and dismayed at the treatment given to Simon and the report of his Commission. He could not understand how the Prime Minister and the Viceroy had, apparently behind the back of the Commission, agreed to a round table conference with Indian politicians and a formal declaration of dominion status as the goal of British policy in India.

Outside Indian affairs, Birkenhead had played a prominent part in the General Strike of 1926. Although his views on labour relations would today be regarded as reactionary in the extreme, he was active behind the scenes in trying to produce a conciliatory formula. His efforts were praised by Labour leaders at the time.[7] By the middle of his term at the India Office Birkenhead had revived the practice of writing articles for the Press and even of commending proprietary articles in advertisements. The Prime Minister was obliged to defend him in the House of Commons

[5] 61 H.L. Deb. 5s. col. 1091.   [6] *F.E.*, p. 515.
[7] *Holmes–Laski Letters* (1953), p. 840.

and an agreement was reached that Birkenhead would not write upon either political or general subjects, but in 1928 the decision to extend the female franchise and grant the vote to 'flappers' brought out his latent dislike of women in politics and he published a strongly worded article attacking the decision. The Prime Minister had once more to explain and try to justify Birkenhead's conduct to the House of Commons, drawing a distinction between mere journalism and writings of a more literary kind.[8] On his side Birkenhead felt angry that he was debarred from earning extra money by his pen. As his son remarked, it is a pity that F.E. recoiled from the drudgery of the pen. For at his best he had an admirable English prose style—clear and vivid, the phrases illuminated by telling adjectives. It is doubtful if F.E. ever in his life wrote a sentence which had to be read a second time for its meaning to be ascertained. (His handwriting was also beautifully firm and clear.) In the years after he left the Woolsack he produced a number of volumes. The later ones are marred by an increasing flatness of style and a reliance on 'ghosts'. It is best to pass in silence over some of them, such as *Fifty Famous Fights* (1932) (which went into a second edition in 1951), and *The World in 2030* (1930), which produced from J. B. S. Haldane serious allegations of plagiarism, refuted not too convincingly.

His financial difficulties had by now become really acute. In April 1927 he wrote to Baldwin that he had been offered £15,000 a year 'in guilt-edged surroundings'[9] but he did not wish to leave the India Office. In March 1928 Baldwin offered him the Woolsack in succession to Cave but this was declined.[1] Birkenhead was by now negotiating for directorships in the City and on 18 October 1928 he wrote to Baldwin finally resigning his office. Four days later he was created G.C.S.I. Birkenhead and Baldwin parted on much more friendly terms than either would have thought possible a few years before. His resignation gave rise to questions in Parliament and discussion in the Press about the annual payment of £5,000 to which an ex-Lord Chancellor not holding any other office of profit under the Crown is entitled under the Lord Chancellor's Pension Act, 1832. It was suggested that Birkenhead was not morally entitled to this sum as he was not obeying the constitutional convention requiring the recipient of such a payment to render unpaid judicial service when called upon to do so. The charges enraged Birkenhead and he made a number of angry replies of a rather contradictory character[2]—that there was no legal or moral obligation to provide continuous, or indeed any, judicial services, and that in any event he proposed to assign the pension to trustees for the benefit of certain hospitals. Birkenhead argued that the object of

[8] 216 H.C. Deb. 5s. col. 356.   [9] Baldwin papers.
[1] See below, p. 468.   [2] *The Times*, 22 November 1928.

the pension was to enable the Government of the day to obtain the services of a man of outstanding eminence at the Bar as Lord Chancellor. Such a man could not be expected to surrender the opportunities of advancement at the Bar merely in return for a position which, however splendid, was liable to be terminated with little or no notice.[3] As etiquette forbade an ex-Lord Chancellor to return to the Bar it was only reasonable to provide him with a sum to compensate him for what he had lost, and Birkenhead stated that by accepting the Woolsack he personally had deprived himself of the opportunity of making eight times the amount of the pension at the Bar. In short, his argument was that the payment was not a pension at all. He also said that if judicial services were expected it was absurd that an ex-Chancellor should be paid less than the Law Lords over whom he would preside on the hearing of an appeal.

It is not easy to come to a decision on all this. There is much to be said in Birkenhead's favour. The object of Parliament in 1832 in providing an annual payment of £5,000 upon retirement from the Woolsack was almost certainly not to establish a pension contingent upon the performance of certain services. The long title of the Act states that its object was 'to abolish certain Sinecure Offices connected with the Court of Chancery and to make provision for the Lord High Chancellor on his Retirement from Office'. It is worth noting that the short title of the Lord Chancellor's Pension Act was only conferred by the Short Titles Act, 1896, and that nowhere in the Act is the term pension used as a definition or description of the payments to be made under it. In 1832 the sinecures which the Act abolished, amounting in value to £24,000, were intended to provide for the family of the Lord Chancellor. The parliamentary debates[4] make it plain that by way of compensation for the abolition of these offices his 'retiring allowance' was to be increased from £4,000 to £5,000 per annum. Section 3 of the Act makes this perfectly clear. After reciting that 'Whereas by reason of the abolition of the said offices the Lord Chancellor . . . will be deprived of patronage' it goes on to provide that 'it is therefore just and equitable that more ample provision should be made for the Lord High Chancellor'. The sum of £5,000 is paid quarterly by the Paymaster-General under Letters Patent issued under the authority of the Act. The first payment is made on the first quarter day after the Lord Chancellor resigns the Great Seal, and the payments are suspended while he again occupies the office of Lord Chancellor or any other office of profit under the Crown. Therefore if any ex-Chancellor should wish to abdicate his right to the whole or any part of his pension all he has to do is to give notice to the Paymaster-General of his intentions. Otherwise the

---

[3] This had also been the view of Peel in 1850: See C. 6617, p. 27.

[4] See Hansard's Parliamentary Debates, Third Series, vol. xiv, col. 1296.

payments would seem to be secured upon him by statute and to be just as much his property as the Post Office pension secured upon the Duke of Marlborough by Parliament in the reign of Queen Anne.

But the fact that the payments made under the Act of 1832 are not in strict law a pension conditional upon the performance of services does not conclude the matter, for a constitutional convention may have grown up requiring such services. Here the testimony seems to be all one way. The constitutional practice of the past century has undoubtedly been for an ex-Chancellor to sit judicially when asked to do so.[5] Conversely, if he should wish neither to sit nor to draw his pension there seems to be no reason why he should not be entitled to act in this way, whatever views may be held as to the propriety of the means which he has adopted to supplement his income.[6] Finally, it may well be that the obligation to sit judicially is in practice less onerous today than at the beginning of the century, when there were only three to five Law Lords as compared with the nine of today, and the Treasury was less willing than it has since become to create new judgeships.

Birkenhead entered the City too late to make much impression upon it or his own waning fortunes. A curious lassitude and quietness seemed to have come over him. He who had once shown so great a zest for life could now sometimes be seen sitting quietly by himself. In the spring of 1930 he fell seriously ill while on holiday at Biarritz. In May he had recovered sufficiently to send two pungent letters to *The Times*[7] on the subject of the Radcliffe Observatory—the future of astronomy being then a subject of controversy at Oxford. The rest of the summer passed quietly at Charlton. After an attack of pneumonia he died at his London house, 32 Grosvenor Gardens, on 30 September 1930. After cremation his ashes were taken to Charlton and buried on 4 October under a finely wrought cross in the small churchyard which looks out over the North Oxfordshire fields. The very large congregation composed of men and women from King George of Greece to a local poacher testified to the extraordinary width of his friendships. Birkenhead was succeeded by his only son, Frederick Winston Furneaux, Viscount Furneaux. His will left everything to his wife absolutely. Birkenhead's estate was valued for probate at £63,223.

---

[5] See 614 H.C. Deb. 5s. col. 1480 (1959), and 220 H.L. Deb. 5s. col. 104 (1959).
[6] For the case of Lord Kilmuir in 1962, see 667 H.C. Deb. 5s. col. 999.
[7] On 15 and 21 May.

APPENDIX

Common Law. In *Fitch* v. *Dewes* [1921] 2 A.C. 158, Birkenhead, in an unreserved judgment, held that a covenant by a solicitor's managing clerk not to practise within seven miles of his employer after the expiry of his contract, without any limit as to time, was not necessarily void as against public policy. Birkenhead pointed out that it was in the public interest that suitably framed restrictive covenants of this kind should be permitted, because otherwise solicitors (especially those without a partner) would be chary of admitting young men to the confidential knowledge to be acquired in the course of business in their offices.

In *D.P.P.* v. *Beard* [1920] A.C. 479, the Lord Chancellor sat with no fewer than seven Law Lords to determine (*a*) the intent required by the law to constitute the felony of murder, (*b*) the effect of drunkenness rendering the prisoner less capable of forming that intent. Birkenhead delivered the unanimous judgment of the House. On point (*a*) he affirmed the traditional view that if death ensued from an act of violence done in the course or furtherance of a felony of violence (e.g. rape), that was murder. On point (*b*) he affirmed that although drunkenness was in general no defence unless actual insanity supervened, evidence of a state of drunkenness rendering the accused incapable of forming the specific intent required for the particular crime might be taken into account in deciding whether the Crown had proved that the accused had the requisite intent. But as it had been proved that Beard had killed a girl in the course of a drunken rape (a felony of violence), it would be necessary for him to show that his mind was so affected by drink that he was unable to form the intention to rape—an impossible task. Beard's conviction for murder was therefore affirmed.

In *Les Affréteurs Réunis Société Anonyme* v. *Walford Ltd.* [1919] A.C. 801, the House held that the commission stipulated to be paid to the brokers who had negotiated a charter-party could be obtained from the ship-owners by the charterers as trustees for the brokers. An equitable principle enabled the common law rule that no third party could sue upon a contract to be evaded.

In an unreserved judgment Birkenhead pointed out that this principle had been clearly established ever since 1853. How was it that the trial judge (Bailhache J., an experienced commercial lawyer) had disregarded this principle? It was on the ground that there was a mercantile custom to the effect that a commission clause embodying such a principle was worthless. Birkenhead dealt with the finding in his customary style (pp. 808-9):

In contrast with the extreme sanctity which the learned judge concedes to this custom . . . I confess that I am somewhat attracted by the tone of his reference to the deliberate contract entered into between the parties. The custom, the learned judge says, is 'irrespective of the form in which the commission clause finds its way into the charter-party'. My Lords, in my experience important clauses do not 'find their way' into important contracts. They are, on the contrary, the fruit of negotiation and consideration. The process is by no means so fortuitous as is supposed. The learned judge, in my judgment . . . has in effect declared that a custom may be given effect to in commercial matters which is entirely inconsistent with the plain words of an agreement into which commercial men, certainly acquainted with so well known a custom, have nevertheless thought proper to enter. Much evidence would be necessary to convince me of the existence of such a custom, and, if it were forthcoming, I should nevertheless hold the custom to be bad on grounds which seem to me to be both notorious and elementary.

The judgment in the *Walford* case was unreserved, as was that in *Friedrich Krupp Aktiengesellschaft* v. *Orcanera Iron Ore Co. Ltd.* [1919] 88 L.J. (Ch.) 304, an appeal heard in the same month, on 30 January 1919 when the Lord Chancellor was still a commoner. (His judgment would therefore appear to be a breach of the convention (above, p. 146) which prohibits the unennobled from utterance.) Unreserved judgments are a rarity in the House of Lords. Although judicial celerity is generally a virtue, it is by no means necessarily so (as Birkenhead's son suggests, *F.E.*, p. 490) for in an appellate tribunal the issues raised are generally so important as to deserve the fullest consideration.

Change for the mere sake of novelty had no appeal to him. In *British and Foreign Insurance Co. Ltd.* v. *Wilson Shipping Co. Ltd.* [1921] 1 A.C. 188, Birkenhead emphasized that a rule of mercantile law which had been acted on by merchants for more than a century should not lightly be disturbed even if the House thought it did not truly represent the law.

Equally he discouraged attempts to raise on appeal points which had not been considered in the courts below: *North Staffordshire Railway Co.* v. *Edge* [1920] A.C. 254, and also arguments which depended on too minute an examination of the language used in a judgment, or which blurred the distinction between *ratio decidendi* and *obiter dictum*: *Manton* v. *Cantwell* [1920] A.C. 781.

In *Rutherford* v. *Richardson* [1923] A.C. 1, he laid bare some of the harsh and inhumane results which followed from a law which, as it then stood, did not permit one spouse to divorce another for insanity.

Equity. His judgment in *Bourne* v. *Keane* [1919] A.C. 815 has already been mentioned. It covers some thirty pages of the Law Reports. Birkenhead persuaded his fellow Law Lords (except Wrenbury) to uphold the validity of a bequest for masses for the souls of the dead. In so doing the House overruled a decision of eighty-four years' standing, and refused to follow dicta going back for 300 years—and this on a matter of Chancery practice, in which certainty is of prime importance. It is one of the most striking examples there is of the 'judicial valour' which Pollock admired. It shows that the House of Lords is not definitely committed to the view that it is better to be consistently wrong than ultimately right. In a characteristic passage at the beginning of his judgment (p. 831), Birkenhead indicated the advantages of a bold policy.

Unwilling as I am to question old decisions, I shall be able, if my view prevails, to reflect that your Lordships will not within a short period of time have pronounced to be valid legacies given for the purpose of denying 'some of the fundamental doctrines of the Christian religion' [Lord Parker of Waddington in *Bowman* v. *Secular Society* [1917] A.C. 406, 445] and have held to be invalid a bequest made for the purpose of celebrating the central sacrament in a creed which commands the assent of many millions of our Christian fellow-countrymen. In the second place, and in the event supposed, your Lordships will have the satisfaction of deciding that the law of England corresponds upon this important point with the law of Ireland, of our great Dominions, and of the United States of America. A decision based, as I believe this to be based, upon a sound view of the law may reasonably appeal to these two powerful considerations of policy as against the admitted impolicy of disturbing old decisions.

Constitutional Law. In *McCawley* v. *The King* [1920] A.C. 691, he delivered an admirable judgment in the Privy Council emphasizing that a broad interpretation must be given to the legislative powers conferred upon colonial legislatures so that they might be masters in their own household. The judgment contains some remarks on the difference between a 'controlled' constitution (such as that of a colonial legislature) and an 'uncontrolled' constitution (such as that of the United Kingdom) which have often been cited by writers on constitutional law.

In *Home Secretary* v. *O'Brien* [1923] A.C. 603, Birkenhead (no longer Lord Chancellor) presided over the House for the purpose of hearing an appeal involving an important question concerning the liberty of the subject. The Court of Appeal had ordered a writ of habeas corpus to issue in respect of the detention of the respondent, and the question was whether the Home Secretary could appeal against this order. O'Brien had been arrested by the Home Secretary and handed over to the Government of the Irish Free State in Dublin. The Home Secretary had acted in good faith but without lawful authority. 'Had the Home Secretary', said

o*

Birkenhead, 'contented himself with one act of illegality—namely, the forcible internment within this country of the respondent—it is admitted that discharge would have been automatic, and consequently there could have been no appeal. But inasmuch as the Home Secretary has added a second illegality to the first—namely, by forcibly handing over the respondent to the Government of the Irish Free State—he has thereby disabled the Court of Appeal from effectively ordering his discharge, so that the respondent, because there were two illegalities instead of one, is deprived of his ancient constitutional privilege.' It is not surprising that the House held that no appeal lay against the issue of a writ of habeas corpus, whether the discharge of the prisoner had actually been ordered or not. Until the law on this point was altered to the disadvantage of the subject by the Administration of Justice Act, 1960, Birkenhead's speech was accepted as an authoritative assertion of the traditional bias of the common law in favour of individual liberty.

In *Viscountess Rhondda's Claim* [1922] 2 A.C. 339, 'the massive irony of Gibbon' was employed to expose the historical fallacies inherent in the belief that a peeress in her own right was entitled to sit and vote in Parliament. In a judgment covering thirty-two pages of the Law Reports Birkenhead held that a peerage held by a peeress in her own right is one to which in law the incident of exercising the right to receive a writ is not and never was attached. By the majority of twenty-two to four the Committee of Privileges (which had previously decided in the opposite sense) rejected Lady Rhondda's claim.

LORD CAVE

CHAPTER I

GEORGE CAVE WAS BORN AT 67 CHEAPSIDE, LONDON, on 23 February 1856 the second son of Thomas Cave by his wife Elizabeth, daughter of Jasper Shallcrass of Banstead.[1] The house in which he was born has been destroyed and the site is now occupied by the Ghana Commercial Bank. Both parents were unusual people. His father, who was descended from a line of farmers in Gloucestershire and Oxfordshire, rose to success in business in the City of London and, after being High Sheriff of the City in 1863–4, entered the House of Commons as Liberal Member for Barnstaple. On the son's birth certificate he is described as 'Managing Director of the Anchor Assurance Company'. His mother was a woman of strong character, possessing deep religious interests of an Evangelical kind, who lived to the age of 96, dying only in 1925 after seeing her son Lord Chancellor. Of the rest of the family two younger brothers achieved eminence, Edmund Cave becoming a Master of the Supreme Court and Basil Cave Consul-General in Zanzibar.

George Cave, in maturity, was a tall, erect man with long legs and keen blue eyes, looking more like a colonel or successful company director than a Chancery lawyer. His father had unusual views on education for a Victorian parent. At the age of 10 he sent George, together with his elder brother Tom, to school in France at the Lycée at Caen in Normandy. This was certainly a curious thing for any parent to have done in the eighteen-sixties. The imagination is strained at the vision of these two small boys leaving Victorian England at the height of its prosperity, and being subjected to the ferocious discipline and concentrated over-work of a French school.

At Caen they stayed for three years, unable to travel home either at Christmas or Easter for holidays. The letters home which have survived from this period indicate that they did not enjoy themselves. They disliked the climate, the food, and above all, their fellow pupils, whom they found to be, in the best tradition of the beliefs of English schoolboys, dirty, given to cheating, and apt to sneak to the masters.

On their return in 1869 the two boys were dispatched by their father on a walking tour of the south country and when they called on the Mayor of Dover he was so taken with the self-possession with which the

---

[1] The primary source for the life of Cave is Sir Charles Mallet's *Lord Cave* (1931). The author had access to family papers which have since been destroyed. Quotations are from this work unless otherwise stated.

two children sent in their visiting cards that he personally showed them around the town and sent them on to do the same at Walmer Castle, where Lord Granville, the Lord Warden, was in residence. Whatever else may be said about Thomas Cave, he certainly believed in instilling a spirit of self-reliance and initiative into his sons.

In September 1869 George Cave was sent as a day boy to Merchant Taylors' school in the City of London, at that date still in rather cramped quarters in Suffolk Lane. The school was not then enjoying the most distinguished period in its long history and Cave received no more than an adequate education on standard Victorian lines—classics, mathematics, a little history and French. Needless to say he was teased by his fellows for his impeccable French accent. When he left school in 1874 he had a scholarship at St. John's College, Oxford (which is closely connected with Merchant Taylors'), of £100 a year for seven years, a Pitt Club exhibition tenable for four years, and a school scholarship tenable for two years. Cave had tried for an open scholarship at New College but was unsuccessful, being beaten by his own future brother-in-law, R. F. Horton, from Shrewsbury. He was then able to fall back on the closed scholarship from Merchant Taylors' to St. John's.

Cave travelled to and from school each day by train or omnibus from the family home in Lancaster Gate, whence the restless Thomas Cave was apt to disappear for long periods on the continent, taking with him his wife and such of his children as happened to be available. At another time the family lived at Brighton, which made it necessary for the boys to travel up to London by a workmen's train at 5.40 a.m. each day. Thomas Cave finally settled on Queensberry Villa at Richmond as a family home, but it rarely happened that they were all together even during the school holidays.

When Cave went up to St. John's in 1874 he found a college which had been little affected by the reforms of the Gladstone Commission of 1852. The President was Dr. Bellamy, whose father had been a headmaster of Merchant Taylors'. He himself is believed to have resided in Oxford with only one year's absence from 1836 to 1905 and was at that date just beginning a presidency of nearly forty years. As the historian of Oxford remarked, 'Dr. Bellamy was a worthy representative of the quiet, conservative traditions of St. John's'.[2]

As an undergraduate Cave was a quiet and hard-working man who was popular enough with his contemporaries to be elected a member of the Archery Club and the King Charles Club. He rowed after a fashion but was just left out of the college boat for Torpids. His father vexed him from time to time by insisting on a most careful standard of economy and

[2] Mallet, p. 62.

PLATE 15

Lord Cave as Chancellor

PLATE 16

Lord Cave in later life

an accurate keeping of accounts. George entered every penny in a note book but was ready to complain to his mother that £170 a year was 'an impossible income for Oxford'. It is not surprising that he owed £100 when he went down but it is indicative of his self-reliance that he refused the help offered by a near relative and paid off his debts out of the first money which he earned.

In 1878 he obtained (together with Oscar Wilde) a first in Greats in a strong year, having previously obtained a first in Honours Moderations in 1875. He had thus achieved in an unspectacular fashion the greatest academic triumphs which Victorian Oxford had to offer. His sole failure at Oxford seems to have been an unsuccessful attempt at the blue ribbon of classical scholarship, the Ireland. Although, after graduation, he also competed unsuccessfully for All Souls and for the Stowell Fellowship at University College, he does not seem to have been in any way disappointed by either of these failures—indeed, for the Stowell Fellowship he had one who was then regarded as a very strong rival in D. D. Rogers of Balliol, whom he never expected to beat. His mother, who had strong Evangelical sympathies, seems to have tried to induce the son to take Holy Orders but he quietly declined the notion.

Meanwhile he had started eating dinners at the Inner Temple, financing his call to the Bar, which took place in June 1880, by the traditional method of teaching, in this case at his old school. He also secured a scholarship in real property awarded by his Inn.

CHAPTER II

CAVE'S CHAMBERS were at 26 Old Buildings, Lincoln's Inn, and he was fortunate enough to receive a brief on the very day he was called to the Bar and in his first year to earn 100 guineas. No doubt it was a help to him that his elder brother, Tom, was by now a qualified solicitor. Cave was a pupil in the Chambers of H. M. R. Pope, who died prematurely.

Cave's orderly and careful mind was admirably suited for work at the Chancery Bar and the fact that he was somewhat slow in thinking on his feet and had a rather poor delivery was of no particular hindrance as the work of a Chancery barrister lies mainly in drafting wills, conveyances, and other documents. On his appearance in court he does not need the eloquence which is essential to someone at the Common Law Bar.

By 1885 he felt secure enough to marry, his bride being Ann Estella, daughter of William Withey Mathews of Chard and North Cadbury, and sister of Sir Lloyd Mathews of Zanzibar, whose name was a household word throughout East Africa for strict justice and honest administration. She was a vivacious lady with some artistic talents who was admirably suited to spur her somewhat slow-moving husband to greater things. In later years Lady Cave published some artless books of reminiscences. In one she recorded a visit to Queensberry House during their engagement:

> The first evening I was there my future father-in-law said to me, 'Do you know you are going to marry a possible future Lord Chancellor?' I replied, 'Yes, I know.' One of the family said, 'Well, the first thing I hope you will do is to make that ugly-looking seat better to look at.'
>
> A few days after we were walking together down St. James's Street, and I was talking of the milestones that must be passed before the Woolsack could be reached, and George said, 'When I take silk, I will give you a diamond necklace.' I said 'No: a pearl necklace when you take silk and a diamond one when you are Lord Chancellor.' A tall man was passing and turned with a charming smile to look at the young people with such lofty aspirations. I asked who it was, as I seemed to know the face. The reply was, 'I expect you do. That is Arthur Balfour.'[1]

The young couple settled down in a small house on Richmond Hill and for some years lived quiet lives while George Cave was building up his practice at the Bar.

He moved to other chambers at 4 New Square where he joined George

[1] Estella Cave, *Odds and Ends of My Life* (1929), pp. 18–19.

Borrett. By 1890 he was earning nearly £1,000 a year and in 1892 he earned £1,494. It was the unsensational, laborious work of a Chancery junior, but once a solicitor had entrusted a brief to Cave he was apt to return many times in the future. Still there were some awkward moments while waiting for the briefs to come in. In later life Lady Cave recalled an occasion when they went with a friend, Reginald Westmacott, to a seaside resort for the weekend:

In those days briefs were not so frequent as later, anyhow we spent too freely. We paid our hotel bill, arranged for our luggage to meet us at the station and passed out with honours, but there was luncheon still to get. We went to a restaurant for a simple meal, but our undoing was a rum omelette. George asked for the bill, glanced at it, and ordered coffee and liqueurs. I was speechless. Saying to Reginald, 'We will stroll out until the coffee is ready', they left me as a hostage hoping to be retrieved. They came back, calm, cool and collected, sat down, had coffee, and tipped the waiter into smiles. On the steps I said: 'How?'; he dangled from his pocket a watchless chain, and put it back without a word![2]

By 1890 they were living at Wardrobe Court, Richmond, a charming brick house near Henry VII's palace. This had been bought for them by Thomas Cave, who at that date had retired from Parliament and was devoting himself solely to his business interests. Characteristically, though, it was not an outright gift, for he insisted on the young couple paying him an economic rent for it. By this time George Cave had begun to take an active part in local government in Richmond and Surrey. Although brought up as a Liberal, he had followed Hartington and Chamberlain on the question of Home Rule in 1886 and by now was indistinguishable from a Unionist. He was a respected member of the Richmond Town Council and later of the Surrey County Council. In particular his grasp of financial detail was welcome. He also acquired a considerable practical knowledge of the licensing question which was later valuable to him in the House of Commons. He soon became Chairman of the Financial Committee of the Surrey County Council and in 1894, at the age of 38, Chairman of Surrey Quarter Sessions, an important position in view of the amount of crime which the nearness of London brought within his jurisdiction.

Meanwhile his practice at the Bar was growing in a steady but unsensational way. In 1895 he earned some £1,600, by 1900, £2,700 and in 1904, the year in which he took silk, he made between £4,000 and £5,000. His manner in court had improved with increasing self-confidence and knowledge of the world but he was still a reserved man known to few outside his intimate circle. 'He was especially to us Lincoln's Inn people

[2] Mallet, pp. 12–13.

a strangely reserved personality: very few of us knew him well, although he was friendly with us all', so wrote Robert Younger, the future Lord Blanesburgh. He had become something of an authority on the law relating to easements (as far back as 1888 he had brought out a new edition of *Gale on Easements*, which followed a new edition of *Sweet's Concise Precedents in Conveyancing* two years before).

His work as Chairman of the Surrey Court of Sessions seemed to many at first sight to be so different from that of a Chancery silk that it was surprising that it should appeal to him, but Cave carried it out with his customary patience and calmness and thoroughness. One case from those years may interest the modern reader. In 1898 women were just beginning to use the bicycle and the Victorians were much exercised about the proper female dress for bicycling. The more advanced cyclists advocated the use of a garment known as 'bloomers', but many thought that a lady in trousers rather than in a skirt was a dreadful sight, so when, in October 1898 a woman of some common sense and independence, Lady Harberton, called for lunch at the Hautboy Hotel, Ockham, after bicycling in bloomers, she was refused admittance to the dining-room by the landlady, who said that she was willing to serve Lady Harberton in the bar parlour (which was full of workmen drinking and smoking), but that it was impossible to admit her to the dining-room in bloomers. Lady Harberton thereupon launched a private prosecution against the innkeeper for the common law misdemeanour of failing to supply a traveller with the necessary food and lodging. The innkeeper was defended by Horace Avory, at that time a rising junior at the criminal Bar. Cave summed up very carefully to the jury to the effect that an innkeeper could not refuse to supply food because of the shape of the traveller's dress but was entitled to offer that food in some room other than the normal room. The sole question left to the jury then was whether the room offered for the lunch was in fact a reasonable and proper place. The jury apparently thought that it was and acquitted the innkeeper. Afterwards a friend told Cave, 'I was talking after luncheon to Horace Avory, and he expressed great admiration for you on the seat of judgment. It was a matter of surprise that the intellect of a Chancery man should rise to the height of Quarter Sessions.'

In 1904 Cave's success as a judge in criminal cases was recognized when he was appointed Recorder of Guildford. The only sadness of those years, but one which went very deep, was the death of their infant child in the summer of 1899. On the other hand, the death of his father in 1894 had brought him another house in Richmond, for he was left Queensberry House, which was the last of Mr. Cave's many dwelling places.

Finally the years of quiet and unostentatious work for local government in Surrey had their reward when, in December 1905, the sitting Conservative Member for Richmond, Sir Thomas Skewes-Cox, unexpectedly announced that he would not stand at the forthcoming election. Cave was unanimously chosen as his successor by the local Conservative association and was returned by a majority of 1,000 over the Liberal candidate, Robert Whyte, in an election in which many safe Conservative seats were lost. Thus at the unusually mature age of 50 George Cave became K.C., M.P.

The newly elected Member and his wife felt it necessary to have somewhere nearer the House of Commons to live than Wardrobe Court. For a short while they lived with a number of other M.P.s at the Westminster Palace Hotel, where they saw the rising Mr. F. E. Smith breakfasting every morning with a noisy, small daughter. A certain amplitude in the Cave attitude to the troubles of daily life can be seen in the fact that he acquired the lease of 'a small house in Piccadilly' (No. 80) because 'it was difficult to get home to Richmond on busy nights'. They shortly afterwards moved once more, to No. 4 Smith Square, which was retained until Cave was appointed a Law Lord in 1918, when the more leisurely pace of life in the House of Lords enabled them to move back to Richmond.

George Cave's maiden speech could not have been more different from that of his fellow Conservative new Member, F. E. Smith. Speaking in the same year (March 1906), he intervened in a quiet way on a Police Pensions Bill.[3]

His other speeches in the House were on equally unemotional and businesslike matters. But the Members liked his quiet, persuasive way of tackling problems and above all the absence of forensic glitter about his style of oratory. The House of Commons' traditional dislike of lawyers did not operate in Cave's case. By April 1908 he had sufficiently established his reputation for the Leader of the Opposition, Balfour, to ask him to undertake the important task of moving the rejection of the Government's Licensing Bill, which was a major attempt to deal justly with the evil of intemperance. Control of the 'liquor traffic' was then a political issue, and the 'Temperance Movement' was closely allied to Liberalism. An observer described the scene: 'He rose in a crowded House, heated with a fine speech from Mr. Asquith, and it says much for Mr. Cave that in these difficult circumstances he made a speech which established his reputation beyond recall. He flooded the Bill with facts, figures, and vivid illustrations. A certain judicial attitude of mind added greatly to the force of incisive argument.' Another observer pronounced him 'the embodiment of Quarter Sessions propriety, a happy combination of the magistrate and the Squire'. Cave's principal point was that although the Conservative

[3] 153 H.C. Deb. 4s. col. 386.

Party supported the reduction of licences in the cause of temperance, there must be adequate compensation for those whose licences had not been renewed, and this he said the Bill failed to give. As is well known, the Lords foolishly refused a Second Reading to the Bill in October. An outburst of Liberal indignation followed. It was discovered that no fewer than 129 peers owned shares in breweries. Attention was also called to the fact that an increasing number of powerful figures in the brewing industry had recently been ennobled by Conservative governments. The refusal of the Lords to pass the Licensing Bill was undoubtedly one of the factors which led to the Parliament Act, 1911. So far as the licensing laws themselves are concerned, the result of the different pressures had produced legislation which is often illogical or obscure. It has been well said that 'The English public house at closing time gives the foreigner a glimpse of the proverbial misery which is supposed to accompany our national temperament for taking pleasure seriously, just as the proliferation of drinking clubs proves further evidence of our proverbial hypocrisy.'[4]

After this speech, Cave's position in the House and in his party was dominant. The Government went so far as to invoke his help on several matters; for example, Mr. Churchill, when Home Secretary, appointed him to hold an inquiry into the conduct of the police in the case of Steinie Morrison, a once notorious London murderer. He was also the subject of attention by the cartoonists of the day who delighted to portray his long legs and his high domed forehead. The more critical cartoons generally showed him in company with 'Mr. Bung the Brewer' as a result of his speech on the Licensing Bill.

At the general election of January 1910 he was helped by the fact that his opponent was one of those obscure men with a German name (in this case Holzapfel) whom the pre-1914 Liberal Party seemed to delight to honour, and Cave was returned by a majority of 5,000 votes. He never again had to contest the Kingston Division.

In the controversy of 1910 and 1911 over the relationship of the two Houses, Cave was prepared in private to admit that the House of Lords had made a mistake in rejecting the budget of 1909 and that some revision of the existing rules was needed. He was prepared to contemplate some reform of the House of Lords and to leave all purely financial matters to be determined by the Commons. But, as in duty bound, he strongly opposed the Parliament Bill in debate in 1911, moving a series of ingenious amendments to the measure. He proposed, for example, a referendum in the case of Bills embodying an important constitutional change and also that a joint committee under the presidency of the Speaker, and not only

[4] J. M. Lee, 'The Political Significance of Licensing Legislation' (1960) 14 Parliamentary Affairs 211, at 212.

the Speaker himself, should be responsible for deciding what constituted a Money Bill.

In the same year, 1911, he was active in supporting Sir Edward Carson in bringing the Archer-Shee case before the House. It will be remembered that justice was eventually done to the young naval cadet who had been wrongly dismissed from Dartmouth. Many observers in the House thought that Cave's moderate statement of the facts was one of the main reasons which induced the Government to agree to a settlement of the case. In the same year he felt obliged by the increasing pressure of work to give up his post as Chairman of Quarter Sessions and the magistrates and other friends in Surrey subscribed for a portrait painted by W. H. Symonds, which was hung in the Justices Room attached to the Quarter Sessions Court.

In June 1913 he had the disagreeable task of moving in the House of Commons a motion in relation to the report of the Select Committee which had investigated the Marconi case. Cave's view represented that of the minority on the Committee which, while condemning the reckless Press charges, declined to accept entirely the defence of the Attorney-General and the Chancellor of the Exchequer and condemned as a grave error of judgment the reticence of those Ministers in regard to their purchases of shares in the American Marconi Company. Cave's power of lucid exposition of complicated facts, his evident sincerity and honesty and gift for moderate statement made him the ideal person to move such a motion in the highly charged atmosphere of the House. He summed up the views of many when he said: 'I am not here to preach a sermon against speculation. . . . But I do not think we like the Chancellor of our Exchequer, the head of the Treasury, who has great financial operations to overlook and control, who desires the respect of the City of London, to go into this kind of transaction.'[5] In 1913 the Government's Home Rule Bill once again passed through the House of Commons but was rejected by the House of Lords. If it passed the Commons once more it would become law under the provisions of the Parliament Act, 1911. Cave held the orthodox view in his party that Ulster must either be coerced to come in under the Bill or else excluded by Parliament itself. He put forward this view on several occasions in the House. In 1913 he went further in a letter to *The Times*[6] which propounded a theory which caused much dispute amongst constitutional lawyers. Cave argued that if the Liberal Government failed to hold something in the nature of a referendum before the Bill passed into law in order to secure the clear

[5] 54 H.C. Deb. 5s. col. 400.

[6] 6 September 1913 (reprinted in Jennings, *Cabinet Government* (3rd ed., 1959), Appendix III).

assent of the electors to such a fundamental change in the constitution, then the King would be entitled to dissolve Parliament under the prerogative without the consent of the Prime Minister. Cave considered and rejected another argument which some Unionist lawyers had put forward to the effect that the King might veto the Bill unless such an election or referendum was held. Cave's letter was supported by both Dicey and Anson, each of whom had in their earlier days preached the orthodox doctrine of the sovereignty of Parliament, but neither of whom now liked to see his words being taken literally by a Liberal parliamentary majority. Both Dicey and Anson argued that the monarch had in the last resort power to safeguard the fundamentals of the constitution by dissolving Parliament to secure the assent of the electors to a fundamental change. But as the wise Lord Esher pointed out, this proposal was in truth a reversal of the constitutional development of nearly two hundred years. For since the Act of Settlement, 1701, it had become plain that the monarch was bound to act on the advice of Ministers responsible to Parliament, and if the monarch refused his assent to a Bill, or dissolved Parliament without the consent of the Prime Minister of the day, he would sooner or later be obliged to find other Ministers to carry on the Government, and at the general election which must inevitably ensue, the King's name would be brought into party politics with consequences which, as Lord Esher remarked, 'No loyal subject could contemplate without misgivings'. As the Irish Secretary, Birrell, wrote to Asquith on 8 September 1913:

Cave's letter was instructive—for of course it is not the *veto*, but the *right* to *dissolve*, which has of late been uppermost in certain '*minds*'. It is odd that a mouldy Equity draftsman and conveyancer should be so *bold*—but was not *Beales* also a Lincoln's Inn man—to say nothing of that anti-Christ, the present Lord Chancellor,[7] whose *sittlichtrecht* seems to be a bastard gospel—not by such preachments will war be put down.[8]

In the same month of September the ex-Lord Chancellor, Loreburn, sent a letter to *The Times* arguing in favour of a constitutional convention but although, as we have seen,[9] this was much discussed in high quarters, nothing came of it. In October Cave delivered a fighting speech at Bedford on which the Chancellor of the Exchequer, Lloyd George, wrote to F. E. Smith on 6 October: 'What is the good of Steel-Maitland talking of rapprochement when he sends Cave to Bedford to start another campaign of pure scurrility? This must mean war to the knife. I

[7] Haldane.
[8] Asquith papers.
[9] See above, pp. 169–72.

know enough of Cave to be able to conclude that he would not be a party to this dirty work unless he had been officially asked to do it. This is certainly not the way to conciliation.'[1]

These years brought to Cave a number of other distinctions outside politics—he was appointed Attorney-General to the Prince of Wales, an office of great antiquity though not of great business or emolument; he became Standing Counsel to Oxford University and he was elected a member of Grillions Club, a dining club for the eminent of Edwardian England.

[1] Earl of Birkenhead, *F.E.* (1959), p. 227.

CHAPTER III

THE OUTBREAK OF WAR found Cave still in practice at the Bar, but he readily surrendered any spare time to government work. In particular, he acted as Chairman of the Contraband Committee which dealt with difficult questions arising out of cargoes captured at sea which were suspected to be destined for German use although consigned to neutral ports.

The reconstruction of the Government in May 1915 did not bring any position to Cave, the two Law Officers appointed being F. E. Smith and Carson. Cave was consoled with a Privy Councillorship in the Honours List which followed—though it was an honour well earned by his work on the Contraband Committee. In the autumn of that year, however, Carson resigned from the Cabinet over the question of giving help to Serbia, which was being simultaneously attacked by Germany, Austria, and Bulgaria. After a full review, the Cabinet decided to leave the unfortunate country to her fate—a hard decision but one which was entirely justifiable in view of the military risks involved. Carson, however, was obstinate to the last and persisted in maintaining his point of view to the extent of resignation. For the vacant post Cave was 'strongly fancied by his Conservative friends and himself'.[1] But the Solicitor-General, F. E. Smith, did not acquiesce in this view and invited Cave to call on him. The two men had twenty minutes private conversation and when Cave came out of the room he had agreed to accept the Solicitor-Generalship under his junior colleague and to wait for the senior post. Both F.E. and Cave voluntarily deprived themselves of £5,000 a year as salaries as a wartime sacrifice. The appointment brought with it the customary knighthood—together with fees amounting to £60. 12s. 0d. payable to the Exchequer. The oath of office which Cave took was in the old form and is perhaps worth reproducing:

I George Cave do declare that well and truly I will serve the King as his Solicitor-General in all His Courts of Record within that part of the United Kingdom of Great Britain and Ireland called Great Britain and truly counsel the King in all His matters when I shall be called and duly and truly administer the King's matters and sue the King's process after the course of the law and after my cunning—For any matter against the King where the King is party I will take no wages or fee of any man—I will duly in convenient time speed such matters as any person shall have to do in law against the King as I may

1 Birkenhead, *F.E.*, p. 283.

lawfully do without long delay tracting or tarrying the party of his lawful process in that that to me belongeth and I will be attendant to the King's matters when I shall be called thereto.

The heavy work of advising the Government in wartime occupied most of Cave's time, but he found time also to introduce a small but necessary piece of reform in the criminal law—the Indictment Act, 1915, which simplified and shortened the form of indictments in criminal cases. Cave showed the House an indictment as it might be under the old system. It was on parchment forming a bundle 9 inches in diameter which when unrolled had twice encircled his private room.

Amongst the cases of the time Cave appeared for the Crown together with the Attorney-General, F. E. Smith, in the prosecution of Roger Casement for high treason, a trial which has already been adequately described elsewhere.[2] Later, in January 1917 when Cave had become Home Secretary, he received the following letter from Duke, the Chief Secretary for Ireland:

I think you are the custodian of the diary of the late Roger Casement. I have been asked, with a view to the pending questions (whether this person was a saint or a sinner), whether the book would be produced to any responsible and trustworthy Roman Catholic dignitary who might desire to satisfy himself of its authenticity and character. Can you tell me?[3]

Cave noted on the letter that he had no objection to showing the diary to such a person if he was vouched for by the Chief Secretary. This incident is, of course, of particular interest in view of the allegation later made by supporters of Casement that the British Government had been party to a gigantic conspiracy to forge the diaries.[4] If there had been the slightest basis for this allegation, it would be very surprising to find Cave, who as Solicitor-General had appeared for the prosecution, informing the Irish Secretary only six months after Casement's execution that the Government had no objection to a properly qualified Irish cleric inspecting the documents in question. It is perhaps a pity that in later years successive Home Secretaries took the view that the Casement diaries were of too confidential a nature to be disclosed. It was not until 1959 that they were opened to inspection, thereby giving support to the foolish theory of an official conspiracy.

In the intrigues which resulted in the fall of Asquith in December 1916 Cave took no part although his position in the Conservative Party entitled him to high office when the new government was formed. He was offered the post of Home Secretary and an immediate reply was demanded. He felt obliged to accept although he had no time to consult

[2] See above, pp. 370–9.   [3] Mallet, p. 183.   [4] See above, p. 373.

anyone except his old friend, Ernest Pollock. Cave's talents were of a kind peculiarly suited to the Home Office, which is a position in which it is possible to make a great reputation but also one in which it is possible to make a small mistake which is seized upon by Parliament, the Press, and the public, and magnified into a major error. Cave's prudence and honesty safeguarded him against a disaster of this kind.

In 1917 Cave had to pilot through the House a vast new Bill relating to the franchise which contained thirty-three clauses and six schedules. It substituted for the seven existing franchise qualifications three only, namely (i) residence, (ii) the occupation of business premises worth £10 per annum, and (iii) university graduation. The Bill in effect doubled the electorate and increased the number of male voters by about 2 million. It also added an entirely new class of voters—women over 30, who numbered at least six million. Finally, amongst a number of other changes, it abolished the time-honoured system whereby a general election was spread over three weeks by providing that all constituencies should poll on the same day. One particular problem gave rise to hours of debate on the committee stage. The Speaker's Conference on which the Bill was founded had unanimously advocated the adoption of the system of proportional representation.

But when it came to selecting the localities for its trial, great cities for instance like London or Liverpool or Birmingham, the representatives affected were generally found to be opposed to the plan. Mr. Austen Chamberlain resisted the application of the scheme to Birmingham and the attempt of the House of Lords to override on that point the decision of the Commons with a warmth of independent Radicalism which Mr. Asquith took occasion to note and to admire. Mr. Asquith, on his side, while lucidly defending the desirability of a valuable experiment, was at least as lucid in explaining its unsuitability to the County of Fife.[5]

In the event the Commons were compelled to agree to a limited experiment in proportional representation and to surrender the alternative vote 'although they had four times decisively rejected the first, and had four times definitely if narrowly affirmed the second'. In the end neither alternative was adopted and the country continued to operate its general elections on the principle of the simple majority vote.

Cave's work on the Franchise Bill was so heavy that he felt obliged to decline an appointment which, as his biographer says, 'would have been specially acceptable to a Chancery lawyer who had never wished to abandon his profession'. The Mastership of the Rolls was about to become vacant due to the failing health of the holder, Lord Cozens-Hardy. The

[5] Mallet, pp. 197–8.

post was being offered to Cave at the end of 1917 on the understanding that he would first see the Franchise Bill through the House of Commons, but when the appointment actually had to be made, early in 1918, at a critical stage of the war, Cave felt it impossible to accept. He wrote to the Prime Minister: 'But now things have changed. The war promises to be long and difficult, and there may be trouble at home. If you think that I can be of service to you in the war, or that my leaving you now might affect to any extent, however slight, the strength of the Government, I would rather stay with you and take my chance of what the future may bring.'[6] So Lord Justice Swinfen Eady was appointed to the position, which he held for little more than a year. Cave's own name was mentioned for other vacant appointments about the same time. The critical military situation in March and April 1918 brought about demands for a change in the Government. As Harcourt wrote to Buckmaster on 24 April:

The clouds gather round this impossible and contemptible Government, but no alternative materializes. The *Morning Post* is reduced to suggesting Sir George Cave. He is only one shade better than the Speaker. In despair, the country will eventually have to take the one man capable, which is Asquith, though the majority of them do not realize it. 'Wait and see' as a phrase—but not as a fact—has soaked into what they think are their souls.[7]

Two days earlier Lord Esher had written more concisely to Derby: 'The *Morning Post* today proposes *Cave* as Prime Minister. Gwynne has no sense of humour.'[8] At the same time there was also much speculation that Cave might succeed to the Speakership when Lowther retired, though in the event this resignation did not occur until 1921.

In June 1918 Cave led an important mission to The Hague to come to an agreement with the German Government over the exchange of prisoners of war and for the better treatment of those who remained. The delegates were much impressed by the fluency and purity of the French which Cave had learned long ago in the lycée at Caen. Before the discussions had reached a successful conclusion Cave was called home to deal with an anti-alien agitation which had sprung up in the Press and which even reached the extent of alleging that the Home Secretary was himself of German sympathies and had a German wife. Scarcely had this problem been disposed of when the country was startled by a police strike in August 1918 when Cave was on holiday at Burnham. On Saturday 31 August it was said that only five police officers were on duty between Westminster and Temple Bar. The Prime Minister, with his

[6] Mallet, p. 207.   [7] Buckmaster papers.
[8] R. Churchill, *Lord Derby* (1959), p. 359.

peculiar flair for negotiating in a delicate situation, intervened and the strike was promptly settled by large concessions. The Commissioner of Police, Sir Edward Henry, resigned and Cave himself as the responsible minister felt obliged to offer his resignation, but it was refused by Lloyd George.

It was not, therefore, surprising that in November of that year, two days after the Armistice, he agreed to succeed Lord Parker of Waddington as a Lord of Appeal. This was work of a kind which was peculiarly suitable to Cave's training and abilities and his appointment was received with general satisfaction. Although he was appointed on 13 November, he did not, in fact, surrender the Seals as Home Secretary until 14 January 1919, for the Prime Minister was, understandably, anxious for him to hold the office until he had an opportunity of reconstructing the Government as a whole after the general election. In the interval he answered several questions in the House of Lords on behalf of the Home Office. The spectacle of a Law Lord exercising the functions of a Cabinet Minister was criticized at the time.[9] Although there was some precedent for it in the case of Haldane,[1] such a fusion of functions is a departure from the normal principles of the Constitution, and can best be justified as due to a temporary exigency. As Cave had been a Secretary of State he was given a Viscounty instead of the normal life-peerage which is conferred on Law Lords. This had the unusual result that when there was no Lord Chancellor present Cave presided at a hearing over many Law Lords who were senior to him.

One of these, Lord Dunedin, has left an admirable summary of Cave as a judge:

He first joined us as a Lord of Appeal in Ordinary, and he shortly afterwards became Lord Chancellor. Whether in equality or in superiority of official position there was no difference. He was the most admirable of colleagues, very eager to give of his best, and with a sincere desire to maintain the high reputation of the judgments of the Supreme Tribunal. He was patient with Counsel, but always anxious for relevancy. In considering cases before judgment he was eminently open to suggestion from others, though he would not allow himself to be over-persuaded to adhere to an opinion which he did not really hold. His judgments will I think take high rank in the books, though there are not enough of them to win him the fame which has been won by some of his predecessors.

Lest however I should be thought to be a mere flatterer, let me add this. I sat on the Tribunals a good many years before he did, and consequently he had frequently appeared before me as Counsel. Now in my judgment he was a very good example of what I think is generally acknowledged to be the case—that the best judge is not always to be found in the ranks of the most brilliant

[9] See (1918) 53 L.J. (N.) 391.   [1] See above, p. 213.

Counsel. Lord Cave at the Bar was a good advocate—none could dare to say the contrary—but I did not, and would not, ascribe to him the highest rank as a pleader. Yet from the very first day that he sat with us it became apparent that he was going to be a first rate judge.[2]

One of the judgments which Cave delivered as a Law Lord in these years may be referred to not merely because of its intrinsic interest, but because it gives a very good example of his strength as a judge.[3] In 1920 civil disorder in Ireland had reached such a pitch that the Lord-Lieutenant issued a proclamation which put the four south-western counties under martial law. In the proclamation there was a provision that after 27 December 1920, any unauthorized person found in possession of arms, ammunition or explosives 'will be liable on conviction by a Military Court to suffer death'. Notwithstanding this statement the ordinary civil courts in Ireland continued to function. Two Irishmen, Clifford and O'Sullivan, who were civilians, were arrested by military forces in the County of Cork in April 1921 and were found with arms and ammunition in their possession. They were sentenced to death by certain officers sitting as a military court, after an admittedly fair trial. In view of certain previous decisions in the Irish Courts to the effect that their jurisdiction to grant the writ of habeas corpus was ousted when a proclamation of martial law was in existence, Clifford and O'Sullivan applied, not for habeas corpus, but for a writ of prohibition against the military court, the Commander-in-Chief and the Military Governor of County Cork to prohibit them from confirming or executing the judgment, on the ground that the military court was illegal and had no jurisdiction over the applicants. The application having been refused in the Irish courts, an appeal was brought to the House of Lords and Cave delivered a judgment which seemed to one of his colleagues 'simply admirable' in its avoidance of statements which might have caused a conflict with the executive of the day. Discretion was desirable, because at the date of the judgment (July 1921) a truce had been proclaimed and peace negotiations were in progress. Cave's point was the simple one that a writ of prohibition could issue only to a body which could properly be described as a court and that the tribunal of military officers before whom the appellants had been convicted was not a court in any sense known to the law. He took up a phrase in the affidavit of the solicitor for the appellants and neatly turned it against them.

In the present case the body which it is sought to prohibit, though called a military court, neither possesses nor claims any such authority . . . In the affidavit of Mr. Skinner, the solicitor for the appellants, upon which the application for a writ of prohibition was founded, the deponent, referring to the

[2] Mallet, p. 226.   [3] *Re Clifford and O'Sullivan* [1921] 2 A.C. 570.

officers before whom the appellants had been charged, says: 'The said officers did not purport to act under any commission from His Majesty to try prisoners, or under any statutory or common law authority or as a Court Martial. They purported to act merely as officers carrying out instructions from Major-General Strickland, the General Officer commanding at Cork'; and this statement correctly describes the position of the officers in question as defined by the appellants and by the respondents, and makes it plain that those officers did not purport to act as a Court in any legal sense.[4]

Cave's relief from the day-to-day routine of party politics did not indicate any lessening in his interests. There were a very wide variety of committees dealing with post-war problems on which he sat. In particular he devoted an immense amount of effort to the fate of missing prisoners . of war and his work in this field won him the gratitude of countless relatives and friends of soldiers throughout the British Empire. One mission in particular led him to South Africa as a result of the decision of the Judical Committee of the Privy Council in 1918 in the Rhodesian lands case.[5]

The decision of the Judicial Committee in 1918 had been to the effect that the British South Africa Company, a relic of the days of Cecil Rhodes's Imperialism, should be entitled to reimbursement for what it had spent on the development of the territory, though as we have seen, the sturdy radical, Lord Loreburn, had vehemently dissented from this part of the decision. As the settlers of Southern Rhodesia naturally objected strongly to finding out of their own pockets the sum of £8,000,000 which was claimed for the benefit of the company's shareholders, it was decided to send out a Commission, under Cave, to settle the matter. Amongst those who accompanied him were the famous Treasury civil servant Lord Chalmers, and also Captain N. G. Howitt, who is generally believed to figure in *Mr. Standfast*, one of John Buchan's novels. Lady Cave also joined the party and produced a pleasantly written diary of the expedition.[6] The Commission, after much delay and argument, in January 1921 announced their award, which was to the effect that the company should be paid some £4,400,000 in place of the £7,800,000 claimed. The award was generally welcomed as a fair solution. For his services on this Commission Cave received from the Government the G.C.M.G. and some time later it was even suggested that he might be willing to succeed Lord Buxton as Governor-General of the Union of South Africa. This, however, Cave, for good reasons of his own, did not feel able to accept.

In 1920, before the Rhodesian Commission had actually reported, Cave went on a long tour of 15,000 miles through Canada and the United

4 [1921] 2 A.C. 570, at 583–4.   5 [1919] A.C. 211.   6 *Three Journeys* (1928).

States. He had accepted the invitation which is customarily issued by the Canadian Bar Association to some distinguished English judge to speak at its annual convention. This was held at Montreal and afterwards the Caves journeyed down across the Great Lakes to St. Louis where they returned to England after another journey through Canada by the middle of October. The ardours and excitements of this were also recorded by Lady Cave.

In April 1922 Cave performed another valuable piece of public service in heading a Commission to report on the Trade Boards. The Committee, set up in September 1921, reported in April 1922, after an inquiry which involved 27 public sittings and the hearing of 113 witnesses. Trade Boards had been set up by Mr. Churchill when President of the Board of Trade in 1909 in order to protect the worker against sweating in under-developed industries. Although they had worked well they were constantly under attack by the employers for various reasons. The Committee found that although the Trade Board system had undoubtedly improved industrial relations and had raised conditions of employment and rates of payment in some unorganized trades, they had also contributed to increased trade depression and unemployment. The recommendation was to the effect that no new Trade Board should be created and those in existence should be continued with reduced powers.

A more controversial matter which arose early in 1922 and on which Cave took, perhaps, a rather surprising stand was the right of Law Lords to take part in debates on political subjects in the House of Lords. As we have seen,[7] Birkenhead as Lord Chancellor felt obliged to rebuke Carson and Finlay for the view that Law Lords were in no way different from other peers; Birkenhead insisted that the judicial function was of such paramount importance that it should not be brought into suspicion by speeches of a political character. On this matter Cave, unwisely, allowed himself to be persuaded, it appears by his wife and mother, to speak on the side of Carson. He opened himself to a particularly effective retort when he stated that he would not sit on any Irish appeal to the Judicial Committee involving the interpretation of clauses in the Treaty to which he had objected in political speeches. Birkenhead pointed out that Cave would thereby be preventing himself from performing the judicial duties for which he was paid by the public.[8]

[7] See above, p. 342.
[8] 49 H.L. Deb. 5s. col. 938, 943.

CHAPTER IV

WHEN CAVE LEFT POLITICS for the position of a Law Lord at the end of 1918 it must have appeared to him that his political career, with its opportunities of the Woolsack, was at an end. There were in the Conservative Party lawyers with a greater public appeal and more professional ability than he possessed. In particular, the fact that F. E. Smith, nearly twenty years Cave's junior, had been appointed Lord Chancellor, must have appeared to foreclose definitely any prospect of further advancement. Other men with claims were Ernest Pollock and Leslie Scott, the Attorney-General and Solicitor-General respectively from March 1922, when Gordon Hewart had been promoted Lord Chief Justice. But the fall of the coalition Government in October 1922 brought about unexpected consequences. The events leading up to the momentous Carlton Club meeting of 19 October have already been considered in the Life of Birkenhead, and it has been seen how Bonar Law was required to form a government from the ranks of the dissident Conservatives, who were not men of much reputation compared to those (Birkenhead, Balfour, Chamberlain) who had remained loyal to Lloyd George. 'Not since the secession of the Peelites had a Conservative leader been confronted by such a dearth of talent in his ranks.'[1] So far as the legal appointments were concerned it was obvious that much would turn on the attitude of the Law Officers. The Attorney-General, Pollock, was a man of complete integrity. His loyalty to the principles of Conservatism was undoubted; but he also held the simple view that he should be loyal to his Prime Minister. He was convinced that no real issue of principle in public affairs separated the two factions of the Tory Party. At the Carlton Club he voted against Bonar Law's proposal to come out of the coalition. The story may be carried on in his own words:

The meeting began to break up when Austen called me over to him and said—'You know, Ernest, I do not ask or expect you Law Officers to resign. That would be too definite a blow to your career and you must not sacrifice your future for me.' I replied that I would stick to what I had said in accepting the course he had laid down and saw no reason to differentiate my position in office from those with whom the Law Officers had worked these several years.

It was nearly 2 o'clock when I left the Carlton Club and went back to the Courts where I had to argue a case before Lawrence J., now my colleague in the Court of Appeal, Lawrence, L.J. The change of atmosphere was not unwelcome

[1] R. Blake, *The Unknown Prime Minister* (1955), p. 461. See above, pp. 387–90.

for I had worked hard to prevent a split and it reminded me that politics were not my only mistress.[2]

That evening Pollock attended a meeting of Chamberlain's supporters at which a manifesto for the press was drafted in defence of their attitude.

As we were leaving the room, Austen called me into his own study and said that he appreciated my support and recognized the disadvantage that I would suffer by resigning the Attorney-Generalship. He added that he hoped I would acquiesce in the proposal which he desired to make to the King that I should have a baronetcy conferred upon me.

Now I had no thought of honours at such a time or of any personal reward. A baronetcy had no attraction for me. There were two in our family[3] and I hesitated. Austen was kindly insistent and said 'Shall I fetch Arthur, perhaps he would convince you?' So Arthur Balfour came in with all that unruffled calm that belonged to him at all times, and we discussed the matter—my own view being that it was not a time for the distribution of benefits or honours, and I quoted the words of Elisha to Gehazi—'Is it a time to receive money, and to receive garments and oliveyards and vineyards?'[4]

Well, answered Arthur Balfour, surely if there are to be any honours at any time, this is an occasion when one is clearly earned and rightly bestowed? Suddenly our grandson came into my mind, and I thought it might help him in his lonely fight in the world to have a handle to his name, and so I consented.

A long day ended with a return to my legal work which always provided a righting lever to restore equilibrium amid the rolling and tossing of politics.[5]

The following day, Friday, Bonar Law was immersed in the intricacies of Cabinet making. He was anxious to obtain the services of Pollock and was even prepared to ignore his vote at the Carlton Club and offer him the Woolsack. This view was supported by Lord Beaverbrook. An emissary was therefore despatched to Pollock in the form of his close friend and cousin, Guy Pollock, a sub-editor on the *Daily Express*.

He came to my room at the Law Courts hot-foot from Bonar Law and Beaverbrook and said—'This is all rot, Ernest, you have got to be Lord Chancellor', and he told me the post was open to me if I would join Bonar Law. My answer was clear and easy. 'How could I vote one way on Thursday, and by a *volte face*, change over to the other side on Friday?' Guy was very kindly persistent and argued at some length. But I saw my path quite clearly then, and in later years, after reflection, I have no hesitation in confirming the view that I then held.

---

[2] Hanworth papers.

[3] i.e. two baronetcies—those conferred on the Lord Chief Baron (Sir Frederick, 1866), and his brother the Field Marshal (Sir George, 1872).

[4] The reference is to 2 Kings v. 26.

[5] Hanworth papers.

So when Guy found that no response was made to his views and that my answer was a definite negative, he discussed the situation and asked me—'Whom would you advise should be made Lord Chancellor, Sumner or Cave?'

I replied—'Cave, for he has had experience in political life.' We further discussed the question who should become the Law Officers, and he made the suggestion that Sir Leslie Scott and I might carry on for the present—perhaps until after the General Election, when the type of Ministry that was to continue would be settled. These and other possibilities were canvassed between us and he then left; and for my part I heard no more on that day as to the Cabinet making.[6]

Lawyers who pursue a political career are sometimes accused of being time-serving and avaricious of office, but Pollock's conduct on this difficult occasion shows that he was capable of putting aside all temptation and adhering steadfastly to a simple but honourable code of conduct.

Pollock's cousin followed up his unsuccessful arguments with a letter of worldly advice which arrived the next day, 21 October.

I went on to Lord Beaverbrook yesterday and found him at 3.30. He said his interest in you was *personal* and so, I think, it is—50 per cent for you and perhaps a percentage for me. I told him your point of view. He said it was a pity and a tragedy and deplored that F.E. should have drawn you into his wilderness. He, like several others who have spoken to me, is persuaded that you were at first with the Under-Secretaries who counted on you. I think there is no doubt that somehow or other you gave that impression. *At all events it exists.*

I emphasized your personal loyalty to Austen. Lord Beaverbrook said that Bonar could not and would not make any offer or accept any suggestion based on Austen's sanction or consultation with Austen. He said, 'Why, why, did he sign the manifesto—after the Carlton Club vote?' That is regarded as in some sort of defiance of Bonar and a pronouncement of disloyalty to *his* leadership. As to the Law Officers suggestion, an immediate dissolution (decided on) obviates the difficulty and Hogg and Rawlinson[7] are ready to take on the jobs.

So I went away sick and sorry, published a new Ministry with your post filled, and sent you a wire to Leamington.

This morning at 10 a.m. Lord Beaverbrook rang me up—much as usual—to discuss the papers and politics. He asked what you meant by your speech at Leamington. I said truthfully that I didn't know. He said again—'What a tragic pity. Even yesterday, if he had grappled with the situation, he had one foot on the Woolsack.' That, of course, was what I told you. To me the significant thing was that he should revert to you again this morning. It struck me that

6 Hanworth papers.

7 J. F. P. Rawlinson, K.C., M.P. (1860–1926). *The Times* (23 October 1922) said M. Macnaghten, K.C., M.P., was favoured for the position. As we shall see, it was also offered to Maugham: below, p. 548.

the iron might not be too cold to strike, though of course I may be wrong. That is why I am writing a long and disgustingly frank letter.

I believe that the 80 odd Austenites of the Carlton are very likely to be found in Bonar's camp on Monday and I am *sure* that Conservatives who fight under any other banner can only lose their seats, and tend to disrupt a party now more united and enthusiastic than for years. And you profess to call yourself Conservative. You say that L.G. has done the obvious thing and that he will lead a Liberal party. Bang, then, goes any possibility of pursuing *that* allegiance.

Why not return at once to the only fold and seek that goal that makes you great and David[8] a peer? Believe me, Ernest, they will all repent the first heat of adventurous resentment and reform ranks—as Robert Horne prepared to do on the very night of the great office-denying ordinance. But you may be left in the cold. Don't be left in the cold for a 'beau geste' which cannot long figure as a principle. Don't mistake where your talents lie, or what your strength and weakness are in politics. And do be sure when you commune with honour that it really does enjoin or entail what you at first believed.[9]

But Pollock was unmoved by his cousin's blandishments and preferred to remain out in the cold.

So far as the Woolsack was concerned the choice now lay between Cave and Sumner. Sumner had throughout his life been an ardent Conservative and although he had never sat in Parliament he had devoted his acute mind and sharp tongue to the furtherance of the party cause. He had been a bitter opponent of the Government's action in the debate upon the proposal to recall General Dyer after the incident at Amritsar in April 1919. Indeed, as we have seen, as far back as 1915 Sumner's claims had been thought strong enough for him to be considered for the Woolsack in preference to Finlay. The biographer of Sumner says: 'When Bonar Law formed his Ministry in October, 1922, it was thought by many that Sumner might become Lord Chancellor. Lord Cave was perhaps a safer choice, but the best friends of that most amiable man would hardly think that he would make as great a Lord Chancellor as Sumner might have been.'[1] Yet Bonar Law's choice, as a result of Pollock's advice, fell on Cave and on Sunday, 22 October, he was offered the Great Seal.

In Lady Cave's diary there is an account of the events of the day; she had been expecting guests to lunch on Sunday at Richmond when the message came from Bonar Law summoning her husband to Onslow Gardens. He drove off at once promising to return in time to greet his guests, but at half past one there was still no sign of him.

I made polite conversation for a quarter of an hour, and as he did not come I thought it was better to go into luncheon. At two o'clock I heard the car; I did

[8] Pollock's grandson and heir. Pollock's only son had been killed in action in 1918.
[9] Hanworth papers.   [1] *D.N.B.*, *1931–1940*, p. 394.

not dare look up for the moment as he entered the room. My heart was beating wildly. When I looked at him, he gave me a little reassuring nod, and quietly apologizing to our guests for being late, began to eat his lunch as if the greatest ambition of my life (not his, for he always did the next thing, whatever it might be) had not come to pass.[2]

Pollock's memorandum supplies an account of the intervening hours. Cave had called on him 'and told me that he had been to Bonar Law at his house in Onslow Gardens and had been offered and accepted the great office of Lord Chancellor. He also told me that Bonar Law wanted me to call upon him at 2 o'clock. Then we drove together in his car, George telling me gleefully that he had now achieved his ambition.'[3] Pollock never thought it necessary to hint to Cave that the offer had first been made to himself, or that it was his advice that had resulted in Cave being made Chancellor. In later life he was apt to regard Cave's rather patronizing attitude to him with mild amusement. In 1923 he had his reward, for Baldwin made him Master of the Rolls.

The evidence shows that Cave protested gently to Baldwin that Lord Justice Bankes would be a more suitable appointment. He was a better lawyer, Cave wrote on 5 October 1923,[4] and he also had the advantage of judicial experience. But two days later Cave wrote to Baldwin again:

Since writing to you on Friday, I have been wondering whether I should have expressed myself so strongly on a matter which it is for you to decide and on which I feel that I may not have done full justice to an old friend.

May I add then (as a postscript) that while all I said about Bankes is true and I should myself have chosen him, yet I believe that Pollock would make an efficient M.R.—and, if you decide for him, I should be quite content.[5]

But Baldwin disregarded the Lord Chancellor's objections and made Pollock Master of the Rolls. The appointment caused some surprise in the profession, but was regarded as being justified in the result.[6] Baldwin's character was in many respects complex and subtle, but it responded warmly to straightforward honesty in others. In this respect there was a link between Baldwin and Pollock as there was to be later between Baldwin and Inskip.

So on Monday, 23 October, Bonar Law was elected Leader of the Party and immediately afterwards kissed hands as Prime Minister. And on Wednesday, the 25th, Cave received the Great Seal.

The new Cabinet was regarded by Bonar Law himself as being something in the nature of a caretaker Government and there is no doubt that the dearth of available talent had produced a team which, on the surface,

[2] Mallet, pp. 254–5.   [3] Hanworth papers.   [4] Baldwin papers.
[5] Ibid.   [6] See Lord Justice Wrottesley in *D.N.B., 1931–1940*, p. 709.

was less glittering than the Conservative ministers in the coalition Government had been. A fair number of peers were necessary because of the die-hard element in the revolt at the Carlton Club. The heavy sarcasm from the dispossessed coalitionists which greated the new team ('a Government second eleven' and 'second-class intellects') was, however, unfair. Three of its members were Fellows of All Souls and Cave himself, if it had been in his nature to do so, might have retorted that although not a Fellow of All Souls he had obtained a First in Greats in the days when this was the greatest academic achievement at Oxford—which was more than the ex-Lord Chancellor had done. But the country was quite simply anxious for a period of peace, tranquillity and honesty after the glittering excesses of the Lloyd George régime. Cave himself admirably suited this new mood in the country as did its finest exponent, Stanley Baldwin himself. As a writer in *The Times* was to observe some years later, Stanley Baldwin 'brought into public life a pleasant savour, freshness and health. It is the fragrance of the fields, the flavour of apple and hazel nut, all the unpretentious, simple, wholesome, homely but essential qualities, suggestions and traditions of England that Mr. Baldwin has substituted for the over-charged, heavy-laden, decadent atmosphere of our post-war years.'[7]

The popularity of the appointment was shown by the large number of letters of congratulation which flowed into Richmond from men of all parties and none. One perhaps may be quoted—from the clever but eccentric Stephen Ronan, a member of the Irish Court of Appeal.

October 25th, 1922

My Dear Lord,

May I just say how glad I am. I suppose no-one has ever so completely proved his fitness for the Office as you have done. Do you remember my telling you after our last case in the Lords that Lord Ashbourne told me you would probably be Speaker? Curious that it should turn out to be in the Lords. So much for this. You have proved yourself to be:

1. an enormously successful barrister
2. „ „ „ parliamentarian
3. „ „ „ Cabinet Minister
4. „ „ „ Lord of Appeal

It must be unique. I trust you will hold the great office for a long time, and wishing you good health and a long life, am

yours as ever,
S. Ronan[8]

Cave's appointment was notable in some other ways. He was the first

---

[7] *The Times*, 12 August 1925.
[8] Mallet, p. 29.

Law Lord since 1876 to be promoted to a higher office,[9] apart from Charles Russell who was made a Law Lord in May 1894 and Lord Chief Justice of England in the following July. (In 1885 Lord FitzGerald, who had been a Law Lord since 1882, was offered but refused the Lord Chancellorship of Ireland.) He was, it seems, the first judge to be made Lord Chancellor since Lord Justice Cairns was given the Great Seal by Disraeli in 1868. He was also, with Haldane, the only Lord Chancellor who, at the time of his appointment, was a peer of a higher rank than a baron.

Cave's tenure of the Woolsack was not marked by any spectacular events either in the political or in the legal field. But for the next eight years he was at the head of the judicial system of the country, for he was re-appointed by Baldwin in May, 1923, and when the Labour Government was formed in 1924 and the Great Seal was given to Haldane, Cave characteristically agreed to carry out the judicial side of the work in order to free Haldane, whose health by then had begun to fail, for the political and administrative tasks of the office. So from October 1922 until March 1928 Cave was for all but nine months of the time in name Lord Chancellor and in substance the true holder of the office.

We may consider first of all some events on the political side before turning to purely legal problems. The Government had hardly been formed before it was nearly shipwrecked on the rock of the American Debt Settlement. The Chancellor of the Exchequer, Baldwin, returned from Washington having made an agreement which was thought by the Prime Minister to be unduly hard on the British taxpayer. Bonar Law had sufficient experience of the difficulties of dealing with North American financiers not to under-rate the problem which faced Baldwin, but he thought that the Chancellor had sacrificed too much, believing that the only fair settlement was one which involved either cancellation all round or payment all round. He thought it most unfair that Britain should be expected to pay the United States nearly £900,000,000 while not receiving payment from her own debtors in Europe. On 30 January the Prime Minister told his colleagues at a Cabinet meeting that he would rather resign than be a party to the Baldwin settlement. The following morning the principal members of the Cabinet met in an agitated state in Cave's room at the House of Lords, Bonar Law being absent. Everyone agreed that however bad the terms of the settlement might appear to be it would be worse to repudiate them. Accordingly the Duke of Devonshire, Baldwin and Cave were asked to wait upon the Prime Minister and to seek to induce him to withdraw his resignation. Their persuasions were successful and at a Cabinet meeting that afternoon, which lasted only

[9] Lord Macmillan compiled a useful table of the 47 Law Lords between 1876 and 1947: see (1947) 97 L.J. News p. 541.

five minutes, Bonar Law informed his colleagues that he would accept the settlement negotiated by Baldwin with the American financiers.[1]

In May 1923 Cave fell seriously ill with peritonitis at his house at Burnham and was unable to attend the House of Lords until November, just before the Government broke up in confusion on the issue of protection which the Prime Minister had suddenly raised. Baldwin for once in his life, startled the country by an unexpected and indeed almost rash action. He dissolved Parliament and at the election which followed on 6 December the Conservatives lost 117 seats to their opponents. Nevertheless, they were still the strongest party in the House and Cave was much perplexed to know whether or not the Government should meet Parliament or resign at once. In the end it was decided, probably rightly, to meet Parliament and face the issue openly in the then customary way upon a no confidence amendment to the Address. The Government was defeated and the King at once sent for Ramsay MacDonald. A Labour Government, let alone a Labour minority Government, was, in 1924 certainly, a novelty to the mass of the British electorate, and especially to a person of Cave's background. There were two points on which he was called upon to advise the King in his capacity of chief constitutional adviser of the monarchy. The first arose from the point that Ramsay MacDonald was not, at that date, a Privy Councillor. On 9 January Cave, still of course the holder of the Great Seal, sent the following memorandum to the Secretary of the Cabinet, Sir Maurice Hankey:

Secret   House of Lords
                                                                  9.1.24
Sir Maurice Hankey.

In my opinion no person should be allowed to kiss hands as Prime Minister or First Lord of the Treasury without first being sworn as a member of the Privy Council. It is the rule that every member of the Cabinet must be a Privy Councillor, and take the oath of secrecy: and *a fortiori* the Prime Minister, who will be *primus inter pares* and will advise the Sovereign as to the persons whom he is to take into his counsels, should be bound by the oath.

It is conceivable—although I know of no precedent for this course—that the King might commission Mr. Ramsay MacDonald to submit names for a Ministry to be formed under his premiership, and postpone the ceremony of kissing hands until he has been sworn of the Privy Council, but in that case he would until he had kissed hands be in the position not of a Prime Minister but of a person negotiating for the formation of a government.

C.[2]

The procedure suggested by Cave was followed and on 22 January, the morning after the House of Commons had carried the amendment

[1] R. Blake, *The Unknown Prime Minister* (1955), pp. 493–4.
[2] Royal Archives, K. 1918 (132).

against the Government, a Privy Council was held at 11.30 a.m., those present being the King, Arthur Henderson, and J. H. Thomas (two Labour leaders who were already Privy Councillors).[3] At the Council Ramsay MacDonald was sworn in and immediately afterwards he was invited by the King to form a government. No fewer than thirteen Privy Councillors were sworn in at this meeting—a number exceeded only in 1852 when seventeen were created when the Derby ('Who-Who') Government took office. That night George V wrote in his diary: 'I had an hour's talk with him, he impressed me very much; he wishes to do the right thing. Today 23 years ago dear Grandmama died. I wonder what she would have thought of a Labour Government!'[4]

A more serious constitutional issue was raised by Buckingham Palace at this time; namely whether, if Ramsay MacDonald was invited to form a government, he could properly extract from the monarch a promise to grant a dissolution if he were defeated at an early date in the House of Commons. The story can be traced in the following correspondence between Lord Stamfordham and Cave:

Confidential.   Buckingham Palace
                                                    27 December 1923

Dear Lord Chancellor,

Mr. Asquith's recent speech at the National Liberal Club has, prematurely, aroused the question of a possible dissolution of Parliament in the near future and, unfortunately, brought the matter into the press arena.

Although the King's action must to a great extent be guided by the circumstances of the situation when it actually arises, His Majesty is looking ahead at possible eventualities and desires me to ask if you will kindly consider his position and advise as to the exercise of the Prerogative, should Mr. Ramsay MacDonald

(a) make his acceptance of office conditional upon a promise that the King would grant a dissolution in the event of his early defeat in the House of Commons:

(b) after a defeat, ask for a dissolution.

H.M. recognizes that the existence of three parties in the House of Commons creates a case for which there is no precedent. Still the prerogative of refusal of dissolution exists subject of course to ministerial responsibility for the exercise of the prerogative being assured.

The King may have to come to grave and momentous decisions and will naturally turn to his Lord Chancellor for guidance and advice. For this reason and realizing that within three weeks Parliament will be opened the King troubles you with this letter.

                                                    Yours very truly,
                                                    Stamfordham[5]

---

[3] J. H. Thomas, *My Story* (1937), p. 75.
[4] H. Nicolson, *King George V* (1952), p. 384.   [5] Royal Archives, K. 1918 (115).

On 29 December Cave replied from St. Anne's, Burnham, to the effect that he would send a considered answer in a few days.

Meanwhile I cannot think that, if under present conditions anyone should attempt to make it a condition of his acceptance of office that the King should promise him an early dissolution, H.M. would be constitutionally bound to give such a promise. A promise of that kind may have been given in a case where a prospective Prime Minister controlled a strong minority in the House and had a good prospect in the event of dissolution of turning it into a majority; but such a precedent would have no application to a case where the statesman concerned has the support of less than one-third of the members of a House which has just been elected, so that an early dissolution would probably make no substantial change in his position. In such a case I feel sure the Sovereign should hold himself free to exercise his prerogative according to his discretion and with due regard to all the circumstances which may exist when the question arises.[6]

Stamfordham on 5 January replied, referring to an article by Ramsay MacDonald in the *New Leader*.

Does he mean that the prerogative of dissolution rests with the Prime Minister? I am glad to see that you entirely dissent from any such doctrine.
But I do most clearly understand and indeed have always recognized that the Sovereign cannot constitutionally refuse dissolution without previously assuring himself of proper ministerial responsibility for such action.[7]

On the same day Cave wrote from Burnham enclosing his promised memorandum on the constitutional position. After a review of the standard text-book authorities on the matter it proceeded:

There is a further consideration to be borne in mind. The present practice in this country has grown up under a two-party system, which ensures that on the election of a new Parliament one party or the other shall command a majority in the House: but in these days, when there are at least three parties, this is no longer the case, and the dissolution and re-election of Parliament may only prolong the position of stalemate.
What then is the conclusion to be drawn from all these considerations? It is clear that the prerogative of dissolution is the prerogative of the Sovereign and not of his ministers. I think it is equally clear that according to modern constitutional practice a dissolution is neither granted nor refused by the King except on the advice of ministers. But this leaves open the question whether and in what cases the King may properly refuse a dissolution on being satisfied that, if the minister advising it resigns in consequence of the refusal, other ministers will be found who will cover the refusal by their retrospective approval and will make themselves responsible for the King's action. In my view this question can best be answered by considering in what cases the Prime Minister may properly advise a dissolution; for when a Prime Minister acts unconsti-

[6] Ibid.   [7] Ibid.

P*

tutionally or improperly in advising a dissolution, it cannot be the constitutional duty of the King to grant it.

Sir William Anson seems to have held[8] that there are only two cases in which a dissolution is rightly demanded, namely (1) where there is reason to suppose that the House of Commons has ceased to represent the opinion of the country, or (2) when a large change has been made in the electoral conditions and it is proper that the newly-enfranchised electors should enjoy their rights at the earliest possible opportunity; but probably this statement is not intended to be exhaustive. The second dissolution of 1910 was granted because it was desired to take the opinion of the country on a proposal for a great constitutional change, and the dissolution of 1923 because the government of the day desired to be relieved from a pledge by which they considered their action to be unduly hampered; and other cases may be conceived in which a dissolution might not unreasonably be claimed. Where any such good reason for dissolution exists, I think that it would be constitutional as well as wise for the Crown to grant the dissolution; but where no such reason exists, then in my opinion the King may, on being satisfied that his action will be covered by the proper ministerial responsibility, decline to exercise his prerogative of dissolution. An instance of improper advice which might be so disregarded would occur if a minister defeated in the House of Commons within a few months after the election of the new Parliament were to advise a dissolution without showing any solid reason for believing that the dissolution and re-election would substantially modify Parliamentary conditions and give him a majority. If in such a case dissolution were refused, the action of the Sovereign might indeed be subjected to attack by the persons disappointed by his decision: but if the decision rested on sound reasons which all could understand, the attack would fail of its effect.

A second question has been raised, namely whether, if a statesman who is asked to assume the reins of government were to make his acceptance of office conditional on a promise by the King to grant a dissolution in the event of the incoming Government being defeated in the House of Commons, such a promise ought to be given. In my opinion no obligation rests upon the King to give such a promise. Clearly he is not constitutionally bound to do so, for *ex hypothesi* the statesman in question is not yet a minister qualified to advise the Crown. On the other hand, it is undesirable that the prerogative, which ought to be exercised on a careful consideration of all the circumstances existing when the question of its exercise arises, should be fettered by a pre-existing promise. Queen Victoria in 1858 refused such a promise to Lord Derby on the ground that the effect might be to bring the name of the Sovereign into the debates in the House of Commons, and this reason still operates. No doubt the King would be justified in giving an assurance of the above character if there were no other way of securing that the King's government shall be carried on; but in the absence of such a compelling circumstance I do not think that it should be given.[9]

[8] *Law and Custom of the Constitution* (5th ed., 1922), vol. i, pp. 327–9.
[9] Royal Archives, K. 1918 (115).

This memorandum, so far unpublished, is well worthy of taking its place amongst the state papers on English constitutional practice. It shows Cave to have a very sound grasp, not merely of the theoretical rules relating to the working of the constitution, but also to the various practical pressures which may arise from political necessity. If it had not been for his years as a Member for Kingston, it is doubtful if Cave, bred at the Chancery Bar, could have produced such a convincing and lucid exposition of constitutional law and practice.

In October 1924 the Labour Government fell from office after its mishandling of the Campbell case. The King granted Ramsay MacDonald a dissolution, somewhat reluctantly, but he had in truth no alternative for neither Baldwin nor Asquith was willing to form an alternative Government and, in any event, the King felt, rightly, that it would be unwise to refuse a Labour Prime Minister the opportunity of appealing to the electorate for a judgment on his tenure of office.

A few years later Cave again crossed the path of the Labour Party on a constitutional problem. The General Strike of 1926 had, of course, greatly estranged relations between the parties and although Baldwin had triumphed to the extent of securing a peaceful settlement of the strike, he was unable to prevent his own back benchers, flushed with triumph, from passing the Trades Disputes Act, 1927, which endeavoured to make a General Strike illegal. In July 1926 when tempers were still strained after the strike, Cave's touch as Speaker of the House of Lords for once seems to have faltered. The House, on 8 July, was considering a Bill to enable the miners to work eight hours a day. When the Bill had reached its third reading, the four peers who represented the Labour Party proceeded to stretch out the debate by means which the Conservative majority did not like. What appears to have happened was simply that the Opposition prevented the House from adjourning at the customary time for dinner. The debate on the Bill began at 6.30 p.m., and seven speeches were made in the following hour; four from the Government side and three from the Opposition. The House customarily adjourned for dinner at 7.30 p.m., but when another Labour peer rose to speak he was interrupted with cries of 'Divide!' Two more Labour peers then spoke before Lord Salisbury, the Leader of the House, after consultation with Cave, rose and interrupted Lord Arnold's speech. 'It is quite obvious what the noble Lord and his friends are trying to do. It is an abuse of the traditions and the privileges of the House. I move that the question be now put.'[1] Cave accepted the motion, and though normally any motion made in the House can be debated, he refused to allow a debate and the motion was carried by a majority of forty-four votes to four despite Labour protests.

[1] 64 H.L. Deb. 5s. col. 994.

The time was then 8.15 p.m., so that the debate had lasted for less than two hours, on a Bill which had required two whole days for the second reading and two more days for the third reading in the House of Commons. It was subsequently alleged by the Lord Chancellor (and supported by many others) that there was 'concerted action' to obstruct the passage of the Bill, though this was not denied by the acting Leader of the Opposition, and in any case four peers could not obstruct for long, especially when three of them had already spoken and the fourth was engaged in making his speech.[2]

A few days later the House, as a whole, debated the propriety of Cave's action. A motion which was in substance a vote of censure was rejected by 113 votes to 10. Lord Ullswater, who as Mr. Speaker Lowther had presided over the House of Commons during the ferocious debates of 1910–13 spoke as 'a pretty good judge of obstruction', and made a great impression on the peers by doubting whether Cave had been wise in adopting the closure procedure. Cave refused to admit that he had made an error on the earlier occasion, but stated that he did not regard his action as constituting a precedent. It has not been followed by a subsequent Lord Chancellor.

In his work as Lord Chancellor, Cave disposed of the administrative side of his task without fuss and won the admiration of the staff of the office. It fell to him to fill an exceptional number of judicial vacancies in the High Court. In five years he appointed almost half of the King's Bench Division Judges—Wright, Talbot, Humphreys, Charles, Fraser, Hawke, and Finlay. These were good appointments; Wright subsequently became one of the most distinguished Law Lords of the twentieth century; Humphreys was an acknowledged master of criminal law who retired in 1950 after an exceptionally lengthy period on the Bench; Talbot was deeply respected and admired by his friends at the Bar. Fraser, Hawke, and Charles were good representatives of the Common Law tradition. Finlay was criticized as a weak appointment, as we have seen,[3] but in the event turned out to be a respectable judge. Cave also appointed two Chancery judges, Tomlin and Clauson, each of whom later rose to be a Law Lord, and one Probate, Divorce, and Admiralty judge, Bateson, a former Attorney-General's devil. (It is perhaps worth noting that when Cave offered Humphreys the judgeship the latter asked for the appointment to be deferred for a few days in order that he might be allowed to complete the police court proceedings in the case of the notorious murderers, Brown and Kennedy in which he had done all the spade work. The request was firmly refused by Cave.) Cave also made a minor but important

2 W. I. Jennings, *Parliament* (2nd ed., 1957), p. 401.
3 See above, p. 332.

change in the method of appointing magistrates which has already been discussed.[4]

So far as other appointments were concerned, Cave's nominations to the rank of K.C. gave rise to favourable comment only. In particular it was noticed that one of his last acts was to grant silk to Henry Slesser, who had been a Law Officer in the Ramsay MacDonald Government of 1924. This absence of political partisanship on the part of a Conservative Lord Chancellor was favourably compared with the actions of some of his predecessors.

In the same year, 1928, he exchanged the following letters with Sir John Simon, who had decided to give up his great practice at the Bar in order to accept the chairmanship of the India Commission. Simon wrote on 13 January 1928:

> You may remember that I wrote to Sir Claud Schuster last month asking if, in view of my absence on the Indian Commission, some of the Appeals pending to the House of Lords in which I was interested might, if necessary, be postponed so as to come on for hearing after next term. You were kind enough to send me a message through Napier that you would do your best to arrange this for me in respect of two Appeals. . . .
>
> I now write, however, to say that I must not ask you this indulgence, as I have come to the conclusion that the best course for me is to give up practice at the Bar. I shall, therefore, not be available to argue these cases, and am telling my clients so. I shall be out of the country for such long periods, and the future is so uncertain that I think my decision is the right one, though it is a great wrench to let my Chambers and terminate the service of Clerks, and break the habits of so many years.[5]

Cave answered:

> It is a shock to hear that you are giving up practice, and from the standpoint of the Bar and Bench I am very sorry; but of course you are the best judge, and I am comforted by the feeling that you will render fine service to the country both in your mission to India and afterwards.
>
> I have often looked forward to getting the Prime Minister to recruit you for our Appeals, but of course I have known that you are still too young for any such 'cushion'.
>
> Good luck to you in the fine work on which you are entering, and in all your (non-political) enterprises in the future.[6]

To this Simon replied:

> Your kind letter reached me just before I left England and you will, I hope, excuse my delay in writing to thank you most sincerely for it.
>
> Yes: it is a great wrench to give up practice at the Bar—if, as you are good enough to hint, I might some day find myself renewing contact with the Law

[4] See above, p. 158.   [5] Simon papers.   [6] Ibid.

in another capacity, there would be much consolation and satisfaction in that for me. But I don't think a man should plan his life to be immersed in forensic disputation *to the end*: and so, if I stop, I would like to stop with the possibility of full time in front of me for other work of some sort. It involves a change of income which is alarming, but I suppose this ought to be an incentive!

Besides, this Indian Commission is a tremendous business and we are starting in a bad atmosphere. Perhaps it may help a bit to show these Indian critics that at any rate I am taking the thing seriously.

For all your constant kindness and consideration I am and always shall be most grateful. I look forward to seeing you and Lady Cave and reporting progress when we return in April.[7]

During Cave's tenure of the Great Seal the largest piece of legislation ever to reach the statute book passed through Parliament—the Law of Property Act, 1925, and six ancillary statutes. As this great piece of legislation, the culmination of years of devoted work by many different people, remodelled the whole intricate structure of English law relating to real property, something must be said of it here although Cave's own part in the process, despite his Chancery background, was small.

The reforming zeal of the nineteenth century had done much to improve English land law, but at the opening of the twentieth century it was still a mass of obscure and technical rules properly known only to a few inhabitants of Lincoln's Inn. The guiding principle of the reformers was to try to make the transfer of land as easy and simple a matter as the transfer of personalty. The obvious analogy was the transfer of shares in a limited company, in which the title passes simply by inscription upon the register of the company. That was the ideal to be aimed at, though no doubt land being in the nature of things a more complex affair than stocks and shares, it could not be completely achieved. We have already seen how Halsbury, not generally thought of as a legal reformer, had succeeded in inducing Parliament to pass the Land Transfer Act of 1897 which set up a system of registration of title. Unfortunately the object of the Act was largely defeated by the pressure brought to bear from the solicitors' profession which depended for its livelihood upon maintaining the old system of conveyancing by deeds and had therefore procured a section in the Act to the effect that compulsory registration of title would apply only if the County Council in a particular area asked for it. But it quickly began to be appreciated that it was foolish to simplify the system of registration of title without, at the same time, simplifying the title to be registered. Here the main difficulty was the complexity of the English strict settlement of land under which the fee simple was split up amongst the various parties to the settlement, so that no one person under it had

[7] Simon papers.

power to convey a clear title to the whole property. The Settled Land Act of 1882, by a brilliant device known as over-reaching, had attempted to solve this by giving to the life tenant a statutory power to convey that which he had not got, i.e. the fee simple. Upon the exercise of this power the interests of the beneficiaries arising under the settlement were over-reached, i.e. transferred from the land to the purchase money representing the land. This money being capital and not income was known as capital money and had to be paid to two trustees of the settlement. The advocates of further reform based their proposals on reducing the number of legal estates to one and maintaining any family and other interests which might subsist in the parcel of land in question behind the curtain of a single conveyable entity known as the fee simple absolute in possession. After the report of the Royal Commission on the Land Transfer Acts in 1911, Lord Haldane set in hand a Bill to reform the law, and Bills were produced in 1913, 1914, and 1915. After the war the energy of Lord Birkenhead procured the renewal of the work and a vast Law of Property Bill was introduced into Parliament in 1922. The Bill was drafted by Sir Benjamin Cherry with the assistance of Sir Frederick Liddell, the Chief Parliamentary Draftsman. Many persons were consulted and many objections quietened before the combined skill of Sir Leslie Scott, the Solicitor-General, and Lord Birkenhead, the Lord Chancellor, procured its passage through Parliament. For example, the files in the Lord Chancellor's office show that on 1 February 1920 Walter Long, the Conservative statesman and Wiltshire squire, wrote for further information: 'You know the importance of this question to those with whom I am especially connected.' This letter is endorsed in the Lord Chancellor's hand 'careful and courteous' and a very full reply following these instructions was sent, which produced an answer from Long showing that he was delighted at the attention paid to his views, but equally clearly showing that he did not understand the first principles of the Settled Land Act.[8]

A number of the Chancery judges were also consulted by the draftsmen, but only Mr. Justice Peterson ventured to make suggestions. Cherry found Mr. Justice Sargant 'charming', but he said as he had not done any conveyancing for twenty-five years he should be excused. When the Law Property Bill received its second reading in the House of Lords on 3 March 1920 speeches were made by Cave and Phillimore in opposition to it[9] which aroused the caustic comments of Cherry and Brickdale. 'A little knowledge is a dangerous thing', they said. Three statements by Cave in particular aroused their irritation. The first was his remark that a title on sale made by a life tenant was the 'easiest, simplest and safest'. Brickdale said that this statement was 'simply astounding' and showed that 'he has

[8] Lord Chancellor's Office, File No. 1912-56.   [9] 39 H.L. Deb. 5s. col. 269, 274.

completely lost touch with conveyancing'. Secondly, Cave suggested that the Bill should be amended so as to permit legal remainders and executory interests to continue to exist. As this proposal struck at the very root of the proposed Bill which was to reduce to one the number of legal interests which might exist it is not surprising that the draftsmen described it as 'reactionary and illogical'. Thirdly, Cave had expressed dislike of the proposed system of mortgages adopted by the Act, but on this point too his views were criticized as being out of date.

Eventually Birkenhead had to agree to withdraw the Bill for further consideration and amendment. In 1922 it was re-introduced and got through the House of Commons largely as a result of a remarkable speech by Sir Leslie Scott, the Solicitor General. Then rose the problem of getting it through the Lords once more and here the supporters of the Bill felt distinct gloom when it was announced Cave had succeeded Birkenhead as Lord Chancellor, for it looked as if all their efforts would now be nullified. But Cave behaved in the noblest fashion; he simply remarked that it was impossible for him to postpone the operation of the Act because he had criticized it; 'I could not do it,' he said, 'having so lately led the opposition to it.' Eventually the seven Acts passed in 1925 came into operation on 1 January 1926.

Another major legislative achievement of the same session was the passage of the Supreme Court of Judicature (Consolidation) Act, 1925, which wholly repealed forty-three Acts and partly repealed and amended forty-two others relating to the administration of the courts. It was a much-needed measure of worthwhile reform.

Cave's qualities as a judge have already been considered. His judgments as Lord Chancellor show the same characteristics of sober learning and accuracy which he had displayed as a Law Lord. In one case, unfortunately, it seemed as if an error had been made. The decision,[1] which concerned the compensation payable to Irish Civil Servants who had retired from office on the creation of the Irish Free State in 1922, undoubtedly caused serious difficulties to both British and Irish Governments at a time when Anglo-Irish relations were in any event not free from tension. The allegation that the decision was vitiated by a serious error of fact was acutely worrying to a man of Cave's temperament, and there is no doubt that his last months and days were clouded by anxiety over the matter.

The question arose out of Article 10 of the Treaty of 1921, under which the Irish Free State Government undertook 'to pay fair compensation on terms not less favourable than those awarded by the [Government of Ireland] Act of 1920' to civil servants transferred to the service of the Irish Government who retired or were discharged in consequence of the change

1 *Wigg and Cochrane* v. *Att.-Gen. of the I.F.S.* [1927] A.C. 674.

of régime. The normal rule of constitutional law is that a Civil Servant has no right to sue for his pension, but in this case the Judicial Committee, composed of Cave, Finlay, Haldane, and Dunedin, held, on appeal from the Supreme Court of the Irish Free State, that the relevant legislation conferred on the appellants legal rights which they could assert by action in the Irish Courts. The main issue, however, was whether a certain bonus payable to the appellants was pensionable, and if so, what was the proper mode of computation of it. The Irish Government argued that the bonus if pensionable at all, was so only according to certain restrictive conditions contained in a Treasury Minute of 20 March 1922. The Judicial Committee, in a judgment delivered by Cave, held that the Minute was not binding upon the appellants: 'the Minute cannot affect the rights of officers who at its date had been transferred to the Government of the Free State'.[2]

The Irish Government stated that it could not accept this judgment. A lengthy dispatch on 9 November 1927 from its Minister for External Affairs (Patrick McGilligan) put its case clearly and forcibly.[3] The Irish Government was anxious to carry out its Treaty obligations, but was 'at a loss to understand how in face of the known and incontrovertible facts such a conclusion could have been arrived at'. The appellants, it stated, so far from having been transferred to its service before the date of the Treasury Minute, were not transferred until 1 April 1922. The judgment, if carried into effect, would result in more favoured treatment being given to transferred officers retired under Article 10 than they would have received if they had remained in the British Civil Service, or if they had transferred to the Irish Civil Service and retired in the normal way.

At first Cave appears to have accepted the Irish view without much demur. He wrote to Lord Lovat, the Under-Secretary of State for Dominion Affairs, on 16 December 1927:

I have now had time to consider this matter, and I will not ask the Dominions Office further to delay taking action in accordance with the minutes of the Cabinet.

The decision of the Judicial Committee in the case of *Wigg* v. *Irish Free State* was founded on their view of the effect of legislation passed by the Parliament of the Free State; and if that Parliament disapproves of the decision, they have a constitutional right to override it by further legislation. No doubt it is reasonable that they should set up a statutory committee to deal with these numerous claims, and the pity is that they did not take that course long ago. At the same time it has never been the practice of our Parliament to deprive parties who have obtained a judicial decision in their favour, of the fruits of the judgment or of the costs of the proceedings; and I have no doubt that the position of the two

[2] [1927] A.C. at 683.   [3] Baldwin papers.

plaintiffs in Wiggs' Case will be carefully considered by the Government of the Free State.

It appears to me that it is unnecessary and most undesirable to propose any legislation in the British Parliament dealing with this matter. Such legislation would be very difficult to pass, and it would appear to be sufficient that the Dominions Secretary should say (if he thinks so) that the Civil Servants in question are in his opinion being justly dealt with,—and this is all that we promised to secure for them. But this matter, of course, need not be settled at the present time.[4]

Lovat expressed polite doubts to the Prime Minister whether Cave had appreciated how undesirable it was for the Irish Free State to be permitted to alter by unilateral action any of the provisions of the Treaty.

The problem continued to vex all parties in the New Year. In March Cave, mortally ill, withdrew to Burnham. Three days before his death he dictated to Lady Cave a letter which was sent to Baldwin:

26th March 1928

My dear Prime Minister,
           My main purpose in my private note was to make it clear
    1. That my opinion in the decision in *Wigg* v. *Pattison* (on the bonus point) was probably wrong in law.
    2. That for this error the persons principally responsible are those who drafted the opinion.
    3. That this being so, the Irish Free State have a constitutional right to amend the error by Irish legislation agreed to by the British Government.
    4. That the duty of the British Government being to see that justice is done to these pensioners, the British Government has a right to approve of the proposed legislation.
    It cannot be unjust that the Irish ex-Civil Servants should be treated in the same way as the English ex-Civil Servants.
    5. That I am prepared to say this at any time when and as you think fit.

Yours,
Cave[5]

In April 1928 the matter was debated in the House of Lords on a motion by Carson. He declared that for the British Government to acquiesce in the Irish Government's proposal for amending legislation without taking into account the views of the Civil Servants who had been the other party to the litigation 'would be an outrage upon decency in relation to the administration of justice in this country'.[6] Several peers spoke, among them Haldane and Dunedin, who had been members of the Judicial Committee in *Wigg's Case*. Dunedin admitted expressly[7] that there had been a mistake on the part of Cave as to the date of transference of the Civil Servants; Haldane, in more cautious terms, thought there was a

[4] Baldwin papers.   [5] Ibid.   [6] 70 H.L. Deb. 5s. col. 818.   [7] 70 H.L. Deb. 5s. col. 835.

proper case for amending legislation. (It is hardly surprising that Lord Danesfort should have asked whether 'there is any precedent that has ever been recorded in history for a member of His Majesty's Privy Council who has taken part in a judgment coming before this House, behind the backs of the parties who were interested in the judgment and in whose favour the judgment was given, and suggesting that the judgment he himself gave was wrong?'[8]) Birkenhead, then Secretary of State for India, defended the Government strongly. He remarked that he had worked with Cave for many years and 'This is the first time that I ever knew him make a mistake'.[9] He also referred to the 'very moving story' that Cave had written on his deathbed to the Prime Minister to state that his opinion was wrong.

Towards the end of the debate a novel suggestion was made by Lord Reading—that as the Judicial Committee was not bound by its own previous decisions the issue should be referred back to it for reconsideration.

Afterwards counsel for the successful appellants not unnaturally took the view that it was being suggested that the judgment had been obtained by some concealment or trickery on their part. A. A. Dickie, K.C., wrote to the Press repudiating the allegation and suggesting that Cave had not made any error but was in truth trying to answer an ingenious argument from Dickie. This drew a characteristic reply from Birkenhead, who, after disclaiming any imputations of dishonourable conduct, remarked, 'I do not question your statement that you addressed such an argument as you describe to the Judicial Committee. I can only say that, if you did, it may have led to the confusion which has followed.'[1]

Reading's suggestion was gratefully adopted by the Government, and a reference was made to the Judicial Committee under section 4 of the Judicial Committee Act, 1833.[2] In November 1928 the Judicial Committee, presided over by Reading himself, with the assistance of Lords Phillimore, Hanworth, and Alness, and Chief Justice Anglin, decided that although an error had been made in the earlier judgment, the decision itself could be upheld on the ground that the sum awarded was 'fair compensation' within the meaning of Article 10 of the Treaty. The end came when the two Governments agreed to a compromise under which the appellants in *Wigg's Case* would be paid the amounts to which they had been judicially held to be entitled, and that a special tribunal would be set up, the members of which would include representatives of the transferred officers, to assess the compensation due to other classes of claimants.[3]

[8] Ibid., col. 830.   [9] Ibid., col. 839.   [1] See (1928) 62 I.L.T. 115.   [2] [1929] A.C. 242.
[3] 72 H.L. Deb. 5s. col. 1013. A year later Dickie wrote to the Press again to say that twenty-four hours before his death Cave had denied that any error had been made: (1929) 63 I.L.T. 41.

Outside his position as Lord Chancellor, Cave, in 1925, was elected Chancellor of the University of Oxford, an honour which gave him keen personal pleasure, although he felt some unhappiness at the way in which it had come to him; for originally there had been a strong movement in the University to nominate Asquith, undoubtedly the most distinguished Oxonian living. But Asquith's enemies, both political and domestic, were powerful within the University, as has been vividly recounted elsewhere.[4] There were many who objected to him on the ground that he had failed to take out his M.A. degree. No doubt as a briefless barrister he had been unable to afford the necessary 10 guineas and in the years of his greatness the matter had slipped his attention. Anyway a don at Corpus Christi College, G. B. Grundy, set to work to nominate a Conservative to oppose him.

One obvious Conservative candidate was Birkenhead, who had been High Steward of the University since 1922 and was most anxious for the position. When it was vacant again three years later, Birkenhead wrote to Halifax that there was 'no one alive who, having regard (1) to his academic career, (2) to his record of achievement in public affairs, (3) to the sustained and constant contact which he had maintained in relation to Oxford, has claims as high as myself'. But neither in 1925 nor in 1928 did an invitation come. Apart from Birkenhead 'Absolutely the only other Oxford candidate of distinction—a quality not absolutely necessary, but very desirable—was Lord Cave.'[5] Grundy asked Cave to stand, and had his offer accepted by return of post. But then Cave was obliged to draw back. 'For pure downright shilly-shallying Lord Cave created a record in my life's experience.'[6] The reason was that the Government was not strong at the time and his colleagues thought his defeat might be a disservice to the state. Grundy begged him to reconsider his decision, and asked that he might be permitted to meet Cave in company with those of his ministerial colleagues who objected to the nomination.

Cave replied fixing 'the somewhat inconvenient hour of 11.30 p.m. in his private room at the House of Lords. I attended at that time. The official private room of the Lord Chancellor of England was filled with furniture which a second-hand dealer would have treated as scrap. It was a debased and dingy form of Early Victorian, rich no doubt in memories of a long historic past, but economically valueless.'[7] Three Cabinet ministers appeared and Grundy pleaded successfully with them that Cave might be allowed to stand. 'Lord Cave was obviously delighted with the decision.' He was elected, receiving 987 votes out of the 1,428 cast. He

[4] R. Harrod, *The Prof.* (1960), pp. 119–33.
[5] G. B. Grundy, *Fifty-five Years at Oxford* (1944), p. 142.
[6] Grundy, p. 143.   [7] Ibid., p. 144.

fulfilled the duties of the office conscientiously and with dignity. One of his first acts may be recorded here. It is the privilege of the Chancellor to nominate a list of candidates for honorary degrees at the first Encaenia after his election. Cave chose, as might have been expected, an unexceptionable list of dignitaries, among whom was John Simon, who felt somewhat hurt that the University had not previously recognized his talents in this way. The following correspondence[8] may be of interest to others beside Oxford men. First comes a letter of 25 May 1926 from the Warden of Wadham, the then Vice-Chancellor:

I am so glad that the Chancellor has added your name to the list of D.C.Ls. to be conferred at the Encaenia. At his request, I put your name before Council yesterday, and it was gladly accepted; and your name will appear in the *University Gazette* on Wednesday. Will it be possible for you and Lady Simon to stay with me for the Encaenia, coming I hope on the Tuesday and remaining for the Christ Church dinner on the Wednesday night? . . . I am so glad that Oxford is forming this further link with you.

Next, a letter from Cave on 1 June:

I have ventured to propose your name for the honorary D.C.L. at Oxford. I hope that this will not be disagreeable to you, and that you will come up and receive the degree on the 23rd June.

Finally, a note of the same date from Birkenhead from the India Office:

I am delighted. You ought to have had it long ago but they never gave it me until they had to when I became H.S. [High Steward]. By that time I had become a Doctor of the other University and being annoyed, actually wrote refusing it, but George Curzon was so upset that I recalled it. I never think that the old men as apart from the young men at Oxford, have treated me very well.

In private life Cave, at this period, was the same simple, straightforward, unostentatious man he had ever been. He spent much of his time between his two houses at Richmond and Burnham; in particular he enjoyed retiring to the West Country for short golfing holidays. Neither he nor his wife went into London society, in the ordinary sense of that term, but they had a wide circle of devoted friends for whom Cave was accustomed to compose verses—in Latin for the adults and in English for the children. In lighter mood he was, before his elevation to the Woolsack, occasionally seen at race meetings and in earlier years he had sometimes visited Monte Carlo in company with old friends from the Bar. But towards the end his health began to fail and he spent increasingly lengthy periods at Burnham.

In February 1928 he was obviously ill and Baldwin, always careful of

[8] Preserved in the Simon papers.

the health of others besides himself, insisted on him taking a holiday. His illness, as we have seen, was aggravated by worry over the judgment of the Judicial Committee of the Privy Council in the case relating to the Irish transferred Civil Servants.[9]

On 22 March he felt obliged to sent the Prime Minister his resignation:

My dear Prime Minister,

When I mentioned my health to you a few weeks ago, you kindly asked me to take a few weeks rest in the hope that it might improve. Since then I have done my best, but my doctors now advise me that there is no probability that I shall be fit within a reasonable period of time to carry on the duties of a Lord Chancellor.

I therefore feel it to be my duty to request you at the most convenient date to ask His Majesty to permit me to return the Great Seal into his hands. It is hardly necessary to add that it will be with the greatest sorrow and regret that I shall retire from an office which I have been proud to hold and shall sever my connection with Colleagues with whom I have worked so happily and with the Chief for whom I shall always feel a grateful and affectionate regard.

Yours very sincerely,

Cave[1]

On the 29th of that month he died quietly at St. Anne's, Burnham. The previous day he had been well enough to appreciate the significance of the following letter from the Prime Minister:

The King was anxious to confer some special recognition on you at this moment and I know you will forgive me for anticipating what would have been yours at the end of Parliament, and advising him that an earldom should be given you on resignation. He gladly and immediately assented.

You must not worry about anything, but stand firm in the knowledge of the confidence and affection which every one of your colleagues has for you.[2]

Cave was buried in the churchyard of St. Mary's Church, Berrow, a few hundred yards from his house at Burnham, with a handsome stone slab on the west wall of the churchyard where the dunes run down to the sea. (The finely wrought inscription unfortunately contains two mistakes.[3]) After his death, it was discovered that the value of his estate, as re-sworn for probate, amounted to no more than £27,832. As this meant that Lady Cave had only £800 a year to live on the new Chancellor, Hailsham, procured a number of friends to subscribe £4000 to buy her an annuity. Nobody could explain how the prudent and cautious George Cave had left so little.

[9] See above, p. 442.

[1] Baldwin papers. The letter is in Lady Cave's hand, except for the signature.

[2] Mallet, p. 323.

[3] He is described as 'George Cave of Richmond', and the epitaph reads: 'A man who neither sought or (sic) shunned greatness but found it in the path of duty.'

APPENDIX

In *Contracts and Commercial Law* there is a good judgment by Cave in *Commonwealth Shipping Co. Ltd.* v. *P. & O.* [1923] A.C. 191 on the meaning of the phrase 'consequences of warlike operations' in a policy of insurance. He also dealt with promises to perform an existing duty owed to a person other than the plaintiff (*Glasbrook Bros.* v. *Glamorgan C.C.* [1925] A.C. 270), and promises which purport to confer a benefit on a third party (*Elder, Dempster & Co.* v. *Paterson, Zochonis & Co.* [1924] A.C. 522). The decision in the latter case has been restricted to its own very special facts; as Lord Simonds said, it 'has been the subject of so much analytical criticism, and so many different conclusions, that one may well despair of finding out what was decided by which of the five noble and learned Lords who took part in it' (*Scruttons, Ltd.* v. *Midland Silicones, Ltd.* [1962] A.C. 446, at 468.

In *Torts* there are useful judgments in *Mersey Docks and Harbour Board* v. *Procter* [1923] A.C. 253 (duty to invitee), and *Sutherland* v. *Stopes* [1925] A.C. 47 (libel).

In *Constitutional Law* there is a very clear judgment in *Duff Development Co.* v. *Kelantan Government* [1924] A.C. 797. The Government was held entitled to claim the immunity from suit to which a foreign sovereign was entitled, although even Cave was moved to disapproval over the moral as distinct from the legal validity of the claim in the circumstances of that case. His judgment in the habeas corpus case of *Re Clifford and O'Sullivan* [1921] 2 A.C. 570 has already been considered.

In *Revenue Law* there is a good judgment in *Russian Commercial Bank* v. *De Mulhouse* [1925] A.C. 112 (foreign nationalization decree). Cave also dealt in two cases with the difficult subject of the residence of a limited company for purposes of taxation—*Bradbury* v. *English Cotton Co.* [1923] A.C. 744, and *Swedish Central Ry. Co.* v. *Thompson* [1925] A.C. 495—the latter decision being one which has given rise to considerable difficulties, and some modification of Cave's views has proved necessary (see *Unit Construction Co. Ltd.* v. *Bullock* [1960] A.C. 351. The difficult subject of residence for revenue purposes was also dealt with (this time in relation to an individual) in *I.R.C.* v. *Levene* [1928] A.C. 217, and *I.R.C.* v. *Lysaght* [1928] A.C. 234. In the latter case Cave's dissenting judgment on the facts has been preferred by several competent authorities.

In *Equity* there is a judgment in the important case of *Attorney-General* v. *National Provincial Bank* [1924] A.C. 262, in which the House of Lords held that the words 'patriotic purposes or objects' were too uncertain to constitute a valid charitable bequest. In *Ward* v. *Laverty* [1925] A.C. 101 Cave affirmed the principle that the welfare of the child was the paramount consideration in cases of custody. In *Ward* v. *Van der Loeff* [1924] A.C. 653 Cave, as might have been expected, said 'It is far too late to question the principle' that a court will not receive evidence to show that a woman is past the age of child-bearing.

LORD HAILSHAM

CHAPTER I

WHEN LORD HAILSHAM RETIRED from the office of Lord Chancellor in 1938 he wrote to a friend:

> I have had no less than four publishers anxious for me to write my reminiscences; but I have explained to them that if I wrote what I really knew I should be very indiscreet and very embarrassing to the Government, and if I didn't include indiscretions the reminiscences would be very dull. Further than that, as you know, I have kept no press cuttings or diaries or records of my life. When the lives of the Lord Chancellors are brought up to date, all they will find to say about me is that I am believed to have been educated at Eton, that I was twice Lord Chancellor, once Secretary of State for War, and subsequently Lord President of the Council, but that further details of my life are wrapt in obscurity.[1]

One is reminded of some remarks made about himself by a former Lord Chancellor, Lyndhurst: 'What have I been but a successful lawyer? I have been three times Chancellor, and I have tried to do something for my country in my place in Parliament. But what is there in that to make the world desire to know anything about me hereafter?'[2] Yet in each case it has been possible for later generations to reconstruct rather more of the lives of Lyndhurst and Hailsham than they themselves would apparently have wished.

The Hoggs are an established family. The ancestors of the Lord Chancellor emigrated from Scotland to Ulster at the end of the seventeenth century when the plantation of that province had been almost completed. William Hogg of Lisburn, Co. Antrim,[3] died in 1824 leaving an elder son, James Weir Hogg; as a youth in Ulster he seems to have been discontented with his lot. A full diary which is still preserved in the family papers records vividly the gloom and depression felt by an ambitious boy in the sad rain-swept surroundings of Co. Antrim. Efforts to study Blackstone's Commentaries on the laws of England were continually frustrated by laziness and depression. Still he did well enough to become a scholar and gold medallist of Trinity College, Dublin, and later emigrated to India. He was obliged to borrow the money for the voyage from an uncle who exacted very stiff terms as to repayment of capital and interest. This ungenerous action was for ever remembered by the young

[1] Hailsham papers.   [2] T. Martin, *Life of Lord Lyndhurst* (1884), p. iii.
[3] The Hogg home was on the site now occupied by Lisburn Town Hall: (1929) 63 I.L.T. 24.

man who rose to become Chairman of the East India Company in the days when 'John Company' was the wealthy and powerful Governor of a vast tract of the Indian sub-continent. He returned home, acquired a seat in Parliament, a baronetcy and a Privy Councillorship, and died in 1876 leaving by his wife Mary, one of the Swintons of Berwick, no less than fourteen children. The fourteenth child and seventh son was Quintin, who, after leaving Eton, joined the firm of sugar merchants, Hogg, Curtis & Campbell, which under his direction prospered greatly until the very end of the nineteenth century, when a sharp fall in the value of sugar was noticeable everywhere. Hogg's main interest, however, was not sugar trading but philanthropy. He is known to history as the founder of the Polytechnic in Regent Street: 'What we wanted to develop our institute into was a place which should recognize that God had given man more than one side to his character, and where we could gratify any reasonable taste, whether athletic, intellectual, spiritual, or social.'[4] The subsequent growth of that remarkable institution is known to all. It branched out into something like a Technical College in the days before the State took a responsibility for the provision of such further education. A branch of the Polytechnic became one of the earliest firms in the field of mass holiday tours. It is now a distinct commercial entity under the name of the Poly Touring Association Ltd. Quintin Hogg sank at least £100,000 of his own fortune in this remarkable venture. He married Alice, the eldest daughter of William Graham, formerly Member of Parliament for Glasgow. Three of her sisters were prominent in the social life of Edwardian England: Lady Horner, Lady Jekyll, and Lady Muir Mackenzie.

The eldest of their three sons, the subject of this biography, was born on 28 February 1872 at 10 Chesham Place, London (then, as now, a solid house in a pleasant corner of Belgravia), and christened Douglas McGarel (the second name was in honour of Charles McGarel, who had married Quintin's sister Mary, and also introduced him to the sugar business). Quintin Hogg's home was always open to the boys of the Polytechnic and Douglas grew up in their company. In later life his ability, unusual in a Conservative politician of pre-1939 days, to understand and sympathize with working-class aspirations was ascribed to the easy and friendly terms on which he had mixed during his childhood with the boys of the Polytechnic. After a period at Cheam School, where his friends remembered him as a small, fat boy, always at the top of his class,[5] Douglas Hogg proceeded to Eton, where he was in R. C. Radcliffe's house. He left after a distinguished career, having been Captain of the Oppidans. In the normal way he might have gone to either Oxford or Cambridge, but Quintin Hogg, like so many philanthropists, was apt to be cautious where

[4] *D.N.B.. 1901–1911*, p. 279.   [5] Information from 9th Earl of Sandwich.

PLATE 17

Lord Hailsham leaving Westminster Abbey

PLATE 18

Lord Hailsham at a point-to-point with (*left to right*) W. W. Grantham, K.C. (son of Mr. Justice Grantham), and Mr. Justice Avory

expenditure on his own family was concerned and he insisted on Douglas joining the family firm and proceeding out to British Guiana to manage a sugar estate there. The sugar trade at the time was in a depressed condition and it was felt that the active young man might do something to restore the state of the business. So Douglas Hogg spent some eight years in a remote and unattractive part of the world meticulously keeping the accounts of the sugar estate and acquiring a knowledge of commerce which was later of considerable value to him in practice at the Bar.

On the outbreak of the Boer War in 1899 Hogg at once volunteered for service, but was rejected because of defective eyesight; but he was not to be deterred from proceeding to South Africa and, invoking the aid of his Scottish relations, he served as a Trooper throughout the War in the Lothian and Berwickshire Yeomanry. On one occasion he was hit by a Boer bullet, but fortunately it was deflected by a heavy silver flask for spirits which he was carrying. (The flask with the indentation is still preserved in the family.) Later he was invalided home after being laid up with an attack of the prevalent dysentry. He thereupon started to read for the Bar and was called by Lincoln's Inn on 27 January 1902. On 3 September 1902 his father wrote to a former member of the Polytechnic:

Douglas has passed his final Bar examination brilliantly and in fact did so much better than anybody else that the scholarship which he was debarred from taking up on account of his age was awarded to no-one else, it being held that there was really no second to him in the exam. He is an enthusiast in his work, has quite a number of briefs already, and I am sure will do uncommonly well. Dr. Warre, the Headmaster of Eton, told me when he was leaving that if I would put him into Law he would undertake that he would become Lord Chancellor, as he was pretty nearly the ablest fellow that had ever passed through his hands. Of course one must take an opinion like this *cum grano*, but making all allowances it was a very flattering description for the Headmaster of Eton to give of any boy.[6]

The authorities at Eton, although at first a little hazy on the matter, finally confirmed in 1928[7] that Douglas Hogg was the fourth Etonian to become Lord Chancellor, though the first for 150 years; the other three were Charles, Lord Talbot, Lord Chancellor 1733-7; Charles, Lord Camden, Lord Chancellor 1766–70; and Henry, Lord Bathurst, Lord Chancellor 1771–8.

Hogg's early years at the Bar were much assisted not merely by his practical knowledge of men and commerce gained in British Guiana and South Africa, but also by the fact that for a few months before being called he had worked in the offices of a firm of city solicitors with a large commercial practice, Messrs. Ashurst, Morris, Crisp & Co., who loyally

[6] Hailsham papers.   [7] Letter from C. K. Marten in Hailsham papers.

provided him with his first brief on 28 January 1902—a watching brief in the Commercial Court for £2. 4s. 6d. He read as a pupil in the Chambers of Harry Dobb, who later became a county court judge, but died on 23 March 1928, only a few days before his former pupil became Lord Chancellor. A few years after call Hogg felt firmly enough established to marry, on 14 August 1905, Elizabeth, the daughter of Judge James Trimble Brown of Nashville, Tennessee, and the widow of his first cousin, Archibald Marjoribanks, a son of Lord Tweedmouth (Lady Tweedmouth had been Quintin Hogg's eldest sister.). The lady had worried about her position as a widow with two young children, and had consulted her friends[8] about the desirability of accepting some wealthier suitor who had appeared. But her own inclinations were in favour of the young barrister and she never regretted the choice.

Hogg now made the traditional attempt of a rising common law junior to acquire a parliamentary seat. He had not far to look, for it so happened that in 1909 his own constituency of Marylebone East was in a state of dissension. The sitting member, Lord Robert Cecil, later Viscount Cecil of Chelwood, whose majority was under 700, was adjudged to hold unsound views on the subject of tariff reform. He appears to have been an ardent free trader, a divergence from the official party standpoint which was all the more obvious because the member for Marylebone West, Sir Samuel Scott (the constituency at that date was divided) was orthodox in his protectionist views. A new Unionist Association was formed as a break-away group from the official body, and in July 1909 it unanimously resolved to recommend Douglas Hogg for adoption as its candidate for the constituency. The prospective candidate wrote to the committee modestly disclaiming any personal ambition:

I had no intention of standing for Parliament at the next election, and there is obviously unpleasantness and difficulty in fighting a Unionist in his own constituency, but I have satisfied myself that the Tariff Reformers in East Marylebone have made every reasonable possible concession to avoid a split in the party, and if in the fight that has been forced upon them they look upon me as the best man available to champion their cause, I don't think I am justified on any grounds of personal convenience in shirking the responsibility.[9]

But the confusion in the affairs of the East Marylebone Conservatives became worse. A stormy General Meeting in October revealed only that Robert Cecil had few supporters:[1] his opponents were divided amongst those who supported Douglas Hogg and those who supported one Richard Jebb. At one stage both Hogg and Jebb appear to have been

8 Hailsham papers.   9 The Times, 24 July 1909.
1 For his views, see Viscount Cecil of Chelwood, All the Way (1949), pp. 107–13.

adopted as prospective anti-Cecil candidates, although all affected to deplore the folly of running two, let alone three, Conservative candidates. In the late autumn Hogg stood down in order to promote party unity in the constituency. (He may also have reflected that it is scarcely wise for anyone who seeks to make a career in the Conservative Party to be discovered in opposition to the House of Cecil.) Lord Robert Cecil then announced that he would not stand again for Marylebone (he was later returned for Hitchin), so the result was that the Tariff Reform section of the East Marylebone Conservatives found themselves with a candidate, Jebb, to whom nobody was deeply attached.

At the general election of January 1910 the official Conservative candidate, (Sir) James Boyton, was returned, with Jebb, standing as an Independent Conservative, at the bottom of the poll. When the two Marylebone constituencies were amalgamated in 1918, the former Member for West Marylebone was returned unopposed for the united constituency.

Hogg, after this unsuccessful venture into politics, devoted himself to his practice at the Bar. His fee-books, which have survived[2] for almost the entire period of his life at the Bar, show that in his first year he made £417. 1s. By 1906 this had risen to some £4,000; by 1912 to some £9,000, and by 1913 to £12,707. In later years he would describe how depressed he had felt waiting for work to come—'I was reduced to reading Smith's *Leading Cases*', he would say. The period could not have been very long. The greatest years of his practice were, however, after the war; he had taken silk in July 1917, being one of the four K.C.s created during the whole period of the war.[3] It had become a necessity for him to do this because he had been laid up for some five months by a severe attack of typhoid fever at the beginning of the year and the strain of a junior practice would have been too much. It was in the years of the boom in litigation after the end of the war that his earnings rose to a height which have seldom been equalled at the English Bar. In the period between 1 May 1920 and 31 December 1920, he earned £27,432, and between 1 January 1921 and 30 April 1921, £13,501, making a total of £40,933. In the following year, from 1 May 1921 to 30 April 1922, the sum rose to £46,541. It is particularly noticeable that most of the fees marked on the various briefs are for comparatively small sums and that they came from an exceptionally wide range of solicitors. It is very doubtful whether any other advocate of the inter-war years could produce authentic evidence of similar earnings in two successive years. In the year

2 In the Hailsham papers.
3 The others were A. M. Dunne and G. R. Lowndes, two specialists in Indian appeals to the Privy Council, and R. A. (later Lord) Wright.

1923 when he was Attorney-General his earnings dropped to £11,420, but in 1924, when he resumed private practice, they rose again to £39,163; in 1925 they were £21,766. It is not surprising that in later years Hogg declared that each step in life had halved his income: 'At the Bar, he would say I made £40,000 a year; as Law Officer, £20,000; as Lord Chancellor, £10,000; and, now, as Lord President of the Council, £5,000.'[4]

Two cases from his great post-war years may be recorded—one just before, and the other just after, his period as Attorney-General. In *Wakeford* v. *Bishop of Lincoln*[5] proceedings had been instituted in the Consistory Court against Archdeacon Wakeford charging certain offences against ecclesiastical law. It was alleged that the Archdeacon, a married man, aged 62 years, had on three separate occasions stayed at the Bull Hotel, Peterborough, with a woman who was not his wife. The Archdeacon appealed to the Judicial Committee from an adverse finding of the Consistory Court. The appeal was before a Board composed of Lord Birkenhead, L.C., and Lords Buckmaster, Dunedin and Shaw, sitting with four assessors (the Bishops of London, Gloucester, Rochester and Ely). The appeal took the form of a re-hearing, much evidence being adduced which was not available in the proceedings before the Consistory Court. The conflict of evidence was acute and the struggle between the parties severe. There was undoubtedly much sympathy, within and without the court room, for the Archdeacon, who was a man of unblemished character holding a distinguished position. But he was also a man described in evidence as having 'a facility for making enemies', and indeed his defence was that he was the victim of a conspiracy, the main parties to which were two local clergymen, Moore and Worthington, the latter being also the Archdeacon's brother-in-law.

As Lord Birkenhead put it in his judgment:

Upon this ill-feeling (on the part of Moore) and animus (on the part of Worthington) the Appellant's counsel has sought to build the theory of a gigantic conspiracy, swiftly designed and skilfully organized, directed to the ruin of the Appellant, conceived by Moore and Worthington and put into execution by King (a sergeant in the Peterborough Police) and the Pughs (who kept the Bull Inn) with the assistance, more or less well informed, of the servants at the hotel, Tuplin, and King's colleagues in the Peterborough police force.

[4] Viscount Mersey, *Journals and Memories* (1952), p. 46.

[5] [1921] 1 A.C. 813. The Law Reports contain only the judgment of the Judicial Committee on the point of law which arose on the application for leave to appeal. Lord Birkenhead's full judgment will be found in *The Times* for 27 April 1921 or in the collection of his judgments edited by Roland Burrows and published by H.M.S.O. in 1923.

The junior counsel for the Bishop, W. N. (later Mr. Justice) Stable, has provided a vivid picture of the proceedings.

The case caused a tremendous stir as Wakeford was an outstanding figure in the Church, and I believe was the next to be appointed as a Bishop. The proceedings at Lincoln were a foregone conclusion as the evidence was all one way, overwhelming. Wakeford appealed to the Privy Council and took in Edward Carson. It was the last case Carson did as he had his appointment as a Lord of Appeal in his pocket. At Lincoln the case had been conducted for the Bishop by William Hansell with such assistance as I could afford. The Privy Council ordered a re-hearing so the Bishop took in Hogg to lead Hansell and myself. Carson's performance was a tour de force: he had not a card in his hand but he decided to dominate the whole proceedings.

I got a very clear impression that the Court was very adverse to the Bishop and would allow Wakeford's appeal if it was possible. Why this was so I don't know, possibly it was felt that Wakeford was such a prominent figure in the Church it would have been wiser for the Bishop to turn a blind eye to what was only a very human frailty—but unbecoming to a future Anglican Bishop. Birkenhead the L.C. was a Liverpool man. Anyhow, whatever the cause, at the conclusion of the whole case when there was nothing left but Hogg's closing speech, Wakeford felt we were a routed army: it was the Bishop who was in the dock, his supporters were malicious men bent on the destruction of a great Christian prelate. You could feel the hostility of the Court. Then Hogg began his closing speech. It was masterly. Quietly, bit by bit, he analysed the evidence, and showed that from every direction the evidence amounted to absolute proof. He stripped the defence of all the fustian in which Carson had arrayed it and exposed it as being non-existent. Slowly the tide ebbed; the quiet logical build-up of every known fact in its appropriate place presented a complete picture, it was unanswerable. I think Lord Birkenhead struggled to the last but eventually was convinced. It was a magnificent example of a great general whose army had been routed re-organizing the troops and snatching victory from disaster.[6]

Hogg's closing speech was delivered on 18 April, and the Lord Chancellor announced that the Board would deliver its judgment on 26 April.

As Mr. Justice Stable said, Birkenhead struggled to the last before conceding that the evidence against the Archdeacon was overwhelming.

A vital point in the case concerned the Archdeacon's signature in the registration book at the Bull Inn, Peterborough. Birkenhead woke his wife at four o'clock in the morning, coming in fully dressed and haggard, with a magnifying glass, a letter with Wakeford's signature, and a photograph of the signature in the book at the Bull Inn. After scrutinizing the two signatures together, they came to the bleak conclusion that there was no difference.[7]

On 26 April Birkenhead read a judgment which is remarkable for its

[6] In a letter of 2 May 1962 to the author.   [7] Birkenhead, *F.E.* (1959), p. 401.

close and penetrating analysis of complicated and controverted facts. The
Board had reluctantly found that the charges were proved and 'the hypothesis of such a conspiracy is utterly untenable'. There was complete
silence throughout the one and a half hours which it took to deliver the
judgment.

After he had ceased to be Attorney-General in January 1924, Hogg
appeared for the petitioner, the respondent to the appeal, in *Russell* v.
Russell,[8] together with Sir Edward Marshall Hall, K.C., R. F. Bayford,
K.C., and V. Russell. The question for the House of Lords was whether
evidence of non-access might be given in divorce proceedings by one
spouse with the result of bastardizing a child of the marriage. The answer
was of great importance, not only to the parties to the suit, the sole
evidence of the wife's adultery being the testimony of the husband that
he did not have access to his wife at any time when the child could have
been conceived, but also to all those who were interested in the proceedings
in the Divorce Court, either as possible parties or as practitioners.

'Sir Douglas Hogg', said Lord Dunedin, 'in the course of as able and
concise a speech as I have ever heard at Your Lordship's Bar, admitted
with perfect frankness that the evidence would be inadmissible in a
legitimacy case.'[9] Hogg's argument was that the rule prohibiting the
introduction of such evidence had never been applied to a case in which
the object of the suit was to dissolve the bond of marriage on the ground
of adultery, it only applied where there was a marriage in existence and
the legitimacy of a child born in wedlock was in question. 'Where the
issue is adultery the birth of a child is mere accident', he argued.[1] This
ingenious argument was rejected by the majority of the House, Lord
Finlay saying: 'To what an extraordinary state would the admission of this
evidence in the present case reduce the law of England! The infant may
be illegitimate for the purpose of proving adultery; but legitimate for the
purpose of succeeding to property or a title!'[2]

It was also argued for the husband that in practice such evidence was
constantly given. The reply was: 'Then as to the practice of the Divorce
Court, Sir Douglas Hogg has probably practised but little in that Court,
but he had with him others who had, and I did not understand him to say
that he could cite any instance of the class of testimony in evidence in this
case which has ever been given.'[3]

In the end the House, Lords Sumner and Carson dissenting, held that on
grounds of decency and public policy the law prohibited the introduction
of such evidence. 'The practice of the Divorce Court must accommodate
itself to the authority of the rule. If the inconvenience (contrary to my

[8] [1924] A.C. 687.   [9] Ibid., at p. 724.   [1] Ibid., at p. 696.   [2] Ibid., at p. 719.
[3] Ibid., at p. 729, per Lord Dunedin.

opinion) proves intolerable, the Legislature, if it thinks proper, may provide a remedy,' said Lord Birkenhead. The inconvenience proved intolerable (at least to practitioners in the Divorce Court) and by the Law Reform (Miscellaneous Provisions) Act, 1949, Section 7 (since repealed and re-enacted by the Matrimonial Causes Act, 1950 section 32 (1)). Parliament abolished the rule in *Russell* v. *Russell*, thus vindicating the position for which Douglas Hogg had argued unsuccessfully in 1924.

CHAPTER II

IN 1922 HOGG'S LIFE seemed as if it had settled into the routine of a prosperous K.C. He was at the top of his profession: he had a wife and family and a country house in Sussex—Carter's Corner Place near Herstmonceux, which he had bought in the same year as he took silk. He had also been adopted as Conservative candidate for Marylebone in succession to the sitting Member, Sir Samuel Scott, who had announced his intention of not seeking re-election. But there was no reason to expect that a K.C. aged 50 years would be able to make an impact on the House of Commons sufficiently great to carry him up the ladder of political and professional advancement. The fall of the coalition Government in October 1922, however, drastically changed the course of his life. It has already been seen that Bonar Law had the task of forming a government without the assistance of some of the most experienced and distinguished members of the Conservative Party.[1] For some time he made efforts to induce the former Law Officers, Ernest Pollock and Leslie Scott, to remain in their positions, although as early as Friday 20 October, the day after Lloyd George had resigned, Pollock had been told that Hogg was ready to take office as Attorney-General.[2] Further efforts to induce Pollock to support Bonar Law were made over the week-end, but after much discussion with both Bonar Law and Austen Chamberlain, Pollock had written to the former on Monday 23 October:

Let me first thank you for the honour you have done to the Law Officers and the Lord Advocate in asking them to retain their posts in your Administration and further to provide one of their number to take the post of Home Secretary in it.

Let me also thank you for the manner in which you have done it and your kindness to me personally.

Needless to say we have most carefully considered the proposition in all its bearings and our decision is that we cannot accept your offer. We cannot see that the cooperation offered to those who have worked and are ready to work with us to attain the common objects of stability and peace at home and abroad and to stem the principles of communism and nationalization is sufficient.

Although we are prepared as Conservatives and Unionists to support the Conservative and Unionist party generally by our votes, we are not prepared to take the responsibility of the position which has, we think, been unwisely created.

[1] See above, pp. 387–9, 424–7.   [2] See below, p. 462.

Perhaps we may add that the result to us personally of the refusal to make (sic), estimates the measure of our convictions.[3]

Upon receiving this letter Bonar Law abandoned all further attempts to persuade Pollock to join the new Government and appointed Hogg to be Attorney-General, with a seat in the Cabinet.

The supplanted Attorney-General, Ernest Pollock, wrote in his memorandum of the events surrounding the break-up of the coalition:

Douglas Hogg was appointed Attorney-General—a really able man who was a great friend of mine. He came to the Bar after a short career in the City, a little later in life than is usually the case, and I had got to know him well as a Junior—a real friendship grew up between us which has continued without a break for these many years. It was, therefore, no hardship to hand over my room and papers to him, even though the departing from the post of Attorney-General did—I must confess it—cause me a pang. To be Head of the Bar of England is a great position, especially to one who like myself was bred in the traditions of the Bench and Bar, and always wished to be a barrister and loved the work as well as the interchange of human interests and intellectual activities. Beyond this too, a Law Officer has some opportunity of helping others and doing acts of friendship among those that he has known all his life.

However, Hogg and I had no difficulty between us. As he had never before been a Law Officer I was able to give him some hints; and early in the next year he showed his appreciation by asking me to go with him before the International Court of Justice at the Hague where an important case as to the rights of persons born in Tunis of British parents was to be decided between France and Britain.[4]

Hogg's solid position in the Conservative Party can be deduced from the speed with which its emissaries attempted to secure his services. (It should be noted that he had not been present at the Carlton Club on Thursday 19 October: normally an adopted Conservative candidate is entitled to attend meetings of the party but the meeting summoned for the 19th by Austen Chamberlain was limited to Conservative Members of Parliament. Tory peers and parliamentary candidates were both excluded, perhaps for the good reason that they would have been even more anti-Lloyd George than the back-bench M.P.s, or perhaps because Chamberlain was only the leader of the Conservative Party in the House of Commons. The party as a whole had been without a leader since the resignation of Balfour in 1911.) Douglas Hogg in October 1922 was not only at the top of his profession but also a well-known figure in the second rank of Conservative politicians. It is necessary to emphasize this fact, because Mr. Randolph Churchill has put into circulation a story designed

[3] Hanworth papers.
[4] Ibid. The case was *Nationality Decrees in Tunis and Morocco* (Series B No. 4).

to show that Douglas Hogg was unknown to the great world at that date. The story in Mr. Churchill's own words is as follows:

The difficulties in which the leading members of the Government found themselves at this time are well illustrated by an anecdote which is still told by two sons-in-law of the Duke of Devonshire.[5] One evening while the Government was being formed Derby went round to Devonshire House. This was only a few months before this splendid building in Piccadilly, with its galaxy of memories of political confabulations extending over two centuries, was to be pulled down and replaced by Lord Rootes' glittering automobile emporium. Devonshire expressed concern about the Government's lack of adequate representation in the Commons, and in particular as to who would be the Government's principal spokesman, Baldwin being at this time utterly unversed in Parliamentary technique. Someone said:
  'Let's get some clever lawyer.'
  'I know the very man,' said Derby. 'Someone was telling me about him the other day, a fellow called Pig.'
  'The only Pig I know,' said Devonshire, 'is James Pigge in Surtees.'
  Thus did that able lawyer, Sir Douglas Hogg, who at that time was probably the leading Silk at the Bar and who was destined as the first Viscount Hailsham to sit on the Woolsack, first come to the attention of the magnificoes of the Tory Party.[6]

There are two objections to this story. The first is that the events which it describes could not have happened. Ernest Pollock's cousin Guy, formerly the Managing Editor of the *Morning Post*, was acting as an intermediary between Bonar Law and Beaverbrook on the one hand and his cousin on the other. In an undated letter received by his cousin on the 21 October (Saturday) Guy Pollock wrote: 'I went to Lord Beaverbrook yesterday [i.e. Friday the 20th] and found him at 3.30. . . . As to the Law Officers suggestion, an immediate dissolution (decided on) obviates the difficulty and Hogg and Rawlinson are ready to take on the jobs.'[7]

So by the afternoon of Friday the 20th Hogg's name and his willingness to accept office were known at least to Bonar Law and Beaverbrook. It follows that if the alleged conversation at Devonshire House ever took place on 'one evening while the Government was being formed', it must have been on Thursday the 19th, or (possibly) Friday the 20th. But the contemporary extracts from Derby's own diary show that on the Thursday evening he dined with Maureen and Oliver Stanley, leaving at

[5] Presumably this refers to the Rt. Hon. Harold Macmillan, M.P., and the Rt. Hon. James Stuart, M.P. (later Lord Stuart of Findhorn).

[6] R. Churchill, *Lord Derby* (1959), pp. 460–1.

[7] Hanworth papers. For the full text of the letter, see above, pp. 426–7. Inskip was eventually appointed Solicitor-General, after consideration of the names of Rawlinson, Macnaghten, and Maugham.

9.30 p.m. to visit Bonar Law, while on the Friday, Derby 'went by night train to Knowsley'.[8]

The second objection to this story is that it is a confused version of

A contemporary after dinner story told with a different point and in a slightly different form in 1922 at pro-Coalition dinner parties in order to make fun of the little known and untried (as they were thought) personalities in the Bonar Law administration. I remember it well at the time, when it was brought home in great glee by my brother Edward Marjoribanks. But originally the story was told without the reference to Surtees and in a different form: for it originally related to Derby and not to Devonshire, and to a point of time after and not *before* the formation of the Bonar Law administration. The story was:

Derby: 'They tell me there is a fellow in the House of Commons called Pig, who is managing the whole thing very well.'[9]

Lord Beaverbrook has emphatically confirmed the accuracy of Guy Pollock's account. He has also stated that Hogg was brought to the notice of Bonar Law by his secretary, the wife of J. B. Melville, who became Solicitor-General in the Labour Government of 1929. Mrs. Melville told Bonar Law of the high esteem in which Hogg was held at the Bar. 'Your father and Bonar Law met at Claridge's Hotel, of all places. And they dine, a most unusual event for Bonar Law. After the dinner Bonar Law told me that he was fascinated by your father, and had asked him to join the Government as Attorney-General and to stand for Parliament, taking his place on the Front Bench from the very moment of his entry into the Chamber.'[1]

So within one month Douglas Hogg became Member of Parliament, Attorney-General, a Privy Councillor (2 November), and a Knight (12 December). The only parallel to this rapid promotion was the career of Richard Webster, who was created Attorney-General by Lord Salisbury in 1885, although he had never sat in the House of Commons. Many congratulatory letters flowed in, including one from his uncle, Sir John Horner:

I am delighted to know that you are going to be the Attorney-General. You will have many congratulations, but I will send you one on my own behalf. Some day when your life is written as a past Lord Chancellor, the author will say of you that he rose to be Attorney-General purely from ability, industry and character in the legal profession without help either from influence outside or from previous distinction in the House of Commons—though no doubt there is plenty of this to come. I will not do the obvious thing, and compare

[8] Churchill, *Lord Derby*, pp. 453, 455.

[9] Letter from the 2nd Viscount Hailsham to the author in April 1962.

[1] In a letter of 24 May 1962 to the 2nd Viscount Hailsham. (But Hogg was already adopted as a Conservative candidate.)

Dick Webster to you, because I am pretty sure that you are a better man than he was. So you must take this letter only as a testimony of the real and very great pleasure that your success gives me.[2]

Another letter from one of the old boys of the Polytechnic recalled his speech in the Polytechnic Parliament, a debating society which Quintin Hogg ran for his boys along strictly parliamentary lines. The father had crept in and hid under the steps of the Speaker's Chair in order to hear his son speak.[3]

Within three days of his introduction to the House Hogg was obliged to make his maiden speech on one of the Government's most controversial measures—the Irish Free State (Constitution) Bill, which was necessary to give effect in English law to the Treaty of 6 December 1921, under which the Irish Free State achieved what was then called Dominion status. It was essential for the Bill to pass through all its parliamentary stages before the anniversary of the signing of the Treaty lest much of the new legal machinery should collapse. It was also essential that the susceptibilities of the back-bench Conservatives, upon whose votes Bonar Law's political life depended, should not be too deeply shocked. The Government told the Attorney-General they were relying on him. It was a lot to ask of a man with an Ulster ancestry, but he performed the task extremely well.[4]

Lord FitzAlan, who as Lord Edmund Talbot had been Chief Whip to the Unionist Party, wrote on 28 November:

My dear Attorney,
    As an old Whip I cannot help writing you a line to congratulate you on your great success last night. I knew well how difficult it is even for practised lawyers like yourself to catch the atmosphere of the House and you just did it at once and apparently quite naturally and without effort. It was really a very fine performance and the manner, tone and substance of what you said, knocked the stuffing completely out of the Opposition. I have often listened with much anxiety to a maiden speech but never with greater admiration and enjoyment than to yours last night.
                                                            Yours sincerely,
                                                            FitzAlan.[5]

In the same month Hogg and Chamberlain were asked by a nervous Cabinet to draft a letter to a deputation of hunger-marchers who had insisted on being received by the Prime Minister personally, rather than 'underlings' in the form of the Ministers of Health and Labour.

In 1923 there were further Irish difficulties. The Home Secretary, W. C. Bridgeman, had sent certain Irish political prisoners over to Dublin. His intentions were honourable but his actions were illegal. The Opposi-

---

[2] Hailsham papers.   [3] Ibid.   [4] 159 H.C. Deb. 5s. col. 371.   [5] Hailsham papers.

tion gleefully pointed out that the Home Secretary had infringed an important provision of the Habeas Corpus Act, 1679, which prohibited sending prisoners out of the jurisdiction with intent to delay the issue of the writ, and had thereby rendered himself liable to the fearsome medieval penalties of premunire—life imprisonment, the forfeiture of all his chattels to the Crown, and his lands to be ploughed up and laid waste. An Act of Indemnity was clearly necessary. Such Acts are never popular with the House, and the burden of conducting it through its Committee and Report stages fell on the Attorney-General.[6]

By now he was recognized by all as the Government's most powerful debater. On 24 January 1923 Bonar Law wrote to Curzon: 'Hogg, as you know, is turning out to be a real discovery. He has an exceptionally good brain and I hope to be able to use him a great deal.'[7] So there was no surprise when he was chosen to wind up the Debate on the Address on 21 January 1924 on which the survival of the Baldwin Government depended.[8] He made a forthright and hard-hitting speech, but Asquith threw the Liberal vote in favour of the Labour Party, and the Government resigned.

As a private member in opposition Hogg took little part in the debates of the 1924 Parliament. There was, however, one curious, perhaps unique, episode in parliamentary history. He was asked to promote the Bill which became the British Museum (No. 2) Act, 1924, and succeeded in procuring its passage throughout all its stages without, so far as the record in Hansard goes, one single word being spoken by Hogg or any other member.

What the Bar thought of Hogg's career as Attorney-General is well indicated from the account of the Annual General Meeting in January 1924 over which he presided, as is customary for the head of the Bar. (It is indicative of the independent air which successful members of the Bar adopt, or used to adopt, towards their own professional organization that Hogg had never attended such a meeting until he was called on to preside over it.) A vote of thanks was moved to him by Sir John Simon in the most cordial terms. Simon said that Hogg, within twelve months, had established himself as one of the great Attorney-Generals of our history and had raised the reputation of the whole profession by the way in which he had discharged his duties in the House of Commons. On one occasion when Hogg had been speaking, a member leant across to Simon and said, 'Who is this who combines the diction of Mr. Winston Churchill with the benevolence of Mr. Pickwick?'[9] The next day Hogg sent Simon a few lines of thanks:

[6] 164 H.C. Deb. 5s. col. 1037.
[7] R. Blake, *The Unknown Prime Minister* (1955), p. 505.
[8] 169 H.C. Deb. 5s. col. 664.   [9] (1924) 157 L.T. News. 76.

Q*

I feel that I must send you these few lines to say how greatly I appreciated your kindness in finding time to attend the Bar Meeting last night with the express purpose of saying what you did about me. I was very greatly touched by your action; it reminds me of how when nearly seven years ago I came back as a junior after five months illness expecting to find my practice vanished and myself nearly forgotten, you were on the doorstep to welcome me and to give me fresh courage. It was the act of a real friend and I am very grateful.[1]

From January to November 1924 Hogg was, of course, out of office during the period of the first Labour Government; but in November Baldwin recalled him to the Attorney-Generalship, granting him in addition the privilege, unusual and somewhat criticized, of a seat in the Cabinet. In answer to a letter of congratulation from Simon, Hogg replied:

Always when I need encouragement I find you at hand; I have not forgotten your welcome back to the Bar after my illness,or your speech at the last Bar General Meeting. I expect in my new job I shall find some colleagues not nearly so close to me in aim and outlook as yourself! I can only promise to do my best to justify your confidence—I hope you know how much I appreciate your kindness and friendship: I shall be quite content if I satisfy your standard as Attorney-General. Many thanks![2]

Hogg's career as Attorney-General in the second Baldwin Government was one of uninterrupted success.

In 1925 he was responsible for piloting through the House two major Government measures—the Administration of Justice (Miscellaneous Provisions) Act, and the Honours (Prevention of Abuses) Act. In later life he used to tell his friends that he had been so sickened by the post-war scramble for honours that he had made it a rule never to ask for an honour for a friend or supporter. (Like all good rules, there were exceptions to this. In 1934 Hailsham, as Leader of the House of Lords, asked that an English peerage should be given to the Earl of Lucan, who had performed much public service, but sat solely as an Irish representative peer.[3] He was naturally most anxious to obtain an English peerage lest his son should be permanently disfranchised, as the machinery for electing Irish representative peers had disappeared in 1922. The request was granted, though perhaps none of the parties concerned foresaw that the son in question would become one of the Labour Party's strongest supporters in the Lords. Hailsham also, as we shall see, asked for a viscounty for Hanworth in 1936.)[4]

One of the important duties of the Attorney-General is to lead for the Crown in revenue appeals. Sometimes there has been criticism of the alleged readiness of the Inland Revenue Commissioners to wear out the

[1] Simon papers.   [2] Ibid.   [3] Baldwin papers.   [4] See below, p. 521.

taxpayer litigant by involving him in a series of lengthy and expensive appeals. When the matter was discussed in the House of Lords in 1930, Hailsham gave an interesting account of the practice when he was Attorney-General,[5] which showed that the Crown did not appeal against unfavourable decisions without careful consideration.

In 1926 he was responsible for securing the passage of the Electricity Supply Act, which established the grid system. The Bill, much of the preparatory work for which had been done under the Labour Government, encountered bitter opposition from a strong group of back-bench Tories. They described as 'outright Socialism' the modest scheme of nationalization of an indispensable public utility which the Bill contained. They found it difficult to argue against the Attorney-General—apart from his professional skill as an advocate, Douglas Hogg was so obviously a man who believed in the virtues of private enterprise. But Hogg had to fight hard all the way—the Second Reading was in March, but all proceedings on the Bill were suspended throughout the summer because of the General Strike, and when they were resumed in the autumn no fewer than twenty-seven days were spent in Committee. It is not surprising that Hogg was accustomed to regard the grid system as almost his own personal invention.

The General Strike itself had called for the fullest exercise of Hogg's talents. He and Joynson-Hicks, the Home Secretary, were the Government's two strong men in the House of Commons. Often they were almost submerged beneath the roar of angry debate. In the Cabinet Baldwin relied much on Hogg—he was entirely sure of what had to be done, and unfaltering in execution of it, but without the provocative flamboyance which was characteristic of Birkenhead and Churchill. It was typical of Hogg's caution that he always refused to express agreement with the proposition of law which formed the basis of Simon's great speech in the Commons on 6 May[6]—namely, that the General Strike was illegal at common law. He agreed that the speech itself had been of great public service in helping to end the strike; but further than that he could not be persuaded to go.

But the following year he was selected by the Government to move the Second Reading of the Trade Disputes Bill[7]—the object of which was to give statutory endorsement to Simon's common law proposition about the illegality of general strikes. Hogg had to fight his hardest against continuous interruption and obstruction. There was never any doubt that the Bill would pass, but the Opposition used every delaying tactic known. The wisdom of the Trade Disputes Act, 1927, has been much criticized

[5] 76 H.L. Deb. 5s. col. 1251.   [6] 195 H.C. Deb. 5s. col. 584.
[7] 205 H.C. Deb. 5s. col. 1305.

by a later generation, and it is generally thought that Baldwin missed an opportunity for a fundamental industrial reconciliation when he allowed his back-benchers to pursue their demand for vengeance.

It was obvious that Hogg had gained the confidence of the Prime Minister and the party to an unusual degree and it was therefore no real surprise when, on the sudden death of Lord Cave on 29 March 1928, following his resignation a day previously, Hogg succeeded him on the Woolsack. The position had indeed been first offered to Birkenhead, then the Secretary of State for India, but had been refused by him on the ground that he still had valuable work to do for India, and 'the ceremonial side of it depressed me.'[8] Baldwin acted with remarkable speed in filling the vacancy. On the 28th, the very day of Cave's resignation, he wrote to the Master of the Rolls, Hanworth:

My dear Ernest
  I have offered Sargant's place to Frank Russell who has accepted.
  The change does not take place till April 14, so for the present I will ask you to keep it secret.
  But I wanted to tell you myself.
  Cave has retired and Hogg goes to the Woolsack.
  Inskip A.-G. and Merriman S.-G.
  These will be in the paper tomorrow.   Yours ever
                                                                          S.B.[9]

Congratulatory letters poured in upon Douglas Hogg; all said the same thing, that the promotion was inevitable, but also that it was a pity that by going to the House of Lords he had deprived himself and the Conservative Party of the chance of becoming Prime Minister. To one correspondent, Lord Stonehaven, an old school fellow, Hogg replied:

Many thanks for your kindness in writing to me to congratulate me on this office. In fact it was a matter of very grave hesitation; but in the long run it really seemed that there was no alternative, and the Prime Minister decided that it was the right thing for me to do. I regret leaving the House of Commons and all that it implies, and I miss the friendliness and companionship of that place very much; the Woolsack is a very solitary substitute. However, it really is an important job that I have to carry out, and I can only do my best to discharge it adequately.[1]

Lord Buckmaster wrote:

I will not repeat the welcome I most cordially offer to you on your accession to the Woolsack but I would like to say that it was no formality when I said I would gladly help you to the full extent of my powers in any way I can.

[8] Earl of Birkenhead, *F.E.* (1959), p. 516.
[9] Hanworth papers. 'Sargant's place' was in the Court of Appeal.
[1] Hailsham papers.

Unfortunately my energies are still under medical control from which I do my best to escape but within these circumscribed limits they are wholly at your service.

I cannot tell you how pleased I am to think that there is every prospect humanly speaking of your holding this office for many years. It gives an opportunity sadly needed and for the last twenty years never enjoyed.[2]

Rayner Goddard, K.C., wrote: 'I hope that for the sake of the Country and the Party you may hold the Seal as long as Lord Eldon.'[3] W. A. Jowitt, K.C., affirmed that 'I cannot imagine a greater tribute to your work than the commonly expressed surprise that you should have taken on the highest office in the law.'[4] Sir Ellis Hume-Williams, K.C., also wrote: 'As I sit here and write, my memory goes back and I see, sitting on the other side of the table, a rather shy youth from Ashurst Morris and Crisp giving instructions to a nervous and apprehensive junior—myself.'[5] A letter also came from the Treasury Solicitor's office:

It is not easy for us to show appreciation of what the Attorney-General has done but we who get up briefs are acutely sensitive to the conduct of them, and no one can know as we do how perfect was the method and how tireless the industry which lay behind that amazing series of victories which you won for the Crown. So forgive me if I say how we are all personally grateful to you, and conscious of the loss which will not be replaced for many generations.[6]

Praise also came from a rather unexpected quarter. On 4 April Harold Laski wrote to Holmes: 'I expect you will have seen that we have a new Lord Chancellor. He is both able and attractive; though he has something of the Old Bailey type of mind. The late Chancellor was a very sober and dignified person, but not, I think, first rate intellectually. He was a man of great courage for he sat for two years with the full knowledge that he was cutting short his own life.'[7]

One who doubted the merits of the promotion was Neville Chamberlain, who wrote to his sister on 31 March:

I regard his promotion as rather a calamity and it was all rushed through in a very unfortunate way. He had always told me that he would want my advice before he decided, but on Friday the 23rd the P.M. sent for him and after telling him that F.E. had refused when it was put that way and though he didn't think he had quite committed himself he admitted when he came to see me on Tuesday that he had not been very definite in saying no. I strongly urged him to delay and said I would ask the P.M. to press F.E. again, but on Wednesday morning I found it was too late as S.B. had already given the Attorney-Generalship to Inskip and made Merriman Solicitor. Poor Douglas was very unhappy

[2] Hailsham papers.   [3] Ibid.   [4] Ibid.   [5] Ibid.   [6] Ibid.
[7] *Holmes–Laski Letters* (1953), p. 1043.

for he had realized that when it came to the point he wanted to continue his political career and of course the tragedy is that he is now barred from the chance of becoming P.M. when S.B. retires. To my mind this is a great misfortune for I believe he would have had a very good chance and I am sure he is the best man we have for such a position. He and I have been very close together on nearly every point that has arisen and I have a very high opinion of his character and judgment. I would gladly serve under him, as I believe he would under me, but I have never regarded him as a rival, having no ambition to become P.M. myself.[8]

Another dissenting voice came from his son Quintin, the second Lord Hailsham, who argued strongly with his father to persuade him to stay in the House of Commons on the ground that he would eventually succeed Baldwin. The father's promotion to the peerage deprived not only him, but also any descendant of his, of the chance of succeeding to the office of Prime Minister, for it had then apparently become a convention of the Constitution that the Prime Minister must be in the House of Commons. On holiday in the south of France, Quintin sent his father a telegram on Thursday, 29 March, the day on which he received the Great Seal: 'Melancholy congratulations. Reform Lords.'[9] He followed this up with a letter:

Dear Father,
      Some are born unto titles: some achieve them and some have them thrust upon them. Pity the poor third class! I fancy the spirit of Edmund Warre hovers satisfied behind the curved backs of the hack writers as they fill their fountain pens before writing once again the story of his true prophecies. By the time this arrives in England Douglas Hogg will be Lord Chancellor. And what title is the most noble going to choose? Might I suggest Lord Hurstmonceux with a U as being slightly the most attractive? I fear Hellingly is not to be considered owing to its social and medical associations. Hailsham is possible. Maghdam Down, pronounced Maumdan, the same as Gilbert and Sullivan's. Polegate is doubtful. (Do you know Polegate? *Such* a nice little man!). Portland Place, though original, is slightly derivative. Warbleton is suburban: but what about Marylebone? I suppose it will be a barony: I shall not be Viscount Sterneaux? As you know, I would have seen you P.M., but having achieved the honour which you have, you are most certainly to be congratulated even by the elder of your sons on having reached a position well in keeping with the family traditions. Chairman of the East India Company, founder of the Polytechnic, Lord Chancellor and Keeper of the King's Conscience . . . *et alors?* You set Neil and me a sufficiently high standard as it is: let me not hanker after anything higher for you, or we will have to heap Pelion on Ossa in order not to dishonour, let alone adorn your greatness. When I am at the age of 56, and earning £3000 a year at the outside on running down cases, if I am lucky—by

[8] I. Macleod, *Neville Chamberlain* (1961), p. 129.   [9] Hailsham papers.

then this may be lucrative—I shall wave my finger at the House of Lords and tell little Douglas: 'If it hadn't been for old grandpa I shouldn't have been here.' But perhaps little Douglas will not be so little by then. Perhaps he will be old enough to answer (*sicut tuus est mos*) *erat hic non nomine tantum Nobilis*.[1]

Some who read this epistle may be fascinated by the contrast between the writer's prophecies and the actual outcome of events. Others may admire and envy the spontaneously happy family atmosphere which this cheerfully irreverent letter reveals. Not every successful lawyer who has a brilliant son is fortunate enough to be on friendly terms with him. The letter is as honourable to the father as it is to the son.

Thirty-four years later the son, having succeeded to his father's peerage, reverted to the topic in a debate in the House of Lords on the problem of the reluctant heir:

It would be difficult, I think, to find four men who differed more completely in temperament or opinion than Lord Hinchingbrooke, Lord Altrincham, Lord Stansgate, and myself. Yet I doubt not that we have one thing in common, which indeed we share with the great majority of mankind: we all loved our fathers and are proud of the stock from which we came. My Lords, this is no snobbery; it is shared by all classes in every age. It is not foolish pride. It is common piety that we honour our fathers and our mothers, that we praise famous men, and the fathers who begat us.

It has fallen, or will fall to us all in a moment of bereavement—and, believe me, the pain of parting is as great for rich and poor alike, and neither age nor long service nor a lifetime full of honours can really blunt the edge of the axe when it falls —to have to leave or else forswear a life we loved, the ordinary healthy normal business of democratic politics as it is lived today in the Commons or on the hustings, and if we have protested to have to seem in so doing to dishonour our heritage and the families which gave us birth.[2]

---

[1] Hailsham papers. The 2nd Viscount Hailsham attained the age of 56 on 9 October 1963. On the following day he announced that he would disclaim his peerage.

[2] 239 H.L. Deb. 5s. col. 380 (10 April 1962).

CHAPTER III

HOGG WAS CREATED A PEER with the title of Lord Hailsham on 5 April and took his seat in the Lords on 19 April. He had been sworn in as Lord Chancellor in the customary way before Lord Hanworth, M.R., in the Court of Appeal on Monday, 2 April, having received the Great Seal on 29 March.

He at once achieved a dominant position in both the legislative and judicial work of the House. When at the end of the year he announced his intention to remarry, his bride being Mildred, daughter of the Rev. F. Parker Dew, and widow of the Hon. Clive Lawrence, formerly Procurator-General and Treasury Solicitor and brother of Lord Trevethin, he received a congratulatory letter from Buckmaster which ended: 'Let me add one more word. I have sat now for nearly 14 years in our judicial work and have served with five Lord Chancellors but I have never passed a term more pleasant than the one just gone by, nor felt my judgments more strongly supported than by agreement with yours.'[1]

In the Long Vacation of 1928 Hailsham had arranged to go to Canada as the guest of the Canadian Bar Association at its annual meeting. But at the last moment a letter came from the Prime Minister and all had to be altered:

4th August, 1928

My dear Lord Chancellor,
        There is nothing I dislike more than putting a friend to such inconvenience and causing him such disappointment as I am obliged to cause you. But I must ask you to give up your visit to Canada and act as my deputy during my absence. Austen's illness is serious. Not only is there no chance of his going to Geneva but it will be probably a matter of months before he will be at work. He has acted for me before and intended to this month. Balfour is useless for this purpose: Salisbury is under medical orders to go away for two months. For obvious though different reasons, neither the Chancellor of the Exchequer[2] nor the Home Secretary[3] can be considered, nor can anyone of lesser rank. The King whom I persuaded to let you leave the country will now be in a fume, with his Foreign Secretary *hors de combat*, so I have no alternative. I am advising him to this effect. If I could get away later I would stay myself now, but my holiday is strictly bound by the Yarmouth Conference of September 27th, and unless I can get a good holiday before that I should be unfit for the strain of the coming year with the General Election. I have never felt more reluctance than in writing this letter but it is clearly your duty to your country and there is no more to be said.

Yours ever, Stanley Baldwin[4]

[1] Hailsham papers.   [2] Churchill.   [3] Joynson-Hicks.   [4] Hailsham papers.

It was unthinkable that Baldwin should give up his own holiday at Aix-en-Provence, so the Lord Chancellor sacrificed his. He wrote an account of his stewardship to Baldwin on 27 August.

My dear Prime Minister
You may like to know how I am discharging the duties of my high office in your absence. The answer is very nearly by doing nothing at all. There have been one or two presentations to livings which I have swallowed blindly from Geoffrey Fry; one or two lunatics whom I have warded off; a question about the use of Portuguese territory by foreign aviation companies where I have approved the unanimous advice of a departmental committee—and that's all. I went to 10 Downing Street when I was in London 10 days ago to see what it was like to be there as P.M., and spent 10 minutes in pleasant conversation with Mr Vincent; and I went to Waterloo to say goodbye to the Delegation to Canada which I was not to accompany.

Of our colleagues I have heard very little. I spent Tuesday at Newick Park with Jix, and persuaded him not to write a letter to the Press as to his motives in keeping McCartney the spy in prison.[5] And in order to preserve the balance of the Cabinet for you, I went to Chartwell last night to dine and sleep, and had a very pleasant evening with Winston: he is to return my visit on Saturday. I had a letter from Leo about protection, but it wound up with an account of his adventures in the high Alps, so I think he is pretty cheerful. Ronnie McNeill phoned on Friday to say that Miss Balfour thought A.J.B. not at all well, but A.J.B. himself took the opposite view; so we arranged that he should be told that there was no need to come to London, that he should carry on as arranged as Foreign Secretary while Ronnie is away, and that if there should be anything urgent I should see Lindsay.

Lady Chamberlain says Austen is very weak, and she is quite wisely protecting him from visitors; and I do hope he will be put right by his voyage and rest: he has been a great asset and a most pleasant and valuable colleague.

You will have read of Haldane's death. I thought it unnecessary to go to Cloan for the funeral, but of course I wrote and sent a wreath. He will be missed very much in the Lords, and I fear the leadership of the Socialists in that House will devolve into much less cautious, and less reasonable, hands. Russell is their best man, but Parmoor is sure to claim the reversion[6] and he is a stupid as well as a tiresome man.

I hope you are having a good time and getting fit for all the hard work in store: this is really only meant to tell you all goes well.

Yours ever
Hailsham[7]

Before Baldwin left for Aix he paid a brief visit to Wales, and reported on his reception in high good humour:

[5] For McCartney, a Russian spy whom Hogg had prosecuted in January 1928, see R. Jackson, *The Case for the Prosecution* (1962), p. 213.
[6] He did so, and held the office until 1931.   [7] Baldwin papers.

11th August 1928

I had a wonderful time in Wales. I drove through 20 miles of mining valleys: the whole population turned out to look at me and see if I had horns and a tail and I think they were agreeably disappointed. Here and there quite a friendly reception. Infinitely better than I had expected: I was looking for half bricks! The children appeared clean, well cared for and no open signs of distress.[8]

In his period out of office Hailsham attracted attention in October 1930 when he delivered a vigorous speech at the Party Conference at Caxton Hall. The issue was the retention of Baldwin as Leader. The Press Lords had made such extravagant claims that Baldwin had behind him the great mass of sensible opinion in the country when he repudiated them in a fighting speech. Hailsham came to his aid and his speech was loudly cheered by the party.

A few months later, though, there was talk of replacing Baldwin by a Hailsham–Chamberlain combination, which 'is what the city would like',[9] but it came to nothing.

When the National Government was formed in August 1931 Hailsham naturally had hopes of resuming the Great Seal, but Sankey's position as one of MacDonald's three supporters was too strong to be disturbed. Nor was Hailsham successful in obtaining one of the four Cabinet places which MacDonald had allocated for distribution amongst the Conservatives, for the Prime Minister stated that the inclusion of Hailsham in this number would be 'particularly obnoxious to the Labour Party'.[1] The reason for this dislike was the spirited and pugnacious manner in which Hailsham when Attorney-General had piloted the Trade Disputes Bill of 1927 through the Commons. But when the Second National Government was formed after the general election in November 1931 room was found for Hailsham as Secretary of State for War, a post which he combined with the Leadership of the House of Lords.

Hailsham was efficient and conscientious at the War Office, but the times were not appropriate for large-scale changes in the army. On one point Hailsham had no doubts. He was convinced that Germany intended war from the moment that country walked out of the Disarmament Conference in 1931. This opinion was fortified by the events of the Hitler régime, and Hailsham repeatedly told his family that war was inevitable.[2] He pressed this view continuously on his colleagues in the Conservative Party and the National Government, but the only one from whom he received support was the Chancellor of the Exchequer, Neville Chamberlain. Whatever was done to maintain our defences between 1931 and 1935 was due to the joint efforts of Chamberlain and Hailsham. The

---

[8] Hailsham papers.   [9] Macleod, *Chamberlain*, p. 142.   [1] Ibid., p. 152.
[2] Information from the 2nd Viscount Hailsham.

adoption of the policy of appeasement in later years has tended to blur this fact.

In the day-to-day work of government Hailsham's role was really the familiar one of being the Government's maid-of-all-work. He was always ready to undertake disagreeable tasks even though they were outside his departmental duties. So we find him taking an active part at the Ottawa Conference on Empire Free Trade in the summer of 1932. In the following year he summarized his thoughts about that experiment as follows:

The British Commonwealth of Nations is a living organism, and living organisms never stand still. They develop in one direction or another, and there were many of us who thought that, when the Statute of Westminster was agreed to in 1930, matters could not stand still with the British Commonwealth. If, in truth, nothing was left to hold us together except our allegiance to the same king occasions would arise of difference of opinion and of strife, in which even that link might easily be broken.[3]

It was therefore proposed that there should be some form of imperial economic union; this was advocated by R. B. Bennett, the Prime Minister of Canada, and his plan was accepted by each one of the Dominions in 1930. But it happened that the Government in the United Kingdom felt itself constrained by its political affiliations, and by its traditions, to refuse to accept the proposals which Bennett put forward. Bennett nevertheless proposed that the meeting should be adjourned for two years until 1932 when it should meet again in Ottawa. Probably he had in mind that the rejection by the British Government of the proposals for greater economic unity did not really represent the minds of the British people and that if time were given it might well happen that the people as a whole might reject the Government's view. This in fact happened, for in October 1931 the English general election returned a National Government by an overwhelming majority and 'the delegation which represented the United Kingdom came with a mandate from the National Government representing the whole nation to say that those proposals which the Government of 1930 had felt then unable to accept, should be not only accepted, but should be developed to a higher degree than Mr. Bennett would have ventured to suggest when he put them forward in 1930.'[4] In addition the world depression had deepened to such an extent that when the conference met the prices of primary products had sunk to a level never reached before.

Here, on the one side, were the Dominions, in the aggregate the greatest producer, of primary products in the world, seeking above all things a market for those products; and, at the same time, consumers to the extent of billions

[3] *Proceedings of the Canadian Bar Association* (1931).   [4] Ibid.

of pounds of foreign manufactures every year. Here, on the other side, was the United Kingdom, hopelessly over-industrialized, depending for the very physical existence of her people on finding markets for industrial products, and offering on the other side the greatest market in the world for those primary products which the Dominions were able to furnish. It looked so simple to arrange matters that the products of the Dominions should come to British markets and that the foreign manufactures which the Dominions needed should be supplied by British factories. It was only when we came closely to grips with the problem that we found how grave the difficulties were.[5]

The difficulties seem to have been the following. First, there was a hopeless over-production of many primary products calling for some organized restriction of supply yet it was difficult to see how this was to be done without 'arousing the innate fear of an Island people against any restriction of their source of supply, and without at the same time arousing an equally deep rooted dislike of a young Dominion against any reduction of its powers of production.'[6] Secondly, although the Dominions produced primary products in large quantities in many cases these quantities were not enough to satisfy the United Kingdom demands. Thirdly, the foreign manufactures which the Dominions consumed were many of them of a class similar to that which the Dominions themselves produced and the Dominion manufacturers were afraid lest the free entry of British products would swamp their markets and drive them out of business. Fourthly, the United Kingdom had to find foreign markets for more than half of its industrial products and the Dominions also had to find foreign markets for large quantities of their wool and wheat. Yet these markets might easily have been closed if the Commonwealth did anything which the foreigner regarded as unfair or unfriendly. The Conference was nevertheless able to agree that the principle of imperial preference should be accepted by each constituent part of the Empire and further that artificial barriers should as far as possible be swept away and tariff preference be given by reducing tariffs on Empire products rather than by raising tariffs on foreign products. It was also agreed that only worthwhile industries should be protected, and finally, that in the United Kingdom so far as possible free entry should be granted to Dominion products against all protective tariffs. This was a great concession on the part of the United Kingdom in refusing any longer to protect its own manufacturers and producers against the Dominion producers. It was also agreed to set up a tribunal to settle quickly any outstanding disputes.

The Ottawa Conference was an exhausting affair[7] and Hailsham returned home a very tired man. In the public service he had placed upon

---

[5] *Proceedings of the Canadian Bar Association* (1931).   [6] Ibid.
[7] Macleod, *Neville Chamberlain*, p. 160.

his health, already weakened by his serious illness in 1917, a burden which it could not properly bear.

One interesting event before the Conference should be recorded, for it displays one of Hailsham's characteristic traits—an aptitude for suggesting an unconventional but workable solution for a difficulty. The Cabinet in the winter of 1931/2 was divided on how far it could recommend Parliament to enact a protective tariff. Some of its free-trade members (Samuel, Sinclair, Maclean, and Snowden) felt the break with their past too much to bring themselves to support a general tariff. It was thought to be an essential principle of Cabinet government, as authoritative as any statutory rule, that the Cabinet must be unanimous in its conclusions. Failing unanimity the offending Minister or Ministers must resign. Only so, it was thought, could the subtle machinery of responsible government be carried on. A break-up of the Cabinet at that date, so soon after its formation, would have had disastrous effects abroad. It was Hailsham's achievement to see that the fundamental principle of unanimity did not necessarily apply to a situation in which the Government was a coalition and the situation confronting it exceptional. 'Why not agree to differ?' he asked his colleagues at a meeting on 22 January.[8] After a moment's surprise, they agreed, and the House of Commons accepted the novelty. The news was received at Windsor with relief. The King wrote to the Prime Minister: 'I heartily congratulate you on staving off what might have been a national crisis, and feel that the greatest credit is due to you and Lord Hailsham for your patience and wisdom in formulating conditions which in the end proved acceptable to the dissentients.'[9] Hailsham had been responsible for a constitutional precedent which is still debated by students of Cabinet government. Characteristically, he saw little to remember in the incident. Lawyers are often very unlegalistic and apt to take short cuts in their conduct of affairs. The dissenting Ministers resigned after Ottawa—rather oddly, perhaps, for having agreed to a general tariff in January it was pedantic to boggle at imperial preference in August.

Ireland was another matter. The refusal of the de Valera Government to pay the Land Annuities to the British Treasury until a final financial settlement between the two countries had been reached had led to one provocative incident after another. The two countries embarked upon an 'economic war', placing discriminatory tariffs on each other's goods. The Dominions Secretary, J. H. Thomas, was a stupid and dishonest plebeian, constitutionally incapable of seeing the Irish point of view. So Hailsham was once more called in to try to re-establish negotiations between London and Dublin. He made several journeys to Dublin, on one travelling rather unconvincingly in disguise, but nothing came of it all. Hailsham's chief

[8] See 83 H.L. Deb. 5s. col. 551.   [9] Nicolson, *King George V* (1952), p. 497.

adviser on Irish matters was Lord Granard, an Irish peer noted both for his nationalist sympathies and for his knowledge of horseflesh. He in turn, as a mass of surviving correspondence reveals,[1] was advised by someone of extreme anti-de Valera views. It is not surprising that little progress was made. On 5 March 1934 Hailsham wrote to Granard:

> Ever since our interviews with de Valera two years ago, I have felt that he was so much obsessed with his own bigoted views of Anglo-Irish relations of the past that there really was no common meeting-ground on which any settlement with him was possible, and that there was no use, therefore, in making a move towards reopening the first session. I only wish I could take a different view, but everything I read of the proceedings from the Irish Free State only tends to confirm that.[2]

Another difficulty in Commonwealth relations, which in retrospect may seem trivial, but at the time gave rise to serious tension, was caused by the adoption of 'body-line' bowling by the English cricket team in the Test Matches against Australia. Hailsham, who had been elected President of M.C.C. in 1933, was obliged to devote many hours to this problem.

Hailsham's loyalty to his friends is illustrated by a letter he wrote to Baldwin in the last days of the MacDonald Government, when people were only waiting for the Silver Jubilee to be over before the Government could be reconstructed. Hailsham wrote on 28 May 1935:

> My dear S.B.,
>   This letter requires no answer. I keep reading in the papers accounts of a Cabinet reconstruction. It is not my business or intention to ask how much truth there is in the rumours; still less do I desire to ask you about my own position, if any; that is a matter which you will tell me about when the proper time comes. But I notice that in almost all these forecasts it is assumed that Charley Londonderry is going to be dropped. Whether you ought to be doing all this is again a matter for your own decision and one on which you can use your own discretion. I would only urge as a friend that he has worked very hard and loyally for four years, and that under him the Air Ministry was able to produce a vast scheme for expansion, which most of the Cabinet professes to believe a reasonable one, at a very short notice. That argument would not justify me in writing. The real reason for this letter is that I am not sure whether you are informed about the position in the House of Lords, and that it had seemed to me, after some considerable anxiety, that it was perhaps not fair to you that I should not tell you what I gather as its leader. Just now the good will of the House of Lords may be very important to us as a government. The old hereditary nobles of the House of Lords do not really regard myself or Sankey as their representatives. We have come to them and they treat us always very kindly and are very good friends but we were not born one of them. Edward

---

[1] Hailsham papers.   [2] Ibid.

Halifax is, to some extent, suspect as being advanced in his views; the one real hereditary peer in the Government is Charley Londonderry who, incidentally, is the great host to the Conservative Party and is the representative of a family which has long been distinguished in British politics. For that reason he has been able to do things for the government, such as the passing of the Petroleum Act, which I doubt if any of us could have done without him. If he is dropped I cannot help fearing that there will be a good deal of resentment—inarticulate, no doubt—but which will show itself in those who do not take a very keen interest in the National Government and who normally would be likely to support us, staying away or joining Salisbury.[3]

In fact Lord Londonderry was dropped, being succeeded by Cunliffe-Lister (Lord Swinton), whose successful tenure of the office is generally conceded to have helped the R.A.F. to victory in 1940. The Air Ministry under Londonderry was weak: in addition he had involved himself in amicable relations with some of the Nazi leaders. Baldwin was right to dispense with him. As Hailsham had predicted, he was an embittered man ('You threw me to the wolves', he wrote later to Baldwin),[4] not consoled by the Leadership of the House of Lords which he held for a few months until the general election of October 1935. On the other hand, the resentment amongst the Peers which Hailsham had feared did not materialize. Here Hailsham may have been influenced by his personal ties with Londonderry House: he was part of a closely knit circle, known to each other by nicknames, which revolved around Lady Londonderry.

The Government was reconstructed on Friday, 7 June 1935. It was the most rapid change-over known in modern politics. At 4.15 p.m. Mac-Donald drove to the Palace; at 6 p.m. the King held a Council at which the new Ministers received their seals. Sankey's position, as we shall see, was not sufficiently strong for him to be retained in office, and he was succeeded by Hailsham.

[3] Hailsham papers.   [4] G. M. Young, *Stanley Baldwin* (1952), p. 184.

CHAPTER IV

So on 7 June 1935 Hailsham received the Great Seal for the second time. He was in his sixty-fourth year. He wrote to his son Neil, then a member of the staff of the Washington Embassy, explanations of the mysteries of the Great Seal which the beginning of the new reign in January had made a matter of interest:

Now as to the Great Seal. Whenever a new seal is put into commission, the old seal is cancelled by two gentle taps from the king, which are carefully calculated to do no possible damage, and the seal thus technically broken becomes the perquisite of the reigning Lord Chancellor. It does not only happen upon the death of a king; for example, I ought to have got one in 1928, when the change in the King's title necessitated a new seal. Unfortunately the Mint took such a long time to get a new one prepared that the change did not actually take place until Sankey was reigning in my stead, so that he got the new one. I don't know how many years it may take the Mint to prepare a seal for King Edward VIII; if I am fortunate enough to be still in office when they have achieved that effort then I shall get the present one, but I think it is by no means a sure thing.[1]

In fact he received a new seal for George VI, not Edward VIII, on 28 February 1938, the old one being damasked in the traditional way. It is now a family heirloom, together with the white wand or staff of office which he bore as Lord High Steward at the de Clifford trial.

It may be of interest to insert here a letter which Hailsham wrote to Lady Cave's solicitors after her death, when it was found that she had bequeathed him a Lord Chancellor's Purse which she had in her possession and which she always described as 'George's Purse'. She bequeathed it to Hailsham, from whom she had in fact received it, subject to the condition that he had not in the meantime acquired a purse from elsewhere. Hailsham was obliged to write:

With regard to the Lord Chancellor's purse I am afraid I cannot truthfully say that the condition has been fulfilled but I should like you and the residuary legatee, whoever she or he may be to know the circumstances. The Lord Chancellor's purse is the purse emblazoned with the royal arms which is carried in procession before him;[2] it is not his property and a special one is not

[1] Hailsham papers. See also above, pp. 31–33.

[2] The purse is now a mere symbol: it never contains the Great Seal, although it is always carried by the Purse Bearer before the Lord Chancellor when in procession, and placed beside him on the Woolsack. The sole occasion on which it is used except for display is on the Opening of Parliament, when it conveys the signed copy of the Queen's Speech from the Robing Room to the steps of the Throne.

provided for each Chancellor but when the purse becomes tarnished or worn a fresh purse is provided[3] and the existing purse then becomes the property of the Lord Chancellor, whomever he may be, at the moment of the change. Shortly after I became Lord Chancellor for the first time it happened that there was a change, and the result was that the old purse became my property and was handed to me. Unfortunately Lady Cave thought that purses were provided for new Lord Chancellors and she always referred to the old purse as 'George's purse'. Naturally I could not distress her with an elaborate explanation or argument about the matter so I gave her the old purse, but I stipulated that she should return it to me at her death. She promised to do this and I've had letters from her even during my present tenure of office referring to the fact that she had provided that the purse should come to me. She never hinted that the legacy was accompanied by the condition providing that I should not receive it if I had received a similar purse in the meantime. In fact there have been two purses in the interval, one which became the property of Lord Sankey when the Silver Jubilee occurred and one became my property on the occasion of the Coronation last May. I was anxious to have two purses as I have two sons and I want very much that each of them has a memento of my office of Lord Chancellor.[4]

As a result of this letter the solicitors released the purse to Hailsham unconditionally.

Within a few days of resuming his seat on the Woolsack Hailsham received a letter of confidential advice from Dunedin—since 1932 retired after many years of distinguished judicial service.

My dear Douglas,
            So you are back again and I am no longer there. I am so sorry! Now for confidences. Here is your team. Blanesburgh. You will *not* as Sankey did, refuse his resignation.[5] Atkin. Clever. And a good common law lawyer. But obstinate if he has taken a view and quite unpersuadable. Tomlin. To my thinking the best of the bunch. Thankerton. Doing well as to work and law, but making himself a veritable nuisance by excessive talking. I was asked to speak to him, and did quite lately. He took it quite well, but I hear (F. W. Greer my informant) that instead of being better he is worse than ever. Russell. Quick, first rate, but occasionally inclined to be narrow in outlook. Macmillan. Very able, but you cannot put your best into law if you have as many irons in the fire as he has. Wright. I think very well of him, but as, of course, I never sat with him, he being my successor, I am not in a position to form a final judgment. All my other views are founded on experience. Don't leave this letter lying on your table open in the House of Lords!!

Yours ever,
Dunedin[6]

---

[3] Until 1873 a purse was provided annually at a cost of £65. But in that year the maker—an elderly lady—died and the Treasury altered the practice.
[4] Hailsham papers.   [5] Blanesburgh resigned in 1937.   [6] Hailsham papers.

The judgments on his fellow Law Lords which Dunedin expressed are in general acceptable. They were a strong team, though they had some peculiarities. Hailsham presided over them with perfect competence, but he had not the deep interest in the analysis of legal principles which marks the great jurist. His judgments were sound and careful but rather unexciting. A practitioner who finds one of Hailsham's judgments in his favour knows a feeling of solid satisfaction; but it is rather different from the feeling of exhilaration with which he reads a judgment by Cairns or Birkenhead, in which the relevant principles will be analysed and restated in language of clarity and distinction.

In December 1935 Hailsham presided over the trial of Lord de Clifford for manslaughter.[7] Until the law was altered by the Criminal Justice Act, 1948, a peer accused of felony (as distinct from misdemeanour) could not be tried on indictment at Assizes in the normal way but had to be tried before his peers in the House of Lords. Each of the 800-odd peers in the House was entitled to attend, and each was a judge both of law and fact. When the verdict had been given there was no right of appeal. This rather cumbrous procedure was known, perhaps oddly, as 'privilege of peerage'.

Trial before the House of Lords, with the Lord High Steward presiding, must be distinguished from trial in the Court of the Lord High Steward, which was the appropriate procedure when Parliament was not in session. Then the Lord High Steward sat with a jury of twenty-three peers and he was the sole judge of law. It is surprising that the authorities did not take advantage of this simpler procedure in the de Clifford case, for Parliament was not sitting when the accused was committed for trial. Perhaps they were influenced by the doubts which existed about the legal and historical authenticity of the Court of the Lord High Steward—or perhaps by the ruling of Jeffreys L. H. S. in 1686 that the court had no power to adjourn for luncheon.

In the de Clifford case the antique and formidable procedure, requiring all the knowledge and skill of Black Rod and Garter to organize, was revived to deal with a simple case of motor manslaughter. (Elaborate researches culminating in a debate in the House itself were required to determine whether peers should wear their cocked hats.) If the case had been tried at Assizes one Treasury counsel would have conducted the prosecution for a fee of 35 guineas.[8] In the event the trial took place in the Royal Gallery of the House of Lords; eighty-five peers attended, assisted by four High Court judges, and the prosecution was conducted by both Law Officers and two Treasury counsel. Hailsham presided over this imposing gathering, not as Lord Chancellor, but as Lord High Steward—

[7] Reported in *Proceedings on the Trial of Lord de Clifford* (H.M.S.O., 1936).
[8] Though the costs of the defence might have been several hundred pounds.

one of the great offices of state, which in medieval times became so powerful that it was not filled after 1399 except specifically for the duration of each trial. After the Commission appointing him had been read, Hailsham moved from the Woolsack to a specially prepared seat beneath the vacant throne, where he received from Garter and Black Rod his white wand of office. The accused was then summoned to the Bar and the trial proceeded—occasionally rather jerkily, but always dignified. Counsel for the accused obtained a ruling that there was no case for him to answer, and the assembled peers then, individually, placed their right hands on their hearts and declared the accused 'Not guilty, upon mine honour'. The Lord High Steward then broke his staff of office over his knee, and the whole colourful assembly wandered vaguely away. In February 1936 the merits of this procedure were discussed in a debate in the Lords instituted by Sankey:[9] but the impetus for reform was not then strong enough, and Privilege of Peerage was not abolished until 1948.

Hailsham was always ready to help Baldwin. In June, 1936, the Prime Minister, in whose constitution there was a streak of vagueness, failed to appreciate the importance of his personal attendance at a City banquet. The merchants and bankers indicated that they expected better things from a Conservative Prime Minister. Hailsham stepped into the breach and received a grateful note from Downing Street on 26 June 1936:

My dear Douglas,
    I must put on record before I retire to bed at Chequers via the Leys School:[1] (a) my asininity in the whole matter of the city dinner. (b) my warm appreciation of your ready help in time of trouble. This note to be published in both our lives and printed in capitals.

Ever yours,
S.B.[2]

27th June 1936

My dear P.M.,
    You shouldn't have added to your labours by writing; but the letter shall be added to the family archives! I was only sorry that on this occasion the willingness of the mouse to help the lion did not avail to set that king of beasts free from one of his entanglements! Do get a rest and come back fit to help us in all these horrid perplexities.

Yours ever,
Hailsham[3]

Hailsham was in the Prime Minister's inner circle. As often happens with men who are seeing each other constantly, and are not in any case

[9] 99 H.L. Deb. 5s. col. 381.   [1] Where he presented the prizes on the 26th.
[2] Hailsham papers.   [3] Baldwin papers.

good correspondents, few letters have survived. But occasionally the veil is lifted. Thus on 20 September 1935 Baldwin wrote:

> 10 Downing Street,
> Whitehall
>
> My dear Douglas,
>   I look forward to seeing you on Tuesday as you suggest. I go to London on Sunday for good but unfortunately it is my turn at Balmoral next week and that falls awkwardly.
>   I have been very worried and shall be glad to have a talk.
>   Ll.G's speech in to-day's Times is so typical!
>   He is a wicked little fellow.
>   'If you want to get into a government' as he observed the other day to a friend of mine 'you must make a nuisance of yourself till they take you in'. He is not an Englishman and underrates the quiet resistance of the English, however stupid.
>
>   Yours ever
>   S.B.[4]

The invasion of the Rhineland was perhaps the event which first made the Baldwin Government as a whole realize the kind of opponent they would have to face. On 10 March 1936 Hailsham wrote to his son Neil:

> I went to Carter's Corner last Saturday for a solitary weekend; no sooner had I got there than I began receiving telephone messages and express messengers and pouches and ultimately I had to come back the next day to read a lot of papers for the Cabinet on Monday morning. It has been and is a very anxious time for us all, and it has kept us very much occupied and concerned. I had never thought that the demilitarized zone would last for ever; but marching into it as Hitler has done is a typical instance of German mentality; it makes one wonder what is the use of negotiating a treaty with a nation which will only observe it so long as it is convenient and will tear it up when it is inconvenient; the 1914 'scrap-of-paper'-attitude seems singularly apposite today.[5]

The major domestic political event of 1936 was the abdication of the new king. Normally the Lord Chancellor, as Keeper of the King's Conscience, would be intimately concerned in such an affair, but in fact Hailsham was somewhat out of touch with events, for a stroke in the late summer had made it necessary for him to obtain leave of absence from all his duties. But in common with well-informed people generally, he knew what was going on and maintained a fairly close contact with Marlborough House. On 17 October 1936 he wrote to his son Neil in Washington:

> I am rather shocked, but not surprised, to hear of the American press exploiting the King's infatuation. So far in England almost everyone seems to be

[4] Hailsham papers.   [5] Ibid.

talking about it, but nothing has appeared in print. I think Rothermere and Beaverbrook and even the *Daily Herald* are really behaving quite well. But it is a little difficult when he flaunts the lady so publicly. When he opened parliament, she was in the 2nd royal car! No one seems to know what is going to happen.[6]

Events thereafter moved with dramatic speed. Baldwin showed an extraordinary skill and assurance and on 10 December Edward VIII abdicated. The previous day Hailsham had written to Halifax:

Incidentally, I suppose that you will have read in the *Times* yesterday the reference to myself, which in effect says that I was clinging to office, although it was in the public interest that I should vacate it,[7] regardless of the fact that I was imposing an undue strain on yourself and on the P.M. I very nearly wrote to you about this, but I decided to see Neville and get him to have a statement sent to the *Times* which would deal with the attack. As a matter of fact I am confident that nothing could be less welcome to the P.M. than having, in addition to the constitutional difficulty, the task of finding a new Cabinet colleague just now. As far as you are concerned, I hope that my absence has not been a real source of trouble to you and I am fortified in that belief owing to the fact that the statements made in the House would of necessity have been made in any event by the leader and no one else, and it would not have been possible for the Lord Chancellor to elaborate or comment on them at all. I imagine that Lothian inspired the paragraph, but I hope that he is as wrong in the last part of this statement as I am sure he is in the earlier sentences; in other words I hope that the Peers have not repented of the leave of absence which they gave me in October last. I think you know that in October I offered my resignation to the P.M. and I only agreed to continue in office on his assurance that he wished it, and on the condition I got the leave of the House of Lords to absent myself until the next session.

The letter continued:

I have followed with the very greatest interest and sympathy the Cabinet's course in the 'crisis'; I think that they have made no mistake at all. I myself anticipated this development as early as May last year and mentioned it to Neville and through him to the P.M., and the advice I then gave as to the constitutional position is exactly the same as that which is embodied in the P.M.'s statement on Friday last. Many thanks for your report on Roche's conversation.[8] One is so apt to hear the disagreeable things that are said about one, that it is very pleasant to get the opposite.

[6] Hailsham papers.
[7] *The Times* had said (8 December) that although everyone had sympathy for the Lord Chancellor in his illness, it was most unfortunate that the House of Lords should be deprived of its chief legal adviser at such an important moment.
[8] In a letter of 3 December Halifax had reported Roche as speaking favourably of Hailsham.

P.S. I have just ascertained that I have suspected Lothian unjustly and that the real culprit is probably a little man called [. . .] who has a grievance against me because he made a number of blunders in reporting the de Clifford Trial and again in commenting upon the constitutional issues which arose on the death of King George V; because I then wrote to Dawson complaining of his mistakes and of the trouble which they caused to us.[9]

A reply came from Halifax on 11 December:

I was greatly vexed by *The Times* note in regard to yourself and have been waiting to see Geoffrey Dawson to reproach him. He is, I think, to blame for letting a thing like that go in before making sure of his facts, quite apart from everything else. I told the P.M. some time ago that, although we naturally miss you very much in the House of Lords, we should, I had no doubt, succeed in carrying on, though we might from time to time get into legal knots! This, however, mercifully has not happened, and, as you know, the House is generous to difficulties which are of no man's making, and I feel sure that if any difficulty of the sort should arise the House will go more than half way to help us out of it. I anticipated that we might have had some constitutional argument this morning from the Law Lords in regard to the preamble of this Abdication Bill and in criticism of the Statute of Westminster. I took the precaution, accordingly, of getting hold of Maugham at the Attorney's suggestion, and, although he was not very happy about the wording, I convinced him that it was too late to alter it, as it had been agreed by all the named Dominions, and that we shall rely on him to make a helpful contribution if anybody else was tiresome. In the event, we negatived the motion for Committee with general assent, and the thing went through in five minutes. It was a dramatic moment when Badeley pronounced the time-honoured formula converting the Sovereign into a Subject. The more I reflect upon it, the more cause for thankfulness I feel there is in the matter having turned out as it has. I do not believe that we could ever have restored the prestige of the Crown without a change, and I do not feel that any of us would have felt secure against repetition of grave trouble if we had weathered this storm. With all the misery of it there has been a good deal in the behaviour of the country, and particularly of Parliament, of which we may be legitimately proud. I fancy the English are the only people who could have behaved with such dignity and restraint.[6]

One of Hailsham's major worries during this period was the Judicial Committee of the Privy Council. The rising tide of nationalism in the Dominions was opposed to the continuance of the right of Appeal to London, and it was a question whether the dominion legislatures had power, either under the Statute of Westminster or otherwise, to abolish it. In two epoch-making decisions the Judicial Committee in 1935, presided over by Sankey, had held that the Irish Free State had power to abolish the appeal generally, and Canada so far as criminal cases were

[9] Hailsham papers.   [1] Ibid.

concerned.[2] But problems remained. Hailsham wrote to Atkin on 17 November 1936:

I think that you and I are both agreed as to the paramount importance of retaining the Appeal to the Privy Council from the Dominions of the Crown and as to the importance of constituting a board which will inspire confidence by its decisions in all parts of the Empire. I am glad to tell you that I have recently heard indirectly that no less than four of the Canadian Counsel which were engaged in the recent Privy Council Appeal[3] have severally expressed the greatest possible satisfaction at the constitution of the Board, so that obviously you were all impressing as I felt sure that you would do. The truth is that we both miss Buckmaster more than ever from the Supreme Tribunals, but nonetheless, I expect the decisions, when given, will carry conviction, which after all is the best test of the strength of the tribunal. I can only say again how sorry I am that I should leave my colleagues to carry the burden of this judicial work unassisted by their official head.

During his term of office Hailsham appointed the following men to the High Court Bench: Macnaghten, Lewis, Wrottesley, Tucker, and Henn Collins to the King's Bench Division; Maugham, Luxmoore, Simonds, and Morton to the Chancery Division; and Hodson to the Probate, Divorce, and Admiralty Division. These were good appointments—they included two future Lord Chancellors (Maugham and Simonds), three Law Lords (Tucker, Morton, Hodson), and two Lords Justices (Luxmoore, Wrottesley).

We shall see that, ardent Conservative politician though he was, Hailsham was adamant on the necessity for making judicial appointments purely on merit.[4] His appointments to the county court and magisterial Benches were also judged sound by competent observers.

One aspect of his work, his editorship of the second edition of Halbury's *Laws of England*, was very carefully supervised. Hailsham refused to treat his connection with that great work as being merely titular, and insisted on scanning the proofs carefully himself.

---

[2] *Moore* v. *Att.-Gen. of the I.F.S.*; *British Coal Corporation* v. *The King*.

[3] This was the very important case of *Att.-Gen. for Canada* v. *Att.-Gen. for Ontario* [1937] A.C. 326, in which the Judicial Committee had given a decision adverse to the power of the Canadian Parliament to give legislative effect to an international treaty.

[4] See below, p. 522.

CHAPTER V

HAILSHAM WAS CONTINUED IN OFFICE by Chamberlain when he succeeded Baldwin in May 1937. Although he was never in Chamberlain's innermost circle, as he had been in Baldwin's, he admired and respected the Prime Minister, but he was not a confidant. This was revealed when Hailsham wrote to his son Neil on 21 February 1938 with reference to the resignation of the Foreign Secretary:

I can't tell you why Anthony resigned because I couldn't make out myself. The actual difference between him and the P.M. and the bulk of the Cabinet was that the P.M. wanted conversations to start with Italy immediately and Anthony wanted to postpone them. But I imagine it must have gone deeper than that. He definitely had agreed to the conversations to start at some time as long ago as last July. I imagine at this moment he is telling the House of Commons why he left; Sam Hoare told me that when he, Sam, went with Anthony to the Foreign Office from the Cabinet on Saturday afternoon he found the Foreign Secretary's room crowded with Left Wingers and pressmen and private secretaries all obviously waiting to support him in a decision already taken; and it is true that the *Daily Express* last week announced that there were grave differences between Anthony and the P.M. and that a Cabinet crisis was imminent and resignations would follow. At that time neither the Cabinet nor, I think, the P.M. had any idea that there was a difference of opinion between Anthony and ourselves[1] and I, therefore, assume that the *Daily Express* had its information from Anthony or somebody in his entourage, and that he had already then decided to break with us. It is a very disagreeable shock for the government because he has great support in the country, and it prejudices the chances of the conversations being successful.[2]

It had now become plain that the burden of the Woolsack was too much for Hailsham in his weakened state of health. Negotiations were set on foot which resulted in the appointment of Maugham. It was agreed that Hailsham should succeed to the sinecure office of Lord President of the Council. (Some twenty years later his son Quintin was to hold this office on two different occasions (1957–9, 1960–3), combining it on the first occasion with the party chairmanship and on the second with the very busy and important post of Minister for Science.) He delivered up the Great Seal on 15 March, only a fortnight after he had received the new Great Seal of George VI together with the damasked Seal of George V. A few days later he wrote to a friend:

[1] The Earl of Avon gives quite a different impression: *The Eden Memoirs* (1962), ch. XIV.   [2] All quotations in this chapter are from the Hailsham papers.

I knew of course that I was going to resign my office, but I did not know who my successor was or what the date will be or whether I should accept the Lord Presidency of the Council or just fade out; and the King's pleasure had not been taken, so that you will understand that I could not put anything in writing. I feel that I am dropping my task unfinished and that I have not stayed the course; but I promised to stay on as Lord President, which is a lighter job, so that I may keep in touch with the government's responsibilities and decisions.

Again he wrote on 16 March:

Last Tuesday I actually resigned from the Woolsack. I was sitting on Monday evening for the Foreign Office statement, and went to the Privy Council on Tuesday to be sworn in as Lord President. Now I am installed in Whitehall with a very nice room and pleasant people to work with, and I think the job will prove quite interesting. I have been continued on my various Cabinet committees. This afternoon in the House there were valedictory speeches and bouquets for me and Halifax and Maugham. I have a nice room in the House of Commons, not of course a suite equal to the Lord Chancellor's, but a room looking out on to King Richard I's statue and practically over my old entrance when I was originally Lord Chancellor.

Hailsham performed his parliamentary duties assiduously. He kept a table showing the comparative attendances at Divisions of himself and other government peers, from which it appears that he was easily top of the list.

On 24 March he wrote again:

I am afraid that you will all have a stiff job to hold the Portuguese to our alliance and prevent them breaking away to the Dictator states; and the folly of the Foreign Office in refusing to recognize Franco and in identifying him with the dictator powers is bearing fruit now that it seems apparent that he will win. If they hadn't taken up the attitude they did, the victory of Franco over the Reds would not have been identified with a victory of the dictator states over the democracies as I am afraid it must be now. However it is no good crying over spilt milk and it remains to try and repair the damage.

Again he wrote on 3 May 1938:

The budget has gone quite extraordinarily well in the House. The Socialists of course are using the 2d. on tea for all they are worth in the constituencies, and they are making a big splash with 'Chamberlain must go', 'Vote for Labour and Peace', 'Arms for Spain'. I expect that they will get away with this in the bye-elections, but I hope that the country will gradually come to realize that the Socialist policy means not peace but war, and that Neville's policy leads to agreements and appeasement. No doubt the Socialists do not realize that they are being wagged by their Communist tail in tune with the orders from Moscow, which detests any agreement with the Fascist powers and which detests anything which prevents the so-called capitalist countries joining in a general war.

R 821321

The great international crisis of the autumn of 1938 found Hailsham a loyal supporter of Chamberlain. He wrote to Londonderry on 27 September:

I have practically no time for my private affairs in these strenuous days. The P.M. is standing up to the strain most wonderfully. And yesterday his Cabinet showed us absolutely united. I wish the Germans could be made to realize that they could have got everything they legitimately wanted from Berchtesgaden, but that the Godesberg demands and the method of force instead of reason are absolutely inadmissible for the future of democracy and civilization.

The following day, 28 September, there was the dramatic scene in the House when Chamberlain's speech was interrupted by the arrival of Hitler's note of invitation to a conference at Munich. A scene of hysterical relief occurred on the floor of the House unparalleled in modern times. Hailsham wrote to a friend on 29 September:

I did not listen to the Prime Minister's speech, I was too tired; but Lord Londonderry heard it in the Lords' library and he said that it was the most moving speech that he had ever heard. It was a curious dramatic touch that Hitler's answer to his final appeal should arrive when he was speaking and he had not seen it until he had read it to the House. I saw him and Anne Chamberlain afterwards. She showed me the draft in his own hand of his telegram which he has sent to Hitler and Mussolini. In his broadcast he sounded a very tired man but he did not show any signs of exhaustion in his face. I think Neville will bring back Peace from Munich and I hope that it will be Peace with Honour.

A few days later he produced as good a brief defence of the melancholy agreement of Munich as could be made.

I still hope that the P.M. will not decide to go to the country; and I am still sceptical about Hitler's good intentions. My defence of the government policy would be not faith in Hitler so much as distrust in our allies and of our preparedness to meet his attack, coupled with the consciousness that nothing that we could have done would have availed Czechoslovakia. It would only have brought worse disaster upon that unfortunate country.

After he had retired Hailsham penned some further thoughts on foreign affairs. On 24 November 1938:

I am afraid the policy of appeasement looks as if it were going to be dished by the Nazis, and I only hope it won't bring down Neville with it. Personally I could not contemplate surrendering any non-Germanic peoples to Nazi rule in existing circumstances. In fact I was thinking of flying out to Tanganyika, meeting the settlers there and then coming back and stumping the country; but I am glad to see that this is no longer necessary.

The question of surrendering Tanganyika ('German East' to an older generation) had first been raised by Halifax after his visit to Hitler in November 1937. It had little support even in the Government.

Later again he wrote:

I always told my colleagues after Munich that the country would be profoundly grateful for peace but very anxious to find a scapegoat for what they would regard as humiliating terms; and unfortunately it seems that I was right. The government are doing quite the right things, and any other government in this country would be infinitely worse, not only for our foreign, but also for our domestic welfare, but I'm afraid people don't think so.

Finally, on 3 May 1939: 'Personally I am more convinced than ever that the policy of guarantees in Eastern Europe and its accompaniment of a Russian alliance is a mistake; if there is one thing that I could hate more than a Nazi hun it is a Bolshevik Communist, so that I am well out of the Government.'

In the lull after Munich Chamberlain decided to reconstruct the Cabinet. He was anxious to bring in Runciman, an elderly Liberal statesman who had been called out of retirement to conduct some thankless negotiations with the Czechs. It was indicated to Hailsham that his place was required. He wrote to Sir Herbert Creedy on 26 October 1938, informing him that he would be resigning his office on the 27th:

The news will be published tomorrow, but I don't want you to get the information from the daily papers, but please keep this confidential until it is published. Please also don't let people say that I am retiring on the grounds of ill-health; the real fact is what I state in my letter of resignation, that the P.M. wants to find a place for Walter Runciman and he is not prepared to take on the administration of a big department, so that it is desirable to make room for him in the comparative sinecure of the Lord Presidency.

On 3 November 1938 Hailsham received a letter from Hoare condoling with him on his departure from the Government: 'Your great services make our loss very conspicuous, but they do more than this, they enhance the patriotic sacrifice you have made in facilitating Neville's re-arrangements.'

There was also a letter from Hankey, expressing sympathy, to which a reply on 7 November runs: 'I was very sorry to give up my job, which I thought I could have carried on certainly throughout this parliament, but as I said in my letter to Neville (though not in these terms!) I felt that my room might be more useful to him than my company.'

In fact Runciman was an exhausted man, and was obliged to resign office because of ill-health the following year.

It might have been thought appropriate that Hailsham should receive another step in the peerage (he had been promoted Viscount in the Dissolution Honours List of 1929). But Chamberlain did no more than offer a G.B.E. on 13 December, which was refused in a letter of the following day: 'Many thanks for your letter; I appreciate your kindly thought and friendliness which prompted it; but under all the circumstances I hope you will forgive my saying that I don't want a G.B.E., and should prefer that my name should not be put forward.'

After he had retired Hailsham wrote to the President of the Primrose League: 'I'm afraid I have made it a rule not to apply for an honour either for myself or for anybody else. When I was at the Bar I had a lurid light cast upon Lloyd George's trafficking in Honours, and when I was a member of the Government I had numberless people trying to persuade me to get them titles; so that I have long decided that I would not have anything to do with such aspirations.'

(It may be recalled that in 1868 Chelmsford, on being dismissed by Disraeli, had angrily refused the G.C.B. on the ground that a step in the peerage was the only honour which could properly be given to a retiring Chancellor: 'They might as well have offered me the Victoria Cross.' Yet in recent times the G.C.B. has been thought appropriate for a Lord Chief Justice retiring after an exceptionally distinguished term of office.)

The gloomy month of October 1938 was lightened for Hailsham by the return of his son Quintin as Member of Parliament for Oxford City. Hailsham made his last public speech in Oxford Town Hall to open his son's campaign. All the opposition to the policy of appeasement was focused on this election, and the fight was severe. Hailsham wrote to his son Neil:

We expected the Liberals and Socialists each to put up a candidate, but now, alas, they have both withdrawn in favour of one Lindsay, the Master of Balliol, and ex-Vice-Chancellor of the University, who is a Bolshy, and who stands as an Independent-Progressive candidate in order to unite the anti-government vote, so Quintin will have quite a stiff fight.

A few days later Hailsham wrote to Quintin:

I noticed Lindsay's speech in which he referred to the government's 'indecision'. The government in fact, in Abyssinia, in Manchuria and in China followed the lead of the League of Nations; in Spain they rigorously observed the non-intervention agreement in which all the powers were associated, including Russia. In Czechoslovakia they certainly were not guilty of any indecision, and they certainly made the position plain both to the Germans and the Czechs long before the crisis. You might get some of your people to turn up the date at which the public announcement was made. I wonder whether Lindsay would be prepared to say the Government ought to have gone to war with Japan about Manchuria and about China, with Italy about Abyssinia and with Germany and Italy about Czechoslovakia, and provoked a general world war about Spain, which I think would be the only 'decision' which they could have been reproached with not making.

The Cabinet were relieved to learn that the pain of departure from office had been softened by his son's success.

Hailsham found enforced inactivity very trying. He had never been idle and he did not enjoy the experience now. Always equable in temper, even under strain, a certain note of petulance now began to creep into his talk and correspondence. He began to quarrel—with the Inland Revenue Commissioners, with local authorities, with Whitehall, with his tenants. One letter from those days is enough to illustrate this sad tendency. It was to Walter Elliot, the Minister of Health:

About a fortnight ago I received from the Hailsham Rural District Council an enquiry as to how many children I was prepared to take at my country home and at a cottage standing in the grounds.

I wrote to them explaining the situation of the house and cottage and asking for some further details of what they wanted. They then professed themselves unable to give the details and asked me whether I would object to their sending my letters up to your Ministry, to which I was very pleased to give my consent. After that, either the Hailsham District Council or the Ministry seems to have published my enquiries and the result has been to let loose upon me a deluge of letters coming from all over the country supporting what they describe as my opposition to the Ministry's compulsory billetting scheme.

I do not propose to accept the rôle of John Hampden for which my correspondents seem anxious to cast me, and I don't imagine that you are prepared to adopt the part of Strafford! But I feel I ought to let you know the intense and widespread feeling which is running through the country against the scheme and the methods adopted to enforce it. I have had pitiful letters from people who have been threatened and who think that there is a compulsory scheme, and that they will be compelled to take the children who are allotted to them. All sorts of objections have been raised with which I do not propose to trouble you. But I am bound in fairness to pass on to you the knowledge I have acquired of the widespread indignation which the scheme is causing and of the element of compulsion which the local authorities are seeking to introduce into it. I don't for a moment suppose that you have any cognisance of the methods which are being used, but in view of the wide areas from which my letters come I find it difficult to believe that the local authorities have simultaneously started using these threats unless somebody at the Ministry is responsible. Voluntary billetting is all very well, although personally I should have thought that hutments or camps and empty houses and public buildings were infinitely preferable, but a voluntary scheme enforced by threats is too closely copied from Communist Russia or from Nazi Germany ever to be popular in this country. To give you an example of what I mean, one correspondent tells me that he was told that if he would not take children then the Government would compel him to take adults in case of war. One old lady who had an old and invalid husband, an ex-Army officer, living alone, asked me whether I could tell her if she did the three months' imprisonment which she understood was the penalty for refusal would her husband be excused from taking the children. I myself was warned or threatened that if I did not volunteer to accept children I should be compelled to take either criminals or prostitutes!

One of Hailsham's interests in retirement was the Polytechnic. Keenly aware of his family responsibilities, he yet felt obliged to refuse the Presidency in 1944 on the death of the second President, Sir Kynaston Studd. But as Chairman of the Board of Governors he was able to secure the appointment of Mr. Bernard Studd.

Hailsham's last years were trying for a man who had been active—paralysed from a second stroke, he lingered on at Carter's Corner Place all through the war and the difficult years of peace. His old political friends were either dead, as with Chamberlain and Londonderry, or themselves incapacitated, as with Baldwin. He took pride in the successful legal and political career of his son Quintin, but in the nature of things his contacts with the younger generation were few. He died at his home on 16 August 1950 and was buried at All Saints, Herstmonceux, a few days later. His grave is at the western boundary of the churchyard looking out over the flat coastal strip to the waters of the English Channel. Beside it is the grave of his stepson Edward Marjoribanks (always 'my son' to Hailsham), who had killed himself in 1930 while temporarily unbalanced by the strain of a career which promised to be one of great brilliance. Hailsham's estate was sworn for probate at £225,032.

Hailsham was a very straightforward and uncomplicated man. He was in many ways a typical representative of English Conservatism of a kind which his fellow-countrymen once admired greatly. Bred in the happy atmosphere of tolerant good-will which marked the comfortable classes of England before 1914 he made no ostentatious display of his great talents, and had considerable reserves of energy upon which to draw when he was called to devote himself to the public service. All that he did was done well, but without strain or show and without any desire for private gain or satisfaction, except for a legitimate pride in duty done.

APPENDIX

In *Contract* there are two good judgments soon after Hailsham became Lord Chancellor—*Reckitt* v. *Barnett, Pembroke, and Slater Ltd.* [1929] A.C. 176, on the true extent of a power of attorney, and *Gosse Millerd Ltd.* v. *Canadian Merchant Marine Ltd.* [1929] A.C. 223, on the effect of negligence on a contract for the carriage of goods by sea. In *The Clan Matheson* [1929] A.C. 514 he dealt clearly with the perennial difficulty of ascertaining whether the events in question constituted the proximate cause of the loss under a policy of marine insurance. In the great case of *Bell* v. *Lever Bros.* [1932] A.C. 161, in which the House of Lords considered the effect of mutual or common mistake upon an otherwise valid contract, Hailsham was content to concur with the judgment of Lord Warrington.

In *Torts* Hailsham delivered an important judgment in *Robert Addie & Sons (Collieries) Ltd.* v. *Dumbreck* [1929] A.C. 358, affirming the common law rule that an occupier of land owes no duty of care to a trespasser other than that of not inflicting intentional injury. Many attempts have been made before and since 1929 to whittle down the rule, especially where, as in Addie's case, the plaintiff is a child. Thus in *Excelsior Wire Rope Co.* v. *Callan* [1930] A.C. 404 a differently constituted House of Lords managed to distinguish Addie's case. The task of reconciling the two decisions has given rise to constant difficulties, but all attempts at reconciliation and explanation have to start from Hailsham's judgment, which occupies a central position as an orthodox exposition of the traditional view. One phrase in his judgment has given rise to difficulties later. In reviewing the general nature of an occupier's liability to his visitors, Hailsham said that to a licensee the duty was no higher than that of preventing damage from a trap 'which is known—or ought to be known—to the occupier'. The suggestion that the licensor was liable for hidden dangers of which he ought to know was criticized on the ground that if it were true there would be no difference between the duty of an invitor and that of a licensor, and in five cases in the Court of Appeal Hailsham's remarks were said to have been made *per incuriam* (see Salmond on Torts, 13th ed., p. 529). But in recent years an alternative explanation which would save the authority of Hailsham's statement has been put forward and generally accepted—namely, that although a licensor is not liable if he has failed to ascertain the existence of the physical facts which constitute the danger, he will not be excused if, knowing those facts, he alleges that he did not appreciate the extent of the risk which they involved: see *Hawkins* v. *Coulsdon and Purley U.D.C.* [1954] 1 Q.B. 319.

In *Swadling* v. *Cooper* [1931] A.C. 1 Hailsham delivered an important judgment on the difficult doctrine of 'last opportunity' in the field of contributory negligence. It was a valiant attempt to provide a simple test instead of the mass of complex and subtle rules which had bedevilled the law on this topic, and as such was welcomed by judges and practitioners, though it was not until the Law Reform (Contributory Negligence) Act, 1945, had changed the whole basis of the law that it was possible to state it in a really satisfactory way.

Two other brief but clear and sensible judgments on torts may be mentioned. In *Arneil* v. *Paterson* [1931] A.C. 560 Hailsham considered the liability of the owners of two dogs for damage done while acting in concert, and in *Tolley* v. *J. S. Fry & Sons* [1931] A.C. 333 he considered the scope of the law relating to an innuendo in an action for libel.

In *Constitutional Law* Hailsham delivered an important judgment in *Eshugbayai Eleko* v. *Government of Nigeria* [1928] A.C. 459 holding that an unsuccessful applicant for the writ of habeas corpus could renew his application before each High Court judge in turn. There was much to be said in support of this judgment both on principle and authority, but it was pointed out that the technical reasoning in the judgment rested on a misinterpretation of the effect of the Judicature Acts (66 L.Q.R. 79), and in *Re Hastings* (No. 2) [1959] 1 Q.B. 358 these criticisms were accepted by the Divisional Court. In consequence the Administration of Justice Act, 1960, section 14(2), reversed the decision in *Eleko* by providing that no application for habeas corpus should be made again on the same grounds to the same or any other court or judge. In *Ecclesiastical Law* Hailsham's judgment in *St. Nicholas Acons* v. *L.C.C.* [1928] A.C. 469 (erection of buildings in churchyards) has been found useful in later cases (see *Re St. Peter the Great, Chichester* [1961] 1 W.L.R. 907). In *Family Law* there is an oft-cited judgment in *Hyman* v. *Hyman* [1929] A.C. 601, holding that a wife cannot contract not to apply to the court for maintenance.

Equity was not a subject which Hailsham would have claimed to be expert in, but in *Inch Noriah* v. *Shaik Allie Bin Omar* [1929] A.C. 127 he delivered a good judgment on the need to uphold the rule that in appropriate cases the presumption of undue influence must be rebutted in the case of voluntary gifts.

LORD SANKEY

CHAPTER I

THE EARLIEST MENTION of the name of Sankey is in 1207, when one Gerard de Sanki (called 'the carpenter') obtained land at Sankey, near Prescot, Lancashire, from Paganus de Vylers, an ancestor of the Earls of Jersey. Some of the family settled in Ireland, but the main branches remained in England, where they spread into many counties. The branch to which the future Lord Chancellor belonged were settled for several generations as yeomen farmers near Harbledown in Kent.[1] But the father of the Lord Chancellor, Thomas Sankey, owned a small general shop in Moreton-in-Marsh. He combined a drapery business with that of an undertaker. The house, with its handsome eighteenth-century bow-front, still exists as an antique shop. There John Sankey was born on 26 October 1866 the eldest child of his parents. His mother was Catalina, daughter of James Dewsbury, clerk, of Manchester, by whom Thomas Sankey had four more children. There was also a half-brother by an earlier marriage. His father died when John was a small boy and the mother, a woman of strong character, removed the young family to Cardiff, where two of her husband's brothers had settled and prospered.

John Sankey attended the local Anglican primary school in Stacey Road before being sent to Lancing College—'a small public-school of ecclesiastical temper on the South Downs', as its most famous old boy has described it in one of his early novels. The expenses of his education were met by a local vicar, Canon Beck. To Lancing Sankey remained devoted for the rest of his life: he actively supported all its activities and organizations, and in later years provided £8,000 to found scholarships to enable boys to go to Oxford.[2]

Sankey himself matriculated at Jesus College in 1885, having obtained an Entrance Scholarship earlier in the year. He was placed in the Second Class in both Honour Moderations and the Final School of Modern History. His Oxford career was in general undistinguished, apart from a mild interest in athletics. As was customary with high-minded undergraduates in those days, he worked in a Stepney Boys' Club during the vacations. He then decided to stay up for a fifth year in order to read for the B.C.L. at the same time as he was eating dinners at the Middle Temple, which he had joined on 28 October 1889. In June 1891 he was placed in the Third Class in the B.C.L. examination. He preserved his examination

[1] The Sankey papers contain an elaborate privately printed family tree.
[2] Sankey papers.

papers carefully and annotated them fully.[3] He was called to the Bar on 29 June 1892.

After being called he spent six months as pupil in the chambers of William Pickford, then in the full tide of a busy commercial practice. In later years Sankey was to succeed to Pickford's position both in the High Court and the Court of Appeal. He also inherited his judicial robes.

For a time he supplemented his income by teaching at St. Paul's Preparatory School, Colet Court. Amongst his pupils was the future Compton Mackenzie.[4] Although there was never very much money, a devoted family somehow found enough to enable him to survive the early difficult years. In any event, Sankey was not an extravagant man. All expenditure, down to the purchase of penny stamps, was entered carefully in one of a series of notebooks which still survive.[5] Jesus was not a college for wealthy men, but even so his battels were noticeably small—e.g. £33. 10s. 4d. for the first quarter of 1889, towards which he was credited with a dividend from his scholarship of £27, leaving a debit balance of only £6.

Almost at once he started to practise on the South Wales circuit. He made Cardiff his centre and his first brief, on 13 December 1892, was at quarter sessions there—a successful defence of one of two prisoners who were accused of robbery with violence. The brief came from Harry Cousins of the firm of Ingledew & Co., and was marked at two guineas. In later years Cousins provided Sankey with many briefs, and he in turn in 1934 procured a knighthood for his old friend. In his first years at the Bar Sankey made 32 guineas. His first civil bill at Assizes was not obtained until 1894, but his Fee Book for those years (which has survived) shows that his earnings rose steadily.

In 1893–4 he made £52. 6d. 0d.; in 1894–5, £188. 10s. 6d.; in 1895–6, £426. 5s. 6d.; in 1896–7, £658. 12s. 0d. The following year, 1897–8, saw a sharp rise to £1,124. 15s. 6d., while for 1898–9 the figure was £1,237. 12s. 0d. A few years later he was earning £5,000 a year.[6]

After the 1897 Act he specialized in Workmen's Compensation cases, and acquired personal knowledge of the hazards and difficulties of the miner's life which was to be of great use in later years when he presided over the Coal Commission.

By now he felt strong enough to consider a move to London with its corollary—an application for a silk gown. He took advice from various people, including Mr. Justice Bigham. The judge strongly supported the proposal. Years later, when Sankey had received the Great Seal, his very first act was to call upon the judge, now, under the title of Lord Mersey,

[3] Sankey papers.   [4] Compton Mackenzie, *Mezzotint* (1958), p. 17.
[5] Sankey papers.   [6] The Sankey papers contain his fee-books for these years.

PLATE 19

Lord Sankey with Miss Edith Sankey leaving St. Paul's on Hospital Sunday

PLATE 20

Lord Sankey in later life

living in retirement, in order to express his gratitude for the advice which had encouraged him to embark upon his successful London career.[7] Amongst his papers he preserved a telegram from the Sub-Treasurer of Lincoln's Inn on 5 March 1907 which ran: 'Application for Chambers Mitre Court buildings accepted.' Sankey endorsed it: 'This telegram completed my intention to go to London.'

Then came the task of persuading Lord Loreburn to grant him silk. After one unsuccessful effort, followed by the lengthy period of deliberation for which Loreburn was famous, the application was granted in May 1909. The list contained only four names in all. In the following month Sankey was appointed Chancellor of the Diocese of Llandaff. The usual letters of congratulation on the double achievement flowed in. With the frankness permitted to a devoted sister, Edith wrote: 'Take exercise, think of your figure in court dress, and shun potatoes!'[8] Hazel, the law tutor of his old college, added to his congratulations the information that if he wished to replace his name on the books (from which he had removed it in 1901) the cost would be £21. 2s. 0d.

The risks involved in moving to London did not materialize: he was soon enjoying a substantial civil practice of the best kind.

Almost his last case at the Bar was an appeal to the House of Lords from Ireland—*Trim School Board* v. *Kelly*[9]—in which the question was whether a master at a school for delinquent boys who had been murdered by his pupils could be said to have suffered 'an accident arising out of and in the course of his employment', so as to entitle his estate to benefit under the Workmen's Compensation Acts. Sankey agreed that 'nobody out of a Court of law would describe an injury which resulted from a deliberately planned assault as the result of an accident,' but was unable to persuade a majority of the House of Lords to agree with him.

In his earlier years his political opinions, so far as they were revealed, seem to have been of an orthodox Conservative kind. In 1910 he was even a candidate at an L.C.C. election in Stepney for the 'Municipal Reform Party'—the name under which the London Conservatives of those days disguised themselves. When Lord Chancellor he showed visitors his framed election address 'as a memorial of the follies of his youth'.

Indeed, his appointment to the High Court Bench in April 1914, at the same time as Montague Shearman, K.C., was regarded at the time as showing Haldane's impartiality. For apart from Sankey's absence of positive Liberal sympathies, he had been a most active opponent of the Welsh Church Disestablishment Bill. Indeed, even if Haldane had wished to appoint a Liberal, it is doubtful if the Cabinet would have permitted

[7] Bigham, *A Picture of my Life*, pp. 343–4.
[8] Sankey papers.   [9] [1914] A.C. 667.

him to do so: for at that time it was known to be anxious to avoid bye-elections. The two Liberal K.C.s in the House, Sir Frederick Low (Norwich) and Llewellyn Williams (Carmarthen Boroughs), each had the misfortune to have an unsafe seat. As we have seen, there are other examples of parliamentary membership being a hindrance rather than a help to a barrister's hopes of promotion. There had also been a large number of recent judicial appointments. Of the thirty judges in April 1914 no fewer than twenty-three had been appointed under the Liberal Government.

There was a large pile of letters to be answered, including one from the Crown Office demanding a cheque for £25. 12s. od. in payment of the necessary fees and stamp duties on the Letters Patent of appointment. R. A. Wright, later to be a Law Lord, wrote that 'I think it is splendid of you to take a judgeship when you are in the full course of your great and increasing success'. Muir Mackenzie, the Permanent Secretary to the Lord Chancellor, wrote on 24 April:

It was a great pleasure to receive so kind a note from you. My own kindness to which you refer consisted of (a) being the Lord Chancellor's postman, and (b) administering the oaths: but those were very satisfactory duties as far as my feelings are concerned. I shall be glad to think that my unknown proceedings had anything to do with your becoming a judge, but I can assure you that you are in that great office for no other reason than that the Lord Chancellor had convinced himself by his own observations that you are the best man, and that he found the same opinion in whatever quarters he made enquiries. With congratulations and good wishes.[1]

Sankey and Shearman were sworn in as Justices of the King's Bench Division on St. George's Day—23 April 1914. For some reason they had not been attired in the customary robes, but in the Court Dress of a King's Counsel. Almost immediately Sankey set out on the Northern Circuit with Mr. Justice Bray. On 13 May 1914 he was elected a Bencher of his Inn.

For the next few years he performed the duties of a King's Bench judge without fuss or notoriety. His main war work was to act as Chairman of the Aliens' Advisory Committee from 1915. He received the thanks of the Home Secretary (Simon), to whom he replied on 29 July 1915.

My dear Home Secretary,
    I am greatly obliged to you for your kind letter and all that you say. It is most gratifying to have a personal letter from so busy a man at so busy a time, and I much appreciate it.

With kind regards,
Yours very truly,
John Sankey

[1] Sankey papers.

This letter was endorsed by Simon: 'Sankey, J. presided over the Internment Committee.'

In this capacity he reviewed the cases of hundreds of Irishmen who had been interned in England after the Rebellion of 1916. For this service he received the G.B.E. in 1917.

Outside the law, Sankey was much concerned with the affairs of the Church in Wales. The Welsh Church Act, 1914, which came into force in March 1920, effected major changes in ecclesiastical organization. The Act itself aroused strong feelings in pre-1914 England, and had to be passed under the special procedure of the Parliament Act, 1911. Without even consulting the Convocation of Canterbury, Parliament had re-arranged the boundaries of six dioceses, three of which, Chester, Hereford and Lichfield, remain in the Province of Canterbury. From the Church in Wales Parliament transferred the majority of its endowments to the county councils and other bodies. The Bishops of the Church in Wales ceased to be members of the House of Lords, although their predecessors had been summoned in 1295 to the Parliament which was the model for all succeeding Parliaments. The Welsh clergy were deprived of their freehold rights in churches, churchyards, and parsonage houses, and of their rights to share in the Bounty of Queen Anne and the revenues of the Ecclesiastical Commissioners. The Church in Wales, which had been associated with the Province of Canterbury before either the Monarchy or Parliament existed, was suddenly told to devise her own Constitution and stand apart.

The task of drafting the Constitution of the Church in Wales was entrusted to Sankey, and the draft measure which he produced for the Convention of 1917 was adopted almost without alteration. Although Sankey had the assistance of Mr. Justice (later Lord) Atkin, and of John Eldon Bankes, K.C. (later Lord Justice), the work was substantially his own and the original drafts in his handwriting are preserved amongst the Welsh National archives. The Constitution has withstood the passage of forty years without giving rise to serious difficulty.

Apart from these activities, it appeared as if his life was about to pursue an even and unexciting course to the date of his retirement—the not too arduous judicial work during the day, and in the evening the tranquil leisure of the bachelor household in Dean's Yard, Westminster, varied only by occasional concerts or, in the vacations, trips to Switzerland. It would have been the life appropriate to the cautious lawyer from Lancing and Jesus who had once been a Conservative member of the L.C.C. But a surprise was in store.

CHAPTER II

IN 1919 AN EVENT OCCURRED which was to change the whole course of Sankey's life. The coalition Government decided that something must be done to improve the coal-mining industry. Britain's greatest capital asset was being wasted away in conditions of brutal squalor and embitterment between owners and men. A Commission was appointed with Sankey as Chairman. There were three to represent the owners and three to represent the men, together with six others nominated by the Government to represent both capital and labour.

The hearings in the King's Robing Room of the House of Lords were long, tedious, and often acrimonious. But Sankey maintained an extraordinary calmness and courtesy which impressed all observers. At moments of strain he was fond of citing the Welsh proverb, 'Digon o waith a chalon i'w wnead'—'Plenty of work and a heart to do it'. It even found a place in the Report as a general recommendation for the industry.

On 23 May 1919, he wrote to Haldane:

I have drawn up a scheme dealing with
              (1) a proposed nationalisation of royalties
              (2) a proposed nationalisation of mines
              (3) the method of purchase
              (4) the working of the industry under the State.

My colleagues here, although very able and anxious to do what they think best in the circumstances, are rather influenced, I do not say unreasonably, by preconceived opinions or desires on the subject, and I should like to have the advantage of discussing it with an independent mind.[1]

The Report was published on 20 June.[2] In sending a copy to Haldane, with thanks for his advice, Sankey wrote: 'I am worn out, but am being allowed no rest, so I am just off to Winchester where I have to start the Assizes tomorrow.'

There were in fact three Reports—one from the owner's representatives, one from the miners', and one from the Chairman. It was this which attracted public attention, for Sankey in forthright terms recommended nationalization as the only possible long-term remedy for the ills of the coal industry. In 1919 this was a startling proposal to come from a person of hitherto conventional views. But at some moment during the lengthy

[1] N.L.S. 5914, f. 124.
[2] Cmd. 82.

sessions of the Commission Sankey seems to have undergone a hidden but fundamental change of mind. His sense of justice, always strong, was outraged by the descriptions of the living conditions of the miners; and his sense of decency was shocked by the cynical and selfish attitude of the owners. Sankey was not blind to the faults of the miners; but he could have remarked with Birkenhead, 'It would be possible to say without exaggeration of the miners' leaders that they were the stupidest men in England if we had not frequent occasion to meet the owners'.[3]

There was some coolness towards Sankey in Conservative quarters in the months after the Report. He said nothing, but he felt deeply hurt at the attitude shown by some old friends. To make things worse, Lloyd George, who was at that moment dependent upon Conservative votes, torpedoed the Report. Nothing was done to implement it.

In the years which followed the publication of the Report Sankey seems to have felt some sense of dissatisfaction. He had been responsible for proposing a great remedy for a great industry, but nothing was being done towards carrying it out. On the surface Sankey remained the calm judge of unadventurous tastes and ideas; beneath, as his letters to his friends show, his dissatisfaction was bringing him closer to the Labour Party.

On 10 July 1919 he wrote to Haldane: 'I am just off to Wells Assizes to sentence 4 gentlemen who plead guilty to bigamy, and to try to discover whether a local dentist has wrongfully dismissed his servant. Rather simple fare after the highly spiced dishes I have lately been sampling, but no doubt very good for me.'[4]

Again he wrote on 10 July 1923: 'I am just off on Circuit again for the nth time this year, and on my return we hope to go to the Tyrol again. For some years now I have done a good deal outside my judicial work; it may be only a July feeling, but my extra efforts do not seem to be very acceptable or beneficial—I don't mean to myself, that I don't want—to anyone, and I think I shall relax somewhat in future.'[5]

It is not surprising that Sankey's name should have been mentioned for the Woolsack when the first Labour Government was formed. The only other possible lawyers were Haldane and Buckmaster. Eventually Ramsay MacDonald chose Haldane, largely because of the wealth of administrative experience which he would bring to the new Cabinet. But as MacDonald wrote to Haldane on 12 January 1924:

I am still very anxious that Sankey might be used, but I am afraid it is absolutely impossible now. I have the best reasons for believing that he wished to come in and help us, and that he is devotedly with us in his heart, though,

[3] Lord Birkenhead, *F.E.* (1959), p. 534. [4] N.L.S. 5914, f. 126.
[5] N.L.S. 5916, ff. 29–30.

believing in all the highest and finest traditions of the Bench, he would never indicate any political leanings. I am drawn very much to that man. I am an absolute outsider to all your legal world, but there is something about Sankey which convinces me that he would find more happiness and welfare with us than where he is. Do pray keep him in mind.[6]

At this time Sankey also struck up a friendship with Harold Laski, who, with an intellectual's pleasure in exchanging ideas with important people about important things, had begun to address to the eminent in law and politics on both sides of the Atlantic lengthy letters on current affairs in which the recipient's own contributions were warmly praised. In November 1921 Laski wrote enthusiastically to Homes: 'Frida and I had a dinner with Sankey and a fine, long talk. Really he is by all odds our best judge, with insight, scholarship and exquisite taste. His one defect is keen churchmanship, but I found that one can placate that sign by hoisting signals of distress at Newman's conversion.'[7] Unfortunately Laski's own letters to Sankey seem to have perished, but some of Sankey's replies[8] are worth printing, because the casual remarks which they contain illustrate his intellectual progress towards Socialism.

23 February 1925

Here I am still in exile & quite minded to compose a 'Tristia'. However this is just a line to thank you for & to congratulate you if I may upon 'The Problem of a Second Chamber'. I have read every word of it & found it not only interesting but, like all your work, inspiring & useful. You are really one of the best of missionaries for the cause I have at heart. I am afraid a serious attack may be brewing but a little beating on the anvil consolidates the metal. The local Evening Paper here is a Wolverhampton one full of Walsall Election news. It has reported at length two really excellent speeches by Maxton. I wish they had been in a paper with a wider circulation. He has a great future before him.

I hope you have been keeping well. I caught the cold of a century at Hereford but am slowly getting better.

These long absences from London are very trying.

8 July 1925

So very many thanks. Again I am your debtor. The Grammar of Politics is indeed a magnum opus. I have not yet had time to read it thro' carefully but I have read eno' to make me decide to take it away with me during the Long Vacation for serious study.

'Socialism and Freedom' however I have read twice with delight. The first time, I marked the passages which specially appealed to me & with which I agreed. The second time I did the same & there is hardly anything now left

[6] N.L.S. 5916, f. 72.   [7] Holmes–Laski Letters (1953), p. 383.
[8] Preserved in the Laski papers.

unmarked. A great & growing party is fortunate in having such a coach. You are at your best in it if I may say so.

I am very much upset about the coal question again. It is only what I expected & what will recur from time to time under the present system, but it is none the less distressing for the country. I should so much like to have a chat with you if you could spare a night.

24 September 1925

I took your 'Grammar of Politics' away with me on the Long & have spent a good deal of time—very pleasantly and very profitably—in reading it.

It is a really wonderful work & I can't imagine how you found the time to write it. The reading was pleasant because I saw so many of my own views so admirably put, and profitable because it has supplied me with many a useful argument. I have however a feeling of envy, because I wish I could have & had written such a book myself.

I do hope it will become a text book for our young men. You will then have rendered a real service to the country. Chapters V & X are among the best.

I shall be back in Town again on Oct. 10th & shall hope to see you soon for a long talk if you have time. The situation becomes interesting.

2 June 1927

I have now had time to read your book on 'Communism' & this is a line to thank you again, not only for sending it to me but for writing it.

I have found it not only interesting but really helpful. I had a general idea of the movement but had never read before such an accurate account of it & such a scientific summing up.

Once more many thanks for a really useful book. I thought the review in the 'New Leader' last week very complimentary. Bosworth is all to the good. Our salvation is getting nearer at hand, but the unfair newspapers make me boil over.

I am here on circuit—a waste of public time & money. Not a single criminal case at the last 3 Assizes & only one civil. Still I am putting in a deal of reading.

As soon as I come back I will come & see you if I may about the Brit. Ins. of Ad. Educ.

In February 1928 a vacancy occurred in the Court of Appeal, and, to Sankey's surprise, it was offered to him by Baldwin. He wrote to Laski on 7 February:

Many thanks for your kind congratulations. They were the first to reach me & none will give me greater pleasure nor shall I value more any that reach me.

I did not expect it from the present régime & tho' I am glad to get it, I have many regrets at leaving the King's Bench, where my work, especially on Circuit, gave me time for extra judicial duties.

I spent last Friday evening at Chequers & had a very pleasant talk with the Prime Minister, who sat with me so long on the Aliens' Advisory Committee.

Things are moving tho somewhat slowly, to the goal which you & I desire. I wish we had an accelerator.[9]

Tomorrow I return to Town, to be sworn in on Thursday & I shall hope to see you at the earliest opportunity.

Later in the month he wrote again:

25 February 1928

My first letter to answer congratulations was to you for your kind telegram. My last shall be also to you for your very welcome letter. I greatly prize your generous words, which have given me real pleasure. It has been a difficult journey for me, this last ten years, & I suspect you do not know what help and encouragement you have given me from time to time. For it, I am, and shall always be, grateful to you. I should like to tell you about my visit to Chequers where the P.M. offered me the appointment, & my sister will write to Mrs. Laski in a day or two to try and find what evenings you are free about the middle of March for we hope to persuade you both to dine with us in honour of the event.

I leave the realities of the King's Bench for the abstractions of the Court of Appeal with regret. I still say I should have preferred politics to the law, M.P. to L.J. & still hope.

Thank you for your two pamphlets 'The British Cabinet' & 'Development of the Representative System'. I don't know which to envy most, your ingenuity or your accuracy; but both are a godsend to the cause we both have at heart.[1]

Following the appointment he was sworn a Privy Councillor in the customary way. (When the Court of Appeal was created in 1875, the new Lords Justices of Appeal were given a choice by the Government whether they would prefer to be distinguished from Justices of the High Court by an extra £1,000 per annum or by an automatic elevation to the Privy Council. They chose the latter honour, and their choice has been held binding on their successors.)

The general election of May 1929 resulted in the defeat of the Baldwin Government. The slogan 'Safety First' had little appeal for the electorate.

Baldwin resigned without meeting Parliament. It was accepted by all that Sankey would be the Lord Chancellor in the new administration, and there was no surprise when on 5 June he was called away in the middle of a case in the Court of Appeal to see MacDonald at his Hampstead house before he left for Windsor. Sankey received the Great Seal on 8 June, and was sworn in at the Law Courts on the 10th, being created a peer the same day.

A huge pile of congratulatory letters from lawyers and politicians of all parties arrived at Dean's Yard. The general tone can be summarized in an extract from a letter from an old friend, Gilbert Stone: 'He who has

[9] Laski papers.   [1] Ibid.

piety and no learning is impracticable. He who has learning and no piety is impossible. He who has both piety and learning becomes Lord Chancellor.'[2] The Lord Chief Justice, Hewart, wrote that 'the news of your appointment was immediately followed by a rise in the price of Consols', and Lady Cave, the widow of the ex-Chancellor, said that 'when I thought of the Woolsack occupied by Parmoor or Slesser I couldn't bear it, and it came to me as such a comfort and relief when I saw your name.'[3] Felix Frankfurter, then a Professor at the Harvard Law School, wrote:

Inasmuch as the Lord-Chancellorship belongs to the spiritual heritage of English speaking lawyers on both sides of the Ocean, perhaps you will permit an American lawyer to greet with respect and admiration the latest incumbent of that great office. Your law reports already amply attest, if you will forgive my saying so, the quality of judgments which will continue to come from you. But the direction given to the administration of justice by the Lord Chancellor is also of great moment to the profession here, particularly in these days when problems of legal administration are, perhaps, the central problems of the law. The foreword which you wrote to Dr. Port's 'Administrative Law' is the latest evidence of your preoccupation with these modern problems and a fruitful impulse which you will lend to their solution.[4]

Sankey was the third man since the beginning of the nineteenth century to reach the Woolsack having first been a puisne judge. The other two were Page Wood, V.-C. (Lord Hatherley) and Rolfe, B. (Lord Cranworth). Since 1929, however, there have been two others—Maugham and Simonds. The appointment was also noteworthy in that Sankey had just completed the fifteen years' service on the Bench which would have qualified him for a pension. Instead of retiring he now took upon himself the burdens of the highest judicial office in the kingdom. It had, however, as we have seen, been his secret ambition for the preceding decade to play a more active part in public life. It is given to few men at the age of 63 to find their ambitions so suddenly gratified. Sankey was a distinct acquisition for the Labour Party. His career reflected solid professional merit untarnished by political adventures, and his appearance and mode of life were both calculated to reassure the ordinary voter, suspicious both of 'intellectuals' and of trade unionists.

Perhaps the strangest feature of Sankey's period of office is the fact that he never spoke in the House (apart from reading the King's Speech on the prorogation in June 1929) from the day of taking his place until 29 April 1930. It is a mystery that the Lord Chancellor, who would normally be one of the Government's chief spokesmen in the Lords, should have been able to keep silent for so long—particularly as the Labour peers

[2] Sankey papers.   [3] Ibid.   [4] Ibid.

in the House were so few on the ground, and Parmoor, the Leader of the House, was not strong. Sankey's speech was to introduce the Coal Mines Bill on its Second Reading.[5] If the House had to wait long to hear it, the delay was worth while. Sankey made an admirable speech, which received the rare compliment of a low mutter of approval (officially described as 'cheers') from an audience renowned for its frigidity and certainly not predisposed towards the merits of the Bill. The speech lasted for almost one hour, but was delivered without notes, Sankey having learnt it by heart. He told the House that although he had not given any public utterance to his views since the Report of 1919, he remained convinced that nationalization was the only cure for the industry. But as he did not feel that a minority government was entitled to enact such a fundamental change he had acquiesced in the milder reforms proposed by the Bill, such as the reduction of the working day. The Bill eventually passed the House at the end of July over the bitter opposition of the coal-owners. The back-bench peers, however, showed themselves more liberal than their leaders, and at last the Bill went through.

Sankey maintained his interest in the Coal Question. He spoke on the matter from time to time after he had left the Woolsack—though it is noticeable that he took no part in the debates on the major Coal Bill of 1938.

In January 1946 he sent Emanuel Shinwell, the Minister of Fuel and Power, a telegram of good wishes on the day before the Second Reading of the Government's Bill to nationalize the mines. He received a grateful acknowledgment from the Minister for the pioneering work done in 1919.[6]

[5] 77 H.L. Deb. 5s. col. 165.
[6] Sankey papers.

CHAPTER III

IN THE CRISIS OF AUGUST 1931 which resulted in the collapse of the second Labour Government, Sankey was throughout a devoted supporter of MacDonald. At a time when there was a public display of ill-temper and jealousy unequalled even in the history of the Labour Party, Sankey somehow escaped the vilification and abuse. He was given a respectful hearing at the otherwise stormy party meeting on 28 August. His reputation was such that it was generally conceded that it was devotion to the welfare of the State alone which impelled him to support the Prime Minister.[1] Sankey found time to send a note of support to Jowitt, the Attorney-General, whose devotion to MacDonald was the subject of particularly severe attack.

30 August 1931

My dear A.G.

   This is just a line to send you my heartiest congratulations. No one had such a difficult task as you had & forgive me saying so you played the man & the hero. You have put the country & personal loyalty before everything else, & your future is safe for you know & everyone will soon recognize that you did the right thing.

  With kind regards & all best wishes to you & Lady Jowitt

Yours very truly
Sankey[2]

Sankey sent Laski some reflections on recent events early in the New Year:

15 February 1932

Many thanks for sending me your last book, 'Studies in Law and Politics'. I have just dipped into it, but see that it is a book which, in the words of Bacon, ought to be 'chewed and digested', and I intend really to study it and to keep it by me for future reference. But I chiefly value the kind words which you have written on the front page. I do not think, however, that my principles, even now, are very different from yours. If I may borrow an analogy from the Law, at the moment I do not see eye to eye with you about practice and procedure. Last August I came to the conclusion, rightly or wrongly, that the country was not only in grave difficulties, but in immediate danger, and that there was need for drastic action. I regret that it was not possible to persuade my colleagues either of the immediate danger or of the necessity for drastic remedies. Time will show which of us was right. Thank Heaven, the immediate danger is, in

---

[1] M. A. Hamilton, *Remembering my Good Friends* (1944), p. 246.   [2] Jowitt papers.

my view, now past, but difficulties still remain, and I shall do my best to assist my country to overcome them. Necessity sometimes has to check progress.

I think one great thing which the Labour Party will have to look to in the immediate future is an amendment of the Constitution under which it works, so as to prevent a situation like that which occurred in August last from occurring again. It would be impertinence for me to make any suggestions, as the Labour Party have expelled me from their ranks, and there, I am afraid, the matter rests. I have, however, given considerable thought to the subject, and I hope that something will be done to prevent such unfortunate divisions in the Labour Party arising in future.[3]

Ireland and India were two topics which occupied much governmental time in the early 'thirties. Sankey acted as Chairman of the Round Table Conference on India, quickly establishing friendly relations with Gandhi. In Ireland Mr. de Valera's Government had been just returned to power in a mood of extreme nationalist self-assertion. One of its first acts was to repudiate liability for the land annuities payable to the British Government for the compulsory acquisition of the landlords' estates until a general settlement of all outstanding financial questions between the two countries had been reached. Mr. de Valera was willing to go back into Irish history no further than the Act of Union, 1800, but he contended that since that date his country had been over-taxed to the extent of many millions. Sankey wrote to Laski on the topic several times in August 1932.

I am very much worried about Ireland, but at the present moment I do not see what can be done. I understand an arbitration by the award of which the parties would consent to be bound, but it is difficult to understand one in which the award is to be merely a basis for further negotiations. The sooner the matter is settled, the better for everybody. Finality is what is wanted.

Many thanks for your letters, and my apologies for the delay in answering them. I have been so overburdened with the work both of my own Department and of the Dominions Office that this is the third successive Monday on which I have found myself in arrears with correspondence—a thing which has not happened to me before since I have held office.

The Irish situation must be causing everyone acute anxiety. Personally, I think that a settlement by negotiation would be preferable to a settlement by arbitration, for I feel pretty confident that if we did offer an arbitration, the result would not be final, but that negotiations would begin when the award was published. I should be glad to hear your views.

With regard to Ireland, the difficulty is that half the Cabinet are in Ottawa and half in England, and mistakes and misunderstandings so easily arise when you have to carry on consultations by cablegrams or long-distance telephone. With one or two exceptions all our colleagues will be back on Saturday, the

[3] Laski papers.

27th, and I hope we shall have a Cabinet on the Monday or Tuesday following, and get a move on.

I note what you say about Mr Norton.[4] He is either mistaken or mis-represented.

Much as I have desired arbitration till a few days ago, I am reaching the conclusion that the difficulties with regard to it are almost insuperable, and that it is impossible to save people's faces on this point. It is not for me to advise our Irish friends, but I should have thought that a legal decision is the last thing they want. I think negotiations are better in the interests of both sides. The difficulty, however, with some people is that they either live in the past or live in the future, and they will not face or try to compose the difficulties of the present.[5]

One of the most difficult problems which have confronted any modern Lord Chancellor occupied much of Sankey's time in 1932 and 1933 — the refusal of the judges to accept the 'cut' of 20 per cent in official salaries authorized by the National Economy Act, 1931. The course of the negotiations illustrates very well how the Lord Chancellor's position as a member of the Cabinet enables him to represent the views of the judges and the Government to each other.

Sankey set out his views in a lengthy memorandum of 15 January 1932 a few days before taking a deputation of the Judges to see the Prime Minister, after private discussions during the autumn of 1931 had failed to produce a solution.

The question here involved is one of very great difficulty. I have had letters from nearly all the judges; I have had private interviews with many of them, and on two occasions have received a semi-official deputation from the judicial body consisting of the Master of the Rolls, representing the Appeal Court, Mr Justice Avory, representing the King's Bench Division (he was present at the first meeting only), Lord Merrivale, representing the Admiralty Division, and Mr Justice Maugham, representing the Chancery Division. It is most unfortunate that the Lord Chief Justice has for many weeks been unable to attend to his official duties. Originally he wrote a letter in which he said, as far as I remember, that the judges would cheerfully comply with the cuts which the Government thought necessary.

It is useless for me to disguise the fact that the judges are . . . rather bent upon giving trouble unless their demands are satisfied.

On the first occasion upon which I saw the deputation, some time before Christmas, their attitude was as follows:

They contended that they had a contract of a very solemn kind under which the Government undertook to pay them £5000 a year, and that, moreover, it was a contract which was confirmed by Statute: that any diminution of salary was a breach of contract and a breach of faith, and so forth.

[4] Leader of the Irish Labour Party.   [5] Laski papers.

When I saw them on the second occasion, namely, the 14th January, they had entirely changed their ground. There was no longer any contention of breach of contract—just the opposite. They admitted that the Government could lower their stipend by Act of Parliament, but the point relied upon is of a somewhat technical character. It is said that the Government have not passed an Act of Parliament; that all that has been done is to authorize Orders in Council applying, amongst other classes, to persons in His Majesty's Service, that constitutionally the judges are not in H.M.'s Service, and that, therefore, there is no Act of Parliament diminishing their stipend; there is no Order in Council authorizing the Government to diminish their stipend, and that the cuts and reductions are illegal.

I need hardly point out that this is an entire departure from their original contention, and it is due to the fact that the judges have now realized that their first point as to breach of contract is not maintainable, and that they are relying upon the point made in the January number of 'The Legal Quarterly'[6] by Professor Holdsworth, the Vinerian Professor of English Law at the University of Oxford, and probably one of the most learned constitutional lawyers in the kingdom.

The fact that the judges have shifted their ground is not one, however, of which we can take any advantage. The question is, are they right in their contentions and, whether right or wrong, what is the Government to do?

Let me here say that other lawyers do not take the same view as Professor Holdsworth, but it would be impossible to deny that the point is a doubtful one. There was no doubt upon the breach-of-contract one, but there *is* a doubt about the Order-in-Council point, and in any event the prestige of the judges must be upheld, whatever one may think about the personal attitude they are adopting at the present crisis of their country's history.

There may be other courses to be pursued, but three at any rate emerge.

1. The Government can sit tight and do nothing.
2. The Government can immediately pass an Act of Parliament reducing the salaries by £1000 a year.
3. The Government can accept their contention and leave the reductions to what each individual may offer.

There are difficulties in the way of all these courses.

As to 1, to do nothing is, I think, impossible. The judges are in a mutinous mood. They have only been restrained from making public pronouncements by personal requests that they should give the Government time to consider the matter. I have not the slightest doubt that if we do nothing the matter will be raised in both Houses of Parliament, and probably outside as well. I therefore reject this as an alternative.

As to 2, this would of course cut the Gordian knot by a single stroke, but we should have to consider how far it would be possible to get a Bill through both Houses.

As to 3, my difficulties are the political ones of the repercussions following

[6] i.e. *The Law Quarterly Review*: see (1931) 46 L.Q.R. 25.

from the feeling of other classes of subjects if the judges are let off altogether, and the (in my view) still more serious point of the unpopularity and odium the judges might incur if it were known that, of all classes of the community, they, who are the best paid, had refused to help the country in her emergency. I put this point before the deputation, but it was turned down with some scorn; they said that what was right was right, and that they would face any unpopularity, although they did not believe they would incur it because they thought the country was on their side.

Their argument was that if we said that the Order did not apply to them we were in effect saying that we had committed an illegality by our reduction of their salaries, and that they ought not to be compelled to consent to a cut—indeed, one judge used the word 'blackmail', and said that they ought not to be blackmailed, which would be the effect of our insisting upon the reduction which we were not entitled to make.

One of the judges offered to let the independent members of the Privy Council decide the matter, but he was alone and the others refused to do anything.

I am sure the Cabinet sympathizes with all people who have suffered cuts—economy, however necessary, is never pleasant or popular. I am equally sure that the Cabinet would do anything to safeguard the constitutional position of the judges. If we could be quite sure that the judges would make a voluntary contribution, I should unhesitatingly advise the withdrawal of the Order as far as it affected them. My only difficulty is that if after the withdrawal of the Order a number of judges refuse to contribute, the last state might be worse than the first from the prestige point of view. They refused to give me any definite indication of what they would do in the event of the withdrawal of the Order, and perhaps they were right, because they do not know themselves, though they think that some of the judges would offer a 20% reduction; the majority would offer 10%, and that two or three would do nothing, and, from the private letters and conversations that I have had from and with them, I think this is about a true estimate.

Although personally I regret the attitude of my colleagues, it may be that we shall have to bend to the storm and adopt the third of my alternatives, but this is a matter which could only be decided after an interchange of views among the Cabinet.[7]

The judges then produced a Memorandum restating their arguments, which the Prime Minister agreed to publish as a White Paper, though without conceding any of the arguments contained in it.[8]

Hailsham wrote to Hanworth about the matter on 29 February 1932:

Since I received your letter I have spoken to Simon and also to Stanley Baldwin and one or two others in the Cabinet; and I have also had the good

---

[7] Sankey papers.
[8] See 88 H.L. Deb. 5s. col. 1208, where the memorandum is printed. The memorandum was drafted by Maugham J. (*At the End of the Day*, p. 356).

fortune to meet Duke and to have a few words with him. I think that probably the Cabinet would be persuaded to publish any memorandum for which the Judges pressed. My own opinion, and I think that also of my political colleagues (including Simon) was that the effect of a memorandum might not be quite so satisfactory to the Judges' own position as they and we should wish. But that is more a matter for them than for me. I personally will do my best to get any statement made which in the opinion of the Judges themselves is necessary to indicate their position.[9]

Unfortunately the argument about judicial salaries continued into 1933. In April the Cabinet was informed that Mr. Justice Macnaghten, one of the King's Bench Judges, and a son of the great Lord Macnaghten, intended to present a Petition of Right against the legality of the cuts. Sankey and Hailsham saw Macnaghten and told him that the Cabinet were prepared, if necessary, to introduce legislation to validate the cuts. Sankey understood Macnaghten to say that the question of salary was no longer of prime importance to him, and that he would be satisfied if any Act which was passed contained a section declaring that the independence of the judiciary had not been compromised. A draft Act was prepared on these lines by Mr. Justice Avory, whom Sankey had consulted.

The story may be continued in Sankey's own words:

At his own request, Mr Justice Macnaghten came to see me again on Saturday, April 29th. At the beginning of the conversation I said that I could only continue my talks with him upon the basis that the cuts in the salaries must remain. He said that he quite agreed with this, and that his concern was to see that the status and independence of the judges should not be thought to have been impaired. I told him that I thought there ought to be no difficulty in coming to an agreement on these lines, and that if necessary I hoped that an Act of Parliament could be passed which would be as satisfactory to him and those with whom he was acting as it would be to the Government. He asked me if I could show him the lines of the proposed Act. I handed him a copy of Mr Justice Avory's draft; he read it hurriedly, and, before I could say anything, he became greatly excited and said that the draft only made matters worse, and that, whereas before the Government had insulted the judges, it now 'wanted to kick their bottoms'. These were his exact words. I then begged him not to be so hasty, and said the draft was one which had been prepared by Mr Justice Avory, with whom he had been in consultation. He replied that Lord Hailsham had told him that I had seen Mr Justice Avory, but he (Mr Justice Macnaghten) could not imagine that Mr Justice Avory agreed with the proposals in the present draft, and that I must have misunderstood him. I said there was no room for any misunderstanding as to what Mr Justice Avory's views were, for I had Mr Justice Avory's original draft in his own handwriting, which I there and then handed to Mr Justice Macnaghten. He then rather quietened down.

[9] Hailsham papers.

I told him that Mr Justice Avory could not of course bind him or anybody else, as Mr Justice Avory himself had very properly said, but at any rate would it not be wise to accept Mr Justice Avory's draft as a basis for discussion, which we proceeded to do.

We went through it very carefully, and Mr Justice Macnaghten appeared then to accept it, but he finally made one objection. He said the result of the draft might be that the public would think that the judges had refused to consent to the cuts, and that therefore they were unpatriotic; that this was not the fact, and he desired that it should be made clear somehow that the judges had always been willing to accept the cuts. I said that I had no doubt that we could come to some satisfactory conclusion on this, which was apparently the only out-standing difficulty. I asked him if he thought it could be overcome by adding a recital to the Bill; something like 'whereas the judges have been always ready and willing to pay the cuts', and if so, would he draft a recital and let me have it for consideration. He then thought for a minute or two, and said there would be a difficulty about this, as he was afraid it was not quite correct, and he did not think that the judges were all ready and willing to accept the cuts—at any rate it pressed very hardly on him, perhaps more hardly than on anybody else. He then said he would like to place his whole position before me, and I said I was prepared to listen.

First, he said he thought he had a mission. The judges had to resist the power of the Crown in Stuart days, and had done so successfully. Now they had to resist the power of the Executive, and he felt it his duty, even if others did not agree with him, to fight the Executive on this point. He added that the legisla-tion of the last fifty or sixty years had made great inroads on the independence of the judges: he particularly instanced two acts in the Seventies, the Judicature and the Life Peerage Acts. He said appointments to the Court of Appeal and to the House of Lords were now in the hands of the Prime Minister; that no judge of first instance had a chance of promotion to the Court of Appeal or to the House of Lords if he displeased the Government or the Prime Minister. I here ventured to stop him, saying that although I was prepared to listen, I could not agree, and thought that on reflection he himself would not press such a point. He then went on to rail against the superior Civil Servants, and said that in any campaign against the Government he should bring out the facts. He contended that, whereas the power and remuneration of the Civil Servants had been increased in the last twenty years, the power and prestige of the judges had been reduced: that they had had no bonus during the War as the Civil Servants had, and that their need was greater than that of Civil Servants. He said the judges were now in the power of the Civil Servants, and that he con-sidered his position was no better than that of an office-boy at the Home Office. I again stopped him and said that I really must protest, and that I was sure he would forgive me for saying that I thought not only was his language extra-vagant, but that it was a travesty of the facts. I then said I had endeavoured to do everything I could to bring about an agreement, but as he appeared to reject every suggestion, it was now his turn to put forward suggestions for a solution of the difficulty. He thought for a minute or two, and then said that he was afraid it was very difficult to separate the question of the cuts from the question of status, but he thought the best way out was that the cuts should continue till April 5th of next year without further protest, but that from April 5th next year the Cabinet should place themselves in the hands of the judges and accept the judges' determination; that he was sure the judges (at any rate, he himself was) would be willing that the cuts should be continued if they thought that financial necessity required it.

This suggestion appeared to me so amazing that I said I was afraid it was useless to continue the conversation, but that I should like to point out to him that he had all along been taking up the position that the question of salary was quite immaterial, and now he was in effect seeking to have the salaries restored, and that I really could not continue to talk to him on the subject. He then said would I see Mr Justice Clauson and Mr Justice Luxmoore, and if they agreed to accept my proposals, he would, but he was just about to go on a fortnight's circuit to Leeds. I thought this was not very helpful, as they would probably say that if Mr Justice Macnaghten agreed, they would. The conclusion of the matter was this:

No petition is to be presented for several weeks, but when he returns from the Leeds Assizes he will see his two brother judges and then he will write to me. If he says that no useful purpose can be served by another interview, he is to be at liberty to take what course he likes, and the Government is to be at liberty to take what course they like. If, on the other hand, he thought he would like to see me again, I should be very glad to see him and resume the conversation, but that we should only proceed upon the basis that the cuts must remain.

I need hardly say that after that our conversation proceeded on the most friendly personal basis for we are friends of many years standing both at the Bar and, subsequently, on the Bench. He asked if he might take away with him the draft of the proposed Act of Parliament, to which I agreed.[1]

A lengthy opinion on the whole matter was obtained from a leading member of the common law Bar. It emphasized that the term 'service' connoted the existence of some measure of control in or subservience to the person served. 'Service is nonetheless service because it is spelt with a capital letter.' A minimum test of the right of control was the existence of a power to terminate the services rendered—which since the Act of Settlement did not exist as between the Crown and the judges, for the generally accepted interpretation of that Act is that the judges can be dismissed either upon an Address from both Houses of Parliament, or by the courts themselves by an order made on *scire facias* proceedings brought at the suit of the Crown itself in respect of conduct which both Houses

[1] Sankey papers. It is strange that nobody recalled that in 1832, when the judges' salaries were reduced from £5,500 to £5,000 per annum, the Government had to concede that the Act should not affect vested interests: see C. 6617, p. 185.

have decided for one reason or another not to treat as misconduct justifying removal by an Address. The essential fact is that the Crown acting
alone cannot since 1701 dismiss a judge. It was the undoubted intention
of the framers of the Act of Settlement to relieve the judges of their former
status of dependence upon the Executive, and it would run contrary to
this declared intention to hold that judges were in the service of the Crown.
In a debate on the subject in November 1933 Sankey reaffirmed the
traditional independence of the judiciary. To meet criticisms advanced
by Lords Rankeillour and Buckmaster he affirmed that the Civil Service
'stood in an entirely different position from the Judiciary. The method of
their appointment was different, their tenure was different, and their
stipend was upon a different basis.'[2] The last parliamentary echo of the
controversy was in December 1935, when Lord Rankeillour moved the
Second Reading of the Judiciary (Safeguarding) Bill, designed to safeguard the tenure and stipend of judges of the superior courts.[3] It failed to
secure a passage.

There is another point which might have been referred to in support
of the judges' arguments. All the modern cases on the relationship of
master and servant emphasize that the criterion of the relationship is the
existence in the master of a power to give directions as to the mode of
performing the service in question. Other factors—e.g. the powers of
appointment and dismissal—are relevant but not decisive. Now it is
perfectly clear that the Crown has never exercised, nor even claimed to
exercise, a power to give directions to the judges as to the mode of
deciding a particular case. Any such direction would be a grave breach of
constitutional propriety and would be ignored completely by a judge,
whose sworn duty it is to administer justice according to law. There can
be little doubt that in the controversy of 1931-3 the judges had the
stronger position in point of law. The wisdom of their attitude from the
broader viewpoint of national policy is a matter on which opinions may
still differ.

In December 1934 there was a most painful open quarrel with the
Lord Chief Justice Hewart, over an apparently innocuous provision in
the Law Reform (Miscellaneous Provisions) Bill, which authorized the
Master of the Rolls to appoint one of the Lords Justices to preside over
Appeal Court II. Until then the practice had been for the senior Lord
Justice to preside automatically. Lord Justice Slesser, who had been
Solicitor-General in the MacDonald Government before being raised to
the Court of Appeal, conceived the idea that this clause was designed to
deprive him of one of the perquisites of the seniority which would shortly

[2] 90 H.L. Deb. 5s. col. 82.
[3] 99 H.L. Deb. 5s. col. 221.

be his.[4] Slesser consulted Hewart, who appears to have suffered something in the nature of a brainstorm on hearing the news. He at once convinced himself that the whole episode was part of an elaborate conspiracy on the part of Whitehall to interfere with the independence of the judiciary. It was another example of the 'Bureaucracy Triumphant' against which he had published a volume under the title in 1929. At the centre of the conspiracy, he believed, was Sir Claud Schuster, the Permanent Secretary to the Lord Chancellor since 1915. Schuster was an able and self-confident man whose wits were rather quicker than those of Hewart. On 11 December the Bill was due to obtain a Second Reading in the Lords. That day the Divisional Court, presided over by Hewart, had before it a case of great importance in the law relating to parliamentary privilege—*R. v. Graham-Campbell, ex parte Herbert*.[5] Hewart dealt with the case in a hasty and perfunctory way. But he was determined to adjourn the court early in order to be in time for the debate in the Lords.

When he rose to speak (it was his maiden speech) Hewart was almost incoherent with rage. In spluttering and menacing words, he developed his attack on Sankey and Schuster.[6] The peers listened in complete silence to a speech so alien to all their traditions. Sankey had not the time to prepare an adequate reply, but a few days later, when the adjourned debate was resumed, he produced a temperate and dignified answer to the sweeping charges made against him. He was supported by Hailsham and Hanworth, and the episode closed with the Lord Chief Justice shaking hands with his fellow-judges.

Sankey's period on the Woolsack showed a novel and sustained effort in the cause of law reform. There is no member of the Cabinet specifically charged with the duty of dealing with this subject, but it is generally understood that the Lord Chancellor is more responsible than any other minister. Still, the whole process of reform was spasmodic and uncertain, depending upon the personality of the Chancellor for the moment and his ability to persuade his Cabinet colleagues to insert the necessary Bills in an overcrowded legislative programme.

One of the first of Sankey's reforms was the appointment in October 1929 of the Committee on Ministers' Powers (known to all who are interested in public law as the Scott-Donoughmore Committee). The exhaustive report of this body, published in 1931,[7] is an authoritative state paper of great value on the related questions of subordinate legislation and the exercise of judicial powers by government departments.

In January 1934 Sankey set up a permanent Law Revision Committee, 'to consider how far, having regard to the Statute Law and to judicial

---

[4] See his account in *Judgment Reserved* (1941).
[5] [1935] 1 K.B. 594.   [6] 95 H.L. Deb. 5s. col. 224.   [7] Cmd. 4060.

decisions, such legal maxims and doctrines as the Lord Chancellor may from time to time refer to them require revision in modern conditions'. The Committee at first was composed of four judges, five barristers, two professors of law, one solicitor, and the Permanent Secretary to the Lord Chancellor. In 1937 two more academic lawyers were added. After the war the Committee was reconstituted in 1952 under the title of the Law Reform Committee. The Committee produced eight valuable Reports before the war, on seven of which amending legislation followed.[8] There can be no doubt that the establishment for the first time of an institution charged with the duty of examining into and recommending specific reforms on legal questions entitles Sankey to a high place amongst the Lord Chancellors. The only person who seems to have disputed this judgment is Hailsham. On 28 October 1935 he wrote to Baldwin asking that Hanworth should be promoted to a viscounty in the New Year Honours List (as was done), not merely because he had been Master of the Rolls for twelve years, but also because

he had been chairman of a variety of legal committees and I think it is no exaggeration to say that all the law reforms which have passed parliament during Sankey's lord-chancellorship have owed their existence to Hanworth and the work he did as the chairman of the various committees which threshed them out. There is also the fact that, if he feels his work has been recognized, I am quite certain that he will come and help us as a volunteer in the judicial work of the Privy Council in the House of Lords as soon as his health has been sufficiently restored. On both grounds therefore, as a reward for service well done, and as a gratitude for favours to come, I should very much like to know that he is included in the New Year's list.[9]

But this opinion seems partial and unfair. There is no doubt that Hanworth had done good work as Chairman of the Business of the Courts Committee. Indeed, it was because he was fully occupied until that Committee had issued its Second Interim Report in December, 1933, that there was some delay in setting up the Law Revision Committee. There had been a debate on the subject in the House of Commons in December 1932,[1] after which Donald Somervell, then a new K.C. and M.P., had sent Schuster a memorandum suggesting the establishment of a committee. He was told that the Lord Chancellor had already decided in favour of such a step. But it is unjust to Sankey to rate Hanworth above him as a law reformer.

To the King's Bench Division Sankey as Lord Chancellor appointed du Parcq, Goddard, Lawrence, Porter, Singleton, Greaves-Lord, Hilbery, and Atkinson. Each of the first four of these rose to be a Law Lord (and

---

[8] See Wade 'The Machinery of Law Reform' (1961) 24 M.L.R. 3.
[9] Hailsham papers.　　[1] 273 H.C. Deb. 5s. col. 1103.

Goddard to be Lord Chief Justice), and Singleton became a Lord Justice. In May 1933 a vacancy occurred to which Atkinson was eventually appointed, but Sankey first consulted Hailsham on the matter, pointing out that as Atkinson sat as Conservative M.P. for Altrincham his appointment would necessitate a bye-election. (We have already seen[2] that in practice membership of the House of Commons may be a hindrance rather than a help to judicial promotion.) Hailsham wrote on 2 May 1933:

With regard to the second document, I should like to say that I have no doubt at all of the soundness of your advice and that personally I agree entirely with the course you took. I would only add that if I were in your place I should destroy every copy except one of the document, and lock the one remaining sample in the innermost recess of Schuster's most secret safe. It is quite astonishing how easily a secret like this gets out; and it would be very distressing if any of the matters to which you refer should become public property. With regard to your first document . . . I think I can safely say that I think either of the two names you mention would be thoroughly satisfactory for an appointment; so far as I can judge they would be amongst the first whom I should have thought it right to consider in your place. The fact of Atkinson's age and that this is his last opportunity of reaching the Bench seem to me to weigh the scales in his favour for the present appointment. If, on the other hand, you'd ask me to agree the letter to the Prime Minister, I have rather more hesitation. I think it right then that, before you make the appointment, you should ascertain from the Prime Minister or the Chief Whip that no grave political consequences are likely to ensue; and since the appointment would involve a bye-election, I think it would be right before making it, to inform the Prime Minister and to ask whether there is any strong political objection, stressing the point which you make in your letter that it is hard on a man to be barred from judicial promotion because of his membership of the House of Commons. A letter on these lines would seem to me to be only fair. My doubt is when you go further and name two persons, one of whom is a member of Parliament and the other is not, and in effect invite the Prime Minister to choose between them. I don't think it is any business of the Prime Minister to have a voice in the selection of a judge, and I don't think it should be relevant for him to know who would get the post, if he objects to the M.P. having it. In the present case, of course, you make it plain that you are only consulting him because of the fact that one of the two possible candidates is a Member of Parliament; but the fact that he is consulted and that he is given the opportunity of deciding that the other man should get the post might conceivably set an example towards a precedent which would give the Prime Minister a voice in these appointments; and I think that you and I both agree that that would be very undesirable. A man ought to be chosen for the judicial bench because he is the best man available and for no other reason. Suppose, for example, the Prime Minister were to write back and ask whether you would consider the claims of some other man; a difficult situation might easily be created. My letter therefore

[2] See above, pp. 21, 51, 58, 325.

would have confined itself to stating the facts with regard to Atkinson and to asking the Prime Minister whether he saw any grave political objections to his appointment. If he did raise a grave objection, then I should appoint Singleton; but I should not have mentioned his name to the Prime Minister, or indeed, have told the Prime Minister what I should do if a political difficulty arose in Atkinson's case.[3]

No more admirable illustration of the spirit of strict impartiality which pervades the making of modern judicial appointments could be found. (It may be added that Singleton was eventually appointed in November 1934.)

To the Chancery Division Sankey appointed Farwell, Bennett, and Crossman, and to the Probate, Divorce, and Admiralty Division Langton and Bucknill. All these were perfectly satisfactory. In addition Sankey appointed thirty-four county court judges, two Official Referees, and two Common Serjeants of the City of London. He also appointed 3,937 J.P.s in England, and 1,799 in Scotland. The party allegiances of the English appointments were as follows:[4]

Labour:	1,166
Conservative:	1,401
Liberal:	620
Independent:	650

For the Scottish magistrates the figures were:

Labour:	378
Conservative:	643
Liberal:	325
Independent:	453

One proposal of great interest which Laski made to Sankey was that an academic lawyer should be appointed to the Bench. Such an appointment is common enough in the United States, but is unknown in England (the first Vinerian Professor, Blackstone, certainly became a judge in 1770, but his Chair was not a full-time professorship as understood today). Laski procured Professor (later Lord) Chorley to write in support of W. C. Gutteridge of London University, a commercial and international lawyer of the highest distinction.

Sankey wrote to Laski on 30 October 1934:

Many thanks for your letter enclosing one from Chorley. You may readily imagine that I do not make appointments off my own bat without consulting anybody. At least a fortnight before you wrote to me I had conversations with four of the most distinguished lawyers, who now hold or have held the biggest

[3] Hailsham papers. [4] Sankey papers.

positions in the law. As a matter of fact I suggested to them the question of appointing an academic lawyer as Judge, and indeed I even suggested the name of the gentleman to whom Chorley refers in his letter. I am afraid, however, that every person whom I consulted was against it. I have since that consulted others with a similar result, except in one case where it was suggested to me that I might ask an academic lawyer to go Commissioner on circuit and see both what he did and how his appointment was received.

I am afraid, therefore, that at the present moment it is quite impossible to do anything along the lines which, as you will see, I have not only thought of but put forward some time before your letter reached me. I do not think that any-body realizes with what opposition legal reforms and legal innovations meet, unless it is the person who puts them forward. I should like to show you some day a list of the reforms contained either in Acts of Parliament or new rules which have been carried since I have been Lord Chancellor. They number between 30 and 40 and I don't think one of them was carried without persistent and sustained opposition at first. It is both discouraging and distressing.

I have marked this letter private and confidential and I would ask you to be good enough to keep it so. You need not, however, imagine that my somewhat disagreeable experience is going to prevent me from pursuing a forward policy.[5]

The letter is a good illustration of Sankey's zeal for law reform, although a critic might say that it was somewhat unrealistic to suggest assessing the judicial capacities of an academic lawyer by appointing him Commissioner of Assize, for that involves work of a kind for which his previous experience would be of only the slightest value.

Ecclesiastical appointments were not a matter in which Sankey took much personal interest—rather surprisingly, in view of his known high-churchmanship. One letter has survived which illustrates vividly the difficulties which the Lord Chancellor often has in filling the Crown livings in his gift, which are very often the least lucrative amongst the patronage of the Crown.

On 3 March 1931 Sankey wrote in reply to a letter from the Bishop of St. Albans complaining of an appointment:

Thank you for your letter. I am sorry to hear I am laid up—I was not aware of it, and, as far as I know, it is not true.

Your letter has caused me much perplexity, owing to the very strong language you use, and I regret that you view Mr Veitch's appointment with dismay and his going to Harpenden as disastrous. I cannot help thinking that the Harpenden parishioners are a very difficult set of people. I offered the living to two of your nominees in turn. For your private information, the parishioners did not want either of them, but indirectly put great pressure upon me to appoint another gentleman, who, however, could not take it.

I am afraid it is very difficult to do anything in the circumstances, but, before

[5] Laski papers.

attempting it, I should like to know categorically what is their objection to Mr Veitch. I need hardly say that personally I have never seen and know nothing about him, except what I gather from his testimonials.

Would you mind answering the following questions:—

  (1) Is he too old?
  (2) Has he an unsatisfactory wife?
  (3) Has he too many children?
  (4) Has he too little money?
  (5) Is his Churchmanship too high, too low, or too Laodicean?
  (6) Is his personal appearance against him?
  (7) Is his manner against him?
  (8) Is it thought that he is not a great preacher?
  (9) Are his politics unacceptable?
  (10) Is he not sufficiently learned?
  (11) Is he out of sympathy with young people?
  (12) Is his wife unable to play the organ?
  (13) Has he a poor singing voice?
  (14) Is he one of the 'vestmented' clergy?

You will, I know, think most of the foregoing questions impertinent and ridiculous, as I do myself, but they are simply those which I have accumulated from various parishes during my tenure, and I am sure that the objection of the parishioners to Mr Veitch must be due to one or other of these causes. If not, I shall have to add a fifteenth to my list.[6]

As a judge Sankey for long periods was unable to sit either in the House of Lords or the Judicial Committee because of his work as Chairman, first of the Inter-Imperial Relations Committee of the Imperial Conference, and later of the Federal Structure Committee of the Indian Round Table Conference. It is notable that none of his judgments are reported in the Appeal Cases for 1932 or 1933. In general Sankey's judgments are clear, careful, and correct, but they do not entitle him to a place among the great English judges. An assessment of them will be found in the Appendix, but one merit of them may be noted now. His long years as a trial judge, who writes his judgments knowing that they may be dissected minutely before an appellate court, had not deprived him of the ability to rise to the heights when necessary. Two examples may be given. In a number of cases in the 1930s (e.g. *Edwards* v. *Att.-Gen.*,[7] *In re the Regulation and Control of Aeronautics in Canada* [1932] A.C. 54 and *British Coal Corporation* v. *The King*[8]), Sankey delivered the judgment of the Judicial Committee on a series of difficult questions arising under the

[6] Sankey papers. Mr. G. S. Veitch (d. 1959) was Rector of Harpenden 1931–58.
[7] [1930] A.C. 124.
[8] [1935] A.C. 500. Judgment was delivered the day before Sankey gave up the Great Seal.

British North America Acts. In each case a broad and liberal interpretation was adopted consistent with the policy of according the fullest independence to the self-governing members of the Commonwealth. The *British Coal Corporation* case contains a passage familiar to lawyers dealing with the true interpretation of sections 4 and 7 of the Statute of Westminster, 1931:

> It is doubtless true that the power of the Imperial Parliament to pass on its own initiative any legislation that it thought fit extending to Canada remains in theory unimpaired; indeed, the Imperial Parliament could, as a matter of abstract law, repeal or disregard sect. 4 of the Statute. But that is theory and has no relation to realities. In truth, Canada is in enjoyment of the full scope of self-government.[9]

The second instance is Sankey's judgment in *Woolmington* v. *D.P.P.*,[1] in which, speaking for a unanimous House of Lords, he affirmed that 'throughout the web of the English criminal law one golden thread is always to be seen, that it is the duty of the prosecution to prove the prisoner's guilt. . . . No matter what the charge or where the trial, the principle that the prosecution must prove the guilt of the prisoner is part of the common law of England and no attempt to whittle it down can be entertained.

The judgment, subject to correction on one minor point,[2] has been consistently cited with approval throughout the common law world. It produced at once an admiring letter from Lord Craigmyle, better known to lawyers as Lord Shaw:

> I wish you to know with what high satisfaction I have just read your judgment in the criminal appeal. From the moment that I read the charge to the Jury, I felt that a new and dangerous turn was being given to an old and abominable English precedent. This impression was deepened when the Criminal Appeal Court failed to rise to a better view, and I strongly approve of the Attorney-General giving his fiat for the House of Lords. And now has come your judgment. I think you must allow me to tell you what I feel about it. It is a great judgment, scholarly, and with that human touch which seeks and finds a high place in law for life and liberty. As you know such things, including questions of constitutional right and practice, are very sacred to me: and I do rejoice in your pronouncement—removing as it does a reproach from the Law of England. Well done, dear friend, bless you.[3]

[9] [1935] A.C. at 520.   [1] [1935] A.C. 462.

[2] See *Mancini* v. *D.P.P.* [1942] A.C. 1, in which the House of Lords emphasized that the trial judge need not leave the issue of manslaughter to the jury in every case, but only where there was evidence justifying such a verdict. It is important to note that Sankey was a member of the House which heard the appeal, and therefore concurred in this amendment of his judgment in *Woolmington*.

[3] Sankey papers.

Despite his loyal support for the Prime Minister in his most difficult hour, Sankey's place in the Cabinet does not seem to have been very strong. The experienced politicians around the table regarded some of Sankey's contributions to debate with a mixture of amusement and contempt. He lacked much of their equipment. Thus his knowledge of geography was faulty and he often was uncertain about the exact relationship of one country to another. So, conscientious as always, he brought a small atlas with him to Cabinet meetings, and when the discussion turned to foreign affairs he would produce it at the table and keep turning the pages to see where this or that country was. It was not surprising that criticism of him began to mount. In February 1934 we hear of Neville Chamberlain, the Chancellor of the Exchequer, plotting to replace him by Hailsham. But Sankey objected strongly to MacDonald ('I gather he wept!' Chamberlain recorded[4]), and nothing was done for the moment.

But in June 1935 the National Government was reconstructed. The Prime Minister's powers had been obviously failing for the past year and there was general relief when he exchanged places with Baldwin, the Lord President of the Council. At such a moment all members of the Cabinet place, or are deemed to place, their seals of office at the disposal of the new Prime Minister. Now Baldwin and his party had no reason to love Sankey. In addition Baldwin had a long friendship for and serious political obligations to his ex-Lord Chancellor, Hailsham. So that unless MacDonald made Sankey's continuance on the Woolsack an indispensable condition of his own membership of the Cabinet, it was plain that Sankey's position was precarious. But in fact MacDonald was anxious to secure a Cabinet post for his son Malcolm. So he jettisoned Sankey.

All these facts appear to have been known and their significance appreciated by everyone except Sankey himself. He surrendered the Great Seal on 7 June 1935 having held it for exactly six years—a longer period than any other Chancellor in this period except Halsbury and Loreburn. The Principal of Jesus, Hazel, wrote on 12 June:

Altogether I think this change on the Woolsack is bad business for the government as a National Government. I suppose when we get down to ultimates, the Tories have never forgiven you the 'Sankey Report'.

I am only an outsider and in no way 'in the know' but it looks as if J.R.M. was so anxious to get Malcolm into the Cabinet (for which he is not yet ripe, albeit an industrious and able person) that he didn't care who else was sacrificed. He ought to have insisted on your staying.[5]

Malcolm MacDonald himself wrote from Lossiemouth on 8 June:

[4] I. Macleod, *Neville Chamberlain* (1961), p. 166.
[5] Sankey papers. All subsequent quotations are from this source.

Dear Lord Sankey,

It was very charming of you at Buckingham Palace on Friday to come and wish me well in the new Cabinet, for I know that you must be feeling that I am only in it because you are out of it. Personally I wish that you were to be a colleague in my first Cabinet, for I have always enjoyed being associated with you in work, and you, despite the fact that you held the very high office of Lord Chancellor, have always been astonishingly kind to me as a young and undistinguished politician. I remember that I had the honour to serve you during the first Indian Round Table Conference, when you showed the very highest statesmanship and were largely responsible for the fact that that crucial conference ended successfully. If the Indian reforms work well, and relations between India and Gt. Britain are close and friendly in future, instead of troubled and bitter, you are one of the first half-dozen men whom we have to thank.

I remember too that you in a great way and I in a small way went together to the Labour Party meeting after the formation of the first National Government, to defend an unpopular cause. I can never tell you how grateful I felt to you for your courage and independence during those difficult times. The rank and file of the Labour Movement liked and trusted you, and your loyalty to the new government, I am certain, persuaded many of them to support it. So you have played a great part in two of the most fateful enterprises of modern times: saving Great Britain from the crisis of 1931, and creating friendship between the new British Empire and the new India.

Yours very sincerely,
Malcolm MacDonald

Hanworth, the Master of the Rolls, wrote on the 8th:

So your 'day of redemption' as you used to call it, has come, and I do not doubt that now that it has arrived you welcome it with mixed feelings. It is not easy to give up a post that has for so many years engaged your energies. I know that from experience. But there is a relief from burdens which have been heavy.

We must all be grateful to you for having faithfully upheld the law and your great position during the Labour Government of 1929–1931: and since then we must not overlook the difficult situation with some of the judges that arose from the 'cut'.

In these you preserved the judiciary from an unfortunate controversy and public disapproval. Then last December there culminated that unhappy outburst of which it is best to say as little as possible. Through these vicissitudes you have not had an easy time, and yet you have carried out several important legal reforms which will always be attached to your name. So I think you may take off your armour with the satisfaction of having done good work.

It has been a pleasure to me to back up where I could, and give such help as was possible, and I have valued the confidence, and the confidences, that you have entrusted to me. Accept my best thanks.

Now you must take a rest and then come back to help in the H.L. and at the Judicial Committee where you are much needed. We are here till Wednesday and then go to Cambridge where they are giving me an Hon: LL.D. on Thursday to my great pleasure.

Sankey managed to send a note of good wishes to his successor, who replied:

My dear Sankey,

I greatly appreciate your generous congratulations. I have very mixed feelings about the move. I was very happy at the War Office, & I liked leading the House: but as you & I know there is plenty of work in my new post & after all it is a very great office which calls for the best one has to give. One great regret is that I should displace you; and I appreciate all the more your letter. Probably you will want a holiday, or I would ask you to come & help over India; but I hope that later on you may return & lend a hand to

Yours,
Hailsham

Reading, the ex-Viceroy and Lord Chief Justice, wrote on the 29th:

I had hoped to see you when I returned for the 2nd Reading Debate on India. Your absence from the Lords disturbs me & makes me wonder whether I know the true facts. In any event you will not need my assurance that I shall always cherish the recollections of the close cordial & confidential relationship between you & me during your term of office—There is more I wish to say but first do let me know how you are & whether there will be an opportunity of our meeting before I have to go away.

Whatever the future regarding India the memories of your invaluable collaboration in the critical days particularly of the 1st Rd. Table Conference will remain with me & more important with all interested in the development of India.

Sankey replied on 4 July:

Next let me thank you for your kind letter which was very welcome and a real help at a time of disappointment and disillusionment. I did not retire from the Lord-Chancellorship, quite the contrary. I was anxious to continue and had actually prepared my speech on the India Bill and also notes for certain amendments which I knew would be made on Committee. However, politicians are queer things, and devoid of gratitude, however hard you work.

He wrote in similar terms to many other sympathizers.

One of the most interesting of the many letters which he received came from Professor A. L. Goodhart, of Oxford University:

May I say with what regret I read the news that you would resign the Lord Chancellorship—a regret which I know is shared by every member of the Oxford Law Faculty. In the long history of the Chancellorship your years of office will stand out as being among the most distinguished. As I see it, three

s*

features in particular will be noted by those who in future will describe the legal history of our time. (1) In no previous Chancellorship has the appointment to the Bench been so obviously based on merit. You have established the tradition that a choice must not be influenced by personal or partisan considerations. (2) Your insistence that legal reform must not be intermittent but should be part of a permanent policy has done much to affect the general attitude to the law. Other Lord Chancellors have favoured reform in particular branches of the law but you were the first one to state it as a general principle. (3) Your interest in the literature and the teaching of the law has materially helped to emphasize the idea that law is a learned profession and not merely a skilled craft. You have insisted that practice based on a mere routine knowledge of individual cases is not enough. These three great contributions which you have made will, I am certain, never be forgotten.

CHAPTER IV

AFTER HIS RETIREMENT Sankey does not seem to have felt entirely bound by the conventional obligation of an ex-Lord Chancellor to earn his pension by sitting judicially when requested to do so. Hailsham once tried to tempt him to do so, and succeeded, no doubt because the tactful terms of his letter were well calculated to soothe wounded feelings:

3 December 1935

First of all let me congratulate you on being Treasurer of the Middle Temple; I think it is such an honour. I calculate that I shall have to live to be well over eighty before my term comes at Lincoln's Inn. That is because you attained distinction so much earlier in life than I did. I understood from what you said last week that you are not coming for the de Clifford trial, and I cannot honestly press you for that, as I think we have already a wealth of judicial and other talent clamorous to be present. There is however a much more urgent need for your help early next sitting. There is in the list for hearing a case called *The County Council of the Parts of Lindsey (Lincolnshire)* v. *Marshall*. I understand from Schuster that it is a pure Common Law point and that the sort of question involved is as to the liability of the County Council which provides a hospital for the illness of some unhappy woman patient which is alleged to have occurred owing to the negligence of the matron or doctors of the hospital. Roche cannot sit, as he was in the Court of Appeal, and I shall normally therefore be only left with Atkin, who is rather apt to take the opportunity of making the law as it ought to be, instead of administering it as it is. I am really rather anxious, as to what may be formulated as the Common Law doctrine; Atkin is naturally apt to be followed by his fellow law lords of the Chancery or Scottish Bar on a Common Law point, and I should really value your assistance, in order to elucidate what the Common Law really is. What I should like best would be for you and me both to sit; but if it were an inducement to you to come I will gladly let you preside and go to the Privy Council.[1]

But after 1935 Sankey does not appear to have sat judicially until 1940.[2]

Sankey always went to great pains to be on friendly personal terms with all in public life, whether friend or foe. He was always ready with

---

[1] Sankey papers. For the case, see [1937] A.C. 97. In fact Hailsham presided.

[2] See *Lethbridge* v. *Independent Order of Foresters* [1940] A.C. 513, and *Apostolic Throne of St. Jacob* v. *Said* [1940] 1 All E.R. 54. In the latter case Sankey, for the Judicial Committee, delivered a full and interesting judgment distinguishing between a gold clause contract and a currency contract, and holding that the respondent, who had satisfied the pressing pecuniary needs of the Apostolic Throne, had been prudent enough to stipulate for a gold clause for the payment of his debt.

a cheerful greeting or an appropriate letter. Thus on 12 October 1940 he wrote to the Marquess of Salisbury to congratulate him upon the appointment of his son, Lord Cranborne, as Secretary of State for the Dominions, and received the following reply:

I have received your most kind letter. It is indeed a great satisfaction that my son should have got this promotion. You have said some very nice things about us, and of course I understand, that though differing from many trained in the same environment as we have been you recognize our good intentions. Some 10 years ago I went round the world with a parliamentary party which included several Labour M.P.s and a delightful Yorkshire Member, a Labour Member from Bradford, discriminated much as you have done. I am not sure that he would have criticized Labour organization but to him it was not the Conservatives of our type that he hated—though of course he differed from us—but the employers, the bad employers from whom he had suffered. I for one learnt a lot from him.[3]

Some believed that he carried this geniality of manner too far. The officials of his department thought it undignified for the Lord Chancellor, when in procession preceded by the Mace and Purse-Bearer, to halt for a word with an acquaintance passed in the corridors of the House. But there was no doubt that this geniality, which had, to the sensitive, perhaps a touch of the Welsh preacher in it, made a favourable impression. Thus when the office of High Steward of Oxford University fell vacant in 1930, it was thought by many that Simon had claims to be appointed by the Chancellor. But the then Vice-Chancellor, Dudden of Pembroke, represented to Grey that Simon's personal unpopularity in Oxford was so great that the appointment should rather be given to Sankey, as was done.[4]

Although Sankey in his retirement took no active part in political or legal life he still retained a sympathetic interest in the Labour Party and its doings. He wrote to Laski on 28 November 1939:

Many thanks for sending me your pamphlet on the Labour Party, the War, and the Future. I have read it with great interest, and may I add with complete approval, especially those parts on the need for vigilance and Labour's urgent tasks. As you know, I was dismissed from the Labour Party some years ago, but I hope I remain one of its best friends, and I have been very much upset recently by observing an attitude of defeatism in its members. I have no doubt this springs from always having to fight an overwhelming majority, but I should very much wish this spirit could be counteracted. Several times lately I have seen

---

[3] Sankey papers.
[4] As High Steward he delivered an admirable lecture on the great ecclesiastical and admiralty judge, Stowell, the brother of Eldon: Sankey, 'Lord Stowell' (1935), 52 L.Q.R. 327.

prominent members of the Party, who say 'We shall never be in again in my lifetime'. 'Well, it does not matter. I would rather be in opposition nowadays than in charge of affairs'. I ventured to tell one of them the other day that the Party would probably be in within a year or two, and the reply was most discouraging. My friend, a very distinguished man, simply smiled and said 'I hope not'.

Well, if the Labour Party do not want to get in, well and good, but personally I look upon the matter from the point of view of the country, and I think the return of the Labour Party is necessary for England, but of course I may be wrong.[5]

In 1942 a Committee headed by Mr. Justice Uthwatt (another old member of the Fabian Society) produced a Report on Compensation and Betterment. It was an integral part of the Government's post-war policy to ensure that the profits arising out of land development should be available for the benefit of the community as a whole, and the far-reaching recommendations to that end of the Uthwatt Committee were largely incorporated in the Town and Country Planning Act, 1947. Sankey wrote to Uthwatt on 16 September 1942:

Just a line to thank you for, and congratulate you upon, your excellent report. It is good that it has had such a splendid reception & I hope, & think, that it will sting some of our post war profiteers.

I trust you are getting a good rest & holiday. You ought to.[6]

In the same year there was some talk of Sankey rejoining the Labour Party, but the matter never came to anything. His last major political speech was in February 1943, when he eloquently urged the adoption of the Beveridge Report on Social Security.[7] It was indeed noticed by his friends that, the nationalization of coal apart, the great achievements of the Attlee Government in the post-war years evoked no interest in him. A certain apathy had begun to prevail.

Life at 13 Albert Place was quiet. It was not a house where people 'dropped in', and Sankey and his sister were not addicted to London social life. Before he went on the Bench he was sometimes to be seen at race meetings, but this was soon dropped. He never went to the cinema or theatre, though there were occasional visits to concerts. Otherwise Sankey's only relaxation was walking on the South Downs between two convenient stations. There were also trips to Switzerland and the Tyrol in August. It was noticed that all letters from his house were on black-edged paper. Surprised correspondents who inquired tactfully about recent bereavements were told that Sankey regarded himself as being in perpetual mourning since the death of his mother in 1921. It was not surprising that the atmosphere of 13 Albert Place was compared to that

[5] Laski papers.   [6] Uthwatt papers.   [7] 126 H.L. Deb. 5s. col. 275.

of Balmoral: in each case an entire household revolved smoothly around the wishes of one rather self-centred individual.

Sankey died at his home on 6 February 1948. His grave is on the southern side of the old churchyard at Moreton-in-Marsh, opposite that of his mother, only 200 yards from the house of his birth. His estate was sworn for probate at £85,588. The three institutions to which he was attached, Lancing, Jesus College, and the Church in Wales, received substantial benefits under his will.

APPENDIX

In *Torts* there are two good judgments produced in the year Sankey spent in the Court of Appeal—*Broome* v. *Agar* (1928) 139 L.T. 521 (innuendo in libel action), and *Lloyd's Bank* v. *Chartered Bank* [1929] 1 K.B. 40 (negligence by collecting bank). Sankey did not produce any major judgment on this subject while he was on the Woolsack, although in *Mechanical Inventions Co.* v. *Austin* [1935] A.C. 346 (infringement of patent; assessment of damages) there are some good dicta emphasizing that counsel as well as the judge owe a duty to the cause of justice, and that it may be broken by protracted and irrelevant cross-examination.

In *Contracts* there is a clear exposition in *Foster* v. *Driscoll* [1929] 1 K.B. 470 of the principles which will govern the question whether a contract should not be enforced on the ground that it is against public policy. Another aspect of this difficult question, appertaining to *Conflict of laws*, was also considered in *De Beéche* v. *South American Stores Ltd.* [1935] A.C. 148, in which the problem was whether an English court would permit a contracting party to refuse performance on the ground that performance would include the doing in a foreign country of something which the law of that country made illegal.

In *Criminal Law* besides the great judgment in *Woolmington* v. *D.P.P.* [1935] A.C. 462, emphasizing that the burden of proof was on the prosecution, there is a good judgment in *Maxwell* v. *D.P.P.* [1935] A.C. 309 on the difficult question of the admission of evidence of previous bad conduct on the part of the prisoner.

In *Constitutional Law* there is a clear treatment of the tests for distinguishing between an administrative and a judicial body in *Shell Co. of Australia* v. *Federal Commissioner of Taxation* [1931] A.C. 275. The two important decisions in *Edwards* v. *Attorney-General* [1930] A.C. 124, and *British Coal Corporation* v. *The King* [1935] A.C. 500, have already been considered.

In *International Law* there is a decision holding, on a special reference to the Judicial Committee, that a frustrated attempt at robbery at sea might amount to piracy: *In re Piracy Jure Gentium* [1934] A.C. 586. It is a full and careful judgment which perhaps goes farther than some authorities on international law would approve.

LORD MAUGHAM

CHAPTER I

FREDERIC HERBERT MAUGHAM was born on 20 October 1866, at
St. Cloud, a small village near Paris. He was the second of the four
surviving sons of Robert Ormond Maugham, by his wife Edith
Mary, the elder daughter of Major Charles Snell of the Indian Army.
Frederic Maugham in later life said that: 'For my part I claim to be one
of the members of that great and distinguished body known as the
English middle class, and like most of them my accurate knowledge does
not go much further back than my grand-parents.'[1] Although an elaborate
family tree has been printed[2] showing that Lord Maugham was the
twenty-third in descent from King Edward I (mainly through daughters
and second marriages) it will be sufficient here to start with his paternal
grandfather, Robert Maugham, whose ancestors had been small farmers
in the Lake District. He was educated at Appleby Grammar School, and
then articled to a firm of solicitors in London, who still carry on business
under the name of Tamplin & Co. in Bishopsgate. Robert Maugham was
an active man, who was one of the principal founders of the Law Society
in 1825, and was Secretary of it from 1831 to 1856. The picture of him
which has survived in the Law Society's Hall shows a man of vigorous
and Victorian character, and this impression is supported by the little
which is known of him. In *Sweet* v. *Maugham* (1840)[3] he was involved in
litigation in the Chancery Division, when the plaintiff, a partner in the well-
known legal publishing firm, claimed that Robert Maugham as Editor of the
Legal Observer (which later became the *Solicitors' Journal*) had infringed the
plaintiff's copyright in an article in *The Jurist*. The decision of the court
was that it was unnecessary for the plaintiff in a bill seeking an injunction
to specify the parts of the works which he alleged had been pirated.
Other legal proceedings involving a claim for breach of copyright in
which Robert Maugham was a party have been traced,[4] but this time he
appeared as plaintiff. He also found time to write a book on the subject of
copyright, as well as a number of other miscellaneous writings. His son,

---

[1] Viscount Maugham, *At the End of the Day* (1954), p. 6. I am grateful to Messrs.
William Heinemann Ltd. for permission to quote from this work.

[2] P. Montague-Smith, 'Two Royal Descents' (1952), II 'The Genealogists' Magazine',
207.

[3] 2 Sim. 51.

[4] See S. Rubinstein, 'Piracy at the Solicitors Final Examination' (1959) 56 The Law
Society's Gazette 619.

Robert Ormond Maugham, settled in Paris as a solicitor, and built up a flourishing practice there amongst the expatriate British community. It is interesting to note that in 1885 a case relating to him came before the Divisional Court of the Queen's Bench Division. The question was whether work done by Robert Maugham as a solicitor in France was liable to taxation in England. The court called for the bill of costs, and 'seeing numerous items of six shillings and eightpence said this had a very English look, and as the Attorney was an English Attorney and employed by British subjects by retainer sent from England, it must be taken that his bill was subject to taxation according to English law.'[5]

As a child Frederic Maugham encountered the excitement of the Franco-Prussian War of 1870 and its aftermath of civil disorder in Paris itself. He was first sent to a French lycée, and like another Lord Chancellor of our period, Lord Cave, acquired a fluent knowledge of French, and an impeccable accent, which remained with him for the rest of his life. With his brothers he was then dispatched to Dover College, which was clearly a convenient place for parents living in Paris to send their children.

My life at Dover was very unhappy for the first year or two, for I was a shy and doubtless an unattractive boy with a slight French accent and no knowledge of games. My brothers and I were at first called 'froggies' since we came from Paris, and, I suspect, wore French clothes. Nor does a boy know of his own peculiarities of speech. It took me many years to acquire an English pronunciation of a good many words derived from the French; I still cannot without deliberation pronounce (or mispronounce) the words 'liqueur' or 'blouse' or 'landau' and other French words as an Englishman does.[6]

Originally it was intended that the Maugham children should proceed from Dover College to Winchester, but their parents were satisfied with Dover, so the children remained there. In later years Maugham appears to have felt a certain resentment at this decision.

At Cambridge and at the Bar, I of course met men from many schools, and I cannot say that I ever felt that they had gained any advantages over me from having been at the more celebrated establishments, except one, which is a very important one. Wherever they go they find friends, probably wearing the same 'school tie', who are willing and anxious to give them a helping hand; and in many cases their kindly words spoken in time may make all the difference between success and failure. I could name several politicians in my time who would never have reached positions in the Government if they had come from small and undistinguished schools.[7]

At Dover Maugham developed a natural aptitude for mathematics.

[5] (1885) 87 L.T. News. 418.   [6] *At the End of the Day*, p. 15.   [7] Ibid., pp. 14–15.

PLATE 21

Lord Maugham as Chancellor

PLATE 22

Lord Maugham in later life

I hope I shall not be thought a prig if I confess that I saw beauty in certain of the theorems and propositions to be found in text books of algebra and Euclid. . . . The geometry of curves filled me with pleasure—conic sections, spirals, cycloids, trochoids and so forth, and I am still amazed at the surprising propositions which have been discovered in reference to these simple figures, and also at the algebraical theorems to which the names of some great men are attached.[8]

Others who have been devoted to mathematics have testified to the aesthetic pleasure which they have found in its study.

The course of Maugham's life was now altered by the death of his parents within a few years of each other. At the age of eighteen together with his three brothers[9] he was thrown on the world with a small capital sum, his sole other resource being an Entrance Scholarship to Trinity Hall of eighty pounds a year, and a school-leaving Scholarship of fifty pounds a year. The children's guardians were a London solicitor, Albert Dixon, and their uncle, Henry Maugham, the vicar of Whitstable. This cleric has been immortalized in the novel *Of Human Bondage* by Somerset Maugham, the youngest brother, who spent his years in the unsympathetic atmosphere of the Rectory, and left such a mordant account of it.

In the Michaelmas Term of 1885 Frederic Maugham went up to Trinity Hall, a young man almost alone in the world, with a tiny capital sum, some reputation for mathematics, and a fair degree of skill at games. 'The railway-station can only be described as dingy and sordid; but never have I emerged from it on a visit to Cambridge without a thrill. Old as I am, it is with a beating heart that I walk along a street with buildings of a lovely grey tint and I do not enter or pass the entrance gates of Colleges without emotion.[1]' All who have been members of the University of Cambridge will echo Maugham's affectionate words, written when he was nearing his ninetieth year. The emotions of this rather solitary and self-contained young man were centred from the first mainly on his college. His rooms

were just under the tiles and were very cold in winter and sometimes unbearably hot in summer, but for me it was Heaven and for three years they were my home. My parents being dead, and there being no relatives who could take me in, I had in truth no other home, and I think that Cambridge from that circumstance meant more to me than it did to anyone else of my acquaintance. All my clothes, my knick-knacks, all my books, in a word, all my scanty belongings were in those two small rooms. I bought the furniture in Cambridge;

[8] Ibid., p. 19.
[9] Two of these brothers, Harry (an author), and Charles (who succeeded to his father's position as a solicitor in Paris), died young.
[1] *At the End of the Day*, p. 23.

I can well remember the shock I received on the arrival of the bill. But the chairs and book-case were of oak and solid enough to withstand any vicissitudes. I still possess some of them hidden away in back regions of my present house, and I think no-one but myself could imagine that they were possessed of the smallest element of romance.[2]

Trinity Hall in those days was a small College famous mainly for its achievements on the river. The Master was the famous Sir Henry Maine, the author of *Ancient Law*, but to Maugham 'He was a tired, overworked man, and such a person finds it very difficult to be light-hearted (*desipere*) even in the right place.'[3]

Maugham confessed in later life that he devoted little time to his mathematical studies; indeed he doubted whether after his first few weeks at Trinity Hall he ever worked more than an hour or two a day, and very often not even that. His energies and enthusiasms were concentrated on rowing. He rowed for the College in three successive years, 1887, 1888, and 1889, in each of which the Hall boat went Head of the River. In 1888 and 1889 he rowed (as number seven) in the successful Cambridge crew in the University Boat Race. He also became Captain of the College rugby fifteen for the years 1887 to 1888, and outside sporting activities, was prominent enough in the University to be elected President of the Union in 1888. All these activities necessarily affected his performance in the Mathematical Tripos. Like another future Lord Chancellor, Buck-master at Christ Church a few years before, he failed to obtain the degree to which his native abilities entitled him. But whereas Buckmaster's failure was due entirely to the strain caused by overwork, Maugham as he candidly admitted in later years, failed to obtain the highest honours simply by reason of his concentration on rowing, and the lack of intellec-tual stimulus provided by a small College to a young man who was not over-anxious to work.

The Tripos examinations of 1888 unfortunately for me came on while I was rowing every evening in the Head of the River boat. The examination was in two parts and I fancy I did pretty well in the first part, known as 'the first three days'. The names of those who passed that mild test were put up in alphabetical order on the Senate House door. Then came after a fortnight's interval the real Tug-of-War—the 'second three days'. Rowing daily, whether in hard practice or in actual racing, is not calculated to improve one's mathematical form. I found I was mentally tired each afternoon after only half an hour's work in answering papers and indeed more than once I was nearly overcome with sleep. One afternoon was little short of a tragedy and my eyes closed. I was therefore not surprised to find when the list came out that I was placed fifth among the 'Senior Optimi', with four 'Senior Ops' above me and seventeen

[2] *At the End of the Day*, p. 22.   [3] Ibid., p. 43.

Wranglers. Had I worked reasonably well at mathematics and also given up rowing, as other men did while the examinations were in progress, I think I could not have failed to be some ten to fifteen places higher; though I could never have been close to the top. It was a very disappointing result; but entirely my own fault. Like most men of my time at Cambridge, I found sports and games were much more attractive than work, and in my case there was no one at any time to urge me to give more time to mathematics. Looking back, however, after the lapse of over half a century I am not sure that I should have got together a practice at the Bar less slowly than I did if I had been, say, tenth Wrangler; and it is the truth, though I dare say not much to my credit, that I was not only proud of getting my Blue for rowing, but greatly encouraged at the time by an illogical feeling that I was capable in some directions at least of climbing to the top.[4]

On 17 November 1890 Maugham was called to the Bar at Lincoln's Inn, on the same day as his college friend Mark Romer, the son of (Sir) Robert Romer, later a Lord Justice, who had himself been appointed a Chancery judge by Lord Halsbury on that very day. Maugham owed a great deal to the Romer family, and constantly confessed his indebtedness to them: 'Being a shy and lonely lad without parents, the unstinted affection of Robert and Betty Romer were of extraordinary value to me in my early days, and to this good fortune I owe to a great extent my future success.'[5] These friends found him lodgings in London in Sydney Street Chelsea (the rent being twenty-five shillings a week). Robert Romer also induced Edward Beaumont, the well-known conveyancer to take on Maugham as a pupil (it will be recalled that Beaumont had as a pupil another future Lord Chancellor, S. O. Buckmaster). The connection with the Romer family became even closer when, on 17 December 1896, Maugham married the only daughter, Helen Mary. Maugham's first appearance in court was before Mr. Justice Stirling, a careful but somewhat slow judge, 'He listened to me with his invariable patience—much to my relief; for I was very nervous, though I hope I concealed the fact.'[6] After leaving Beaumont, Maugham was a pupil with J. G. Butcher, for a year, and after leaving Butcher (for whom he had no great regard) he was taken by Charles Macnaghten, into his chambers at 3 New Square as a 'devil'. Macnaghten was a son of Lord Macnaghten, and a good deal of work flowed into his chambers. In fact at first there was no room for Maugham at 3 New Square, and he was obliged to take a small set of chambers at 14 Old Square. This, as he said,[7] was not a satisfactory arrangement for he lost chances for meeting Macnaghten's clients, whilst devilling their work. But in 1895 a vacancy occurred at 3 New Square and Maugham moved in. 'I remained there for no less than thirty-three

[4] Ibid., pp. 49–50.   [5] Ibid., pp. 25–26.   [6] Ibid., p. 32.   [7] Ibid., p. 59.

years, and only left in 1928 to cross Carey Street and to occupy a Judge's room in the Royal Courts.'[8]

Maugham undoubtedly found his early years at the Bar exceptionally hard. He knew little or nothing of conditions of life in London in general and at the Bar in particular, and in later years was accustomed to say that he would have been wise if he had first served a year in a solicitor's office before being called to the Bar. The wearisome business of waiting for work to come in undoubtedly helped to accentuate his natural reserve, and the somewhat supercilious impression which he created may well be traced back to the lonely years of waiting for briefs in Lincoln's Inn. He left a vivid account of it himself:

When I was sitting at work in my room I could, of course, hear the door to the chambers being opened and some person entering the clerk's room, usually a client. Was it by a remote chance a set of papers coming for me? I could not help but hear the conversation with at times a disturbed heart. The necessity of getting briefs especially if one has a wife and children to support is of a very poignant kind. How often, how distressingly often, the papers were for Macnaghten or Watson! A day, sometimes a whole week, would go by without any of these glorious sheets of paper tied up with red tape arriving with my name on the back. The waiting for work is a terrible drawback to a young barrister's life and tends to sour his whole existence.

I shall never forget those unhappy days. Years after, when I was Lord Chancellor, I had to make a speech at an annual meeting of that great institution the Barristers' Benevolent Society in Lincoln's Inn Hall at which the Duchess of Kent was kind enough to preside. Amongst other things I pointed out how many and great are the difficulties which beset the career of the young barrister. I tried to express his troubled fate under the simile of a large number of little sailing yachts being launched on the bank of a large piece of water, and to narrate how some of them seem to catch a slight breeze pretty quickly and do get on, and others were becalmed and appeared to be unable to advance, and how the unlucky drifted to and fro without ever reaching the middle of the stream where there was generally some chance of a favourable wind. And I naturally added that if some of us had managed to reach the distant shore it was mainly through the operations of chance, a circumstance which ought to persuade us to be generous to the unlucky, who had been becalmed or had met with other mishaps, and had never reached the other side. I think I touched some generous minds.[9]

Maugham's fee-books have not survived, but he has himself left an account of his earnings in his early years. In his first two years he earned about £70, in the third £93, in his fourth £108, in his fifth £230. In

---

[8] *At the End of the Day*, p. 59.

[9] Ibid., pp. 59–60. In his will Maugham left the Barristers' Benevolent Association the sum of £100.

his sixth year after call there was a distinct improvement for his fees amounted to £691.

But that sum included some payments of arrears made by two well-disposed firms who had heard of my approaching marriage. In 1897, my first year of married life, I received only £290, a most disheartening result, which made it not very easy to sleep soundly at night. But there came a turn for the better, and in the next year I made £694. In 1899 the total was £897. After 1900 I began to forge steadily ahead, and by 1911 I was making between £4000 and £5000 a year, a very good income for a Junior at the Chancery Bar.[1]

[1] Ibid., p. 60.

CHAPTER II

IN THE SUMMER OF 1913 Maugham was pressed by his friends and several of the Chancery judges to apply for silk. He duly did so, and was called within the Bar by Lord Chancellor Haldane. The move was a success. 'I found that I thoroughly enjoyed being in charge of a case, with a duty to examine and cross-examine witnesses myself and to address the Judge in my own way. Briefs as a Leader began to come in at once, and in the course of a few months I felt confident that I was giving satisfaction to solicitors and litigants, and that Judges approved of my method of conducting my cases.'[1] Two years later in 1915 Maugham was made a Bencher of Lincoln's Inn. During this period Maugham appeared in some of the heaviest litigation at the Chancery Bar. In particular he was concerned with the proceedings arising out of the winding-up of the Law Guarantee Trust and Accident Society Limited, which had been formed as far back as 1888 by a number of eminent practitioners and for some years had carried on business with apparent success, until the directors, who comprised some of the most eminent members of the solicitors' profession, allowed the manager, one Ronald, too large a hand in the conduct of business.

By the end of 1909 the Society had become insolvent, and very heavy claims were pending against its members. Although the capital was large the shares were only partly paid up, and a number of persons including Sir Edward Clarke found themselves with very heavy calls for unpaid capital. A scheme of arrangement was sanctioned by the court in 1910, but there were legal difficulties of almost every kind arising out of claims against the directors, against the shareholders for calls, against the re-insurers and other persons. Maugham was substantially in charge of the legal side of the litigation and his chambers were piled high with papers dealing with the affairs of the Law Guarantee Society. For some years, indeed, he was so busy with it that he was obliged to refuse much other business. Eventually a case which if fought out might well have lasted as long as the Tichborne case was compromised, and by 1916 the affairs of the Society had been finally wound up.

Maugham was also concerned with the lengthy proceedings which followed the death of Lord Northcliffe and the struggle for the acquisition of his shares in *The Times*.[2] On the one hand there was Northcliffe's

---

[1] *At the End of the Day*, p. 67.
[2] See *The History of The Times* (1952), vol. iv, chap. 19.

brother Rothermere, and on the other hand there was the family of John Walter which had printed and published *The Times* for several generations, and was now anxious to regain control in order to conduct the newspaper on traditional lines. Rothermere possessed the advantage of having a large sum in ready money wherewith to purchase the shares, but Walter had the advantage of having an option under the will of Northcliffe. The option itself, however, was of somewhat dubious value, because the will could or might have been contested on several grounds. In addition time was running against Walter because the break-up of the coalition Government, a few months after Northcliffe's death, had vastly increased the value of the shares, and in consequence, the sum to be found by him. It so happened that the fate of *The Times* was decided on the same day as the fate of the coalition Government itself, Thursday, 19 October 1922. By lunch-time it was known throughout London that the Government was out of office as a result of the vote at the Carlton Club meeting that morning. At 2 p.m. all parties appeared in court before Sir Henry Duke, the President of the Probate, Admiralty, and Divorce Division. Maugham appeared for Sir George Sutton, the administrator of Northcliffe's estate. It was known that Rothermere was prepared to offer an exceedingly high sum for the shares. After a lengthy argument Maugham rose to say that it had occurred to Sutton and his advisers that Walter's option might be recognized in this sense, that instead of having three months in which to make up his mind, he should be obliged to decide within a very short period.

Of course, if it is asked why he should do that, the answer is, because it is not certain that he has any rights at all. If there is to be any dealing with this interest at all, it is a case where, it seems to me, both sides may very well be advised to make something in the nature of a concession to the other. If, by reason of any opposition, the thing should not go through, it may be that Mr. Walter will lose all his rights. That is, to some extent, a matter of gamble, of which I know nothing.

What I was going to propose was this: if Lord Rothermere exchanges with the administrator, subject to your Lordship thinking that it is a proper course, a contract conditional to the sanction of your Lordship of the contract for the purchase of the whole of the shares at the price in question—there is no objection to my stating the figure:[3]

A breathless moment then ensued in court; no objection was stated, and Maugham proceeded, with according to the official historian of *The Times*, 'a sentence that astounded the Court': 'The figure suggested is £1,350,000 payable according to the terms of the document before me, as to £500,000 within fourteen days of the Order approving this agreement, and the

[3] *The History of the Times*, p. 760.

balance at certain other dates.'[4] This was indeed a stupendous sum and the time stipulated for finding the money was short in the extreme. Nevertheless, with the assistance of the Astor family, the money was found by John Walter and the shares of *The Times* passed out of the control of the Northcliffe interest. A great national institution had been saved.

It so happened that in the middle of conducting this heavy litigation, Maugham's own career reached a turning point. He was offered the Solicitor-Generalship in the new Conservative administration to be formed under Bonar Law. The offer was conveyed to him through Douglas Hogg, the Attorney-General-Elect, who, as we have already seen,[5] had been appointed to the position within a day or so of the fall of the coalition. Maugham recorded later:

This agreeable prospect sent me post-haste down to the Conservative Central Office to see what seat or seats were still vacant; but the persons in charge said it was too late, and that there was not a chance of a vacant seat. I made one or two other inquiries and then had to give up the project. It is true that I had the compensatory feeling that I was saving a large amount of income; but I should have greatly welcomed a year or two in the Commons in an official position. My friend Tom Inskip (afterwards Lord Caldecote) profited by my bad luck; he became the Solicitor-General and began his career to the Woolsack.[6]

A few days after his rebuff by the Central Office, Maugham received a letter from Lord Justice Younger, whose brother Sir George Younger was the Chief Whip of the Conservative Party.

I.11.22

My dear Freddy,

I am in tears over you. What an opportunity missed by the Government. It is enough to make a cat cry.

Are you going to my brother. If you are, let me know, and he shall have an introduction from me as well.

I am only refraining from writing him as it is because he is, I fancy, very hard pressed and there is no advantage in writing to him, so to speak, in the air at such a moment.

But I *am* sorry.

Yours always, R.Y.[7]

The fact that this offer was made to Maugham at all may be taken to indicate both the lack of parliamentary legal talent at the disposal of the Bonar Law Government and his high standing at the Bar. For although

---

[4] *The History of the Times*, p. 760.
[5] See above, pp. 460–3.
[6] *At the End of the Day*, pp. 85–86.
[7] Maugham papers.

an undoubted supporter of the Conservative Party his career in politics had so far been limited to speaking (unsuccessfully) in support of his friend Ellis Hume-Williams, K.C., at North Kensington at the general election of 1906. Maugham had taken no part in public life, and his career had been entirely confined to the Chancery Bar. His war work had been of a somewhat restricted kind. Aged nearly 50 when the war broke out he was able to do no more than act as a member of a body of special constables sworn in to patrol the grounds of Buckingham Palace.

Maugham reverted to his practice as a leading Chancery silk. There was more than enough to do. The manner which some found cold and forbidding can be ascribed as much to the fact that he was thoroughly over-worked as to the reactions of a shy and reserved man to the hardships of his early years. He also seems to have felt some dissatisfaction, perhaps only temporary, at the progress of his professional career. Around 1924 he confessed to Gavin Simonds, K.C., that he felt he had been passed by in the struggle for success at the Bar. But in 1928, when he was aged 61, he was offered a puisne judgeship in the Chancery Division, in succession to Mr. Justice P. O. Lawrence, who had been promoted to the Court of Appeal. The vacancy had been pending for some weeks, but it so happened that it had to be filled in the very first days of Douglas Hogg's tenure of the Woolsack, even before the new Lord Chancellor had been created a peer. Maugham was at first inclined to refuse. He told Hogg, 'That if I had been offered the position some years before at a time when I might have had some hope of a distinguished judicial career, my feelings would have been very different.'[8] He also pointed out that his income would fall by four-fifths, and that before he would have earned his pension by 15 years' service he would have been obliged to retire by reason of incapacity. Hogg pressed him with 'some flattering arguments' and Maugham took a voyage to Gibraltar to think it over. On his return, with the help of some pressure from his wife, he decided to accept.

The new Lord Chancellor wrote on 31 March:

I have just heard by telephone that you have decided to accept; and I write this note to say how glad I am, and to be the first to congratulate the new Judge. I was so anxious that my first appointment should be a good one and one that would commend itself to the profession; and now I know that I need have no fears on that score.

You may like to know that when I was discussing this matter some weeks ago with poor Cave, he agreed with me that you were obviously the right man and he had intended to offer you the vacancy.

May you have many years in which to adorn and enjoy the office, and to render service to the State.[9]

[8] *At the End of the Day*, p. 334.   [9] Maugham papers.

A number of congratulatory letters arrived. Sir Frederick Pollock wrote:

April 16 1928

My best congratulations on your accession to the Bench of the Chancery Division. Common sense and knowledge of mankind have been a great asset to our modern equity decisions, though the public don't understand it, and you will contribute a full share of those qualities as well as of good law. [1]

Simon, who had just left for India as Chairman of the Statutory Commission, also sent his congratulations. Maugham replied:

15th April 1928

Very many thanks for your kind note.

When you sailed on the mission (so well begun, if I may say so), I never intended to become a Judge: but I found that circumstances including the persuasive tongue of Douglas Hogg were too strong for me.

And now—so vain is man—all the nice letters I have received, including yours, have gone a long way to making me happy. . . .[2]

Another letter came from Fergus Morton (later Lord Morton of Henryton):

16.4.28

I want to send you my best congratulations, and best wishes for a long and happy time on the Bench. I don't see any reason for wishing you *success*, because it is perfectly obvious that you have achieved it all through your life and will go on achieving it. But I do hope that you will thoroughly enjoy the more dignified and (may I say it) more restful position which you have now attained, for you must have led a terribly hard life for many years, and I for one, felt grieved to see how tired you looked at the end of each term.

I should like to take this chance of saying how much I have appreciated your unvarying friendliness to me ever since I returned from the War, entirely briefless and rather hopeless of ever getting a brief. Treatment of that kind from the leaders of the Bar does make a difference to an unknown Junior.[3]

Maugham was a success as a Chancery judge. His reported judgments show that he had a mind of formidable analytical power. A full assessment of his judgments will be found in the Appendix. In the meantime it is enough to say that in *Re Askew*[4] he dealt with one of the more difficult problems in the field of conflict of laws (renvoi) in a masterly manner. Like all Maugham's judgments, but unlike many Chancery Division judgments, it is written in a crisp and lucid style which is a pleasure to

[1] Maugham papers.
[2] Simon papers.
[3] Maugham papers.
[4] [1930] 2 Ch. 259.

read. A year after his appointment he received a letter from Lord Buckmaster:

12.12.29

A case you tried with patience I admire but cannot imitate received rough
handling in the C.A.

I thought therefore you might like to see our judgment which, though not
yet delivered, will certainly not be altered and which unless I sent it to you might
not come to your notice.

It is I think fair to say that the C.A. suffered from the incomparable incapacity
of the gentleman who is now a member of their august tribunal.[5]

It has already been seen that Maugham took an active part in the
dispute between the judges and the Cabinet in 1931–2 over the cuts in
judicial salaries.[6] He drafted the memorandum of protest which the
judges submitted, and was a member of the deputation which had an
interview with Sankey. It is a tribute to all parties that these activities did
not interfere with his professional advancement. In January 1934 the
Prime Minister, Ramsay MacDonald, appointed him to the place in the
Court of Appeal left vacant by the resignation of Lord Justice Lawrence.

Sir John Astbury, the retired Chancery judge, wrote to Maugham:

9th January 1934

Just a line to tell you how pleased I was to hear that you have been put in
the Court of Appeal. It seems only the other day, that I was pressing you to
take silk, which you obstinately refused to do; now you have been given the
almost impossible task of keeping Hanworth somewhere near the rails. I hope
you will have a happy time where you are going and not find it too exasperating
never to be quite your own master.[7]

This letter was annotated by Maugham:

(The statement in this letter is true. I was quite content as a busy and successful
Junior.)

Two of the Law Lords also wrote in similar terms. Lord Russell of
Killowen wrote:

6/1/34

A line of warm congratulations from all here on your appointment. There
are pros and cons in the berth as compared with the autocracy of your own
Court, but the balance is I think on the right side. Anyway all will rejoice at
the strengthening of the M.R.'s Court!

As you succeeded to my ermine so must you insert yourself into my black

[5] Maugham papers. The letter is annotated in Maugham's handwriting: The House of
Lords were about to overrule the C.A. and to restore my judgment. The case was
Jonesco v. *Beard* [1930] A.C. 298.

[6] See above, pp. 513–19.   [7] Maugham papers.

and gold which lies at Ravenscrofts' awaiting your wishes: and no delicate questions of waist measurements can arise, so a perfect fit is guaranteed. If you agree let R's state a sum; and if you like I will throw in a frock coat on loan for the occasion of your Privy Council swearing in. Good luck to you and our loves to Nellie and yourself.[8]

Lord Macmillan wrote:

8th January 1934

We are delighted that you enter upon the New Year with added dignity and status and we send our warm and hearty congratulations to the new Lord Justice. If Hanworth has his way it will be a case of *moriturum te salutamus*! But it remains to be seen whether his project will prove acceptable and in any event it will be a distinction to have been the last of the Lords Justices![9] I hope the promotion—so admirably earned and in which all your friends rejoice—will mean less strenuous work for you.[1]

[8] Maugham papers.
[9] This is a reference to some unsuccessful proposals for the reform of the Court of Appeal which were the subject of a bitter debate in the House of Lords: see above, pp. 519–20.
[1] Maugham papers.

CHAPTER III

AUGHAM'S PERIOD IN THE COURT OF APPEAL was brief. In October 1935, on the death of Lord Tomlin, he was appointed to the House of Lords to fill the vacant place. But scarcely had he become accustomed to the pleasant life of a Chancery Law Lord than his career was further interrupted. In March 1938 Lord Hailsham resigned in circumstances which have already been explained,[1] and the Prime Minister, Neville Chamberlain, to the astonishment of the political and legal world, offered the Woolsack to Maugham. Apart from his unsuccessful attempt to secure a parliamentary seat in October 1922 Maugham was entirely without political experience, either local or national. Indeed so divorced was he from the world of affairs that he had never even met the Prime Minister before their interview at No. 10 Downing Street on 9 March 1938. In addition he was aged 71 years—the oldest member of a Cabinet which (apart from Anthony Eden) was not notable for its youth. It is true that Eldon, Campbell, and Finlay had each been appointed to the Woolsack at a greater age, but then each of them had also had considerable parliamentary experience. It was a remarkable appointment at a time when a succession of grave crises, foreign and domestic, were threatening the stability of the Government. Maugham himself always confessed that he had no idea how his name had been placed before the Prime Minister; but those entitled to judge expressed the view that Sir Claud Schuster had had much to do with it. The only other candidates whom the Conservative Party might have favoured for the Woolsack were the Law Officers: Sir Donald Somervell, the Attorney-General and Sir Terence O'Connor, the Solicitor-General. There was also the former Attorney-General, Sir Thomas Inskip, at that moment holding the office of Minister for the Co-ordination of Defence. The Prime Minister or his advisers may have thought that neither of the Law Officers carried sufficient legal weight to compensate for their political skill, and that it was inexpedient politically to disturb Inskip's position at that moment in his newly formed Ministry. Maugham himself asked the Prime Minister to reassure him about the position of Inskip:

I asked him what he was doing about my friend Inskip, and said plainly that I should be unwilling to become Lord Chancellor if he was being left out in the cold. The Prime Minister at once assured me that 'all that was settled' and that Inskip was quite content with what had been arranged. He also gave me

[1] See p. 488 above.

to understand that affairs were in such a curious state that I might be asked to give up my position before the Government went out of office. I quite understood that and said that in that event I should like to be re-appointed as a Lord of Appeal if there should be a vacancy at an early date. He agreed to do that if it could be done.[2]

The interview at No. 10 ended with Maugham, after the fashion of his generation, producing an apt classical quotation:

As I rose to go it occurred to me to explain why I did not say anything about my want of political experience, and I asked him if he remembered the story of the Roman soldier to whom Julius Caesar had given a high command. When the brothers in arms of the soldier expressed some surprise at his appointment, he replied: 'Cur me posse negem, posse quod ille putat?' I translated this as meaning: 'Why should I doubt whether I am fit for the job, if *he* thinks I can tackle it?'[3]

The Attorney-General, Somervell, may have felt some disappointment at being passed over in this way, but he always concealed it and spoke with affection of Maugham: 'Better be a man of Munich than a man of Yalta', he once remarked.[4]

Maugham received the Great Seal on 15 March 1938. On the following day he was sworn in before the Master of the Rolls and took his seat on the Woolsack to the accompaniment of polite speeches from both sides of the House. In reply Maugham said that he spoke with some embarrassment, 'nonetheless because I have spent the greater part of my life in a profession in which embarrassment is generally avoided and always disguised.'[5] Maugham entered upon his work with enthusiasm. Any expectations that the former Chancery judge would be reserved or shy in his manner of controlling the House were at once disappointed. In May 1938 the Coal Bill received its Second Reading. It was met with determined opposition extending over ten parliamentary days and 850 columns of Hansard from some of the most experienced and skilful debaters in England. The object of the Bill was to 'unify' (the word nationalization was carefully avoided) the royalties of the coal owners. The separate ownership of royalties had been found to be a deterrent to the proper working of the industry, and while the ownership of coal was to vest in an independent statutory body, it was proposed to buy out the royalty owners by distributing to them as compensation a global sum. The sum in question represented 15 years purchase of the average annual income and amounted to £66,450,000. Maugham adopted a somewhat hectoring tone which the peers resented. In particular they objected to being given

2 *At the End of the Day*, p. 341.   3 Ibid., pp. 341–2.
4 To the author in 1959.   5 108 H.L. Deb. 5s. col. 127.

what one of them described as a lecture on the importance of not voting according to private pecuniary interests.[6] Lord Stanhope, then Leader of the House, recorded later that he felt irritation at Maugham's attitude, which often succeeded in irritating peers whom Stanhope had pacified by delicate negotiation behind the scenes.[7] Maugham appears to have been happily unconscious of the feelings which he aroused. In his auto-biography he stated:

On a retrospect I think Lords Stanhope, Munster and I are entitled to some credit in the arduous work of improving a very complex and difficult Bill. On a rough estimate I must have made over a hundred speeches. The early ones were received with a good deal of opposition and even hostility, for the Bill greatly reduced the incomes from coal royalties which some of their Lordships were enjoying, but the instinct for fair play which is evident in most of our debates came to my assistance and my remarks were accepted as a true statement of existing law, and they appreciated the fact that I had nothing to do with fixing the global sum which would be distributable among the royalty owners, and was trying to make the Bill a fairer document. In the end I made some good friends in the course of the debates, including a number who were opposed to the Bill.[8]

Maugham also took a leading part in steering through a number of major Acts during the next year. For example the Inheritance (Family Provision) Act, the Limitation Act, the Administration of Justice Act, the Prevention of Fraud (Investments) Act, and the Official Secrets Act.

Perhaps the most important piece of legislation for which Maugham was responsible, personally as well as officially, was the Evidence Act of 1938. This effected a major change in an important part of the law and has been of benefit to numerous litigants ever since. It was an important practical piece of law reform which rightly reflects great credit on Maugham. As he himself remarked later: 'If I shall have left any footprint on the sands of time it will perhaps turn out to be the Act to amend the Law of Evidence.'[9] The Act dealt with the hearsay rule, a judge-made rule which prohibited the courts from receiving in evidence oral or written statements made by persons not present in court and giving evidence on oath, or made by such persons on some prior occasion. The rule was subject to exceptions, some of them not very logical, and was itself based on a fundamental fallacy in that it confused the admissibility of evidence with its weight. The true view, as Bentham long ago pointed out, was that all evidence should be admissible for what it is worth; the question of the weight to be attached to such evidence when admitted is another matter. No doubt the fact that the statements in question were

[6] 108 H.L. Deb. 5s. col. 860.   [7] In a letter to the author in 1959.
[8] *At the End of the Day*, p. 396.   [9] Ibid., p. 340.

not made by a party under the sanction of an oath is a reason for placing less weight upon them, but it is not a reason for refusing entirely to receive such statements in evidence. Maugham's interest in this matter had gone back a considerable way, for he had first suggested the reform at the Annual Meeting of the judges in 1931. There does not seem to be any other recorded example of a puisne judge of the Chancery Division suggesting and attempting to carry into effect an important legal reform. As a result of Maugham's arguments in 1931, a Committee was formed consisting of Lord Justice Greer, Mr. Justice Avory, Mr. Justice Langton, Mr. Justice Roche, and Maugham. The committee considered a Bill drafted by Maugham and after receiving comments from the General Council of the Bar and the Law Society, an attempt was made to secure its passage into law. Despite the valuable nature of the proposed reform, and the fact that on the recommendation of the General Council of the Bar in order to avoid controversy the Bill was limited in its effect to civil as distinct from criminal law proceedings, it was impossible to find parliamentary time for it. The matter then lapsed until Maugham himself became a peer in October 1935, when he attempted unsuccessfully to persuade the Government to take the matter up. Later he himself introduced the Bill in the House of Lords on 2 February 1938, shortly before he became Lord Chancellor. On 22 February he briefly but cogently stated the reasons for the Bill in his Second Reading speech. He gave an example from his own experience of the hardships which existed under the present law, but which would be cured by the Bill. An eminent engineer was sent abroad to examine and report upon a mine. He made an elaborate report to his employers. Litigation subsequently arose and his evidence was urgently required. But he was in a distant country and declined to return to England or to give evidence on commission. His written report was available, but could not according to the existing law be put in evidence.[1] The Bill passed the House of Lords and in May was given a passage by the House of Commons without amendment. On 26 May 1938 Maugham, by now Lord Chancellor, had the pleasure of hearing the royal assent being given to the Bill. The Evidence Act of 1938 has worked well in practice. Indeed the Committee on Supreme Court Practice and Procedure which sat under the Chairmanship of Lord Evershed and issued its report in 1953[2] recommended that the Act should be used as widely and as vigorously as possible, and that some amendments should be made in it to cure difficulties in its working which the

[1] 107 H.L. Deb. 5s. col. 804. Maugham later published an interesting account of the genesis of the Act: 'Observations on the Law of Evidence' (1939) 17 Can. Bar Rev. 469. See also *At the End of the Day*, pp. 336–40.

[2] Cmd. 8878. See also R. Cross, *Evidence*, chap. 20.

passage of time had revealed. In particular, the provision in Section 1(3) excluding statements made by 'a person interested', had given rise to a body of very difficult case-law. The provision was not really necessary for as the whole object of the Act was to make the document in question admissible for what it was worth, the fact that it had been made by a person interested should have been a factor to be taken into account by the court in assessing the value to be placed upon it.

There are certainly other respects in which the Law of Evidence might be reformed—for example the hearsay rule in so far as it is related to criminal proceedings still remains in its full exclusionary rigour. There might also, as Maugham himself pointed out,[3] be machinery for enabling witnesses to be called even though neither party to the litigation wished it, if the judge thought it desirable in the interests of justice. Thus, in the Tichborne case, there were living in England the brother and two sisters of Arthur Orton, yet neither party dared to call these persons to say whether or not the claimant was in truth Arthur Orton. Yet if the evidence had been placed before the court, it is possible that the interminable proceedings would have ended much more speedily.

Apart from his work as a reformer, Maugham as Lord Chancellor displayed all the qualities of clarity and efficiency for which he had achieved a reputation. It fell to him in 1938 to make elaborate arrangements for the removal of the courts from London in time of war. It so happened that nothing had to be done to carry these arrangements into effect, but there is no doubt that they constituted an effective emergency scheme. Maugham's judicial appointments were entirely satisfactory. In March 1938 he appointed Cyril Asquith, K.C., to the King's Bench Division to succeed Mr. Justice Porter, who had been promoted to the House of Lords. Asquith was a man whose reputation and work at the Bar had not been outstanding, but on the Bench he was an instantaneous success, being promoted successively Lord Justice of Appeal and a Law Lord. The higher he went the better he became, and his early death deprived the House of Lords of one of its most distinguished authorities on Common Law. In October 1938 Maugham appointed three more King's Bench judges: R. G. Oliver, K.C., R. P. Croom-Johnson, K.C., and W. N. Stable, K.C. In March 1939 two further vacancies were filled by the appointment of J. D. Cassels, K.C., and H. I. P. Hallett, K.C.

Apart from his legal and parliamentary duties Maugham took an active interest in the course of the severest crisis in the field of foreign affairs which Britain was called upon to undergo in the twentieth century —the Munich settlement. One point should be made clear at the outset:

[3] (1939) 17 Can. Bar Rev. 469.

Maugham was an ardent supporter of the Prime Minister's policy through-out. He defended that policy by speech and action and in 1944 published what is still perhaps the best short account of the Chamberlain point of view, *The Truth about the Munich Crisis*. He returned to the matter again in his autobiography written in extreme old age. The fact that his views coincided with those of the Prime Minister and that they were expressed with such clarity and pungency led several people to think that Maugham must have been partly responsible for the formation and execution of the foreign policy of those years. That is not so. When Sir John Wheeler-Bennett stated, in reference to the events of September 1938, that

> Meanwhile Mr. Chamberlain and his intimate advisers Sir John Simon, Sir Samuel Hoare, Sir Thomas Inskip and the Lord Chancellor, Lord Maugham, pursued the path of appeasement with unruffled complacency, perverse intransigence, and complete disregard of every warning of disaster.[4]

he was answered by Maugham, who said that,

> As far as I am concerned I have a complete answer to the charge, for I was never an intimate adviser in the matter, or indeed in any other purely political matter, and had no opportunity of displaying complacency or intransigence or disregard of warnings, with or without the opprobrious adjectives which the author's imagination has attached to these distressing qualities. I was not at any time a member of any inner group of the Cabinet if there was one.[5]

The great merit of Maugham's approach to the tragedies, national and personal, involved in the Munich settlement is that he tried to view the events of 1938 from the standpoint of 1938, without the benefit of either hindsight or foresight. Maugham was fully prepared to admit that rearmament had been neglected in the earlier years. Indeed he cited Sir Winston Churchill's arguments on this point with the comment that they were 'unanswerable'. But Maugham insisted that it would be necessary to look at affairs from the standpoint of 1938, and to consider how Chamberlain had tried to deal with them. From that point of view, 'I was presenting to the best of my ability an argument to show that Neville Chamberlain, far from deserving the violent abuse of political opponents, had in circumstances of unexampled difficulty deserved well of his country.'[6] The first point that Maugham made was that the Sudeten Germans had a genuine grievance in Czechoslovakia. The state, Maugham

---

[4] *Munich, Prologue to Tragedy* (1948), p. 297.
[5] *At the End of the Day*, p. 383.
[6] Ibid., p. 368.

argued, had been an artificial creation after the Treaty of Versailles due to the persuasiveness of Masaryk and Benes. 'With fair play from the Czechs within a year or two after the Treaty which created the State there would probably have been no Munich.'[7] In any event, Maugham believed Czechoslovakia had become indefensible against a German onslaught after the Anschluss with Austria, and was internally a country divided by violent political faction. These arguments could hardly expect to be received with a favourable hearing in England, where the desertion of Czechoslovakia in the autumn of 1938 naturally, and by an easily explicable reaction, led to an enthusiastic endorsement of all the Czech claims. It is indicative of Maugham's honesty and integrity that he should have put them forward. It followed logically from this view that Maugham extended a hearty approval to the famous leading article in *The Times* of 7 September 1938 suggesting that the cession of the Sudeten districts to Germany should not be excluded from consideration. 'The article was prescient though perhaps premature, for it is always unfortunate in a difficult negotiation if some well intentioned person suggests a course which the negotiator is keeping in reserve as his final offer.'[8] Maugham further answered the critics of Chamberlain, who suggested that contact should have been made with Russia, by pointing out that Russian policy was at that date unpredictable in every respect and dictated entirely by self-interest. If we had indeed brought in Russia at that time, the ultimate result might not have been very different. Furthermore, both France and the Dominions were unreliable allies in any possible war against Germany, and if France had indeed remained neutral no obligation, legal or moral, would have rested upon Great Britain to come to the aid of Czechoslovakia. It was made a matter of complaint against Chamberlain that he had placed too much faith in Hitler's word. Maugham answered this criticism frankly: 'In that we turned out to be wrong, and we can only say that we did not then recognize a new kind of political reptile in human shape when we met him in the way.'[9]

Maugham always had the courage of his convictions. In a speech at the Constitutional Club on 14 December 1938 he combined a vehement defence of Chamberlain's policy with a bitter attack on the activities of (Sir) Winston Churchill. At that stage in our history Churchill's views and policies were anathema to the innermost section of the Conservative Party, and Maugham's speech was greeted with applause. He received a note of congratulations from the Chancellor of the Exchequer:

[7] *At the End of the Day*, p. 362.
[8] Ibid., p. 370.
[9] Ibid., p. 379.

11 Downing St.,
Whitehall, S.W.
16 December

My dear L.C.,
Well done: your speech at the Constitutional Club was first rate
and the trouncing of Churchill could not have been better. Many many thanks.

Yours ever,
John Simon[1]

Some commentators professed themselves to be shocked at the truculence
of Maugham's language, and in particular at his suggestion that politicians
(i.e. Churchill) who advocated war against another country without
considering the probable results, ought to be impeached. Years later
Maugham remarked about this incident: 'I might have expressed myself
with less vigour if I had known that reporters were present; and as it
happens I spoke without notes. The phrase about impeachment is almost
a cliché, for there is no other word in English to express punishment for
a crime by a minister against the State.'[2] Maugham remained unrepentant
on the matter, and carefully preserved a letter which he received in
July 1939 from the veteran Liberal, F. W. Hirst.

July 4th, 1939
Churchill has a wonderful press agency, and seems to have persuaded half a
dozen of the owners of the newspapers to say that 'the nation' wants him in the
Cabinet! Nearly all my friends and acquaintances in all parties distrust him
and think that his inclusion would make peace even more precarious than it is.
You will remember that, after nearly losing the war through Antwerp,
Dardanelles, etc., he was ejected from the Admiralty by the Unionist leaders
in May, 1915, and that after the Armistice he prolonged the war against
Bolshevik Russia and tried to entangle us in a war against Turkey. His judgment
has always been bad, and I do not know of anything that he has done well
except as a writer and rhetorician. His action at the time of the Constitutional
crisis would alone have justified your speech about impeachment.
Please forgive my writing these lines. I have had a number of communications
on the subject, which confirm my very strong feeling that the Prime Minister
will lose the confidence of the country if he united with a man who (as everyone
knows) is spoiling for war.[3]

In August 1939 Maugham was on a visit to Canada for the Annual
Meeting of the Canadian Bar Association. It was for this meeting that he
prepared but did not deliver his paper on the Evidence Act of 1938, which
was later published in the Canadian Bar Review.[4] On Friday, 26 August
he opened the 61st Canadian Exhibition at Toronto. In a speech listened

[1] Maugham papers.   [2] At the End of the Day, p. 384n.
[3] Maugham papers.   [4] See above, p. 556.

to by a wide audience he said that he regarded the Exhibition as a symbol of a united Empire. The address, delivered in a 'voice shaken with emotion', evoked some admiring telegrams from persons in Canada and the United States. The news of the non-aggression pact between Russia and Germany on 23 August caused Maugham to see that war was inevitable. He cut short his Canadian arrangements, and returned home immediately, arriving at Southampton on 1 September.

I had considered for some months the question of my giving up my office in the event of war, not (to be honest) because I thought myself incapable of carrying on, but because I was sure that ordinary people would think that at the age of nearly 73 I ought to give way in time of war to a younger man. And I personally to some extent welcomed a resolution of the Cabinet which involved my retirement. I was glad my friend Caldecote was to hold the position of Lord Chancellor, for I, who had known him for many years, had long held the opinion that few men equally full of moral strength, good sense, and good temper could be found, and he was as straight as a die—not bad qualities in a Minister in time of war.[5]

Maugham surrendered the Great Seal on Monday, 4 September, and was created a Viscount in recognition of his services on the 22nd of the same month. Hereditary honours meant little to Maugham (he had told Chamberlain in 1938 that he was content with his life peerage), but he was glad to have his work recognized in a manner which avoided the mistake made in Buckmaster's case.[6] In answer to a letter of sympathy from Simon, Maugham wrote:

5 September 1939

My dear Simon,
         Very many thanks. Your letter means a lot to me, because though I have reason to think that Bench and Bar are not dissatisfied with my actions as L.C. I have more than a suspicion that my political conduct and speeches have not altogether pleased some of my colleagues, who would have preferred to have a stronger party note in my utterances. I thought and think that—at least when you have a good case—a calm, judicial, spirit carries more weight than the eloquence of an advocate—so I adopted the role which was natural to me.
    I am a little sad at leaving my great position so soon, and should be sadder if I thought it was perhaps because I had done my job badly; but I am greatly cheered by your letter, for there is no one whose opinion I value so much. With many thanks and kindest regards to you and your wife from us both.

Yours ever,
Maugham[7]

[5] *At the End of the Day*, p. 397.   [6] See above, p. 301.   [7] Simon papers.

T*

ALMOST IMMEDIATELY AFTER his surrender of the Great Seal Maugham was re-appointed a Lord of Appeal in Ordinary to fill the vacancy caused by the resignation of Lord Macmillan when the latter was appointed to be Minister of Information. This was a difficult task for anyone at that period, and it was not the happiest episode in Macmillan's long career of public service. After a few months it became clear that another Minister of Information would have to be found, and unfortunately difficulties arose as to the work which Macmillan was now able to do. The new Lord Chancellor, Caldecote, noted in his diary in January 1940.

When Maugham ceased to be L.C. he expressed a hope that he might perhaps resume his work as Lord of Appeal at the next opportunity. When Macmillan became Minister of Information and (after some demur) resigned his post, Maugham was re-appointed. He refused to give any promise to resign in the event of Macmillan ceasing to be M. of Information. He told me, however, and Schuster, that he should—after his appointment—tell Macmillan privately that such would be his intention. This, however, was to be quite private between himself and Macmillan, and only done *after* Macmillan had burnt his boats. Now the P.M.—who was told (I think wrongly) of Maugham's letter to Macmillan, wants Maugham to resign. Maugham refuses, and says his only bargain was to go at the end of the war. He adds, 'my present intention is to keep to this position'. The P.M.'s Secretary—Rucker,—thinks Maugham will (and intends to) alter his intention and will resign in favour of Macmillan. I think it is very hard on both of them.[1]

On 10 January Caldecote recorded:

I had lunch with Macmillan on Monday. Schuster was under the impression that Maugham had told Macmillan that he would resign (after a decent interval), if Macmillan gave up his post in the Govt. Schuster told the P.M.'s Secretary on September 20th in a letter, that Maugham had told him this. Now Maugham tells the P.M. that his 'present intention' is to keep his position till the end of the war, and according to Macmillan, who must be right in his recollection, Maugham never gave him the assurance which Schuster thought. In any case Maugham could not be bound by the assurance even if he gave it, because he expressly said to the P.M. he would give no promise of any sort, except to resign at the end of the war, if Macmillan was free to return and be re-appointed. Macmillan did not say any single thing to complain of the P.M. or Maugham

[1] Caldecote papers.

or anyone else, and said he would go into the country and rest. My opinion of him rose very much. He referred to Sam Hoare's scuttling from the Ministry of Information after having got together a lot of left wing people with no idea of loyalty, and a large heterogeneous collection of people.

I spoke to S. Hoare this morning and asked what was the true story about Hore-Belisha. S. H. said there was no story. The P.M. found the Higher Command in France thoroughly distrusted H. B. He had also fallen out with Ironside. He was inattentive to detail and only interested himself in matters for which there was publicity. (This of course was my experience at the C.I.D. and I told the P.M. so when he appointed H. B.) S. H. had thought the P.M. was going to make a number of changes in the Government at the same time as Belisha's and Macmillan's removals. The P.M.'s Secretary gave me the same impression as late as Friday last when I saw him.[2]

Maugham thereupon resumed his work as a Law Lord, and did not resign his position until July 1941. One appeal which he heard during these years must be mentioned. In *Liversidge* v. *Anderson*[3] the question for the House of Lords was whether certain words in Regulation 18B, made under the Emergency Powers Act, 1939, conferred upon the Home Secretary the power to imprison a person without giving reasons. The words in question were:

If the Secretary of State has reasonable cause to believe any person to be of hostile origin or associations or to have been recently concerned in acts prejudicial to the public safety or the defence of the realm or in the preparation or instigation of such acts and that by reason thereof it is necessary to exercise control over him, he may make an order against that person directing that he be detained.

Under this regulation Sir John Anderson, then the Home Secretary, had in May 1940 issued a detention order against one Jack Perlzweig, alias Robert Liversidge. Liversidge was accordingly detained in Brixton prison, and in 1941 he began an action for false imprisonment against Sir John Anderson, and also Mr. Herbert Morrison, who had succeeded Anderson in September 1940. The question was whether Liversidge was entitled to particulars of the grounds upon which the Home Secretary had reasonable cause to believe him to be a person of hostile associations. The House of Lords held that no such particulars need be furnished by the Home Secretary. It held, Lord Atkin dissenting, that the power conferred by Regulation 18B was a power the limits of which could not be inquired into by the courts, provided that the Home Secretary acted in good faith. Lord Atkin dissented on the grounds that the words 'have reasonable cause to believe', had always been held in the

[2] Caldecote papers.   [3] [1942] A.C. 206.

past to imply an objective power of a justiciable nature. In a much cited passage he remarked that he viewed

with apprehension the attitude of Judges who on a mere question of construction when face to face with claims involving the liberty of the subject show themselves more executive-minded than the executive. . . . It has always been one of the pillars of freedom, one of the principles of liberty for which on recent authority we are now fighting, that the Judges are no respecters of persons and stand between the subject and any attempted encroachment on his liberty by the executive, alert to see that any coercive action is justified in law. In this case I have listened to arguments which might have been addressed acceptably to the Court of King's Bench in the time of Charles I.[4]

It so happened that the presiding Law Lord on the hearing of the Appeal was Maugham (the Lord Chancellor Simon did not preside, no doubt because as Home Secretary as far back as 1915 he had signed a similar detention order which had given rise to the great case of *R. v. Halliday, ex parte Zadig*)[5]. Some days after the judgment had been delivered Maugham took a remarkable step. He wrote a letter to *The Times* to say that owing to the exigencies of printing in war-time he had not seen an advance copy of Lord Atkin's judgment and therefore had not been able in his own judgment to 'make any protest about what I took to be an offensive remark in relation to the Attorney-General and his eminent Junior.'[6] Maugham later said that Atkin during the argument had given no indication that he was about to say such a thing, and that if he had done so, he, Maugham, would have felt obliged to intervene to 'protect the Attorney-General'.[7] A debate of a rather inconclusive character took place in the House of Lords itself as to the propriety of one noble and learned Lord writing to the public press to correct or comment upon the judicial utterances of one of his colleagues.[8]

It seems, however, that Maugham acted rather impulsively in feeling that it was his duty to protect Sir Donald Somervell, the Attorney-General, from the comparison drawn between himself and the Attorney-General of Charles I. If an answer is to be sought to Lord Atkin's criticisms it can best be found in Maugham's own judgment in *Liversidge* v. *Anderson*. For after stressing that the question was in essence one of statutory interpretation, namely, what had Parliament meant by these words in this

[4] [1942] A.C. at 244. The case which Lord Atkin had in mind was *Darnel's Case* (1627) 3 St. Tr. 1, in which the Court of King's Bench had held that at common law it was a good return to a writ of habeas corpus that the applicant was detained *per speciale mandatum domini regis.*
[5] [1917] A.C. 260.   [6] *The Times*, 4 November 1941.   [7] 121 H.L. Deb. 5s. col. 71.
[8] 121 H.L. Deb. 5s. col. 67. See also the memoir of Lord Atkin by his daughter in G.L.I.M. Summer, 1957, p. 13.

context, Maugham pointed out that in such a case one should approach the construction of the regulation without any general presumption as to its meaning,

except the universal presumption that if there was a reasonable doubt as to the meaning of the words used, we should prefer a construction which will carry into effect the plain intention of those responsible for the Order in Council rather than one which will defeat that intention. I am not disposed to deny that in the absence of a context the prima facie meaning of such a phrase as, 'if AB has reasonable cause to believe' a certain circumstance or thing, it should be construed as meaning, 'if there is in fact reasonable cause for believing' that thing and if AB believes it. But I am quite unable to take the view that the words can only have that meaning.[9]

Maugham pointed out several factors which indicated that in the context of this particular regulation Parliament had not intended to provide an objective justiciable power, but rather a power the limits to the exercise of which could be determined by the Home Secretary himself. The factors in question were the nature of the power, the nature of the person over whom it was to be exercised, the way in which it was to be exercised, and, finally, the person who was to exercise it. 'It is to be noted that the person who is primarily entrusted with these most important duties is one of the principal Secretaries of State, and a member of the Government answerable to Parliament for a proper discharge of his duties. I do not think he is at all in the same position as, for example, a police constable.'[1] Some critics have found in these words an exception to Dicey's principle of equality before the Law, but this is to misunderstand Maugham's view. The question is at bottom one of statutory interpretation: what had Parliament meant by these words? It is obvious that one of the factors to be taken into account in answering this question is the kind of person who is to exercise the power. The fact that the person is a Secretary of State answerable to Parliament, indicates that Parliament may have been content to leave the matter to the unfettered discretion of the Minister, and by its use of the words 'have reasonable cause to believe' signified only that it intended the Home Secretary personally to give attention to the matter. There is after all a great difference between 1628 and 1941. In 1628 there was no Parliament in existence and no Minister responsible to Parliament for the way in which Charles I exercised his discretionary powers. In 1941 Parliament was sitting and questions could be addressed to the Home Secretary on his administration of Regulation 18B. In a word, whereas Charles I lost his head, Sir John Anderson only lost his portfolio. After a period of uncertainty it is now perfectly clear that

[9] [1942] A.C. at 221–222.   [1] [1942] A.C. at 222.

Maugham's judgment in *Liversidge* v. *Anderson* was a masterly piece of constitutional law. There is no ground for suggesting he in any way departed from the judicial desire to do justice impartially between Crown and subject. Lord Atkin's judgment, though obviously attractive to anyone who believes in personal liberty, suffers from the flaw that it erects a question of fact into a question of law. Atkin started from the belief that words in a statute must always have one particular meaning, but as Maugham's judgment showed, the true question is what is the meaning of these words in this context.

Shortly before giving judgment in *Liversidge* v. *Anderson*, Maugham had resigned his position as a Law Lord. He continued to assist occasionally, however, in the disposal of appeals to the House of Lords, and in 1946 delivered a most interesting judgment in *Searle* v. *Wallbank*,[2] which contains an authoritative exposition of the rule that there is no duty to prevent domestic animals not known to be dangerous from straying on to the highway. Maugham's wide reading showed to considerable advantage in this judgment, for it contains a good discussion of the history of English roads.

Outside the law Maugham took an active interest in various activities connected with the war. He was much concerned to see that sailors at Scapa Flow had satisfactory accommodation for rest and recreation on shore. He was also concerned with the development of tanks and a good deal of trouble was taken by the authorities to persuade him that all that was necessary was being done.[3] In 1941 his activities were noticed by the Fourth Marquess of Salisbury, who although retired from active politics, maintained a close watch on affairs.

9.1.41.

There is an organization which has been in existence for some months which calls itself the Watching Committee. It consists of a few men—some 20—from both Houses who hope that by their influence and experience they may be useful in watching the conduct of the War and may be able to make suggestions and even exercise a certain amount of pressure in respect of War administration. It has consisted mostly of ex-Cabinet Ministers and men of that status and has indeed furnished a good many of the Ministers as they have developed.

Would you care to join it?

Swinton and Trenchard are members of it amongst others. We are at present much concerned about Shelters and Parcels for British prisoners.[4]

Maugham became so immersed in public affairs that he was even prepared to give up his turn as Treasurer of Lincoln's Inn when that office was offered to him in 1940. He wrote to the Under Treasurer:

[2] [1947] A.C. 341.   [3] Maugham papers.   [4] Ibid.

6th November, 1940

My hesitation as to accepting the Honourable Office of Treasurer of the Inn, so delightful in peace-time, is due to my fear that I may not be able adequately to perform the duties which may fall upon the Treasurer next year in the uncertain and distressing circumstances of War. Moreover, I have my work at Westminster, and I wish to continue my attendance at the House of Lords debates during the War.

But one never knows the future. I should have pleasure in accepting the office on this understanding that if I find I cannot give sufficient time to it to enable me to perform the duties of the office to my own satisfaction, I should then be entitled to retire.

I do not want to put the Council in any difficulty, and I recognize that if I should retire my successor might be prejudiced. If then the Council would prefer me to take the course of declining this Honourable Office, I shall be quite ready to do so, and of course I shall not feel in the least aggrieved.

Please communicate this letter to my fellow Benchers, with my apology for causing any difficulty in the matter.[5]

This communication was not well received by the Benchers. There were indeed some precedents for permitting a Treasurer to act in a titular or honorary capacity, but they mostly related to members of the Royal Family, and it was felt that Maugham was not quite in that category. It was resolved to elect Sir Herbert Cunliffe, K.C., Treasurer in place of Maugham, and the Under Treasurer wrote to inform Maugham of the decision.

We held a Council on Monday [14 November 1940] to consider your letter. The clear and unanimous view of the Benchers was that, since the exigencies of the present situation make it necessary that the Treasurer should give up a great deal of the time to the work of the Inn, it is not desirable in the interests of the Inn, nor would it be fair to a prospective successor in the Treasurership, that there should be any avoidable chance of a change of Treasurer in the course of the year, and in the result, the resolution a copy of which I will forward was passed unanimously: and we elected Cunliffe as Treasurer for 1941, and we elected Atkinson to succeed you as Master of the Library.

I was however asked, in writing to you, to emphasize, how real is the regret of us all that we are not to have the services as Treasurer of a very dear friend, who has done so much good service for the Inn, and figures as by no means the least eminent on our long and distinguished list of Lincoln's Inn Chancellors.[6]

Again in 1946 Maugham refused an offer of the Treasurership on the plea of public duties. His behaviour puzzled his old friends at the Chancery Bar, who could not understand why he had turned down an opportunity of serving in an office which it is the ambition of every loyal member of an Inn to hold. But there was some consolation: it was resolved to place

[5] Black Book of Lincoln's Inn.   [6] Maugham papers.

his arms, together with those of Hailsham, another Lord Chancellor who had failed to become Treasurer, in the window of the Council Room.[7]

In later years Maugham's interest in grand strategy and the conduct of the war became something of an obsession, and when in 1954 he published his autobiography, many of his friends regretted that he had been permitted to occupy more than half of a very lengthy book with a detailed account of the military problems of both World Wars. The account is, as with everything Maugham wrote, clearly written and trenchantly argued. It is certainly a remarkable performance for a man aged 88 years, but the verdict must be that it is not a permanent contribution to military history. Maugham's interest in war and the law had a happier outcome in a little volume which he published in 1951, with a preface by Lord Hankey, entitled *U.N.O. and War Crimes*. It is perhaps the best short account in existence of the arguments which may be advanced against the validity of the Nuremberg trials in international law. Maugham concluded that the judgment of the tribunal at Nuremberg may have been lawful in Germany so long as it was under allied occupation, but that there was no rule of international law justifying the Charter and the Code at the time of their creation. Maugham's most serious criticisms were directed against Articles 6 and 8 of the Charter of Nuremberg. Article 6 conferred upon the tribunal jurisdiction to try (*a*) crimes against peace, (*b*) war crimes, and (*c*) crimes against humanity. Article 8 provided that: 'The fact that the defendant acted pursuant to an order of his Government or of a superior shall not free him from responsibility, but it may be considered in mitigation of punishment if the Tribunal determines that justice so requires.' There is no doubt that Maugham was correct in stressing the novelty of crimes against peace and crimes against humanity. Yet it should be noted that of the twenty-one accused at Nuremberg only one was found guilty of crimes against peace alone, and only two of crimes against humanity alone. All the other accused who were sentenced by the Tribunal were found guilty in addition to other crimes of ordinary war crimes as defined in the Charter in full conformity with existing law. Maugham was perhaps on stronger ground in drawing attention to the weaknesses of Article 8 providing that superior orders were no defence, and his other point was buttressed by some serious practical considerations of a military character advanced by Lord Hankey. Much of what Maugham said about the substantive issues in international law involved in the Nuremberg trial will be debated until the end of time. On one point, however, he appears to have done an injustice to those who were responsible for framing the Charter. He made an accusation of undue haste,

[7] Information from Lord Justice Danckwerts.

which at once brought forth a firm reply from Lord Jowitt, the then Lord Chancellor.

28th November, 1951

I have been reading your book 'U.N.O. and War Crimes' in the light of the newspaper reviews.

I need hardly say that certain organs of the Press, anxious to discredit me and not in the least concerned to deal with the serious arguments involved, have fastened on the suggestion that the Nuremberg Treaty was in an unsatisfactory form simply because I was in a hurry. For any defects there may have been I am, therefore, made solely responsible.

Reading your book (page 36), the implication is plainly made that Articles 6, 7, and 8 of the Charter 'were never properly considered owing to the need for hurry'. I feel that, quite unwittingly, you have done me a grievous injury by making this statement. May I explain to you exactly what my position was. I received a telegram from the Prime Minister, who was at Potsdam, dated 30th July, asking me to try to resolve the few outstanding points that remained with the least possible delay. Accordingly, on the 31st July, 1945, I got in touch with Sir David Maxwell Fyfe, who had been in charge of the negotiations which had been proceeding for several weeks, and the Treasury Solicitor. I then discovered that there were very few points outstanding and these were largely of a drafting nature. On the 1st August I saw Mr. Justice Jackson and further reduced the outstanding difficulties, and on the 2nd August I presided, for the first time, over the meeting of delegates. I did not attempt to start the work de novo, I was merely concerned to get rid of the outstanding difficulties.

It was the fact that I had to be present in the House of Lords at 2 o'clock on the 2nd August, because that was the day on which I myself was to be made a peer, and I had to sit to enable the Lords to take the Oath. But, as you will see from page 417 of Jackson's book, I offered to come back at 5.30 p.m. that day, or the next day at 2.30 p.m.

Anticipating that the discussion on Article 6 might take some time and not wanting to have to break off in the middle of the discussion, I suggested that we should pass it over for the time being (see Jackson, page 402). On Articles 7 and 8 there were no outstanding points (Jackson, page 402). It is, therefore, wholly incorrect to say that these Articles were never properly considered owing to the need for hurry. It would be accurate to say they were not considered at all at the meeting of the 2nd August because no outstanding points arose on them.

Having cleared away all other difficulties we then took up the question of Article 6 (Jackson, page 415). I then had a quarter of an hour left before I had to break off. But at Jackson's request we went on with the discussion during this time. When I had to leave I left David Maxwell Fyfe to take the Chair, and you will see from page 418 of Jackson's book that the remaining discussion under Fyfe's chairmanship lasted only a few minutes.

I am not in the least concerned at present to discuss the force of the substantive criticism which you develop in your book; I merely state that I find myself in agreement with Jackson's observations on page 437 of his book. I am, however, concerned with the suggestion made on page 36 of your book that it was owing to my need for hurry that proper consideration was not given to the Charter. If any such allegation was to be made you surely should have called my attention to the fact that I offered to come back to the meeting later that afternoon and that in the meantime I left Maxwell Fyfe in the Chair with my complete authority to do what was necessary.[8]

Maugham's literary interests also found an outcome in three successful volumes. One dealt with the judicial error in the case of Jean Calas in France in 1761. Maugham followed Voltaire in holding that Calas was quite innocent and the victim of religious intolerance. The work is a clear and valuable account which was written mainly in the intervals of Maugham's heavy work as a Chancery silk. After he became a judge his interest in the conflict of human testimony was awakened by the Tichborne case, and in 1936 he published what is still the best short account of that extraordinary affair. Maugham's skill in the elucidation of complicated facts and his ability to analyse with clarity a complicated chain of evidence is here shown at its very best. In addition there are some interesting remarks not merely about the conduct of the various judges and Counsel engaged in the trial (Maugham had a poor opinion of Coleridge as a cross-examiner), but also on the reasons why the public at large should have believed for so long in the incredible case put forward by the claimant. Maugham said:

It is to be doubted whether the hypnotic effect of repeated statements however ill-founded has ever been sufficiently appreciated in this country. Suggestion of a falsehood acts like a cumulative poison dropped into the ears of the victims, until at length reception of the unwelcome truth becomes for some people almost impossible. . . . In view of documentary evidence which could not be disputed, and of the claimant's own mistakes and foolishness, it is really impossible to explain these long-drawn-out trials except on the hypothesis that at least half the world was so hypnotized before the civil case began into a belief in the genuineness of this imposture that no one could be certain that a unanimous verdict would be obtained from either of the juries.[9]

Maugham also contributed an interesting chapter to a work edited by Sir George Clark entitled *The Campden Wonder*.[1] In 1661 three persons were tried and executed for the murder of the steward of Lady Campden at Chipping Campden in Gloucestershire. The three persons concerned were the steward's fellow-servant, together with his mother and brother, and the conviction was obtained mainly on the confession of the fellow-servant. Two years later the murdered man returned to Chipping Campden with an extraordinary story of having been kidnapped and

[8] Jowitt papers.   [9] *The Tichborne Case* (1936), pp. 18–19.
[1] Published in 1959 by the O.U.P.

sold into slavery in Turkey. The problem of the proof of murder in the absence of a corpse is one well known to criminal lawyers, but Maugham was also fascinated by the conflict of human testimony involved, as he had been earlier by a similar conflict in the Tichborne case. He was also of the opinion that in 1661 there was no settled rule against the reception of hearsay evidence.

Maugham also wrote, but did not publish, a number of miscellaneous works. His papers contain a sketch for a play, and a short essay of interest to Dickensians entitled 'Was Edwin Drood murdered?' He also wrote, and occasionally published in *Blackwood's Magazine*, short stories under the pen name Ormond Greville. Their plot is a trifle slow-moving and elaborate for modern tastes but the interest is maintained throughout, and on the whole they are not unworthy to be compared with the more famous productions of his brother, Somerset Maugham. Maugham's relations with his brother were distant. He permitted himself only one brief reference to him in his lengthy autobiography. When the present author wrote to Mr. Somerset Maugham in 1959 to ask if he had any reminiscences of his brother, he received the following reply:

7th September 1959

I am very much afraid that I cannot be of any help to you. My brother was a very strange, reticent and difficult man. I saw him very seldom, and if it hadn't been for my sister-in-law, his wife, I should not have seen him from years end to years end.

I don't suppose you have ever read a novel of mine called 'The Painted Veil'. I used my brother as my model for the doctor in that story.

My nephew Robin can tell you much more about his father than I can, and on the whole what he tells you can be relied on. You probably know that he was very unpopular in the House of Lords, because, as one member told me, he treated the Peers as hostile witnesses.

The impression of Maugham as a cold, difficult and supercilious man was one which spread beyond the bounds of his own family, but there is also evidence the other way. Harold Laski, a severe critic, met Maugham at a dinner party in 1928 and described him as 'charming'.[2] Those who knew him at the Savile Club or in the Bencher's Room at Lincoln's Inn found an agreeable and relaxed companion. Something can often be learnt of a man's character from the way in which he writes of his friends. After Sir Frederick Pollock, the great jurist, had died in 1937 Maugham along with a number of others contributed to the *Law Quarterly Review* a brief biographical notice.[3] Pollock had himself the reputation of being a difficult man, and Maugham may have been conscious of his own reputation in this respect when he wrote the following words:

[2] *Holmes–Laski Letters* (1953), p. 1063.   [3] (1937) 53 L.Q.R. 168.

This Review he started in 1885, and it was as a humble contributor that I first made his acquaintance. Having only recently come down from Cambridge, I am afraid I anticipated a somewhat 'donnish' attitude from my editor; for in those far-off days (I say nothing of the present) many tutors and lecturers had only rudimentary notions as to how young, diffident and often foolish undergraduates should be addressed if you wanted to get anything into or out of them; but Pollock was an agreeable surprise, for he was shy as I was and not more confident in his manner. . . . .

When I got to know him later as a brother bencher of Lincoln's Inn and met him almost daily at lunch, I found him singularly taciturn. He followed the principle, more suited to others than himself, of not speaking unless he was spoken to. If, however, anyone wanted to know the source of a quotation, or some recondite historical detail, he used to ask Pollock, and, after a few minutes' cogitation and some rather strange sounds, the answer was generally forthcoming. We all realized that he was a man blessed with a very remarkable memory, and, unlike so many of us, it was not a general recollection of the facts, but a recollection which was accurate in all its details. Every now and then he would come out of his shell. I remember one night after dinner at the Inn some benchers, who were in singularly good spirits, proposed to indict a fellow bencher for an imaginary crime. (I know it was imaginary, for I was the supposed criminal.) A number of eloquent speeches were delivered for the prosecution, not without much interruption, and a few for the defence. Pollock had remained silent and it might have been thought that he deprecated what was going on; but he suddenly rose and delivered a remarkable speech (for the defence!) full of humour, law, and antiquarian learning, which was greeted with much applause. None of us had imagined that he could speak so well.[4]

In personal appearance Maugham was a handsome man with beautifully formed hands, which with a little human vanity he was not above displaying to the best advantage. He maintained to the end of his long life the trim figure and athletic build of his youth—unlike many other rowing men. Lady Maugham died in October 1950 and thenceforward Maugham lived on in increasing isolation. He was devotedly looked after by the eldest of his four children, Mrs. Kate Mary Bruce, a lady of warm and vigorous personality whose death all too soon after her father was regretted by many friends. Maugham died at his house, 73 Cadogan Gardens, on 23 March 1958 and was buried at Hartfield Parish Church in Sussex three days later. The grave lies in the new part of the churchyard looking across the Sussex countryside to Tye House, Hartfield, in which he had enjoyed the pleasures of country life for many years. His estate was sworn for probate at £91,000. He was succeeded as 2nd Viscount by his only son, Robert Cecil Romer (Robin) Maugham, an author.

[4] (1937) 53 L.Q.R. 168, pp. 168-9.

APPENDIX

Maugham was versatile and the sweep of his learning and the clarity of his style show to peculiar advantage in his judgments on common law topics, even though he had been trained on the chancery side. His power of disentangling a complicated set of facts is well displayed in *Myers* v. *Elman* [1940] A.C. 282 (unprofessional conduct by solicitor). In *Milne* v. *Commissioner of Police* [1940] A.C. 1, an appeal from the Court of Criminal Appeal, the House considered the question of what amounted to an unlawful use of premises under the Gaming Act, 1835. In his judgment Maugham considered Halsbury's well-known remarks on the subject in the *Kempton Park Case* [1899] A.C. 143, and succeeded in distinguishing them convincingly. Maugham's judgment contains some valuable obiter dicta on the folly of the legal habit of treating the words of a judgment as if they were contained in a statute. It is the principle behind the judicial words which is important. Statutory interpretation was considered in another criminal appeal, *Jennings* v. *Kelly* [1940] A.C. 206, in which there are some wise remarks on the proper interpretation of a proviso.

Some very technical learning relating to deeds is well considered in *Naas* v. *Westminster Bank* [1940] A.C. 366. Maugham emphasized the fundamental point that a deed has no necessary connection with a consensual contract as we know it today. Hence it operates from the moment of execution by the covenantor (unless it be an escrow) even though the covenantee be unaware of the fact. Some equally technical learning of an unfamiliar kind is admirably deployed in *Potts* v. *Hickman* [1941] A.C. 212, in which it was held that a distress for rates was not an execution within the Act of 1709 and so not subject to the lessor's preferential claim for unpaid rent, even though the opposite view had been current in the profession for 230 years.

Judgments on more familiar common law points will be found in *Sedleigh-Denfield* v. *O'Callaghan* [1940] A.C. 880 (nuisance); *Joseph Constantine, Ltd.* v. *Imperial Smelting Corporation* [1942] A.C. 154 (burden of proof in frustration cases); *Crofter Harris Tweed Co.* v. *Veitch* [1942] A.C. 435 (conspiracy); *Digby* v. *General Accident Co.* [1943] A.C. 121 (meaning of 'third party' in policy); and *Searle* v. *Wallbank* [1947] A.C. 341 (liability for animals).

In Equity Maugham's best judgments will be found in *Knightsbridge Estates Trust* v. *Byrne* [1940] A.C. 613, in which he considered how far a mortgage might be made irredeemable, and restated the old law in the light of changed commercial conditions; *Wolstanton, Ltd.* v. *Newcastle-under-Lyme Corporation* [1940] A.C. 860, in which an alleged custom for the lord of a manor to let down the surface without paying compensation was held unreasonable; *King Features Syndicate, Inc.* v. *O. & M. Kleeman, Ltd.* [1941] A.C. 417 (infringement of copyright); and *Aristoc, Ltd.* v. *Rystoc, Ltd.* [1945] A.C. 68 (registration of trade-mark).

LORD CALDECOTE

CHAPTER I

THE VILLAGE OF CALDECOTE near Baldock in Hertfordshire is a little cluster of houses in the middle of large fields of root crops. Near the village there stands a large red brick house on the western slope of a small hill, and in the yard behind this farmhouse there is a tiny fifteenth-century church. The churchyard is enclosed on two sides by barn walls. In this scene of rustic English simplicity, on the far side of the churchyard against the eastern end of the church, there lies the grave of Thomas Walker Hobart Inskip, first Viscount Caldecote. Near by is the grave of his grandfather, Thomas Flint Inskip. Thomas's son James became a solicitor in Bristol and a well-known supporter of Evangelical activities in the West Country. The Imperial Tobacco Company was one of James Inskip's major clients, and for a time he was also Chairman of the Taff Vale Railway Company, which gave its name to several leading cases in the law reports.[1] James Inskip married first in 1865 a cousin, Elizabeth Inskip, by whom he had two children, the elder of whom became the Suffragan Bishop of Barking.[2] By his second wife, Constance Hampden, of Shockerwick, near Bath, whom he married in 1872, three years after the death of Elizabeth, he had issue two sons and four daughters. The elder of these two sons, the future Lord Chancellor, was born on 5 March 1876 at Clifton Park House, Clifton, the pleasant residential suburb of Bristol. (The younger son, John, a man of lively mind, carried on his father's practice in Bristol and was created K.B.E. in 1937.)

After a period at Clifton College, Thomas went up to King's College, Cambridge, where he was placed in the Third Class in the Classical Tripos in 1897. At King's the deeply sincere religious outlook which marked the whole of Inskip's life first became evident. He had been brought up in a strict atmosphere of old-fashioned Victorian piety (his parents did not permit him to attend either dances or theatres) which today would seem excessive in its severity, although it is worth noting that none of the six children reacted against it. One of Inskip's contemporaries at Cambridge, E. J. Woods, the future Bishop of Lichfield, wrote later:[3]

When I came up to Trinity College, Cambridge, as a freshman, he was in his second year at King's; his size and strength had already made him a redoubtable rugger player, he played regularly for King's and received a Varsity trial-

---

[1] *Vaughan* v. *Taff Vale Ry. Co.* (1860) 5 H. & N. 679; *Taff Vale Ry. Co.* v. *A.S.R.S.* [1901] A.C. 426.

[2] Rt. Rev. James Inskip (1868–1949).   [3] Caldecote papers.

cap, though not a 'blue'; and in the region of work and examinations he was beginning to show those powers of intellect and application which were to bring him eminence in years to come. He was also taking a quite definite public stand as a Christian man; which demanded no little courage and resolution in a College where the intellectual climate was traditionally critical and sceptical, and where there persisted an almost 18th-century dislike of any suggestion of religious 'enthusiasm' . . .

I can see him also standing in a circle with myself and others, in the market place on a Sunday evening, at a very informal service of hymns and prayers at which one of us would, in crude and halting fashion, proclaim the truth of the Gospel as we saw it. For my part I wished more than once that the paving stones would open and swallow me up when I saw in the crowd the faces, derisively smiling, of men rowing in the same boat with me! I don't know that Tom was ever 'ragged' by his rugger friends on account of his pious activities; but anyhow I think he was made of sterner stuff than many of us.

Another contemporary later recalled how Inskip objected to the language used by his fellow forwards in the scrum, and how his objections met with a surprisingly respectful hearing.[4] Inskip's first ambition in life at that time was to be a lay missionary and to that end he devoted much of his vacations to work in boys' clubs. But his father persuaded him to go to the Bar, and on 26 April 1899 he was called at the Inner Temple. His father arranged for him to become a pupil in the chambers of John Eldon Bankes, the future Lord Justice of Appeal. Shortly before he was called Inskip recorded in his diary:

I have actually been in London a whole year. Time goes so quickly that month after month slips by without much advance in one's life. What a puzzle it would all be unless one felt sure of the Lord's over-ruling and controlling hand.

I spent last week with Willie Holland[5] at Birmingham; it was splendid seeing him again. If I call any man 'my father in God' it is Bill Holland.[6]

Inskip joined the Western Circuit. His chambers were at 3 Hare Court. His family connections assured him of a reasonable supply of briefs at Bristol; elsewhere his patent honesty of character and good presence made him known. (Inskip was six feet three inches tall, and like many men so blessed by nature, was apt to regard those under six feet high as disagreeably deformed.) 'He had the reputation of telling a client exactly what he thought and of never letting him down', said *The Times* after his death[7]—words which Lord Salisbury thought were the finest epitaph

---

[4] Caldecote papers.

[5] W. Holland, brother of Sir Henry Holland, a medical missionary in India. His wife was the daughter of Inskip's half-sister.

[6] Caldecote papers.   [7] 13 October 1947.

PLATE 23

Lord Caldecote as Chancellor

PLATE 24

(*left to right*) John Inskip, Lady Augusta Inskip, Sir Thomas Inskip, Hon. Mrs. Inskip, Stanley Baldwin, Mrs. Baldwin, Constance, Hampden, and Marta Inskip

A FAMILY GROUP IN 1929

Inskip could have desired.[8] In due course Inskip became a Bencher of his Inn, and in 1943 he served his turn as Treasurer.

At Cambridge Inskip had made friends with some members of the great East Anglian families of Barclay and Buxton, noted for their combination of Christian idealism and worldly success. In his early years at the Bar, and later, these friendships (together with one Sir Arthur (later Lord) Hazlerigg and his wife Dorothy[9]) meant much to Inskip. For many years he lived a bachelor existence in the rather bleak surroundings of the National Club, seldom travelling home, and the opportunities of escape to East Anglia in the winter or Scotland in the summer were eagerly taken. In a more relaxed and expansive world Inskip, while abandoning none of his principles, began to discover new pleasures in life. In particular he became a keen follower of field sports, especially shooting. To one of these friends Inskip wrote when he was on the Woolsack, on 5 March 1940:

It is not easy to reckon up the years since you and I first met; 45 years is a lifetime and it has slipped by. I don't suppose I am the first person who has felt this about the years of one's life. Some people talk about having their life over again. I don't hanker after that, and though I know I have wasted many years when all the hours and days are added up and have misused others, I don't feel sure that I should do any better if I had my chance over again. No one could have had more undeserved blessings than I, neither more in number nor more in lack of merit on the part of the recipient, and I can only think as I look back on these years, that I can trust the love that has bought me and redeemed me to make me perfect and fit for Himself.

It was a happy day for me when you and Harry came into my life, and all those years you have been the best friend anyone ever had. That has been a major mercy to me.[1]

It was in the north that Inskip met his future wife, Lady Augusta, daughter of David, 7th Earl of Glasgow, and widow of Charles Orr Ewing, M.P., who had died young leaving her with three children. The marriage took place on 30 July 1914. In later years Inskip lived in the holidays at Knockinaam, near Portpatrick in Wigtownshire, a house belonging to his wife's family, and spent as much time there as he could manage, shooting, fishing, and sailing. In London his home was at 10 Eaton Square.

Inskip's practice at the Bar was not very substantial before 1914. He was still going the Western Circuit and had not established himself permanently in London. He was a busy but not a fashionable junior, although in 1914 his position was strong enough for him to take silk in

[8] 151 H.L. Deb. 5s. col. 1473.   [9] Lady Hazlerigg was a Buxton.
[1] Caldecote papers.

the last batch of K.C.s created before the war. His political career had begun to develop at an earlier stage. At the age of 30 he had fought Berwick-on-Tweed against Sir Edward Grey himself in the general elections of January 1906 and January 1910. A few months later he obtained the offer of a better seat hoped for by every candidate who fights a hopeless constituency for his party. An offer came from his native Bristol. Inskip noted in his diary on 26 April 1910:

> Invited to stand as M.P. for S. Bristol. Difficulty about money.
> However it is so entirely a thing I don't care two pins about if I cannot do something to help on God's work, that it is very easy and pleasant to wait for Him to make His plans for me.
> I was reading Carlyle's Oliver Cromwell again lately and I came across a passage[2] that I sent on to D. for the baptism of her boy, but I remembered it also for myself. O.C. writing to Lord Wharton who had a son and heir born to him, said 'I rejoice in your particular mercy and I hope it is so to you, for then you will not plot and strive to make the young Baron some great one, but you will say "he is God's to dispose of and guide for" and there you will leave him'.[3]

The plan to stand for Parliament in Bristol seems to have been disapproved of by James Inskip (who had himself twice unsuccessfully fought Bristol East), for his son did not stand at all at the second general election of 1910, at which the Conservative candidate was in fact returned for Bristol South.

Inskip served in the Naval Intelligence Branch of the Admiralty from 1915 to 1918. He was head of the Naval Law Branch in 1918 and in the same year was the Admiralty representative on the War Crimes Committee. In 1918 the political ambitions which he had held for more than twelve years were at last successful when he was returned for Bristol Central at the general election in December. He obtained 12,232 votes against the 7,137 of Ernest Bevin.

Inskip's first big opportunity in politics came with the fall of the coalition Government in October 1922. It has already been seen how the meeting at the Carlton Club affected the fortunes of Birkenhead, Cave, Hailsham, and Maugham.[4] To Inskip it brought an offer of the Solicitor-Generalship from Bonar Law, whose difficulties in finding new Law Officers have already been described.[5] The offer was made despite the fact that Inskip had voted for Austen Chamberlain at the Carlton Club, and even though two other Conservatives in Parliament (Macnaghten and Rawlinson) and one outside (Maugham) had been favourably considered

---

[2] T. Carlyle, *Oliver Cromwell* (1897 ed.), vol. i, pp. 361–2. (Inskip's quotation varies slightly from the original.)
[3] Caldecote papers.   [4] See above, pp. 424–7.   [5] See above, pp. 460–3.

for the post. Inskip served with Douglas Hogg as Law Officer until the Labour Government was formed in January 1924, and together they were reappointed when Baldwin returned to office in November of that year. Almost at once he was offered a puisne judgeship in the King's Bench Division—one of two sanctioned by the House of Commons to meet the increase in business. Inskip refused. There were indeed some precedents for a Solicitor-General accepting a puisne judgeship. Page Wood, Keating, and Brett had been so appointed in Victorian times. But Inskip shared the prevalent view that a Law Officer might legitimately hope for a better appointment. In addition there is reason to believe that he looked upon the work of a puisne judge rather as Lord Campbell had done— although he would not have dreamt of using the same language.

I have no taste for the pleasure which Mr. Justice Alan Park relished so intensely to the last portion of his existence, in meeting the sheriff and being trumpeted into the assize town; in walking up a cathedral clothed in scarlet, under the gaze of boys and old women; or in lecturing the grand jury; and my spirit almost dies away when I think I am to pass the remainder of my days in hearing witnesses swear that the house was all secure when they went to bed, and next morning they discovered that the window had been broken and their bacon was gone.[6]

Inskip worked well with Hogg, and when the latter was appointed Lord Chancellor in March 1928 Inskip succeeded him until the Conservative Government was replaced by the Labour administration of Ramsay MacDonald in June 1929. During this period Inskip consolidated his position in the House of Commons and in the country. Foreign affairs were never a major interest of his, and in any event they were quiescent in the peaceful period after Locarno; but in home affairs two issues attracted his attention. The first was the Trade Disputes Act, 1927, whose object was to render general strikes illegal. Inskip wound up for the Government on the Second Reading of the Bill,[7] which was marked by a continuous series of interruptions from the Labour benches. Although the uproar was so great that he could hardly utter two consecutive sentences which were audible he was generally adjudged to have had a first-class parliamentary success.[8] Later he always expressed his gratitude to Douglas Hogg for having waived his claim to wind up the debate. He also was concerned with the preliminary stages of the attempts to amend the law relating to civil proceedings by and against the Crown.[9]

[6] *Life of Lord Campbell*, ed. J. Hardcastle (1881), vol. ii, p. 295.
[7] 205 H.C. Deb. 5s. col. 1879.
[8] Information from Lord Somervell of Harrow, and from Lord Dunrossil.
[9] See Inskip, 'Proceedings by and against the Crown' (1930) 4 Camb. L.J. 1.

The second debate in which Inskip took a prominent part was on the motion to approve the new Prayer Book on 15 December 1927.[1] The motion was rejected on the ground that the proposed Book went too far in the direction of placating the Anglo-Catholics and so disturbed the traditional Anglicanism of the Church of England. The Protestant Members of the House of Commons, Inskip foremost among them, displayed an unsuspected talent for impassioned oratory. In a debate marked by some outstanding speeches Inskip's was one of the greatest.[2] He wrote afterwards on 20 December:

Thursday the Prayer Book Debate was to take place. I was wondering what to do. I was better but my voice hardly any better. I got Dr. Brydone and he said if I whispered all day and he sprayed my vocal cords, I might be able to make myself heard. Well, the day came and it was a day; I have never known anything like it. I must keep my account of it till I see you. Meanwhile I send various cuttings which Morrison[3] had got or told me of. You will see the references to my unworthy self. Everyone has been very kind. When I sat down, between the P.M. and Winston, the P.M. said nothing but Winston—who had announced he would vote for the measure—said to me as I sat down, 'Well, Solicitor, that's a very fine speech, a fine massive speech'—and he didn't vote. Will you bring these cuttings home: I am also enclosing the Hansard Report: it will serve for some light reading. F. E. Smith has written today a most violent letter to *The Times*, deliberately insulting. Jix and Douglas Hogg—who is now a tremendous enthusiast—are furious and I don't wonder. I don't think the Archbishop will like his new ally.[4] It has been a wonderful week and people have talked of hardly anything else.[5]

A letter came from Simon on 20 December:

I must really congratulate you on your winding-up speech in the Prayer Book Debate. It was far the most solid and powerful piece of pleading from inside the Church of England that I have come across in the whole controversy. I look at these things from outside, as I said, and only try to form a conclusion as a citizen who does not want to be a party to an injustice which would be inflicted on a great body of quiet and sincere religious opinion.

But will you allow me, as a sympathizer, to urge on you most strongly that the newspaper protests and comments must not all come from one side if you want to hold what you have gained. For example, *The Times* this morning contains a number of letters all deploring the House of Commons' decision as a disaster or denouncing it as a folly. Manifestly Birkenhead has not read the debate with attention or else he deliberately avoids meeting the argument. *The*

---

[1] 211 H.C. Deb. 5s. col. 2531.   [2] 211 H.C. Deb. 5s. col. 2637-48.

[3] W. S. Morrison, later Inskip's P.P.S. and eventually Lord Dunrossil.

[4] This was Birkenhead's own view: see Birkenhead, *F.E.*, p. 542. The letter suggested that parsons would be entitled to use the new Book despite the Commons vote against it.

[5] Caldecote papers.

Times cannot refuse to publish a letter from you and from Douglas Hogg—and surely it is important that your point of view should be supported and demonstrated in the press. In the same way, though I have had a very large bundle of letters approving of what I have done to help you, most of them come from a shrieking kind of Protestant who does not really represent the sound, sane point of view which you put forward. Are you and your friends seeing to it that the *Spectator* and the *Observer* get a fair view? If the impression is now created that the House of Commons' vote is a mere piece of obscurantism and it is a denial to the Church of what Church laymen want, your success will be short-lived. On the other hand, newspapers as such have no religious convictions and this demonstration against the House of Commons vote is largely the result of their estimate of who is demonstrating most effectively. I regard the House of Commons vote as an effort by the popular chamber to give the mass of ordinary churchmen, who undoubtedly share your view, another chance. If they allow the House of Laymen to be nobbled a second time and do not set out their case for the ordinary public in plain and reasonable terms now, they certainly will not get the House of Commons to give them the same opportunity again. I distrust the priestly element in our national life so much that I should be sorry to see it ultimately prevail. But though people of my way of thinking can help to give churchmen and churchwomen of your way of thinking another chance, we cannot fight the battle as you can at this stage.

I have no doubt that you have been thinking of all these things and acting accordingly, but you won't mind a friend of yours affected by the stand you took making a perhaps unnecessary comment in a private letter. What I would like to see would be a series of letters appearing and articles being written which state the broad view that there has been in this Prayer Book controversy a mixing-up of the wholly laudable object of modernizing the service and providing additional prayers with the highly controversial and disputable effort to give a new licence to people who hate to be called Protestants to promote what is really a Romanist view by obscure and ingenious juggling with the Communion Service. Can you not get your friends to represent to the Archbishops and Bishops your willingness to co-operate in changes for the first purpose as long as the suspicion of doctrinal change in a Roman direction is effectively removed?

I do not think it has been brought to the mind of the ordinary church-goer that the thing you objected to in the new Book was not any part of the original alternative Book, was not any part of the amendments made in the alternative Book by the House of Laymen or even by the House of Clergy; but that it appears for the first time in a version emanating from the House of Bishops, which to say the least of it, did not in this respect appear to be in the nature of a combination of previous suggestions. Wolmer's fatuous observation that the Communion Service was the only thing that mattered should be rubbed in, and your own observation about the effect of all this on children in school is of the first importance.[6]

[6] For Wolmer's fatuous observation, see 211 H.C. Deb. col. 2651.

The plain truth is that while a great number of lookers-on are being led to believe that the changes would only give to those who liked them greater latitude, they would really have secured that within the next thirty years all the children that passed through church schools (and in hundreds of parishes this is the only school which gets the support of rates and taxes) would have been exposed to the drift toward the view which you and I do not like and which the mass of English people hate. It is not without reason that the Roman Catholic Church says that if you will give them a child up to the age of ten years you may do what you like with him afterwards.[7]

The arguments so skilfully stated in this letter (one of the most lengthy ever written by Simon which has survived) had a considerable effect on the tactics adopted by the Protestant party in the Church during the next few months. The struggle was not finally ended until June of the following year, when the House rejected a modified compromise measure. Inskip recorded on 18 January 1928: 'I went to the Archbishop today. I told him it was hopeless to expect Reservation to go through the House of Commons. He helplessly said, 'Well, what would you do?' I said I thought the first thing was to face facts and cut your coat according to your cloth and put forward the Book without Reservation. There is no doubt the old man begins at least to see that he will have to think out something beside the old measure.'[8]

Inskip appears to have thought that he had made it plain to the Archbishop that he, Hailsham, and Joynson-Hicks would give support, albeit reluctantly, to a revised Measure if the provisions for Perpetual Reservation were dropped, and when he spoke in the Debate in June he was able, 'with icy effect'[9] to suggest that the Archbishop had rejected a reasonable compromise. In fact the Archbishop had not so understood Inskip. In any event, the provisions for Perpetual Reservation were essential to the Measure.

If the old saying that wise men do not reveal their religion is true, Inskip was not a wise man. He was an unashamed representative of the West Country Evangelical tradition which has played such a significant part in English Church history. Throughout his life he was sustained and directed by the simple unreflecting Protestantism which King George V shared with so many of his middle-class subjects. Inskip differed only in the active part he took in many Evangelical causes. For many years he was President of the Lord's Day Observance Society, the Crusaders' Union, and the Y.M.C.A. The body in which he perhaps took the deepest interest was the Church Pastoral Aid Society (C.P.A.S.). From 1917 he

[7] Caldecote papers.   [8] Ibid.
[9] G. K. A. Bell, *Randall Davidson* (3rd ed., 1952), p. 1350. For Inskip's speech, see 218 H.C. Deb. 5s. col. 1299–1312.

was its President, and from 1939 to his death the Chairman of the Patronage Trustees. He was assiduous in attendance at meetings and took great
pains to secure that suitable men were found for the many livings in the
Society's gift. Much of the business of the C.P.A.S. was transacted at
lunch-time prayer meetings in Inskip's chambers in the Temple, or even,
after he became Lord Chief Justice, in his rooms at the Law Courts.[1]
His letters and diaries are full of references to his interest in Evangelical
activities. One example from his years as Lord Chief Justice may be given.
On 25 November 1943 he wrote to an old friend:

I wonder whether you think the Church is making any headway? Sometimes
things look better, then everything seems as dead as ever. I think the time has
come for lay folk to take to heart their shortcomings. We have all blamed the
Parsons for their failure to give a lead. The fact is that we are many of us so
wrapped up in our engagements and pleasures that we don't give any time for
service. Which of us can say that he gives an hour a week to doing something to
make our Faith known? My Father used to go off every Sunday afternoon to
superintend a Sunday School, besides a Men's Bible Class every Monday night,
and other things like C.M.S., etc.

The money question seems to engage more attention now than personal
service![2]

Inskip's religious beliefs as they were manifested in his daily life and
conduct were sometimes misinterpreted. Some people thought him
pompous or lacking in a sense of humour. For many years a legal after-
dinner story was in circulation which made Inskip the butt of one of Lord
Chancellor Birkenhead's more devastating retorts on an occasion when
Inskip had attempted to explain the proper mode of playing roulette.[3]
But these criticisms seem to rest on the fallacious assumption that Inskip
must have shared the weaknesses which are characteristic of evangelical
Protestants as a class rather than on observance of Inskip himself. It is true
that Inskip was an advocate of Sunday observance, a non-smoker, and a
very moderate consumer of alcohol (though not a teetotaller); he was also
not noticeably interesting in conversation, or particularly gifted with wit
or the power of repartee. But despite the rather censorious note which
sometimes crept into his voice, he was in truth a tolerant man who became
more mellow with the passage of time. It was noticed that he viewed
with increasing distaste the activities of the more belligerent Protestants
with whom he was sometimes associated.[4]

---

[1] See *Church and People* (1948), vol. lvi, p. 7 (Rev. Canon Mohan).
[2] Caldecote papers.   [3] R. E. Megarry, *Miscellany-at-Law* (1955), p. 49.
[4] Rt. Rev. E. J. Woods in unpublished memoir in Caldecote papers.

CHAPTER II

Inskip's standing in the house of commons after the Prayer Book Debate is shown by the fact that he was asked if he would accept the Conservative Party's nomination for the Speakership vacant by the death of Speaker Whitley. Inskip, however, refused—partly because of his own distaste for the position ('A lonely life', he said to his wife), and partly because the claims of Major E. FitzRoy, the successful candidate, were advanced with unusual vigour.

The general election of 1929 brought a setback. Not only was the Baldwin Government defeated, but Inskip lost his own seat, being beaten by J. A. Alpass (Lab.), who obtained 20,749 votes as against Inskip's 16,524. In reply to a letter of sympathy from Sir Ernest Pollock, the Master of the Rolls, Inskip wrote on 5 June 1929:

It was very good of you to write. There are many things more important in life than the loss of a seat, and already it is fading into its proper place in the past; but it was a disappointment because it means a break with Bristol which after all is my natural home.

I find a great deal of depression as to the Party's chances in the next ten years but I can't believe the Socialists are going to escape all the rocks.[1]

Inskip was out of the House until 1931, when a seat was found for him at Fareham at the general election of that year, where he was returned unopposed and retained it in 1935, beating the Labour candidate (R. Mack) by 11,233 votes.

In the National Government he was appointed Solicitor-General, the Attorney-Generalship being held by Sir William Jowitt, the Labour nominee. It was characteristic of Inskip that he made no complaint when the exigencies of party politics required him to revert to the junior office and serve under a younger man. But the period was brief. In January Jowitt was obliged to resign, being unable to find a constituency to accept him, and Inskip was appointed to succeed him. On 26 January Inskip wrote to Jowitt:

It seems all wrong not to be writing to you as Attorney and I wish I was. I am only writing a line to wish you both a good holiday and to thank you once more for all your kind words and deeds. It has been a really happy incident in my life to have worked under you.

[1] Hanworth papers.

I am looking forward to seeing you when you come back, so will very many others.

I saw the P.M. this morning. You will probably have heard that it is settled about me and Merriman.[2]

A few days later Inskip was sworn a Privy Councillor. (It is not customary for the Solicitor-General to be made a Privy Councillor, though Pollock in 1922 had been so honoured, but it is surprising that Inskip had not been sworn in when he had held the Attorney-Generalship in 1928.) The new Solicitor-General, Merriman, had held the same office under Inskip in 1928. In the following year Merriman accepted the office of President of the Probate, Divorce, and Admiralty Division, after it had been refused by Inskip,[3] and his place was filled by Donald Somervell, K.C., later Lord Somervell of Harrow, who became one of Inskip's few intimate friends. At the outset of their partnership as Law Officers Somervell thought that as he was the Junior he might help his Leader by writing in full the reasons for his Opinions.[4] But he soon discovered that this was not what Inskip wanted. His theory was that the Government Departments simply wanted an 'Aye' or 'No' answer to the question posed. The only occasion on which Inskip and Somervell wrote a lengthy Opinion was with reference to Mr. Justice Macnaghten's proposed Petition of Right[5] challenging the legality of the deductions in the judges' salaries in 1931. Somervell recorded later: 'There have been subtler lawyers. I think lawyers tend to overwork subtlety. All points have no doubt to be considered, but he was master of the direct approach to the heart of a problem. . . . I remember his talking of a prosecution which he had authorized under the Official Secrets Act which had caused apprehension in some quarters. Tom had taken what he regarded as the straightforward course and was commending this to me. He used words which I remembered because they seemed to imply that he had arrived at this principle by the method of trial and error! "I have found", he said, "that in this sort of matter the straightforward course is generally the best." '[6]

Few of the cases in which Inskip appeared for the Crown during his eleven years as Law Officer would be called sensational by the general reader. He prosecuted in the notorious Bywaters and Thompson murder trial in 1923[7] (to the end of his life he was convinced that Edith Thompson had been rightly convicted of the murder of her husband), and also in the Pepper case of 1936,[8] which attracted public attention at the time.

[2] Jowitt papers.   [3] See below, p. 600.
[4] Unpublished memorandum by Lord Somervell in Caldecote papers.
[5] See above, p. 513.   [6] Caldecote papers.
[7] See *The Trial of Bywaters and Thompson*, ed. F. Young (1923).
[8] See H. Montgomery Hyde, *Sir Patrick Hastings* (1960), pp. 307–12.

The political side of his work during his second term as Law Officer was not as interesting as the first; there was no issue like the Trade Disputes Bill or the Prayer Book.

The most important work we had together in the House of Commons was in the long Committee stage of the Government of India Bill, which became the Act of 1935. The major issues were of course dealt with by the Secretary of State, now Lord Templewood, and the Under Secretary, Mr. R. A. Butler. We had a considerable number of constitutional and legal issues to deal with. At the preliminary discussions with Ministers and officials, I enjoyed and bene-fited by watching him at work. He took it all in, never decided in a hurry, but his judgment, so far as I can remember, always became even more clearly right as it was subjected to the ordeal of debate.[9]

In 1935 Lord Hanworth retired from the office of Master of the Rolls, and Baldwin offered the position to Inskip. But the offer was made and received in a curious way. Baldwin accompanied the offer with an intimation that it was made only because Inskip's services as Law Officer entitled him to the first refusal, and that the Prime Minister would much prefer it if Inskip kept himself available for high political office later. Inskip on his side had grave doubts whether his tastes and abilities were suited to the work of an appellate judge, and found the way of escape indicated by Baldwin not unwelcome. He refused the offer, and the vacancy was filled by the unusual step of asking one of the Law Lords, Lord Wright, to accept the appointment.

Less than a year later the high political office which the Prime Minister had suggested might be open to Inskip became available, but in a form which probably neither of them had imagined. In March 1936 the Prime Minister decided to create a new ministerial post—that of Minister for the Co-ordination of Defence. The decision was made as part of the general policy of re-armament in face of the German menace. Baldwin was firmly opposed to either a Ministry of Defence or a Ministry of Supply but felt obliged to take some step in face of growing parliamentary pressure. He offered the new ministry to Inskip. The offer came as a complete surprise. Inskip knew the perils of the position; but he asked only if Neville Chamberlain approved of the appointment. On being assured that he did, Inskip thought it his duty to accept. It is now clear that a dominating factor in the appointment was the desire on the part of the Prime Minister and his inner circle to exclude Winston Churchill from any share in the defence or foreign policy of the country.[1] It is not easy today to remember the dislike and hostility which the senior members of the Conservative

<hr/>

[9] Memorandum by Lord Somervell in Caldecote papers.
[1] See I. Macleod, *Neville Chamberlain* (1961), p. 193.

Party showed towards Churchill in the nineteen-thirties. The dislike extended beyond politicians; it was shared by many members of the official and governing classes. Thus on 27 March 1936 General Ellison wrote to Sir Charles Harris, another survivor of Haldane's time at the War Office: 'As regards the Inskip appointment I have only one comment, and that is "Thank God we are preserved from Winston Churchill." '[2]

But other comments were less favourable. Churchill himself remarked that Baldwin had necessarily to appoint a man of abilities inferior to himself.[3] Mr. Michael Foot gave wide currency to a quip that no such surprising appointment had been made since the Emperor Caligula appointed his horse a consul.[4] The *Annual Register* in more measured language stated that Inskip's abilities 'had never been regarded as more than mediocre, nor could he lay claim to any great administrative experience'.[5] Inskip's difficult position was not improved by the revelation by Hailsham in the House of Lords that the staff of the new Ministry consisted of only two civil servants, though there was a right to ask for more.[6] It was stated that Inskip's functions were to exercise, on behalf of the Prime Minister, day-to-day supervision of the Committee of Imperial Defence. He was empowered to consult with the Chiefs of Staff, and to convene the Chiefs of Staff Committee under his own chairmanship whenever he or they thought it desirable. The Treasury also hoped that Inskip would help it to allocate funds between the three services.

For the next three years Inskip was at the centre of affairs in one of the most critical periods of British history. It is possible to distinguish his work at the Ministry from his general responsibility as one of the more important members of the Cabinet for the Munich settlement. At the Ministry most of Inskip's work was conducted through an endless series of committees making the preparations for war. It attracted little publicity because it was the policy of the Government to minimize in every way the news of these preparations in case the public should be unnecessarily alarmed. But it is generally agreed that Inskip was responsible for a major decision which contributed to survival in 1940. Strategic thinking in the R.A.F. was dominated by the need to build up Bomber Command. It was Inskip who insisted, against much opposition, that proper provision should also be made for Fighter Command.[7] There were not many Spitfires and Hurricanes available in 1940, but Inskip must be given a large share of the credit for the few there were. He was also responsible

---

[2] Harris papers.   [3] *History of The Times*, vol. iv, part II, p. 902.
[4] Cato, *Guilty Men* (1939), p. 76.   [5] Annual Register, 1936, p. 16.
[6] 100 H.L. Deb. 5s. col. 218.
[7] C. Webster and N. Frankland, *The Strategic Air Offensive against Germany* (1961), vol. i, pp. 76–77.

for the settlement of a tiresome inter-Service dispute about the control of the Fleet Air Arm: his decision in favour of the Admiralty was vindicated by the test of war-time experience. Inskip was less successful in solving Britain's major weakness in 1939, the inadequate system of supply. But in the absence of a Ministry of Supply which could act as a central buying agency for the three Services, and still more in the absence of the compulsory powers which came only with the War itself, there was little Inskip could do except build up and maintain (as he did) an atmosphere of confidence and good-will between the Services and the leading industrialists.[8] 'The root of the matter was that no living man—not even Winston Churchill—could have made a success of the appointment, unless he had been given not only a clear mandate that the rearmament programme was to have the highest priority, regardless of the dislocation of peace-time industry, but also an assurance that he would have the whole-hearted support of the Prime Minister and his colleagues in the Cabinet in any steps which he thought necessary.'[9] In short, it was a position of great responsibility but little authority.

So far as Inskip's general and particular responsibility for the policy of appeasement is concerned, he was a firm supporter of Chamberlain, and convinced that it was possible to detach the dictators from each other. On 19 January 1938 Eden was pained to see that Inskip, seated beside him in Cabinet, had written on top of his papers: 'Eden's policy to line up the U.S.A., Great Britain, and France, result war.'[1] The story of Inskip's part in the Munich crisis is best told by a series of extracts, necessarily abbreviated, from the exceptionally full diary which he kept for the whole period from August 1938 to September 1939.[2]

26 August 1938

I received a request to attend a 'meeting of ministers' on Tuesday, 30 August, and I left Abernyte on Monday night. Almost the whole Cabinet was present. Hailsham (who is no more than a passenger now)[3] was absent on a cruise to South America. Edward Stanley[4] was in Canada and Burgin[5] in Switzerland. Sir Nevile Henderson,[6] who had been summoned from Berlin, was called into the meeting. Halifax[7] gave a long account of the events of the last three weeks

[8] Information from Lord Ismay and Lord Dunrossil.
[9] Lord Ismay, *Memoirs* (1960), p. 75.
[1] Earl of Avon, *The Eden Memoirs* (1962), vol. ii, p. 560.
[2] Caldecote papers. All future extracts are from this diary unless otherwise stated.
[3] Lord Hailsham was Lord President of the Council from March to October 1938.
[4] Edward, Lord Stanley, Secretary of State for Dominion Affairs, May-October, 1938; to be distinguished from his younger brother, Oliver, who was President of the Board of Trade, 1937-40.
[5] L. Burgin, Minister of Transport, 1937-39.
[6] H.M. Ambassador in Berlin, 1937-39.
[7] Earl of Halifax, Foreign Secretary, 1938-40.

... Germany was clearly planning actively for the possibility of war in the near future. ...

Halifax then weighed up the facts. Hitler was thought by some to have made up his mind to intervene by force. Others thought he had not yet reached this point, but he was undoubtedly taking measures to be ready to use force. Henderson thought it was most unlikely that Germany would attack France. This opinion became more and more widely held, both by Ministers and by the Chiefs of Staff, but up to the middle of September it never seems to have occurred to the public that Germany would force France and possibly Great Britain into the position that they would have to begin the war, so far as Germany and themselves were concerned. Winston Churchill had been very busy with his favourite plan of a joint Note by several (unnamed) Powers. He wanted to say a great deal more than was said by Simon[8] at Lanark on 29 August. (John Simon had only repeated the P.M.'s March 24th warning that war once begun would almost certainly involve Great Britain.)

The P.M. was opposed to making any further statement, largely because it would be bluff if it went beyond Lanark. Simon clung hopefully to Benes'[9] good intentions. I shared his opinion as to the importance of getting Benes' proposals before the world in order to show what a good offer Benes was making. Henderson was very insistent also on this point. Later events showed that the value of Benes' successive proposals was always diminished by the fact that they were running after—but not quite catching up—the increasing demands of the Sudeten Germans.

There was no real difference of opinion, although Duff Cooper[1] and Oliver Stanley both professed to want to force the issue with Hitler. While professing this view, they each had a 'but' at the end of their observations. In the end it was decided not to repeat our warning to Hitler. In other words, we were to keep Hitler guessing, while we pressed Benes to get on with the negotiations.

During the first week of September the Prime Minister was maturing in his mind the plan to make a personal visit to Hitler. The proposal was revealed to Inskip on 7 September. After stating that Sir Robert Vansittart,[2] 'whose position at the Foreign Office is quite anomalous (a legacy from Anthony Eden) had become thoroughly worked up', had suggested a Note to Hitler to the effect that Great Britain would come in if France honoured her obligations to Czechoslovakia, Inskip recorded:

The P.M. then broached a proposal to me, which he has discussed with Halifax and Simon. He thought something dramatic was needed to get out of the rut of exchange of Notes. What did I think of the idea of an offer by him to go to Germany and see Hitler? Vansittart had fought the idea tooth and nail.

[8] Sir J. Simon, Chancellor of the Exchequer, 1938–40.
[9] Eduard Benes, President of Czechoslovakia.
[1] A. Duff Cooper, First Lord of the Admiralty, 1937–8.
[2] P.U.S. at Foreign Office, 1930–8; Chief Diplomatic Adviser, 1938–41.

'It was Henry IV going to Canossa over again.' I was a little tepid about the proposal, and merely said it could do no harm. I was pledged to secrecy, as surprise and timing were vital to its success. Later the same day the P.M. asked Kingsley Wood[3] the same question and I think also Malcolm MacDonald.[4]

On Monday, 12 September, there was another long Cabinet meeting. It was decided not to deliver any further Note to Hitler but to await his Nuremberg speech. Nothing was said in Cabinet about the Prime Minister's proposal to visit Hitler (Plan 2, as it was officially called).

Meanwhile the Chiefs of Staff were asked by me at the request of the Cabinet to make a report as to the military position in the event of a coup by Hitler— in other words, what action could we take. Oliver Stanley made the request that the C.O.S. should also say what the position would be next year if Germany made her coup and later attempted to advance by a coup in other directions. Oliver Stanley's idea was [that] a preventive war now is better than a war in twelve months. He wanted a report from the C.O.S. to support this view, from which he has apparently never receded, though he has never insisted on it. Oliver Stanley has his ears on the political and parliamentary rails: he wants to be ready for what is coming along: in other words he wants to lay off his commitments. For a man who is genuinely brave and very able, he has a most astonishing liking for sitting on the fence, or at any rate for only coming down off the fence provided the gate is open.

The next two days saw important developments. The reports of Hitler's Nuremberg speech began to come in on the Tuesday.

About 3 o'clock things began rattling down to war. German troop movements, fighting in Czechoslovakia, fiercer German and Sudeten propaganda. Phipps[5] reported that Bonnet[6] was in a state of collapse . . . Daladier[7] tried to telephone to P.M. who would not speak to him . . . Everything showed that the French didn't want to fight, were not fit to fight, and wouldn't fight. . . . In these circumstances the P.M. thought the time had come for Plan 2. There was no time to tell the Cabinet. He sent a telegram to Hitler offering to come to Berchtesgaden to see him.

On the Wednesday the Cabinet met in the morning. There was some anxiety in Chamberlain's inner circle. Apart from worry about how the Cabinet would receive the news of the offer, no reply had yet come from Hitler himself.

The P.M. told the Cabinet all about Plan 2. Almost everyone spoke with admiration of the P.M.'s bold stroke. Walter Elliot[8] was inclined to complain

[3] Sir K. Wood, Secretary of State for Air, 1938–40.
[4] Malcolm MacDonald, Secretary of State for the Colonies, May–October, 1938.
[5] Sir E. Phipps, H.M. Ambassador in Paris.
[6] G. Bonnet, French Foreign Minister.   [7] E. Daladier, French Prime Minister.
[8] Walter Elliot, Minister of Health, 1938–40.

that he had not been consulted. He expressed his difficulty in approving or disapproving the P.M.'s plan. He was very querulous, and also rather obscure. No one else took that line. Winterton[9], however, anxious to display his own rectitude, said our present position was due to the failure of the Government during the last three years to take rearmament seriously. The only excuse for the P.M.'s plan was that he might tell Hitler that sooner or later we should be in a position to resist his aggression policy, and were going to redouble our efforts. Duff Cooper later pointed out the absurdity of Winterton's idea. Nobody takes Winterton seriously. He is vain and pugnacious, and incapable of weighing his words, so that even when he says wise things, he spoils them by repetition and over-statement. His pose as the man who alone in the Cabinet has no responsibility for our relative military weakness, makes Winterton look a little foolish to everyone but himself. With all his obvious faults Winterton has a sense of loyalty, and would not willingly desert anyone in a tight place. He has little or no sense of humour, though for ever engaging in rather noisy laughter while he dilates upon his long experience of affairs. . . . Simon finished by his usual shower of compliments to P.M.—all fully deserved, but somehow or other coming from Simon's lips they give an impression of soapiness and flattery which they do not deserve. 'Brilliant'—his absence 'grievous' even for 48 hours. If he came back with seeds of peace with honour 'a remarkable achievement', and so on. I don't think the P.M. relishes such butterings, but he was plainly touched—as he said—by the confidence placed in him.

The Cabinet separated at 3.30 p.m., still without a definite reply from Hitler. But later in the afternoon the Führer telephoned to say that he would expect Chamberlain the following day. By Friday the 16th the Prime Minister was back in London and on the 19th, 'astonishingly fresh and alert', he gave the Cabinet an account of his journey to Berchtesgaden and of his meeting with Hitler ('the commonest looking little dog he had ever seen').

The impression made by the P.M.'s story was a little painful. Hitler had made him listen to a boast that the German military machine was a terrible instrument, ready to move now, and once put in motion could not be stopped. The P.M. said more than once to us that he was just in time. It was plain that Hitler had made all the running: he had in fact blackmailed the P.M.

We had a long discussion, lasting all day. Everyone expressed his views on the question of self-determination and a plebiscite. Duff Cooper, Oliver Stanley, and Winterton as before argued against giving in to Hitler and then gave their assent. Winterton was even more than usually truculent in the manner of his remarks. (He had written that day to Halifax to say that there would be two—if not three—resignations if we tried to force a plebiscite on Czechoslovakia. Halifax showed me the letter.) Winterton showed no signs of any resignation. It was quite clear that he would agree to anything: his views as stated were a kite, but nobody felt inclined to go up into the air after it.

[9] Earl Winterton, Chancellor of the Duchy of Lancaster, 1937–9.

U*

On Sunday the 18th Bonnet and Daladier came over to London and a joint Anglo-French Note was drafted to be dispatched to Czechoslovakia. The substance of the Note was that if the Sudeten areas were given up Great Britain and France would guarantee Czechoslovakia against un-provoked aggression. This Note was approved at a Cabinet meeting on the 19th, at which 'Winterton said it was very satisfactory to find the Cabinet entirely united, and Duff Cooper added the comment that any differences had only been as to emphasis and not as to substance'. The Munich Agreement itself was signed on 29 September.

Inskip's account is corroborated throughout by the other members of the Chamberlain Cabinet who have left their stories behind them,[1] though naturally there are differences of emphasis. (Few could imitate the bland detachment of Halifax,[2] who said of the policy which he himself both executed and largely conceived, that if he had been in opposition he would have opposed it.) The novelty in Inskip's story is the vivid and mordant picture of the dissident group (Duff Cooper, Winterton, Stanley) within the Cabinet.

The months after Munich found the public anxious to discover a scapegoat for the humiliation which Great Britain had suffered. Much of the criticism fastened on Inskip. A typical example can be found in Sir Arthur Salter's book *Security*, published in the spring of 1939:

> Massive in figure, impressive in his delivery and imperturbable in manner, no weakness in the case he was defending embarrassed the confident flow of his argument; no strength in the attack disturbed his equanimity. He was helped too by his transparent sincerity, and the unquestionable honesty and integrity of the whole of his personal and public record. Others might be suspected of deceiving their audience, but not Sir Thomas. What he said, he patently believed. Others might be suspected of a partially deliberate self-deception, of shutting or half-shutting their eyes to unpleasing truths; but not Sir Thomas. He did not need to shut his eyes. He could look with frank and fearless gaze at any prospect, however appalling—and fail to see it.[3]

These remarks may not be thought to be particularly acute or cogent: Inskip's diaries show that he regarded the appalling prospects of 1938 with eyes which were a good deal keener than either his friends or his enemies may have suspected. But their tone is typical of the criticisms made at the time by anti-Chamberlain observers, many of whom were less well informed than Salter. In December 1938 R. S. Hudson, together

---

[1] See Viscount Templewood, *Nine Troubled Years* (1954); Earl of Halifax, *Fulness of Days* (1957); Viscount Maugham, *At the End of the Day* (1954); Viscount Simon, *Retrospect* (1952): I. Macleod, *Neville Chamberlain* (1961); R. J. Minney, *The Private Papers of Hore-Belisha* (1960), chaps. 15–16.

[2] *Fulness of Days*, p. 197.   [3] *Security*, p. 208.

with some other junior Ministers, went to Chamberlain to protest against the continuance in office of Hore-Belisha and Inskip.[4] These criticisms had their effect on Inskip's position. In January 1939 Chamberlain transferred him to the Dominions Office. Inskip had allowed his diary to lapse after Munich, but on this occasion he took it up again and inserted a detailed account of his conversation with the Prime Minister.

17 January 1939

P.M. saw me today. After general talk about his Italian trip and a discussion about a committee on disarmament, the following conversation took place:

P.M.: I want to talk to you about your future. (Pause.) I have no criticism of anything you have done or not done in your position. You took on a thankless job, and you have done a great deal of important work. You have made some big decisions which we have accepted, and they have been most valuable. (Pause.) You have been in your job nearly three years. Now I want to make a proposal to you. Don't say anything till I have told you the whole plan.

 If you give up your post the question arises where you ought to go, and I suggest the Dominions. Malcolm MacDonald can't go as he is: he has his hands full with the Colonies and somebody must take the Dominions. It isn't a very absorbing Department and I regard that as important. You will be available for committees, and moreover we haven't many first class debaters and I find difficulty sometimes in ringing the changes. You have told me more than once that you are ready to put yourself in my hands, and that was very good of you. That is why I hope you won't think that I am treating you unfairly. If you think it is a humiliation tell me, and I will reconsider it. I haven't made up my mind but I want to know how you feel about it.

 Then the question comes who will take your place. I can't put a junior Minister in the position, and I can't see anyone in the Cabinet that will do the job as well as you have done it. I can only think of one man.

 (I rapidly thought—or tried to think—of someone, but I failed, and neither Anthony Eden nor Winston came into my mind.)

P.M.: I propose Chatfield.[5]

 (My mouth opened, or my eyes.)

P.M.: I know what you are going to say: 'He belongs to one of the Services.'

 (I wasn't going to say this. I was thinking of his position in the House of Lords.)

But I think he can hold the scales: he has been out of the Admiralty for some time now, and I think he will give the public confidence.

 Then I have to think of how to deal with the position in the House of Commons. This business of the House of Lords and the House of

[4] Inskip always regarded Hudson's criticism as founded on the breach of a private confidence and spoke of him with contempt.
[5] Admiral of the Fleet Lord Chatfield.

Commons is for ever embarrassing me. I think I can find a way out and I have one or two ideas. I don't want to be obliged to legislate so as to appoint another Secretary and I must find some other plan. (Long pause.)

P.M.: Your position in the House of Commons and in the country and in the press has gone back lately.

I: Yes, I think it has.

P.M.: Well now, perhaps you would like time to think about it.

I: No, I don't feel that is necessary. When S. B. asked me to do the job, I told him it was no good thinking over it. If he had made up his mind that I was the only man he could get, I would do my best. So now, if you have decided it is in the public interest for me to go, of course I am not going to object. As to humiliation, it will be represented in the press and in some quarters in Parliament as such, but I should not look at it like that.

P.M.: I am sure there wouldn't be any great exultation at your departure as there would be if Hore-Belisha[6] was to be going. There will be comment, but it won't be unfriendly.

I: I don't very much mind if it is. I suppose the Dominions will not feel they are being fobbed off with a failure?

P.M.: I am sure they will not. They were delighted to get Malcolm. They didn't know who they might get.

(I thought this an odd statement if it was intended to reassure me.)

I: Well, if you think it best, of course I am in your hands.

The interview concluded with further expressions of gratitude by the Prime Minister for the attitude which Inskip had adopted. Before the end, however, Chamberlain touched on the matter of Inskip's future career once more:

I don't propose to ask Maugham to resign so that I could offer you the Lord Chancellorship. He has done very well, and though I gave him no promise I should not like to turn him out before the election.[7] In the ordinary way I should propose—if we come back after the election and I am P.M.—to offer you the Lord Chancellorship then. That will save you from having to make the decision now as to whether you will go to the Lords or continue in the House of Commons. You can then keep open—if you like—your chance of being P.M. It is the choice Hailsham had to make, and I think he always regretted afterwards that he became Lord Chancellor.[8]

I.: Do you mean that you want to keep my way open to become P.M. if I want to take it?

P.M.: Yes, that is what I mean.

Inskip's family and friends were angry at the decision. Kingsley Wood 'said something about an awful example of ingratitude in politics'. Inskip

---

[6] L. Hore-Belisha, Secretary of State for War, 1937–40.
[7] See above, p. 554.   [8] See above, pp. 469–70.

himself summarized the position: 'My feelings at present are chiefly of a loss of interest in my current work, and a desire to get it all over and out. I have a broad back, and I have had blows before this one, and it will be rather fun standing at bay with the jackals—who can't really bite me, though I have little doubt they will snarl.'

In retrospect it is perhaps easier to do justice to Chamberlain. The right of the Prime Minister to make ministerial changes is undoubted, as Inskip himself quite recognized. Nor can it be denied that Chamberlain had reasons for making the change in this particular case. The fact that Inskip had done the best he could in an almost impossible position supplied a reason for sympathetic treatment but not for postponing action which the public interest demanded. All who serve the Crown in a civil or military capacity know that they may be asked to perform difficult tasks and judged by the highest standards if they fail. It is a risk which is known to be incident to the public service. It could be said on behalf of Chamberlain that he did not dismiss Inskip from the Government but offered him an alternative office of respectable status. Chamberlain also gave a very good reason why it was not possible to appoint Inskip to the Woolsack at that moment, and coupled it with a promise to appoint him thereafter, at the same time indicating that Inskip was a likely successor to himself. On this point Chamberlain could be represented as taking a benevolent and prudent interest in Inskip's future. But Chamberlain does seem to have been somewhat lacking in tact in the manner in which he made the change, as the mordant tone of Inskip's account recognized. Inskip was also entitled to take the view that he was being replaced by a not noticeably better qualified person.

A letter of sympathy from Simon arrived, to which Inskip replied on 31 January:

My dear John

Your very kind letter of course gave me great pleasure. It has been a hard row to hoe, and I am not sorry to give it up for a most interesting but less exposed position. I have nothing but gratitude to all my colleagues but you have been extraordinarily helpful at all times. I think I can see some of your difficulties, and of course I will help in every way I can.

Yours ever,

Tom Inskip

You were the first to give me a hint of what S. B. was going to ask me to do, when I met you in the hall at No. 10![9]

Inskip was sworn in as Secretary of State on 2 February 1939. One of his officials recorded later:

[9] Simon papers.

Sir Thomas was an agreeable man to work for. He had common sense, a clear head and never fussed. He was cheerful and unfailingly polite. He was an orderly worker who got through his papers rapidly. He did not try to do the work of officials but confined himself to broad issues.

But he was not an inspiring Secretary of State. I don't think he had much interest in external relations in general and the Commonwealth in particular and his outlook was rather that of a competent barrister dealing with his briefs coolly and efficiently. . . .

In the Spring of 1939 Sir Nevile Henderson was sending very serious warnings of the utter unreliability of Hitler and his aggressive intentions. Before he went to Cabinet one morning where the German question was to be discussed, Sir Thomas read one of the Ambassador's rather hair-raising reports, and, giving it back to me, dismissed it as crying wolf: he described Sir Nevile as a pessimist whose views had to be discounted.[1]

One of Inskip's tasks at the Dominions Office was to hold a daily conference with the High Commissioners who represented the various Dominions in London. By these conferences and a flood of daily telegrams London maintained the constant contact and consultation with the capitals of the Dominions which had been a feature of Commonwealth policy since the Imperial Conference of 1926. As war drew nearer Inskip resumed his very full diary, in which there are many references to these daily meetings with the High Commissioners.

At the Cabinet (on 22 August to consider the Russo-German Pact) the P.M. seemed 'under the weather'. Halifax was quite calm. The only discussion was as to whether the P.M. should write to Hitler, telling him he must not mistake our position, and whether this should go by a special emissary, or through Henderson. In the end the latter was decided. . . .

Having said at Connel Ferry on August 3rd that 'war was now unlikely' I watch with interest the movements. I still find it difficult to believe that war is 'likely': there is, however, an obviously grave and tense situation, which may result in an explosion. . . . I saw the High Commissioners last night. Bruce[2] and Dulanty[3] both thought the reaffirmation of our position was most dangerous, as it would only encourage Beck[4] to be intransigent. We ought to find out Beck's position first, and then make our pronouncement to fit the position. Bruce felt very strongly, and he went in to see the P.M. and the Foreign Secretary, who made a very slight change—scarcely more than verbal—in the Press statement with regard to the Moscow Pact. Bruce was a little melodramatic. I was not greatly impressed. He didn't seem to have thought of the danger of letting the world think we are going to 'run out'. Dulanty—representing a country that never helps—thinks it consistent with his detached position to offer comments about our policy.

[1] Information from Hon. Sir F. E. Cumming-Bruce, K.C.M.G.
[2] S. M. Bruce, High Commissioner for Australia, 1933–45.
[3] J. W. Dulanty, High Commissioner for Eire, 1930–50.
[4] E. Beck, Foreign Minister of Poland.

The next day passed in further discussion of the implications of the Moscow Pact. On 25 August

Halifax saw the High Commissioners in my room at 10.15 p.m. He stayed nearly an hour. Bruce was again rather excitable on the same lines as 2 or 3 days ago. Te Water[5] made a long and interesting (but for its sententious expression) proposal that the Peace Front Nations should, as a last statesmanlike effort, make a 'great declaration' of their position towards constructive proposals. He proposed that Roosevelt should make an appeal to the nations to join in a great conference to resettle the peace of the world. Halifax was rather attracted by this idea, and promised to think over it. Halifax, after a long day, including a speech in the House of Lords, and a broadcast at 9.30 p.m., seemed as calm as usual, with the air of rather languid weariness which never quite deserts him, unless he has found something to tickle his sense of humour, which is never far off.

The next few days were occupied with efforts to save Poland from the fate that was obviously about to overtake her. On 30 August Hitler demanded the presence of a Polish delegate with full powers in Berlin within 24 hours. He was told that this was impossible and during the morning the Cabinet met to approve a draft Note in reply.

Before the Cabinet the High Commissioners came with their customary readiness to offer their ideas as to our draft. 'It should be friendly', 'it should make a clear statement of our position', etc. etc. At the Cabinet Halifax produced a draft which we discussed rather disjointedly. There are some people in the Cabinet—Ernest Brown and Burgin, and sometimes Elliot—who see the ghosts of Munich in every sentence that comes from Germany. They put the worst interpretation on everything. Burgin is omniscient, and acts as a sort of chorus to the P.M. 'Yes, Prime Minister', 'I entirely agree', and, sotto voce, approving comments.

The fruitless efforts continued during the next few days.

This morning (1 September) I was met by an unshaven fellow who told me Hitler had broadcast to his army saying he had only one alternative—to meet force with force. When I entered the office I was told Germany had bombed Warsaw.

[5] C. T. te Water, High Commissioner for South Africa, 1923–39.

CHAPTER III

THE OUTBREAK OF WAR brought a change to Inskip's own position. The Prime Minister asked him to leave the Dominions Office and offered him the Woolsack. On Friday 1 September Inskip recorded:

After yesterday's Cabinet the P.M., who has asked us all for our resignations, told me that he would in any case want to make a change at the Dominions Office (he gave no reason), and if he were able to offer me the Lord Chancellorship, or as an alternative the Lord Presidency, which would I prefer. I said Lord Chancellor: it was my own profession. P.M. said that was what he hoped. I imagine he wants to put someone else in the War Cabinet than myself (*sic*) as Dominions Secretary. Also he wants to give himself another vacancy by my going to the Lord Chancellorship.

I don't like the P.M.'s methods. He is a 'faux ami', and I think I shall be glad to be out of his inner circle. . . . I was at least entitled to be taken into his confidence as to why I should leave the Dominions Office. But, as I say, I shall be glad to be out of reach of him if I become Lord Chancellor, and for that reason I am not sorry to become Lord Chancellor. Eddy Devonshire asked me to realize that a good many people in both Houses wanted me to succeed Neville. I told Eddy that I would think about it, but there was no certainty that Neville would ask the King to make me P.M., and in any case I had no ambition to be P.M. Eddy said that was one reason why so many people thought I was the man they wanted.

I have refused more places than I ever deserved to have offered to me. (1) A puisne Judgeship in 1924 by S. B. (He afterwards re-appointed me Solicitor-General.) (2) Speaker by S. B. in 1928. (3) President of Probate Division by Ramsay MacDonald in 1935 [? 1933], and (4) Master of the Rolls in 1935 by S. B. If I refused Lord Chancellorship and Lord President it would seem more than presumptuous.

The fact that Inskip was being seriously considered in the inner circles of the Conservative Party as a possible successor to Chamberlain is not generally known. But there is corroboration of Inskip's own account in a letter of 13 October 1947 from the 7th Duke of Devonshire to Lady Caldecote.[1]

My dear Lady Caldecote
            This is just one line to say how very deeply grieved I was, and how much I sympathized with you, when I heard of your loss. My relations with Tom were strange, if not unique, in that I respected and revered him as one might a Father or indeed a Grand-father and at the same time loved him as one

[1] Caldecote papers.

might a brother, and a younger one at that. From the first time I ever knew him at all, on the National Assembly, I was strongly drawn towards him and I was never so happy as when I was his Under-Secretary.

I wonder if he ever told you about the time when he was made Lord Chancellor and I went and begged him* not to take the appointment because I looked to him to lead the Conservative Party. He pulled a face and said that it was strange that when all his friends at the Bar were congratulating him, his own Under-Secretary should come into his room and accuse him of being barely better than a traitor. I said that I had not meant that at all, but that there were lots of others beside myself, who looked to him, because of his solid qualities of judgment, honesty, reliability and sound common sense. Tom pulled another face and made a very characteristic remark: 'Well, Eddy, I am grateful for your confidence in me, but I do not think I am the man you want. When the war is over I shall be getting old, and after wars people are highly strung and want someone young and exciting to be their leader. Now, Eddy, I may, or may not, have the qualities you ascribe to me, but you cannot possibly hope that five or six years from now I shall be a glamour-girl. Therefore I think I am right to serve the Law rather than the Party'.

He was a truly good and great man. He did a great deal of good in his life and England is a better place for his years of service. I loved him very dearly and can, I think, understand the extent of your loss.

Yours very sincerely,
Eddy Devonshire

(*) In, perhaps, unduly strong terms.

Inskip's diary contains a record of the interview at No. 10 Downing Street at which he was actually offered the Woolsack.

On Monday, September 4th, P.M. asked me to see him about 7.30 p.m.[2] after his return from the House, where he declared War. I went over: he said, 'I won't keep you a moment, I want you to become Lord Chancellor.' I said 'Very well' and in 60 seconds was out of the room. I returned in five minutes to ask his approval of a telegram from him to Hertzog.[3] He approved it, and I left again. The telegram to Hertzog was to try and get him in on our side. On Tuesday Clark[4] told us it was too late as the Cabinet was split. Smuts[5] and Denys Reitz[6] with five others (English) against Hertzog and five others (Afrikaans). 7 for war against 6 for peace.

In the course of the day the War Cabinet was announced, and later my appointment and one or two others. I said goodbye to my people at the D.O. I think they were more than officially sorry. So was I.

[2] Inskip's memory must be at fault here. Chamberlain announced to the House of Commons that war had been declared at 12.6 p.m. on Sunday, 3 September (351 H.C. Deb. 5s. col. 291). See also below, p. 602.

[3] J. B. M. Hertzog, Prime Minister of South Africa, 1924–39.

[4] Sir W. Clark, U.K. High Commissioner in South Africa, 1934–9.

[5] Jan C. Smuts, Minister of Justice.

[6] Denys Reitz, Deputy Prime Minister.

On Saturday, 2 September, Inskip described how he went over to 10 Downing Street late in the evening to hear the news.

Everyone was out, but as I was coming away the P.M. met me. He said he had had a most unpleasant task,[7] and the House had been very restless. When the House had risen he found a number of members of the Cabinet had been meeting and complaining the statement was not what we had agreed, and they were in a state of semi-revolt. He sent for them; they came in looking very sullen, and Simon made their point clear. The P.M. told them the French wouldn't agree and he had to make some statement. The P.M. seemed a little rattled and his face was deeply lined: it may have had a bad effect on a man who is past 70, and has borne a very heavy burden. Moreover he seemed to be conducting the Foreign Policy, and I wonder if Halifax will stand it. The P.M. *is* a man of peace. He spoke to me tonight about the hundreds of thousands of children in France that would be killed if war came. I told him not to be too much upset by all this. . . .

I got Kingsley Wood to tell me the names of the Cabinet members who were in the state of 'semi-revolt' last night. He said 'the usual people'—Oliver Stanley, Walter Elliot, Burgin (not so strong), and Ernest Brown (ditto).

Inskip received the Great Seal at a Council held at 11.15 a.m. on Monday 4 September, and was sworn in before the Master of the Rolls (Sir Wilfrid Greene) the following day. He was created a peer under the title of Viscount Caldecote, of Bristol, on 6 September. (As a former Secretary of State, convention entitled him to a viscounty instead of the usual barony.) He wrote to Simon on 13 September:

I do most truly value your letter. You have always been the most true and kind friend to me for many years, and it is very kind now once more to send me out on my new work with encouraging words.

Of course my Father has often been in my thoughts. I am glad you remember him so well.

My warmest thanks and good luck to you in your War Cabinet.[8]

Caldecote's term as Lord Chancellor (eight months) was brief, but not exceptionally so. Halsbury had been Chancellor for eight months in 1885, and Herschell for six months in 1886. St. Leonards was Lord Chancellor for ten months in 1852.[9] He discharged the legal and political duties of his office in a manner which gave his officials and others entire satisfaction, but the brevity of his tenure of the Great Seal and the accompanying circumstances of war time prevented Caldecote from leaving any significant memorial behind him. So far as judicial appointments were concerned, no vacancies in the High Court had to be filled. His private

---

[7] 'A short but very fierce debate': W. S. Churchill, *The Gathering Storm* (1948), vol. i, p. 318. See also R. J. Minney, *The Private Papers of Hore-Belisha*, pp. 226–27.

[8] Simon papers.   [9] Erskine had been Lord Chancellor for 14 months in 1806–7.

diary during this period reflected only the general uncertainties and puzzlements of the first months of the war. The lack of definite news and the fact that he was not in the War Cabinet often reduced him to chronicling the table-talk of the day. So, dining one evening at Buckingham Palace ('short coats and black ties were the order of the day') he found the King in a state of irritation at the activities of his exiled brother. In particular, a demand from the Duke of Windsor that his military uniforms should be forwarded to him produced a royal refusal.

The fall of the Chamberlain Government in May 1940 inevitably affected Caldecote's own position. In the confusion of the time it was for some days uncertain what his future would be; but one evening Sir Claud Schuster telephoned shortly before the nine o'clock news to say that it was about to be announced that Simon was to succeed him on the Woolsack.[1] Caldecote was offered, and thought it right to accept, his old post at the Dominions Office, together with the Leadership of the House of Lords. He surrendered the Great Seal on 12 May. Five months later to the day he was appointed (12 October) Lord Chief Justice in succession to Lord Hewart.

In his brief second tenure of the Dominions Office Caldecote left behind him a striking impression. Although he could not be described as an outstanding Secretary of State in a company which included (at that time) Malcolm MacDonald, Eden, Attlee, and Salisbury, he had the qualities necessary for success in the dark days of 1940. Caldecote's complete self-confidence and imperturbability inspired all who had to work with him at that time. Each day the High Commissioners came for their conference, and each day during that summer the news was worse than the last. Yet the Dominions never faltered. One of Caldecote's officials recalled afterwards[2] the day when it was announced that the exigencies of war had required the Royal Navy to fire on the French Fleet at Oran, and how the Secretary of State, in a calm and efficient way, set himself to the task of communicating the news to the Dominions. Caldecote succeeded where a more intellectual and highly strung Minister might have failed. His qualities were those of a pre-1914 English Conservative of the type of Walter Long. He was solid, honest, unintellectual, and right. At that time and place they were the qualities which were needed.

When he became Lord Chief Justice in October Caldecote succeeded to a great office which had become somewhat tarnished during the occupancy of his predecessor. Hewart was perhaps the worst Lord Chief Justice of England since the seventeenth century. Although no imputation of corruption or dishonesty could be brought against him, as against

[1] Information from Dowager Viscountess Caldecote.
[2] Information from Sir Savile Garner and Sir Eric Machtig.

Scroggs and Jeffreys, on the bench he rivalled them in arbitrary and unjudicial behaviour. The author of the famous dictum that 'justice must not only be done, but manifestly and obviously be seen to be done'[3] was incapable of securing its observance in his own court. Towards the end of his career he was also constantly in bad health and the routine administration of the courts began to suffer. One day he was informed by telephone from Downing Street that his resignation was expected,[4] and although he had once publicly stated that he would never retire,[5] he felt it wise to comply with the request. It was fortunate for the reputation of the Bench that Caldecote was available to succeed him.

Caldecote was the first ex-Lord Chancellor to be appointed Lord Chief Justice, although the opposite process is not unknown, as the careers of Jeffreys, Hardwicke, and Campbell demonstrate. Caldecote discharged the duties of his office with dignity and efficiency. In criminal trials he was (unlike his predecessor) a model of fairness and impartiality. His sense of duty made him choose the more difficult and unpopular circuits for himself instead of leaving them to the junior judge. He also took an active interest in the affairs of the Council of Legal Education, of which he was Chairman from 1942 to 1946.[6] Caldecote did not regard the office as a tiresome formality. He thought, rightly, that the Inns were not spending enough on legal education and procured an increase in their annual contributions to the Council. He improved the accommodation available for lectures and recreation. The changes for which he was responsible were of great value when the post-war flood of students arrived. But in the nature of things no man could have gained an outstanding reputation as Lord Chief Justice in war time.

Something of his private thoughts may be gathered from a few of the many letters to an old friend which he wrote during this time.

15 June 1941

As to the war, I think the only way to look at it is a part of chastening for us all.

A great deal of our national life has been shallow; now surprising qualities are being revealed. Hardness where one thought only to find softness, a sense of duty where excitement and pleasure seemed the chief objects in life. All of us who ought to have known better let things drift complacently as if it wasn't our fault that so many things were wrong, and as long as we kept fairly straight, other people might go wrong if they wished.

I think we have all been afraid of speaking out. Our grandparents used to talk of a separated life, but we think that is rather out of date and narrow, but

---

[3] *R. v. Sussex JJ.* [1924] 1 K.B. 256, 259.   [4] R. Jackson, *The Chief* (1959), p. 335.
[5] R. M. Jackson, *The Machinery of Justice in England* (3rd ed., 1960), p. 239.
[6] Information from W. C. Cleveland-Stevens, K.C.

I am sure that our grandparents and our parents were the people who made the stock of the Nation so sound and instinctively wise in their outlook on the world.

23 March 1942

In spite of this appalling war, not to speak of the last one, I have had a very happy life; I was going to say 'fortunate', which is quite true in the ordinary sense of the word. I have had more than I deserved of some things that people think a great deal of. I don't know that those are the things that have made me much happier. The real things have been, all the affection of my friends and of mine for them, and the sense of the goodness of God in everything, and my home. This must all be as true of you as of me. Anyhow I don't regret the years as they pass; they are too happy for that.

27 April 1943

More than ever we seem to me to be just living on the remnants of our Christian heritage. To all intents and purposes the younger generation does not find any use for Christian practice or teachings. Air Cadet Force Census of churchgoers taken in Scotland shows that 80% never enter a Church or Religious Service and don't show any sign of wanting to do so. Even if they did, I don't know what they would get. The average sermon has no message for young or old, unless I am very unfortunate in my experience. Most Preachers talk to their congregations as if they were all that needed any ministration—a sort of company of the Elect who may be trusted to keep heart if they are reminded of their duty. The Archbishop,[7] who has, I think, great qualities, seems much more in earnest about Social Reform than in making the Church of our Nation a Missionary Church. I would like to think I am pessimistic, but lately everything has seemed to be going downhill and nothing but a miracle can stop it.

Towards the end of the war Caldecote's health began to fail, and after some months of rest in 1945 he returned to the bench a visibly older man. His resignation on 21 January 1946 was not unexpected. Caldecote died at his home, Greystones, Enton Green, Godalming, on 11 October 1947, and was buried at Baldock as already described.[8]

Caldecote's career is notable for two reasons. First, because it affords an example of unostentatious Christian integrity in a series of high public offices. Secondly, because although he was one of the very few lawyers to hold each of the offices of Lord Chancellor and Lord Chief Justice, he will be remembered not as an advocate or a judge but as the holder of a vital Cabinet post at a critical moment in the nation's history. It is natural to make comparison with Haldane. But even a man of Haldane's intellectual stature could not have made a success of the Ministry for the Co-ordination of Defence in the years from 1936 to 1939. Before the Kaiser's War the First Sea Lord[9] was accustomed to declaim that

[7] Most Rev. W. Temple, Archbishop of Canterbury.
[8] See above, p. 577.   [9] Admiral Fisher.

> Time and the ocean and some fostering star
> In high cabal have made us what we are.

Twenty years later the position of Great Britain had declined both absolutely and relatively. No longer the richest country in the world, her own Government was weaker and her allies less dependable. She was also required to deal with an enemy of unexampled ruthlessness and evil. The material is not yet available for writing a full history of the defence policy of those years. At present it is at least clear that Caldecote's part was entirely straightforward and creditable.

Some people thought him lucky, and indeed it has been seen that he twice referred to his own good fortune.[1] So *The Times* obituary notice said of him that 'in view of the winding path of his approaches to the higher offices of the law he might well be described as a lucky man, for, judged by the intellectual standards of many of his contemporaries, he was not an outstanding figure: but few grudged him his good luck'.[2] Yet an exceptionally shrewd and well-qualified observer thought otherwise; Sir Claud Schuster wrote to Lady Caldecote on 13 October 1947:[3]

I have always thought Tom the very model and example of what a lawyer in public life should be. He was not, I suppose, without a decent ambition, and desired to put his great gifts of character and sound judgment and industry at the service of his country. But, as it happened, I saw most of him at the great crises of his life, at the time of the debate on the Prayer Book, when he was forced into the Ministry of Defence, when he had to abandon the idea of becoming Master of the Rolls, when he became and when he ceased to be Lord Chancellor, when he, almost reluctantly, was persuaded to sacrifice the rest and retirement which he desired and to become Chief Justice. On all these occasions his own personal advancement and prestige were the last things which, for him, counted in the decision. *The Times* says that he was lucky. I have always thought him the opposite. If he had received the Chancellorship, as was his due, when Maugham was appointed; if he had become Chief Justice earlier in times when he would not have been hampered by war conditions, he might have had, indeed I am sure he would have had, in either office a long and fruitful reign. In each case fate was against him. And in addition he had to bear, as he did in silence, the burden of reproaches from ignorant people for the impossible task set him in the Ministry of Coordination of Defence.

Caldecote was succeeded by his only son, Robin Andrew, who had obtained the D.S.C. as a Lieutenant Commander in the Royal Navy and afterwards became a distinguished engineer and a Fellow of King's College, Cambridge, who has inherited his father's interest in the C.P.A.S., of which he is Treasurer. Caldecote died a poor man, his fortune dissipated by anonymous charitable gifts. His estate was valued for probate at £17,079.

[1] See above, pp. 600, 605.   [2] 10 October 1947.   [3] Caldecote papers.

APPENDIX

In *Constitutional Law* Caldecote delivered judgments in *Wallace-Johnson* v. *R.* [1940] A.C. 231, in which the Privy Council had to deal with a colonial statute on the subject of sedition. In *Lethbridge* v. *Independent Order of Foresters* [1940] A.C. 513 there is a full and careful judgment on the question whether an Act of the Alberta legislature reducing the rate of interest on provincial debentures was *ulta vires* on the ground that its 'pith and substance' dealt with a dominion subject-matter, as was held to be the case. In *Murray* v. *Parkes* [1942] 2 K.B. 123 Caldecote considered the inter-relationship of British and Irish nationality.

In *Revenue Law* there are a number of good judgments, which no doubt reflect the experience Caldecote had gained when as Law Officer he had led for the Crown in revenue appeals. Examples are *Cameron* v. *Prendergast* [1940] A.C. 549 (payment to director for retention of office); *Hughes* v. *B. G. Utting & Co. Ltd.* [1940] A.C. 463 (value of ground rent as trading profit); *United Steel Companies Ltd.* v. *Cullington* [1940] A.C. 812 (wear and tear allowances); *Lowry* v. *Consolidated African Selection Trust Ltd.* [1940] A.C. 648.

In *Workmens' Compensation* there is a good judgment on the difficult topic of whether a particular incapacity is due to disease in *Fife Coal Co. Ltd.* v. *Young* [1940] A.C. 479.

In *Torts* Caldecote delivered judgment in *McLeod* v. *Buchanan* [1940] 2 All E.R. 79, in which the House of Lords impliedly approved the important case of *Monk* v. *Warbey* [1935] 1 K.B. 75, in which it was held that a breach of the statutory duty on a car-owner to take out third-party insurance gives rise to a civil action. There is also a good judgment from his years as Lord Chief Justice in *Winstanley* v. *Bampton* [1943] K.B. 321, dealing with the scope of qualified privilege in defamation.

In *Criminal Law* Caldecote naturally delivered many judgments in the war-time years when he presided over the Divisional Court. But the nature of the business before that court calls for rapidity of decision; fully matured and considered judgments are always rare, and in any case the cast of Caldecote's mind was not such as to make such judgments congenial to him. But a good judgment will be found in *Owens* v. *Minoprio* [1942] 1 K.B. 193 (autrefois acquit), and in *D.P.P.* v. *Kent & Sussex Contractors Ltd.* [1944] K.B. 149, and *Moore* v. *Bresler Ltd.* [1944] 2 All E.R. 515 he delivered two important judgments on the criminal liability of corporations. A corporation may be liable criminally if it is possible to impute to it, as an artificial entity, the acts or omissions of its servants or agents, if those servants or agents are in a position to influence the direction of the company. The liability is not truly vicarious. As Caldecote said in the *Kent & Sussex Contractors* case 'The officers are the company for this purpose'. There is some doubt whether this principle was properly applied in *Moore* v. *Bresler,* where the officials in question were merely the general manager and sales manager of one of the branches of the company, but the principle itself is of undoubted validity.

In *R.* v. *Leckey* [1944] K.B. 80 a robust judgment by Caldecote affirmed the principle that a person accused of a crime is entitled to refuse to answer questions; such a refusal may be commented upon by the judge at the trial, but even he must do so in moderate terms; no inference of guilt is to be drawn from the accused's silence. In *R.* v. *Young* (1944) Cr. App. Rep. 57 Caldecote considered the scope of the common law misdemeanour of public mischief. In *Joyce* v. *D.P.P.* [1946] A.C. 247 the House of Lords affirmed the judgment of the Court of Criminal Appeal [1945] 2 All E.R. 673 delivered by Caldecote.

TABLE OF CASES

INDEX